EPICTETUS

II

LCL 218

EPICTETUS

THE DISCOURSES

BOOKS III–IV

FRAGMENTS · ENCHEIRIDION

WITH AN ENGLISH TRANSLATION BY

W. A. OLDFATHER

HARVARD UNIVERSITY PRESS

CAMBRIDGE, MASSACHUSETTS
LONDON, ENGLAND

First published 1928

LOEB CLASSICAL LIBRARY® is a registered trademark
of the President and Fellows of Harvard College

ISBN 978-0-674-99240-5

*Printed on acid-free paper and bound by
Edwards Brothers, Ann Arbor, Michigan*

CONTENTS

ARRIAN'S DISCOURSES
OF EPICTETUS

ΑΡΡΙΑΝΟΥ
ΤΩΝ ΕΠΙΚΤΗΤΟΥ ΔΙΑΤΡΙΒΩΝ

$\overline{\text{Α}}$ $\overline{\text{Β}}$ $\overline{\text{Γ}}$ $\overline{\text{Δ}}$

$\overline{\text{Γ}}$

ΚΕΦΑΛΑΙΑ ΤΟΥ $\overline{\text{Γ}}$ ΒΙΒΛΙΟΥ

---

[1] s : πλαττομένους S.

[2] The entire title supplied from Ch. X. by s.

2

ARRIAN'S DISCOURSES
OF EPICTETUS

IN FOUR BOOKS

BOOK III

Chapters of the Third Book

Γ

α΄. Περὶ καλλωπισμοῦ.

1 Εἰσιόντος τινὸς πρὸς αὐτὸν νεανίσκου ῥητορικοῦ περιεργότερον ἡρμοσμένου τὴν κόμην καὶ τὴν ἄλλην περιβολὴν κατακοσμοῦντος Εἰπέ μοι, ἔφη, εἰ οὐ δοκοῦσίν σοι κύνες τ᾽ εἶναι καλοί τινες καὶ ἵπποι καὶ οὕτως τῶν ἄλλων ζῴων ἕκαστον ;—
2 Δοκοῦσιν, ἔφη.—Οὐκοῦν καὶ ἄνθρωποι οἱ μὲν καλοί, οἱ δ᾽ αἰσχροί ;—Πῶς γὰρ οὔ ;—Πότερον οὖν κατὰ τὸ αὐτὸ ἕκαστα τούτων ἐν τῷ αὐτῷ γένει καλὰ προσαγορεύομεν ἢ ἰδίως ἕκαστον ;
3 οὕτως δ᾽ ὄψει αὐτό. ἐπειδὴ πρὸς ἄλλο μὲν ὁρῶμεν κύνα πεφυκότα, πρὸς ἄλλο δ᾽ ἵππον, πρὸς

4

CHAPTER I

Of personal adornment

ONCE, when he was visited by a young student of rhetoric whose hair was somewhat too elaborately dressed, and whose attire in general was highly embellished, Epictetus said : Tell me if you do not think that some dogs are beautiful, and some horses, and so every other creature.—I do, said the young man.—Is not the same true also of men, some of them are handsome, and some ugly?—Of course.—Do we, then, on the same grounds, pronounce each of these creatures in its own kind beautiful, or do we pronounce each beautiful on special grounds? I shall show you what I mean. Since we see that a dog is born to do one thing, and a horse another, and, if you will, a nightingale for something else, in general

5

ἄλλο δ' εἰ οὕτως τύχοι ἀηδόνα, καθόλου μὲν οὐκ
ἀτόπως ἀποφήναιτ' ἄν τις ἕκαστον τηνικαῦτα
καλὸν εἶναι, ὁπότε κατὰ τὴν αὑτοῦ φύσιν κράτιστ'
ἔχοι· ἐπεὶ δ' ἡ φύσις ἑκάστου διάφορός ἐστιν,
διαφόρως εἶναί μοι δοκεῖ ἕκαστον αὐτῶν καλόν·
4 ἢ γὰρ οὔ ;—Ὡμολόγει.—Οὐκ οὖν ὅπερ κύνα
ποιεῖ καλόν, τοῦτο ἵππον αἰσχρόν, ὅπερ δ' ἵππον
καλόν, τοῦτο κύνα αἰσχρόν, εἴ γε διάφοροι αἱ
5 φύσεις εἰσὶν αὐτῶν ;—Ἔοικεν.—Καὶ γὰρ τὸ
παγκρατιαστὴν οἶμαι ποιοῦν καλὸν τοῦτο παλαι-
στὴν οὐκ ἀγαθὸν ποιεῖ, δρομέα δὲ καὶ γελοιότα-
τον· καὶ ὁ πρὸς πενταθλίαν καλὸς ὁ αὐτὸς οὗτος
6 πρὸς πάλην αἴσχιστος ;—Οὕτως, ἔφη.—Τί οὖν
ποιεῖ ἄνθρωπον καλὸν ἢ ὅπερ τῷ γένει καὶ κύνα καὶ
ἵππον ;—Τοῦτο, ἔφη.—Τί οὖν ποιεῖ κύνα καλόν ; ἡ
ἀρετὴ ἡ κυνὸς παροῦσα. τί ἵππον ; ἡ ἀρετὴ ἡ¹
ἵππου παροῦσα. τί οὖν ἄνθρωπον ; μή ποθ' ἡ
7 ἀρετὴ ἡ ἀνθρώπου παροῦσα ; καὶ σὺ οὖν εἰ θέλεις
καλὸς εἶναι, νεανίσκε, τοῦτο ἐκπόνει, τὴν ἀρετὴν
8 τὴν ἀνθρωπικήν.—Τίς δ' ἐστὶν αὕτη ;—Ὅρα, τίνας
αὐτὸς ἐπαινεῖς, ὅταν δίχα πάθους τινὰς ἐπαινῇς·
πότερα τοὺς δικαίους ἢ τοὺς ἀδίκους ;—Τοὺς
δικαίους.—Πότερον τοὺς σώφρονας ἢ τοὺς ἀκο-
λάστους ;—Τοὺς σώφρονας.—Τοὺς ἐγκρατεῖς δ'
9 ἢ τοὺς ἀκρατεῖς ;—Τοὺς ἐγκρατεῖς.—Οὐκοῦν
τοιοῦτόν τινα ποιῶν σαυτὸν ἴσθι ὅτι καλὸν

¹ ἡ added by s.

---

¹ One who specialized in the *pancratium*, a combination of
boxing, wrestling, and plain " fighting."

it would not be unreasonable for one to declare that each of them was beautiful precisely when it achieved supreme excellence in terms of its own nature ; and, since each has a different nature, each one of them, I think, is beautiful in a different fashion. Is that not so?—He agreed.—Does it not follow, then, that precisely what makes a dog beautiful, makes a horse ugly, and precisely what makes a horse beautiful, makes a dog ugly, if, that is, their natures are different?—So it appears.—Yes, for, to my way of thinking, what makes a pancratiast [1] beautiful does not make a wrestler good, and, more than that, makes a runner quite absurd : and the same man who is beautiful for the pentathlon [2] is very ugly for wrestling?—That is so, said he.—What, then, makes a man beautiful other than just that which makes a dog or a horse beautiful in its kind?—Just that, said he.—What is it, then, that makes a dog beautiful? The presence of a dog's excellence. What makes a horse beautiful? The presence of a horse's excellence. What, then, makes a man beautiful? Is it not the presence of a man's excellence? Very well, then, young man, do you too, if you wish to be beautiful, labour to achieve this, the excellence that characterizes a man.—And what is that?—Observe who they are whom you yourself praise, when you praise people dispassionately ; is it the just, or the unjust?—The just ;—is it the temperate, or the dissolute ?—The temperate ;—and is it the self-controlled, or the uncontrolled?—The self-controlled.—In making yourself that kind of person, therefore, rest assured that you will be making your-

[2] An all-round competition in running, jumping, wrestling, and hurling the discus and the javelin.

ποιήσεις· μέχρις δ' ἂν τούτων ἀμελῇς, αἰσχρόν
σ' εἶναι ἀνάγκη, κἂν πάντα μηχανᾷ ὑπὲρ τοῦ
φαίνεσθαί σε[1] καλόν.

10 Ἐντεῦθεν οὐκέτι ἔχω σοι πῶς εἴπω· ἄν τε γὰρ
λέγω ἃ φρονῶ, ἀνιάσω σε καὶ ἐξελθὼν τάχα οὐδ'
εἰσελεύσῃ· ἄν τε μὴ λέγω, ὅρα οἷον ποιήσω, εἰ
σὺ μὲν ἔρχῃ πρὸς ἐμὲ ὠφεληθησόμενος, ἐγὼ[2] δ'
οὐκ ὠφελήσω σ' οὐδέν, καὶ σὺ μὲν ὡς πρὸς
φιλόσοφον, ἐγὼ δ' οὐδὲν ἐρῶ σοι ὡς φιλόσοφος.

11 πῶς δὲ καὶ οὐκ[3] ὠμόν ἐστι πρὸς αὐτόν σε τὸ
περιιδεῖν ἀνεπανόρθωτον; ἄν ποθ' ὕστερον

12 φρένας σχῇς, εὐλόγως μοι ἐγκαλέσεις· "τί εἶδεν
ἐν ἐμοὶ ὁ Ἐπίκτητος, ἵνα βλέπων με τοιοῦτον
εἰσερχόμενον πρὸς αὐτὸν οὕτως αἰσχρῶς ἔχοντα
περιίδῃ καὶ[4] μηδέποτε μηδὲ ῥῆμα εἴπῃ; οὕτως

13 μου ἀπέγνω; νέος οὐκ ἤμην; οὐκ ἤμην λόγου
ἀκουστικός; πόσοι δ' ἄλλοι νέοι ἐφ' ἡλικίας πολ-

14 λὰ τοιαῦτα διαμαρτάνουσιν; τινά ποτ' ἀκούω
Πολέμωνα ἐξ ἀκολαστοτάτου νεανίσκου τοσαύτην μεταβολὴν μεταβαλεῖν. ἔστω, οὐκ ᾤετό με
Πολέμωνα ἔσεσθαι· τὴν μὲν κόμην ἠδύνατό μου
διορθῶσαι, τὰ μὲν περιάμματά μου περιελεῖν,
ψιλούμενόν με παῦσαι ἠδύνατο, ἀλλὰ βλέπων

15 με—τίνος εἴπω;—σχῆμα ἔχοντα ἐσιώπα." ἐγὼ
οὐ λέγω, τίνος ἐστὶ τὸ σχῆμα τοῦτο· σὺ δ' αὐτὸ

---

[1] Or perhaps γε, Oldfather.   [2] s: ἔργωι S.
[3] οὐκ added by Koraes.   [4] καί supplied by s.

---

[1] Once when drunk he burst in upon Xenocrates, but was
converted by him and eventually succeeded him in the head-

8

self beautiful; but so long as you neglect all this, you must needs be ugly, no matter if you employ every artifice to make yourself look beautiful.

Beyond that I know not what more I can say to you; for if I say what I have in mind, I shall hurt your feelings, and you will leave, perhaps never to return; but if I do not say it, consider the sort of thing I shall be doing. Here you are coming to me to get some benefit, and I shall be bestowing no benefit at all; and you are coming to me as to a philosopher, and I shall be saying nothing to you as a philosopher. Besides, is it anything but cruel for me to leave you unreformed? If some time in the future you come to your senses, you will have good reason to blame me: "What did Epictetus observe in me," you will say to yourself, "that, although he saw me in such a condition and coming to him in so disgraceful a state, he should let me be so and say never a word to me? Did he so completely despair of me? Was I not young? Was I not ready to listen to reason? And how many other young fellows make any number of mistakes of the same kind in their youth? I am told that once there was a certain Polemo[1] who from being a very dissolute young man underwent such an astonishing transformation. Well, suppose he did not think that I should be another Polemo; he could at least have set my hair right, he could have stripped me of my ornaments, he could have made me stop plucking my hairs; but although he saw me looking like—what shall I say?—he held his peace." As for me, I do not say what it is you look

ship of the Academy. See below IV. 11. 30; Diogenes Laertius, 4, 16; and Horace, *Sat.* II. 3, 253-7.

ἐρεῖς τόθ', ὅταν εἰς σαυτὸν ἔλθῃς, καὶ γνώσει,
οἷόν ἐστι καὶ τίνες αὐτὸ ἐπιτηδεύουσι.

16   Τοῦτό μοι ὕστερον ἂν ἐγκαλῇς, τί ἔξω ἀπολογή-
σασθαι ; ναί· ἀλλ' ἐρῶ καὶ οὐ πεισθήσεται.
τῷ γὰρ Ἀπόλλωνι ἐπείσθη ὁ Λάϊος ; οὐκ ἀπελθὼν καὶ μεθυσθεὶς χαίρειν εἶπεν τῷ χρησμῷ ; τί
οὖν ; παρὰ τοῦτο οὐκ εἶπεν αὐτῷ ὁ Ἀπόλλων τὰς
17 ἀληθείας ; καίτοι ἐγὼ μὲν οὐκ οἶδα οὔτ' εἰ πει-
σθήσῃ μοι οὔτ' εἰ μή· ἐκεῖνος δ' ἀκριβέστατα ᾔδει
18 ὅτι οὐ πεισθήσεται, καὶ ὅμως εἶπεν.—Διὰ τί δ'
εἶπεν ;—Διὰ[1] τί δὲ Ἀπόλλων ἐστίν ; διὰ τί δὲ
χρησμῳδεῖ ; διὰ τί δ' εἰς ταύτην τὴν χώραν
ἑαυτὸν κατατέταχεν, ὥστε μάντις εἶναι καὶ πηγὴ
τῆς ἀληθείας καὶ πρὸς αὐτὸν ἔρχεσθαι τοὺς ἐκ
τῆς οἰκουμένης ; διὰ τί δὲ προγέγραπται τὸ γνῶθι
σαυτὸν μηδενὸς αὐτὸ νοοῦντος ;

19   Σωκράτης πάντας ἔπειθε τοὺς προσιόντας[2]
ἐπιμελεῖσθαι ἑαυτῶν ; οὐδὲ τὸ χιλιοστὸν μέρος.
ἀλλ' ὅμως ἐπειδὴ εἰς ταύτην τὴν τάξιν ὑπὸ τοῦ
δαιμονίου, ὥς φησιν αὐτός, κατετάχθη, μηκέτι
ἐξέλιπεν. ἀλλὰ καὶ πρὸς τοὺς δικαστὰς τί
20 λέγει· "ἄν μ' ἀφῆτε," φησίν, "ἐπὶ τούτοις, ἵνα
μηκέτι ταῦτα πράσσω ἃ νῦν, οὐκ ἀνέξομαι οὐδ'
ἀνήσω· ἀλλὰ καὶ νέῳ καὶ πρεσβυτέρῳ καὶ ἁπλῶς
ἀεὶ τῷ ἐντυγχάνοντι προσελθὼν πεύσομαι ταῦτα
ἃ καὶ νῦν πυνθάνομαι, πολὺ δὲ μάλιστα ὑμῶν,

---

[1] διά supplied by *s*.
[2] *s* : προσίοντας or προσανόντας *S*.

---

[1] Who warned him not to beget a son, the ill-starred Oedipus.

like, but *you* will say it, when you come to yourself, and will realize what it is and the kind of people those are who act this way.

If you bring this charge against me some day, what shall I be able to say in my own defence? Yes; but suppose I speak and he not obey. And did Laius obey Apollo?[1] Did he not go away and get drunk and say good-bye to the oracle? What then? Did that keep Apollo from telling him the truth? Whereas I do not know whether you will obey me or not. Apollo knew perfectly well that Laius would not obey, and yet he spoke.—But why did he speak?—And why is he Apollo? And why does he give out oracles? And why has he placed himself in this position,[2] to be a prophet and a fountain of truth, and for the inhabitants of the civilized world to come to him? And why are the words "Know thyself" carved on the front of his temple, although no one pays attention to them?

Did Socrates succeed in prevailing upon all his visitors to keep watch over their own characters? No, not one in a thousand. Nevertheless, once he had been assigned this post, as he himself says, by the ordinance of the Deity,[3] he never abandoned it. Nay, what does he say even to his judges? "If you acquit me," he says, "on these conditions, namely, that I no longer engage in my present practices, I will not accept your offer, neither will I give up my practices, but I will go up to young and old, and, in a word, to everyone that I meet, and put to him the same question that I put now, and beyond all others I will especially interrogate you," he says, "who are

[2] For the expression compare II. 4, 3; IV. 10, 16.
[3] Based upon the *Apology*, 28 E.

φησί, τῶν πολιτῶν, ὅτι ἐγγυτέρω μου γένει ἐστέ."

21 οὕτως περίεργος εἶ, ὦ Σώκρατες, καὶ πολυπράγμων; τί δέ σοι μέλει, τί ποιοῦμεν; "οἷον καὶ
λέγεις; κοινωνός μου ὢν καὶ συγγενὴς ἀμελεῖς
σεαυτοῦ καὶ τῇ πόλει παρέχεις πολίτην κακὸν

22 καὶ τοῖς συγγενέσι συγγενῆ καὶ τοῖς γείτοσι
γείτονα." "σὺ οὖν τίς εἶ;" ἐνταῦθα μέγα
ἐστὶ τὸ εἰπεῖν ὅτι "οὗτός εἰμι, ᾧ δεῖ μέλειν
ἀνθρώπων." οὐδὲ γὰρ λέοντι τὸ τυχὸν βοΐδιον
τολμᾷ ἀντιστῆναι αὐτῷ· ἂν δ' ὁ ταῦρος προσελθὼν ἀνθίστηται, λέγε αὐτῷ, ἄν σοι δόξῃ,
"σὺ δὲ τίς εἶ;" καὶ "τί σοὶ μέλει;" ἄνθρωπε,

23 ἐν παντὶ γένει φύεταί τι ἐξαίρετον· ἐν βουσίν,
ἐν κυσίν, ἐν μελίσσαις, ἐν ἵπποις. μὴ δὴ λέγε
τῷ ἐξαιρέτῳ "σὺ οὖν τί εἶ;" εἰ δὲ μή, ἐρεῖ
σοι φωνήν ποθεν λαβὸν "ἐγώ εἰμι τοιοῦτον οἷον
ἐν ἱματίῳ πορφύρα· μή μ' ἀξίου ὅμοιον εἶναι τοῖς
ἄλλοις ἢ τῇ φύσει μου ¹ μέμφου, ὅτι με διαφέροντα
παρὰ τοὺς ἄλλους ἐποίησεν."

24 Τί οὖν; ἐγὼ τοιοῦτος; πόθεν; σὺ γὰρ
τοιοῦτος οἷος ἀκούειν τἀληθῆ; ὤφελεν. ἀλλ' ὅμως
ἐπεί πως κατεκρίθην πώγωνα ἔχειν πολιὸν καὶ
τρίβωνα καὶ σὺ εἰσέρχῃ πρὸς ἐμὲ ὡς πρὸς φιλόσοφον, οὐ χρήσομαί σοι ὠμῶς οὐδ' ἀπογνωστικῶς,

---

¹ Deleted by Kronenberg, and "nature" rather than
"my nature" would seem to be more logical here (cf. Grant's
note on Aristotle's *Ethics*, 2.1.3). But μου is supported by
the precisely similar σου of § 30, which is if anything even
more illogical. In the original remark of Diogenes, whom
Epictetus is clearly quoting in § 30 (see the note at that
point), ἐγκαλεῖν τῇ φύσει is used as it is normally in Greek.
Apparently we have in these two locutions a form of
expression peculiar to Epictetus.

my fellow-citizens, inasmuch as you are nearer akin to me." [1] Are you so inquisitive, O Socrates, and meddlesome? And why do you care what we are about? "Why, what is that you are saying? You are my partner and kinsman, and yet you neglect yourself and provide the State with a bad citizen, and your kin with a bad kinsman, and your neighbours with a bad neighbour." "Well, who are you?" Here it is a bold thing to say, "I am he who must needs take interest in men." For no ordinary ox dares to withstand the lion himself; [2] but if the bull comes up and withstands him, say to the bull, if you think fit, "But who are you?" and "What do you care?" Man, in every species nature produces some superior individual, among cattle, dogs, bees, horses. Pray do not say to the superior individual, "Well, then, who are you?" Or if you do, it will get a voice from somewhere and reply to you, "I am the same sort of thing as red in a mantle; [3] do not expect me to resemble the rest, and do not blame my nature [4] because it has made me different from the rest."

What follows? Am I that kind of person? Impossible. Are you, indeed, the kind of person to listen to the truth? I would that you were! But nevertheless, since somehow or other I have been condemned to wear a grey beard and a rough cloak, [5] and you are coming to me as to a philosopher, I shall not treat you cruelly, nor as though I despaired of

---

[1] A free paraphrase of the *Apology*, 29 C, E, and 30 A. Compare also I. 9, 23.

[2] Compare I. 2, 30.

[3] Compare I. 2, 17 (and note, where read " bright red ") and 22 ; the reference is to the stripe in the *toga praetexta*.

[4] See critical note.

[5] External symbols of a philosopher.

ἀλλ' ἐρῶ· νεανίσκε, τίνα θέλεις καλὸν ποιεῖν;
25 γνῶθι πρῶτον τίς εἶ καὶ οὕτως κόσμει σεαυτόν.
ἄνθρωπος εἶ· τοῦτο δ' ἐστὶ θνητὸν ζῷον
χρηστικὸν φαντασίαις λογικῶς. τὸ δὲ λογικῶς
τί ἐστιν; φύσει ὁμολογουμένως καὶ τελέως.
26 τί οὖν ἐξαίρετον ἔχεις; τὸ ζῷον; οὔ. τὸ θνητόν; οὔ. τὸ χρηστικὸν φαντασίαις; οὔ. τὸ
λογικὸν ἔχεις ἐξαίρετον· τοῦτο κόσμει καὶ
καλλώπιζε· τὴν κόμην δ' ἄφες τῷ πλάσαντι
27 ὡς αὐτὸς ἠθέλησεν. ἄγε, τίνας ἄλλας ἔχεις
προσηγορίας; ἀνὴρ εἶ ἢ γυνή;—Ἀνήρ.—Ἄνδρα
οὖν καλλώπιζε, μὴ γυναῖκα. ἐκείνη φύσει λεία
γέγονε καὶ τρυφερά· κἂν ἔχῃ τρίχας πολλάς,
τέρας ἐστὶ καὶ ἐν τοῖς τέρασιν ἐν Ῥώμῃ δείκνυται.
28 ταὐτὸ[1] δ' ἐπ' ἀνδρός ἐστι τὸ μὴ ἔχειν· κἂν μὲν
φύσει μὴ ἔχῃ, τέρας ἐστίν, ἂν δ' αὐτὸς ἑαυτοῦ
ἐκκόπτῃ καὶ ἀποτίλλῃ, τί αὐτὸν ποιήσωμεν; ποῦ
αὐτὸν δείξωμεν καὶ τί προγράψωμεν; "δείξω
ὑμῖν ἄνδρα, ὃς θέλει μᾶλλον γυνὴ εἶναι ἢ ἀνήρ."
29 ὦ δεινοῦ θεάματος· οὐδεὶς οὐχὶ θαυμάσει τὴν
προγραφήν· νὴ τὸν Δία, οἶμαι ὅτι αὐτοὶ οἱ τιλ-
λόμενοι οὐ παρακολουθοῦντες, ὅτι τοῦτ' αὐτό
30 ἐστιν, ὃ ποιοῦσιν, ποιοῦσιν. ἄνθρωπε, τί ἔχεις
ἐγκαλέσαι σου τῇ φύσει; ὅτι σε ἄνδρα ἐγέννη-
σεν; τί οὖν; πάσας ἔδει γυναῖκας γεννῆσαι; καὶ

---

[1] Wolf and Blass: τοῦτο S.

you, but I shall say: Young man, whom do you wish to make beautiful? First learn who you are, and then, in the light of that knowledge, adorn yourself. You are a human being; that is, a mortal animal gifted with the ability to use impressions rationally. And what is "rationally"? In accordance with nature and perfectly. What element of superiority, then, do you possess? The animal in you? No. Your mortality? No. Your ability to use impressions? No. Your reason is the element of superiority which you possess; adorn and beautify that; but leave your hair to Him who fashioned it as He willed. Come, what other designations apply to you? Are you a man or a woman?—A man.—Very well then, adorn a man, not a woman. Woman is born smooth and dainty by nature, and if she is very hairy she is a prodigy, and is exhibited at Rome among the prodigies. But for a man *not* to be hairy is the same thing, and if by nature he has no hair he is a prodigy, but if he cuts it out and plucks it out of himself, what shall we make of him? Where shall we exhibit him and what notice shall we post? "I will show you," we say to the audience, "a man who wishes to be a woman rather than a man." What a dreadful spectacle! No one but will be amazed at the notice; by Zeus, I fancy that even the men who pluck out their own hairs do what they do without realizing what it means. Man, what reason have you to complain against your nature?[1] Because it brought you into the world as a man?[2] What then? Ought it to have brought all persons into the world

[1] Compare the critical note on § 23.
[2] An almost verbatim quotation from Diogenes the Cynic. See Athenaeus, XIII. 565 C.

τί ἂν ὄφελος ἦν σοι τοῦ κοσμεῖσθαι ; τίνι ἂν
31 ἐκοσμοῦ, εἰ πάντες ἦσαν γυναῖκες ; ἀλλ᾽ οὐκ
ἀρέσκει σοι τὸ πραγμάτιον ; ὅλον δι᾽ ὅλων αὐτὸ
ποίησον· ἆρον—τί ποτ᾽ ἐκεῖνο ;—τὸ αἴτιον τῶν
τριχῶν· ποίησον εἰς ἅπαντα σαυτὸν γυναῖκα, ἵνα
μὴ πλανώμεθα, μὴ τὸ μὲν ἥμισυ ἀνδρός, τὸ δ᾽
32 ἥμισυ γυναικός. τίνι θέλεις ἀρέσαι ; τοῖς γυναι-
καρίοις ; ὡς [1] ἀνὴρ αὐτοῖς ἄρεσον. "ναί· ἀλλὰ
τοῖς λείοις χαίρουσιν." οὐκ ἀπάγξῃ ; καὶ εἰ τοῖς
33 κιναίδοις ἔχαιρον, ἐγένου ἂν κίναιδος ; τοῦτό σοι
τὸ ἔργον ἐστίν, ἐπὶ τοῦτο ἐγεννήθης, ἵνα σοι αἱ
34 γυναῖκες αἱ ἀκόλαστοι χαίρωσιν ; τοιοῦτόν σε
θῶμεν πολίτην Κορινθίων, κἂν οὕτως τύχῃ, ἀστυ-
νόμον ἢ ἐφήβαρχον ἢ στρατηγὸν ἢ ἀγωνοθέτην ;
35 ἄγε καὶ γαμήσας τίλλεσθαι μέλλεις ; τίνι καὶ
ἐπὶ τί ; καὶ παιδία ποιήσας εἶτα κἀκεῖνα τιλλόμενα
ἡμῖν εἰσάξεις εἰς τὸ πολίτευμα ; καλὸς πολίτης
καὶ βουλευτὴς καὶ ῥήτωρ. τοιούτους δεῖ νέους
εὔχεσθαι ἡμῖν φύεσθαι καὶ ἀνατρέφεσθαι ;

36   Μή, τοὺς θεούς σοι, νεανίσκε· ἀλλ᾽ ἅπαξ
ἀκούσας τῶν λόγων τούτων ἀπελθὼν σαυτῷ εἰπέ·
"ταῦτά μοι Ἐπίκτητος οὐκ εἴρηκεν· πόθεν γὰρ
ἐκείνῳ ; ἀλλὰ θεός τίς ποτ᾽ εὐμενὴς δι᾽ ἐκείνου.
οὐδὲ γὰρ ἂν ἐπῆλθεν Ἐπικτήτῳ ταῦτα εἰπεῖν

---

[1] *Sb* ; ὦ *S*.

---

[1] Compare I. 29, 16 together with note on that passage,
and for a more extended discussion *Trans. of the Amer.
Philol. Assoc.*, 52 (1921), 46.
[2] The interlocutor must have been a Corinthian.

as women? And if that had been the case, what
good would you be getting of your self-adornment?
For whom would you be adorning yourself, if all
were women? Your paltry body[1] doesn't please
you, eh? Make a clean sweep of the whole matter;
eradicate your—whatshall I call it?—the cause of your
hairiness; make yourself a woman all over, so as not
to deceive us, not half-man and half-woman. Whom
do you wish to please? Frail womankind? Please
them as a man. "Yes, but they like smooth men."
Oh, go hang! And if they liked sexual perverts,
would you have become such a pervert? Is this
your business in life, is this what you were born for,
that licentious women should take pleasure in you?
Shall we make a man like you a citizen of Corinth,[2]
and perchance a warden of the city, or superintendent of ephebi,[3] or general, or superintendent of the
games? Well, and when you have married are you
going to pluck out your hairs? For whom and to
what end? And when you have begotten boys, are
you going to introduce them into the body of
citizens as plucked creatures too? A fine citizen
and senator and orator! Is this the kind of young
men we ought to pray to have born and brought up
for us?

By the gods, young man, may such not be your fate!
But once you have heard these words go away and say
to yourself, "It was not Epictetus who said these
things to me; why, how could they have occurred to
him? but it was some kindly god or other speaking
through him. For it would not have occurred to
Epictetus to say these things, because he is not in

[3] Young men completing their education and serving their
term in the army.

37 οὐκ εἰωθότι λέγειν πρὸς οὐδένα. ἄγε οὖν τῷ θεῷ
πεισθῶμεν, ἵνα μὴ θεοχόλωτοι ὦμεν." οὔ· ἀλλ'
ἂν μὲν κόραξ κραυγάζων σημαίνῃ σοί τι, οὐχ ὁ
κόραξ ἐστὶν ὁ σημαίνων, ἀλλ' ὁ θεὸς δι' αὐτοῦ·
ἂν δὲ δι' ἀνθρωπίνης φωνῆς σημαίνῃ τι, τὸν
ἄνθρωπον προσποιήσῃ [1] λέγειν σοι ταῦτα, ἵν'
ἀγνοῇς [2] τὴν δύναμιν τοῦ δαιμονίου, ὅτι τοῖς μὲν
οὕτως, τοῖς δ' ἐκείνως σημαίνει, περὶ δὲ τῶν
μεγίστων καὶ κυριωτάτων διὰ [3] καλλίστου ἀγ-
38 γέλου σημαίνει; τί ἐστιν ἄλλο, ὃ λέγει ὁ ποιη-
τής;

ἐπεὶ πρό οἱ εἴπομεν [4] ἡμεῖς,
Ἑρμείαν πέμψαντε διάκτορον [5] ἀργειφόντην,
μήτ' αὐτὸν κτείνειν μήτε μνάασθαι ἄκοιτιν.

39 ὁ Ἑρμῆς καταβὰς ἔμελλεν Αἰγίσθῳ [6] λέγειν ταῦτα
καὶ σοὶ νῦν λέγουσιν οἱ θεοὶ ταῦτα,

Ἑρμείαν πέμψαντε [7] διάκτορον ἀργειφόντην,

μὴ ἐκστρέφειν τὰ καλῶς ἔχοντα μηδὲ περιεργάζε-
σθαι, ἀλλ' ἀφεῖναι τὸν ἄνδρα ἄνδρα, τὴν γυναῖκα
γυναῖκα, τὸν καλὸν ὡς ἄνθρωπον καλόν, [8] τὸν
40 αἰσχρὸν ὡς ἄνθρωπον αἰσχρόν. ὅτι οὐκ εἶ κρέας
οὐδὲ τρίχες, ἀλλὰ προαίρεσις· ταύτην ἂν σχῇς
41 καλήν, τότ' ἔσει καλός. μέχρι δὲ νῦν οὐ τολμῶ

---

[1] Blass : ποιήσει S.   [2] Blass : ἵνα γνοίης S.
[3] διά supplied by Sb.
[4] Upton from Homer : ἐπεὶ οἱ προείπομεν S.
[5] Oldfather : πέμψαντες εὔσκοπον S. The reading restored
is that of Zenodotus and Aristophanes, which has left some
traces in two MSS., one scholium, and a papyrus of the 3rd
cent. after Christ, and especially in § 39 below. See my note
in Class. Philol., vol. 22, for a full discussion of this passage.
[6] Bentley : αὐτῷ S. For arguments in favour of Bentley's
emendation see Trans. Am. Philol. Ass. 52 (1921) 49.

the habit of speaking to anyone. Come then, let us obey God, that we rest not under His wrath." Nay, but if a raven gives you a sign by his croaking, it is not the raven that gives the sign, but God through the raven ; whereas if He gives you a sign through a human voice, will you pretend that it is the man who is saying these things to you, so that you may remain ignorant of the power of the divinity, that He gives signs to some men in this way, and to others in that, but that in the greatest and most sovereign matters He gives His sign through His noblest messenger? What else does the poet mean when he says :

> Since ourselves we did warn him,
> Sending down Hermes, the messenger god, the
>   slayer of Argus,
> Neither to murder the husband himself, nor make
>   love to his consort ?[1]

As Hermes descended to tell Aegisthus that, so now the gods tell you the same thing,

> Sending down Hermes, the messenger god, the
>   slayer of Argus,

not to distort utterly nor to take useless pains about that which is already right, but to leave the man a man, and the woman a woman, the beautiful person beautiful as a human being, the ugly ugly as a human being. Because *you* are not flesh, nor hair, but moral purpose; if you get that beautiful, then *you* will be beautiful. So far I do not have the

---

[1] Homer, *Odyssey*, a, 37-9.

[7] πέμψαντες S ; see note 5 above.
[8] Oldfather : τὸν καλὸν ἄνθρωπον ὡς καλὸν ἄνθρωπον S.

19

σοι λέγειν, ὅτι αἰσχρὸς εἶ· δοκεῖς γάρ μοι πάντα
42 θέλειν ἀκοῦσαι ἢ τοῦτο. ἀλλ᾽ ὅρα, τί λέγει
Σωκράτης τῷ καλλίστῳ πάντων καὶ ὡραιοτάτῳ
Ἀλκιβιάδῃ· "πειρῶ οὖν καλὸς εἶναι." τί αὐτῷ
λέγει; "πλάσσε σου τὴν κόμην καὶ τίλλε σου
τὰ σκέλη"; μὴ γένοιτο· ἀλλὰ "κόσμει σου τὴν
43 προαίρεσιν, ἔξαιρε τὰ φαῦλα δόγματα." τὸ
σωμάτιον οὖν πῶς; ὡς πέφυκεν. ἄλλῳ τούτων
44 ἐμέλησεν· ἐκείνῳ ἐπίτρεψον.[1]—Τί οὖν; ἀκάθαρτον δεῖ εἶναι;—Μὴ γένοιτο· ἀλλ᾽ ὃς εἶ καὶ πέφυκας, τοῦτον κάθαιρε, ἄνδρα ὡς ἄνδρα καθάριον
45 εἶναι, γυναῖκα ὡς γυναῖκα, παιδίον ὡς παιδίον. οὔ·
ἀλλὰ καὶ τοῦ λέοντος ἐκτίλωμεν τὴν κόμην, ἵνα μὴ
ἀκάθαρτος ᾖ, καὶ τοῦ ἀλεκτρυόνος τὸν λόφον· δεῖ
γὰρ καὶ τοῦτον καθάριον εἶναι. ἀλλ᾽ ὡς ἀλεκτρυόνα καὶ ἐκεῖνον ὡς λέοντα καὶ τὸν κυνηγετικὸν
κύνα ὡς κυνηγετικόν.

β΄. Περὶ τίνα ἀσκεῖσθαι δεῖ τὸν προκόψοντα καὶ
ὅτι τῶν κυριωτάτων ἀμελοῦμεν.

1 Τρεῖς εἰσὶ τόποι, περὶ οὓς ἀσκηθῆναι δεῖ τὸν
ἐσόμενον καλὸν καὶ ἀγαθόν· ὁ περὶ τὰς ὀρέξεις
καὶ τὰς ἐκκλίσεις, ἵνα μήτ᾽ ὀρεγόμενος ἀποτυγχάνῃ
2 μήτ᾽ ἐκκλίνων περιπίπτῃ· ὁ περὶ τὰς ὁρμὰς καὶ

---

¹ ἐπίστρεψον S originally.

---

[1] An inexact quotation of Plato, *Alcib.* I. 131 D.
[2] Compare I, 25, 13 ; 30, 1 ; II. 5, 22.
[3] The implication is that the interlocutor's conception of
"cleanliness" has to do merely with things external.
[4] Compare II. 17, 15 ff. This triple division of philosophy
is the one original element in the teaching of Epictetus, and
even it is rather a pedagogical device than an innovation in

courage to tell you that you are ugly, for it looks to me as though you would rather hear anything than that. But observe what Socrates says to Alcibiades, the most handsome and youthfully beautiful of men : "Try, then, to be beautiful."[1] What does he tell him? "Dress your locks and pluck the hairs out of your legs?" God forbid! No, he says, "Make beautiful your moral purpose, eradicate your worthless opinions." How treat your paltry body, then? As its nature is. This is the concern of Another;[2] leave it to Him.—What then? Does the body have to be left unclean?—God forbid! but the man that you are and were born to be, keep that man clean, a man to be clean as a man, a woman as a woman, a child as a child. No, but let's pluck out also the lion's mane, so that he may not fail to be "cleaned up," and the cock's comb, for he too ought to be "cleaned up"![3] Clean? Yes, but clean as a cock, and the other clean as a lion, and the hunting dog clean as a hunting dog!

CHAPTER II

The fields of study in which the man who expects to make progress will have to go into training ; and that we neglect what is most important

THERE are three fields of study[4] in which the man who is going to be good and excellent must first have been trained. The first has to do with desires and aversions, that he may never fail to get what he desires, nor fall into what he avoids ; the second

thought. Compare Vol. I. p. xxi, and the literature there cited.

ἀφορμὰς καὶ ἁπλῶς ὁ περὶ τὸ καθῆκον, ἵνα τάξει,
ἵνα εὐλογίστως, ἵνα μὴ ἀμελῶς· τρίτος ἐστὶν ὁ περὶ
τὴν ἀνεξαπατησίαν καὶ ἀνεικαιότητα καὶ ὅλως ὁ
3 περὶ τὰς συγκαταθέσεις. τούτων κυριώτατος καὶ
μάλιστα ἐπείγων ἐστὶν ὁ περὶ τὰ πάθη· πάθος
γὰρ ἄλλως οὐ γίνεται εἰ μὴ ὀρέξεως ἀποτυγχανού-
σης ἢ ἐκκλίσεως περιπιπτούσης. οὗτός ἐστιν ὁ
ταραχάς, θορύβους, ἀτυχίας, ὁ δυστυχίας ἐπι-
φέρων, ὁ πένθη, οἰμωγάς, φθόνους, ὁ φθονερούς,[1] ὁ
ζηλοτύπους ποιῶν, δι' ὧν οὐδ' ἀκοῦσαι λόγου
4 δυνάμεθα. δεύτερός ἐστιν ὁ περὶ τὸ καθῆκον·
οὐ δεῖ γάρ με εἶναι ἀπαθῆ ὡς ἀνδριάντα, ἀλλὰ
τὰς σχέσεις τηροῦντα τὰς φυσικὰς καὶ ἐπιθέτους
ὡς εὐσεβῆ, ὡς υἱόν, ὡς ἀδελφόν, ὡς πατέρα, ὡς
πολίτην.

5 Τρίτος ἐστὶν ὁ ἤδη τοῖς προκόπτουσιν ἐπι-
βάλλων, ὁ περὶ τὴν αὐτῶν τούτων ἀσφάλειαν,
ἵνα μηδ' ἐν ὕπνοις λάθῃ τις ἀνεξέταστος παρελ-
θοῦσα φαντασία μηδ' ἐν οἰνώσει μηδὲ μελαγ-
χολῶντος.—Τοῦτο ὑπὲρ ἡμᾶς, φησίν, ἐστίν.—
6 Οἱ δὲ νῦν φιλόσοφοι ἀφέντες τὸν πρῶτον τόπον
καὶ τὸν δεύτερον καταγίνονται περὶ τὸν τρίτον·
μεταπίπτοντας, τῷ[2] ἠρωτῆσθαι περαίνοντας,

---

[1] φόβους (" fears ") conjectured by Reiske, very plausibly.
[2] τῷ added by Oldfather after the similar correction by s in
I. 7, 1 (where the fact that τῷ is due to s should have been
recorded).

---

[1] A briefer definition is given in I. 27, 10.
[2] See critical note.
[3] The expression is not logical, for the *field of study*

with cases of choice and of refusal, and, in general, with duty, that he may act in an orderly fashion, upon good reasons, and not carelessly; the third with the avoidance of error and rashness in judgement, and, in general, about cases of assent. Among these the most important and especially pressing is that which has to do with the stronger emotions; for a strong emotion does not arise except a desire fails to attain its object, or an aversion falls into what it would avoid.[1] This is the field of study which introduces to us confusions, tumults, misfortunes and calamities; and sorrows, lamentations, envies;[2] and makes[3] us envious and jealous—passions which make it impossible for us even to listen to reason. The second field of study deals with duty; for I ought not to be unfeeling like a statue, but should maintain my relations, both natural and acquired, as a religious man, as a son, a brother, a father, a citizen.

The third belongs only to those who are already making progress; it has to do with the element of certainty in the matters which have just been mentioned, so that even in dreams, or drunkenness, or a state of melancholy-madness, a man may not be taken unawares by the appearance of an untested sense-impression.—This, says someone, is beyond us.—But philosophers nowadays pass by the first and second fields of study, and concentrate upon the third, upon arguments which involve equivocal premises, which derive syllogisms by the process of interrogation, which involve hypothetical premises,[4]

obviously can do nothing of the kind, but the fault is probably not in the MS. tradition.

[4] See I. 7, 1, and note for these first three.

7 ὑποθετικούς, Ψευδομένους.[1]—Δεῖ γάρ, φησίν, καὶ
ἐν ταῖς ὕλαις ταύταις γενόμενον διαφυλάξαι τὸ
ἀνεξαπάτητον.—Τίνα ;—τὸν καλὸν καὶ ἀγαθόν.—

8 σοὶ οὖν τοῦτο λείπει ; τὰς ἄλλας ἐκπεπόνηκας ;
περὶ κερμάτιον ἀνεξαπάτητος εἶ ; ἐὰν ἴδῃς
κοράσιον καλόν, ἀντέχεις τῇ φαντασίᾳ ; ἂν ὁ
γείτων σου κληρονομήσῃ, οὐ δάκνῃ ; νῦν οὐδὲν

9 ἄλλο σοι λείπει ἢ ἡ ἀμεταπτωσία ; τάλας, αὐτὰ
ταῦτα τρέμων μανθάνεις καὶ ἀγωνιῶν, μή τίς σου
καταφρονήσῃ, καὶ πυνθανόμενος, μή τίς τι περὶ

10 σοῦ λέγει. κἄν τις ἐλθὼν εἴπῃ σοι ὅτι "λόγου
γινομένου, τίς ἄριστός ἐστι τῶν φιλοσόφων,
παρών τις ἔλεγεν, ὅτι εἷς φιλόσοφος ὁ δεῖνα,"
γέγονέ σου τὸ ψυχάριον ἀντὶ δακτυλιαίου δίπηχυ.
ἂν δ' ἄλλος παρὼν εἴπῃ "οὐδὲν εἴρηκας, οὐκ
ἔστιν ἄξιον τοῦ δεῖνος ἀκροᾶσθαι· τί γὰρ οἶδεν ;
τὰς πρώτας ἀφορμὰς ἔχει, πλέον δ' οὐδέν,"
ἐξέστηκας, ὠχρίακας, εὐθὺς κέκραγας "ἐγὼ αὐτῷ

11 δείξω, τίς εἰμί, ὅτι μέγας φιλόσοφος." βλέπεται
ἐξ αὐτῶν τούτων. τί θέλεις ἐξ ἄλλων δεῖξαι ;
οὐκ οἶδας, ὅτι Διογένης τῶν σοφιστῶν τινὰ οὕτως
ἔδειξεν ἐκτείνας τὸν μέσον δάκτυλον, εἶτα ἐκμα-
νέντος αὐτοῦ "Οὗτός ἐστιν," ἔφη, "ὁ δεῖνα·

12 ἔδειξα ὑμῖν αὐτόν" ; ἄνθρωπος γὰρ δακτύλῳ οὐ

---

[1] Oldfather : ψευδομένους vulg. See explanatory note.

---

[1] *i.e.*, if a man says he is lying, is he really lying, or telling
the truth? See II. 17, 34, and note. Ψευδομένους is used
without the article, as in II. 21, 17.

[2] Literally, "from a finger's breadth (·7 in.) to two cubits."

[3] See Diogenes Laertius, 6, 34, who says that Demosthenes
was the man thus pointed at.

and sophisms like *The Liar*.[1]—Of course, he says, even when a man is engaged in subjects of this kind he has to preserve his freedom from deception.—But what kind of a man ought to engage in them?— Only the one who is already good and excellent.— Do you, then, fall short in this? Have you already attained perfection in the other subjects? Are you proof against deception in handling small change? If you see a pretty wench, do you resist the sense-impression? If your neighbour receives an inheritance, do you not feel a twinge of envy? And is security of judgement now the only thing in which you fall short? Wretch, even while you are study-ing these very topics you tremble and are worried for fear someone despises you, and you ask whether anybody is saying anything about you. And if someone should come and say, "A discussion arising as to who was the best of the philosophers, someone who was there said that So-and-so was the only real philosopher," immediately your poor little one-inch soul shoots up a yard high.[2] But if another party to the discussion says, "Nonsense, it's a waste of time to listen to So-and-so. Why, what does he know? He has the rudiments, but nothing else," you are beside yourself, you grow pale, immediately you shout, "I'll show him who I am, that I am a great philosopher!" Yet we see what a man is by just such conduct. Why do you wish to show it by any-thing else? Do you not know that Diogenes[3] showed one of the sophists thus, pointing out his middle finger at him,[4] and then when the man was furious with rage, remarked, "That's So-and-so; I've pointed him out to you." For a man is not some-

---

[4] Regarded in antiquity as an insulting gesture.

δείκνυται ὡς λίθος ἢ ὡς ξύλον, ἀλλ' ὅταν τις τὰ
δόγματα αὐτοῦ δείξῃ, τότε αὐτὸν ὡς ἄνθρωπον
ἔδειξεν.

13 Βλέπωμεν καὶ σοῦ τὰ δόγματα. μὴ γὰρ οὐ
δῆλόν ἐστιν, ὅτι σὺ τὴν προαίρεσιν τὴν σαυτοῦ
ἐν οὐδενὶ τίθεσαι, ἔξω δὲ βλέπεις εἰς τὰ ἀπροαίρετα, τί ἐρεῖ ὁ δεῖνα καὶ τίς εἶναι δόξεις, εἰ
φιλόλογος, εἰ Χρύσιππον ἀνεγνωκὼς[1] ἢ ᾿Αντίπα-
τρον ; εἰ μὲν γὰρ καὶ ᾿Αρχέδημον, ἀπέχεις
14 ἅπαντα. τί ἔτι ἀγωνιᾷς, μὴ οὐ δείξῃς ἡμῖν, τίς
εἶ ; θέλεις σοι εἴπω, τίνα ἡμῖν ἔδειξας ; ἄνθρωπον
παριόντα[2] ταπεινόν, μεμψίμοιρον, ὀξύθυμον,
δειλόν, πάντα μεμφόμενον, πᾶσιν ἐγκαλοῦντα,
μηδέποτε ἡσυχίαν ἄγοντα, πέρπερον· ταῦτα
15 ἡμῖν ἔδειξας. ἄπελθε νῦν καὶ ἀναγίγνωσκε
᾿Αρχέδημον· εἶτα μῦς ἂν καταπέσῃ καὶ ψοφήσῃ,
ἀπέθανες. τοιοῦτος γάρ σε μένει θάνατος, οἷος[3]
καὶ τὸν—τίνα ποτ᾿ ἐκεῖνον ;—τὸν Κρῖνιν.[4] καὶ
16 ἐκεῖνος μέγα ἐφρόνει, ὅτι ἐνόει ᾿Αρχέδημον. τάλας
οὐ θέλεις ἀφεῖναι ταῦτα τὰ μηδὲν πρὸς σέ ;
πρέπει ταῦτα τοῖς δυναμένοις δίχα ταραχῆς αὐτὰ
μανθάνειν, οἷς ἔξεστιν εἰπεῖν " οὐκ ὀργίζομαι, οὐ
λυποῦμαι, οὐ φθονῶ, οὐ κωλύομαι, οὐκ ἀναγ-
κάζομαι. τί μοι λοιπόν ; εὐσχολῶ, ἡσυχίαν
17 ἄγω. ἴδωμεν, πῶς περὶ τὰς μεταπτώσεις τῶν

---

[1] Kronenberg: ἀνέγνως S.
[2] ἀνθρωπάριον ("a mean little person") very plausibly
suggested by Reiske.
[3] Menage: οἷον S. [4] Reiske: κρίνειν S.

---

[1] See critical note.
[2] A Stoic philosopher of no great prominence, who must be
supposed to have died from an apoplectic stroke occasioned by

thing like a stone or a stick of wood to be pointed out with a finger, but when one shows a man's judgements, then one shows him as a man.

Let us take a look at your judgements too. Is it not evident that you set no value on your own moral purpose, but look beyond to the things that lie outside the province of the moral purpose, namely, what So-and-so will say, and what impression you will make, whether men will think you a scholar, or that you have read Chrysippus or Antipater? Why, if you have read them and Archedemus too, you have everything! Why are you any longer worried for fear you will not show us who you are? Do you wish me to tell you what kind of a man you have shown us that you are? A person who comes into our presence[1] mean, hypercritical, quick-tempered, cowardly, finding fault with everything, blaming everybody, never quiet, vain-glorious; these are the qualities which you have exhibited to us. Go away now and read Archedemus; then if a mouse falls down and makes a noise, you are dead with fright. For the same kind of death awaits you that carried off—what's his name?—oh, yes, Crinus.[2] He, too, was proud of himself because he could understand Archedemus. Wretch, are you not willing to let alone those things that do not concern you? They are appropriate for those who can study them without disturbance of spirit, who have the right to say, "I do not yield to anger, or sorrow, or envy; I am not subject to restraint, or to compulsion. What do I yet lack? I enjoy leisure, I have peace of mind. Let us see how we ought to deal with equivocal

fright at a mouse falling down from the wall. See Von Arnim in the *Real-Encyclopädie*,[2] *s.v.*

λόγων δεῖ ἀναστρέφεσθαι· ἴδωμεν, πῶς ὑπόθεσίν
τις λαβὼν εἰς οὐδὲν ἄτοπον ἀπαχθήσεται."
18 ἐκείνων ἐστὶ ταῦτα. τοῖς εὖ παθοῦσι πρέπει
πῦρ καίειν, ἀριστᾶν, ἂν οὕτως τύχῃ, καὶ ᾄδειν
καὶ ὀρχεῖσθαι· βυθιζομένου δὲ τοῦ πλοίου σύ μοι
παρελθὼν ἐπαίρεις τοὺς σιφάρους.

γ΄. Τίς ὕλη τοῦ ἀγαθοῦ καὶ πρὸς τί μάλιστ'
ἀσκητέον.

1 "Ὕλη τοῦ καλοῦ καὶ ἀγαθοῦ τὸ ἴδιον ἡγεμονικόν, τὸ σῶμα δ' ἰατροῦ καὶ ἰατραλείπτου,[1] ὁ
ἀγρὸς γεωργοῦ ὕλη· ἔργον δὲ καλοῦ καὶ ἀγαθοῦ
2 τὸ χρῆσθαι ταῖς φαντασίαις κατὰ φύσιν. πέφυκεν δὲ πᾶσα ψυχὴ ὥσπερ τῷ ἀληθεῖ ἐπινεύειν,
πρὸς τὸ ψεῦδος ἀνανεύειν, πρὸς τὸ ἄδηλον
ἐπέχειν, οὕτως πρὸς μὲν τὸ ἀγαθὸν ὀρεκτικῶς
κινεῖσθαι, πρὸς δὲ τὸ κακὸν ἐκκλιτικῶς, πρὸς
3 δὲ τὸ μήτε κακὸν μήτ' ἀγαθὸν οὐδετέρως. ὡς
γὰρ τὸ τοῦ Καίσαρος νόμισμα οὐκ ἔξεστιν ἀπο-
δοκιμάσαι τῷ τραπεζίτῃ οὐδὲ τῷ λαχανοπώλῃ,
ἀλλ' ἂν δείξῃς, θέλει οὐ θέλει, προέσθαι αὐτὸν
δεῖ τὸ ἀντ' αὐτοῦ πωλούμενον, οὕτως ἔχει καὶ ἐπὶ
4 τῆς ψυχῆς. τὸ ἀγαθὸν φανὲν εὐθὺς ἐκίνησεν ἐφ'
αὑτό, τὸ κακὸν ἀφ' αὑτοῦ. οὐδέποτε δ' ἀγαθοῦ
φαντασίαν ἐναργῆ ἀποδοκιμάσει ψυχή, οὐ μᾶλ-

[1] Schweighäuser: ἀπαλείπτου S.

premises in arguments; let us see how a person may adopt an hypothesis and yet not be led to an absurd conclusion." These things belong to men of that type. When men are prospering it is appropriate to light a fire, to take luncheon, and, if you will, even to sing and dance; but when the ship is already sinking you come up to me and start to hoist the topsails!

CHAPTER III

What is the subject-matter with which the good man has to deal; and what should be the chief object of our training?

THE subject-matter with which the good and excellent man has to deal is his own governing principle, that of a physician and the masseur is the body, of a farmer is his farm; but the function of the good and excellent man is to deal with his impressions in accordance with nature. Now just as it is the nature of every soul to assent to the true, dissent from the false, and to withhold judgement in a matter of uncertainty, so it is its nature to be moved with desire toward the good, with aversion toward the evil, and feel neutral toward what is neither evil nor good. For just as neither the banker nor the greengrocer may legally refuse the coinage of Caesar, but if you present it, whether he will or no, he must turn over to you what you are purchasing with it, so it is also with the soul. The instant the good appears it attracts the soul to itself, while the evil repels the soul from itself. A soul will never refuse a clear sense-impression of good,

λον ἢ τὸ Καίσαρος νόμισμα. ἔνθεν ἐξήρτηται
πᾶσα κίνησις καὶ ἀνθρώπου καὶ θεοῦ.
5 Διὰ τοῦτο πάσης οἰκειότητος προκρίνεται τὸ
ἀγαθόν. οὐδὲν ἐμοὶ καὶ τῷ πατρί, ἀλλὰ τῷ
ἀγαθῷ. "οὕτως εἶ σκληρός;" οὕτως γὰρ
πέφυκα· τοῦτό μοι τὸ νόμισμα δέδωκεν ὁ θεός·
6 διὰ τοῦτο, εἰ τοῦ καλοῦ καὶ δικαίου τὸ ἀγαθὸν
ἕτερόν ἐστιν, οἴχεται καὶ πατὴρ καὶ ἀδελφὸς καὶ
7 πατρὶς καὶ πάντα τὰ πράγματα. ἀλλ' ἐγὼ τὸ
ἐμὸν ἀγαθὸν ὑπερίδω, ἵνα σὺ σχῇς, καὶ παρα-
χωρήσω σοι; ἀντὶ τίνος; "πατήρ σου εἰμί."
ἀλλ' οὐκ ἀγαθόν. "ἀδελφός σου εἰμί." ἀλλ'
8 οὐκ ἀγαθόν. ἐὰν δ' ἐν ὀρθῇ προαιρέσει θῶμεν,
αὐτὸ τὸ¹ τηρεῖν τὰς σχέσεις ἀγαθὸν γίνεται καὶ
λοιπὸν ὁ τῶν ἐκτός τινων ἐκχωρῶν, οὗτος τοῦ
9 ἀγαθοῦ τυγχάνει. "αἴρει τὰ χρήματα ὁ πατήρ."
ἀλλ' οὐ βλάπτει. "ἕξει τὸ πλέον τοῦ ἀγροῦ ὁ
ἀδελφός."² ὅσον καὶ θέλει. μή τι οὖν τοῦ
αἰδήμονος, μή τι τοῦ πιστοῦ, μή τι τοῦ φιλα-
10 δέλφου; ἐκ ταύτης γὰρ τῆς οὐσίας τίς δύναται
ἐκβαλεῖν; οὐδ' ὁ Ζεύς. οὐδὲ γὰρ ἠθέλησεν, ἀλλ'
ἐπ' ἐμοὶ αὐτὸ ἐποίησεν καὶ ἔδωκεν οἷον εἶχεν
αὐτός, ἀκώλυτον, ἀνανάγκαστον, ἀπαραπόδιστον.
11 Ὅταν οὖν ἄλλῳ ἄλλο τὸ νόμισμα ᾖ, ἐκεῖνό
τις³ δείξας ἔχει τὸ ἀντ' αὐτοῦ πιπρασκόμενον.
12 ἐλήλυθεν εἰς τὴν ἐπαρχίαν κλέπτης ἀνθύπατος.
τίνι νομίσματι χρῆται; ἀργυρίῳ. δεῖξον καὶ
ἀπόφερε ὃ θέλεις. ἐλήλυθεν μοιχός. τίνι νομίσ-

¹ τό added by Reiske.
² ὁ ἀδελφός added by Schweighäuser.
³ Sb (or Sa): ἐκεῖνος S.

any more than a man will refuse the coinage of
Caesar. On this concept of the good hangs every
impulse to act both of man and of God.

That is why the good is preferred above every
form of kinship. My father is nothing to me, but
only the good. "Are you so hard-hearted?" Yes,
that is my nature. This is the coinage which God
has given me. For that reason, if the good is something different from the noble and the just, then
father and brother and country and all relationships
simply disappear. But shall I neglect my good, so
that you may have it, and shall I make way for you?
What for? "I am your father." But not a good.
"I am your brother." But not a good. If, however, we define the good as consisting in a right
moral purpose, then the mere preservation of the
relationships of life becomes a good; and furthermore, he who gives up some of the externals achieves
the good. "My father is taking away my money."
But he is doing you no harm. "My brother is going
to get the larger part of the farm." Let him have
all he wants. That does not help him at all to get
a part of your modesty, does it, or of your fidelity, or
of your brotherly love? Why, from a possession of
this kind who can eject you? Not even Zeus. Nay,
nor did He even wish to, but this matter He put
under my control, and He gave it to me even as
He had it Himself, free from hindrance, compulsion,
restraint.

When, therefore, different persons have different
pieces of coinage, a man offers the coin and gets what
is bought by it. A thief has come to the province
as Proconsul. What coinage does he use? Silver.
Offer it and carry away what you wish. An adulterer

ματι χρῆται; κορασιδίοις. "λάβε," φησίν, "τὸ
νόμισμα καὶ πώλησόν μοι τὸ πραγμάτιον." δὸς

13 καὶ ἀγόραζε. ἄλλος περὶ παιδάρια ἐσπούδακεν.
δὸς αὐτῷ τὸ νόμισμα καὶ λάβε ὃ θέλεις. ἄλλος
φιλόθηρος. δὸς ἱππάριον καλὸν ἢ κυνάριον·
οἰμώζων καὶ στένων πωλήσει ἀντ' αὐτοῦ ὃ θέλεις.
ἄλλος γὰρ αὐτὸν ἀναγκάζει ἔσωθεν, ὁ τὸ νόμισμα
τοῦτο τεταχώς.

14 Πρὸς τοῦτο μάλιστα τὸ εἶδος αὐτὸν γυμναστέον. εὐθὺς ὄρθρου προελθὼν ὃν ἂν ἴδῃς, ὃν ἂν
ἀκούσῃς, ἐξέταζε, ἀποκρίνου ὡς πρὸς ἐρώτημα.
τί εἶδες; καλὸν ἢ καλήν; ἔπαγε τὸν κανόνα.
ἀπροαίρετον ἢ προαιρετικόν; ἀπροαίρετον· αἶρε

15 ἔξω. τί εἶδες; πενθοῦντ'[1] ἐπὶ τέκνου τελευτῇ;
ἔπαγε τὸν κανόνα. ὁ θάνατός ἐστιν ἀπροαίρετον·
αἶρε ἐκ τοῦ μέσου. ἀπήντησέ σοι ὕπατος; ἔπαγε
τὸν κανόνα. ὑπατεία ποῖόν τί ἐστιν; ἀπροαίρετον ἢ προαιρετικόν; ἀπροαίρετον· αἶρε καὶ
τοῦτο, οὐκ ἔστι δόκιμον· ἀπόβαλε, οὐδὲν πρὸς

16 σέ. καὶ τοῦτο εἰ ἐποιοῦμεν καὶ πρὸς τοῦτο
ἠσκούμεθα καθ' ἡμέραν ἐξ ὄρθρου μέχρι νυκτός,

17 ἐγίνετο ἄν τι, νὴ τοὺς θεούς. νῦν δ' εὐθὺς ὑπὸ
πάσης φαντασίας κεχηνότες λαμβανόμεθα καὶ
μόνον, εἴπερ ἄρα, ἐν τῇ σχολῇ μικρόν τι διεγει-
ρόμεθα· εἶτ' ἐξελθόντες ἂν ἴδωμεν πενθοῦντα,
λέγομεν "ἀπώλετο"· ἂν ὕπατον, "μακάριος."

¹ s: πενθοῦν S.

---

¹ The reference is to God, who has ordained that every
man should prefer what he regards as "good" to everything
else. See § 5 above. The fault consists in making a wrong

has come. What coinage does he use? Frail wenches.
"Take," says one, "the coin and sell me the little
baggage." Give, and buy. Another is interested in
boys. Give him the coin and take what you wish.
Another is fond of hunting. Give him a fine horse
or dog; with sighs and groans he will sell for it what
you wish; for Another constrains him from within,
the one who has established this currency.[1]

It is chiefly with this principle in mind that a man
must exercise himself. Go out of the house at early
dawn, and no matter whom you see or whom you
hear, examine him and then answer as you would to
a question. What did you see? A handsome man
or a handsome woman? Apply your rule. Is it outside the province of the moral purpose, or inside?
Outside. Away with it. What did you see? A
man in grief over the death of his child? Apply
your rule. Death lies outside the province of the
moral purpose. Out of the way with it. Did a
Consul meet you? Apply your rule. What sort of
thing is a consulship? Outside the province of the
moral purpose, or inside? Outside. Away with it, too,
it does not meet the test; throw it away, it does not
concern you. If we had kept doing this and had exercised ourselves from dawn till dark with this principle
in mind,—by the gods, something would have been
achieved! But as it is, we are caught gaping straightway at every external impression that comes along, and
we wake up a little only during the lecture, if indeed
we do so even then. After that is over we go out,
and if we see a man in grief, we say, "It is all over
with him"; if we see a Consul, we say, "Happy

choice of what is to be considered "good." For "Another"
as a reverent form of reference to Zeus, see I. 25, 13 and note.

ἂν ἐξωρισμένον, "ταλαίπωρος"· ἂν πένητα,
18 "ἄθλιος, οὐκ ἔχει πόθεν φάγῃ." ταῦτ' οὖν
ἐκκόπτειν δεῖ τὰ πονηρὰ δόγματα, περὶ τοῦτο
συντετάσθαι. τί γάρ ἐστι τὸ κλαίειν καὶ οἰμώζειν ; δόγμα. τί δυστυχία ; δόγμα. τί στάσις,
τί διχόνοια, τί μέμψις, τί κατηγορία, τί ἀσέβεια,
19 τί φλυαρία ; ταῦτα πάντα δόγματά ἐστι καὶ
ἄλλο οὐδὲν καὶ δόγματα περὶ τῶν ἀπροαιρέτων
ὡς ὄντων ἀγαθῶν καὶ κακῶν. ταῦτά τις ἐπὶ τὰ
προαιρετικὰ μεταθέτω, κἀγὼ αὐτὸν ἐγγυῶμαι ὅτι
εὐσταθήσει, ὡς ἂν ἔχῃ τὰ περὶ αὑτόν.

20 Οἷόν ἐστιν ἡ λεκάνη τοῦ ὕδατος, τοιοῦτον ἡ
ψυχή, οἷον ἡ αὐγὴ ἡ προσπίπτουσα τῷ ὕδατι,
21 τοιοῦτόν αἱ φαντασίαι. ὅταν οὖν τὸ ὕδωρ κινηθῇ,
δοκεῖ μὲν καὶ ἡ αὐγὴ κινεῖσθαι, οὐ μέντοι κινεῖται.
22 καὶ ὅταν τοίνυν σκοτωθῇ τις, οὐχ αἱ τέχναι καὶ
αἱ ἀρεταὶ συγχέονται, ἀλλὰ τὸ πνεῦμα, ἐφ' οὗ
εἰσίν· καταστάντος δὲ καθίσταται κἀκεῖνα.

δ΄.   Πρὸς τὸν ἀκόσμως ἐν θεάτρῳ σπουδάσαντα.

1   Τοῦ δ' ἐπιτρόπου τῆς Ἠπείρου ἀκοσμότερον
σπουδάσαντος κωμῳδῷ τινὶ καὶ ἐπὶ τούτῳ δημοσίᾳ λοιδορηθέντος, εἶτα ἑξῆς ἀπαγγείλαντος πρὸς

man"; if we see an exile, "Poor fellow"; or a
poverty-stricken person, "Wretched man, he has
nothing with which to get a bite to eat." These,
then, are the vicious judgements which we ought to
eradicate; this is the subject upon which we ought
to concentrate our efforts. Why, what is weeping
and sighing? A judgement. What is misfortune?
A judgement. What are strife, disagreement, fault-
finding, accusing, impiety, foolishness? They are all
judgements, and that, too, judgements about things
that lie outside the province of moral purpose,
assumed to be good or evil. Let a man but transfer
his judgements to matters that lie within the
province of the moral purpose, and I guarantee that
he will be steadfast, whatever be the state of things
about him.

The soul is something like a bowl of water, and
the external impressions something like the ray of
light that falls upon the water. Now when the
water is disturbed, it looks as though the ray of
light is disturbed too, but it is not disturbed. And
so, therefore, when a man has an attack of vertigo,
it is not the arts and the virtues that are thrown
into confusion, but the spirit in which they exist;
and when this grows steady again, so do they too.

CHAPTER IV

*To the man who took sides, in an undignified manner,
while in a theatre*

The Procurator of Epirus took the side of a comic
actor in a somewhat undignified manner and was
reviled by the people for doing so. Thereupon he
brought word to Epictetus that he had been reviled,

αὐτόν, ὅτι ἐλοιδορήθη, καὶ ἀγανακτοῦντος πρὸς
τοὺς λοιδορήσαντας Καὶ τί κακόν, ἔφη, ἐποίουν;
2 ἐσπούδαζον καὶ οὗτοι ὡς καὶ σύ. εἰπόντος δ᾽
ἐκείνου Οὕτως οὖν τις σπουδάζει; Σέ, ἔφη,
βλέποντες τὸν αὐτῶν ἄρχοντα, τοῦ Καίσαρος
φίλον καὶ ἐπίτροπον, οὕτως σπουδάζοντα οὐκ
3 ἔμελλον καὶ αὐτοὶ οὕτως σπουδάζειν; εἰ γὰρ μὴ δεῖ
οὕτως σπουδάζειν, μηδὲ σὺ σπούδαζε· εἰ δὲ δεῖ, τί
χαλεπαίνεις, εἴ σε ἐμιμήσαντο; τίνας γὰρ ἔχουσιν μιμήσασθαι οἱ πολλοὶ ἢ τοὺς ὑπερέχοντας
ὑμᾶς; εἰς τίνας ἀπίδωσιν ἐλθόντες εἰς τὰ θέατρα
4 ἢ ὑμᾶς; " ὅρα πῶς ὁ ἐπίτροπος τοῦ Καίσαρος
θεωρεῖ· κέκραγεν· κἀγὼ τοίνυν κραυγάσω. ἀνα-
πηδᾷ· κἀγὼ ἀναπηδήσω. οἱ δοῦλοι αὐτοῦ δια-
κάθηνται κραυγάζοντες· ἐγὼ δ᾽ οὐκ ἔχω δούλους·
ἀντὶ πάντων αὐτὸς ὅσον δύναμαι κραυγάσω."
5 εἰδέναι σε οὖν δεῖ, ὅταν εἰσέρχῃ εἰς τὸ θέατρον,
ὅτι κανὼν εἰσέρχῃ καὶ παράδειγμα τοῖς ἄλλοις,
6 πῶς αὐτοὺς δεῖ θεωρεῖν. τί οὖν σε ἐλοιδόρουν;
ὅτι πᾶς ἄνθρωπος μισεῖ τὸ ἐμπόδιζον. ἐκεῖνοι
στεφανωθῆναι ἤθελον τὸν δεῖνα, σὺ ἕτερον·
ἐκεῖνοι σοὶ ἐνεπόδιζον καὶ σὺ ἐκείνοις. σὺ
εὑρίσκου ἰσχυρότερος· ἐκεῖνοι ὃ ἐδύναντο ἐποίουν,
7 ἐλοιδόρουν τὸ ἐμπόδιζον. τί οὖν θέλεις; ἵνα σὺ
μὲν ποιῇς ὃ θέλεις, ἐκεῖνοι δὲ μηδ᾽ εἴπωσιν [1] ἃ

[1] s: θέλωσιν S.

and gave expression to his indignation at the men
who had so reviled him. Why, what wrong were
they doing? said Epictetus. They too were taking
sides, just as you yourself were. But when the
other asked, Is that the way, then, in which a man
takes sides? he replied, Yes, they saw you, their
Governor, the friend and Procurator of Caesar,
taking sides in this way, and weren't they likely to
take sides themselves in the same way? Why, if
people should not take sides in this way, you had
better not do so yourself; but if they should, why
are you angry if they imitated you? For whom have
the people to imitate but you, their superior?
Whom do they look to but you, when they go to the
theatres? "See," says one of them, "how the
Procurator of Caesar acts in the theatre; he
shouts; very well, I'll shout too. He jumps up and
down; I'll jump up and down too. His claque of
slaves sit in different parts of the house and shout,
whereas I haven't any slaves; very well, I'll shout
as loud as I can to make up for all of them." You
ought to know, then, that when you enter the
theatre, you enter as a standard of behaviour and as
an example to the rest, showing them how they
ought to act in the theatre. Why, then, did they
revile you? Because every man hates what stands
in his way. They wanted So-and-so to get the
crown, while you wanted the other man to get it.
They were standing in your way, and you in theirs.
You turned out to be the stronger; they did what
they could, and reviled what was standing in their
way. What, then, do you wish? That you should
be able to *do* what you wish, but that they should
not even *say* what they wish? And what is there

θέλουσιν; καὶ τί θαυμαστόν; οἱ γεωργοὶ τὸν
Δία οὐ λοιδοροῦσιν, ὅταν ἐμποδίζωνται ὑπ'
αὐτοῦ; οἱ ναῦται οὐ λοιδοροῦσι; τὸν Καίσαρα
παύονται λοιδοροῦντες; τί οὖν; οὐ γιγνώσκει ὁ
8 Ζεύς; τῷ Καίσαρι οὐκ ἀπαγγέλλονται τὰ λεγό-
μενα; τί οὖν ποιεῖ; οἶδεν ὅτι, ἂν πάντας τοὺς
9 λοιδοροῦντας κολάζῃ, οὐχ ἕξει τίνων ἄρξει. τί
οὖν; ἔδει εἰσερχόμενον εἰς τὸ θέατρον τοῦτο
εἰπεῖν " ἄγε ἵνα Σώφρων στεφανωθῇ"; ἀλλ'
ἐκεῖνο " ἄγε ἵνα τηρήσω τὴν ἐμαυτοῦ προαίρεσιν
ἐπὶ ταύτης τῆς ὕλης κατὰ φύσιν ἔχουσαν."
10 ἐμοὶ παρ' ἐμὲ φίλτερος οὐδείς· γελοῖον οὖν, ἵν'
11 ἄλλος νικήσῃ κωμῳδῶν, ἐμὲ βλάπτεσθαι.—Τίνα
οὖν θέλω νικῆσαι ;—Τὸν νικῶντα· καὶ οὕτως ἀεὶ
νικήσει, ὃν θέλω.—Ἀλλὰ θέλω στεφανωθῆναι
Σώφρονα.—Ἐν οἴκῳ ὅσους θέλεις ἀγῶνας ἄγων
ἀνακήρυξον αὐτὸν Νέμεα, Πύθια, Ἴσθμια, Ὀλύμ-
πια· ἐν φανερῷ δὲ μὴ πλεονέκτει μηδ' ὑφάρπαζε
12 τὸ κοινόν. εἰ δὲ μή, ἀνέχου λοιδορούμενος· ὡς,
ὅταν ταὐτὰ ποιῇς τοῖς πολλοῖς, εἰς ἴσον ἐκείνοις
καθιστᾷς σαυτόν.

ε΄. Πρὸς τοὺς διὰ νόσον ἀπαλλαττομένους.[1]

1 Νοσῶ, φησίν, ἐνθάδε καὶ βούλομαι ἀπιέναι
2 εἰς οἶκον.—Ἐν οἴκῳ γὰρ ἄνοσος ἦς σύ; οὐ
σκοπεῖς, εἴ τι ποιεῖς ἐνθάδε τῶν πρὸς τὴν

---

[1] 8: πλαττομένους S.

---

[1] The word "school" does not, of course, appear in the
Greek, but such was the nature of the educational institution
which Epictetus conducted, and that is clearly what is meant
here. See in particular Ivo Bruns: De Schola Epicteti (1897),

surprising in all that? Don't the farmers revile
Zeus, when he stands in their way? Don't the
sailors revile Zeus? Do men ever stop reviling
Caesar? What then? Doesn't Zeus know about
it? Isn't Caesar informed of what is said? What,
then, does he do? He knows that if he punishes
all who revile him he will have no one left to rule
over. What then? Ought you upon entering the
theatre to say, "Come, let's see that Sophron gets
the crown"? and not rather, "Come, let me in this
subject-matter maintain my moral purpose in accord
with nature"? No one is dearer to me than myself; it is absurd, therefore, for me to let myself be
hurt in order that another man may win a victory as a
comic actor.—Whom, then, do I wish to win the
victory? The victor; and so the one whom I wish
to win the victory will always win it.—But I wish
Sophron to get the crown.—Stage as many contests
as you will in your own house, and proclaim him
victor in the Nemean, Pythian, Isthmian, and
Olympic games; but out in public do not arrogate
to yourself more than your due, and do not filch
away a public privilege. Otherwise you must
put up with being reviled; because, when you do
the same things that the people do, you are putting
yourself on their level.

CHAPTER V

To those who leave school[1] *because of illness*

I AM ill here, says one of the students, and want
to go back home.—What, were you free from illness

and the studies by Colardeau, Halbauer, and Hartmann, listed
in Vol. I, *Introduction*.

προαίρεσιν τὴν σαυτοῦ φερόντων, ἵν' ἐπανορ-
θωθῇ; εἰ μὲν γὰρ μηδὲν ἀνύεις, περισσῶς καὶ
3 ἦλθες. ἄπιθι, ἐπιμελοῦ τῶν ἐν οἴκῳ. εἰ γὰρ
μὴ δύναταί σου τὸ ἡγεμονικὸν σχεῖν κατὰ φύσιν,
τό γ' ἀγρίδιον δυνήσεται·¹ τό γε κερμάτιον
αὐξήσεις, τὸν πατέρα γηροκομήσεις, ἐν τῇ ἀγορᾷ
ἀναστραφήσῃ, ἄρξεις· κακὸς κακῶς τί ποτε
4 ποιήσεις τῶν ἑξῆς. εἰ δὲ παρακολουθεῖς σαυτῷ,
ὅτι ἀποβάλλεις τινὰ δόγματα φαῦλα καὶ ἄλλ'
ἀντ' αὐτῶν ἀναλαμβάνεις καὶ τὴν σαυτοῦ
στάσιν μετατέθεικας ἀπὸ τῶν ἀπροαιρέτων ἐπὶ
τὰ προαιρετικά, κἄν ποτ' εἴπῃς "οἴμοι," οὐ
λέγεις διὰ τὸν πατέρα, τὸν ἀδελφόν, ἀλλὰ
5 "δι' ἐμέ," ἔτι ὑπολογίζῃ νόσον; οὐκ οἶδας,
ὅτι καὶ νόσος καὶ θάνατος καταλαβεῖν ἡμᾶς
ὀφείλουσίν τί ποτε ποιοῦντας; τὸν γεωργὸν
γεωργοῦντα καταλαμβάνουσι, τὸν ναυτικὸν
6 πλέοντα. σὺ τί θέλεις ποιῶν καταληφθῆναι;
τί ποτε μὲν γὰρ ποιοῦντά σε δεῖ καταληφθῆναι.
εἴ τι ἔχεις τούτου κρεῖσσον ποιῶν καταληφθῆναι, ποίει ἐκεῖνο.

7 Ἐμοὶ μὲν γὰρ καταληφθῆναι γένοιτο μηδενὸς
ἄλλου ἐπιμελουμένῳ ἢ τῆς προαιρέσεως τῆς
ἐμῆς, ἵν' ἀπαθής, ἵν' ἀκώλυτος, ἵν' ἀνανάγκαστος,
8 ἵν' ἐλεύθερος. ταῦτα ἐπιτηδεύων θέλω εὑρε-

¹ εὐθενήσεται (will prosper) Elter rather plausibly.

---

¹ See the critical note.

at home? Do you not raise the question whether
you are doing here any of the things that have a
bearing upon your moral purpose, so that it shall be
improved? For if you are not accomplishing anything, it was no use for you to have come in the first
place. Go back and tend to your affairs at home.
For if your governing principle cannot be brought
into conformity with nature, no doubt your paltry
piece of land can be made to conform with it.[1] You
will increase the amount of your small change; you
will care for your father in his old age, you will walk
up and down in the market, you will hold office; a
poor wretch yourself, you will do wretchedly whatever comes next. But if you understand yourself,
namely, that you are putting away certain bad
judgements and taking on others in their place, and
that you have transferred your status from what lies
outside the province of the moral purpose to what
lies inside the same, and that if ever you say
" Alas!" you are speaking, not for your father's sake,
or your brother's sake, but " for my own sake," then
why take account of illness any longer? Do you
not know that disease and death needs must over-
take us, no matter what we are doing? They over-
take the farmer at his work in the fields, the sailor
on the sea. What do you wish to be doing when it
overtakes you? For no matter what you do you will
have to be overtaken by death. If you have anything better to be doing when you are so overtaken,
get to work on that.

As for me, I would fain that death overtook me
occupied with nothing but my own moral purpose,
trying to make it tranquil, unhampered, uncon-
strained, free. This is what I wish to be engaged in

θῆναι, ἵν᾿ εἰπεῖν δύνωμαι τῷ θεῷ " μή τι παρέβην σου τὰς ἐντολάς; μή τι πρὸς ἄλλα
ἐχρησάμην ταῖς ἀφορμαῖς ἃς ἔδωκας; μή τι
ταῖς αἰσθήσεσιν ἄλλως, μή τι ταῖς προλήψεσιν;
μή τί σοί ποτ᾿ ἐνεκάλεσα; μή τι ἐμεμψάμην
9 σου τὴν διοίκησιν; ἐνόσησα, ὅτε ἠθέλησας· καὶ
οἱ ἄλλοι, ἀλλ᾿ ἐγὼ ἑκών. πένης ἐγενόμην σου
θέλοντος, ἀλλὰ χαίρων. οὐκ ἦρξα, ὅτι σὺ οὐκ
ἠθέλησας· οὐδέποτ᾿ ἐπεθύμησα ἀρχῆς. μή τί
με τούτου ἕνεκα στυγνότερον εἶδες; μὴ οὐ
προσῆλθόν σοί ποτε φαιδρῷ τῷ προσώπῳ,
10 ἕτοιμος εἴ τι ἐπιτάσσεις, εἴ τι σημαίνεις; νῦν
με θέλεις ἀπελθεῖν ἐκ τῆς πανηγύρεως· ἄπειμι,
χάριν σοι ἔχω πᾶσαν, ὅτι ἠξίωσάς με συμπανη-
γυρίσαι σοι καὶ ἰδεῖν ἔργα τὰ σὰ καὶ τῇ διοικήσει
11 σου συμπαρακολουθῆσαι.[1] ταῦτά με ἐνθυμού-
μενον, ταῦτα γράφοντα, ταῦτα ἀναγιγνώσκοντα
καταλάβοι ὁ θάνατος.
12 Ἀλλ᾿ ἡ μήτηρ μου τὴν κεφαλὴν νοσοῦντος οὐ
κρατήσει.— Ἄπιθι τοίνυν πρὸς τὴν μητέρα·
ἄξιος γὰρ εἶ τὴν κεφαλὴν κρατούμενος νοσεῖν.—
13 Ἀλλ᾿ ἐπὶ κλιναρίου κομψοῦ ἐν οἴκῳ κατεκείμην.
— Ἄπιθί σου ἐπὶ τὸ κλινάριον· ἢ[2] ὑγιαίνων
ἄξιος εἶ ἐπὶ τοιούτου κατακεῖσθαι. μὴ τοίνυν
ἀπόλλυε, ἃ δύνασαι ἐκεῖ ποιεῖν.
14 Ἀλλ᾿ ὁ Σωκράτης τί λέγει; "ὥσπερ ἄλλος
τις," φησίν, "χαίρει[3] τὸν ἀγρὸν τὸν αὑτοῦ
ποιῶν κρείσσονα, ἄλλος τὸν ἵππον, οὕτως ἐγὼ
καθ᾿ ἡμέραν χαίρω παρακολουθῶν ἐμαυτῷ

---

[1] σοί after this word deleted in s.
[2] Upton: ἢ S.

when death finds me, so that I may be able to say to God, "Have I in any respect transgressed Thy commands? Have I in any respect misused the resources which Thou gavest me, or used my senses to no purpose, or my preconceptions? Have I ever found any fault with Thee? Have I blamed Thy governance at all? I fell sick, when it was Thy will; so did other men, but I willingly. I became poor, it being Thy will, but with joy. I have held no office, because Thou didst not will it, and I never set my heart upon office. Hast Thou ever seen me for that reason greatly dejected? Have I not ever come before Thee with a radiant countenance, ready for any injunctions or orders Thou mightest give? And now it is Thy will that I leave this festival; I go, I am full of gratitude to Thee that Thou hast deemed me worthy to take part in this festival with Thee, and to see Thy works, and to understand Thy governance." Be this my thought, this my writing, this my reading, when death comes upon me.

But my mother will not hold my head in her arms when I am ill.—Very well, go back to your mother; you are just the sort of person that deserves to have his head held in somebody's arms when he is ill!—But at home I used to have a nice bed to lie on.—Go back to your bed; without doubt you deserve to lie on such a fine bed even when you are well! Pray, then, do not lose by staying here what you can do there.

But what does Socrates say? "As one man rejoices," remarks he, "in improving his own farm, and another his own horse, so I rejoice day by day

---

⁸ *s*: χαίρειν *S*.

15 βελτίονι γινομένῳ."—Πρὸς τί; μή τι πρὸς
λεξείδια;—Ἄνθρωπε, εὐφήμει.—Μή τι πρὸς
16 θεωρημάτια;—Τί ποιεῖς;—Καὶ μὴν οὐ βλέπω,
τί ἐστιν ἄλλο, περὶ ὃ ἀσχολοῦνται οἱ φιλόσοφοι.
—Οὐδέν σοι δοκεῖ εἶναι τὸ μηδέποτε ἐγκαλέσαι
τινί, μὴ θεῷ, μὴ ἀνθρώπῳ· μὴ μέμψασθαι
μηδένα· τὸ αὐτὸ πρόσωπον ἀεὶ καὶ ἐκφέρειν καὶ
17 εἰσφέρειν; ταῦτα ἦν, ἃ ᾔδει ὁ Σωκράτης, καὶ
ὅμως οὐδέποτε εἶπεν, ὅτι οἰδέν τι ἢ διδάσκει.
εἰ δέ τις λεξείδια ᾔτει ἢ θεωρημάτια, ἀπῆγεν
πρὸς Πρωταγόραν, πρὸς Ἱππίαν. καὶ γὰρ εἰ
λάχανά τις ζητῶν ἐληλύθει, πρὸς τὸν κηπουρὸν ἂν αὐτὸν ἀπήγαγεν· τίς οὖν ὑμῶν ἔχει
18 ταύτην τὴν ἐπιβολήν; ἐπεί τοι εἰ εἴχετε,[1] καὶ
ἐνοσεῖτε ἂν ἡδέως καὶ ἐπεινᾶτε καὶ ἀπεθνήσκετε.[2]
19 εἴ τις ὑμῶν ἠράσθη κορασίου κομψοῦ, οἶδεν ὅτι
ἀληθῆ λέγω.

ϛʹ. Σποράδην τινά.

1   Πυθομένου δέ τινος, πῶς[3] νῦν μᾶλλον ἐκπε-
πονημένου τοῦ λόγου πρότερον μείζονες προ-
2 κοπαὶ ἦσαν, Κατὰ τί, ἔφη, ἐκπεπόνηται καὶ
κατὰ τί μείζους αἱ προκοπαὶ τότε ἦσαν; καθὸ

---

[1] Sc: ἔχετε S.   [2] Sc: πεινᾶτε and ἀποθνήσκετε S.
[3] Schweighäuser: τῶν S.

---

[1] The closest parallels from Xenophon (*Mem.* I. 6. 8 and
14) and Plato (*Prot.* 318 A) express the idea so differently
that we have here probably (through Chrysippus) a fragment
from one of the lost Socratic dialogues, of which there was a
large body.

in following the course of my own improvement."[1]
In what respect; in little philosophic phrases?—
Man, hold your tongue.—In little philosophic
theories, then?—What are you doing?—Well, I
don't see anything else that the philosophers spend
their time on.—Is it nothing in your eyes never to
bring accusation against anyone, be it God or man?
Never to blame anyone? Always to wear the same
expression on one's face, whether one is coming out
or going in?[2] These are the things which Socrates
knew, and yet he never said that he either knew or
taught anything. But if someone called for little
philosophic phrases or theories, he used to take him
over to Protagoras or Hippias. It was just as though
someone had come to him for fresh vegetables, and
he would have taken him over to the market
gardener. Who, then, among you makes this purpose of Socrates the purpose of his own life? Why,
if you did, you would have been glad even to be ill,
and to go hungry, and to die. If any one of you was
ever in love with a pretty wench, he knows that
what I say is true.

CHAPTER VI

Some scattered sayings

WHEN someone asked how it was that, despite
the greater amount of work which was done nowadays in logic, there was more progress made in
former times, Epictetus replied, On what has labour
been expended in our time, and in what was the
progress greater in those days? For in that upon

[2] See also about Socrates in Aelian, *Var. Hist.* 9, 7.

γὰρ νῦν ἐκπεπόνηται, κατὰ τοῦτο καὶ προκοπαὶ
3 νῦν εὑρεθήσονται. καὶ νῦν μὲν ὥστε συλλογισμοὺς ἀναλύειν ἐκπεπόνηται καὶ προκοπαὶ
γίνονται· τότε δ' ὥστε τὸ ἡγεμονικὸν κατὰ
φύσιν ἔχον τηρῆσαι καὶ ἐξεπονεῖτο καὶ προκοπαὶ
4 ἦσαν. μὴ οὖν ἐνάλλασσε μηδὲ ζήτει, ὅταν ἄλλο
ἐκπονῇς, ἐν ἄλλῳ προκόπτειν. ἀλλ' ἴδε, εἴ τις
ἡμῶν πρὸς τούτῳ ὤν, ὥστε κατὰ φύσιν ἔχειν καὶ
διεξάγειν, οὐ προκόπτει. οὐδένα γὰρ εὑρήσεις.

5   Ὁ σπουδαῖος ἀήττητος· καὶ[1] γὰρ οὐκ ἀγωνί-
6 ζεται, ὅπου μὴ κρείσσων[2] ἐστίν. " εἰ τὰ[3] κατὰ
τὸν ἀγρὸν θέλεις, λάβε·[4] λάβε τοὺς οἰκέτας,
λάβε τὴν ἀρχήν, λάβε τὸ σωμάτιον. τὴν δ'
ὄρεξιν οὐ ποιήσεις ἀποτευκτικὴν οὐδὲ τὴν
7 ἔκκλισιν περιπτωτικήν." εἰς τοῦτον μόνον τὸν
ἀγῶνα καθίησιν τὸν περὶ τῶν προαιρετικῶν· πῶς
οὖν οὐ μέλλει ἀήττητος εἶναι;

8   Πυθομένου δέ τινος, τί ἐστιν ὁ κοινὸς νοῦς,
"Ὥσπερ, φησίν, κοινή τις ἀκοὴ λέγοιτ' ἂν ἡ
μόνον φωνῶν διακριτική, ἡ δὲ τῶν φθόγγων
οὐκέτι κοινή, ἀλλὰ τεχνική, οὕτως ἐστί τινα,
ἃ οἱ μὴ παντάπασιν διεστραμμένοι τῶν ἀνθρώπων κατὰ τὰς κοινὰς ἀφορμὰς ὁρῶσιν. ἡ
τοιαύτη κατάστασις κοινὸς νοῦς καλεῖται.

---

[1] Upton's "codex": ἢ S.
[2] The words that follow in S, εἰ μὴ ὅπου κρείσσων, are omitted in s.
[3] τά added by Sb.   [4] λάβε added by Upton.

---

[1] On the use of the term κοινὸς νοῦς in Epictetus one may compare Bonhöffer, *Epiktet und die Stoa*, 121 and 224. It means simply the intellectual faculty that any normal man possesses.

which labour has been expended in our time,
progress also will be found in our time. The fact is
that in our time labour has been expended upon the
solution of syllogisms, and there is progress along
that line; but in the early days not only had labour
been expended upon maintaining the governing
principle in a state of accord with nature, but there
was also progress along that line. Do not, therefore, substitute one thing for the other, and do not
expect, when you devote labour to one thing, to be
making progress in another. But see whether any
one of us who is devoting himself to keeping in a
state of conformity with nature, and to spending his
life so, fails to make progress. For you will find
that there is none of whom that is true.

The good man is invincible; naturally, for he
enters no contest where he is not superior. "If you
want my property in the country," says he, "take it;
take my servants, take my office, take my paltry
body. But you will not make my desire fail to get
what I will, nor my aversion fall into what I would
avoid." This is the only contest into which the good
man enters, one, namely, that is concerned with the
things which belong in the province of the moral
purpose; how, then, can he help but be invincible?

When someone asked him what "general perception"[1] was, he replied, Just as a sense of hearing
which distinguishes merely between sounds would
be called "general," but that which distinguishes
between tones is no longer "general," but "technical," so there are certain things which those men
who are not altogether perverted see by virtue of
their general faculties. Such a mental constitution
is called "general perception."

9 Τῶν νέων τοὺς μαλακοὺς οὐκ ἔστι προτρέψαι
ῥᾴδιον· οὐδὲ γὰρ τυρὸν[1] ἀγκίστρῳ λαβεῖν· οἱ
δ᾽ εὐφυεῖς, κἂν ἀποτρέπῃς, ἔτι μᾶλλον ἔχονται
10 τοῦ λόγου. διὸ καὶ ὁ Ροῦφος τὰ πολλὰ ἀπέ-
τρεπεν τούτῳ δοκιμαστηρίῳ χρώμενος τῶν εὐ-
φυῶν καὶ ἀφυῶν. ἔλεγε γὰρ ὅτι " ὡς ὁ λίθος, κἂν
ἀναβάλῃς, ἐνεχθήσεται κάτω ἐπὶ γῆν κατὰ[2] τὴν
αὑτοῦ κατασκευήν, οὕτως καὶ ὁ εὐφυής, ὅσῳ
μᾶλλον ἀποκρούεταί τις αὐτόν, τοσούτῳ μᾶλλον
νεύει ἐφ᾽ ὃ πέφυκεν."

ζ΄. Πρὸς τὸν διορθωτὴν τῶν ἐλευθέρων
πόλεων, Ἐπικούρειον ὄντα.

1 Τοῦ δὲ διορθωτοῦ εἰσελθόντος πρὸς αὐτὸν
(ἦν δ᾽ οὗτος Ἐπικούρειος) Ἄξιον, ἔφη, τοὺς
ἰδιώτας ἡμᾶς παρ᾽ ὑμῶν τῶν φιλοσόφων πυν-
θάνεσθαι, καθάπερ τοὺς εἰς ξένην πόλιν ἐλθόντας
παρὰ τῶν πολιτῶν καὶ εἰδότων, τί κράτιστόν
ἐστιν ἐν κόσμῳ, ἵνα καὶ αὐτοὶ ἱστορήσαντες
μετίωμεν, ὡς ἐκεῖνοι τὰ ἐν ταῖς πόλεσι, καὶ
2 θεώμεθα. ὅτι μὲν γὰρ τρία ἐστὶ περὶ τὸν
ἄνθρωπον, ψυχὴ καὶ σῶμα καὶ τὰ ἐκτός, σχεδὸν
οὐδεὶς ἀντιλέγει· λοιπὸν ὑμέτερόν ἐστιν ἀπο-

---

[1] See note to the translation.
[2] γῆν κατά added by Schweighäuser.

---

[1] A proverb; see Diog. Laert. 4, 47, where the adjective
ἀπαλός ("soft") is used of the cheese, which Wolf and Upton,
perhaps with good reason, wanted to add here. At all events
that is the kind of cheese which is meant.

κρίνασθαι, τί ἐστὶ τὸ κράτιστον. τί ἐροῦμεν
3 τοῖς ἀνθρώποις; τὴν σάρκα; καὶ διὰ ταύτην
Μάξιμος ἔπλευσεν μέχρι Κασσιόπης χειμῶνος
μετὰ τοῦ υἱοῦ προπέμπων, ἵν᾽ ἡσθῇ τῇ σαρκί;
4 ἀρνησαμένου δ᾽ ἐκείνου καὶ εἰπόντος Μὴ γέ-
νοιτο· Οὐ προσήκει περὶ τὸ κράτιστον ἐσπου-
δακέναι;—Πάντων μάλιστα προσήκει.—Τί οὖν
κρεῖσσον ἔχομεν τῆς σαρκός;—Τὴν ψυχήν, ἔφη.
—Ἀγαθὰ δὲ τὰ τοῦ κρατίστου κρείττονά ἐστιν ἢ
5 τὰ τοῦ φαυλοτέρου;—Τὰ τοῦ κρατίστου.—
Ψυχῆς δὲ ἀγαθὰ πότερον προαιρετικά ἐστιν ἢ
ἀπροαίρετα;—Προαιρετικά.—Προαιρετικὸν οὖν
ἐστιν ἡ ἡδονὴ ἡ ψυχική;—Ἔφη.—Αὕτη δ᾽ ἐπὶ
6 τίσιν γίνεται; πότερον ἐφ᾽ αὑτῇ; ἀλλ᾽ ἀδιανόη-
τόν ἐστιν· προηγουμένην γάρ τινα ὑφεστάναι
δεῖ οὐσίαν τοῦ ἀγαθοῦ, ἧς τυγχάνοντες ἡσθησό-
7 μεθα κατὰ ψυχήν.—Ὡμολόγει καὶ τοῦτο.—Ἐπὶ
τίνι οὖν ἡσθησόμεθα ταύτην τὴν ψυχικὴν
ἡδονήν; εἰ γὰρ ἐπὶ τοῖς ψυχικοῖς[1] ἀγαθοῖς,
εὕρηται ἡ οὐσία τοῦ ἀγαθοῦ. οὐ γὰρ δύναται
ἄλλο μὲν εἶναι ἀγαθόν, ἄλλο δ᾽ ἐφ᾽ ᾧ εὐλόγως
ἐπαιρόμεθα, οὐδὲ τοῦ προηγουμένου μὴ ὄντος
ἀγαθοῦ τὸ ἐπιγέννημα ἀγαθὸν εἶναι. ἵνα γὰρ
εὔλογον ᾖ τὸ ἐπιγέννημα, τὸ προηγούμενον δεῖ
8 ἀγαθὸν εἶναι. ἀλλ᾽ οὐ μὴ εἴπητε φρένας ἔχοντες·
ἀνακόλουθα γὰρ ἐρεῖτε καὶ Ἐπικούρῳ καὶ τοῖς

---

[1] ψυχικοῖς added by Schenkl (from the scholium).

---

[1] There were at least two distinguished men of the name
at this time, but it is not clear that either one is meant.
[2] More likely the headland and harbour on the northern
end of Corcyra than the almost wholly unknown town near
Nicopolis, which some have thought of.

answer the question, Which is the best? What are we going to tell men? The flesh? And was it for this that Maximus [1] sailed all the way to Cassiope [2] during the winter with his son, to see him on his way? Was it to have pleasure in the flesh? When the other had denied that and said "God forbid!" Epictetus continued: Is it not proper to have been very zealous for that which is best?—It is certainly most proper.—What have we better, then, than the flesh?—The soul, said he.—Are the goods of the best thing better, or those of the inferior?—Those of the best thing.—Do goods of the soul belong in the sphere of the moral purpose, or do they not?—To the sphere of the moral purpose.—Is the pleasure of the soul, therefore, something that belongs in this sphere?—He agreed.—At what is this produced? At itself? [3] But that is inconceivable. For we must assume that there is already in existence a certain antecedent essence of the good, by partaking of which we shall feel pleasure of soul.—He agreed to this also.—At what, then, are we going to feel this pleasure of soul? If it is at the goods of the soul, the essence of the good has already been discovered. For it is impossible that one thing be good, and yet that it is justifiable for us to take delight in something else; nor again, that when the antecedent is not good the consequent be good; because, in order to justify the consequent, the antecedent must be good. But say not so, you Epicureans, if you are in your right mind; for you will be saying what is inconsistent both with Epicurus and with the rest of

---

[3] "*An ex se ipsa?* Id est, *an delectamur, quia delectamur?*" Schweighäuser.

9 ἄλλοις ὑμῶν δόγμασιν. ὑπολείπεται λοιπὸν
ἐπὶ τοῖς σωματικοῖς ἥδεσθαι τὴν κατὰ ψυχὴν
ἡδονήν· πάλιν ἐκεῖνα γίνεται προηγούμενα καὶ
οὐσία τοῦ ἀγαθοῦ.

10 Διὰ τοῦτο ἀφρόνως ἐποίησε Μάξιμος, εἰ δι᾽
ἄλλο τι ἔπλευσεν ἢ διὰ τὴν σάρκα, τοῦτ᾽ ἔστι
11 διὰ τὸ κράτιστον. ἀφρόνως δὲ ποιεῖ καὶ εἰ
ἀπέχεται τῶν ἀλλοτρίων δικαστὴς ὢν καὶ
δυνάμενος λαμβάνειν. ἀλλ᾽ ἄν σοι δόξῃ, ἐκεῖνο
μόνον σκεπτώμεθα, ἵνα κεκρυμμένως, ἵν᾽ ἀσφα-
12 λῶς, ἵνα μή τις γνῷ. τὸ γὰρ κλέψαι οὐδ᾽ αὐτὸς
Ἐπίκουρος ἀποφαίνει κακόν, ἀλλὰ τὸ ἐμπεσεῖν·
καὶ ὅτι πίστιν περὶ τοῦ λαθεῖν λαβεῖν ἀδύνατον,
13 διὰ τοῦτο λέγει "μὴ κλέπτετε." ἀλλ᾽ ἐγώ σοι
λέγω, ὅτι ἐὰν κομψῶς καὶ περιεσταλμένως γίνηται,
λησόμεθα· εἶτα καὶ φίλους ἐν τῇ Ῥώμῃ ἔχομεν
δυνατοὺς καὶ φίλας[1] καὶ οἱ Ἕλληνες ἀδρανεῖς
εἰσιν· οὐδεὶς τολμήσει ἀναβῆναι τούτου ἕνεκα.
14 τί ἀπέχῃ τοῦ ἰδίου ἀγαθοῦ; ἄφρον ἐστὶ τοῦτο,
ἠλίθιόν ἐστιν. ἀλλ᾽ οὐδ᾽ ἂν λέγῃς μοι, ὅτι
15 ἀπέχῃ, πιστεύσω σοι. ὡς γὰρ ἀδύνατόν ἐστι
τῷ ψευδεῖ φαινομένῳ συγκαταθέσθαι καὶ ἀπὸ
τοῦ ἀληθοῦς ἀπονεῦσαι, οὕτως ἀδύνατόν ἐστι
τοῦ φαινομένου ἀγαθοῦ ἀποστῆναι. ὁ πλοῦτος
δ᾽ ἀγαθὸν καὶ οἱονεὶ[2] τὸ ποιητικώτατόν γε
16 τῶν ἡδονῶν. διὰ τί μὴ περιποιήσῃ αὐτόν; διὰ
τί δὲ μὴ τὴν τοῦ γείτονος γυναῖκα διαφθείρωμεν,

[1] Wolf : φιλίας S.

52

your doctrines. The only thing left for you to say
is that pleasure of soul is pleasure in the things of
the body, and then *they* become matters of prime
importance, and the true nature of the good.

That is why Maximus acted foolishly if he made
his voyage for the sake of anything but the flesh,
that is, for the sake of anything but the best   And
a man acts foolishly too, if, when he is judge and
able to take the property of other men, he keeps
his hands off it. But, if you please, let us consider
this point only, that the stealing be done secretly,
safely, without anybody's knowledge. For even
Epicurus himself does not declare the act of theft
evil, but only getting caught, and merely because
it is impossible to feel certain that one will not be
detected, he says, "Do not steal." But I tell you
that if it is done adroitly and circumspectly, we shall
escape detection; besides that, we have influential
friends in Rome, both men and women; and the
Greeks are a feeble folk, none of them will have the
courage to go up to Rome for that purpose. Why
refrain from your own good? This is foolish, it is
silly. And again, I shall not believe you, even if
you tell me that you do refrain. For just as it is
impossible to assent to what is seen to be false, and
to reject what is true, so it is impossible to reject
what is seen to be good. Now wealth is a good, and
when it comes to pleasures is, so to speak, the thing
most productive of them. Why should you not
acquire it? And why should we not seduce our
neighbour's wife, if we can escape detection? And

---

² Schenkl (the word seems to be known hitherto only
from glosses, but it seems practically certain here): οἷον ἂν
ἦι (or ἦς) S.

ἂν δυνώμεθα λαθεῖν, ἂν δὲ φλυαρῇ ὁ ἀνήρ, καὶ
17 αὐτὸν προσεκτραχηλίσωμεν; εἰ θέλεις εἶναι
φιλόσοφος οἷος δεῖ, εἴ γε τέλειος, εἰ ἀκολουθῶν
σου τοῖς δόγμασιν· εἰ δὲ μή, οὐδὲν διοίσεις ἡμῶν
τῶν λεγομένων Στωικῶν· καὶ αὐτοὶ γὰρ ἄλλα
18 λέγομεν, ἄλλα δὲ ποιοῦμεν. ἡμεῖς λέγομεν τὰ
καλά, ποιοῦμεν τὰ αἰσχρά· σὺ τὴν ἐναντίαν
διαστροφὴν ἔσῃ διεστραμμένος δογματίζων τὰ
αἰσχρά, ποιῶν τὰ καλά.[1]
19   Τὸν θεόν σοι, ἐπινοεῖς Ἐπικουρείων πόλιν·
"ἐγὼ οὐ γαμῶ." "οὐδ' ἐγώ· οὐ γὰρ γαμητέον."
ἀλλ' οὐδὲ παιδοποιητέον, ἀλλ' οὐδὲ πολιτευτέον.
τί οὖν γένηται; πόθεν οἱ πολῖται; τίς αὐτοὺς
παιδεύσει; τίς ἐφήβαρχος, τίς γυμνασίαρχος;
τί δὲ καὶ παιδεύσει αὐτούς; ἃ Λακεδαιμόνιοι
20 ἐπαιδεύοντο ἢ Ἀθηναῖοι; λάβε μοι νέον, ἄγαγε
κατὰ τὰ δόγματά σου. πονηρά ἐστι τὰ δόγματα,
ἀνατρεπτικὰ πόλεως, λυμαντικὰ οἴκων, οὐδὲ
21 γυναιξὶ πρέποντα. ἄφες ταῦτ', ἄνθρωπε. ζῇς
ἐν ἡγεμονούσῃ πόλει· ἄρχειν σε δεῖ, κρίνειν
δικαίως, ἀπέχεσθαι τῶν ἀλλοτρίων, σοὶ καλὴν
γυναῖκα φαίνεσθαι μηδεμίαν ἢ τὴν σήν, καλὸν
παῖδα μηδένα, καλὸν ἀργύρωμα μηδέν, χρύσωμα
22 μηδέν. τούτοις σύμφωνα δόγματα ζήτησον, ἀφ'
ὧν ὁρμώμενος ἡδέως ἀφέξῃ πραγμάτων οὕτως
23 πιθανῶν[2] πρὸς τὸ ἀγαγεῖν καὶ νικῆσαι. ἂν δὲ
πρὸς τῇ πιθανότητι τῇ ἐκείνων καὶ φιλοσοφίαν

---

[1] Wolf (after Schegk) and Upton's "codex": δογματίζων
τὰ καλά· ποιῶν τὰ αἰσχρά S.
[2] Shaftesbury: πιθανῶς S.

---

[1] See note on I. 1, 34.

if her husband talks nonsense, why should we not break his neck to boot? That is, if you wish to be a proper sort of philosopher, a perfect one, consistent with your own doctrines. If not, you will be no better than we who bear the name of Stoics; for we too talk of one thing and do another. We talk of the noble and do the base; but you will be perverse in the opposite way, laying down base doctrines, and doing noble deeds.

In the name of God, I ask you, can you imagine an Epicurean State? One man says, "I do not marry." "Neither do I," says another, "for people ought not to marry." No, nor have children; no, nor perform the duties of a citizen. And what, do you suppose, will happen then? Where are the citizens to come from? Who will educate them? Who will be superintendent of the ephebi,[1] or gymnasium director? Yes, and what will either of these teach them? What the young men of Lacedaemon or Athens were taught? Take me a young man; bring him up according to your doctrines. Your doctrines are bad, subversive of the State, destructive to the family, not even fit for women. Drop these doctrines, man. You live in an imperial State; it is your duty to hold office, to judge uprightly, to keep your hands off the property of other people; no woman but your wife ought to look handsome to you, no boy handsome, no silver plate handsome, no gold plate. Look for doctrines consistent with these principles of conduct, doctrines which will enable you to refrain gladly from matters so persuasive to attract and to overpower a man. If, however, in addition to the persuasive power of the things just mentioned, we shall have gone

τινά ποτε ταύτην ἐξευρηκότες ὦμεν συνεπω-
θοῦσαν ἡμᾶς ἐπ' αὐτὰ καὶ ἐπιρρωννύουσαν, τί
γένηται;

24 Ἐν τορεύματι [1] τί κράτιστόν ἐστιν, ὁ ἄργυρος
ἢ ἡ τέχνη; χειρὸς οὐσία μὲν ἡ σάρξ, προηγού-
25 μενα δὲ τὰ χειρὸς ἔργα. οὐκοῦν καὶ καθήκοντα
τρισσά· τὰ μὲν πρὸς τὸ εἶναι, τὰ δὲ πρὸς τὸ ποιά
εἶναι, τὰ δ' αὐτὰ τὰ προηγούμενα. οὕτως καὶ
ἀνθρώπου οὐ τὴν ὕλην δεῖ τιμᾶν, τὰ σαρκίδια,
26 ἀλλὰ τὰ προηγούμενα. τίνα ἐστὶ ταῦτα; πολι-
τεύεσθαι, γαμεῖν, παιδοποιεῖσθαι, θεὸν σέβειν,
γονέων ἐπιμελεῖσθαι, καθόλου ὀρέγεσθαι, ἐκκλίνειν, ὁρμᾶν, ἀφορμᾶν, ὡς ἕκαστον τούτων δεῖ
27 ποιεῖν, ὡς πεφύκαμεν. πεφύκαμεν δὲ πῶς; ὡς
ἐλεύθεροι, ὡς γενναῖοι, ὡς αἰδήμονες. ποῖον γὰρ
ἄλλο ζῷον ἐρυθριᾷ, ποῖον αἰσχροῦ φαντασίαν
28 λαμβάνει; τὴν ἡδονὴν δ' ὑπόταξαι τούτοις ὡς
διάκονον, ὡς ὑπηρέτην, ἵνα προθυμίας ἐκκαλέση-
ται, ἵν' ἐν τοῖς κατὰ φύσιν ἔργοις παρακρατῇ.
29 Ἀλλ' ἐγὼ πλούσιός εἰμι καὶ οὐδενὸς χρεία μοί
ἐστιν.—Τί οὖν ἔτι προσποιῇ φιλοσοφεῖν; ἀρκεῖ

---

[1] Wolf: ἐν τῶι ῥεύματι S.

---

[1] The classification of duties in this sentence is obscure,
and the commentators have ever been in straits both to
elucidate it, and to explain what bearing it has upon the
context. The first two classes (which are essentially one)
deal with outward existence; the last touches our higher
nature. A full discussion of this matter will be found in
A. Bonhöffer; *Die Ethik des Stoikers Epiktet*, p. 205–6. A
very similar Stoic division of duties into five classes, where
the third class of Epictetus is triply divided, will be found in
Cicero, *De Finibus*, III. 16 and 20. I believe that the sentence,
though probably going back to Epictetus, did not belong

ahead and invented also some such doctrine as this
of yours, which helps to push us on into them, and
gives them additional strength, what is going to
happen?

In a piece of plate what is the best thing, the
silver or the art? The substance of the hand is
mere flesh, but the important thing is the works of
the hand. Now duties are of three kinds; first,
those that have to do with mere existence, second,
those that have to do with existence of a particular
sort, and third, the principal duties themselves.[1] So
also in the case of man, it is not his material substance that we should honour, his bits of flesh, but
the principal things. What are these? The duties
of citizenship, marriage, begetting children, reverence to God, care of parents,[2] in a word, desire,
avoidance, choice, refusal, the proper performance
of each one of these acts, and that is, in accordance
with our nature. And what is our nature? To act
as free men, as noble, as self-respecting. Why,
what other living being blushes, what other compre-
hends the impression of shame? And it is our
nature to subordinate pleasure to these duties as
their servant, their minister, so as to arouse our
interest and keep us acting in accordance with
nature.

But I am rich and need nothing.—Why, then,
do you still pretend to be a philosopher? Your

here originally (so also Bonhöffer, it seems), but derived
from a marginal note upon τὰ προηγούμενα, just below, and
the sentence immediately following.

[2] After the *Golden Verses of Pythagoras*, 3–4:

τούς τε καταχθονίους σέβε δαίμονας, ἔννομα ῥέζων·
τούς τε γόνεις τίμα, τούς τ' ἄγχιστ' ἐκγεγαῶτας.

τὰ χρυσώματα καὶ τὰ ἀργυρώματα· τί σοι
30 χρεία δογμάτων;—᾿Αλλὰ καὶ κριτής εἰμι τῶν
Ἑλλήνων.—Οἶδας κρίνειν; τί σε ἐποίησεν εἰδέναι;—Καῖσάρ μοι κωδίκελλον ἔγραψεν.—Γρα-
31 ψάτω σοι, ἵνα κρίνῃς περὶ τῶν μουσικῶν· καὶ τί
σοι ὄφελος; ὅμως δὲ πῶς κριτὴς ἐγένου; τὴν
τίνος χεῖρα καταφιλήσας, τὴν Συμφόρου ἢ τὴν
Νουμηνίου; τίνος πρὸ τοῦ κοιτῶνος κοιμηθείς;
τίνι πέμψας δῶρα; εἶτα οὐκ αἰσθάνῃ, ὅτι τοσούτου ἄξιόν ἐστι κριτὴν εἶναι ὅσου Νουμήνιος;—
᾿Αλλὰ δύναμαι ὃν θέλω εἰς φυλακὴν βαλεῖν.—
32 Ὡς λίθον.—᾿Αλλὰ δύναμαι ξυλοκοπῆσαι ὃν
θέλω.—Ὡς ὄνον. οὐκ ἔστι τοῦτο ἀνθρώπων
33 ἀρχή. ὡς λογικῶν ἡμῶν ἄρξον δεικνὺς ἡμῖν τὰ
συμφέροντα καὶ ἀκολουθήσομεν· δείκνυε τὰ
34 ἀσύμφορα καὶ ἀποστραφησόμεθα. ζηλωτὰς
ἡμᾶς κατασκεύασον σεαυτοῦ ὡς Σωκράτης ἑαυτοῦ. ἐκεῖνος ἦν ὁ ὡς ἀνθρώπων ἄρχων, ὁ
κατεσκευακὼς ὑποτεταχότας αὑτῷ τὴν ὄρεξιν
τὴν αὐτῶν, τὴν ἔκκλισιν, τὴν ὁρμήν, τὴν ἀφορμήν.
35 "τοῦτο ποίησον, τοῦτο μὴ ποιήσῃς· εἰ δὲ μή, εἰς
φυλακήν σε βαλῶ." οὐκέτι ὡς λογικῶν ἡ ἀρχὴ
36 γίνεται. ἀλλ᾿ "ὡς ὁ Ζεὺς διέταξεν, τοῦτο ποίη-
σον· ἂν δὲ μὴ ποιήσῃς, ζημιωθήσῃ, βλαβήσῃ."
ποίαν βλάβην; ἄλλην οὐδεμίαν, ἀλλὰ τὸ μὴ
ποιῆσαι ἃ δεῖ· ἀπολέσεις τὸν πιστόν, τὸν αἰδή-

---

[1] Otherwise unknown, but obviously freedmen influential
at court.
[2] That is, so as to be able to salute him the very first thing
in the morning.

gold and silver plate are enough to satisfy you;
what do you need doctrines for?—Yes, but I sit too
as judge over the Hellenes.—Do you know how to
sit as judge? What has brought you to know that?
—Caesar wrote credentials for me.—Let him write
you credentials that will allow you to sit as a judge
in music and literature; and what good will it do
you? However this may be, there is another
question, and that is, how did you come to be
a judge? Whose hand did you kiss—that of
Symphorus or that of Numenius?[1] In front of
whose bedroom door did you sleep?[2] To whom did
you send presents? After all, don't you recognize
that the office of judge is worth exactly as much as
Numenius is?—But I can throw whom I will into
prison.—As you can a stone.—But I can have
beaten to death with a club whom I will.—As you
can an ass.—That is not governing men. Govern us
as rational beings by pointing out to us what is
profitable, and we will follow you; point out what
is unprofitable, and we will turn away from it.
Bring us to admire and emulate you, as Socrates
brought men to admire and emulate him. He was
the one person who governed people as men, in that
he brought them to subject to him their desire,
their aversion, their choice, their refusal. "Do
this; do not do this; otherwise I will throw you
into prison." Say that, and yours ceases to be a
government as over rational beings. Nay, rather,
say, "As Zeus has ordained, do this; if you do not
do so, you will be punished, you will suffer injury."
What kind of injury? No injury but that of not
doing what you ought; you will destroy the man of
fidelity in you, the man of honour, the man of

59

μονα, τὸν κόσμιον. τούτων ἄλλας βλάβας μεί-
ζονας μὴ ζήτει.

η'. Πῶς πρὸς τὰς φαντασίας γυμναστέον;

1 Ὡς πρὸς τὰ ἐρωτήματα τὰ σοφιστικὰ γυμνα-
ζόμεθα, οὕτως καὶ πρὸς τὰς φαντασίας καθ'
2 ἡμέραν ἔδει γυμνάζεσθαι· προτείνουσι γὰρ ἡμῖν
καὶ αὗται ἐρωτήματα. ὁ υἱὸς ἀπέθανε τοῦ δεῖνος.
ἀπόκριναι "ἀπροαίρετον, οὐ κακόν." ὁ πατὴρ
τὸν δεῖνα ἀποκληρονόμον ἀπέλιπεν. τί σοι
δοκεῖ; "ἀπροαίρετον, οὐ κακόν." Καῖσαρ αὐτὸν
3 κατέκρινεν. "ἀπροαίρετον, οὐ κακόν." ἐλυπήθη
ἐπὶ τούτοις. "προαιρετικόν, κακόν." γενναίως
4 ὑπέμεινεν. "προαιρετικόν, ἀγαθόν." κἂν οὕτως
ἐθιζώμεθα, προκόψομεν· οὐδέποτε γὰρ ἄλλῳ
συγκαταθησόμεθα ἢ οὗ φαντασία καταληπτικὴ
5 γίνεται. ὁ υἱὸς ἀπέθανε. τί ἐγένετο; ὁ υἱὸς
ἀπέθανεν. ἄλλο οὐδέν; οὐδὲ ἕν.[1] τὸ πλοῖον
ἀπώλετο. τί ἐγένετο; τὸ πλοῖον ἀπώλετο. εἰς
φυλακὴν ἀπήχθη. τί γέγονεν; εἰς φυλακὴν
ἀπήχθη. τὸ δ' ὅτι "κακῶς πέπραχεν" ἐξ αὐτοῦ

---

[1] Schweighäuser: ἄλλο οὐδὲ ἕν S. ἄλλο οὐδέν; οὐδέν Trincavelli and most editors.

---

[1] The φαντασία καταληπτική, a term peculiar to Stoic
psychology, is "an impression so distinct and vivid and
consistent and permanent as to carry its own conviction of
certainty and to be its own criterion of truth" (P. E. More,
Hellenistic Philosophies, 85). See Bonhöffer, *Epiktet und die
Stoa*, 160–7, 228–32. Among recent writers E. R. Bevan,
Stoics and Sceptics, 36, renders the phrase "grasping impression"; G. Murray, *The Stoic Philosophy*, 27 and 44,
"comprehensive sense-impression." Cf. R. M. Wenley,

decent behaviour. You need not look for greater injuries than these.

CHAPTER VIII

How ought we to exercise ourselves to deal with the impressions of our senses ?

As we exercise ourselves to meet the sophistical interrogations, so we ought also to exercise ourselves daily to meet the impressions of our senses, because these too put interrogations to us. So-and-so's son is dead. Answer, "That lies outside the sphere of the moral purpose, it is not an evil." His father has disinherited So-and-so; what do you think of it? "That lies outside the sphere of the moral purpose, it is not an evil." Caesar has condemned him. "That lies outside the sphere of the moral purpose, it is not an evil." He was grieved at all this. "That lies within the sphere of the moral purpose, it is an evil." He has borne up under it manfully. "That lies within the sphere of the moral purpose, it is a good." Now if we acquire this habit, we shall make progress; for we shall never give our assent to anything but that of which we get a convincing sense-impression.[1] His son is dead. What happened? His son is dead. Nothing else? Not a thing. His ship is lost. What happened? His ship is lost. He was carried off to prison. What happened? He was carried off to prison. But the observation: "He has fared ill," is an addition that

---

Stoicism, 87, for the metaphor in the adjective: "Conviction of truth must . . . involve an unshakable grip upon the actual."

6 ἕκαστος προστίθησιν. "ἀλλ' οὐκ ὀρθῶς ταῦτα
ὁ Ζεὺς ποιεῖ." διὰ τί; ὅτι σε ὑπομενητικὸν
ἐποίησεν, ὅτι μεγαλόψυχον, ὅτι ἀφεῖλεν αὐτῶν
τὸ εἶναι κακά, ὅτι ἔξεστίν σοι πάσχοντι ταῦτα
εὐδαιμονεῖν, ὅτι σοι τὴν θύραν ἤνοιξεν, ὅταν σοι
μὴ ποιῇ; ἄνθρωπε, ἔξελθε καὶ μὴ ἐγκάλει.

7 Πῶς ἔχουσι Ῥωμαῖοι πρὸς φιλοσόφους ἂν
θέλῃς γνῶναι, ἄκουσον. Ἰταλικὸς ὁ μάλιστα
δοκῶν αὐτῶν φιλόσοφος εἶναι παρόντος ποτέ μου
χαλεπήνας τοῖς ἰδίοις, ὡς ἀνήκεστα πάσχων,
"Οὐ δύναμαι," ἔφη, "φέρειν· ἀπόλλυτέ με,
ποιήσετέ με τοιοῦτον γενέσθαι," δείξας ἐμέ.

θ'. Πρός τινα ῥήτορα ἀνιόντα εἰς Ῥώμην
ἐπὶ δίκῃ.

1 Εἰσελθόντος δέ τινος πρὸς αὐτόν, ὃς εἰς Ῥώμην
ἀνῄει δίκην ἔχων περὶ τιμῆς τῆς αὐτοῦ, πυθό-

---

1 Compare I. 9, 20 ; III. 13, 14, and Vol. I. p. xxv f.
2 For the particular expression here, see II. 6, 22.
3 The sense of this curious and apparently quite detached
anecdote, which has puzzled some scholars, seems to be that
the otherwise quite unknown Italicus, who was clearly not a
philosopher *propria persona*, but merely enjoyed some local
reputation among people at Rome for dabbling in philosophy,
was being urged by his friends to submit to some hardship
in a truly philosophic manner, and resented the implication
that he actually *was* a philosopher like the mean and humble
slave or freedman Epictetus. Roman popular feeling about

each man makes on his own responsibility. "But," you say, "Zeus does not do right in all this." What makes you think so? Because He has made you capable of patient endurance, and high-minded, because He has taken from these things the quality of being evils, because you are permitted to suffer these things and still to be happy, because He has opened for you the door,[1] whenever they are not to your good?[2] Man, go out, and do not complain.

Hear how the Romans feel about philosophers, if you care to know. Italicus, who has a very great reputation among them as a philosopher, once, when I was present, got angry at his friends, as though he were suffering something intolerable, and said, "I cannot bear it: you are the death of me! you will make me just like him," and pointed at me![3]

CHAPTER IX

To a certain rhetorician who was going to Rome for a lawsuit

THERE came in to visit Epictetus one day a man who was on his way to Rome, where he was engaged in a lawsuit involving an honour to be bestowed on him.[4]

philosophy is probably not greatly overdrawn in the well-known advice of Ennius (frag. sc. 376 Vahlen) to taste of philosophy, but not to gorge oneself upon it; and the jest of Plautus (*Captivi*, 284), apropos of a reckless romancer, that "he is not simply lying now, he is philosophizing."

[4] The situation seems a bit strange to us, but the famous lawsuit between Aeschines and Ctesiphon, in which Demosthenes delivered the oration *De Corona*, technically, indeed, in behalf of Ctesiphon, but actually in his own cause, offers a close parallel.

μενος τὴν αἰτίαν, δι' ἣν ἄνεισιν, ἐπερωτήσαντος
ἐκείνου, τίνα γνώμην ἔχει περὶ τοῦ πράγματος,
2 Εἴ μου πυνθάνῃ, τί πράξεις ἐν Ῥώμῃ, φησίν,
πότερον κατορθώσεις ἢ ἀποτεύξῃ, θεώρημα πρὸς
τοῦτο οὐκ ἔχω· εἰ δὲ[1] πυνθάνῃ, πῶς πράξεις,
τοῦτο εἰπεῖν, ὅτι, εἰ μὲν ὀρθὰ δόγματα ἔχεις,
καλῶς, εἰ δὲ φαῦλα, κακῶς. παντὶ γὰρ αἴτιον
τοῦ πράσσειν πως τὸ[2] δόγμα. τί γάρ ἐστιν,
3 δι'[3] ὃ ἐπεθύμησας προστάτης χειροτονηθῆναι
Κνωσίων; τὸ δόγμα. τί ἐστίν, δι' ὃ νῦν εἰς
Ῥώμην ἀνέρχῃ; τὸ δόγμα. καὶ μετὰ χειμῶνος
καὶ κινδύνου καὶ ἀναλωμάτων;—Ἀνάγκη γάρ
4 ἐστιν.—Τίς σοι λέγει τοῦτο; τὸ δόγμα. οὐκοῦν
εἰ πάντων αἴτια τὰ δόγματα, φαῦλα δέ τις ἔχει
δόγματα, οἷον ἂν ᾖ τὸ αἴτιον, τοιοῦτον καὶ τὸ
5 ἀποτελούμενον. ἆρ' οὖν πάντες ἔχομεν ὑγιῆ
δόγματα καὶ σὺ καὶ ὁ ἀντίδικός σου; καὶ πῶς
διαφέρεσθε; ἀλλὰ σὺ μᾶλλον ἢ ἐκεῖνος; διὰ
τί; δοκεῖ σοι. κἀκείνῳ καὶ τοῖς μαινομένοις.
6 τοῦτο πονηρὸν κριτήριον. ἀλλὰ δεῖξόν μοι, ὅτι
ἐπίσκεψίν τινα καὶ ἐπιμέλειαν πεποίησαι τῶν
σαυτοῦ δογμάτων. καὶ ὡς νῦν εἰς Ῥώμην πλεῖς
ἐπὶ τῷ προστάτης εἶναι Κνωσίων καὶ οὐκ ἐξαρκεῖ
σοι μένειν ἐν οἴκῳ τὰς τιμὰς ἔχοντι ἃς εἶχες,
ἀλλὰ μείζονός τινος ἐπιθυμεῖς καὶ ἐπιφανεστέρου,
πότε οὕτως ἔπλευσας ὑπὲρ τοῦ τὰ δόγματα
7 ἐπισκέψασθαι τὰ σαυτοῦ καὶ εἴ τι φαῦλον ἔχεις,

---

[1] Schenkl: εἰμ. S, or ἐμέ (Allen).

[2] πωςτό Oldfather: πράσσειν τι δόγμα S. The sharp contrast
between τί πράξεις and πῶς πράξεις above, which is the whole
point in the present passage, is completely falsified by the
reading in S.

[3] δι' added by Shaftesbury.

64

Epictetus asked what the reason was for the trip
to the Capital, and the man proceeded to ask
what opinion he had about the matter. If you
ask me *what* you are going to *do* in Rome, says
Epictetus, whether you will succeed or fail, I have
no precept to offer. If, however, you ask *how* you
are going to *fare*, I have this to say : If you have
sound judgements, you will fare well ; if unsound
judgements, ill ; since in every case the way a man
fares is determined by his judgement.[1] For what is
it that made you eager to be elected patron of the
people of Cnossos?[2] Your judgement. What is it
that impels you now to go up to Rome? Your
judgement. And that in stormy weather, in danger,
and at expense ?—Yes, but I have to.—Who tells you
that? Your judgement. Very well, then, if a man's
judgements determine everything, and if a man has
unsound judgements, whatever be the cause such also
will be the consequence. Do we all, then, have sound
judgements, both you and your opponent? If so,
then how do you come to disagree? But do you
have sound judgements rather than he? Why?
You think so. So does he, and so do madmen.
This is a poor criterion. But show me that you have
made any study of your own judgements and have
paid attention to them. And as now you are sailing to
Rome so as to become patron of the men of Cnossos,
and you are not satisfied to stay at home and keep
the honours which you had, but you have set your
heart upon something greater and more conspicuous,
so did you ever make a voyage for the purpose of
studying your own judgements, and of rejecting one,

[1] See critical note.
[2] The principal city of Crete.

ἐκβαλεῖν ; τίνι προσελήλυθας τούτου ἕνεκα ;
ποῖον χρόνον ἐπέταξας σαυτῷ, ποίαν ἡλικίαν ;
ἔπελθέ σου τοὺς χρόνους, εἰ ἐμὲ αἰσχύνῃ, αὐτὸς
8 πρὸς σαυτόν. ὅτε παῖς ἦς, ἐξήταζες τὰ σαυτοῦ
δόγματα ; οὐχὶ δ' ὡς πάντα ποιεῖς, ἐποίεις ἃ
ἐποίεις ; ὅτε δὲ μειράκιον ἤδη καὶ τῶν ῥητόρων
ἤκουες καὶ αὐτὸς ἐμελέτας, τί σοι λείπειν ἐφαν-
9 τάζου ; ὅτε δὲ νεανίσκος καὶ ἤδη ἐπολιτεύου καὶ
δίκας αὐτὸς ἔλεγες καὶ εὐδοκίμεις, τίς σοι ἔτι
ἴσος ἐφαίνετο ; ποῦ δ' ἂν ἠνέσχου ὑπό τινος
10 ἐξεταζόμενος, ὅτι πονηρὰ ἔχεις δόγματα ; τί οὖν
σοι θέλεις εἴπω ;—Βοήθησόν μοι εἰς τὸ πρᾶγμα.
—Οὐκ ἔχω πρὸς τοῦτο θεωρήματα· οὐδὲ σύ, εἰ
τούτου ἕνεκα ἐλήλυθας πρὸς ἐμέ, ὡς πρὸς φιλόσοφον ἐλήλυθας, ἀλλ' ὡς πρὸς λαχανοπώλην,
11 ἀλλ' ὡς πρὸς σκυτέα.—Πρὸς τί οὖν ἔχουσιν οἱ
φιλόσοφοι θεωρήματα ;—Πρὸς τοῦτο, ὅ τι ἂν
ἀποβῇ, τὸ ἡγεμονικὸν ἡμῶν κατὰ φύσιν ἔχειν
καὶ διεξάγειν. μικρόν σοι δοκεῖ τοῦτο ;—Οὔ·
ἀλλὰ τὸ μέγιστον.—Τί οὖν ; ὀλίγου χρόνου
χρείαν ἔχει καὶ ἔστι παρερχόμενον αὐτὸ λαβεῖν ;
εἰ δύνασαι, λάμβανε.

12   Εἶτ' ἐρεῖς " συνέβαλον Ἐπικτήτῳ ὡς λίθῳ, ὡς
ἀνδριάντι." εἶδες γάρ με καὶ πλέον οὐδέν.
ἀνθρώπῳ δ' ὡς ἀνθρώπῳ συμβάλλει ὁ τὰ

if it is unsound? Whom have you ever visited for this purpose? What time have you set yourself, what period of your life? Review the periods of your life, all to yourself, if you are ashamed to do so before me. When you were a boy were you in the habit of examining your judgements? Did you not habitually do what you then did just as you do everything now? And when you grew to be a youth and were attending the lectures of the rhetoricians, and were yourself practising, what did you fancy that you yet lacked? And when you were a young man and began to take part in politics, and to plead cases yourself, and to have a good reputation, who any longer seemed in your eyes to be your equal? Would you under any circumstances have submitted to be put through an examination on the charge that you had wretched judgements? Very well then, what do you wish me to say to you?—Help me in this affair.—I have no precepts to offer for this; and you too, if you came to me for this purpose, have not come to me as to a philosopher, but as to a vegetable-dealer, as to a cobbler.—To what end, then, do philosophers have precepts to offer?—To this end, that whatever happen, our governing principle shall be, and abide to the end, in accord with nature. Do you regard that as a trifle?—No; it is of the utmost moment.—What then? Does this require only a little time, and is it possible to acquire it on a passing visit? Acquire it, then, if you can!

Then you will say, "When I met Epictetus it was like meeting a stone, a statue." Yes, for you took a look at me, and nothing more. The person who meets a man as a man is one who learns to

67

δόγματα αὐτοῦ καταμανθάνων καὶ ἐν τῷ μέρει
13 τὰ ἴδια δεικνύων. κατάμαθέ μου τὰ δόγματα,
δεῖξόν μοι τὰ σὰ καὶ οὕτως λέγε συμβεβληκέναι
μοι. ἐλέγξωμεν ἀλλήλους· εἴ τι ἔχω κακὸν
δόγμα, ἄφελε αὐτό· εἴ τι ἔχεις, θὲς εἰς τὸ μέσον.
14 τοῦτό ἐστι φιλοσόφῳ συμβάλλειν. οὔ· ἀλλὰ
"πάροδός ἐστι καὶ ἕως τὸ πλοῖον μισθούμεθα,
δυνάμεθα καὶ Ἐπίκτητον ἰδεῖν· ἴδωμεν, τί ποτε
λέγει." εἶτ' ἐξελθὼν "οὐδὲν ἦν ὁ Ἐπίκτητος,
ἐσολοίκιζεν, ἐβαρβάριζεν." τίνος γὰρ ἄλλου
κριταὶ εἰσέρχεσθε ;
15   "Ἀλλ' ἂν πρὸς τούτοις," φησίν, "ὦ, ἀγρὸν
οὐχ ἔξω ὡς οὐδὲ σύ, ποτήρια ἀργυρᾶ οὐχ
ἔξω ὡς οὐδὲ σύ, κτήνη καλὰ ὡς οὐδὲ σύ."
16 πρὸς ταῦτα ἴσως ἀρκεῖ ἐκεῖνο εἰπεῖν ὅτι
"ἀλλὰ χρείαν αὐτῶν οὐκ ἔχω· σὺ δ' ἂν πολλὰ
κτήσῃ, ἄλλων χρείαν ἔχεις, θέλεις οὐ θέλεις,
17 πτωχότερός μου."—Τίνος οὖν ἔχω χρείαν ;—Τοῦ
σοὶ μὴ παρόντος· τοῦ εὐσταθεῖν, τοῦ κατὰ φύσιν
18 ἔχειν τὴν διάνοιαν, τοῦ μὴ ταράττεσθαι. πάτρων, οὐ πάτρων, τί μοι μέλει ; σοὶ μέλει. πλουσιώτερός σού εἰμι· οὐκ ἀγωνιῶ, τί φρονήσει περὶ
ἐμοῦ ὁ Καῖσαρ· οὐδένα κολακεύω τούτου ἕνεκα.
ταῦτα ἔχω ἀντὶ τῶν ἀργυρωμάτων, ἀντὶ τῶν
χρυσωμάτων. σὺ χρυσᾶ σκεύη, ὀστράκινον τὸν
λόγον, τὰ δόγματα, τὰς συγκαταθέσεις, τὰς
19 ὁρμάς, τὰς ὀρέξεις. ὅταν δὲ ταῦτα ἔχω κατὰ
φύσιν, διὰ τί μὴ φιλοτεχνήσω καὶ περὶ τὸν

understand the other's judgements, and in his turn
exhibits his own. Learn to know my judgements;
show me your own, and then say you have met me.
Let us put one another to the test; if I cherish any
evil judgement, take it away; if you cherish one,
bring it forward. That is what it means to meet a
philosopher. Oh no; but your way is: "We are
passing, and while we are hiring our ship, we have a
chance to take a look at Epictetus; let's see what in
the world he has to say." Then you leave with the
remark: "Epictetus was nothing at all, his language
was full of solecisms and barbarisms." What else
were you capable of judging, when you came in like
that?

"But," says someone, "if I devote myself to these
things, I shall not own a farm any more than you do,
I shall not have silver goblets any more than you, or
fine cattle any more than you." To all this it is
perhaps enough to answer: "I do not need them;
but you, even if you acquire many possessions, need
still others, and whether you will or not, are more
poverty-stricken than I am."—What, then, do I
need?—What you do not have; steadfastness, your
mind in a state of conformity with nature, freedom
from vexation of spirit. Patron or not patron, what
do I care? But you care. I am richer than you
are; I am not worried about what Caesar is going to
think of me; I flatter no man for that purpose. All
this is what I have as an offset to your silver plate,
and your gold plate. You have furnishings of gold,
but your reason, your judgements, your assent, your
choice, your desire—of earthenware. But when I
have these in a state of conformity with nature, why
should I not take up logic also as a sort of hobby?

λόγον; εὐσχολῶ γάρ· οὐ περισπᾶταί μου ἡ
διάνοια. τί ποιήσω μὴ περισπώμενος; τούτου
τί ἀνθρωπικώτερον ἔχω; ὑμεῖς ὅταν μηδὲν ἔχητε,
20 ταράσσεσθε, εἰς θέατρον εἰσέρχεσθε ἢ ἀναλύετε·
διὰ τί ὁ φιλόσοφος μὴ ἐξεργάσηται τὸν αὑτοῦ
21 λόγον; σὺ κρυστάλλινα, ἐγὼ τὰ τοῦ Ψευδομένου·
σὺ μούρρινα, ἐγὼ τὰ τοῦ Ἀποφάσκοντος. σοὶ
πάντα μικρὰ φαίνεται ἃ ἔχεις, ἐμοὶ τὰ ἐμὰ πάντα
μεγάλα. ἀπλήρωτός σού ἐστιν ἡ ἐπιθυμία, ἡ
22 ἐμὴ πεπλήρωται. τοῖς παιδίοις[1] εἰς στενό-
βρογχον κεράμιον καθιεῖσιν τὴν χεῖρα καὶ
ἐκφέρουσιν ἰσχαδοκάρυα ταὐτὸ[2] συμβαίνει· ἂν
πληρώσῃ τὴν χεῖρα, ἐξενεγκεῖν οὐ δύναται, εἶτα
κλάει. ἄφες ὀλίγα ἐξ αὐτῶν καὶ ἐξοίσεις. καὶ
σὺ ἄφες τὴν ὄρεξιν· μὴ πολλῶν ἐπιθύμει καὶ
οἴσεις.[3]

ιʹ. Πῶς φέρειν δεῖ τὰς νόσους;

1   Ἑκάστου δόγματος ὅταν ἡ χρεία παρῇ, πρόχειρον αὐτὸ ἔχειν δεῖ· ἐπ' ἀρίστῳ τὰ περὶ ἀρίστου,
ἐν βαλανείῳ τὰ περὶ βαλανείου, ἐν κοίτῃ τὰ περὶ
κοίτης.

---

[1] ταιδίοις supplied by Wolf.   [2] Capps: τοῦτο S.
[3] Wolf plausibly suggested εὑροήσεις, " you will prosper,"
for this extremely abrupt and obscure locution.

---

[1] See note in II. 17, 34.
[2] Highly coloured and very expensive glass.

For, I have plenty of leisure; my mind is not being dragged this way and that. What shall I do, seeing there is nothing that disturbs me? What have I which more becomes a man than this? You and your kind when you have nothing to do are restless, go to the theatre, or wander up and down aimlessly. Why should not the philosopher develop his own reason? You turn to vessels of crystal, I to the syllogism called "The Liar";[1] you to myrrhine ware,[2] I to the syllogism called "The Denyer."[3] Everything that you already have seems small in your sight, but everything that I have seems important to me. Your strong desire is insatiate, mine is already satisfied. The same thing happens to the children who put their hand down into a narrow-necked jar and try to take out figs and nuts: if they get their hand full, they can't get it out, and then they cry. Drop a few and you will get it out. And so do you too drop your desire; do not set your heart upon many things and you will obtain.[4]

CHAPTER X

How ought we to bear our illnesses?

WHEN the need arises for each separate judgement, we ought to have it ready; at lunch our judgements about lunch, at the bath our judgements about a bath, in bed our judgements about a bed.

---

[3] The exact nature of this argument is unknown, although Chrysippus wrote two works on the subject (Diog. Laert. 7, 197), and it is casually mentioned also by Clement of Alexandria, *Strom.* 5, 11.

[4] See critical note.

2 μηδ' ὕπνον μαλακοῖσιν ἐπ' ὄμμασι προσδέ-
    ξασθαι,
   πρὶν τῶν ἡμερινῶν[1] ἔργων λογίσασθαι ἕκαστα·
3 "πῇ παρέβην; τί δ' ἔρεξα; τί μοι δέον οὐ
    τετέλεσται;"[2]
   ἀρξάμενος δ' ἀπὸ τούτου[3] ἐπέξιθι· καὶ μετέ-
    πειτα
   δειλὰ μὲν οὖν[4] ῥέξας ἐπιπλήσσεο, χρηστὰ δὲ
    τέρπου.

4 καὶ τούτους τοὺς στίχους κατέχειν χρηστικῶς,
οὐχ ἵνα δι' αὐτῶν ἀναφωνῶμεν, ὡς διὰ τοῦ Παιὰν
5 Ἄπολλον. πάλιν ἐν πυρετῷ τὰ πρὸς τοῦτο·
μή, ἂν πυρέξωμεν, ἀφιέναι πάντα καὶ ἐπιλανθά-
νεσθαι· "ἂν ἐγὼ ἔτι φιλοσοφήσω, ὃ θέλει
γινέσθω. πού ποτ' ἀπελθόντα τοῦ σωματίου
ἐπιμελεῖσθαι δεῖ."[5] εἴ γε[6] καὶ πυρετὸς οὐκ
6 ἔρχεται. τὸ δὲ φιλοσοφῆσαι τί ἐστιν; οὐχὶ
παρασκευάσασθαι πρὸς τὰ συμβαίνοντα; οὐ
παρακολουθεῖς οὖν, ὅτι τοιοῦτόν τι λέγεις· "ἂν
ἔτι ἐγὼ παρασκευάσωμαι πρὸς τὸ πράως φέρειν
τὰ συμβαίνοντα, ὃ θέλει γινέσθω"; οἷον εἴ τις

---

[1] Corrected from the ordinary text by Schweighäuser:
ἡμερινῶν S.

[2] C. Schenkl: ἐκτετέλεσται S; but the ordinary text οὐκ
ἐτελέσθη appears also below in iv. 6, 35.

[3] H. Schenkl: τοῦδε S: πρώτου the ordinary text (and
Bentley).

[4] οὖν added by C. Schenkl: ἐκπρήξας the ordinary text (and
Bentley).

"Also allow not sleep to draw nigh to your
    languorous eyelids,
Ere you have reckoned up each several deed of
    the daytime:
'Where went I wrong? Did what? And what
    to be done was left undone?'
Starting from this point review, then, your acts,
    and thereafter remember:
Censure yourself for the acts that are base, but
    rejoice in the goodly."[1]

And keep these verses on hand to use, not by
way of exclamations, as we cry, "Paean Apollo!"
Again, in a fever have ready the judgements which
apply to that. Let us not, if we fall into a fever,
abandon and forget all our principles, saying: "If I
ever study philosophy again, let anything happen that
will! I'll have to go away somewhere and take care of
my poor body." Yes indeed, if fever does not go
there too![2] But what is philosophy? Does it not mean
making preparation to meet the things that come
upon us? Do you not understand, then, that what
you are saying amounts to something like this: "If
I ever again prepare to bear quietly the things that
come upon me, let anything happen that will"?

[1] The *Golden Verses*, vulgarly ascribed to Pythagoras, 40-
44, with several variations in detail.
[2] The sense of this difficult and corrupt passage seems to
be that Epictetus sarcastically approves the plan, with,
however, the proviso, that there be no fever where his
interlocutor plans to go; which was impossible, because
there was no such place. In other words, one cannot avoid
hardships by changing one's residence; therefore, prepare to
meet them wherever you are.

---

⁵ δεῖ added by Upton.   ⁶ Schweighäuser: τε S.

πληγὰς λαβὼν ἀποσταίη τοῦ παγκρατιάζειν.
7 ἀλλ' ἐκεῖ μὲν ἔξεστι καταλῦσαι καὶ μὴ δέρεσθαι,
ἐνθάδε δ' ἂν καταλύσωμεν φιλοσοφοῦντες, τί
ὄφελος ; τί οὖν δεῖ λέγειν πρὸς αὐτὸν [1] ἐφ'
ἑκάστου τῶν τραχέων ; ὅτι "ἕνεκα τούτου ἐγυμ-
8 ναζόμην, ἐπὶ τοῦτο ἤσκουν." ὁ θεός σοι λέγει
" δός μοι ἀπόδειξιν, εἰ νομίμως ἤθλησας, εἰ
ἔφαγες ὅσα δεῖ, εἰ ἐγυμνάσθης, εἰ τοῦ ἀλείπτου
ἤκουσας." εἶτ' ἐπ' αὐτοῦ τοῦ ἔργου καταμα-
λακίζῃ ; νῦν τοῦ πυρέττειν καιρός ἐστιν, τοῦτο
καλῶς γινέσθω· τοῦ διψᾶν, δίψα καλῶς· τοῦ
9 πεινᾶν, πείνα καλῶς. οὐκ ἔστιν ἐπὶ σοί ; τίς
σε κωλύσει ; ἀλλὰ πιεῖν μὲν κωλύσει ὁ ἰατρός,
καλῶς δὲ διψᾶν οὐ δύναται· καὶ φαγεῖν μὲν
κωλύσει, πεινᾶν δὲ καλῶς οὐ δύναται.

10   'Αλλ' οὐ φιλολογῶ· — Τίνος δ' ἕνεκα φιλο-
λογεῖς ; ἀνδράποδον, οὐχ ἵνα εὐροῇς ; οὐχ ἵνα
εὐσταθῇς ; οὐχ ἵνα κατὰ φύσιν ἔχῃς καὶ διεξά-
11 γῃς ; τί κωλύει πυρέσσοντα κατὰ φύσιν ἔχειν
τὸ ἡγεμονικόν ; ἐνθάδ' ὁ ἔλεγχος τοῦ πράγματος,
ἡ δοκιμασία τοῦ φιλοσοφοῦντος. μέρος γάρ ἐστι
καὶ τοῦτο τοῦ βίου, ὡς περίπατος, ὡς πλοῦς, ὡς
12 ὁδοιπορία, οὕτως καὶ πυρετός. μή τι περιπατῶν
ἀναγιγνώσκεις ; — Οὔ. — Οὕτως οὐδὲ πυρέσσων.
ἀλλ' ἂν καλῶς περιπατῇς, ἔχεις τὸ τοῦ περιπα-

---

[1] Kronenberg (after Schegk) : λέγειν αὖ τόν S.

---

[1] See note on III. 1, 5.
[2] The same phrase appears in 2 Timothy ii. 5.
[3] At Olympia, for example, men had to practise under
supervision and observe a strict diet for one whole month
before the games.

74

It is just as if a man should give up the pancratium [1] because he has received blows. The only difference is that in the pancratium a man may stop, and so avoid a severe beating, but in life, if we stop the pursuit of philosophy, what good does it do? What, then, ought a man to say to himself at each hardship that befalls him? "It was for *this* that I kept training, it was to meet *this* that I used to practise." God says to you, "Give Me proof, whether you have striven lawfully,[2] eaten what is prescribed,[3] taken exercise, heeded your trainer." After that, do you flinch when the time for action arrives? Now it is time for your fever, let it come upon you in the right way; for thirst, bear your thirst in the right way; to go hungry, bear hunger in the right way. It is not in your power, you say? Who is there to prevent you? Nay, your physician will prevent you from drinking, but he cannot prevent you from thirsting in the right way; and he will prevent you from eating, but he cannot prevent you from bearing hunger in the right way.

But am I not a scholar?—And for what purpose do you devote yourself to scholarship? Slave, is it not that you may be happy? Is it not that you may be secure? Is it not that you may conform to nature and live your life in that way. What prevents you, when you have a fever, from having your governing principle conform with nature? Here is the proof of the matter, the test of the philosopher. For this too is a part of life; like a stroll, a voyage, a journey, such is also a fever. I presume you do not read while taking a stroll, do you?—No.—No more than when you have a fever. But if you stroll in the right way, you perform what is expected of a stroller;

75

τοῦντος· ἂν καλῶς πυρέξῃς, ἔχεις τὰ τοῦ πυρέσ-
13 σοντος. τί ἐστι καλῶς πυρέσσειν; μὴ θεὸν
μέμψασθαι, μὴ ἄνθρωπον, μὴ θλιβῆναι ὑπὸ τῶν
γινομένων, εὖ καὶ καλῶς προσδέχεσθαι τὸν θάνατον, ποιεῖν τὰ προστασσόμενα· ὅταν ὁ ἰατρὸς
εἰσέρχηται, μὴ φοβεῖσθαι, τί εἴπῃ, μηδ' ἂν εἴπῃ
"κομψῶς ἔχεις," ὑπερχαίρειν· τί γάρ σοι ἀγαθὸν
14 εἶπεν; ὅτε γὰρ ὑγίαινες, τί σοι ἦν ἀγαθόν;
μηδ' ἂν εἴπῃ "κακῶς ἔχεις," ἀθυμεῖν· τί γάρ
ἐστι τὸ κακῶς ἔχειν; ἐγγίζειν τῷ διαλυθῆναι
τὴν ψυχὴν ἀπὸ τοῦ σώματος. τί οὖν δεινόν
ἐστιν; ἐὰν νῦν μὴ ἐγγίσῃς, ὕστερον οὐκ ἐγγιεῖς;
ἀλλὰ ὁ κόσμος μέλλει ἀνατρέπεσθαι σοῦ ἀποθα-
15 νόντος; τί οὖν κολακεύεις τὸν ἰατρόν; τί λέγεις
"ἐὰν σὺ θέλῃς, κύριε, καλῶς ἔξω"; τί παρέχεις
αὐτῷ ἀφορμὴν τοῦ ἐπᾶραι ὀφρῦν; οὐχὶ δὲ τὴν
αὐτοῦ ἀξίαν αὐτῷ ἀποδίδως, ὡς σκυτεῖ περὶ τὸν
πόδα, ὡς τέκτονι περὶ τὴν οἰκίαν, οὕτως καὶ τῷ
ἰατρῷ περὶ τὸ σωμάτιον, τὸ οὐκ ἐμόν, τὸ φύσει
νεκρόν; τούτων ὁ καιρός ἐστι τῷ πυρέσσοντι·
16 ἂν ταῦτα ἐκπληρώσῃ, ἔχει τὰ αὑτοῦ. οὐ γάρ
ἐστιν ἔργον τοῦ φιλοσόφου ταῦτα τὰ ἐκτὸς
τηρεῖν, οὔτε τὸ οἰνάριον οὔτε τὸ ἐλάδιον οὔτε
τὸ σωμάτιον, ἀλλὰ τί; τὸ ἴδιον ἡγεμονικόν. τὰ
δ' ἔξω πῶς; μέχρι τοῦ μὴ ἀλογίστως κατὰ
17 ταῦτα ἀναστρέφεσθαι. ποῦ οὖν ἔτι καιρὸς τοῦ

---

[1] That is, matter which is only temporarily endowed with
life by virtue of union for a short while with the soul.

76

if you have fever in the right way, you perform the
things expected of the man who has a fever. What
does it mean to have fever in the right way? Not
to blame God, or man, not to be overwhelmed by
what happens to you, to await death bravely and in
the right way, to do what is enjoined upon you;
when your physician comes to see you, not to be
afraid of what he will say, and at the same time not
to be carried away with joy, if he says, "You are
doing splendidly"; for what *good* to you lay in
that remark? Why, when you were well, what *good*
was it to you? It means not to be downhearted, too,
if he says, "You are in a bad way." For what does
it mean to be in a bad way? That you are close to
a separation of the soul from the body. What, then,
is terrifying about that? If you do not draw near
now, will you not draw near later? And is the
universe going to be upset when you die? Why,
then, do you wheedle your physician? Why do you
say, "If you wish, Master, I shall get well"? Why
do you give him occasion to put on airs? Why not
give him just what is his due? As I give the shoemaker his due about my foot, the builder his due
about my house, so also the physician his due about
my paltry body, something that is not mine, something that is by nature dead.[1] These are the things
that the moment demands for a man who is in a
fever; if he meets these demands, he has what
properly belongs to him. For it is not the business
of the philosopher to guard these external matters
—neither his paltry wine, nor his paltry oil, nor his
paltry body—but what? His own governing principle.
And how treat externals? Only so far as not to act
thoughtlessly about them. What proper occasion is

φοβεῖσθαι ; ποῦ οὖν ἔτι καιρὸς ὀργῆς ; ποῦ φόβου
18 περὶ τῶν ἀλλοτρίων, περὶ τῶν μηδενὸς ἀξίων ;
δύο γὰρ ταῦτα πρόχειρα ἔχειν δεῖ· ὅτι ἔξω τῆς
προαιρέσεως οὐδέν ἐστιν οὔτε ἀγαθὸν οὔτε κακὸν
καὶ ὅτι οὐ δεῖ προηγεῖσθαι τῶν πραγμάτων, ἀλλ'
19 ἐπακολουθεῖν. "οὐκ ἔδει οὕτως μοι προσε-
νεχθῆναι τὸν ἀδελφόν." οὔ· ἀλλὰ τοῦτο μὲν
ἐκεῖνος ὄψεται. ἐγὼ δ', ὡς ἂν προσενεχθῇ, αὐτὸς
20 ὡς δεῖ χρήσομαι τοῖς πρὸς ἐκεῖνον. τοῦτο γὰρ
ἐμόν ἐστιν, ἐκεῖνο δ' ἀλλότριον· τοῦτο οὐδεὶς
κωλῦσαι δύναται, ἐκεῖνο κωλύεται.

ια'. Σποράδην τινά.

1   Εἰσί τινες ὡς ἐκ νόμου διατεταγμέναι κολάσεις
2 τοῖς ἀπειθοῦσι τῇ θείᾳ διοικήσει· "ὃς ἂν ἄλλο
τι ἡγήσηται ἀγαθὸν παρὰ τὰ προαιρετικά, φθονείτω, ἐπιθυμείτω, κολακευέτω, ταρασσέσθω· ὃς
ἂν ἄλλο κακόν, λυπείσθω, πενθείτω, θρηνείτω,
3 δυστυχείτω." καὶ ὅμως οὕτως πικρῶς κολαζό-
μενοι ἀποστῆναι οὐ δυνάμεθα.

4   Μέμνησο, τί λέγει ὁ ποιητὴς περὶ τοῦ ξένου·

ξεῖν', οὔ μοι θέμις ἔστ',[1] οὐδ' εἰ κακίων σέθεν
ἔλθοι,

ξεῖνον ἀτιμῆσαι· πρὸς γὰρ Διός εἰσιν ἅπαντες[2]
ξεῖνοί τε πτωχοί τε.

[1] s: ἔστι καί S.
[2] ἔλθοι . . . ἅπαντες supplied by Schenkl: σεθέντες S.

78

there, then, any longer for fear? What proper
occasion, then, any longer for anger? Or for fear
about things that are not his own concern, worthless things? For here are the two principles that
you ought to have ready at hand: Outside the
sphere of the moral purpose there is nothing either
good or bad; and, We ought not to lead events, but
to follow them. "My brother ought not to have
treated me so." No; but it is for him to look to
that. As for me, no matter how he behaves, I shall
observe all my relations to him as I ought. For this
is my part, the other does not belong to me; in
this nobody can hinder me, the other is subject to
hindrance.

CHAPTER XI

Some scattered sayings

THERE are certain punishments, assigned as it were
by law, for those who are disobedient to the divine
dispensation. "Whoever shall regard as good anything but the things that fall within the scope of his
moral purpose, let him envy, yearn, flatter, feel
disturbed; whoever shall regard anything else as
evil, let him sorrow, grieve, lament, be unhappy."
Nevertheless, for all that we are so severely punished,
we cannot desist.

Remember what the poet [1] says about the stranger:

Stranger, I may not with right dishonour a
    stranger, not even
Worse man were he than art thou; for of God
    are all strangers and beggars.

---

[1] Homer (frequently so designated, especially in late
antiquity), in the *Odyssey*, XIV. 56–8.

5 τοῦτο οὖν καὶ ἐπὶ πατρὸς πρόχειρον ἔχειν· οὔ
μοι θέμις ἔστ᾽ οὐδ᾽ εἰ κακίων σέθεν ἔλθοι, πατέρ'[1]
ἀτιμῆσαι· πρὸς γὰρ Διός εἰσιν ἅπαντες τοῦ Πα-
6 τρῴου· καὶ ἐπ᾽ ἀδελφῷ· πρὸς γὰρ Διός εἰσιν
ἅπαντες τοῦ Ὁμογνίου. καὶ οὕτως κατὰ τὰς
ἄλλας σχέσεις εὑρήσομεν ἐπόπτην τὸν Δία.

ιβ'. Περὶ ἀσκήσεως.

1 Τὰς ἀσκήσεις οὐ δεῖ διὰ τῶν παρὰ φύσιν καὶ
παραδόξων ποιεῖσθαι, ἐπεί τοι τῶν θαυματο-
ποιῶν οὐδὲν διοίσομεν οἱ λέγοντες φιλοσοφεῖν.
2 δύσκολον γάρ ἐστι καὶ τὸ ἐπὶ σχοινίου περιπατεῖν καὶ οὐ μόνον δύσκολον, ἀλλὰ καὶ ἐπικίνδυνον. τούτου ἕνεκα δεῖ καὶ ἡμᾶς μελετᾶν
ἐπὶ σχοινίου περιπατεῖν ἢ φοίνικα ἱστάνειν ἢ
3 ἀνδριάντας περιλαμβάνειν; οὐδαμῶς. οὐκ ἔστι
τὸ δύσκολον πᾶν καὶ ἐπικίνδυνον ἐπιτήδειον
πρὸς ἄσκησιν, ἀλλὰ τὸ πρόσφορον τῷ προκει-
4 μένῳ ἐκπονηθῆναι. τί δ᾽ ἐστὶ τὸ προκείμενον
ἐκπονηθῆναι; ὀρέξει καὶ ἐκκλίσει ἀκωλύτως
ἀναστρέφεσθαι. τοῦτο δὲ τί ἐστιν; μήτε ὀρε-
γόμενον ἀποτυγχάνειν μήτ᾽ ἐκκλίνοντα περιπίπτειν. πρὸς τοῦτο οὖν καὶ τὴν ἄσκησιν ῥέπειν

---

[1] Schweighäuser : πάτερ S.

---

[1] For this aspect of Zeus see O. Gruppe, *Griech. Mythol.
etc.*, p. 1116; and especially A. B. Cook, *Zeus* (index).
[2] "Setting up a palm" may possibly mean climbing a pole
with only the hands and the feet, like the climbers of palms, as
Upton and Schweighäuser (after Bulinger) suggest. There was

This, then, is what one should have ready to use in the case of a father: " I may not rightfully dishonour a father, not even if a worse man than art thou should come ; for of Zeus, the God of Fathers,[1] are they all " ; and so in the case of a brother : " For of Zeus, the God of Kindred, are they all." And similarly, in the other social relations, we shall find Zeus overseeing them all.

CHAPTER XII

Of training

WE ought not to take our training in things that are unnatural or fantastic, since in that case we who profess to be philosophers will be no better than the mountebanks. For it is a hard thing also to walk a tight-rope, and not merely hard but dangerous too. Ought we also for this reason to practise walking a tight-rope, or setting up a palm, or throwing our arms about statues?[2] Not a bit of it. Not every difficult and dangerous thing is suitable for training, but only that which is conducive to success in achieving the object of our effort. And what is the object of our effort? To act without hindrance in choice and in aversion. And what does this mean? Neither to fail to get what we desire, nor to fall into what we would avoid. Toward this end, therefore, our

a " palm-bearer " (φοινεικοφόρος, or σπαδεικοφόρος) connected with the gymnasium at Tegea in Arcadia (*I.G.* V. 2, Nos. 47, 48, 50, 53), who possibly had charge of the exercise referred to here, whatever its exact character may have been. As for embracing statues, Diogenes was said to have done that nude in cold weather, so as to harden himself. Diog. Laert. 6, 23.

5 δεῖ. ἐπεὶ γὰρ οὐκ ἔστιν ἀναπότευκτον σχεῖν τὴν
ὄρεξιν καὶ τὴν ἔκκλισιν ἀπερίπτωτον ἄνευ μεγάλης καὶ συνεχοῦς ἀσκήσεως, ἴσθι ὅτι, ἐὰν ἔξω
ἐάσῃς ἀποστρέφεσθαι αὐτὴν ἐπὶ τὰ ἀπροαίρετα,
οὔτε τὴν ὄρεξιν ἐπιτευκτικὴν ἕξεις οὔτε τὴν
6 ἔκκλισιν ἀπερίπτωτον. καὶ ἐπεὶ τὸ ἔθος ἰσχυρὸν
προηγῆται πρὸς μόνα ταῦτα εἰθισμένων ἡμῶν
χρῆσθαι ὀρέξει καὶ ἐκκλίσει, δεῖ τῷ ἔθει τούτῳ
ἐναντίον ἔθος ἀντιθεῖναι καὶ ὅπου ὁ πολὺς ὄλισθος
τῶν φαντασιῶν, ἐκεῖ ἀντιτιθέναι τὸ ἀσκητικόν.

7 Ἑτεροκλινῶς ἔχω πρὸς ἡδονήν· ἀνατοιχήσω[1]
ἐπὶ τὸ ἐναντίον ὑπὲρ τὸ μέτρον τῆς ἀσκήσεως
ἕνεκα. ἐκκλιτικῶς ἔχω πόνου· τρίψω μου καὶ
γυμνάσω πρὸς τοῦτο τὰς φαντασίας ὑπὲρ τοῦ
ἀποστῆναι τὴν ἔκκλισιν ἀπὸ παντὸς τοῦ τοιού-
8 του. τίς γάρ ἐστιν ἀσκητής; ὁ μελετῶν ὀρέξει
μὲν μὴ[2] χρῆσθαι, ἐκκλίσει δὲ πρὸς μόνα τὰ
προαιρετικὰ χρῆσθαι, καὶ μελετῶν μᾶλλον ἐν
τοῖς δυσκαταπονήτοις. καθ᾽ ὃ καὶ ἄλλῳ πρὸς
9 ἄλλα μᾶλλον ἀσκητέον. τί οὖν ὧδε ποιεῖ τὸ
φοίνικα στῆσαι ἢ τὸ στέγην δερματίνην καὶ
10 ὅλμον καὶ ὕπερον περιφέρειν; ἄνθρωπε, ἄσκη-

---

[1] Bentley (anticipating Schweighäuser): ἂν ἀ . . . . ήσω S.
[2] μή supplied by Gataker.

---

[1] For the "palm tree," see above, note on § 2. As for the
other items, it is conceivable that some Cynics may have
carried about with them such equipment ostentatiously to
indicate that they had all they needed for life; that is,
shelter and the simplest utensils to prepare grain for food,
somewhat as Diogenes was content with his *pithos* and a cup
(although eventually he discarded even the latter). But it
must be confessed that the passage is very obscure. Seneca,
De ira, 2, 12, speaks somewhat disparagingly of *ille qui*

training also should tend. For since it is impossible
without great and constant training to secure that our
desire fail not to attain, and our aversion fall not into
what it would avoid, be assured that, if you allow
training to turn outwards, towards the things that
are not in the realm of the moral purpose, you will
have neither your desire successful in attaining what
it would, nor your aversion successful in avoiding
what it would. And since habit is a powerful in-
fluence, when we have accustomed ourselves to employ
desire and aversion only upon these externals, we
must set a contrary habit to counteract this habit,
and where the very slippery nature of sense-impressions is in play, there we must set our training as a
counteracting force.

I am inclined to pleasure; I will betake myself to
the opposite side of the rolling ship, and that beyond
measure, so as to train myself. I am inclined to
avoid hard work; I will strain and exercise my
sense-impressions to this end, so that my aversion
from everything of this kind shall cease. For who
is the man in training? He is the man who
practises not employing his desire, and practises
employing his aversion only upon the things that
are within the sphere of his moral purpose, yes, and
practises particularly in the things that are difficult
to master. And so different men will have to
practise particularly to meet different things. To
what purpose is it, then, under these conditions, to
set up a palm tree, or to carry around a leather tent,
or a mortar and pestle?[1] Man, practise, if you are

meditatus est . . . _sarcinae ingenti cervices supponere_ (that is,
"the man who has practised carrying about enormous
burdens on his back"), pretty clearly in reference to this
same custom, but without throwing much light upon it.

σον, εἰ γοργὸς εἶ, λοιδορούμενος ἀνέχεσθαι, ἀτι-
μασθεὶς μὴ ἀχθεσθῆναι. εἶθ᾽ οὕτως προβήσῃ,
ἵνα, κἂν πλήξῃ σέ τις, εἴπῃς αὐτὸς πρὸς αὑτὸν
11 ὅτι "δόξον ἀνδριάντα περιειληφέναι." εἶτα καὶ
οἰναρίῳ κομψῶς χρῆσθαι, μὴ εἰς τὸ πολὺ πίνειν
(καὶ γὰρ περὶ τοῦτο ἐπαρίστεροι ἀσκηταί εἰσιν),
ἀλλὰ πρῶτον εἰς τὸ ἀποσχέσθαι, καὶ κορασιδίου
ἀπέχεσθαι καὶ πλακουνταρίου. εἶτά ποτε ὑπὲρ
δοκιμασίας, εἰ ἄρα, καθήσεις εὐκαίρως αὐτὸς
σαυτὸν ὑπὲρ τοῦ γνῶναι, εἰ ὁμοίως ἡττῶσίν σε
12 αἱ φαντασίαι. τὰ πρῶτα δὲ φεῦγε μακρὰν ἀπὸ
τῶν ἰσχυροτέρων. ἄνισος ἡ μάχη κορασιδίῳ
κομψῷ πρὸς νέον ἀρχόμενον φιλοσοφεῖν· χύτρα,
φασί, καὶ πέτρα οὐ συμφωνεῖ.

13 Μετὰ τὴν ὄρεξιν καὶ τὴν ἔκκλισιν δεύτερος
τόπος[1] ὁ περὶ τὴν ὁρμὴν καὶ ἀφορμήν· ἵν᾽[2]
εὐπειθὴς τῷ λόγῳ, ἵνα μὴ παρὰ καιρόν, μὴ
παρὰ τόπον, μὴ παρὰ ἄλλην τινὰ τοιαύτην
συμμετρίαν.[3]

14 Τρίτος ὁ περὶ τὰς συγκαταθέσεις, ὁ πρὸς τὰ
15 πιθανὰ καὶ ἑλκυστικά. ὡς γὰρ ὁ Σωκράτης
ἔλεγεν ἀνεξέταστον βίον μὴ ζῆν, οὕτως ἀνεξέταστον φαντασίαν μὴ παραδέχεσθαι, ἀλλὰ λέγειν
"ἔκδεξαι, ἄφες ἴδω, τίς εἶ καὶ πόθεν ἔρχῃ," ὡς
οἱ νυκτοφύλακες "δεῖξόν μοι τὰ συνθήματα."

---

[1] S (but only the first letter is by the first hand;
τρόπος, which was probably the original reading, s).
[2] ἵν᾽ supplied by Shaftesbury.
[3] Reiske: ἀσυμμετρίαν S.

---

[1] Compare the fable about the earthenware pot and the
bronze jar in Babrius 193 (Crusius) = Aesop 422 (Halm),
Avianus 11, etc.

arrogant, to submit when you are reviled, not to be
disturbed when you are insulted. Then you will
make such progress, that, even if someone strikes
you, you will say to yourself, "Imagine that you
have thrown your arms about a statue." Next train
yourself to use wine with discretion, not with a view
to heavy drinking (for there are some clumsy fools
who practise with this in mind), but first for the
purpose of achieving abstention from wine, and keeping your hands off a wench, or a sweet-cake. And
then some day, if the occasion for a test really comes,
you will enter the lists at a proper time for the sake
of discovering whether your sense-impressions still
overcome you just as they did before. But first of
all flee far away from the things that are too strong
for you. It is not a fair match that, between a pretty
wench and a young beginner in philosophy. "A
pot," as they say, "and a stone do not go together." [1]
     After your desire and your aversion the next
topic [2] has to do with your choice and refusal. Here
the object is to be obedient to reason, not to choose
or to refuse at the wrong time, or the wrong place,
or contrary to some other similar propriety.
     The third topic has to do with cases of assent;
it is concerned with the things that are plausible
and attractive. For, just as Socrates used to tell us
not to live a life unsubjected to examination,[3] so
we ought not to accept a sense-impression unsubjected to examination, but should say, "Wait,
allow me to see who you are and whence you come" [4]
(just as the night-watch say, "Show me your

<hr />

[2] Upon this division of the field of philosophy, which
appears to be peculiar to Epictetus, see note on III. 2, 1.
[3] See note on I. 26, 18.   [4] Compare II. 18, 24.

"ἔχεις τὸ παρὰ τῆς φύσεως σύμβολον, ὃ δεῖ τὴν
16 παραδεχθησομένην ἔχειν φαντασίαν;" καὶ λοιπὸν ὅσα τῷ σώματι προσάγεται ὑπὸ τῶν γυμνα-
ζόντων αὐτό, ἂν μὲν ὧδέ που ῥέπῃ πρὸς ὄρεξιν
καὶ ἔκκλισιν, εἴη ἂν καὶ αὐτὰ ἀσκητικά· ἂν δὲ
πρὸς ἐπίδειξιν, ἔξω νενευκότος[1] ἐστὶ καὶ ἄλλο
τι θηρωμένου καὶ θεατὰς ζητοῦντος τοὺς ἐροῦντας
17 "ὢ[2] μεγάλου ἀνθρώπου." διὰ τοῦτο καλῶς ὁ
Ἀπολλώνιος ἔλεγεν ὅτι "ὅταν θέλῃς σαυτῷ
ἀσκῆσαι, διψῶν ποτὲ καύματος ἐφέλκυσαι
βρόγχον ψυχροῦ καὶ ἔκπτυσον καὶ μηδενὶ
εἴπῃς."

ιγʹ. Τί ἐρημία καὶ ποῖος ἔρημος.

1   Ἐρημία ἐστὶ κατάστασίς τις ἀβοηθήτου. οὐ
γὰρ ὁ μόνος ὢν εὐθὺς καὶ ἔρημος, ὥσπερ οὐδ' ὁ
2 ἐν πολλοῖς ὢν οὐκ ἔρημος. ὅταν γοῦν ἀπολέσω-
μεν ἢ ἀδελφὸν ἢ υἱὸν ἢ φίλον, ᾧ προσαναπαυό-
μεθα, λέγομεν ἀπολελεῖφθαι ἔρημοι, πολλάκις ἐν
Ῥώμῃ ὄντες, τοσούτου ὄχλου ἡμῖν ἀπαντῶντος

---

[1] Wolf: νενευκός S.   [2] Wolf: ὡς S.

---

[1] A token or mark of identification was frequently called
for in ancient times by the police (especially at night), much
as in some of the occupied and annexed districts of Europe
since the Great War.

tokens").[1] "Do you have your token from nature, the one which every sense-impression which is to be accepted must have?" And, in conclusion, all the methods which are applied to the body by the persons who are giving it exercise, might also themselves be conducive to training, if in some such way as this they tend toward desire and aversion; but if they tend toward display, they are characteristic of a man who has turned toward the outside world, and is hunting for something other than the thing itself which he is doing, and is looking for spectators who will say, "Ah, what a great man!" It is this consideration which renders admirable the remark that Apollonius used to make: "When you wish to train for your own sake, then when you are thirsty some hot day take a mouthful of cold water, and spit it out—[2] and don't tell anybody about it!"

CHAPTER XIII

The meaning of a forlorn state, and the kind of person a forlorn man is

A FORLORN state is the condition of one who is without help. For a man is not forlorn merely because he is alone, any more than a man in the midst of a crowd is necessarily not forlorn. At all events, when we have lost a brother, or a son, or a friend with whom we have shared the same bed, we say that we have been left forlorn, though often we are in Rome, with such large crowds meeting us in the streets, and so many people living in the same

[2] Something of the same sort is said, but upon somewhat dubious authority, to have been an exercise often practised by Plato (Stobaeus, *Flor.* III. 17, 35).

καὶ τοσούτων συνοικούντων, ἔσθ' ὅτε καὶ[1] πλῆ-
θος δούλων ἔχοντες. θέλει γὰρ ὁ ἔρημος κατὰ
τὴν ἔννοιαν ἀβοήθητός τις εἶναι καὶ ἐκκείμενος
3 τοῖς βλάπτειν βουλομένοις. διὰ τοῦτο, ὅταν
ὁδεύωμεν, τότε μάλιστα ἐρήμους λέγομεν ἑαυ-
τούς, ὅταν εἰς λῃστὰς ἐμπέσωμεν. οὐ γὰρ
ἀνθρώπου ὄψις ἐξαιρεῖται ἐρημίας, ἀλλὰ πιστοῦ
4 καὶ αἰδήμονος καὶ ὠφελίμου. ἐπεὶ εἰ τὸ μόνον
εἶναι ἀρκεῖ πρὸς τὸ ἔρημον εἶναι, λέγε ὅτι καὶ
ὁ Ζεὺς ἐν τῇ ἐκπυρώσει ἔρημός ἐστι καὶ κατα-
κλαίει αὐτὸς ἑαυτοῦ· "τάλας ἐγώ, οὔτε τὴν
"Ηραν ἔχω οὔτε τὴν Ἀθηνᾶν οὔτε τὸν Ἀπόλλωνα
οὔτε ὅλως ἢ ἀδελφὸν ἢ υἱὸν ἢ ἔγγονον ἢ συγ-
5 γενῆ." ταῦτα καὶ λέγουσί τινες ὅτι ποιεῖ μόνος
ἐν τῇ ἐκπυρώσει. οὐ γὰρ ἐπινοοῦσι διεξαγωγὴν
μόνου[2] ἀπό τινος φυσικοῦ ὁρμώμενοι, ἀπὸ τοῦ
φύσει κοινωνικοῦ εἶναι καὶ φιλαλλήλου καὶ ἡδέως
6 συναναστρέφεσθαι ἀνθρώποις. ἀλλ' οὐδὲν ἧττον
δεῖ τινὰ καὶ πρὸς τοῦτο παρασκευὴν ἔχειν τὸ
δύνασθαι αὐτὸν ἑαυτῷ ἀρκεῖν, δύνασθαι αὐτὸν
7 ἑαυτῷ συνεῖναι· ὡς ὁ Ζεὺς αὐτὸς ἑαυτῷ σύνεστιν
καὶ ἡσυχάζει ἐφ' ἑαυτοῦ καὶ ἐννοεῖ τὴν διοίκησιν
τὴν ἑαυτοῦ οἵα ἐστὶ καὶ ἐν ἐπινοίαις γίνεται πρε-
πούσαις ἑαυτῷ, οὕτως καὶ ἡμᾶς δύνασθαι αὐτοὺς
ἑαυτοῖς λαλεῖν, μὴ προσδεῖσθαι ἄλλων, διαγωγῆς

---

[1] καί added by Schegk.
[2] καί after this word was deleted by Reiske.

---

[1] The periodic consumption of the universe by fire, and its
rebirth, a doctrine which the Stoics inherited from Heracleitus. Even the deities, with the exception of Zeus, succumb
in the *Götterdämmerung*. Precisely the same situation as

house with us, and sometimes even though we have
a multitude of slaves. For according to the nature of
the concept the 'forlorn' means the person who is
without help, and exposed to those who wish to
injure him. That is why, when we go on a journey,
we call ourselves forlorn most especially at the
moment that we encounter robbers. For it is not
the sight of a human being as such which puts an
end to our forlorn condition, but the sight of a
faithful, and unassuming, and helpful human
being. Why, if being alone is enough to make one
forlorn, you will have to say that even Zeus himself
is forlorn at the World-Conflagration,[1] and bewails
himself: "Wretched me! I have neither Hera,
nor Athena, nor Apollo, nor, in a word, brother, or
son, or grandson, or kinsman." There are even
those who say that this is what he does when left
alone at the World-Conflagration; for they cannot
conceive of the mode of life of one who is all alone,
starting as they do from a natural principle, namely,
the facts of natural community of interest among
men, and mutual affection, and joy in intercourse.
But one ought none the less to prepare oneself for
this also, that is, to be able to be self-sufficient, to be
able to commune with oneself; even as Zeus communes
with himself, and is at peace with himself, and contemplates the character of his governance, and
occupies himself with ideas appropriate to himself,
so ought we also to be able to converse with ourselves,
not to be in need of others, not to be at a loss for

that described here is referred to by Seneca, *Ep. Mor.* 9,16:
Qualis est Iovis (vita), cum resoluto mundo et dis in unum con-
fusis paulisper cessante natura adquiescit sibi cogitationibus suis
traditus.

8 μὴ ἀπορεῖν· ἐφιστάνειν τῇ θείᾳ διοικήσει, τῇ
αὐτῶν πρὸς τἆλλα σχέσει· ἐπιβλέπειν, πῶς
πρότερον εἴχομεν πρὸς τὰ συμβαίνοντα, πῶς νῦν·
τίνα ἐστὶν ἔτι τὰ θλίβοντα· πῶς ἂν θεραπευθῇ
καὶ ταῦτα, πῶς ἐξαιρεθῇ· εἴ τινα ἐξεργασίας
δεῖται τούτων,[1] κατὰ τὸν αὐτῶν [2] λόγον ἐξεργάζεσθαι.

9 Ὁρᾶτε γάρ, ὅτι εἰρήνην μεγάλην ὁ Καῖσαρ
ἡμῖν δοκεῖ παρέχειν, ὅτι οὐκ εἰσὶν οὐκέτι πόλεμοι
οὐδὲ μάχαι οὐδὲ λῃστήρια μεγάλα οὐδὲ πειρα-
τικά, ἀλλ' ἔξεστιν πάσῃ ὥρᾳ ὁδεύειν, πλεῖν ἀπ'
10 ἀνατολῶν ἐπὶ δυσμάς. μή τι οὖν καὶ ἀπὸ
πυρετοῦ δύναται ἡμῖν εἰρήνην παρασχεῖν, μή τι
καὶ ἀπὸ ναυαγίου, μή τι καὶ ἀπὸ ἐμπρησμοῦ ἢ
ἀπὸ σεισμοῦ ἢ ἀπὸ κεραυνοῦ; ἄγε ἀπ' ἔρωτος;
οὐ δύναται. ἀπὸ πένθους; οὐ δύναται. ἀπὸ
φθόνου; οὐ δύναται. ἀπ' οὐδενὸς ἁπλῶς τού-
11 των· ὁ δὲ λόγος ὁ τῶν φιλοσόφων ὑπισχνεῖται
καὶ ἀπὸ τούτων εἰρήνην παρέχειν. καὶ τί λέγει;
"ἄν μοι προσέχητε, ὦ ἄνθρωποι, ὅπου ἂν ἦτε,
ὅ τι ἂν ποιῆτε, οὐ λυπηθήσεσθε, οὐκ ὀργισθή-
σεσθε, οὐκ ἀναγκασθήσεσθε, οὐ κωλυθήσεσθε,
ἀπαθεῖς δὲ καὶ ἐλεύθεροι διάξετε ἀπὸ πάντων."
12 ταύτην τὴν εἰρήνην τις ἔχων κεκηρυγμένην οὐχ
ὑπὸ τοῦ Καίσαρος (πόθεν γὰρ αὐτῷ ταύτην
κηρύξαι;), ἀλλ' ὑπὸ τοῦ θεοῦ κεκηρυγμένην διὰ
13 τοῦ λόγου οὐκ ἀρκεῖται, ὅταν ᾖ [3] μόνος, ἐπι-
βλέπων καὶ ἐνθυμούμενος "νῦν ἐμοὶ κακὸν οὐδὲν
δύναται συμβῆναι, ἐμοὶ λῃστὴς οὐκ ἔστιν, ἐμοὶ
σεισμὸς οὐκ ἔστιν, πάντα εἰρήνης μεστά, πάντα

---

[1] Schenkl: τῶν S.   [2] Reiske (after Schegk): αὐτοῦ S.
[3] ᾖ supplied by Sb.

some way to spend our time; we ought to devote ourselves to the study of the divine governance, and of our own relation to all other things; to consider how we used to act toward the things that happen to us, and how we act now; what the things are that still distress us; how these too can be remedied, or how removed; if any of these matters that I have mentioned need to be brought to perfection, to perfect them in accordance with the principle of reason inherent in them.

Behold now, Caesar seems to provide us with profound peace, there are no wars any longer, nor battles, no brigandage on a large scale, nor piracy, but at any hour we may travel by land, or sail from the rising of the sun to its setting. Can he, then, at all provide us with peace from fever too, and from shipwreck too, and from fire, or earthquake, or lightning? Come, can he give us peace from love? He cannot. From sorrow? From envy? He cannot—from absolutely none of these things. But the doctrine of the philosophers promises to give us peace from these troubles too. And what does it say? "Men, if you heed me, wherever you may be, whatever you may be doing, you will feel no pain, no anger, no compulsion, no hindrance, but you will pass your lives in tranquillity and in freedom from every disturbance." When a man has this kind of peace proclaimed to him, not by Caesar—why, how could *he* possibly proclaim it?—but proclaimed by God through the reason, is he not satisfied, when he is alone? When he contemplates and reflects, "Now no evil can befall me, for me there is no such thing as a brigand, for me there is no such thing as an earthquake, everything is full of peace, everything

ἀταραξίας· πᾶσα ὁδός, πᾶσα πόλις, πᾶς [1] σύνο-
δος, γείτων, κοινωνὸς ἀβλαβής. ἄλλος παρέχει
τροφάς, ᾧ μέλει, ἄλλος ἐσθῆτα, ἄλλος αἰσθήσεις
14 ἔδωκεν, ἄλλος προλήψεις. ὅταν δὲ μὴ παρέχῃ
τἀναγκαῖα, τὸ ἀνακλητικὸν σημαίνει, τὴν θύραν
ἤνοιξεν καὶ λέγει σοι 'ἔρχου.' ποῦ; εἰς οὐδὲν
δεινόν, ἀλλ' ὅθεν ἐγένου, εἰς τὰ φίλα καὶ συγ-
15 γενῆ, εἰς τὰ στοιχεῖα. ὅσον ἦν ἐν σοὶ πυρός,
εἰς πῦρ ἄπεισιν, ὅσον ἦν γῃδίου, εἰς γῄδιον, ὅσον
πνευματίου, εἰς πνευμάτιον, ὅσον ὑδατίου, εἰς
ὑδάτιον. οὐδεὶς Ἅιδης οὐδ' Ἀχέρων οὐδὲ Κω-
κυτὸς οὐδὲ Πυριφλεγέθων, ἀλλὰ πάντα θεῶν
16 μεστὰ καὶ δαιμόνων." ταῦτά τις ἐνθυμεῖσθαι
ἔχων καὶ βλέπων τὸν ἥλιον καὶ σελήνην καὶ
ἄστρα καὶ γῆς ἀπολαύων καὶ θαλάσσης ἔρημός
17 ἐστιν οὐ μᾶλλον ἢ καὶ ἀβοήθητος. "τί οὖν;
ἄν τις ἐπελθών μοι μόνῳ ἀποσφάξῃ με;" μωρέ,
σὲ οὔ, ἀλλὰ τὸ σωμάτιον.

18 Ποία οὖν ἔτι ἐρημία, ποία ἀπορία; τί χείρονας
ἑαυτοὺς ποιῶμεν τῶν παιδαρίων; ἅ τινα ὅταν
ἀπολειφθῇ μόνα, τί ποιεῖ; ἄραντα ὀστράκια καὶ
σποδὸν οἰκοδομεῖ τί ποτε, εἶτα καταστρέφει καὶ
πάλιν ἄλλο οἰκοδομεῖ· καὶ οὕτως οὐδέποτε ἀπο-
19 ρεῖ διαγωγῆς. ἐγὼ οὖν, ἂν πλεύσητε ὑμεῖς, μέλλω
καθήμενος κλαίειν ὅτι μόνος ἀπελείφθην καὶ
ἔρημος οὕτως; οὐκ ὀστράκια ἔξω, οὐ σποδόν;

---

[1] Schweighäuser (as in II. 14, 8 ; IV. 1, 97) : πᾶσα S.

---

[1] A reverent expression for God. See note on III. 1, 43.

full of tranquillity; every road, every city, every fellow-traveller, neighbour, companion, all are harmless. Another,[1] whose care it is, supplies food; Another supplies raiment; Another has given senses; Another preconceptions. Now whenever He does not provide the necessities for existence, He sounds the recall; He has thrown open the door and says to you, "Go." Where? To nothing you need fear, but back to that from which you came, to what is friendly and akin to you, to the physical elements.[2] What there was of fire in you shall pass into fire, what there was of earth into earth, what there was of spirit into spirit, what there was of water into water. There is no Hades, nor Acheron, nor Cocytus, nor Pyriphlegethon, but everything is filled with gods and divine powers." [3] A man who has this to think upon, and who beholds the sun, and moon, and stars, and enjoys land and sea, is no more forlorn than he is without help. "Why, what then? What if someone should attack me when I am alone and murder me?" Fool, not murder *you*, but your trivial body.

What kind of forlornness is left, then, to talk about? What kind of helplessness? Why make ourselves worse than little children? When they are left alone, what do they do? They gather up sherds and dust and build something or other, then tear it down and build something else again; and so they are never at a loss as to how to spend their time. Am I, then, if you set sail, to sit down and cry because I am left alone and forlorn in *that* fashion? Shan't I have sherds, shan't I have dust? But they

[2] Compare the Introduction, p. xxv f.
[3] A doctrine ascribed to Thales, Diog. Laert. 1, 27.

ἀλλ' ἐκεῖνα ὑπ' ἀφροσύνης ταῦτα ποιεῖ, ἡμεῖς δ'
ὑπὸ φρονήσεως δυστυχοῦμεν ;

20 Πᾶσα μεγάλη δύναμις ἐπισφαλὴς τῷ ἀρχο-
μένῳ. φέρειν οὖν δεῖ τὰ τοιαῦτα κατὰ δύναμιν,
ἀλλὰ κατὰ φύσιν . . .[1] ἀλλ' οὐχὶ τῷ φθισικῷ.
21 μελέτησόν ποτε διαγωγὴν ὡς ἄρρωστος, ἵνα ποθ'
ὡς ὑγιαίνων διαγάγῃς. ἀσίτησον, ὑδροπότησον·
ἀπόσχου ποτὲ παντάπασιν ὀρέξεως, ἵνα ποτὲ καὶ
εὐλόγως ὀρεχθῇς. εἰ δ' εὐλόγως, ὅταν ἔχῃς τι
22 ἐν σεαυτῷ ἀγαθόν, εὖ ὀρεχθήσῃ. οὔ· ἀλλ'
εὐθέως ὡς σοφοὶ διάγειν ἐθέλομεν καὶ ὠφελεῖν
ἀνθρώπους. ποίαν ὠφέλειαν ; τί ποιεῖς ; σαυτὸν
γὰρ ὠφέλησας ; ἀλλὰ προτρέψαι αὐτοὺς θέλεις.
σὺ γὰρ προτέτρεψαι ; θέλεις αὐτοὺς ὠφελῆσαι ;
23 δεῖξον αὐτοῖς ἐπὶ σεαυτοῦ, οἵους ποιεῖ φιλοσοφία,
καὶ μὴ φλυάρει. ἐσθίων τοὺς συνεσθίοντας
ὠφέλει, πίνων τοὺς πίνοντας, εἴκων πᾶσι, παρα-
χωρῶν, ἀνεχόμενος, οὕτως αὐτοὺς ὠφέλει καὶ μὴ
κατεξέρα αὐτῶν τὸ σαυτοῦ φλέγμα.

---

[1] Reiske indicated the lacuna.

---

[1] The change in subject-matter is so abrupt that something may perhaps have fallen out in some ancestor of S, or
perhaps the next chapter-heading has become displaced by a
few lines. Yet there are similarly abrupt transitions in III.
8, 7 and III. 15, 14.
[2] Something like "Give food (or wine) to the healthy man"
(Reiske), or "Wrestling is very good for the healthy man"
(Schenkl), has probably fallen out at this point.

act thus out of folly, and are we miserable out of wisdom?

[1] Great power is always dangerous for the beginner. We ought, therefore, to bear such things according to our power—nay, in accordance with nature . . . [2] but not for the consumptive. Practise at some one time a style of living like an invalid, that at some other time you may live like a healthy man. Take no food, drink only water; refrain at some one time altogether from desire, that at some other time you may exercise desire, and then with good reason. And if you do so with good reason, whenever you have some good in you, you will exercise your desire aright.[3] No, that's not our way, but we wish to live like wise men from the very start, and to help mankind. Help indeed! What are you about? Why, have you helped yourself? But you wish to help them progress. Why, have you made progress yourself? Do you wish to help them? Then show them, by your own example, the kind of men philosophy produces, and stop talking nonsense. As you eat, help those who are eating with you; as you drink, those who are drinking with you; by yielding to everybody, giving place, submitting—help men in this way, and don't bespatter them with your own sputum.[4]

[3] "It is one of the paradoxes of conduct that a man cannot will to do good until in a sense he has become good, but Epictetus would doubtless admit that the will must from the first have exercise." Matheson, I. 32.

[4] Referring, no doubt, to the sputtering of excessively ardent lecturers.

ιδ΄. Σποράδην τινά.

1 Ὡς οἱ καλοὶ[1] τραγῳδοὶ μόνοι ᾷσαι οὐ δύνανται,
ἀλλὰ μετὰ πολλῶν, οὕτως ἔνιοι μόνοι περιπα-
2 τῆσαι οὐ δύνανται. ἄνθρωπε, εἴ τις εἶ, καὶ
μόνος περιπάτησον καὶ σαυτῷ λάλησον καὶ μὴ
3 ἐν τῷ χορῷ κρύπτου. σκώφθητί ποτε, περί-
βλεψαι, ἐνσείσθητι, ἵνα γνῷς, τίς εἶ.

4 Ὅταν τις ὕδωρ πίνῃ ἢ ποιῇ τι ἀσκητικόν, ἐκ
πάσης ἀφορμῆς λέγει αὐτὸ πρὸς πάντας· "ἐγὼ
5 ὕδωρ πίνω." διὰ γὰρ τοῦτο ὕδωρ πίνεις, διὰ
γὰρ τὸ ὕδωρ πίνειν; ἄνθρωπε, εἴ σοι λυσιτελεῖ
6 πίνειν, πῖνε· εἰ δὲ μή, γελοίως ποιεῖς. εἰ δὲ
συμφέρει σοι καὶ πίνεις, σιώπα πρὸς τοὺς δυσα-
ρεστοῦντας τοιούτοις[2] ἀνθρώποις. τί οὖν; αὐτοῖς
τούτοις ἀρέσκειν θέλεις;

7 Τῶν πραττομένων τὰ μὲν προηγουμένως πράττεται, τὰ δὲ κατὰ περίστασιν, τὰ δὲ κατ᾽ οἰκονο-
μίαν, τὰ δὲ κατὰ συμπεριφοράν, τὰ δὲ κατ᾽
ἔνστασιν.

8 Δύο ταῦτα ἐξελεῖν τῶν ἀνθρώπων, οἴησιν καὶ
ἀπιστίαν. οἴησις μὲν οὖν ἐστὶ τὸ δοκεῖν μηδενὸς
προσδεῖσθαι, ἀπιστία δὲ τὸ ὑπολαμβάνειν μὴ

---

[1] This has been read uniformly κακοί ever since the time
of Wolf. But it is clear from Aristotle, *Pol.* 3. 13, 21, that
superior solo voices were not used in the chorus, and it is a
notorious fact that excellent choral effects are secured with
voices which are not suitable for solo performance.
[2] Meibom : τοῖς *S.*

CHAPTER XIV

Some scattered sayings

As the good chorus-singers in tragedy cannot render solos, but can sing perfectly well with a number of other voices, so some men cannot walk around by themselves. Man, if you are anybody, both walk around by yourself, and talk to yourself, and don't hide yourself in the chorus. Let yourself be laughed at sometimes, look about you, shake yourself up, so as to find out who you actually are.

Whenever a man drinks water only, or has some ascetic practice, he takes every opportunity to talk about it to everybody: "I drink water only." Why, do you drink water just for the sake of drinking water? Man, if it is good for you to drink water, drink it! Otherwise your conduct is absurd. But if it does you good and you drink water only, don't say a word about it to the people who are annoyed by such persons. Why, what's your object? Are these just the ones you wish to please?[1]

Among actions some are performed primarily on their own account, others on occasion, or as a matter of good management, or as required by tact, or as part of a formal plan.

Here are two things of which one must rid men, conceit and diffidence. Now conceit is to fancy that one needs nothing further. And diffidence is to assume that one cannot enjoy a life of serenity

---

[1] That is: If you drink water only, do it to please yourself, and not for the sake of impressing others; above all, not for the sake of trying to impress those who dislike teetotalers.

δυνατὸν εἶναι εὑροεῖν[1] τοσούτων περιεστηκότων.
9 τὴν μὲν οὖν οἴησιν ἔλεγχος ἐξαιρεῖ, καὶ τοῦτο
πρῶτον ποιεῖ Σωκράτης . . .[2] ὅτι δ' οὐκ ἀδύνατόν ἐστι τὸ πρᾶγμα, σκέψαι καὶ ζήτησον — οὐδέν
10 σε βλάψει ἡ ζήτησις αὕτη· καὶ σχεδὸν τὸ φιλοσοφεῖν τοῦτ' ἔστι, ζητεῖν, πῶς ἐνδέχεται ἀπαραποδίστως ὀρέξει χρῆσθαι καὶ ἐκκλίσει.

11 " Κρείσσων εἰμὶ σοῦ· ὁ γὰρ πατήρ μου ὑπατικός
12 ἐστιν." ἄλλος λέγει " ἐγὼ δεδημάρχηκα, σὺ δ'
οὔ." εἰ δ' ἵπποι ἦμεν, ἔλεγες ἂν ὅτι " ὁ πατήρ
μου ὠκύτερος ἦν," ἢ[3] ὅτι " ἐγὼ ἔχω πολλὰς
κριθὰς καὶ χόρτον," ἢ ὅτι " κομψὰ περιτρα-
χήλια." τί οὖν εἰ[4] ταῦτά σου λέγοντος εἶπον ὅτι
13 " ἔστω ταῦτα, τρέχωμεν οὖν " ; ἄγε, ἐπ' ἀνθρώπου οὖν οὐδέν ἐστι τοιοῦτον οἷον ἐφ' ἵππου
δρόμος, ἐξ οὗ γνωσθήσεται ὁ χείρων καὶ ὁ
κρείττων ; μήποτ' ἐστὶν αἰδώς, πίστις, δικαιο-
14 σύνη ; τούτοις δείκνυε κρείττονα σεαυτόν, ἵν' ὡς
ἄνθρωπος ᾖς[5] κρείττων. ἄν μοι λέγῃς ὅτι
" μεγάλα λακτίζω," ἐρῶ σοι κἀγὼ ὅτι " ἐπὶ ὄνου
ἔργῳ μέγα φρονεῖς."

---

[1] Schenkl (after Wolf): εὑρεῖν σ̔ S (mostly by Sc in an
erasure).
[2] Reiske observed the lacuna.
[3] ἢ supplied by Hense.
[4] τί οὖν εἰ Oldfather: εἰ οὖν S. εἶτ' οὖν or τί οὖν Reiske.

98

under so many adverse circumstances. Now conceit is removed by cross-examination, and this is what Socrates starts with. . . .[1] But that the matter is not impossible, consider and search—this kind of search will do you no harm ; and, indeed, to philosophize practically amounts to this, that is, to search how it is possible to employ desire and aversion without hindrance.

"I am superior to you, for my father has consular rank."[2] Another says, "I have been a tribune, and you have not." And if we were horses, you would be saying : "My sire was swifter than yours," or, "I have quantities of barley and fodder," or, "I have pretty neck-trappings." What then, if, when you were talking like this, I said, "Granted all that, let's run a race, then"? Come now, is there, then, nothing in man like running in the case of a horse, whereby the worse and the better will be recognized? Isn't there such a thing as reverence, faith, justice? Prove yourself superior in these points, in order to be superior as a human being. If you tell me, "I can deliver a mighty kick,"[3] I shall say to you in my turn, "You are proud over what is the act of an ass."

---

[1] There is no clear connection here with the preceding, and the topic of the removal of diffidence could scarcely have been passed over.

[2] The subject-matter of this is closely paralleled in frag. 18, *Encheiridion* 44, and in the florilegia. It was clearly a commonplace.

[3] Much practised by the pancratiasts, who struck both with the heel and with the knee.

---

[5] In Schweighäuser without comment, after Schegk : ᾗ S.

ιε'. "Οτι δεῖ περιεσκεμμένως ἔρχεσθαι ἐφ'
ἕκαστα.

1   Ἑκάστου ἔργου σκόπει τὰ καθηγούμενα καὶ τὰ
ἀκόλουθα καὶ οὕτως ἔρχου ἐπ' αὐτό. εἰ δὲ μή,
τὴν μὲν πρώτην ἥξεις προθύμως ἅτε μηδὲν τῶν
ἑξῆς ἐντεθυμημένος, ὕστερον δ' ἀναφανέντων
2   τινῶν αἰσχρῶς ἀποστήσῃ. "θέλω Ὀλύμπια
νικῆσαι." ἀλλὰ σκόπει τὰ καθηγούμενα αὐτοῦ καὶ
τὰ ἀκόλουθα· καὶ οὕτως ἄν σοι λυσιτελῇ, ἅπτου
3   τοῦ ἔργου. δεῖ σε εὐτακτεῖν, ἀναγκοφαγεῖν, ἀπέχεσθαι πεμμάτων, γυμνάζεσθαι πρὸς ἀνάγκην, ὥρᾳ
τεταγμένῃ, ἐν καύματι, ἐν ψύχει· μὴ ψυχρὸν πίνειν,
μὴ οἶνον ὅτ' ἔτυχεν· ἁπλῶς ὡς ἰατρῷ[1] παραδε-
4   δωκέναι σεαυτὸν τῷ ἐπιστάτῃ· εἶτα ἐν τῷ ἀγῶνι
παρορύσσεσθαι, ἔστιν ὅτε χεῖρα ἐκβαλεῖν, σφυρὸν[2] στρέψαι, πολλὴν ἀφὴν καταπιεῖν, μαστι-
γωθῆναι· καὶ μετὰ τούτων πάντων ἔσθ' ὅτε
5   νικηθῆναι. ταῦτα λογισάμενος, ἂν ἔτι θέλῃς,
ἔρχου ἐπὶ τὸ ἀθλεῖν· εἰ δὲ μή, ὅρα ὅτι ὡς τὰ
παιδία ἀναστραφήσῃ, ἃ νῦν μὲν ἀθλητὰς παίζει,
νῦν δὲ μονομάχους, νῦν δὲ σαλπίζει, εἶτα τρα-
6   γῳδεῖ ὅ τι ἂν[3] ἴδῃ καὶ θαυμάσῃ. οὕτως καὶ σὺ

---

[1] The text of the *Encheiridion*: ἁπλῶς ἰατρῷ γάρ S
(originally).
[2] The text of the *Encheiridion*: ὀφρύν S (originally),
changed to ὀσφύν.   [3] Reiske: ὅταν S.

---

[1] Repeated with slight variations in *Encheiridion*, 29.
[2] See note on *Ench.* 29, 2.
[3] A technical term (Diog. Laert. 6, 27) of somewhat
uncertain meaning, but probably referring to a preliminary
wallowing in dust or mud before the wrestling match at the
pancratium.

CHAPTER XV [1]

That we ought to approach each separate thing with circumspection

IN each separate thing that you do consider the matters which come first, and those which follow after, and only then approach the thing itself. Otherwise, at the start you will come to it enthusiastically because you have never reflected upon any of the subsequent steps, but later on, when some of them appear, you will give up disgracefully. "I wish to win an Olympic victory." But consider the matters which come before that and those which follow after; and only when you have done that, then, if it profits you, put your hand to the task. You have to submit to discipline, follow a strict diet, give up sweet-cakes, train under compulsion, at a fixed hour, in heat or in cold; you must not drink cold water,[2] nor wine just whenever you feel like it; you must have turned yourself over to your trainer precisely as you would to a physician. Then when the contest comes on, you have to "dig in" beside [3] your opponent, sometimes dislocate your wrist, sprain your ankle, swallow quantities of sand, take a scourging;[4] yes, and then sometimes get beaten along with all that. After you have counted up these points, go on into the games, if you still wish to; otherwise, I would have you observe that you will be turning back like children. Sometimes they play athletes, again gladiators, again they blow trumpets, and then act a play about anything that they have seen and admired. So you too are now

---

[4] That is, for any foul committed.

νῦν μὲν ἀθλητής, νῦν δὲ μονομάχος, εἶτα φιλόσοφος, εἶτα ῥήτωρ, ὅλῃ δὲ τῇ ψυχῇ οὐδέν, ἀλλ' ὡς ὁ
πίθηκος πᾶν ὃ ἂν ἴδῃς μιμῇ καὶ ἀεί σοι ἄλλο ἐξ
7 ἄλλου ἀρέσκει, τὸ σύνηθες δ' ἀπαρέσκει. οὐ γὰρ
μετὰ σκέψεως ἦλθες ἐπί τι οὐδὲ περιοδεύσας
ὅλον τὸ πρᾶγμα οὐδὲ βασανίσας, ἀλλ' εἰκῇ καὶ
κατὰ ψυχρὰν ἐπιθυμίαν.

8   Οὕτως τινὲς ἰδόντες φιλόσοφον καὶ ἀκούσαντές
τινος οὕτως λέγοντος, ὡς Εὐφράτης λέγει (καίτοι
τίς οὕτως δύναται εἰπεῖν ὡς ἐκεῖνος;), θέλουσιν
9 καὶ αὐτοὶ φιλοσοφεῖν. ἄνθρωπε, σκέψαι πρῶτον
τί ἐστὶ τὸ πρᾶγμα, εἶτα καὶ τὴν σαυτοῦ φύσιν, τί
δύνασαι βαστάσαι. εἰ παλαιστής, ἰδού σου
10 τοὺς ὤμους, τοὺς μηρούς, τὴν ὀσφύν. ἄλλος γὰρ
πρὸς ἄλλο τι πέφυκεν. δοκεῖς ὅτι ταῦτα
ποιῶν δύνασαι φιλοσοφεῖν; δοκεῖς ὅτι δύνασαι
ὡσαύτως ἐσθίειν, ὡσαύτως πίνειν, ὁμοίως ὀργίζε-
11 σθαι, ὁμοίως δυσαρεστεῖν; ἀγρυπνῆσαι δεῖ,
πονῆσαι, νικῆσαί τινας ἐπιθυμίας, ἀπελθεῖν ἀπὸ
τῶν οἰκείων, ὑπὸ παιδαρίου καταφρονηθῆναι, ὑπὸ
τῶν ἀπαντώντων καταγελασθῆναι, ἐν παντὶ
12 ἔλασσον ἔχειν, ἐν ἀρχῇ, ἐν τιμῇ, ἐν δίκῃ. ταῦτα
περισκεψάμενος, εἴ σοι δοκεῖ, προσέρχου, εἰ θέλεις
ἀντικαταλλάξασθαι τούτων ἀπάθειαν, ἐλευθερίαν,
ἀταραξίαν. εἰ δὲ μή, μὴ πρόσαγε, μὴ ὡς τὰ

---

[1] Although the expression (lit. "with cold desire") seems
a bit strange, because the fault seems to lie especially in the
lack of forethought and circumspection, still it is supported
by the version in the *Encheiridion*, and particularly by the
phrase, "yet with your whole soul nothing," in § 6 above.
Mere desire, without reason and deliberation, is apparently
regarded by Epictetus as a weak thing.

an athlete, now a gladiator, then a philosopher,
after that a rhetorician, yet with your whole soul
nothing, but like an ape you imitate whatever you
see, and one thing after another is always striking
your fancy, but what you are accustomed to bores
you. For you have never gone out after anything
with circumspection, nor after you have examined
the whole matter all over and tested it, but you act
at haphazard and half-heartedly.[1]

In the same way, when some people have seen a
philosopher and heard someone speaking like
Euphrates[2] (though, indeed, who can speak like
him?), they wish to be philosophers themselves.
Man, consider first what the business is, and then
your own natural ability, what you can bear. If
you wish to be a wrestler, look to your shoulders,
your thighs, your loins. For one man has a natural
talent for one thing, another for another. Do you
suppose that you can do the things you do now, and
yet be a philosopher? Do you suppose that you can
eat in the same fashion, drink in the same fashion, give
way to anger and to irritation, just as you do now?
You must keep vigils, work hard, overcome certain
desires, abandon your own people, be despised by
a paltry slave, be laughed to scorn by those who
meet you, in everything get the worst of it, in
office, in honour, in court. Look these drawbacks
over carefully, and then, if you think best, approach
philosophy, that is, if you are willing at the price
of these things to secure tranquillity, freedom, and
calm. Otherwise, do not approach; don't act like

[2] An eminent Stoic lecturer, highly praised by Pliny
(*Ep.* I. 10), and a bitter enemy of Apollonius of Tyana.
A specimen of his eloquence is given below, IV. 8, 17-20.

παιδία νῦν μὲν φιλόσοφος, ὕστερον δὲ τελώνης,
13 εἶτα ῥήτωρ, εἶτα ἐπίτροπος Καίσαρος. ταῦτα οὐ
συμφωνεῖ· ἕνα σε δεῖ ἄνθρωπον εἶναι ἢ ἀγαθὸν ἢ
κακόν· ἢ τὸ ἡγεμονικόν σε δεῖ ἐξεργάζεσθαι τὸ
σαυτοῦ ἢ τὰ ἐκτός· ἢ περὶ τὰ ἔσω φιλοπονεῖν[1] ἢ
περὶ τὰ ἔξω· τοῦτ' ἔστι φιλοσόφου στάσιν ἔχειν
ἢ ἰδιώτου.

14   Ῥούφῳ τις ἔλεγεν Γάλβα σφαγέντος ὅτι
"Νῦν προνοίᾳ ὁ κόσμος διοικεῖται;" ὁ δὲ "Μὴ
παρέργως ποτ'," ἔφη, "ἀπὸ Γάλβα κατεσκεύασα,
ὅτι προνοίᾳ ὁ κόσμος διοικεῖται;"

ιϛ'. Ὅτι εὐλαβῶς δεῖ συγκαθιέναι εἰς
συμπεριφοράν.

1   Ἀνάγκη τὸν συγκαθιέντα τισὶν ἐπιπλέον ἢ εἰς
λαλιὰν ἢ εἰς συμπόσια ἢ ἁπλῶς εἰς συμβίωσιν ἢ
αὐτὸν ἐκείνοις ἐξομοιωθῆναι ἢ ἐκείνους μετα-
2 θεῖναι ἐπὶ τὰ αὑτοῦ. καὶ γὰρ ἄνθρακα ἀπεσβεσ-
μένον ἂν θῇ παρὰ τὸν καιόμενον, ἢ αὐτὸς ἐκεῖνον
3 ἀποσβέσει[2] ἢ ἐκεῖνος τοῦτον ἐκκαύσει. τηλικούτου οὖν τοῦ κινδύνου ὄντος εὐλαβῶς δεῖ τοῖς
ἰδιώταις συγκαθίεσθαι εἰς τὰς τοιαύτας συμπερι-
φορὰς μεμνημένους, ὅτι ἀμήχανον τὸν συναντρι-

----

[1] Meibom: φιλοπόνει S.
[2] ἀποσβέσει supplied by the Salamanca edition, after Schegk.

----

[1] See note on III. 13, 20.
[2] The Roman emperor; the incident took place in A.D. 69.

a child—now a philosopher, later on a tax-gatherer,
then a rhetorician, then a procurator of Caesar.
These things do not go together. You must be
one person, either good or bad; you must labour to
improve either your own governing principle or
externals; you must work hard either on the inner
man, or on things outside; that is, play the rôle
of a philosopher, or else that of a layman.[1]

When Galba[2] was assassinated, someone said to
Rufus,[3] "Is the universe governed *now* by Providence?" But he replied, "Did I ever, even in
passing, take the case of Galba as the basis for an
argument that the universe is governed by Providence?"

CHAPTER XVI

That one should enter cautiously into social intercourse

THE man who consorts frequently with one person
or another either for conversation, or for banquets,
or for social purposes in general, is compelled either
to become like them himself, or else to bring them
over to his own style of living; for if you put by
the side of a live coal one that has gone out, either
the dead coal will put the live one out, or the latter
will kindle the former. Since the risk, then, is so
great, we ought to enter cautiously into such social
intercourse with the laymen, remembering that it
is impossible for the man who brushes up against

---

[3] Musonius Rufus, the distinguished philosopher and
teacher of Epictetus, to whom the latter was greatly indebted.
See the indices to the two vols. of this translation, and Vol. I,
Introduction, p. viii.

βόμενον τῷ ᾐσβολωμένῳ μὴ καὶ αὐτὸν ἀπολαῦσαι
4 τῆς ἀσβόλης. τί γὰρ ποιήσεις, ἂν περὶ μονο-
μάχων λαλῇς,[1] ἂν περὶ ἵππων, ἂν περὶ ἀθλητῶν,
ἂν τὸ ἔτι τούτων χεῖρον περὶ ἀνθρώπων· " ὁ δεῖνα
κακός, ὁ δεῖνα ἀγαθός· τοῦτο καλῶς ἐγένετο,
τοῦτο κακῶς"· ἔτι ἂν σκώπτῃ, ἂν γελοιάζῃ, ἂν
5 κακοηθίζηται ; ἔχει τις ὑμῶν παρασκευὴν οἵαν ὁ
κιθαριστικὸς τὴν λύραν λαβών, ὥστ' εὐθὺς
ἁψάμενος τῶν χορδῶν γνῶναι τὰς ἀσυμφώνους
καὶ ἁρμόσασθαι τὸ ὄργανον ; οἵαν εἶχεν δύναμιν
Σωκράτης, ὥστ' ἐν πάσῃ συμπεριφορᾷ[2] ἄγειν ἐπὶ
6 τὸ αὑτοῦ τοὺς συνόντας ; πόθεν ὑμῖν ; ἀλλ'
ἀνάγκη ὑπὸ τῶν ἰδιωτῶν ὑμᾶς περιάγεσθαι.

7 Διὰ τί οὖν ἐκεῖνοι ὑμῶν ἰσχυρότεροι ; ὅτι
ἐκεῖνοι μὲν τὰ σαπρὰ ταῦτα ἀπὸ δογμάτων
λαλοῦσιν, ὑμεῖς δὲ τὰ κομψὰ ἀπὸ τῶν χειλῶν·
διὰ τοῦτο ἄτονά ἐστι καὶ νεκρά, καὶ σικχᾶναι
ἔστιν ἀκούοντα ὑμῶν τοὺς προτρεπτικοὺς καὶ τὴν
ἀρετὴν τὴν ταλαίπωρον, ἣ ἄνω κάτω θρυλεῖται.
8 οὕτως ὑμᾶς οἱ ἰδιῶται νικῶσιν. πανταχοῦ γὰρ
9 ἰσχυρὸν τὸ δόγμα, ἀνίκητον τὸ δόγμα. μέχρις
ἂν οὖν παγῶσιν ἐν ὑμῖν αἱ κομψαὶ ὑπολήψεις
καὶ δύναμίν τινα περιποιήσησθε πρὸς ἀσφάλειαν,
συμβουλεύω ὑμῖν εὐλαβῶς τοῖς ἰδιώταις συγ-
καταβαίνειν· εἰ δὲ μή, καθ' ἡμέραν ὡς κηρὸς ἐν
ἡλίῳ διατακήσεται, ὑμῶν εἴ τινα ἐν τῇ σχολῇ
10 ἐγγράφετε. μακρὰν οὖν ἀπὸ τοῦ ἡλίου πού ποτε
ὑπάγετε, μέχρις ἂν κηρίνας τὰς ὑπολήψεις ἔχητε.
11 διὰ τοῦτο καὶ τῶν πατρίδων συμβουλεύουσιν

---

[1] Schweighäuser : λαλῇις S.
[2] Wolf, after Schegk : συμφορᾷ S.

the person who is covered with soot to keep from getting some soot on himself. For what are you going to do if he talks about gladiators, or horses, or athletes, or, worse still, about people: "So-and-so is bad, So-and-so is good; this was well done, this ill"; or again, if he scoffs, or jeers, or shows an ugly disposition? Has any of you the capacity of the expert lyre-player when he takes up his lyre, which enables him, the instant he touches the strings, to recognize the ones which are off pitch, and to tune the instrument? Or the power that Socrates had, which enabled him in every kind of social intercourse to bring over to his own side those who were in his company? How could you have? But you must necessarily be converted by the laymen.

Why, then, are they stronger than you are? Because their rotten talk is based on judgements, but your fine talk comes merely from your lips; that's why what you say is languid and dead, and why a man may well feel nausea when he hears your exhortations and your miserable "virtue," which you babble to and fro. And thus the laymen get the better of you; for everywhere judgement is strong, judgement is invincible. Therefore, until these fine ideas of yours are firmly fixed within you, and you have acquired some power which will guarantee you security, my advice to you is to be cautious about joining issue with the laymen; otherwise whatever you write down in the lecture-room will melt away by day like wax in the sun.[1] Retire, then, to some spot or other far away from the sun, so long as the ideas which you have are waxen. It is for this reason that the philosophers advise us to leave even

---

[1] Such lecture-notes were written on wax tablets.

ἀποχωρεῖν οἱ φιλόσοφοι, ὅτι τὰ παλαιὰ ἔθη
περισπᾷ καὶ οὐκ ἐᾷ ἀρχὴν γενέσθαι τινὰ ἄλλου
ἐθισμοῦ, οὐδὲ φέρομεν τοὺς ἀπαντῶντας καὶ λέγον-
τας "ἴδ᾽ ὁ δεῖνα φιλοσοφεῖ, ὁ τοῖος καὶ ὁ τοῖος."

12 οὕτως καὶ οἱ ἰατροὶ τοὺς μακρονοσοῦντας ἐκπέμ-
πουσιν εἰς ἄλλην χώραν καὶ ἄλλα ἀέρα καλῶς

13 ποιοῦντες. καὶ ὑμεῖς ἀντεισαγάγετε ἄλλα ἔθη·
πήξατε ὑμῶν τὰς ὑπολήψεις, ἐναθλεῖτε αὐταῖς.

14 οὔ· ἀλλ᾽ ἔνθεν ἐπὶ θεωρίαν, εἰς μονομαχίαν, εἰς
ξυστόν,[1] εἰς κίρκον· εἶτ᾽ ἐκεῖθεν ὧδε καὶ πάλιν

15 ἔνθεν ἐκεῖ οἱ αὐτοί. καὶ ἔθος κομψὸν οὐδέν, οὔτε
προσοχὴ οὔτ᾽ ἐπιστροφὴ ἐφ᾽ αὑτὸν καὶ παρα-
τήρησις "πῶς χρῶμαι ταῖς προσπιπτούσαις
φαντασίαις; κατὰ φύσιν ἢ παρὰ φύσιν; πῶς
ἀποκρίνωμαι πρὸς αὐτάς; ὡς δεῖ ἢ ὡς οὐ δεῖ;
ἐπιλέγω τοῖς ἀπροαιρέτοις, ὅτι οὐδὲν πρὸς ἐμέ;"

16 εἰ γὰρ μήπω οὕτως ἔχητε, φεύγετε ἔθη τὰ πρότερον, φεύγετε τοὺς ἰδιώτας, εἰ θέλετε ἄρξασθαί
ποτέ τινες εἶναι.

ιζ'. Περὶ προνοίας.

1 Ὅταν τῇ προνοίᾳ ἐγκαλῇς, ἐπιστράφηθι καὶ
2 γνώσῃ, ὅτι κατὰ λόγον γέγονεν. "ναί, ἀλλ᾽ ὁ

---

[1] Where the athletes exercised in winter, or in bad
weather.

our own countries, because old habits distract
us and do not allow a beginning to be made of
another custom, and we cannot bear to have men
meet us and say, "Look, So-and-so is philosophizing,
although he is this sort of a person or that."
Thus also physicians send away to a different
region and a different climate those who are suffering from chronic disorders, and that is well.
Do you also introduce different habits; fix your
ideas, exercise yourselves in them. But no, you go
from the class-room to a show, a gladiatorial combat,
a gymnasium-colonnade,[1] a circus; and then you
come back here from these places, and you go back
there again from here, and remain the same persons
all the time.[2] And so you acquire no fine habit;
you pay no regard or attention to your own self;
you do not observe: "How do I deal with the
external impressions which befall me? In accordance
with nature, or contrary to it? How shall I respond
to these impressions? As I should, or as I should
not? Do I declare to the things which lie outside
the sphere of my moral purpose that they mean
nothing to me?" Why, if you have not yet acquired
this state of mind, flee from your former habits, flee
from the laymen, if you would begin to be somebody
some time.

CHAPTER XVII

Of Providence

WHENEVER you find fault with Providence, only
consider and you will recognize that what happens
is in accordance with reason. "Yes," you say,

[2] Cf. " . . . But evermore came out by the same door
where in I went."—Omar Khayyám (Fitzgerald), 27.

ἄδικος πλέον ἔχει." ἐν τίνι; ἐν ἀργυρίῳ· πρὸς
γὰρ τοῦτό σου κρείττων ἐστίν, ὅτι[1] κολακεύει,
3 ἀναισχυντεῖ, ἀγρυπνεῖ. τί θαυμαστόν; ἀλλ᾽
ἐκεῖνο βλέπε, εἰ ἐν τῷ πιστὸς εἶναι πλέον σου
ἔχει, εἰ ἐν τῷ αἰδήμων. οὐ γὰρ εὑρήσεις· ἀλλ᾽
ὅπου κρείττων, ἐκεῖ σαυτὸν εὑρήσεις πλέον
4 ἔχοντα. κἀγώ ποτ᾽ εἶπόν τινι ἀγανακτοῦντι,
ὅτι Φιλόστοργος εὐτυχεῖ, "Ἤθελες ἂν σὺ μετὰ
Σούρα κοιμᾶσθαι;"—"Μὴ γένοιτο," φησίν, "ἐ-
5 κείνη ἡ ἡμέρα."—Τί οὖν ἀγανακτεῖς, εἰ λαμβάνει
τι ἀνθ᾽ οὗ πωλεῖ; ἢ πῶς μακαρίζεις τὸν διὰ
τούτων, ἃ σὺ ἀπεύχῃ, κτώμενον ἐκεῖνα; ἢ τί
κακὸν ποιεῖ ἡ πρόνοια, εἰ τοῖς κρείττοσι τὰ
κρείττω δίδωσιν; ἢ οὐκ ἔστι κρεῖττον αἰδήμονα
6 εἶναι ἢ πλούσιον; Ὡμολόγει. Τί οὖν ἀγανακτεῖς, ἄνθρωπε, ἔχων τὸ κρεῖττον; μέμνησθε
οὖν ἀεὶ καὶ πρόχειρον ἔχετε, ὅτι νόμος οὗτος
φυσικὸς τὸν κρείττονα τοῦ χείρονος πλέον ἔχειν,
ἐν ᾧ κρείττων ἐστί, καὶ οὐδέποτ᾽ ἀγανακτήσετε.
7 "ἀλλ᾽ ἡ γυνή μοι κακῶς χρῆται." καλῶς. ἄν
τίς σου πυνθάνηται, τί ἐστὶ τοῦτο, λέγε "ἡ
γυνή μοι κακῶς χρῆται." "ἄλλο οὖν οὐδέν;"
8 οὐδέν. "ὁ πατήρ μοι οὐδὲν δίδωσιν." . . .[2] ὅτι
δὲ κακόν ἐστιν, τοῦτο ἔσωθεν αὐτῷ δεῖ προσ-

---

[1] Wolf and Upton's "codex": ὃ S.
[2] Lacuna observed by Wolf.

---

[1] Probably the Palfurius Sura who had been expelled from
the Senate under the Flavian emperors. Suet. *Dom.* 13, 2.

"but the wicked man is better off." In what respect? In money; for in respect to that he is superior to you, because he flatters, is shameless, lies awake nights. What is surprising in that? But look rather and see if he is better off than you are in being faithful, and considerate. For you will not find that to be the case; but where you are superior, there you will find that you are better off than he is. And so I once asked a man who was complaining about the prosperity of Philostorgus, "Would you have been willing to cohabit with Sura?"[1] "May that day never come!" said he. Why, then, are you indignant if he gets something for what he sells? Or how can you deem him blessed who acquires what he has by means which you abhor? Or what harm does Providence do if it gives the better thing to the better men? Or is it not better to be considerate than to be rich? He agreed that it was. Why, then, are you indignant, man, when you have the better part? I would have the rest of you always remember, then, and be ready to apply the following truth: That this is a law of nature for the superior to have the better of the inferior, in the respect in which he is superior; and then you will never be indignant. "But my wife treats me badly." Very well; if someone asks you what this amounts to, say, "My wife treats me badly." "Nothing else, then?" Nothing. "My father doesn't give me anything" . . .[2] But is it necessary in your own mind to add to the preceding statement, that to receive nothing from your father

---

[2] The lacuna is probably to be filled out thus: What does this amount to? Merely that your father doesn't give you anything.

9 θεῖναι καὶ προσκαταψεύσασθαι; διὰ τοῦτο οὐ
δεῖ τὴν πενίαν ἐκβάλλειν, ἀλλὰ τὸ δόγμα τὸ
περὶ αὐτῆς, καὶ οὕτως εὐροήσομεν.

ιη΄. Ὅτι οὐ δεῖ πρὸς τὰς ἀγγελίας
ταράσσεσθαι.

1   Ὅταν σοί τι προσαγγελθῇ ταρακτικόν, ἐκεῖνο
ἔχε πρόχειρον, ὅτι ἀγγελία περὶ οὐδενὸς προαι-
2 ρετικοῦ γίνεται. μή τι γὰρ δύναταί σοί τις
ἀγγεῖλαι, ὅτι κακῶς ὑπέλαβες ἢ κακῶς ὠρέχθης;
—Οὐδαμῶς.—Ἀλλ᾽ ὅτι ἀπέθανέν τις· τί οὖν
πρὸς σέ; ὅτι σε κακῶς τις λέγει· τί οὖν πρὸς
3 σέ; ὅτι ὁ πατὴρ τάδε τινὰ ἑτοιμάζεται· ἐπὶ
τίνα; μή τι ἐπὶ τὴν προαίρεσιν; πόθεν δύναται;
ἀλλ᾽ ἐπὶ τὸ σωμάτιον, ἐπὶ τὸ κτησείδιον·
4 ἐσώθης, οὐκ ἐπὶ σέ.[1] ἀλλ᾽ ὁ κριτὴς ἀποφαίνεται
ὅτι ἠσέβησας. περὶ Σωκράτους δ᾽ οὐκ ἀπε-
φήναντο οἱ δικασταί; μή τι σὸν ἔργον ἐστὶ τὸ
ἐκεῖνον ἀποφήνασθαι; — Οὔ. — Τί οὖν ἔτι σοι
5 μέλει; ἔστι τι τοῦ πατρός σου ἔργον, ὃ ἂν μὴ
ἐκπληρώσῃ, ἀπώλεσεν τὸν πατέρα, τὸν φιλό-
στοργον, τὸν ἥμερον. ἄλλο δὲ μηδὲν ζήτει
τούτου ἕνεκα αὐτὸν ἀπολέσαι.[2] οὐδέποτε γὰρ
ἐν ἄλλῳ μέν τις ἁμαρτάνει, εἰς ἄλλο δὲ βλάπ-

---

[1] οὐκοῦν after σέ is omitted in s.
[2] Wolf: ἀπολέσθαι S.

is an evil, and at that to add a lie too? For this reason we ought not to cast out poverty, but only our judgement about poverty, and so we shall be serene.

CHAPTER XVIII

That we ought not to allow any news to disturb us

WHENEVER some disturbing news is reported to you, you ought to have ready at hand the following principle: News, on any subject, never falls within the sphere of the moral purpose. Can anyone bring you word that you have been wrong in an assumption or in a desire?—By no means.—But he can bring you word that someone is dead. Very well, what is that to you? That someone is speaking ill of you. Very well, what is that to you? That your father is making certain preparations. Against whom? Surely not against your moral purpose, is it? Why, how can he? But against your paltry body, against your paltry possessions; you are safe, it is not against you. But the judge condemns you on the charge of impiety. And did not the judges similarly condemn Socrates? Surely it is no concern of yours that the judge pronounced you guilty, is it? —No.—Why, then, are you any further concerned? Your father has a certain function, and if he does not perform it, he has destroyed the father in him, the man who loves his offspring, the man of gentleness within him. Do not seek to make him lose anything else on this account. For it never happens that a man goes wrong in one thing, but is injured in

6 τεται. πάλιν σὸν ἔργον τὸ ἀπολογηθῆναι
εὐσταθῶς, αἰδημόνως, ἀοργήτως. εἰ δὲ μή,
ἀπώλεσας καὶ σὺ τὸν υἱόν, τὸν αἰδήμονα, τὸν
7 γενναῖον. τί οὖν; ὁ κριτὴς ἀκίνδυνός ἐστιν;
οὔ· ἀλλὰ κἀκείνῳ τὰ ἴσα κινδυνεύεται. τί οὖν
ἔτι φοβῇ, τί ἐκεῖνος κρινεῖ;[1] τί σοὶ καὶ τῷ
8 ἀλλοτρίῳ κακῷ; σὸν κακόν ἐστι τὸ κακῶς
ἀπολογηθῆναι· τοῦτο φυλάσσου μόνον· κριθῆναι
δ' ἢ μὴ κριθῆναι ὥσπερ ἄλλου ἐστὶν ἔργον,
9 οὕτως κακὸν ἄλλου ἐστίν. "ἀπειλεῖ σοι ὁ
δεῖνα." ἐμοί; οὔ. "ψέγει σε." αὐτὸς ὄψεται,
πῶς ποιεῖ τὸ ἴδιον ἔργον. "μέλλει σε κατα-
κρινεῖν ἀδίκως." ἄθλιος.

ιθ'. Τίς στάσις ἰδιώτου καὶ φιλοσόφου;

1 Ἡ πρώτη διαφορὰ ἰδιώτου καὶ φιλοσόφου·
ὁ μὲν λέγει "οὐαί μοι διὰ τὸ παιδάριον, διὰ τὸν
ἀδελφόν, οὐαὶ διὰ τὸν πατέρα," ὁ δ', ἄν ποτ'
εἰπεῖν ἀναγκασθῇ, "οὐαί μοι" ἐπιστήσας λέγει
2 "δι' ἐμέ." προαίρεσιν γὰρ οὐδὲν δύναται κωλῦσαι
3 ἢ βλάψαι ἀπροαίρετον εἰ μὴ αὐτὴ ἑαυτήν. ἂν
οὖν ἐπὶ τοῦτο ῥέψωμεν καὶ αὐτοί, ὥσθ' ὅταν

---

[1] Koraes after Schegk : κρίνῃ S.

[1] On this point see the Introduction, Vol. I, p. xx :
"Every man bears the exclusive responsibility himself for
his own good or evil, since it is impossible to imagine a
moral order in which one person does the wrong and another,
the innocent, suffers"; or, as here, where a person might do
wrong in the moral sphere, and yet not suffer also in the
moral sphere. Compare also the note on I. 28, 10, in Vol. I.

another.[1]   Again, it is your function to defend yourself firmly, respectfully, without passion.   Otherwise, you have destroyed within you the son, the
respectful man, the man of honour.   What then?
Is the judge secure?   No; but he too runs just as
great a risk.   Why, then, are you afraid of what
decision he is going to render?   What have you to
do with another man's evil?   Your own evil is to
make a bad defence; only guard against that, but
just as being condemned or not being condemned is
another's function, so it is another's evil.   "So-and-
so threatens you."   Me?   No.   "He blames you."
He himself will attend to how he is performing his
own proper function.   "He is on the point of con-
demning you unjustly."   Poor devil!

CHAPTER XIX

*What is the position of the layman, and what that of
the philosopher?*

THE first difference between a layman and a
philosopher: The one says, "Woe is me because
of my child, my brother, woe because of my father";
and the other, if he can ever be compelled to say,
"Woe is me," adds, after a pause, "because of myself."   For nothing outside the sphere of the moral
purpose can hamper or injure the moral purpose; it
alone can hamper or injure itself.   If, then, we too tend
in this latter direction so that, whenever we go amiss,

This general position, which as an unverifiable postulate
underlies the whole Stoic philosophy, and is the very starting-
point of their whole system of thinking, is what might
be styled the πρῶτον ψεῦδος of Stoicism.

δυσοδῶμεν, αὐτοὺς αἰτιᾶσθαι καὶ μεμνῆσθαι, ὅτι
οὐδὲν ἄλλο ταραχῆς ἢ ἀκαταστασίας αἴτιόν
ἐστιν ἢ δόγμα, ὀμνύω ὑμῖν πάντας θεούς, ὅτι
4 προεκόψαμεν.¹ νῦν δ' ἄλλην ὁδὸν ἐξ ἀρχῆς
ἐληλύθαμεν. εὐθὺς ἔτι παίδων ἡμῶν ὄντων ἡ
τιτθή, εἴ ποτε προσεπταίσαμεν χάσκοντες,
οὐχὶ ἡμῖν ἐπέπλησσεν, ἀλλὰ τὸν λίθον ἔτυπτεν.
τί γὰρ ἐποίησεν ὁ λίθος ; διὰ τὴν τοῦ παιδίου
5 σου μωρίαν ἔδει μεταβῆναι αὐτόν ; πάλιν ἂν μὴ
εὕρωμεν φαγεῖν ἐκ βαλανείου, οὐδέποθ' ἡμῶν
καταστέλλει τὴν ἐπιθυμίαν ὁ παιδαγωγός, ἀλλὰ
δέρει τὸν μάγειρον. ἄνθρωπε, μὴ γὰρ ἐκείνου
σε παιδαγωγὸν κατεστήσαμεν ; ἀλλὰ τοῦ παιδίου
6 ἡμῶν· τοῦτο ἐπανόρθου, τοῦτο ὠφέλει. οὕτως
καὶ αὐξηθέντες φαινόμεθα παιδία. παῖς γὰρ ἐν
μουσικοῖς ὁ ἄμουσος, ἐν γραμματικοῖς ὁ ἀγράμ-
ματος,² ἐν βίῳ ὁ ἀπαίδευτος.

κ'. Ὅτι ἀπὸ πάντων τῶν ἐκτὸς ἔστιν
ὠφελεῖσθαι.

1 Ἐπὶ τῶν θεωρητικῶν φαντασιῶν πάντες
σχεδὸν τὸ ἀγαθὸν καὶ τὸ κακὸν ἐν ἡμῖν ἀπέ-
2 λιπον, οὐχὶ δ' ἐν τοῖς ἐκτός. οὐδεὶς λέγει
ἀγαθὸν τὸ ἡμέραν εἶναι, κακὸν τὸ νύκτα εἶναι,
μέγιστον δὲ κακῶν τὸ τρία τέσσαρα εἶναι.
3 ἀλλὰ τί ; τὴν μὲν ἐπιστήμην ἀγαθόν, τὴν δ'
ἀπάτην κακόν, ὥστε καὶ περὶ αὐτὸ τὸ ψεῦδος
ἀγαθὸν³ συνίστασθαι, τὴν ἐπιστήμην τοῦ ψεύδος

---

¹ Wolf : προέκοψεν S.   ² s : ἀγραμμάτικος S.

we blame ourselves, and bear in mind that nothing
but judgement is responsible for the disturbance of
our peace of mind and our inconstancy, I swear to
you by all the gods that we have been making progress. But as it is, we have taken a different course
from the start. Even while we were still children,
our nurse, if ever we bumped into something, when
we were going along with our mouths open, did not
scold us, but used to beat the stone. Why, what
did the stone do? Ought it to have moved out of
the road because of your childish folly? And again,
if we when children don't find something to eat
after our bath, our attendant never checks our
appetite, but he cudgels the cook. Man, we didn't
make you the cook's attendant, did we? but our
child's. Correct him, help him. So, even when we
have grown up, we look like children. For it is
being a child to be unmusical in things musical, to
be unlettered in things literary, to be uneducated in
life.

CHAPTER XX

That it is possible to derive advantage from everything external

In the case of our intellectual impressions practically all men have agreed that the good and the
evil are in ourselves, and not in externals. Nobody
calls the statement that it is day, good, or that it is
night, bad, and the greatest of evils, the statement
that three is four. But what? They call knowledge
good, and error evil; so that even in regard to what
is false there arises a good, that is, the knowledge

---

[3] Schweighäuser : ἀπάτην S.

4 εἶναι αὐτό. ἔδει οὖν οὕτως καὶ ἐπὶ τοῦ βίου.
ὑγεία ἀγαθόν, νόσος δὲ κακόν; οὔ, ἄνθρωπε.
ἀλλὰ τί; τὸ καλῶς ὑγιαίνειν ἀγαθόν, τὸ κακῶς
κακόν. — Ὥστε καὶ ἀπὸ νόσου ἔστιν ὠφεληθῆναι; — Τὸν θεόν σοι,[1] ἀπὸ θανάτου γὰρ οὐκ
5 ἔστιν; ἀπὸ πηρώσεως γὰρ οὐκ ἔστιν; μικρά
σοι δοκεῖ ὁ Μενοικεὺς ὠφεληθῆναι, ὅτ᾽ ἀπέ-
θνησκεν; — Τοιαῦτά τις εἰπὼν ὠφεληθείη[2] οἷα
ἐκεῖνος ὠφελήθη. — Ἔα, ἄνθρωπε, οὐκ ἐτήρησεν
τὸν φιλόπατριν, τὸν μεγαλόφρονα, τὸν πιστόν,
τὸν γενναῖον; ἐπιζήσας δὲ οὐκ ἂν[3] ἀπώλλυεν
6 ταῦτα πάντα; οὐ περιεποιεῖτο τὰ ἐναντία; τὸν
δειλὸν οὐκ ἀνελάμβανεν, τὸν ἀγεννῆ, τὸν μισό-
πατριν, τὸν φιλόψυχον; ἄγε δοκεῖ σοι μικρὰ
7 ὠφεληθῆναι ἀποθανών; οὔ· ἀλλ᾽ ὁ τοῦ Ἀδμήτου
πατὴρ μεγάλα ὠφελήθη ζήσας οὕτως ἀγεννῶς
8 καὶ ἀθλίως; ὕστερον γὰρ οὐκ ἀπέθανεν; παύσασθε, τοὺς θεοὺς ὑμῖν,[4] τὰς ὕλας θαυμάζοντες,
παύσασθ᾽ ἑαυτοὺς δούλους ποιοῦντες πρῶτον τῶν
πραγμάτων, εἶτα δι᾽ αὐτὰ καὶ τῶν ἀνθρώπων
τῶν ταῦτα περιποιεῖν ἢ ἀφαιρεῖσθαι δυναμένων.

9 Ἔστιν οὖν ἀπὸ τούτων ὠφεληθῆναι; — Ἀπὸ
πάντων. — Καὶ ἀπὸ τοῦ λοιδοροῦντος; — Τί δ᾽
ὠφελεῖ τὸν ἀθλητὴν ὁ προσγυμναζόμενος; τὰ

---

[1] Bentley: σου S.
[2] ἢ after this word is deleted by s.
[3] ἄν added by Upton, after Schegk.
[4] Bentley and Shaftesbury, about the same time:
ὑμῶν S.

that the false *is* false. So it ought to be, then, also with our life. Is health a good, and illness an evil? No, man. What then? To be well for a good end is good, to be well for an evil end is evil.—So that it is possible to derive advantage even from illness, you mean?—Why, I call God to witness, isn't it possible to derive advantage from death? Why, isn't it possible from lameness?[1] Do you think that Menoeceus[2] derived but little good when he died?— May the one who says anything like that derive the same sort of good that he did!—Ho, there, man, did he not maintain the patriot that he was, the high-minded man, the man of fidelity, the man of honour? And had he lived on, would he not have lost all these? Would he not have won the very opposite? Would he not have acquired the character of the coward, the ignoble man, the disloyal, the lover of his own life? Come now, do you think that Menoeceus derived but little good by his death? Oh, no! But the father of Admetus derived great good from living so ignobly and wretchedly, did he? Why, didn't he die later? Make an end, I adjure you by the gods, of admiring material things, make an end of turning yourselves into slaves, in the first place, of things, and then, in the second place, on their account, slaves also of the men who are able to secure or to take away these things.

Is it possible, then, to derive advantage from these things?—Yes, from everything.—Even from the man who reviles me?—And what good does his wrestling-companion do the athlete? The very

---

[1] Perhaps a reference to his own case. See Introd. p. ix. f., in Vol. I.

[2] Who gave his life to save his native city, Thebes.

μέγιστα. καὶ οὗτος ἐμοῦ προγυμναστὴς γίνεται·
τὸ ἀνεκτικόν μου γυμνάζει, τὸ ἀόργητον, τὸ
10 πρᾷον. οὔ· ἀλλ' ὁ μὲν τοῦ τραχήλου καθάπτων
καὶ τὴν ὀσφύν μου καὶ τοὺς ὤμους καταρτίζων
ὠφελεῖ με καὶ ὁ ἀλείπτης καλῶς ποιῶν λέγει
"ἆρον ὕπερον ἀμφοτέραις,"[1] καὶ ὅσῳ βαρύτερός
ἐστιν ἐκεῖνος, τοσούτῳ μᾶλλον ὠφελοῦμαι ἐγώ·
εἰ δέ τις πρὸς ἀοργησίαν με γυμνάζει, οὐκ
11 ὠφελεῖ με; τοῦτ' ἔστι τὸ μὴ εἰδέναι ἀπ'
ἀνθρώπων ὠφελεῖσθαι. κακὸς γείτων; αὑτῷ·
ἀλλ' ἐμοὶ ἀγαθός· γυμνάζει μου τὸ εὔγνωμον,
τὸ ἐπιεικές. κακὸς πατήρ; αὑτῷ· ἀλλ' ἐμοὶ
12 ἀγαθός. τοῦτ' ἔστι τὸ τοῦ Ἑρμοῦ ῥαβδίον·
"οὗ θέλεις," φασίν,[2] "ἅψαι καὶ χρυσοῦν ἔσται."
οὔ· ἀλλ' ὃ θέλεις φέρε κἀγὼ αὐτὸ ἀγαθὸν
ποιήσω. φέρε νόσον, φέρε θάνατον, φέρε ἀπορίαν, φέρε λοιδορίαν, δίκην τὴν περὶ τῶν ἐσχά-
των· πάντα ταῦτα τῷ ῥαβδίῳ τοῦ Ἑρμοῦ
13 ὠφέλιμα ἔσται. "τὸν θάνατον τί ποιήσεις;"
τί γὰρ ἄλλο ἢ ἵνα σε κοσμήσῃ ἢ ἵνα δείξῃς[3]
ἔργῳ δι' αὐτοῦ, τί ἐστιν ἄνθρωπος τῷ βουλήματι
14 τῆς φύσεως παρακολουθῶν; "τὴν νόσον τί
ποιήσεις;" δείξω αὐτῆς τὴν φύσιν, διαπρέψω
ἐν αὐτῇ, εὐσταθήσω, εὑρήσω, τὸν ἰατρὸν οὐ
15 κολακεύσω, οὐκ εὔξομαι ἀποθανεῖν. τί ἔτι
ἄλλο ζητεῖς; πᾶν ὃ ἂν δῷς, ἐγὼ αὐτὸ ποιήσω
μακάριον, εὐδαιμονικόν, σεμνόν, ζηλωτόν.

---

[1] Schweighäuser: ὑπὲρ ἀμφοτέρας S.
[2] Upton: φησίν S. Cicero, Off. I. 158: Quod si omnia
nobis . . . quasi virgula divina, ut aiunt, suppeditarent, shows
clearly that this is a proverbial saying.
[3] Reiske: δείξῃ σε S.

greatest. So also my reviler becomes one who prepares me for my contest; he exercises my patience, my dispassionateness, my gentleness. You say: No. But the man who lays hold of my neck and gets my loins and my shoulders into proper shape helps me, and the rubber does well when he says, "Lift the pestle with both hands,"[1] and the heavier it is, the more good I get out of doing so; whereas, if a man trains me to be dispassionate, does he do me no good? Your attitude means that you do not know how to derive advantage from men. Is your neighbour bad? Yes, for himself; but for me he is good; he exercises my good disposition, my fair-mindedness. Is your father bad? Yes, for himself; but for me he is good. This is the magic wand of Hermes. "Touch what you will," the saying goes, "and it will turn into gold." Nay, but bring whatever you will and *I* will turn it into a good. Bring disease, bring death, bring poverty, reviling, peril of life in court; all these things will become helpful at a touch from the magic wand of Hermes. "What will you make of death?" Why, what else but make it your glory, or an opportunity for you to show in deed thereby what sort of person a man is who follows the will of nature. "What will you make of disease?" I will show its character, I will shine in it, I will be firm, I will be serene, I will not fawn upon my physician, I will not pray for death. What else do you still seek? Everything that you give I will turn into something blessed, productive of happiness, august, enviable.

---

[1] The physical exercise referred to in III. 12, 9.

16 Οὔ· ἀλλὰ " βλέπε μὴ νοσήσῃς· κακόν ἐστιν."
οἷον εἴ τις ἔλεγεν " βλέπε μὴ λάβῃς ποτὲ φαντασίαν τοῦ τὰ τρία τέσσαρα εἶναι· κακόν ἐστιν."
ἄνθρωπε, πῶς κακόν; ἂν ὃ δεῖ περὶ αὐτοῦ
ὑπολάβω, πῶς ἔτι με βλάψει; οὐχὶ δὲ μᾶλλον
17 καὶ ὠφελήσει; ἂν οὖν περὶ πενίας ὃ δεῖ ὑπολάβω,
ἂν περὶ νόσου, ἂν περὶ ἀναρχίας, οὐκ ἀρκεῖ μοι;
οὐκ ὠφέλιμα ἔσται; πῶς οὖν ἔτι ἐν τοῖς ἐκτὸς
τὰ κακὰ καὶ τἀγαθὰ δεῖ με ζητεῖν;
18 Ἀλλὰ τί; ταῦτα μέχρι ὧδε, εἰς οἶκον δ' οὐδεὶς
ἀποφέρει· ἀλλ' εὐθὺς πρὸς τὸ παιδάριον πόλεμος, πρὸς τοὺς γείτονας, πρὸς τοὺς σκώψαντας,
19 πρὸς τοὺς καταγελάσαντας. καλῶς γένοιτο
Λεσβίῳ, ὅτι με καθ' ἡμέραν ἐξελέγχει μηδὲν
εἰδότα.

κα΄. Πρὸς τοὺς εὐκόλως ἐπὶ τὸ σοφιστεύειν
ἐρχομένους.

1 "Οτι οἱ[1] τὰ θεωρήματα ἀναλαβόντες ψιλὰ
εὐθὺς αὐτὰ ἐξεμέσαι θέλουσιν ὡς οἱ στομαχικοὶ
2 τὴν τροφήν. πρῶτον αὐτὰ[2] πέψον, εἶθ' οὕτως
οὐ[3] μὴ ἐξεμέσῃς· εἰ δὲ μή, ἔμετος τῷ ὄντι
3 γίνεται, πρᾶγμ' ἀκάθαρτον[4] καὶ ἄβρωτον. ἀλλ'

[1] οἱ added by Schenkl.　　[2] Richards: αὐτό S.
[3] Kronenberg: οὕτω μή S.
[4] Wolf: καθαρόν S. But possibly the reading can be
retained (with Schegk) in the sense: "What was clean
food becomes mere vomit and unfit to eat."

[1] That is, no farther than the class-room.
[2] Presumably some scoffer or irritating person known to
the audience.

ἀπ' αὐτῶν ἀναδοθέντων δεῖξόν τινα ἡμῖν μεταβολὴν τοῦ ἡγεμονικοῦ τοῦ σεαυτοῦ, ὡς οἱ ἀθληταὶ
τοὺς ὤμους, ἀφ' ὧν ἐγυμνάσθησαν καὶ ἔφαγον,
ὡς οἱ τὰς τέχνας ἀναλαβόντες, ἀφ' ὧν ἔμαθον.
4 οὐκ ἔρχεται ὁ τέκτων καὶ λέγει " ἀκούσατέ μου
διαλεγομένου περὶ τῶν τεκτονικῶν," ἀλλ' ἐκμισ-
θωσάμενος οἰκίαν ταύτην κατασκευάσας δείκ-
5 νυσιν, ὅτι ἔχει τὴν τέχνην. τοιοῦτόν τι καὶ σὺ
ποίησον· φάγε ὡς ἄνθρωπος, πίε ὡς ἄνθρωπος,
κοσμήθητι, γάμησον, παιδοποίησον, πολίτευσαι·
ἀνάσχου λοιδορίας, ἔνεγκε ἀδελφὸν ἀγνώμονα,
6 ἔνεγκε πατέρα, ἔνεγκε υἱόν, γείτονα, σύνοδον.
ταῦτα ἡμῖν δεῖξον, ἵν' ἴδωμεν, ὅτι μεμάθηκας ταῖς
ἀληθείαις τι τῶν φιλοσόφων. οὔ· ἀλλ' " ἐλθόντες ἀκούσατέ μου σχόλια λέγοντος." ὕπαγε,
7 ζήτει τίνων κατεξεράσεις. " καὶ μὴν ἐγὼ ὑμῖν
ἐξηγήσομαι τὰ Χρυσίππεια ὡς οὐδείς, τὴν λέξιν
διαλύσω καθαρώτατα, προσθήσω ἄν που καὶ
Ἀντιπάτρου καὶ Ἀρχεδήμου φοράν."

8   Εἶτα τούτου ἕνεκα ἀπολίπωσιν οἱ νέοι τὰς
πατρίδας καὶ τοὺς γονεῖς τοὺς αὑτῶν, ἵν' ἐλθόντες
9 λεξείδιά σου ἐξηγουμένου ἀκούσωσιν; οὐ δεῖ
αὐτοὺς ὑποστρέψαι ἀνεκτικούς, συνεργητικούς,
ἀπαθεῖς, ἀταράχους, ἔχοντάς τι ἐφόδιον τοιοῦτον
εἰς τὸν βίον, ἀφ' οὗ ὁρμώμενοι φέρειν δυνήσονται
τὰ συμπίπτοντα καλῶς καὶ κοσμεῖσθαι ὑπ'
10 αὐτῶν; καὶ πόθεν σοι μεταδιδόναι τούτων ὧν
οὐκ ἔχεις; αὐτὸς γὰρ ἄλλο τι ἐποίησας ἐξ ἀρχῆς

---

[1] Called *principes dialecticorum* by Cicero, *Acad.* II.
143.

ou have digested these principles, show us some
change in your governing principle that is due to
them; as the athletes show their shoulders as the
results of their exercising and eating, and as those
who have mastered the arts can show the results of
their learning. The builder does not come forward
and say, "Listen to me deliver a discourse about the
art of building"; but he takes a contract for a
house, builds it, and thereby proves that he possesses
the art. Do something of the same sort yourself
too; eat as a man, drink as a man, adorn yourself,
marry, get children, be active as a citizen; endure
revilings, bear with an unreasonable brother, father,
son, neighbour, fellow-traveller. Show us that you
can do these things, for us to see that in all truth
you have learned something of the philosophers.
No, but "Come and listen to me deliver my com-
ments," you say. Go to! Look for people on
whom to throw up! "Yes, but I will set forth to
you the doctrines of Chrysippus as no one else can;
his language I will analyse so as to make it perfectly
clear; possibly I will throw in a bit of the vivacity of
Antipater and Archedemus." [1]

And then it's for this, is it, that the young men
are to leave their fatherlands and their own parents,
—to come and listen to you interpreting trifling
phrases? Ought they not to be, when they return
home, forbearing, ready to help one another, tranquil,
with a mind at peace, possessed of some such provision
for the journey of life, that, starting out with it,
they will be able to bear well whatever happens, and
to derive honour from it? And where did you get
the ability to impart to them these things which you
do not possess yourself? Why, from the first did

ἢ περὶ ταῦτα κατετρίβης, πῶς οἱ συλλογισμοὶ
ἀναλυθήσονται, πῶς οἱ μεταπίπτοντες, πῶς οἱ
τῷ ἠρωτῆσθαι περαίνοντες; " ἀλλ' ὁ δεῖνα
11 σχολὴν ἔχει· διὰ τί μὴ κἀγὼ σχῶ;" οὐκ εἰκῆ
ταῦτα γίνεται, ἀνδράποδον, οὐδ' ὡς ἔτυχεν, ἀλλὰ
12 καὶ ἡλικίαν εἶναι δεῖ καὶ βίον καὶ θεὸν ἡγεμόνα.
οὔ· ἀλλ' ἀπὸ λιμένος[1] μὲν οὐδεὶς ἀνάγεται μὴ
θύσας τοῖς θεοῖς καὶ παρακαλέσας αὐτοὺς βοη-
θοὺς οὐδὲ σπείρουσιν ἄλλως οἱ ἄνθρωποι εἰ μὴ
τὴν Δήμητρα ἐπικαλεσάμενοι· τηλικούτου δ'
ἔργου ἀψάμενός τις ἄνευ θεῶν ἀσφαλῶς ἅψεται
13 καὶ οἱ τούτῳ προσιόντες εὐτυχῶς προσελεύσονται; τί ἄλλο ποιεῖς, ἄνθρωπε, ἢ τὰ μυστήρια
ἐξορχῇ καὶ λέγεις " οἴκημά ἐστι καὶ ἐν Ἐλευσῖνι,
ἰδοὺ καὶ ἐνθάδε. ἐκεῖ ἱεροφάντης· καὶ ἐγὼ
ποιήσω ἱεροφάντην. ἐκεῖ κῆρυξ· κἀγὼ κήρυκα
καταστήσω. ἐκεῖ δᾳδοῦχος· κἀγὼ δᾳδοῦχον.
14 ἐκεῖ δᾷδες· καὶ ἐνθάδε. αἱ φωναὶ αἱ αὐταί· τὰ
γινόμενα τί διαφέρει ταῦτα ἐκείνων;"; ἀσε-
βέστατε ἄνθρωπε, οὐδὲν διαφέρει; καὶ παρὰ
τόπον ταῦτα[2] ὠφελεῖ καὶ παρὰ καιρόν; οὐ·
ἀλλὰ[2] καὶ μετὰ θυσίας δὲ καὶ μετ' εὐχῶν καὶ
προηγνευκότα καὶ προδιακείμενον τῇ γνώμῃ, ὅτι

---

[1] Wolf: ἀπολιπόμενος S.

[2] Oldfather: καὶ παρὰ τόπον ταῦτα ὠφελεῖ καὶ παρὰ καιρόν·
καὶ μετὰ θυσίας S and all editors, except Upton, who saw
that the passage was corrupt, but not how to heal it.
ταῦτα is ambiguous and misses the obvious point. Besides,
within eight lines, to have exactly the same phrases, παρὰ
τόπον and παρὰ καιρόν, in a diametrically opposite sense,
where the text is certainly sound, seems to me intolerable.
The plain sense of the entire context appears to require
these changes, the first of which is the slightest imaginable,
and the second, not absolutely necessary perhaps, in the

you ever do anything but wear yourself out over the
question how solutions can be found for syllogisms,
for the arguments that involve equivocal premises,
and those which derive syllogisms by the process
of interrogation?[1] "But So-and-so lectures; why
shouldn't I too?" Slave, these things are not done
recklessly, nor at random, but one ought to be of a
certain age, and lead a certain kind of life, and have
God as his guide. You say: No. But no man sails
out of a harbour without first sacrificing to the gods
and invoking their aid, nor do men sow hit-or-miss,
but only after first calling upon Demeter; and yet
will a man, if he has laid his hand to so great a task
as this without the help of the gods, be secure in so
doing, and will those who come to him be fortunate
in so coming? What else are you doing, man, but
vulgarizing the Mysteries, and saying, "There is a
chapel at Eleusis; see, there is one here too. There
is a hierophant there; I too will make a hierophant.
There is a herald there; I too will appoint a herald.
There is a torch-bearer there; I too will have a
torch-bearer. There are torches there; and here too.
The words said are the same; and what is the
difference between what is done here and what is
done there?"? Most impious man, is there no
difference? Are the same acts helpful, if they are
performed at the wrong place and at the wrong time?
Nay, but a man ought to come also with a sacrifice,
and with prayers, and after a preliminary purification,
and with his mind predisposed to the idea that he

---

[1] See note on I. 7, 1.

---

abrupt and dramatic style of Epictetus, but probably what
would have been written, had he been writing instead of
speaking.

ἱεροῖς προσελεύσεται καὶ ἱεροῖς παλαιοῖς. οὕτως
15 ὠφέλιμα γίνεται τὰ μυστήρια, οὕτως εἰς φαντασίαν ἐρχόμεθα, ὅτι ἐπὶ παιδείᾳ καὶ ἐπανορθώσει
τοῦ βίου κατεστάθη πάντα ταῦτα ὑπὸ τῶν πα-
16 λαιῶν. σὺ δ' ἐξαγγέλλεις αὐτὰ καὶ ἐξορχῇ παρὰ
καιρόν, παρὰ τόπον, ἄνευ θυμάτων, ἄνευ ἁγνείας·[1]
οὐκ ἐσθῆτα ἔχεις ἣν δεῖ τὸν ἱεροφάντην, οὐ κόμην,
οὐ στρόφιον οἷον δεῖ, οὐ φωνήν, οὐχ ἡλικίαν, οὐχ
ἥγνευκας ὡς ἐκεῖνος, ἀλλ' αὐτὰς μόνας τὰς φωνὰς
ἀνειληφὼς λέγεις. ἱεραί εἰσιν αἱ φωναὶ αὐταὶ
καθ' αὑτάς ;
17 Ἄλλον τρόπον δεῖ ἐπὶ ταῦτα ἐλθεῖν· μέγα
ἐστὶ τὸ πρᾶγμα, μυστικόν ἐστιν, οὐχ ὡς ἔτυχεν
18 οὐδὲ τῷ τυχόντι δεδομένον. ἀλλ' οὐδὲ σοφὸν
εἶναι τυχὸν ἐξαρκεῖ πρὸς τὸ ἐπιμεληθῆναι νέων·
δεῖ δὲ καὶ προχειρότητά τινα εἶναι καὶ ἐπιτη-
δειότητα πρὸς τοῦτο, νὴ τὸν Δία, καὶ σῶμα ποιὸν
καὶ πρὸ πάντων τὸν θεὸν συμβουλεύειν ταύτην
19 τὴν χώραν κατασχεῖν, ὡς Σωκράτει συνεβού-
λευεν τὴν ἐλεγκτικὴν χώραν ἔχειν, ὡς Διογένει
τὴν βασιλικὴν καὶ ἐπιπληκτικήν, ὡς Ζήνωνι τὴν
20 διδασκαλικὴν καὶ δογματικήν. σὺ δ' ἰατρεῖον
ἀνοίγεις ἄλλο οὐδὲν ἔχων ἢ φάρμακα, ποῦ δὲ ἢ
πῶς ἐπιτίθεται ταῦτα, μήτε εἰδὼς μήτε πολυ-
21 πραγμονήσας. "ἰδοὺ ἐκεῖνος ταῦτα τὰ[2] κολ-
λύρια· κἀγὼ ἔχω." μή τι οὖν καὶ τὴν δύναμιν
τὴν χρηστικὴν αὐτοῖς ; μή τι οἶδας καὶ πότε

---

[1] s (and Bentley): ὑγιείας S.
[2] τά added by Koraes.

will be approaching holy rites, and holy rites of great
antiquity. Only thus do the Mysteries become
helpful, only thus do we arrive at the impression
that all these things were established by men of
old time for the purpose of education and for the
amendment of our life. But you are publishing the
Mysteries abroad and vulgarizing them, out of time,
out of place, without sacrifices, without purification;
you do not have the dress which the hierophant
ought to wear, you do not have the proper head of
hair, nor head-band, nor voice, nor age; you have
not kept yourself pure as he has, but you have
picked up only the words which he utters, and
recite them. Have the words a sacred force all by
themselves?

One ought to approach these matters in a different
fashion; the affair is momentous, it is full of mystery,
not a chance gift, nor given to all comers. Nay, it
may be that not even wisdom is all that is needed
for the care of the young; one ought also to have a
certain readiness and special fitness for this task, by
Zeus, and a particular physique, and above all the
counsel of God advising him to occupy this office,
as God counselled Socrates to take the office of
examining and confuting men, Diogenes the office of
rebuking men in a kingly manner, and Zeno that of
instructing men and laying down doctrines. But you
are opening up a doctor's office although you possess
no equipment other than drugs, but when or how
these drugs are applied you neither know nor have
ever taken the trouble to learn. "See," you say,
"that man has these eye-salves, and so have I."
Have you, then, at all the faculty of using them
aright? Do you know at all when and how and for

22 καὶ πῶς ὠφελήσει καὶ τίνα ; τί οὖν κυβεύεις ἐν
τοῖς μεγίστοις, τί ῥᾳδιουργεῖς, τί ἐπιχειρεῖς
πράγματι μηδέν σοι προσήκοντι ; ἄφες αὐτὸ τοῖς
δυναμένοις, τοῖς κοσμοῦσι. μὴ προστρίβου καὶ
αὐτὸς αἶσχος φιλοσοφίᾳ διὰ σαυτοῦ, μηδὲ γίνου
23 μέρος τῶν διαβαλλόντων τὸ ἔργον. ἀλλὰ εἴ σε
ψυχαγωγεῖ τὰ θεωρήματα, καθήμενος αὐτὰ
στρέφε αὐτὸς ἐπὶ σεαυτοῦ· φιλόσοφον δὲ μηδέποτ' εἴπῃς σεαυτὸν μηδ' ἄλλου ἀνάσχῃ λέγοντος, ἀλλὰ λέγε "πεπλάνηται· ἐγὼ γὰρ οὔτ'
ὀρέγομαι ἄλλως ἢ πρότερον οὐδ' ὁρμῶ ἐπ' ἄλλα
οὐδὲ συγκατατίθεμαι ἄλλοις οὐδ' ὅλως ἐν χρήσει
φαντασιῶν παρήλλαχά τι ἀπὸ τῆς πρότερον
24 καταστάσεως." ταῦτα φρόνει καὶ λέγε περὶ
σεαυτοῦ, εἰ θέλεις τὰ κατ' ἀξίαν φρονεῖν· εἰ δὲ
μή, κύβευε καὶ ποίει ἃ ποιεῖς. ταῦτα γάρ σοι
πρέπει.

κβ'. Περὶ Κυνισμοῦ.

1 Πυθομένου δὲ τῶν γνωρίμων τινὸς αὐτοῦ, ὃς
ἐφαίνετο ἐπιρρεπῶς ἔχων πρὸς τὸ κυνίσαι, Ποῖόν
τινα εἶναι δεῖ τὸν κυνίζοντα καὶ τίς ἡ πρόληψις ἡ τοῦ πράγματος, Σκεψόμεθα κατὰ
2 σχολήν· τοσοῦτον δ' ἔχω σοι εἰπεῖν, ὅτι ὁ δίχα

---

[1] The Cynics were the intransigent and uncompromising
moralists, resembling the holy men, ascetics, and dervishes
of the Orient. Epictetus idealizes them somewhat in this
discourse, regarding them as a kind of perfected wise men,

whom they will do good? Why, then, do you play at hazard in matters of the utmost moment, why do you take things lightly, why do you put your hand to a task that is altogether inappropriate for you? Leave it to those who are able to do it, and do it with distinction. Do not yourself by your own actions join the number of those who bring disgrace upon philosophy, and do not become one of those who disparage the profession. If, however, you find the principles of philosophy entertaining, sit down and turn them over in your mind all by yourself, but don't ever call yourself a philosopher, and don't allow anyone else to say it of you, but say, rather, "He is mistaken; for my desire is no different from what it used to be, nor my choice, nor my assent, nor, in a word, have I changed at all, in my use of external impressions, from my former state." Think this and say this about yourself, if you wish to think aright. If not, keep on playing at hazard and doing what you are doing now; for it becomes you.

CHAPTER XXII

On the calling of a Cynic [1]

WHEN one of his acquaintances, who seemed to have an inclination to take up the calling of a Cynic, asked him what sort of a man the Cynic ought to be, and what was the fundamental conception of his calling, Epictetus said: We will consider it at leisure; but I can tell you this much, that the man who lays

like some of the early Christian anchorites, but points out very clearly that their style of life was not practicable for every man, indeed not even for one so humble and frugal as he himself was.

θεοῦ τηλικούτῳ πράγματι ἐπιβαλλόμενος θεο-
χόλωτός ἐστι καὶ οὐδὲν ἄλλο ἢ δημοσίᾳ θέλει
3 ἀσχημονεῖν. οὐδὲ γὰρ ἐν οἰκίᾳ καλῶς οἰκουμένῃ
παρελθών τις αὑτῷ ἑαυτῷ λέγει "ἐμὲ δεῖ οἰκο-
νόμον εἶναι." εἰ δὲ μή, ἐπιστραφεὶς ὁ κύριος
καὶ ἰδὼν αὐτὸν σοβαρῶς διατασσόμενον, ἑλκύσας
4 ἔτεμεν. οὕτως γίνεται καὶ ἐν τῇ μεγάλῃ ταύτῃ
πόλει. ἔστι γάρ τις καὶ ἐνθάδ' οἰκοδεσπότης
5 ἕκαστα ὁ διατάσσων. "σὺ ἥλιος εἶ· δύνασαι
περιερχόμενος ἐνιαυτὸν ποιεῖν καὶ ὥρας καὶ τοὺς
καρποὺς αὔξειν καὶ τρέφειν καὶ ἀνέμους κινεῖν
καὶ ἀνιέναι καὶ τὰ σώματα τῶν ἀνθρώπων θερ-
μαίνειν συμμέτρως· ὕπαγε, περιέρχου καὶ οὕτως
διακίνει ἀπὸ τῶν μεγίστων ἐπὶ τὰ μικρότατα.
6 σὺ μοσχάριον εἶ· ὅταν ἐπιφανῇ λέων, τὰ σαυτοῦ
πρᾶσσε· εἰ δὲ μή, οἰμώξεις. σὺ ταῦρος εἶ, προσελθὼν μάχου· σοὶ γὰρ τοῦτο ἐπιβάλλει καὶ
7 πρέπει καὶ δύνασαι αὐτὸ ποιεῖν. σὺ δύνασαι
ἡγεῖσθαι τοῦ στρατεύματος ἐπὶ Ἴλιον· ἴσθι
Ἀγαμέμνων. σὺ δύνασαι τῷ Ἕκτορι μονο-
8 μαχῆσαι· ἴσθι Ἀχιλλεύς." εἰ δὲ Θερσίτης
παρελθὼν ἀντεποιεῖτο τῆς ἀρχῆς, ἢ οὐκ ἂν
ἔτυχεν ἢ τυχὼν ἂν ἠσχημόνησεν ἐν πλείοσι
μάρτυσι.
9   Καὶ σὺ βούλευσαι[1] περὶ τοῦ[2] πράγματος ἐπι-
10 μελῶς· οὐκ ἔστιν οἷον δοκεῖ σοι. "τριβώνιον
καὶ νῦν φορῶ καὶ τόθ'[3] ἕξω,[4] κοιμῶμαι καὶ νῦν
σκληρῶς καὶ τότε κοιμήσομαι, πηρίδιον προσ-
λήψομαι καὶ ξύλον καὶ περιερχόμενος αἰτεῖν

---

[1] Upton from his "codex": συμβουλεῦσαι S.
[2] τοῦ added by Reiske.   [3] Schenkl: τότ' S.
[4] Salmasius: ἔξω S.

his hand to so great a matter as this without God, is hateful to Him, and his wish means nothing else than disgracing himself in public. For in a well-ordered house no one comes along and says to himself, "I ought to be manager of this house"; or if he does, the lord of the mansion, when he turns around and sees the fellow giving orders in a high and mighty fashion, drags him out and gives him a dressing down. So it goes also in this great city, the world; for here also there is a Lord of the Mansion who assigns each and every thing its place. "*You* are the sun; you have the power, as you make the circuit of the heavens, to produce the year and the seasons, to give increase and nourishment to the fruits, to stir and to calm the winds, and to give warmth in moderation to the bodies of men; arise, make the circuit of the heavens, and so set in motion all things from the greatest to the least. *You* are a calf; when a lion appears, do what is expected of you; otherwise you will smart for it. *You* are a bull; come on and fight, for this is expected of you, it befits you, and you are able to do it. *You* are able to lead the host against Ilium; be Agamemnon. *You* are able to fight a duel with Hector; be Achilles." But if Thersites came along and claimed command, either he would not have got it, or if he had, he would have disgraced himself in the presence of a multitude of witnesses.

So do you also think about the matter carefully; it is not what you think it is. "I wear a rough cloak even as it is, and I shall have one then; I have a hard bed even now, and so I shall then; I shall take to myself a wallet and a staff,[1] and I shall

---

[1] Quite like modern dervishes.

ἄρξομαι τοὺς ἀπαντῶντας, λοιδορεῖν· κἂν ἴδω
τινὰ δρωπακιζόμενον, ἐπιτιμήσω αὐτῷ, κἂν
τὸ κόμιον πεπλακότα ἢ ἐν κοκκίνοις περιπα-
11 τοῦντα." εἰ τοιοῦτόν τι φαντάζῃ τὸ πρᾶγμα,
μακρὰν ἀπ' αὐτοῦ· μὴ προσέλθῃς, οὐδέν ἐστι
12 πρὸς σέ. εἰ δ' οἷόν ἐστι φανταζόμενος οὐκ
ἀπαξιοῖς σεαυτόν, σκέψαι ἡλίκῳ πράγματι
ἐπιχειρεῖς.
13   Πρῶτον ἐν τοῖς κατὰ σαυτὸν οὐκέτι δεῖ σε
ὅμοιον ἐν οὐδενὶ φαίνεσθαι οἷς νῦν ποιεῖς, οὐ θεῷ
ἐγκαλοῦντα, οὐκ ἀνθρώπῳ· ὄρεξιν ἆραί σε[1] δεῖ
παντελῶς, ἔκκλισιν ἐπὶ μόνα μεταθεῖναι τὰ
προαιρετικά· σοὶ μὴ ὀργὴν εἶναι, μὴ μῆνιν, μὴ
φθόνον, μὴ ἔλεον· μὴ κοράσιόν σοι φαίνεσθαι
καλόν, μὴ δοξάριον, μὴ παιδάριον, μὴ πλακουν-
14 τάριον. ἐκεῖνο γὰρ εἰδέναι σε δεῖ, ὅτι οἱ ἄλλοι
ἄνθρωποι τοὺς τοίχους προβέβληνται καὶ τὰς
οἰκίας καὶ τὸ σκότος, ὅταν τι τῶν τοιούτων
ποιῶσιν, καὶ τὰ κρύψοντα πολλὰ ἔχουσιν.
κέκλεικε τὴν θύραν, ἔστακέν[2] τινα πρὸ τοῦ
κοιτῶνος· "ἄν τις ἔλθῃ, λέγε ὅτι ἔξω ἐστίν, οὐ
15 σχολάζει." ὁ Κυνικὸς δ' ἀντὶ πάντων τούτων
ὀφείλει τὴν αἰδῶ προβεβλῆσθαι· εἰ δὲ μή, γυμνὸς
καὶ ἐν ὑπαίθρῳ ἀσχημονήσει. τοῦτο οἰκία ἐστὶν
αὐτῷ, τοῦτο θύρα, τοῦτο οἱ ἐπὶ τοῦ κοιτῶνος,
16 τοῦτο σκότος. οὔτε γὰρ θέλειν τι δεῖ ἀποκρύπτειν
αὐτὸν τῶν ἑαυτοῦ (εἰ δὲ μή, ἀπῆλθεν, ἀπώλεσε

1 Wolf: ἀρέσαι S.   Wolf: ἔστακέν S.

begin to walk around and beg from those I meet, and revile them; and if I see someone who is getting rid of superfluous hair by the aid of pitch-plasters, or has a fancy cut to his hair, or is strolling about in scarlet clothes, I will come down hard on him." If you fancy the affair to be something like this, give it a wide berth; don't come near it, it is nothing for you. But if your impression of it is correct, and you do not think too meanly of yourself, consider the magnitude of the enterprise that you are taking in hand.

First, in all that pertains to yourself directly you must change completely from your present practices, and must cease to blame God or man; you must utterly wipe out desire, and must turn your aversion toward the things which lie within the province of the moral purpose, and these only; you must feel no anger, no rage, no envy, no pity; no wench must look fine to you, no petty reputation, no boy-favourite, no little sweet-cake. For this you ought to know: Other men have the protection of their walls and their houses and darkness, when they do anything of that sort, and they have many things to hide them. A man closes his door, stations someone at the entrance to his bedroom: "If anyone comes, tell him 'He is not at home, he is not at leisure.'" But the Cynic, instead of all these defences, has to make his self-respect his protection; if he does not, he will be disgracing himself naked and out of doors. His self-respect is his house, his door, his guards at the entrance to his bedroom, his darkness. For neither ought he to wish to keep concealed anything that is his (otherwise he is lost, he has destroyed the Cynic

ARRIAN'S DISCOURSES OF EPICTETUS

τὸν Κυνικόν, τὸν ὕπαιθρον, τὸν ἐλεύθερον, ἦρκται
τι τῶν ἐκτὸς¹ φοβεῖσθαι, ἦρκται χρείαν ἔχειν
τοῦ ἀποκρύψοντος) οὔτε ὅταν θέλῃ δύναται. ποῦ
17 γὰρ αὐτὸν ἀποκρύψῃ ἢ πῶς; ἂν δ' ἀπὸ τύχης²
ἐμπέσῃ ὁ παιδευτὴς ὁ κοινός, ὁ παιδαγωγός, οἷα
18 πάσχειν ἀνάγκη; ταῦτ' οὖν δεδοικότα ἐπιθαρρεῖν
οἷόν τ' ἔτι ἐξ ὅλης ψυχῆς ἐπιστατεῖν τοῖς ἄλλοις
ἀνθρώποις; ἀμήχανον, ἀδύνατον.

19   Πρῶτον οὖν τὸ ἡγεμονικόν σε δεῖ τὸ σαυτοῦ
20 καθαρὸν ποιῆσαι καὶ τὴν ἔνστασιν ταύτην· "νῦν
ἐμοὶ ὕλη ἐστὶν ἡ ἐμὴ διάνοια, ὡς τῷ τέκτονι τὰ
ξύλα, ὡς τῷ σκυτεῖ τὰ δέρματα· ἔργον δ' ὀρθὴ
21 χρῆσις τῶν φαντασιῶν. τὸ σωμάτιον δὲ οὐδὲν
πρὸς ἐμέ· τὰ τούτου μέρη οὐδὲν πρὸς ἐμέ. θάνατος; ἐρχέσθω, ὅταν θέλῃ, εἴτε ὅλου εἴτε μέρους
22 τινός. φυγή;³ καὶ ποῦ δύναταί τις ἐκβαλεῖν;
ἔξω τοῦ κόσμου οὐ δύναται. ὅπου δ' ἂν ἀπέλθω,
ἐκεῖ ἥλιος, ἐκεῖ σελήνη, ἐκεῖ ἄστρα, ἐνύπνια,
οἰωνοί, ἡ πρὸς θεοὺς ὁμιλία."

23   Εἶθ' οὕτως παρεσκευασμένον οὐκ ἔστι τούτοις
ἀρκεῖσθαι τὸν ταῖς ἀληθείαις Κυνικόν, ἀλλ'
εἰδέναι δεῖ, ὅτι ἄγγελος ἀπὸ τοῦ Διὸς ἀπέσταλται

¹ Wolf: ἐντός S.   ² τύχης S.
³ Upton: φεῦγε S.

¹ That is, the trusted servant who attended constantly the
boys of the well-to-do families, and in particular watched
over their deportment and morals.
² ἐμπεσεῖν seems to me to be used as in III. 7, 12. This is
a rare meaning, indeed, but supported to some extent also
by the gloss in Hesychius: ἐμπεσεῖν· εἰς δεσμωτήριον ἀχθῆναι.
The word is also used of getting caught in a trap, Xenophon
Mem. II. 1, 4: τοῖς θηράτροις ἐμπίπτουσι. That is probably the

136

within him, the man of outdoor life, the free man;
he has begun to fear something external, he has
begun to need something to conceal him), nor can
he keep it concealed when he wishes to do so.   For
where will he conceal himself, or how?   And if
this instructor of us all, this "pedagogue,"[1] chance
to get caught,[2] what must he suffer!   Can, then, a
man who is afraid of all this continue with all his
heart to supervise the conduct of other men?   It
cannot be done, it is impossible.

In the first place, then, you must make your
governing principle pure, and you must make
the following your plan of life: "From now on my
mind is the material with which I have to work, as
the carpenter has his timbers, the shoemaker his
hides; my business is to make the right use of my
impressions.   My paltry body is nothing to me;
the parts of it are nothing to me.   Death?   Let
it come when it will, whether it be the death of
the whole or some part.   Exile?   And to what place
can anyone thrust me out?   Outside the universe he
cannot.   But wherever I go, there are sun, moon,
stars, dreams, omens, my converse with gods."

In the next place, the true Cynic, when he is
thus prepared, cannot rest contented with this, but
he must know that he has been sent by Zeus to men,

---

original form of expression from which the intransitive use
derives.   Schenkl (not Schweighäuser, to whom I owe the
above references to Hesychius and Xenophon) appears to me
to be wrong in rendering the word "decipior," although
Matheson is inclined to follow him.   Capps suggests that
"the κοινὸς παιδευτής is God," and that ἐμπέσῃ means "break
in upon."   But that might be somewhat inconsistent with
ἀπὸ τυχῆς, which seems hardly appropriate of an action on
the part of God.

καὶ πρὸς τοὺς ἀνθρώπους περὶ ἀγαθῶν καὶ κακῶν
ὑποδείξων αὐτοῖς, ὅτι πεπλάνηνται καὶ ἀλλαχοῦ
ζητοῦσι τὴν οὐσίαν τοῦ ἀγαθοῦ καὶ τοῦ κακοῦ,
ὅπου οὐκ ἔστιν, ὅπου δ' ἔστιν, οὐκ ἐνθυμοῦνται,

24 καὶ ὡς ὁ Διογένης ἀπαχθεὶς πρὸς Φίλιππον μετὰ
τὴν ἐν Χαιρωνείᾳ μάχην κατάσκοπος εἶναι. τῷ
γὰρ ὄντι κατάσκοπός ἐστιν ὁ Κυνικὸς τοῦ τίνα

25 ἐστὶ τοῖς ἀνθρώποις φίλα καὶ τίνα πολέμια·
καὶ δεῖ αὐτὸν ἀκριβῶς κατασκεψάμενον ἐλθόντ'
ἀπαγγεῖλαι τἀληθῆ μήθ' ὑπὸ φόβου ἐκπλαγέντα,
ὥστε τοὺς μὴ ὄντας πολεμίους δεῖξαι, μήτε τινὰ
ἄλλον τρόπον ὑπὸ τῶν φαντασιῶν παραταραχ-
θέντα ἢ συγχυθέντα.

26 Δεῖ οὖν αὐτὸν δύνασθαι ἀνατεινάμενον, ἂν
οὕτως τύχῃ, καὶ ἐπὶ σκηνὴν τραγικὴν ἀνερχό-
μενον λέγειν τὸ τοῦ Σωκράτους " ἰὼ ἄνθρωποι,[1]
ποῖ φέρεσθε ; τί ποιεῖτε, ὦ ταλαίπωροι ; ὡς
τυφλοὶ ἄνω καὶ κάτω κυλίεσθε· ἄλλην ὁδὸν
ἀπέρχεσθε τὴν οὖσαν ἀπολελοιπότες, ἀλλαχοῦ
ζητεῖτε τὸ εὔρουν καὶ τὸ εὐδαιμονικόν,[2] ὅπου οὐκ

27 ἔστιν, οὐδ' ἄλλου δεικνύοντος πιστεύετε. τί αὐτὸ
ἔξω ζητεῖτε ; ἐν σώματι οὐκ ἔστιν. εἰ ἀπιστεῖτε,
ἴδετε Μύρωνα, ἴδετε Ὀφέλλιον. ἐν κτήσει οὐκ
ἔστιν. εἰ δ' ἀπιστεῖτε, ἴδετε Κροῖσον, ἴδετε τοὺς
νῦν πλουσίους, ὅσης οἰμωγῆς ὁ βίος αὐτῶν
μεστός ἐστιν. ἐν ἀρχῇ οὐκ ἔστιν. εἰ δὲ μή γε,

---

[1] Schweighäuser : ἰώνθρωποι S : ὤνθρωποι Leopold.
[2] Shaftesbury : ἡγεμονικόν S.

partly as a messenger, in order to show them that
in questions of good and evil they have gone astray,
and are seeking the true nature of the good and
the evil where it is not, but where it is they never
think; and partly, in the words of Diogenes, when
he was taken off to Philip, after the battle of
Chaeroneia, as a scout.[1] For the Cynic is truly a
scout, to find out what things are friendly to men
and what hostile; and he must first do his scouting
accurately, and on returning must tell the truth, not
driven by fear to designate as enemies those who
are not such, nor in any other fashion be distraught
or confused by his external impressions.

He must, accordingly, be able, if it so chance,
to lift up his voice, and, mounting the tragic stage,
to speak like Socrates: "Alas! men, where are you
rushing?[2] What are you doing, O wretched people?
Like blind men you go tottering all around. You
have left the true path and are going off upon
another; you are looking for serenity and happiness
in the wrong place, where it does not exist, and
you do not believe when another points them out
to you. Why do you look for it outside? It does
not reside in the body. If you doubt that, look
at Myron, or Ophellius.[3] It is not in possessions.
If you doubt that, look at Croesus, look at the rich
nowadays, the amount of lamentation with which
their life is filled. It is not in office. Why, if it

---

[1] Compare I. 24, 3-10. The philosopher is a sort of spy
sent on in advance into this world, to report to the rest of us
what things are good and what evil.

[2] [Plato], *Cleitophon*, 407 A—B.

[3] Probably famous athletes or gladiators of the day;
otherwise unknown.

ἔδει τοὺς δὶς καὶ τρὶς ὑπάτους εὐδαίμονας εἶναι·
28 οὐκ εἰσὶ δέ. τίσιν περὶ τούτου πιστεύσομεν;
ὑμῖν τοῖς ἔξωθεν τὰ ἐκείνων βλέπουσιν καὶ ὑπὸ
τῆς φαντασίας περιλαμπομένοις ἢ αὐτοῖς ἐκείνοις;
29 τί λέγουσιν; ἀκούσατε αὐτῶν, ὅταν οἰμώζωσιν,
ὅταν στένωσιν, ὅταν δι᾽ αὐτὰς τὰς ὑπατείας καὶ
τὴν δόξαν καὶ τὴν ἐπιφάνειαν ἀθλιώτερον οἴωνται
30 καὶ ἐπικινδυνότερον ἔχειν. ἐν βασιλείᾳ οὐκ
ἔστιν. εἰ δὲ μή, Νέρων ἂν εὐδαίμων ἐγένετο καὶ
Σαρδανάπαλλος. ἀλλ᾽ οὐδ᾽ Ἀγαμέμνων εὐδαίμων
ἦν καίτοι κομψότερος ὢν Σαρδαναπάλλου καὶ
Νέρωνος, ἀλλὰ τῶν ἄλλων ῥεγκόντων ἐκεῖνος τί
ποιεῖ;

πολλὰς ἐκ κεφαλῆς προθελύμνους ἕλκετο χαίτας.

καὶ αὐτὸς τί λέγει;

πλάζομαι ὧδε,

φησίν, καὶ

ἀλαλύκτημαι· κραδίη δέ μοι ἔξω
στηθέων ἐκθρῴσκει.

31 τάλας, τί τῶν σῶν ἔχει κακῶς; ἡ κτῆσις; οὐκ
ἔχει· ἀλλὰ πολύχρυσος εἶ καὶ πολύχαλκος. τὸ
σῶμα; οὐκ ἔχει.[1] τί οὖν σοι κακόν ἐστιν; ἐκεῖνο,
ὅ τί ποτε[2] ἠμέληταί σου καὶ κατέφθαρται, ᾧ
ὀρεγόμεθα, ᾧ ἐκκλίνομεν, ᾧ ὁρμῶμεν καὶ ἀφορ-
32 μῶμεν. πῶς ἠμέληται; ἀγνοεῖ τὴν οὐσίαν τοῦ

---

[1] Capps transfers to this position τὸ σῶμα; οὐκ ἔχει, which
in S precede ἀλλὰ . . . πολύχαλκος.
[2] τὸ τίποτε Blass, perhaps rightly.

---

[1] Iliad, X. 15.

ἀγαθοῦ πρὸς ἣν πέφυκε καὶ τὴν τοῦ κακοῦ καὶ
τί ἴδιον ἔχει καὶ τί ἀλλότριον. καὶ ὅταν τι τῶν
ἀλλοτρίων κακῶς ἔχῃ, λέγει "οὐαί μοι, οἱ γὰρ
33 Ἕλληνες κινδυνεύουσι." ταλαίπωρον ἡγεμονικὸν
καὶ μόνον ἀτημέλητον καὶ ἀθεράπευτον. "μέλλουσιν ἀποθνήσκειν ὑπὸ τῶν Τρώων ἀναιρεθέντες."
ἂν δ' αὐτοὺς οἱ Τρῶες μὴ ἀποκτείνωσιν, οὐ μὴ
ἀποθάνωσιν; "ναί, ἀλλ' οὐχ ὑφ' ἓν πάντες." τί
οὖν διαφέρει; εἰ γὰρ κακόν ἐστι τὸ ἀποθανεῖν, ἄν
τε ὁμοῦ ἄν τε καθ' ἕνα ὁμοίως κακόν ἐστιν. μή
τι ἄλλο τι μέλλει γίνεσθαι ἢ τὸ σωμάτιον χωρίζε-
34 σθαι καὶ ἡ ψυχή; "οὐδέν." σοὶ δὲ ἀπολλυ-
μένων τῶν Ἑλλήνων ἡ θύρα κέκλεισται; οὐκ
ἔξεστιν ἀποθανεῖν; "ἔξεστιν." τί οὖν πενθεῖς;
οὐαί,[1] βασιλεὺς καὶ τὸ τοῦ Διὸς σκῆπτρον ἔχων.
ἀτυχὴς βασιλεὺ οὐ γίνεται· οὐ μᾶλλον ἢ
35 ἀτυχὴς θεός. τί οὖν εἶ; ποιμὴν ταῖς ἀληθείαις·
οὕτως γὰρ κλάεις ὡς οἱ ποιμένες, ὅταν λύκος
ἁρπάσῃ τι τῶν προβάτων αὐτῶν· καὶ οὗτοι δὲ
36 πρόβατά εἰσιν οἱ ὑπὸ σοῦ ἀρχόμενοι. τί δὲ καὶ

[1] Oldfather : οὐᾶ S.

[1] Specifically alluding to the position of Agamemnon in the situation referred to above.

[2] This is a distinct over-statement of the case. Obviously it makes a great deal of difference for a State (and it is in his capacity as head of a State that Agamemnon is here appearing), whether its fighting men are killed all at once, or die one at a time in the course of nature.

[3] Presumably a king is expected to commit suicide before becoming "unfortunate," as suggested in § 34. If he survived under the circumstances here described, he certainly must be "unfortunate," at least as a man, in any ordinary sense of the term. Capps, however, thinks the meaning of Epictetus to be that a king qua king, that is, while really holding the sceptre of Zeus, is blessed of fortune. If "unfortunate" he is simply not such a king. This refinement

the true nature of the good, to which it was born, and of the true nature of the evil, and of what is its own proper possession, and what is none of its own concern. And whenever some one of these things that are none of its own concern is in a bad way, it says, "Woe is me, for the Greeks are in danger."[1] Ah, miserable governing principle, the only thing neglected and uncared for! "They are going to perish, slain by the Trojans." But if the Trojans do not kill them, will they not die anyway? "Yes, but not all at once." What difference does it make, then? For if death is an evil, whether they die all at once, or die one at a time, it is equally an evil.[2] Nothing else is going to happen, is it, but the separation of the paltry body from the soul? "Nothing." And is the door closed for you, if the Greeks perish? Are you not permitted to die? "I am." Why, then, do you grieve? "Woe is me, a king, and holding the sceptre of Zeus!" A king does not become unfortunate any more than a god becomes unfortunate.[3] What are you, then? Truly a shepherd![4] for you wail as the shepherds do when a wolf carries off one of their sheep; and these men over whom you rule are sheep. But why did you come here[5] in the first

would be similar to the well-known argument concerning the "ruler *qua* ruler," in the first book of Plato's *Republic*. The more common-sense view of the case is well expressed by the Scholiast on Homer's *Odyssey* XI. 438, thus: "A king is unfortunate when his subjects fare ill."

[4] Referring to the common Homeric designation of a ruler as the "shepherd of the folk."

[5] Capps proposes the novel view that ἤρχου is from ἄρχομαι, and "takes up ἀρχόμενοι [35] . . . Agamemnon, by allowing himself to be dominated by an ἀλλότριον πρᾶγμα, has become a subject, a sheep."

ἤρχου ; μή τι ὄρεξις ὑμῖν ἐκινδυνεύετο, μή τι
ἔκκλισις, μή τι ὁρμή, μή τι ἀφορμή ; "οὔ," φησίν,
"ἀλλὰ τοῦ ἀδελφοῦ μου τὸ γυναικάριον ἡρπάγη."

37 οὐκ οὖν [1] κέρδος μέγα στερηθῆναι μοιχικοῦ γυναι-
καρίου ; "καταφρονηθῶμεν οὖν ὑπὸ τῶν Τρώων ;"
τίνων ὄντων ; φρονίμων ἢ ἀφρόνων ; εἰ φρονίμων,
τί αὐτοῖς πολεμεῖτε ; εἰ ἀφρόνων, τί ὑμῖν μέλει ;

38 " 'Εν τίνι οὖν ἔστι τὸ ἀγαθόν, ἐπειδὴ ἐν τούτοις
οὐκ ἔστιν ; εἰπὲ ἡμῖν, κύριε ἄγγελε καὶ κατά-
σκοπε." "ὅπου οὐ δοκεῖτε οὐδὲ θέλετε ζητῆσαι
αὐτό. εἰ γὰρ ἠθέλετε, εὕρετε ἂν αὐτὸ ἐν ὑμῖν ὂν
οὐδ' ἂν ἔξω ἐπλάζεσθε οὐδ' ἂν ἐζητεῖτε τὰ

39 ἀλλότρια ὡς ἴδια. ἐπιστρέψατε αὐτοὶ ἐφ' ἑαυ-
τούς, καταμάθετε τὰς προλήψεις ἃς ἔχετε. ποῖόν
τι φαντάζεσθε τὸ ἀγαθόν ; τὸ εὔρουν, τὸ εὐδαιμονικόν, τὸ ἀπαραπόδιστον. ἄγε, μέγα [2] δ' αὐτὸ
φυσικῶς οὐ φαντάζεσθε ; ἀξιόλογον οὐ φαν-

40 τάζεσθε ; ἀβλαβὲς οὐ φαντάζεσθε ; ἐν ποίᾳ οὖν
ὕλῃ δεῖ ζητεῖν τὸ εὔρουν καὶ ἀπαραπόδιστον ; ἐν
τῇ δούλῃ ἢ ἐν τῇ ἐλευθέρᾳ ;" "ἐν τῇ ἐλευθέρᾳ."
"τὸ σωμάτιον οὖν ἐλεύθερον ἔχετε ἢ δοῦλον ;"
"οὐκ ἴσμεν." "οὐκ ἴστε ὅτι πυρετοῦ δοῦλόν
ἐστιν, ποδάγρας, ὀφθαλμίας, δυσεντερίας, τυράννου, πυρός, σιδήρου, παντὸς τοῦ ἰσχυροτέρου ;"

41 "ναὶ δοῦλον." "πῶς οὖν ἔτι ἀνεμπόδιστον εἶναί
τι δύναται τῶν τοῦ σώματος ; πῶς δὲ μέγα ἢ
ἀξιόλογον τὸ φύσει νεκρόν, ἢ γῆ, ὁ πηλός ; τί οὖν ;

42 οὐδὲν ἔχετε ἐλεύθερον ;" "μήποτε οὐδέν." "καὶ

---

[1] οὐκοῦν S.   [2] Wolf : μετά S.

---

[1] See sections 24 and 25 above, and note there.

place? Your desire was not in danger, was it, or your avoidance, your choice, or your refusal? " No," he answers, " but my brother's frail wife was carried off." Was it not, then, a great gain to lose a frail and adulterous wife? " Shall we, then, be despised by the Trojans?" Who are they? Wise men or foolish? If wise, why are you fighting with them? If foolish, why do you care?

" In what, then, is the good, since it is not in these things? Tell us, Sir messenger and scout." [1] " It is where you do not expect it, and do not wish to look for it. For if you had wished, you would have found it within you, and you would not now be wandering outside, nor would you be seeking what does not concern you, as though it were your own possession. Turn your thoughts upon yourselves, find out the kind of preconceived ideas which you have. What sort of a thing do you imagine the good to be? Serenity, happiness, freedom from restraint. Come, do you not imagine it to be something naturally great? Something precious? Something not injurious? In what kind of subject-matter for life ought one to seek serenity, and freedom from restraint? In that which is slave, or in that which is free?" "In the free." "Is the paltry body which you have, then, free or is it a slave?" "We know not." "You do not know that it is a slave of fever, gout, ophthalmia, dysentery, a tyrant, fire, iron, everything that is stronger?" "Yes, it is their servant." "How, then, can anything that pertains to the body be unhampered? And how can that which is naturally lifeless, earth, or clay, be great or precious? What then? Have you nothing that is free?" " Per-

τίς ὑμᾶς ἀναγκάσαι δύναται συγκαταθέσθαι τῷ
ψευδεῖ φαινομένῳ;" "οὐδείς." "τίς δὲ μὴ συγκαταθέσθαι τῷ φαινομένῳ ἀληθεῖ;" "οὐδείς."
"ἐνθάδ᾽ οὖν ὁρᾶτε, ὅτι ἔστι τι ἐν ὑμῖν ἐλεύθερον

43 φύσει. ὀρέγεσθαι δ᾽ ἢ ἐκκλίνειν ἢ ὁρμᾶν ἢ ἀφορμᾶν ἢ παρασκευάζεσθαι ἢ προτίθεσθαι τίς ὑμῶν
δύναται μὴ λαβὼν φαντασίαν λυσιτελοῦς ἢ μὴ
καθήκοντος;" "οὐδείς." "ἔχετε οὖν καὶ ἐν

44 τούτοις ἀκώλυτόν τι[1] καὶ ἐλεύθερον. ταλαίπωροι, τοῦτο ἐξεργάζεσθε, τούτου ἐπιμέλεσθε, ἐνταῦθα ζητεῖτε τὸ ἀγαθόν."

45 Καὶ πῶς ἐνδέχεται μηδὲν ἔχοντα, γυμνόν,
ἄοικον, ἀνέστιον, αὐχμῶντα, ἄδουλον,[2] ἄπολιν

46 διεξάγειν εὐρόως; ἰδοὺ ἀπέσταλκεν ὑμῖν ὁ θεὸς

47 τὸν δείξοντα ἔργῳ, ὅτι ἐνδέχεται. "ἴδετέ με,
ἄοικός εἰμι, ἄπολις, ἀκτήμων, ἄδουλος· χαμαὶ
κοιμῶμαι· οὐ γυνή, οὐ παιδία, οὐ πραιτωρίδιον,
ἀλλὰ γῆ μόνον καὶ οὐρανὸς καὶ ἓν τριβωνάριον.

48 καὶ τί μοι λείπει; οὔκ εἰμι ἄλυπος, οὔκ εἰμι
ἄφοβος, οὔκ εἰμι ἐλεύθερος; πότε ὑμῶν εἶδέν μέ
τις ἐν ὀρέξει ἀποτυγχάνοντα, πότ᾽ ἐν ἐκκλίσει
περιπίπτοντα; πότ᾽ ἐμεμψάμην ἢ θεὸν ἢ ἄνθρωπον, πότ᾽ ἐνεκάλεσά τινι; μή τις ὑμῶν ἐσκυθρω-

49 πακότα με εἶδεν; πῶς δ᾽ ἐντυγχάνω τούτοις, οὓς
ὑμεῖς φοβεῖσθε καὶ θαυμάζετε; οὐχ ὡς ἀνδρα-
πόδοις; τίς με ἰδὼν οὐχὶ τὸν βασιλέα τὸν ἑαυτοῦ
ὁρᾶν οἴεται καὶ δεσπότην;"

---

[1] τι added by Wolf, after Schegk.
[2] Upton : δοῦλον S.

haps nothing." "And who can compel you to assent to that which appears to you to be false?" "No one." "And who to refuse assent to that which appears to you to be true?" "No one." "Here, then, you see that there *is* something within you which is naturally free. But to desire, or to avoid, or to choose, or to refuse, or to prepare, or to set something before yourself—what man among you can do these things without first conceiving an impression of what is profitable, or what is not fitting?" "No one." "You have, therefore, here too, something unhindered and free. Poor wretches, develop this, pay attention to this, seek here your good."

And how is it possible for a man who has nothing, who is naked, without home or hearth, in squalor, without a slave, without a city, to live serenely? Behold, God has sent you the man who will show in practice that it is possible. "Look at me," he says, "I am without a home, without a city, without property, without a slave; I sleep on the ground; I have neither wife nor children, no miserable governor's mansion, but only earth, and sky, and one rough cloak. Yet what do I lack? Am I not free from pain and fear, am I not free? When has anyone among you seen me failing to get what I desire, or falling into what I would avoid? When have I ever found fault with either God or man? When have I ever blamed anyone? Has anyone among you seen me with a gloomy face? And how do I face those persons before whom you stand in fear and awe? Do I not face them as slaves? Who, when he lays eyes upon me, does not feel that he is seeing his king and his master?"

50 Ἴδε κυνικαὶ φωναί, ἴδε χαρακτήρ, ἴδ' ἐπιβολή.
οὔ· ἀλλὰ πηρίδιον καὶ ξύλον καὶ γνάθοι μεγάλαι·
καταφαγεῖν πᾶν ὃ ἂν [1] δῷς ἢ ἀποθησαυρίσαι ἢ
τοῖς ἀπαντῶσι λοιδορεῖσθαι ἀκαίρως ἢ καλὸν
51 τὸν ὦμον δεικνύειν. τηλικούτῳ πράγματι ὁρᾷς
πῶς μέλλεις ἐγχειρεῖν; ἔσοπτρον πρῶτον λάβε,
ἴδε σου τοὺς ὤμους, κατάμαθε τὴν ὀσφύν, τοὺς
μηρούς. Ὀλύμπια μέλλεις ἀπογράφεσθαι, ἄνθρωπε, οὐχί τινά ποτε ἀγῶνα ψυχρὸν καὶ ταλαί-
52 πωρον. οὐκ ἔστιν ἐν Ὀλυμπίοις νικηθῆναι
μόνον καὶ ἐξελθεῖν, ἀλλὰ πρῶτον μὲν ὅλης τῆς
οἰκουμένης βλεπούσης δεῖ ἀσχημονῆσαι, οὐχὶ
Ἀθηναίων μόνον ἢ Λακεδαιμονίων ἢ Νικοπολι-
τῶν, εἶτα καὶ δέρεσθαι δεῖ τὸν εἰκῆ ἐξελθόντα,[2]
πρὸ δὲ τοῦ δαρῆναι διψῆσαι, καυματισθῆναι,
πολλὴν ἀφὴν καταπιεῖν.
53 Βούλευσαι ἐπιμελέστερον, γνῶθι σαυτόν, ἀνά-
κρινον τὸ δαιμόνιον, δίχα θεοῦ μὴ ἐπιχειρήσῃς.
ἂν γὰρ συμβουλεύσῃ, ἴσθι ὅτι μέγαν σε θέλει
54 γενέσθαι ἢ πολλὰς πληγὰς λαβεῖν. καὶ γὰρ
τοῦτο λίαν κομψὸν τῷ Κυνικῷ παραπέπλεκται·
δέρεσθαι αὐτὸν δεῖ ὡς ὄνον καὶ δερόμενον φιλεῖν
αὐτοὺς τοὺς δέροντας ὡς πατέρα πάντων, ὡς
55 ἀδελφόν. οὔ· ἀλλ' ἄν τίς σε δέρῃ, κραύγαζε
στὰς ἐν τῷ μέσῳ "ὦ Καῖσαρ, ἐν τῇ σῇ εἰρήνῃ

---

[1] Schenkl: ἐάν S.
[2] εἰσελθόντα Meibom. Compare explanatory note.

---

[1] Meibom's conjecture, εἰσελθόντα, which is sometimes
accepted, would mean, "The man who carelessly enters the
contest." But the punishment of flogging would probably be
reserved for the person who failed to appear finally in the
lists, since everyone had to have a month's preliminary

Lo, these are words that befit a Cynic, this is his character, and his plan of life. But no, you say, what makes a Cynic is a contemptible wallet, a staff, and big jaws; to devour everything you give him, or to stow it away, or to revile tactlessly the people he meets, or to show off his fine shoulder. Do you see the spirit in which you are intending to set your hand to so great an enterprise? First take a mirror, look at your shoulders, find out what kind of loins and thighs you have. Man, it's an Olympic contest in which you are intending to enter your name, not some cheap and miserable contest or other. In the Olympic games it is not possible for you merely to be beaten and then leave; but, in the first place, you needs must disgrace yourself in the sight of the whole civilized world, not merely before the men of Athens, or Lacedaemon, or Nicopolis; and, in the second place, the man who carelessly gets up and leaves[1] must needs be flogged, and before he is flogged he has to suffer thirst, and scorching heat, and swallow quantities of wrestler's sand.

Think the matter over more carefully, know yourself, ask the Deity, do not attempt the task without God. For if God so advises you, be assured that He wishes you either to become great, or to receive many stripes. For this too is a very pleasant strand woven into the Cynic's pattern of life; he must needs be flogged like an ass, and while he is being flogged he must love the men who flog him, as though he were the father or brother of them all. But that is not your way. If someone flogs you, go stand in the midst and shout, "O Caesar, what do I

training on the spot, during which time those who had entered would suffer the inconveniences described below.

οἷα πάσχω; ἄγωμεν ἐπὶ τὸν ἀνθύπατον."
56 Κυνικῷ δὲ Καῖσαρ τί ἐστιν ἢ ἀνθύπατος ἢ ἄλλος
ἢ ὁ καταπεπομφὼς αὐτὸν καὶ ᾧ λατρεύει, ὁ
Ζεύς ; ἄλλον τινὰ ἐπικαλεῖται ἢ ἐκεῖνον ; οὐ
πέπεισται δ', ὅ τι ἂν πάσχῃ τούτων, ὅτι ἐκεῖνος
57 αὐτὸν γυμνάζει ; ἀλλ' ὁ μὲν Ἡρακλῆς ὑπὸ
Εὐρυσθέως γυμναζόμενος οὐκ ἐνόμιζεν ἄθλιος
εἶναι, ἀλλ' ἀόκνως ἐπετέλει πάντα τὰ προστατ-
τόμενα·[1] οὗτος δ' ὑπὸ τοῦ Διὸς ἀθλούμενος
καὶ γυμναζόμενος μέλλει κεκραγέναι καὶ ἀγανακ-
τεῖν, ἄξιος φορεῖν τὸ σκῆπτρον τὸ Διογένους ;
58 ἄκουε, τί λέγει ἐκεῖνος πυρέσσων πρὸς τοὺς
παριόντας· "κακαί," ἔφη, "κεφαλαί, οὐ μενεῖτε ;
ἀλλ' ἀθλητῶν μὲν ὀλέθρων[2] μάχην ὀψόμενοι
ἄπιτε ὁδὸν τοσαύτην εἰς Ὀλυμπίαν· πυρετοῦ δὲ
59 καὶ ἀνθρώπου μάχην ἰδεῖν οὐ βούλεσθε ;" ταχύ
γ' ἂν ὁ τοιοῦτος ἐνεκάλεσεν τῷ θεῷ καταπεπομ-
φότι αὐτὸν ὡς παρ' ἀξίαν αὐτῷ χρωμένῳ, ὅς
γε ἐνεκαλλωπίζετο ταῖς περιστάσεσι καὶ θέαμα
εἶναι ἠξίου τῶν παριόντων. ἐπὶ τίνι γὰρ ἐγκα-
λέσει ; ὅτι εὐσχημονεῖ ; τί[3] κατηγορεῖ ; ὅτι
λαμπροτέραν ἐπιδείκνυται τὴν ἀρετὴν τὴν ἑαυ-

---

[1] Meibom : πραττόμενα S.
[2] Blass : ὀλέθρον ἢ μάχην S.   [3] Elter : ὅτι S.

---

[1] Referred to also by Jerome, *Adv. Jovinianum*, 2, 14.
[2] An ancient scholiast, probably Arethas (cf. Schenkl[2],
p. lxxx), remarks at this point, that Epictetus had probably
read the Gospels and Jewish literature. But this particular
passage does not furnish any very cogent argument, for the
evidence adduced, namely the injunctions about "turning
the other cheek" and "loving your enemies" (*Matth.* 5, 39
and 44), has nothing in common with the somewhat vain-

have to suffer under your peaceful rule? let us go
before the Proconsul." But what to a Cynic is
Caesar, or a Proconsul, or anyone other than He
who has sent him into the world, and whom he
serves, that is, Zeus? Does he call upon anyone
but Zeus? And is he not persuaded that whatever
of these hardships he suffers, it is Zeus that is exercising him? Nay, but Heracles, when he was being
exercised by Eurystheus, did not count himself
wretched, but used to fulfil without hesitation everything that was enjoined upon him: and yet is this
fellow, when he is being trained and exercised by
Zeus, prepared to cry out and complain? Is he a
man worthy to carry the staff of Diogenes? Hear *his*
words to the passers-by as he lies ill of a fever:[1]
"Vile wretches," he said, "are you not going to
stop? Nay, you are going to take that long, long
journey to Olympia, to see the struggle of worthless
athletes; but do you not care to see a struggle
between fever and a man?"[2] No doubt a man of
that sort would have blamed God, who had sent him
into the world, for mistreating him! Nay, *he* took
pride in his distress, and demanded that those who
passed by should gaze upon him. Why, what will
he blame God *for*? Because he is living a decent
life? What charge does he bring against Him?
The charge that He is exhibiting his virtue in a more

glorious speech of Diogenes. Probably, however, the
scholium actually belongs at § 54, where there is, indeed, a
certain resemblance. Fairly apposite, also, is the citation
of *James* 1, 2 : πᾶσαν χαρὰν ἡγήσασθε, ἀδελφοί, ὅταν πειρασμοῖς
περιπέσητε ποικίλοις, in connection with the next sentence.
But even at the best, these words from the *New Testament*
are only parallels, certainly not sources. On the general
question, see Introd., Vol. I., p. xxvi f.

60 τοῦ ; ἄγε, περὶ πενίας δὲ τί λέγει, περὶ θανάτου, περὶ πόνου ; πῶς συνέκρινεν τὴν εὐδαιμονίαν τὴν αὑτοῦ τῇ μεγάλου βασιλέως ; μᾶλλον δ'
61 οὐδὲ συγκριτὸν ᾤετο εἶναι. ὅπου γὰρ ταραχαὶ καὶ λῦπαι καὶ φόβοι καὶ ὀρέξεις ἀτελεῖς καὶ ἐκκλίσεις περιπίπτουσαι καὶ φθόνοι καὶ ζηλοτυπίαι, ποῦ ἐκεῖ πάροδος εὐδαιμονίας ; ὅπου δ' ἂν ᾖ σαπρὰ δόγματα, ἐκεῖ πάντα ταῦτα εἶναι ἀνάγκη.

62 Πυθομένου δὲ τοῦ νεανίσκου, εἰ νοσήσας ἀξιοῦντος φίλου πρὸς αὐτὸν ἐλθεῖν ὥστε νοσοκομηθῆναι ὑπακούσει, Ποῦ δὲ φίλον μοι δώσεις Κυνικοῦ ;
63 ἔφη. δεῖ γὰρ αὐτὸν ἄλλον εἶναι τοιοῦτον, ἵν' ἄξιος ᾖ φίλος αὐτοῦ ἀριθμεῖσθαι. κοινωνὸν αὐτὸν εἶναι δεῖ τοῦ σκήπτρου καὶ τῆς βασιλείας καὶ διάκονον ἄξιον, εἰ μέλλει φιλίας ἀξιωθήσεσθαι, ὡς Διογένης Ἀντισθένους ἐγένετο, ὡς
64 Κράτης Διογένους. ἢ¹ δοκεῖ σοι, ὅτι, ἂν χαίρειν αὐτῷ λέγῃ προσερχόμενος, φίλος ἐστὶν αὐτοῦ
65 κἀκεῖνος αὐτὸν ἄξιον ἡγήσεται τοῦ πρὸς αὐτὸν εἰσελθεῖν ; ὥστε ἄν σοι δοκῇ καὶ ἐνθυμηθῇς τι² τοιοῦτον, κοπρίαν μᾶλλον περιβλέπου κομψήν, ἐν ᾗ πυρέξεις,³ ἀποσκέπουσαν τὸν βορέαν, ἵνα
66 μὴ περιψυγῇς. σὺ δέ μοι δοκεῖς θέλειν εἰς οἶκόν τινος ἀπελθὼν διὰ χρόνου χορτασθῆναι. τί οὖν σοι καὶ ἐπιχειρεῖν πράγματι τηλικούτῳ ;
67 Γάμος δ', ἔφη, καὶ παῖδες προηγουμένως παρα-

¹ Schegk : ᾖ S.   ² Reiske : ἐνθυμήθητι S.
³ Schweighäuser : πῦρ ἕξεις S.

---

¹ Of Persia.
² The word means also "staff," as in 57.

brilliant style? Come, what says Diogenes about poverty, death, hardship? How did he habitually compare his happiness with that of the Great King?[1] Or rather, he thought there was no comparison between them. For where there are disturbances, and griefs, and fears, and ineffectual desires, and unsuccessful avoidances, and envies, and jealousies —where is there in the midst of all this a place for happiness to enter? But wherever worthless judgements are held, there all these passions must necessarily exist.

And when the young man asked whether he, as a Cynic, should consent, if, when he had fallen ill, a friend asked him to come to his house, so as to receive proper nursing, Epictetus replied: But where will you find me a Cynic's friend? For such a person must be another Cynic, in order to be worthy of being counted his friend. He must share with him his sceptre[2] and kingdom, and be a worthy ministrant, if he is going to be deemed worthy of friendship, as Diogenes became the friend of Antisthenes, and Crates of Diogenes. Or do you think that if a man as he comes up greets the Cynic, he is the Cynic's friend, and the Cynic will think him worthy to receive him into his house? So if that is what you think and have in mind, you had much better look around for some nice dunghill, on which to have your fever, one that will give you shelter from the north wind, so that you won't get chilled. But you give me the impression of wanting to go into somebody's house for a while and to get filled up. Why, then, are you even laying your hand to so great an enterprise?

But, said the young man, will marriage and children

153

λοφθήσονται ὑπὸ τοῦ Κυνικοῦ ;—Ἂν μοι σοφῶν,
ἔφη, δῷς πόλιν, τάχα μὲν οὐδ᾽ ἥξει τις ῥᾳδίως
ἐπὶ τὸ κυνίζειν. τίνων γὰρ ἕνεκα ἀναδέξηται[1]
68 ταύτην τὴν διεξαγωγήν; ὅμως δ᾽ ἂν ὑποθώμεθα,
οὐδὲν κωλύσει καὶ γῆμαι αὐτὸν καὶ παιδοποιή-
σασθαι. καὶ γὰρ ἡ γυνὴ αὐτοῦ ἔσται ἄλλη
τοιαύτη καὶ ὁ πενθερὸς ἄλλος τοιοῦτος καὶ τὰ
69 παιδία οὕτως ἀνατραφήσεται. τοιαύτης δ᾽ οὔσης
καταστάσεως, οἵα νῦν ἔστιν, ὡς ἐν παρατάξει,
μή ποτ᾽ ἀπερίσπαστον εἶναι δεῖ τὸν Κυνικόν,
ὅλον πρὸς τῇ διακονίᾳ τοῦ θεοῦ, ἐπιφοιτᾶν ἀνθρώποις δυνάμενον, οὐ προσδεδεμένον καθήκουσιν
ἰδιωτικοῖς οὐδ᾽ ἐμπεπλεγμένον σχέσεσιν, ἃς
παραβαίνων οὐκέτι σώσει τὸ τοῦ καλοῦ καὶ
ἀγαθοῦ πρόσωπον, τηρῶν δ᾽ ἀπολεῖ τὸν ἄγγελον
70 καὶ κατάσκοπον καὶ κήρυκα τῶν θεῶν; ὅρα γάρ,
ὅτι αὐτὸν ἀποδεικνύαι δεῖ[2] τινὰ τῷ πενθερῷ,
ἀποδιδόναι τοῖς ἄλλοις συγγενέσι τῆς γυναικός,
αὐτῇ τῇ γυναικί· εἰς νοσοκομίας λοιπὸν ἐκκλείε-
71 ται, εἰς πορισμόν. ἵνα τἆλλα ἀφῶ, δεῖ αὐτὸν
κουκκούμιον, ὅπου θερμὸν ποιήσει τῷ παιδίῳ,
ἵν᾽ αὐτὸ λούσῃ εἰς σκάφην· ἐρίδια τεκούσῃ τῇ
γυναικί, ἔλαιον, κραβάττιον, ποτήριον (γίνεται
72 ἤδη πλείω σκευάρια)· τὴν ἄλλην ἀσχολίαν,
τὸν περισπασμόν. ποῦ μοι λοιπὸν ἐκεῖνος ὁ
βασιλεὺς ὁ τοῖς κοινοῖς προσευκαιρῶν,

ᾧ λαοί τ᾽ ἐπιτετράφαται καὶ τόσσα μέμηλεν·

---

[1] Schenkl : ἂν δξηται S.
[2] δεῖ added by Schenkl : Sc (?) has it after ὅτι.

---

[1] Homer, *Iliad*, II. 25.

be undertaken by the Cynic as a matter of prime
importance?—If, replied Epictetus, you grant me a
city of wise men, it might very well be that no one
will lightly adopt the Cynic's profession. For in
whose interest would he take on this style of life?
If, nevertheless, we assume that he does so act, there
will be nothing to prevent him from both marrying
and having children; for his wife will be another
person like himself, and so will his father-in-law, and
his children will be brought up in the same fashion.
But in such an order of things as the present, which
is like that of a battle-field, it is a question, perhaps,
if the Cynic ought not to be free from distraction,
wholly devoted to the service of God, free to go
about among men, not tied down by the private
duties of men, nor involved in relationships which
he cannot violate and still maintain his rôle as
a good and excellent man, whereas, on the other
hand, if he observes them, he will destroy the
messenger, the scout, the herald of the gods, that
he is. For see, he must show certain services to
his father-in-law, to the rest of his wife's relatives,
to his wife herself; finally, he is driven from his
profession, to act as a nurse in his own family and to
provide for them. To make a long story short, he
must get a kettle to heat water for the baby, for
washing it in a bath-tub; wool for his wife when
she has had a child, oil, a cot, a cup (the vessels get
more and more numerous); not to speak of the rest
of his business, and his distraction. Where, I beseech
you, is left now our king, the man who has leisure
for the public interest,

Who hath charge of the folk and for many a thing
    must be watchful?[1]

ὃν δεῖ τοὺς ἄλλους ἐπισκοπεῖν, τοὺς γεγαμηκότας,
τοὺς πεπαιδοποιημένους, τίς καλῶς χρῆται τῇ
αὑτοῦ γυναικί, τίς κακῶς, τίς διαφέρεται, ποία
οἰκία εὐσταθεῖ, ποία οὔ, ὡς ἰατρὸν περιερχόμενον
73 καὶ τῶν σφυγμῶν ἁπτόμενον; "σὺ πυρέττεις,
σὺ κεφαλαλγεῖς, σὺ ποδαγρᾷς· σὺ ἀνάτεινον, σὺ
φάγε, σὺ ἀλούτησον· σὲ δεῖ τμηθῆναι, σὲ δεῖ
74 καυθῆναι." ποῦ σχολὴ τῷ εἰς τὰ ἰδιωτικὰ
καθήκοντα ἐνδεδεμένῳ; ἄγε,[1] οὐ δεῖ αὐτὸν πορίσαι
ἱματίδια τοῖς παιδίοις; πρὸς γραμματιστὴν ἀπο-
στεῖλαι πινακίδια ἔχοντα, γραφεῖα, τιτλάρια,[2]
κἀπὶ[3] τούτοις κραβάττιον ἑτοιμάσαι; οὐ γὰρ
ἐκ τῆς κοιλίας ἐξελθόντα δύναται Κυνικὰ εἶναι·
εἰ δὲ μή, κρεῖσσον ἦν αὐτὰ γενόμενα ῥῖψαι ἢ
75 οὕτως ἀποκτεῖναι. σκόπει, ποῦ κατάγομεν τὸν
76 Κυνικόν, πῶς αὐτοῦ τὴν βασιλείαν ἀφαιρούμεθα.
—Ναί· ἀλλὰ Κράτης ἔγημεν.—Περίστασίν μοι
λέγεις ἐξ ἔρωτος γενομένην καὶ γυναῖκα τιθεὶς
ἄλλον Κράτητα. ἡμεῖς δὲ περὶ τῶν κοινῶν γάμων
καὶ ἀπεριστάτων ζητοῦμεν καὶ οὕτως ζητοῦντες
οὐχ εὑρίσκομεν ἐν[4] ταύτῃ τῇ καταστάσει
προηγούμενον τῷ Κυνικῷ τὸ πρᾶγμα.
77 Πῶς οὖν ἔτι, φησίν, διασώσει τὴν κοινωνίαν;
—Τὸν θεόν σοι[5] μείζονα δ' εὐεργετοῦσιν ἀνθρώ-

---

[1] Transposed to this position by Upton from the beginning
of the next sentence.
[2] Du Cange : τιλλάρια S.
[3] Elter, after Schegk : καί S.
[4] ἐν added by Upton.
[5] Upton : σου S.

---

[1] That ancient marriages (which would appear to have
been quite as successful as any other) were very seldom con-

Where, pray, is this king, whose duty it is to over-see the rest of men; those who have married; those who have had children; who is treating his wife well, and who ill; who quarrels; what household is stable, and what not; making his rounds like a physician, and feeling pulses? "You have a fever, you have a headache, you have the gout. You must abstain from food, you must eat, you must give up the bath; you need the surgeon's knife, you the cautery." Where is the man who is tied down to the duties of everyday life going to find leisure for such matters? Come, doesn't he have to get little cloaks for the children? Doesn't he have to send them off to a school-teacher with their little tablets and writing implements, and little note-books; and, besides, get the little cot ready for them? For *they* can't be Cynics from the moment they leave the womb. And if he doesn't do all this, it would have been better to expose them at birth, rather than to kill them in this fashion. See to what straits we are reducing our Cynic, how we are taking away his kingdom from him.—Yes, but Crates married.— You are mentioning a particular instance which arose out of passionate love, and you are assuming a wife who is herself another Crates. But our inquiry is concerned with ordinary marriage apart from special circumstances,[1] and from this point of view we do not find that marriage, under present con-ditions, is a matter of prime importance for the Cynic.

How, then, said the young man, will the Cynic still be able to keep society going?—In the name of God, sir, who do mankind the greater service?

cerned with romantic passion, is well known, but seldom so explicitly stated as here.

πους οἱ ἢ δύο ἢ τρία κακόρυγχα παιδία ἀνθ᾽
αὑτῶν εἰσάγοντες ἢ οἱ ἐπισκοποῦντες πάντας
κατὰ δύναμιν ἀνθρώπους, τί ποιοῦσιν, πῶς
διάγουσιν, τίνος ἐπιμελοῦνται, τίνος ἀμελοῦσι
78 παρὰ τὸ προσῆκον; καὶ Θηβαίους μείζονα ὠφέ-
λησαν ὅσοι τεκνία αὑτοῖς κατέλιπον Ἐπαμι-
νώνδου τοῦ ἀτέκνου ἀποθανόντος; καὶ Ὁμήρου
πλείονα τῇ κοινωνίᾳ συνεβάλετο Πρίαμος ὁ
πεντήκοντα γεννήσας περικαθάρματα ἢ Δαναὸς
79 ἢ Αἴολος; εἶτα στρατηγία μὲν ἢ σύνταγμά τινα
ἀπείρξει γάμου ἢ παιδοποιίας καὶ οὐ δόξει οὗτος
ἀντ᾽ οὐδενὸς ἠλλάχθαι τὴν ἀτεκνίαν, ἡ δὲ τοῦ
80 Κυνικοῦ βασιλεία οὐκ ἔσται ἀνταξία; μήποτε
οὐκ αἰσθανόμεθα τοῦ μεγέθους αὐτοῦ οὐδὲ
φανταζόμεθα κατ᾽ ἀξίαν τὸν χαρακτῆρα τὸν
Διογένους, ἀλλ᾽ εἰς τοὺς νῦν ἀποβλέπομεν, τοὺς
τραπεζῆας[1] πυλαωρούς, οἳ οὐδὲν μιμοῦνται
ἐκείνους ἢ εἴ τι[2] ἄρα πόρδωνες γίνονται, ἄλλο
81 δ᾽ οὐδέν; ἐπεὶ οὐκ ἂν ἡμᾶς ἐκίνει ταῦτα οὐδ᾽
ἂν ἐπεθαυμάζομεν, εἰ μὴ γαμήσει ἢ παιδοποιή-
σεται. ἄνθρωπε, πάντας ἀνθρώπους πεπαιδο-
ποίηται, τοὺς ἄνδρας υἱοὺς ἔχει, τὰς γυναῖκας
θυγατέρας· πᾶσιν οὕτως προσέρχεται, οὕτως
82 πάντων κήδεται. ἢ σὺ δοκεῖς ὑπὸ περιεργίας
λοιδορεῖσθαι τοῖς ἀπαντῶσιν; ὡς πατὴρ αὐτὸ
ποιεῖ, ὡς ἀδελφὸς καὶ τοῦ κοινοῦ πατρὸς ὑπηρέτης τοῦ Διός.
83   Ἄν σοι δόξῃ, πυθοῦ μου καὶ εἰ πολιτεύσεται.

---

[1] Upton: τραπεζῆς S.
[2] Schenkl: ὅτι S.

---

[1] Homer, *Iliad*, XXII. 69.

Those who bring into the world some two or three ugly-snouted children to take their place, or those who exercise oversight, to the best of their ability, over all mankind, observing what they are doing, how they are spending their lives, what they are careful about, and what they undutifully neglect? And were the Thebans helped more by all those who left them children than by Epaminondas who died without offspring? And did Priam, who begot fifty sons, all rascals, or Danaus, or Aeolus, contribute more to the common weal than did Homer? What? Shall high military command or writing a book prevent a man from marrying and having children, while such a person will not be regarded as having exchanged his childlessness for naught, and yet shall the Cynic's kingship not be thought a reasonable compensation? Can it be that we do not perceive the greatness of Diogenes, and have no adequate conception of his character, but have in mind the present-day representatives of the profession, these "dogs of the table, guards of the gate,"[1] who follow the masters not at all, except it be in breaking wind in public, forsooth, but in nothing else? Otherwise such points as these you have been raising would never have disturbed us, we should never have wondered why a Cynic will never marry or have children. Man, the Cynic has made all mankind his children; the men among them he has as sons, the women as daughters; in that spirit he approaches them all and cares for them all. Or do you fancy that it is in the spirit of idle impertinence he reviles those he meets? It is as a father he does it, as a brother, and as a servant of Zeus, who is Father of us all.

If you will, ask me also if he is to be active in

84 σαννίων, μείζονα πολιτείαν ζητεῖς, ἧς πολιτεύε-
ται ; ἢ¹ ἐν ᾿Αθηναίοις παρελθὼν ἐρεῖ τις περὶ
προσόδων ἢ πόρων, ὃν δεῖ πᾶσιν ἀνθρώποις
διαλέγεσθαι, ἐπίσης μὲν ᾿Αθηναίοις, ἐπίσης δὲ
Κορινθίοις, ἐπίσης δὲ ῾Ρωμαίοις οὐ περὶ πόρων
οὐδὲ περὶ προσόδων οὐδὲ περὶ εἰρήνης ἢ πο-
λέμου, ἀλλὰ περὶ εὐδαιμονίας καὶ κακοδαιμονίας,
περὶ εὐτυχίας καὶ δυστυχίας, περὶ δουλείας καὶ
85 ἐλευθερίας ; τηλικαύτην πολιτείαν πολιτευο-
μένου ἀνθρώπου σύ μου πυνθάνῃ εἰ πολιτεύσεται;
πυθοῦ μου καί, εἰ ἄρξει· πάλιν ἐρῶ σοι· μωρέ,
ποίαν ἀρχὴν μείζονα, ἧς ἄρχει ;

86 Χρεία μέντοι καὶ σώματος ποιοῦ τῷ τοιούτῳ.
ἐπεί τοι ἂν φθισικὸς προέρχηται, λεπτὸς καὶ
ὠχρός, οὐκέτι ὁμοίαν ἔμφασιν ἡ μαρτυρία αὐτοῦ
87 ἔχε ι. δεῖ γὰρ αὐτὸν οὐ μόνον τὰ τῆς ψυχῆς
ἐπιδεικνύοντα παριστάνειν τοῖς ἰδιώταις ὅτι
ἐνδέχεται δίχα τῶν θαυμαζομένων ὑπ᾿ αὐτῶν
εἶναι² καλὸν καὶ ἀγαθόν, ἀλλὰ καὶ διὰ τοῦ
σώματος ἐνδείκνυσθαι, ὅτι ἡ ἀφελὴς καὶ λιτὴ
καὶ ὕπαιθρος δίαιτα οὐδὲ τὸ σῶμα λυμαίνεται·
88 "ἰδοὺ καὶ τούτου μάρτυς εἰμὶ ἐγὼ καὶ τὸ σῶμα
τὸ ἐμόν." ὡς Διογένης ἐποίει· στίλβων γὰρ
περιήρχετο καὶ κατ᾿³ αὐτὸ τὸ σῶμα ἐπέστρεφε
89 τοὺς πολλούς. ἐλεούμενος δὲ Κυνικὸς ἐπαίτης

¹ Schweighäuser : εἰ S.
² The Salamanca ed., Wolf, and Salmasius : εἶναι ὑπ᾿
αὐτῶν S.
³ Wolf : καθ᾿ S.

¹ Said by the Scholiast to be a reference to the otherwise
unknown philosopher Sannio ; but this note certainly, as
Capps suggests, belongs back at § 84, and is there a false

politics. You ninny, are you looking for any nobler politics than that in which he is engaged? Or would you have someone in Athens step forward and discourse about incomes and revenues, when he is the person who ought to talk with all men, Athenians, Corinthians, and Romans alike, not about revenues, or income, or peace, or war, but about happiness and unhappiness, about success and failure, about slavery and freedom? When a man is engaging in such exalted politics, do *you* ask me if he is to engage in politics? Ask me also, if he will hold office. Again I will tell you: Fool, what nobler office will he hold than that which he now has?

And yet such a man needs also a certain kind of body, since if a consumptive comes forward, thin and pale,[1] his testimony no longer carries the same weight. For he must not merely, by exhibiting the qualities of his soul, prove to the laymen that it is possible, without the help of the things which they admire, to be a good and excellent man, but he must also show, by the state of his body, that his plain and simple style of life in the open air does not injure even his body : "Look," he says, "both I and my body are witnesses to the truth of my contention." That was the way of Diogenes, for he used to go about with a radiant complexion,[2] and would attract the attention of the common people by the very appearance of his body. But a Cynic who excites pity is regarded as a beggar ;

inference from the word σαννίων, which is addressed to the young man. For a similar dislocation of a scholium, see the note on § 58.

[2] Due in part at least to his regular use of oil for anointing. Diogenes Laertius, 6, 81.

δοκεῖ· πάντες ἀποστρέφονται, πάντες προσκόπ-
τουσιν. οὐδὲ γὰρ ῥυπαρὸν αὐτὸν δεῖ φαίνεσθαι,
ὡς μηδὲ κατὰ τοῦτο τοὺς ἀνθρώπους ἀποσοβεῖν,
ἀλλ' αὐτὸν τὸν αὐχμὸν αὐτοῦ δεῖ καθαρὸν εἶναι
καὶ ἀγωγόν.

90   Δεῖ δὲ καὶ χάριν πολλὴν προσεῖναι φυσικὴν
τῷ Κυνικῷ καὶ ὀξύτητα (εἰ δὲ μή, μύξα γίνεται,
ἄλλο δ' οὐδέν), ἵνα ἑτοίμως δύνηται καὶ παρα-
91 κειμένως πρὸς τὰ ἐμπίπτοντα ἀπαντᾶν. ὡς
Διογένης πρὸς τὸν εἰπόντα " σὺ εἶ ὁ Διογένης
ὁ μὴ οἰόμενος εἶναι θεούς; " " καὶ πῶς," ἔφη,
92 " σὲ θεοῖς ἐχθρὸν νομίζω; " πάλιν Ἀλεξάν-
δρῳ ἐπιστάντι αὐτῷ κοιμωμένῳ καὶ εἰπόντι

" οὐ χρὴ παννύχιον εὕδειν βουληφόρον ἄνδρα "

ἔνυπνος ἔτι ὢν ἀπήντησεν

" ᾧ λαοί τ' ἐπιτετράφαται καὶ τόσσα μέμηλεν."

93   Πρὸ πάντων δὲ τὸ ἡγεμονικὸν αὐτοῦ καθαρώτερον εἶναι τοῦ ἡλίου· εἰ δὲ μή, κυβευτὴν ἀνάγκη
καὶ ῥᾳδιουργόν, ὅστις ἐνεχόμενός τινι αὐτὸς
94 κακῷ ἐπιτιμήσει τοῖς ἄλλοις. ὅρα γάρ, οἷόν
ἐστιν. τοῖς βασιλεῦσι τούτοις καὶ τυράννοις οἱ
δορυφόροι καὶ τὰ ὅπλα παρεῖχε τὸ [1] ἐπιτιμᾶν

---

[1] Schweighäuser : παρείχετο S.

---

[1] See Diogenes Laertius, 6, 42; the same joke appears
already in Aristophanes (*Eq.* 32–4), as Capps remarks.
[2] The same account in Theon, *Progymn.* 5 (Stengel, II.
p. 98). The famous meeting of these two men is pretty
clearly apocryphal, at least in certain details. See Natorp
in the *Real-Encyclopädie*[2], V. 767.

everybody turns away from him, everybody takes
offence at him. No, and he ought not to look dirty
either, so as not to scare men away in this respect
also ; but even his squalor ought to be cleanly and
attractive.

Furthermore, the Cynic ought to possess great
natural charm and readiness of wit—otherwise he
becomes mere snivel, and nothing else—so as to be
able to meet readily and aptly whatever befalls ;
as Diogenes answered the man who said : " Are you
the Diogenes who does not believe in the existence
of the gods ? " by saying, " And how can that be ?
You I regard as hated by the gods ! " [1] Or again,
when Alexander [2] stood over him as he was sleeping
and said,

> Sleeping the whole night through beseems not
> the giver of counsel,

he replied, still half asleep,

> Who hath charge of the folk, and for many a
> thing must be watchful.[3]

But above all, the Cynic's governing principle
should be purer than the sun ; if not, he must
needs be a gambler and a man of no principle,
because he will be censuring the rest of mankind,
while he himself is involved in some vice. For see
what this means. To the kings and tyrants of this
world their bodyguards and their arms used to

[3] Homer, *Iliad*, II. 24 and 25. The only point in the
anecdote seems to be that Diogenes could say something
more or less apposite even when only half awake ; for the
completion of the quotation is in no sense a real answer to
the reproach.

ARRIAN'S DISCOURSES OF EPICTETUS

τισὶν καὶ¹ δύνασθαι καὶ κολάζειν τοὺς ἁμαρ-
τάνοντας καὶ αὐτοῖς οὖσι κακοῖς, τῷ δὲ²
Κυνικῷ ἀντὶ τῶν ὅπλων καὶ τῶν δορυφόρων
τὸ συνειδὸς τὴν ἐξουσίαν ταύτην παραδίδωσιν.
95 ὅταν ἴδῃ,³ ὅτι ὑπερηγρύπνηκεν ὑπὲρ ἀνθρώπων
καὶ πεπόνηκεν καὶ καθαρὸς μὲν κεκοίμηται,
καθαρώτερον δ' αὐτὸν ἔτι ὁ ὕπνος ἀφῆκεν,
ἐντεθύμηται δ', ὅσα ἐντεθύμηται ὡς φίλος τοῖς
θεοῖς, ὡς ὑπηρέτης, ὡς μετέχων τῆς ἀρχῆς τοῦ
Διός, πανταχοῦ δ' αὐτῷ πρόχειρον τὸ

　　　ἄγου δέ μ', ὦ Ζεῦ, καὶ σύ γ' ἡ Πεπρωμένη,

καὶ ὅτι εἰ ταύτῃ τοῖς θεοῖς φίλον, ταύτῃ γινέσθω·
96 διὰ τί μὴ θαρρήσῃ παρρησιάζεσθαι πρὸς τοὺς
ἀδελφοὺς τοὺς ἑαυτοῦ, πρὸς τὰ τέκνα, ἁπλῶς
πρὸς τοὺς συγγενεῖς ;
97 Διὰ τοῦτο οὔτε περίεργος οὔτε πολυπράγμων
ἐστὶν ὁ οὕτω διακείμενος· οὐ γὰρ τὰ ἀλλότρια
πολυπραγμονεῖ, ὅταν τὰ ἀνθρώπινα ἐπισκοπῇ,
ἀλλὰ τὰ ἴδια. εἰ δὲ μή, λέγε καὶ τὸν στρατηγὸν
πολυπράγμονα, ὅταν τοὺς στρατιώτας ἐπισκοπῇ
καὶ ἐξετάζῃ καὶ παραφυλάσσῃ καὶ τοὺς ἀκοσ-
98 μοῦντας κολάζῃ. ἐὰν δ' ὑπὸ μάλης ἔχων
πλακουντάριον ἐπιτιμᾷς ἄλλοις, ἐρῶ σοι· οὐ
θέλεις μᾶλλον ἀπελθὼν εἰς γωνίαν καταφαγεῖν
99 ἐκεῖνο ὃ κέκλοφας ; τί δὲ σοὶ καὶ τοῖς ἀλλοτρίοις ;

¹ Blass very reasonably suspected this word, although the
text as it stands can be translated after a fashion.
² δέ added by Upton from his "codex."
³ Upton from his "codex": ἴδῃς S.

¹ The rather curious imperfect tense here (at which several
scholars have taken offence) may be due to an attempt to
164

afford[1] the privilege of censuring certain persons,
and the power also to punish those who do wrong,
no matter how guilty they themselves were; whereas
to the Cynic it is his conscience which affords him
this power, and not his arms and his bodyguards.
When he sees that he has watched over men, and
toiled in their behalf; and that he has slept in
purity, while his sleep leaves him even purer than
he was before; and that every thought which he
thinks is that of a friend and servant to the gods,
of one who shares in the government of Zeus; and
has always ready at hand the verse

> Lead thou me on, O Zeus, and Destiny,[2]

and "If so it pleases the gods, so be it,"[3] why
should he not have courage to speak freely to his
own brothers, to his children, in a word, to his
kinsmen?

That is why the man who is in this frame of
mind is neither a busybody nor a meddler; for he
is not meddling in other people's affairs when he
is overseeing the actions of men, but these are his
proper concern. Otherwise, go call the general a
meddler when he oversees and reviews and watches
over his troops, and punishes those who are guilty
of a breach of discipline. But if you censure other
men while you are hiding a little sweet-cake under
your arm, I'll say to you: Wouldn't you rather go
off into a corner and eat up what you have stolen?
What have you to do with other people's business?

---

avoid the suggestion that the Roman emperors might also be
evil men themselves.

[2] See note on II. 23, 42, in Vol. I.

[3] Plato, *Crito,* 43 D.

τίς γὰρ εἶ; ὁ ταῦρος εἶ ἢ ἡ βασίλισσα τῶν
μελισσῶν; δεῖξόν μοι τὰ σύμβολα τῆς ἡγεμονίας,
οἷα ἐκείνη ἐκ φύσεως ἔχει. εἰ δὲ κηφὴν εἶ ἐπι-
δικαζόμενος τῆς βασιλείας τῶν μελισσῶν, οὐ
δοκεῖς ὅτι καὶ σὲ καταβαλοῦσιν οἱ συμπολι-
τευόμενοι, ὡς αἱ μέλισσαι τοὺς κηφῆνας;

100   Τὸ μὲν γὰρ ἀνεκτικὸν τοσοῦτον ἔχειν δεῖ τὸν
Κυνικόν, ὥστ' αὐτὸν ἀναίσθητον δοκεῖν τοῖς
πολλοῖς καὶ λίθον· οὐδεὶς αὐτὸν λοιδορεῖ, οὐδεὶς
τύπτει, οὐδεὶς ὑβρίζει· τὸ σωμάτιον δ' αὐτοῦ
δέδωκεν αὐτὸς χρῆσθαι τῷ θέλοντι ὡς βούλεται.

101 μέμνηται γάρ, ὅτι τὸ χεῖρον ἀνάγκη νικᾶσθαι
ὑπὸ τοῦ κρείττονος, ὅπου χεῖρόν ἐστιν, τὸ δὲ
σωμάτιον τῶν πολλῶν χεῖρον, τὸ ἀσθενέστερον

102 τῶν ἰσχυροτέρων. οὐδέποτ' οὖν εἰς τοῦτον κατα-
βαίνει τὸν ἀγῶνα, ὅπου δύναται νικηθῆναι, ἀλλὰ
τῶν ἀλλοτρίων εὐθὺς ἐξίσταται, τῶν δούλων οὐκ

103 ἀντιποιεῖται. ὅπου δὲ προαίρεσις καὶ χρῆσις
τῶν φαντασιῶν, ἐκεῖ ὄψει, ὅσα ὄμματα ἔχει, ἵν'
εἴπῃς, ὅτι Ἄργος τυφλὸς ἦν πρὸς αὐτόν.

104 μή που συγκατάθεσις προπετής, μή που ὁρμὴ
εἰκαία, μή που ὄρεξις ἀποτευκτική, μή που
ἔκκλισις περιπτωτική, μή που[1] ἐπιβολὴ ἀτελής,
μή που μέμψις, μή που ταπείνωσις ἢ φθόνος;

105 ὧδε ἡ πολλὴ προσοχὴ καὶ σύντασις, τῶν δ'
ἄλλων ἕνεκα ὕπτιος ῥέγκει· εἰρήνη πᾶσα.
λῃστὴς προαιρέσεως οὐ γίνεται, τύραννος οὐ

106 γίνεται. σωματίου δέ; ναί. καὶ κτησειδίου;

[1] μή που supplied by Schenkl.

[1] That is, actually or effectually, for the mere act without
any effect is as nothing.

Why who are you? Are you the bull in the herd,
or the queen bee of the hive? Show me the tokens
of your leadership, like those which nature gives
the queen bee. But if you are a drone and lay
claim to the sovereignty over the bees, don't you
suppose your fellow-citizens will overthrow you, just
as the bees so treat the drones?

Now the spirit of patient endurance the Cynic must
have to such a degree that common people will think
him insensate and a stone; nobody reviles[1] him,
nobody beats him, nobody insults him; but his body
he has himself given for anyone to use as he sees
fit. For he bears in mind that the inferior, in that
respect in which it is inferior, must needs be
overcome by the superior, and that his body is
inferior to the crowd—the physically weaker, that
is, inferior to the physically stronger. Therefore,
he never enters this contest where he can be
beaten, but immediately gives up what is not his
own; he makes no claim to what is slavish.[2] But
in the realm of the moral purpose, and the use
of his sense-impressions, there you will see he
has so many eyes that you will say Argus was blind
in comparison with him. Is there anywhere rash
assent, reckless choice, futile desire, unsuccessful
aversion, incompleted purpose, fault-finding, self-
disparagement, or envy? Here is concentrated his
earnest attention and energy; but, as far as other
things go, he lies flat on his back and snores; he is
in perfect peace. There rises up no thief of his
moral purpose, nor any tyrant over it. But of his
body? Certainly. And of his paltry possessions?

[2] Like the body, his own or that of another. His rule is
over the mind and the moral purpose.

ναί· καὶ ἀρχῶν καὶ τιμῶν. τί οὖν αὐτῷ τούτων μέλει; ὅταν οὖν τις διὰ τούτων αὐτὸν
ἐκφοβῇ, λέγει αὐτῷ "ὕπαγε, ζήτει τὰ παιδία·
ἐκείνοις τὰ προσωπεῖα φοβερά ἐστιν, ἐγὼ δ'
οἶδα, ὅτι ὀστράκινά ἐστιν, ἔσωθεν δὲ οὐδὲν
ἔχει."

107   Περὶ τοιούτου πράγματος βουλεύῃ. ὥστε ἐὰν
σοι δόξῃ, τὸν θεόν σοι, ὑπέρθου καὶ ἰδού σοι
108 πρῶτον τὴν παρασκευήν. ἰδοὺ γάρ, τί καὶ ὁ
"Εκτωρ λέγει τῇ Ἀνδρομάχῃ· "ὕπαγε," φησίν,
"μᾶλλον εἰς οἶκον καὶ ὕφαινε·

πόλεμος δ' ἄνδρεσσι μελήσει
πᾶσι, μάλιστα δ' ἐμοί." [1]

109 οὕτως καὶ τῆς ἰδίας παρασκευῆς συνῄσθετο καὶ
τῆς ἐκείνης ἀδυναμίας.

κγ'. Πρὸς τοὺς ἀναγιγνώσκοντας καὶ διαλεγο-
μένους ἐπιδεικτικῶς.

1   Τίς εἶναι θέλεις, σαυτῷ πρῶτον εἰπέ· εἶθ'
οὕτως ποίει ἃ ποιεῖς. καὶ γὰρ ἐπὶ τῶν ἄλλων
2 σχεδὸν ἁπάντων οὕτως ὁρῶμεν γινόμενα. οἱ
ἀθλοῦντες πρῶτον κρίνουσιν, τίνες εἶναι θέλουσιν,
εἶθ' οὕτως τὰ ἑξῆς ποιοῦσιν. εἰ δολιχοδρόμος,
τοιαύτη τροφή, τοιοῦτος περίπατος, τοιαύτη
τρῖψις, τοιαύτη γυμνασία· εἰ σταδιοδρόμος,
πάντα ταῦτα ἀλλοῖα· εἰ πένταθλος, ἔτι ἀλλοιό-

---

[1] πᾶσιν, ἐμοὶ δὲ μάλιστα the MSS. of Homer.

[1] Homer, *Iliad*, VI. 492–3.

Certainly; and of his offices and honours. Why, then, does he pay any attention to these? So when anyone tries to terrify him by means of these things, he says to him, " Go to, look for children; *they* are scared by masks; but I know that they are made of earthenware, and have nothing inside."

Such is the nature of the matter about which you are deliberating. Wherefore, in the name of God I adjure you, put off your decision, and look first at your endowment. For see what Hector says to Andromache. " Go," says he, " rather into the house and weave;

> but for men shall war be the business,
> Men one and all, and mostly for me." [1]

So did he recognize not only his own special endowment, but also her incapacity.

CHAPTER XXIII

To those who read and discuss for the purpose of display

TELL yourself, first of all, what kind of man you want to be; and then go ahead with what you are doing. For in practically every other pursuit we see this done. The athletes first decide what kind of athletes they want to be, and then they act accordingly. If a man wants to be a distance-runner, he adopts a suitable diet, walking, rubbing, and exercise; if he wants to be a sprinter, all these details are different; if he wants to contend in the pentathlon, they are still more different

3 τερα. οὕτως εὑρήσεις καὶ ἐπὶ τῶν τεχνῶν. εἰ
τέκτων, τοιαῦτα ἕξεις· εἰ χαλκεύς, τοιαῦτα.
ἕκαστον γὰρ τῶν γινομένων ὑφ' ἡμῶν ἂν μὲν
ἐπὶ μηδὲν ἀναφέρωμεν, εἰκῆ ποιήσομεν· ἐὰν δ'
4 ἐφ' ὃ μὴ δεῖ, διεσφαλμένως. λοιπὸν ἡ μέν τίς
ἐστι κοινὴ ἀναφορά, ἡ δ' ἰδία. πρῶτον ἵν' ὡς
ἄνθρωπος. ἐν τούτῳ τί περιέχεται; μὴ ὡς
πρόβατον, εἰκῆ¹ ἐπιεικῶς· μὴ βλαπτικῶς² ὡς
5 θηρίον. ἡ δ' ἰδία πρὸς τὸ ἐπιτήδευμα ἑκάστου
καὶ τὴν προαίρεσιν. ὁ κιθαρῳδὸς ὡς κιθαρῳδός,
ὁ τέκτων ὡς τέκτων, ὁ φιλόσοφος ὡς φιλόσοφος,
6 ὁ ῥήτωρ ὡς ῥήτωρ. ὅταν οὖν λέγῃς "δεῦτε καὶ
ἀκούσατέ μου ἀναγιγνώσκοντος ὑμῖν," σκέψαι
πρῶτον μὴ εἰκῆ αὐτὸ ποιεῖν. εἶτ' ἂν εὕρῃς, ὅτι
7 ἀναφέρεις, σκέψαι, εἰ ἐφ' ὃ δεῖ. ὠφελῆσαι
θέλεις ἢ ἐπαινεθῆναι; εὐθὺς ἀκούεις λέγοντος
"ἐμοὶ δὲ τοῦ παρὰ τῶν πολλῶν ἐπαίνου τίς
λόγος;" καὶ καλῶς λέγει. οὐδὲ γὰρ τῷ
μουσικῷ, καθὸ μουσικός ἐστιν, οὐδὲ τῷ γεωμε-
8 τρικῷ. οὐκοῦν ὠφελῆσαι θέλεις; πρὸς τί;
εἰπὲ καὶ ἡμῖν, ἵνα καὶ αὐτοὶ τρέχωμεν εἰς τὸ
ἀκροατήριόν σου. νῦν δύναταί τις ὠφελῆσαι
ἄλλους μὴ αὐτὸς ὠφελημένος; οὔ. οὐδὲ γὰρ
εἰς τεκτονικὴν ὁ μὴ τέκτων οὐδ' εἰς σκυτικὴν
ὁ μὴ σκυτεύς.
9 Θέλεις οὖν γνῶναι, εἰ ὠφέλησαι; φέρε σου
τὰ δόγματα, φιλόσοφε. τίς ἐπαγγελία ὀρέξεως;

---

¹ εἰκῆ added by Reiske. Compare § 6.
² Schenkl: πρόβατον, εἰ βλαπτικῶς καὶ ἐπιεικῶς, ὡς S.

---

¹ See on I. 29, 59, in Vol. I.

You will find the same thing in the arts. If you
want to be a carpenter, you will have such and
such exercises; if a blacksmith, such and such other.
For in everything that we do, if we do not refer
it to some standard, we shall be acting at random;
but if we refer it to the wrong standard, we shall
make an utter failure. Furthermore, there are two
standards to go by, the one general, the other
individual. First of all, I must act as a man. What
is included in this? Not to act as a sheep, gently
but without fixed purpose; nor destructively, like
a wild beast. The individual standard applies to
each man's occupation and moral purpose. The
citharoede is to act as a citharoede,[1] the carpenter
as a carpenter, the philosopher as a philosopher,
the rhetor as a rhetor. When, therefore, you say,
"Come and listen to me as I read you a lecture,"
see to it first that you are not acting without fixed
purpose. And then, if you find that you *are* using
a standard of judgement, see if it is the right one.
Do you wish to do good or to be praised? you ask.
Immediately you get the answer, "What do I care
for praise from the mob?" And that is an excellent
answer. Neither does the musician, in so far as he
is a musician, nor the geometrician. Do you wish
to do good, then? To what end? men reply. Tell
us, also, that we too may run to your lecture-room.
Now can anybody do good to others unless he has
received good himself? No more than the non-
carpenter can help others in carpentry, or the non-
cobbler in cobbling.

Do you wish, then, to know whether you have
received any good? Produce your judgements,
philosopher. What does desire promise? Not to

10 μὴ ἀποτυγχάνειν. τίς ἐκκλίσεως ; μὴ περιπίπτειν. ἄγε, πληροῦμεν αὐτῶν τὴν ἐπαγγελίαν ; εἰπέ μοι τἀληθῆ· ἂν δὲ ψεύσῃ, ἐρῶ σοι "πρῴην ψυχρότερόν σου τῶν ἀκροατῶν συνελθόντων καὶ μὴ ἐπιβοησάντων σοι τεταπεινωμένος ἐξῆλθες·

11 πρῴην ἐπαινεθεὶς περιήρχου καὶ πᾶσιν ἔλεγες 'τί σοι ἔδοξα ;' 'θαυμαστῶς, κύριε, τὴν ἐμήν σοι σωτηρίαν.' 'πῶς δ' εἶπον ἐκεῖνο ;' 'τὸ ποῖον ;' 'ὅπου διέγραψα τὸν Πᾶνα καὶ τὰς

12 Νύμφας.' 'ὑπερφυῶς.'" εἶτά μοι λέγεις, ἐν ὀρέξει καὶ ἐκκλίσει κατὰ φύσιν ἀναστρέφῃ ;

13 ὕπαγε, ἄλλον πεῖθε. τὸν δεῖνα δὲ πρῴην οὐκ ἐπῄνεις παρὰ τὸ σοὶ φαινόμενον ; τὸν δεῖνα δ' οὐκ ἐκολάκευες τὸν συγκλητικόν ; ἤθελές σου

14 τὰ παιδία εἶναι τοιαῦτα ;—Μὴ γένοιτο.—Τίνος οὖν ἕνεκα ἐπῄνεις καὶ περιεῖπες αὐτόν ;—Εὐφυὴς νεανίσκος καὶ λόγων ἀκουστικός.—Πόθεν τοῦτο ; —Ἐμὲ θαυμάζει.—Εἴρηκας τὴν ἀπόδειξιν.

Εἶτα τί δοκεῖ σοι ; αὐτοί σου οὗτοι οὐ κατα-
15 φρονοῦσιν λεληθότως ; ὅταν οὖν ἄνθρωπος συνειδὼς ἑαυτῷ μηθὲν ἀγαθὸν μήτε πεποιηκότι μήτ' ἐνθυμουμένῳ εὕρῃ φιλόσοφον τὸν λέγοντα "μεγαλοφυὴς καὶ ἁπλοῦς καὶ ἀκέραιος," τί δοκεῖς ἄλλο αὐτὸν λέγειν ἢ "οὗτός τινά ποτέ

16 μου χρείαν ἔχει" ; ἢ εἰπέ μοι, τί μεγαλοφυοῦς ἔργον ἐπιδέδεικται ; ἰδοὺ σύνεστί σοι τοσούτῳ χρόνῳ, διαλεγομένου σου ἀκήκοεν, ἀναγιγνώσ-

fail in getting. What does aversion? Not to fall
into what we are avoiding. Well, do we fulfil their
promise? Tell me the truth; but if you lie, I will
say to you: "The other day, when your audience
gathered rather coolly, and did not shout applause,
you walked out of the hall in low spirits. And
again the other day, when you were received with
applause, you walked around and asked everybody,
'What did you think of me?' 'It was marvellous,
sir, I swear by my life.' 'How did I render that
particular passage?' 'Which one?' 'Where I drew
a picture of Pan and the Nymphs?' 'It was
superb.'" And after all this you tell me that you
follow nature in desire and aversion? Go to; try
to get somebody else to believe you! Didn't you,
just the other day, praise So-and-so contrary to your
honest opinion? And didn't you flatter So-and-so,
the senator? Did you want your children to be
like that?—Far from it!—Why then did you praise
him and palaver over him?—He is a gifted young
man and fond of listening to discourses.—How do
you know that?—He is an admirer of mine.—There
you gave your proof!

After all, what do you think? Don't these very
same persons secretly despise you? When, therefore, a person who is conscious of never having
either thought or done a good thing finds a
philosopher who tells him, "You are a genius,
straightforward and unspoiled," what else do you
suppose the man says to himself but, "This man
wants to use me for something or other"? Or else
tell me; what work of genius has he displayed?
Look, he has been with you all this time, he has
listened to your discourse, he has heard you lecture.

κοντος ἀκήκοεν. κατέσταλται, ἐπέστραπται ἐφ'
αὑτόν; ἦσθηται, ἐν οἵοις κακοῖς ἐστίν; ἀπο-
17 βέβληκεν οἴησιν; ζητεῖ τὸν διδάξοντα;—Ζητεῖ,
φησί.—Τὸν διδάξοντα, πῶς δεῖ βιοῦν; οὔ, μωρέ·
ἀλλὰ πῶς δεῖ φράζειν· τούτου γὰρ ἕνεκα καὶ
σὲ θαυμάζει. ἄκουσον αὐτοῦ, τίνα λέγει.
" οὗτος ὁ ἄνθρωπος πάνυ τεχνικώτατα γράφει,
18 Δίωνος πολὺ κάλλιον." ὅλον ἄλλο ἐστί. μή
τι λέγει " ὁ ἄνθρωπος αἰδήμων ἐστίν, οὗτος πιστός
ἐστιν, οὗτος ἀτάραχός ἐστιν"; εἰ δὲ καὶ ἔλεγεν,
εἶπον ἂν αὐτῷ "ἐπειδὴ οὗτος πιστός ἐστιν,
οὗτος ὁ πιστὸς τί ἐστιν;" καὶ εἰ μὴ εἶχεν εἰπεῖν,
προσέθηκα ἂν ὅτι " πρῶτον μάθε, τί λέγεις, εἶθ'
οὕτως λέγε."

19 Οὕτως οὖν κακῶς διακείμενος καὶ χάσκων περὶ
τοὺς ἐπαινέσοντας καὶ ἀριθμῶν τοὺς ἀκούοντάς
σου θέλεις ἄλλους ὠφελεῖν· " σήμερόν μου πολλῷ
πλείονες ἤκουσαν." " ναί, πολλοί." " δοκοῦμεν
ὅτι πεντακόσιοι." " οὐδὲν λέγεις· θὲς αὐτοὺς
χιλίους." " Δίωνος οὐδέποτ' ἤκουσαν τοσοῦτοι."
" πόθεν αὐτῷ;" " καὶ κομψῶς αἰσθάνονται λόγων." " τὸ καλόν, κύριε, καὶ λίθον κινῆσαι
20 δύναται." ἰδοὺ φωναὶ φιλοσόφου, ἰδοὺ διάθεσις
ὠφελήσοντος ἀνθρώπους· ἰδοὺ ἀκηκοὼς ἄνθρωπος

---

[1] Probably the famous lecturer of the day, Dio Chrysostom,
of Prusa.

[2] To be taken as intended for a serious compliment, and
probably a popular saying (as Upton suggested) like our
" Music hath charms," or, " The very stones would cry out."
The idea behind it would be familiar from the story of how
the trees followed Orpheus, in order to hear his beautiful
music, or the stones arranged themselves in the walls of
Thebes, to the strains of Amphion. Capps, however, thinks

Has he settled down? Has he come to himself?
Has he realized the evil plight in which he is?
Has he cast aside his self-conceit? Is he looking
for the man who will teach him?—He *is* looking,
the man says.—The man who will teach him how he
ought to live? No, fool, but only how he ought
to deliver a speech; for that is why he admires even
you. Listen to him, and hear what he says. "This
fellow has a most artistic style; it is much finer
than Dio's."[1] That's altogether different. He
doesn't say, does he, "The man is respectful, he
is faithful and unperturbed"? And even if he had
said this, I would have replied: "Since this man is
faithful, what is your definition of the faithful man?"
And if he had no answer to give, I would have added:
"First find out what you are talking about, and
then do your talking."

When you are in such a sorry state as this, then,
gaping for men to praise you, and counting the
number of your audience, is it your wish to do good
to others? "To-day I had a much larger audience."
"Yes, indeed, there were great numbers." "Five
hundred, I fancy." "Nonsense, make it a thousand." "Dio never had so large an audience."
"How could you expect him to?" "Yes, and they
are clever at catching the points." "Beauty, sir, can
move even a stone."[2] There are the words of a
philosopher for you! That's the feeling of one who
is on his way to do good to men! There you have

that "$\tau \grave{o} \kappa \alpha \lambda \acute{o} \nu$ means 'honour'" here, and that the remark
is "cynical." He would translate: "Talk of honour, sir,"
etc., adding the explanatory note: "That is, the speaker
would have had no success with his audience if he had
preached honour and virtue (as the true philosopher should)."

λόγου, ἀνεγνωκὼς τὰ Σωκρατικὰ ὡς Σωκρατικά,
οὐχὶ δ' ὡς Λυσίου καὶ Ἰσοκράτους. "πολλάκις
ἐθαύμασα, τίσιν ποτὲ λόγοις. οὔ· ἀλλὰ τίνι
21 ποτὲ λόγῳ· τοῦτ' ἐκείνου λειότερον." μὴ γὰρ
ἄλλως αὐτὰ ἀνεγνώκατε ἢ ὡς ᾠδάρια; ὡς εἴ
γε ἀνεγιγνώσκετε ὡς δεῖ, οὐκ ἂν πρὸς τούτοις
ἐγίνεσθε, ἀλλ' ἐκεῖνο μᾶλλον ἐβλέπετε "ἐμὲ δ'
Ἄνυτος καὶ Μέλητος ἀποκτεῖναι μὲν δύνανται,
βλάψαι δ' οὔ," καὶ ὅτι "ὡς ἐγὼ ἀεὶ τοιοῦτος
οἷος μηδενὶ¹ προσέχειν τῶν ἐμῶν ἢ τῷ λόγῳ, ὃς
22 ἄν μοι σκοπουμένῳ βέλτιστος φαίνηται." διὰ
τοῦτο τίς ἤκουσέ ποτε Σωκράτους λέγοντος ὅτι
"οἶδά τι καὶ διδάσκω"; ἀλλὰ ἄλλον ἀλλαχοῦ
ἔπεμπεν. τοιγαροῦν ἤρχοντο πρὸς αὐτὸν ἀξιοῦντες φιλοσόφοις ὑπ' αὐτοῦ συσταθῆναι κἀκεῖνος
23 ἀπῆγεν καὶ συνίστανεν. οὔ· ἀλλὰ προσπέμπων
ἔλεγεν "ἄκουσόν μου σήμερον διαλεγομένου ἐν
τῇ οἰκίᾳ τῇ Κοδράτου."

Τί σου ἀκούσω; ἐπιδεῖξαί μοι θέλεις, ὅτι
κομψῶς συντιθεῖς τὰ ὀνόματα; συντιθεῖς, ἄν-
θρωπε· καὶ τί σοι ἀγαθόν ἐστιν; "ἀλλ' ἐπαί-

---

¹ Wolf : μηδέν S.

---

¹ The rhetors must have disputed whether the opening
words of Xenophon's *Memorabilia* might not have been
improved upon by using the singular λόγῳ instead of the
plural λόγοις.
² Plato, *Apol.* 30 C.
³ Slightly modified from Plato, *Crito*, 46 B.
⁴ *i.e.* to different authorities on special subjects.
⁵ Actual instances of such introductions are recorded in
the *Protagoras*, 310 E, and the *Theaetetus*, 151 B. Compare
also Maximus Tyrius, 38, 4, *b*. The personal relations
between Socrates and the Sophists in general were clearly
not strained.

a man who has listened to reason, who has read the accounts of Socrates as coming from Socrates, not as though they were from Lysias, or Isocrates! "' I have often wondered by what arguments ever '—no, but 'by what argument ever'—this form is smoother than the other!'" [1] You have been reading this literature just as you would music-hall songs, haven't you? Because, if you had read them in the right way, you would not have lingered on these points, but this is the sort of thing rather that would have caught your eye: "Anytus and Meletus can kill me, but they cannot hurt me"; [2] and: "I have always been the kind of man to pay attention to none of my own affairs, but only to the argument which strikes me as best upon reflection." [3] And for that reason who ever heard Socrates saying, "I know something and teach it"? But he used to send one person here and another there. [4] Therefore men used to go to him to have him introduce them to philosophers, [5] and he used to take them around and introduce them. But no, *your* idea of him, no doubt, is that, as he was taking them along, he used to say, "Come around to-day and hear me deliver a discourse in the house of Quadratus"! [6]

Why should I listen to you? Do you want to exhibit to me the clever way in which you put words together? You do compose them cleverly, man; and what good is it to you? "But praise me."

[6] The practice of letting a popular or distinguished scholar lecture in one's house was particularly common in Greek and Roman times. Several distinguished persons by the name of Quadratus were contemporaries of Epictetus (*Prosopographia Imperii Romani*, Vol. III, nos. 600 ff.), but it is not certain that any one of them is meant, because they resided regularly at Rome, and this discourse was held at Nicopolis.

24 νεσόν με." τί λέγεις τὸ ἐπαίνεσον ; "εἰπέ μοι
'οὐᾶ' καὶ 'θαυμαστῶς.'" ἰδοὺ λέγω. εἰ δ'
ἐστὶν ἔπαινος ἐκεῖνο, ὅ τι ποτὲ λέγουσιν οἱ
φιλόσοφοι τῶν ἐν τῇ[1] τοῦ ἀγαθοῦ κατηγορίᾳ,[2]
τί σε ἔχω ἐπαινέσαι ; εἰ ἀγαθόν ἐστι τὸ φράζειν
25 ὀρθῶς, δίδαξόν με καὶ ἐπαινέσω. τί οὖν ; ἀηδῶς
δεῖ τῶν τοιούτων ἀκούειν ; μὴ γένοιτο. ἐγὼ μὲν
οὐδὲ κιθαρῳδοῦ ἀηδῶς ἀκούω· μή τι οὖν τούτου
ἕνεκα κιθαρῳδεῖν με δεῖ στάντα ; ἄκουσον, τί
λέγει Σωκράτης· "οὐδὲ γὰρ ἂν πρέποι, ὦ ἄνδρες,
τῇδε τῇ ἡλικίᾳ ὥσπερ μειρακίῳ πλάττοντι λόγους
εἰς ὑμᾶς εἰσιέναι." "ὥσπερ μειρακίῳ" φησίν.
26 ἔστι γὰρ τῷ ὄντι κομψὸν τὸ τεχνίον ἐκλέξαι
ὀνομάτια καὶ ταῦτα συνθεῖναι καὶ παρελθόντα
εὐφυῶς ἀναγνῶναι ἢ εἰπεῖν καὶ μεταξὺ ἀναγιγνώσκοντα ἐπιφθέγξασθαι ὅτι "τούτοις οὐ πολλοὶ δύνανται παρακολουθεῖν, μὰ τὴν ὑμετέραν
σωτηρίαν."
27 Φιλόσοφος δ' ἐπ' ἀκρόασιν παρακαλεῖ ; —
Οὐχὶ δ' ὡς ὁ ἥλιος ἄγει αὐτὸς ἐφ' ἑαυτὸν τὴν
τροφήν, οὕτως δὲ καὶ οὗτος ἄγει τοὺς ὠφελη-
θησομένους ; ποῖος ἰατρὸς παρακαλεῖ, ἵνα τις
ὑπ' αὐτοῦ θεραπευθῇ ; καίτοι νῦν ἀκούω ὅτι
καὶ οἱ ἰατροὶ παρακαλοῦσιν ἐν Ῥώμῃ· πλὴν ἐπ'
28 ἐμοῦ παρεκαλοῦντο. "παρακαλῶ σε ἐλθόντα

---

[1] Upton (in part after Wolf): τῶν τοῦ ἀγαθοῦ S.
[2] κατηγορία S.

---

[1] Plato, *Apology*, 17 C.
[2] According to Stoic doctrine the so-called "rays" of the
sun were thought to be lines of vapour drawn to the sun in
order to feed its fires. Zeno, frag. 35 ; Cleanthes, frag. 501 ;

What do you mean by "praise"? "Cry out to me, 'Bravo!' or 'Marvellous!'" All right, I'll say it. But if praise is some one of those things which the philosophers put in the category of the good, what praise can I give you? If it is a good thing to speak correctly, teach me and I will praise you. What then? Ought one to take no pleasure in listening to such efforts? Far from it. I do not fail to take pleasure in listening to a citharoede; surely I am not bound for that reason to stand and sing to my own accompaniment on the harp, am I? Listen, what does Socrates say? "Nor would it be seemly for me, O men of Athens, at my time of life to appear before you like some lad, and weave a cunning discourse."[1] "Like some lad," he says. For it is indeed a dainty thing, this small art of selecting trivial phrases and putting them together, and of coming forward and reading or reciting them gracefully, and then in the midst of the delivery shouting out, "There are not many people who can follow this, by your lives, I swear it!"

Does a philosopher invite people to a lecture?—Is it not rather the case that, as the sun draws its own sustenance to itself,[2] so he also draws to himself those to whom he is to do good? What physician ever invites a patient to come and be healed by him? Although I am told that in these days the physicians in Rome *do* advertise; however, in my time they were called in[3] by their patients. "I invite you to

Chrysippus, frags. 579, 652, 658–663, all in Von Arnim's *Stoicorum Veterum Fragmenta.*

[3] The three slightly varying translations for παρακαλεῖν, "invite," "advertize," and "call in," seem to be required by our idiom.

ἀκοῦσαι, ὅτι σοι κακῶς ἐστὶ καὶ πάντων μᾶλλον
ἐπιμελῇ ἢ οὗ δεῖ σε ἐπιμελεῖσθαι καὶ ὅτι ἀγνοεῖς
τὰ ἀγαθὰ καὶ τὰ κακὰ καὶ κακοδαίμων εἶ καὶ
δυστυχής." κομψὴ παράκλησις. καὶ μὴν ἂν
μὴ ταῦτα ἐμποιῇ ὁ τοῦ φιλοσόφου λόγος, νεκρός
29 ἐστι καὶ αὐτὸς καὶ ὁ λέγων. εἴωθε λέγειν ὁ
Ῥοῦφος "εἰ εὐσχολεῖτε ἐπαινέσαι με, ἐγὼ δ'
οὐδὲν λέγω." τοιγαροῦν οὕτως ἔλεγεν, ὥσθ'
ἕκαστον ἡμῶν καθήμενον οἴεσθαι, ὅτι τίς ποτε
αὐτὸν διαβέβληκεν· οὕτως ἥπτετο τῶν γιγνομένων, οὕτως πρὸ ὀφθαλμῶν ἐτίθει τὰ ἑκάστου
κακά.

30 Ἰατρεῖόν ἐστιν, ἄνδρες, τὸ τοῦ φιλοσόφου
σχολεῖον· οὐ δεῖ ἡσθέντας ἐξελθεῖν, ἀλλ' ἀλγή-
σαντας. ἔρχεσθε γὰρ οὐχ ὑγιεῖς, ἀλλ' ὁ μὲν
ὦμον ἐκβεβληκώς, ὁ δ' ἀπόστημα ἔχων, ὁ δὲ
31 σύριγγα, ὁ δὲ κεφαλαλγῶν. εἶτ' ἐγὼ καθίσας
ὑμῖν λέγω νοημάτια καὶ ἐπιφωνημάτια, ἵν' ὑμεῖς
ἐπαινέσαντές με ἐξέλθητε, ὁ μὲν τὸν ὦμον
ἐκφέρων οἷον εἰσήνεγκεν, ὁ δὲ τὴν κεφαλὴν
ὡσαύτως ἔχουσαν, ὁ δὲ τὴν σύριγγα, ὁ δὲ τὸ
32 ἀπόστημα; εἶτα τούτου ἕνεκα ἀποδημήσωσιν
ἄνθρωποι νεώτεροι καὶ τοὺς γονεῖς τοὺς αὐτῶν
ἀπολίπωσιν[1] καὶ τοὺς φίλους καὶ τοὺς συγγενεῖς
καὶ τὸ κτησίδιον, ἵνα σοι "οὐᾶ" φῶσιν ἐπιφωνημάτια λέγοντι; τοῦτο Σωκράτης ἐποίει, τοῦτο
Ζήνων, τοῦτο Κλεάνθης;

[1] Koraes: ἀπολείπουσιν S.

[1] At greater length in Gellius, 5, 1, 1.
[2] So it had, indeed, become in his time. Compare Introd.
p. xxiv. Thus also one of the great libraries at Alexandria is
said to have had over its portal: ἰατρεῖον τῆς ψυχῆς. If the

come and hear that you are in a bad way, and that you are concerned with anything rather than what you should be concerned with, and that you are ignorant of the good and the evil, and are wretched and miserable." That's a fine invitation ! And yet if the philosopher's discourse does not produce this effect, it is lifeless and so is the speaker himself. Rufus used to say, " If you have nothing better to do than to praise me, then I am speaking to no purpose." [1] Wherefore he spoke in such a way that each of us as we sat there fancied someone had gone to Rufus and told him of our faults ; so effective was his grasp of what men actually do, so vividly did he set before each man's eyes his particular weaknesses.

Men, the lecture-room of the philosopher is a hospital ; [2] you ought not to walk out of it in pleasure, but in pain. For you are not well when you come ; one man has a dislocated shoulder, another an abscess, another a fistula, another a head-ache. And then am I to sit down and recite to you dainty little notions and clever little mottoes, so that you will go out with words of praise on your lips, one man carrying away his shoulder just as it was when he came in, another his head in the same state, another his fistula, another his abscess ? And so it's for this, is it, that young men are to travel from home, and leave their parents, their friends, their relatives, and their bit of property, merely to cry " Bravo ! " as you recite your clever little mottoes? Was this what Socrates used to do, or Zeno, or Cleanthes?

story is true (which I very much doubt), the inscription surely belongs to the decadence, for such was clearly not the conception of science which prevailed in the great days of Alexandria.

33 Τί οὖν; οὐκ ἔστιν ὁ προτρεπτικὸς χαρακτήρ;
— Τίς γὰρ οὐ λέγει; ὡς ὁ¹ ἐλεγκτικός, ὡς ὁ
διδασκαλικός. τίς οὖν πώποτε τέταρτον εἶπεν
34 μετὰ τούτων τὸν ἐπιδεικτικόν; τίς γάρ ἐστιν ὁ
προτρεπτικός; δύνασθαι καὶ ἐνὶ καὶ πολλοῖς
δεῖξαι τὴν μάχην ἐν ᾗ κυλίονται· καὶ ὅτι μᾶλλον
πάντων φροντίζουσιν ἢ ὧν θέλουσιν. θέλουσι
μὲν γὰρ τὰ πρὸς εὐδαιμονίαν φέροντα, ἀλλαχοῦ
35 δ' αὐτὰ ζητοῦσι. τοῦτο ἵνα γένηται, δεῖ τεθῆναι
χίλια βάθρα καὶ παρακληθῆναι τοὺς ἀκουσο-
μένους καὶ σὲ ἐν κομψῷ στολίῳ ἢ τριβωναρίῳ
ἀναβάντα ἐπὶ πούλβινον διαγράφειν, πῶς Ἀχιλ-
λεὺς ἀπέθανεν; παύσασθε, τοὺς θεοὺς ὑμῖν,
καλὰ ὀνόματα καὶ πράγματα καταισχύνοντες,
36 ὅσον ἐφ' ἑαυτοῖς. οὐδὲν προτρεπτικώτερον ἢ
ὅταν ὁ λέγων ἐμφαίνῃ τοῖς ἀκούουσιν ὅτι χρείαν
37 αὐτῶν ἔχει. ἢ εἰπέ μοι, τίς ἀκούων ἀναγιγνώσ-
κοντός σου ἢ διαλεγομένου περὶ αὐτοῦ ἠγωνίασεν
ἢ ἐπεστράφη εἰς αὐτὸν ἢ ἐξελθὼν εἶπεν ὅτι
" καλῶς μου ἥψατο ὁ φιλόσοφος· οὐκέτι δεῖ
38 ταῦτα ποιεῖν "; οὐχὶ δ', ἂν λίαν εὐδοκιμῇς, λέγει
πρός τινα " κομψῶς ἔφρασεν τὰ περὶ τὸν Ξέρξην,"
ἄλλος " οὔ· ἀλλὰ τὴν ἐπὶ Πύλαις μάχην ";
τοῦτό ἐστιν ἀκρόασις φιλοσόφου;

---

¹ ὁ added by a modern hand in S.

¹ That is, as a style appropriate to philosophers, for the
epideictic, or style of display, was a well-recognized branch
of oratory in general—and not entirely unknown, perhaps,
among certain popular preachers even to-day.

² As God needs the universe in which to exercise and display His power, so the teacher needs pupils, the speaker an
audience. There is a mutual need, therefore, each of the
other.

Well! But isn't there such a thing as the right style for exhortation?—Why yes, who denies that? Just as there is the style for refutation, and the style for instruction. Who, then, has ever mentioned a fourth style along with these, the style of display?[1] Why, what *is* the style for exhortation? The ability to show to the individual, as well as to the crowd, the warring inconsistency in which they are floundering about, and how they are paying attention to anything rather than what they truly want. For they want the things that conduce to happiness, but they are looking for them in the wrong place. To achieve that must a thousand benches be placed, and the prospective audience be invited, and you put on a fancy cloak, or dainty mantle, and mount the speaker's stand, and paint a word-picture of—how Achilles died? By the gods, I beseech you, have done with discrediting, as far as it is in your power to discredit, words and actions that are noble! There is nothing more effective in the style for exhortation than when the speaker makes clear to his audience that he has need of them.[2] Or tell me, who that ever heard you reading a lecture or conducting a discourse felt greatly disturbed about himself, or came to a realization of the state he was in, or on going out said, "The philosopher brought it home to me in fine style; I must not act like this any longer"? But doesn't he say to a companion, if you make an unusually fine impression, "That was beautiful diction in the passage about Xerxes"; and doesn't the other answer, "No, I preferred the one about the battle of Thermopylae"?[3] Is this what listening to a philosopher amounts to?

[3] A typical *rhetorum campus,* as Cicero calls it (*De Officiis,* 1, 61).

κδ'. Περὶ τοῦ μὴ δεῖν προσπάσχειν τοῖς οὐκ ἐφ᾽ ἡμῖν.

1 Τὸ ἄλλου παρὰ φύσιν σοὶ κακὸν μὴ γινέσθω· οὐ γὰρ συνταπεινοῦσθαι πέφυκας οὐδὲ συνα-

2 τυχεῖν, ἀλλὰ συνευτυχεῖν. ἂν δέ τις ἀτυχῇ, μέμνησο, ὅτι παρ᾽ αὑτὸν ἀτυχεῖ. ὁ γὰρ θεὸς πάντας ἀνθρώπους ἐπὶ τὸ εὐδαιμονεῖν, ἐπὶ τὸ

3 εὐσταθεῖν ἐποίησεν. πρὸς τοῦτο ἀφορμὰς ἔδωκεν, τὰ μὲν ἴδια δοὺς ἑκάστῳ, τὰ δ᾽ ἀλλότρια· τὰ μὲν κωλυτὰ καὶ ἀφαιρετὰ καὶ ἀναγκαστὰ οὐκ ἴδια, τὰ δ᾽ ἀκώλυτα ἴδια· τὴν δ᾽ οὐσίαν τοῦ ἀγαθοῦ καὶ τοῦ κακοῦ, ὥσπερ ἦν ἄξιον τὸν κηδόμενον ἡμῶν καὶ πατρικῶς προϊστάμενον, ἐν τοῖς ἰδίοις.

4 "ἀλλ᾽ ἀποκεχώρηκα τοῦ δεῖνος καὶ ὀδυνᾶται." διὰ τί γὰρ τὰ ἀλλότρια ἴδια ἡγήσατο ; διὰ τί, ὅτε σε βλέπων ἔχαιρεν, οὐκ ἐπελογίζετο ὅτι θνητὸς εἶ, ἀποδημητικὸς εἶ ; τοιγαροῦν τίνει

5 δίκας τῆς αὑτοῦ μωρίας. σὺ δ᾽ ἀντὶ τίνος ; ἐπὶ τί κλάεις[1] σεαυτόν ; ἢ οὐδὲ σὺ ταῦτα ἐμελέτησας, ἀλλ᾽ ὡς τὰ γύναια τὰ οὐδενὸς ἄξια πᾶσιν οἷς ἔχαιρες ὡς ἀεὶ συνεσόμενος συνῇς, τοῖς τόποις, τοῖς ἀνθρώποις, ταῖς διατριβαῖς ; καὶ νῦν κλαίων ἐκάθισας, ὅτι μὴ τοὺς αὐτοὺς βλέπεις καὶ ἐν τοῖς

6 αὐτοῖς τόποις διατρίβεις. τούτου γὰρ ἄξιος εἶ,

---

[1] Salmasius, after Schegk : κλαισ S.

---

[1] That is, is produced by himself, or is his own fault ; and really affects no one but himself.

CHAPTER XXIV

That we ought not to yearn for the things which are not under our control

L<small>ET</small> not that which in the case of another is contrary to nature become an evil for you ; for you are born not to be humiliated along with others, nor to share in their misfortunes, but to share in their good fortune. If, however, someone is unfortunate, remember that his misfortune concerns himself.[1] For God made all mankind to be happy, to be serene. To this end He gave them resources, giving each man some things for his own, and others not for his own. The things that are subject to hindrance, deprivation, and compulsion are not a man's own, but those which cannot be hindered are his own. The true nature of the good and the evil, as was fitting for Him who watches over and protects us like a father, He gave to man to be among his own possessions. " But I have parted from So-and-so, and he is stricken with grief." Yes, but why did he regard what was not his own as his own ? Why, when he was glad to see you, did he not reflect that you are mortal, and likely to go on a journey ? And therefore he is paying the penalty for his own folly. But why are *you* bewailing yourself, and to what end ? Or did you also neglect to study this matter, but, like worthless women, did you enjoy everything in which you took delight as though you were to enjoy it for ever, your surroundings, human beings, your ways of life ? And now you sit and wail because you no longer lay eyes upon the same persons, and do not spend your life in the same places. Yes, for that's what you

ἵνα καὶ τῶν κοράκων καὶ κορωνῶν ἀθλιώτερος
ἦς, οἷς ἔξεστιν ἵπτασθαι, ὅπου θέλουσιν, καὶ
μετοικοδομεῖν τὰς νεοσσιὰς καὶ τὰ πελάγη δια-
περᾶν μὴ στένουσιν μηδὲ ποθοῦσι τὰ πρῶτα. —
7 Ναί· ἀλλ' ὑπὸ τοῦ ἄλογα εἶναι πάσχει αὐτά. —
Ἡμῖν οὖν λόγος ἐπὶ ἀτυχίᾳ καὶ κακοδαιμονίᾳ
δέδοται ὑπὸ τῶν θεῶν, ἵν' ἄθλιοι, ἵνα πενθοῦντες
8 διατελῶμεν; ἢ πάντες ἔστωσαν ἀθάνατοι καὶ
μηδεὶς ἀποδημείτω,[1] ἀλλὰ μένωμεν ὡς τὰ φυτὰ
προσερριζωμένοι· ἂν δέ τις ἀποδημήσῃ τῶν
συνήθων, καθήμενοι κλαίωμεν καὶ πάλιν, ἂν
ἔλθῃ, ὀρχώμεθα καὶ κροτῶμεν ὡς τὰ παιδία;
9 Οὐκ ἀπογαλακτίσομεν ἤδη ποθ' ἑαυτοὺς καὶ
μεμνησόμεθα ὧν ἠκούσαμεν παρὰ τῶν φιλο-
10 σόφων; εἴ γε μὴ ὡς ἐπαοιδῶν αὐτῶν ἠκούομεν,
ὅτι ὁ κόσμος οὗτος μία πόλις ἐστὶ καὶ ἡ οὐσία, ἐξ
ἧς δεδημιούργηται, μία καὶ ἀνάγκη περίοδόν τινα
εἶναι καὶ παραχώρησιν ἄλλων ἄλλοις καὶ τὰ μὲν
διαλύεσθαι, τὰ δ' ἐπιγίνεσθαι, τὰ μὲν μένειν ἐν
11 τῷ αὐτῷ, τὰ δὲ κινεῖσθαι. πάντα δὲ φίλων
μεστά, πρῶτα μὲν θεῶν, εἶτα καὶ ἀνθρώπων
φύσει πρὸς ἀλλήλους ᾠκειωμένων· καὶ δεῖ τοὺς
μὲν παρεῖναι ἀλλήλοις, τοὺς δ' ἀπαλλάττεσθαι,
τοῖς μὲν συνοῦσι χαίροντας, τοῖς δ' ἀπαλλαττο-
12 μένοις μὴ ἀχθομένους. ὁ δ' ἄνθρωπος πρὸς τῷ
φύσει μεγαλόφρων εἶναι καὶ πάντων τῶν ἀπροαιρέτων καταφρονητικὸς ἔτι κἀκεῖνο ἔσχηκε τὸ μὴ
ἐρριζῶσθαι μηδὲ προσπεφυκέναι τῇ γῇ, ἀλλὰ

---

[1] The clause, μηδ' ἡμεῖς που ἀποδημῶμεν, which follows
here in S, is deleted by Oldfather as a doublet of the preceding three words. It arose probably as a superfluous
attempt either to gloss or to emend.

deserve, to be more wretched than crows and ravens, which can fly away wherever they please, and change their nests, and cross the seas, without groaning or longing for their first home.—Yes, but they feel that way because they are irrational creatures.—Has, then, reason been given us by the gods for misfortune and misery, so that we may spend our lives in wretchedness and mourning? Or shall all men be immortal, and no one leave home, but shall we stay rooted in the ground like the plants? And if any one of our acquaintances leaves home, shall we sit down and wail, and then again, if he comes back, dance and clap our hands as the children do?

Shall we not wean ourselves at last, and call to mind what we have heard from the philosophers?—if, indeed, we did not listen to them as to enchanters—when they said that this universe is but a single state, and the substance out of which it has been fashioned is single, and it needs must be that there is a certain periodic change and a giving place of one thing to another, and that some things must be dissolved and others come into being, some things to remain in the same place and others to be moved. Further, that all things are full of friends, first gods, and then also men, who by nature have been made of one household with one another; and that some men must remain with each other, while others must depart, and that though we must rejoice in those who dwell with us, yet we must not grieve at those who depart. And man, in addition to being by nature high-minded and capable of despising all the things that are outside the sphere of his moral purpose, possesses also this further quality, that, namely, of not being rooted nor growing in the

ἄλλοτ' ἐπ' ἄλλους ἵεσθαι τόπους ποτὲ μὲν
χρειῶν τινῶν ἐπειγουσῶν, ποτὲ δὲ καὶ αὐτῆς τῆς
θέας ἕνεκα.

13 Καὶ τῷ Ὀδυσσεῖ τὸ συμβὰν τοιοῦτόν τι ἦν·

πολλῶν δ' ἀνθρώπων ἴδεν ἄστεα καὶ νόον ἔγνω·

καὶ ἔτι πρόσθεν τῷ Ἡρακλεῖ περιελθεῖν τὴν
οἰκουμένην ὅλην

ἀνθρώπων ὕβριν τε καὶ εὐνομίην ἐφορῶντα,

καὶ τὴν μὲν ἐκβάλλοντα καὶ καθαίροντα, τὴν δ'
14 ἀντεισάγοντα. καίτοι πόσους οἴει φίλους ἔσχεν
ἐν Θήβαις, πόσους ἐν Ἀθήναις, πόσους δὲ περιερχόμενος ἐκτήσατο, ὅς γε καὶ ἐγάμει, ὅπου
καιρὸς ἐφάνη αὐτῷ, καὶ ἐπαιδοποιεῖτο καὶ τοὺς
παῖδας ἀπέλειπεν [1] οὐ στένων οὐδὲ ποθῶν οὐδ' ὡς
15 ὀρφανοὺς ἀφιείς; ᾔδει γάρ, ὅτι οὐδείς ἐστιν
ἄνθρωπος ὀρφανός, ἀλλὰ πάντων ἀεὶ καὶ διηνε-
16 κῶς ὁ πατήρ ἐστιν ὁ κηδόμενος. οὐ γὰρ μέχρι
λόγου ἠκηκόει, ὅτι πατήρ ἐστιν ὁ Ζεὺς τῶν
ἀνθρώπων, ὅς γε καὶ αὑτοῦ πατέρα ᾤετο αὐτὸν
καὶ ἐκάλει καὶ πρὸς ἐκεῖνον ἀφορῶν ἔπραττεν ἃ
ἔπραττεν. τοιγάρτοι πανταχοῦ ἐξῆν αὐτῷ διάγειν
17 εὐδαιμόνως. οὐδέποτε δ' ἔστιν οἷόν τ' εἰς τὸ
αὐτὸ ἐλθεῖν εὐδαιμονίαν καὶ πόθον τῶν οὐ παρόντων. τὸ γὰρ εὐδαιμονοῦν ἀπέχειν δεῖ πάντα ἃ

---

[1] Koraes : ἀπέλιπεν S.

---

[1] Homer, *Odyssey*, I. 3.
[2] Homer, *Odyssey*, XVII. 487 (slightly modified).
[3] This is about the most drastic bit of idealisation of the
Heracles myths which the Stoics, for whom Heracles was a
kind of Arthurian knight, ever achieved. The comic poets

earth, but of moving now to one place and now to
another, at one time under the pressure of certain
needs, and at another merely for the sake of the
spectacle.

Now it was something of this sort which fell to the
lot of Odysseus:

> Many the men whose towns he beheld, and he
> learned of their temper.[1]

And even before his time it was the fortune of
Heracles to traverse the entire inhabited world,

> Seeing the wanton behaviour of men and the
> lawful,[2]

casting forth the one and clearing the world of it,
and introducing the other in its place. Yet how
many friends do you suppose he had in Thebes, in
Argos, in Athens, and how many new friends he
made on his rounds, seeing that he was even in the
habit of marrying when he saw fit, and begetting
children, and deserting his children, without either
groaning or yearning for them, or as though leaving
them to be orphans?[3] It was because he knew that no
human being is an orphan, but all men have ever and
constantly the Father, who cares for them. Why, to
him it was no mere story which he had heard, that
Zeus is father of men, for he always thought of Him
as his own father, and called Him so, and in all that
he did he looked to Him. Wherefore he had the
power to live happily in every place. But it is
impossible that happiness, and yearning for what is
not present, should ever be united. For happiness

naturally presented this aspect of his career in a somewhat
different light.

θέλει, πεπληρωμένῳ τινὶ ἐοικέναι· οὐ δίψος δεῖ
18 προσεῖναι αὐτῷ, οὐ λιμόν.—'Αλλ' ὁ[1] 'Οδυσσεὺς
ἐπεπόνθει πρὸς τὴν γυναῖκα καὶ ἔκλαιεν ἐπὶ
πέτρας καθεζόμενος.—Σὺ δ' Ὁμήρῳ πάντα
προσέχεις καὶ τοῖς μύθοις αὐτοῦ; ἢ εἰ ταῖς ἀληθείαις ἔκλαεν, τί ἄλλο ἢ ἐδυστύχει; τίς δὲ
19 καλός τε καὶ ἀγαθὸς δυστυχεῖ; τῷ ὄντι κακῶς
διοικεῖται τὰ ὅλα, εἰ μὴ ἐπιμελεῖται ὁ Ζεὺς τῶν
ἑαυτοῦ πολιτῶν, ἵν' ὦσιν ὅμοιοι αὐτῷ, εὐδαίμονες.
ἀλλὰ ταῦτα οὐ θεμιτὰ οὐδ' ὅσια ἐνθυμηθῆναι,
20 ἀλλ' ὁ 'Οδυσσεύς, εἰ μὲν ἔκλαεν καὶ ὠδύρετο, οὐκ
ἦν ἀγαθός. τίς γὰρ ἀγαθός ἐστιν ὁ οὐκ εἰδώς,
ὅς ἐστιν; τίς δ' οἶδεν ταῦτα ἐπιλελησμένος,
ὅτι φθαρτὰ τὰ γενόμενα καὶ ἄνθρωπον ἀνθρώπῳ
21 συνεῖναι οὐ δυνατὸν ἀεί; τί οὖν; τῶν μὴ δυνα-
τῶν ἐφίεσθαι ἀνδραποδῶδες, ἠλίθιον, ξένου θεο-
μαχοῦντος, ὡς μόνον οἷόν τε, τοῖς δόγμασι τοῖς
ἑαυτοῦ.
22   'Αλλ' ἡ μήτηρ μου στένει μὴ ὁρῶσά με.—Διὰ
τί γὰρ οὐκ ἔμαθεν τούτους τοὺς λόγους; καὶ οὐ
τοῦτό φημι, ὅτι οὐκ ἐπιμελητέον τοῦ μὴ οἰμώζειν
αὐτήν, ἀλλ' ὅτι οὐ δεῖ θέλειν τὰ ἀλλότρια ἐξ
23 ἅπαντος. λύπη δ' ἡ ἄλλου ἀλλότριόν ἐστιν, ἡ δ'
ἐμὴ ἐμόν. ἐγὼ οὖν τὸ μὲν ἐμὸν παύσω ἐξ ἅπαντος, ἐπ' ἐμοὶ γάρ ἐστιν· τὸ δ' ἀλλότριον πειράσο-
μαι κατὰ δύναμιν, ἐξ ἅπαντος δ' οὐ πειράσο-
24 μαι. εἰ δὲ μή, θεομαχήσω, ἀντιθήσω πρὸς τὸν

---

[1] δ added by Schenkl : ἀλλ' ὀδυσσεύς S.

---

[1] Homer, *Odyssey*, V. 82.

must already possess everything that it wants; it must resemble a replete person: he cannot feel thirst or hunger.—Still, Odysseus felt a longing for his wife, and sat upon a rock and wept.[1]—And do you take Homer and his tales as authority for everything? If Odysseus really wept, what else could he have been but miserable? But what good and excellent man is miserable? In all truth the universe is badly managed, if Zeus does not take care of His own citizens, that they be like Him, that is, happy. Nay, it is unlawful and unholy to think of such an alternative, but if Odysseus wept and wailed, he was not a good man. Why, what man could be good who does not know who he is? And who knows that, if he has forgotten that the things which come into being are corruptible, and that it is impossible for one human being always to live with another? What then? To reach out for the impossible is slavish and foolish; it is acting like a stranger in the universe, one who is fighting against God with the only weapons at his command, his own judgements.

But my mother mourns because she does not see me.—Yes, but why did she not learn the meaning of these words of the philosophers? And I am not saying that you ought to take no pains to keep her from lamenting, but only that a person ought not to want at all costs what is not his own. Now another's grief is no concern of mine, but my own grief is. Therefore, I will put an end at all costs to what is my own concern, for *it* is under my control: and that which is another's concern I will endeavour to check to the best of my ability, but my effort to do so will not be made at all costs. Otherwise I shall be fighting against

Δία, ἀντιδιατάξομαι αὐτῷ πρὸς τὰ ὅλα. καὶ
τἀπίχειρα τῆς θεομαχίας ταύτης καὶ ἀπειθείας
οὐ παῖδες παίδων ἐκτίσουσιν, ἀλλ' αὐτὸς ἐγὼ
μεθ' ἡμέραν, νυκτὸς διὰ τῶν ἐνυπνίων ἐκπηδῶν,
ταρασσόμενος, πρὸς πᾶσαν ἀπαγγελίαν τρέμων,
ἐξ ἐπιστολῶν ἀλλοτρίων ἠρτημένην ἔχων τὴν
25 ἐμαυτοῦ ἀπάθειαν.[1] ἀπὸ Ῥώμης τις ἥκει. " μόνον μή τι κακόν." τί δὲ κακὸν ἐκεῖ σοι συμβῆναι
δύναται, ὅπου μὴ εἶ; ἀπὸ τῆς Ἑλλάδος· " μόνον
μή τι κακόν." οὕτως σοι πᾶς τόπος δύναται
26 δυστυχίας εἶναι αἴτιος. οὐχ ἱκανὸν ἐκεῖ σε ἀτυχεῖν, ὅπου αὐτὸς εἶ, ἀλλὰ καὶ πέραν θαλάσσης
καὶ διὰ γραμμάτων; οὕτως ἀσφαλῶς σοι τὰ
27 πράγματα ἔχει ;—Τί οὖν, ἂν ἀποθάνωσιν οἱ ἐκεῖ
φίλοι ;—Τί γὰρ ἂν ἄλλο ἢ οἱ θνητοὶ ἀπέθανον ;
ἢ πῶς ἅμα μὲν γηρᾶσαι θέλεις, ἅμα δὲ μηδενὸς
28 τῶν στεργομένων μὴ ἰδεῖν θάνατον ; οὐκ οἶσθ',
ὅτι ἐν τῷ μακρῷ χρόνῳ πολλὰ καὶ ποικίλα ἀπο-
βαίνειν ἀνάγκη, τοῦ μὲν πυρετὸν γενέσθαι κρείτ-
29 τονα, τοῦ δὲ λῃστήν, τοῦ δὲ τύραννον ; τοιοῦτο
γὰρ τὸ περιέχον, τοιοῦτον οἱ συνόντες, ψύχη καὶ
καύματα καὶ τροφαὶ ἀσύμμετροι καὶ ὁδοιπορίαι
καὶ πλοῦς καὶ ἄνεμοι καὶ περιστάσεις ποικίλαι·
τὸν μὲν ἀπώλεσαν, τὸν δ' ἐξώρισαν, τὸν δ' εἰς
πρεσβείαν, ἄλλον δ' εἰς στρατείαν ἐνέβαλον.
30 κάθησο τοίνυν πρὸς πάντα ταῦτα ἐπτοημένος,
πενθῶν, ἀτυχῶν, δυστυχῶν, ἐξ ἄλλου ἠρτημένος

---

[1] Schweighäuser : εὐπείθειαν S.

---

[1] The phrase in quotation marks is a verbal reminiscence
of Homer, *Iliad*, XX. 308.

God, I shall be setting myself in opposition to
Zeus, I shall be arraying myself against Him in
regard to His administration of the universe. And
the wages of this fighting against God and this
disobedience will not be paid by "children's
children," [1] but by me myself in my own person, by
day and by night, as I start up out of dreams and am
disturbed, trembling at every message, with my own
peace of mind depending upon letters not my own.
Someone has arrived from Rome. " If only there
is no bad news!" But how can anything bad for
you happen in a place, if you are not there? Someone arrives from Greece. " If only there is no bad
news!" In this way for *you* every place can cause
misfortune. Isn't it enough for you to be miserable
where you are? Must you needs be miserable
even beyond the seas, and by letter? Is this the
fashion in which all that concerns you is secure?
—Yes, but what if my friends over there die?—Why,
what else than that mortal men died? Or how can
you wish to reach old age yourself, and at the same
time not behold the death of any that you love?
Do you not know that in the long course of time
many different things must needs happen; fever
must overcome one man, a brigand another, a
tyrant a third? Because such is the character of the
air about us, such that of our associates; cold and
heat and unsuitable food, and journeys by land and
by sea, and winds and all manner of perils; this
man they destroy, that man they drive into exile,
another they send on an embassy, and yet another
on a campaign. Sit down, therefore, and get all
wrought up at each one of these events, mourning,
unfortunate, miserable, depend on something other

καὶ τούτου οὐχ ἑνός, οὐ δυεῖν, ἀλλὰ μυρίων ἐπὶ μυρίοις.

31 Ταῦτα ἤκουες παρὰ τοῖς φιλοσόφοις, ταῦτ᾽ ἐμάνθανες; οὐκ οἶσθ᾽, ὅτι στρατεία τὸ χρῆμά ἐστιν; τὸν μὲν δεῖ φυλάττειν, τὸν δὲ κατασκοπήσοντα ἐξιέναι, τὸν δὲ καὶ πολεμήσοντα· οὐχ οἷόν τ᾽ εἶναι πάντας ἐν τῷ αὐτῷ οὐδ᾽ ἄμεινον.

32 σὺ δ᾽ ἀφεὶς ἐκτελεῖν τὰ προστάγματα τοῦ στρατηγοῦ ἐγκαλεῖς, ὅταν τί σοι προσταχθῇ τραχύτερον, καὶ οὐ παρακολουθεῖς, οἷον ἀποφαίνεις, ὅσον ἐπὶ σοί, τὸ στράτευμα, ὅτι ἄν σε πάντες μιμήσωνται, οὐ τάφρον σκάψει τις, οὐ χάρακα περιβαλεῖ, οὐκ ἀγρυπνήσει, οὐ κινδυνεύσει, ἀλλὰ ἄχρηστος

33 δόξει στρατεύεσθαι. πάλιν ἐν πλοίῳ ναύτης ἂν πλέῃς, μίαν χώραν κάτεχε καὶ ταύτην προσλιπάρει· ἂν δ᾽ ἐπὶ τὸν ἱστὸν ἀναβῆναι δέῃ, μὴ θέλε, ἂν εἰς τὴν πρῴραν διαδραμεῖν, μὴ θέλε. καὶ τίς ἀνέξεταί σου κυβερνήτης; οὐχὶ δ᾽ ὡς σκεῦος ἄχρηστον ἐκβαλεῖ, οὐδὲν ἄλλο ἢ ἐμπόδιον καὶ

34 κακὸν παράδειγμα τῶν ἄλλων ναυτῶν; οὕτως δὲ καὶ ἐνθάδε· στρατεία τίς ἐστιν ὁ βίος ἑκάστου καὶ αὕτη μακρὰ καὶ ποικίλη. τηρεῖν σε δεῖ τὸ τοῦ στρατιώτου καὶ τοῦ στρατηγοῦ πρὸς νεῦμα [1]

35 πράσσειν ἕκαστα· εἰ οἷόν τε, μαντευόμενον [2] ἃ θέλει. οὐδὲ γὰρ ὅμοιος ἐκεῖνος ὁ στρατηγὸς καὶ οὗτος οὔτε κατὰ τὴν ἰσχὺν οὔτε κατὰ τὴν τοῦ

33 ἤθους ὑπεροχήν. τέταξαι ἐν πόλει ἡγεμόνι [3] καὶ οὐκ ἐν ταπεινῇ τινι χώρᾳ, οὐκ ἐπέτειος ἀλλ᾽

---

[1] Schweighäuser: στρατιώτου πρόσνευμα. καὶ τοῦ στρατηγεῖν S.

[2] Reiske: μαντευόμενος S.

than yourself, and that not one thing or two, but tens upon tens of thousands of things!

Is that what you used to hear when you sat at the feet of the philosophers? Is that what you learned? Do you not know that the business of life is a campaign? One man must mount guard, another go out on reconnaissance, and another out to fight. It is not possible for all to stay in the same place, nor is it better so. But you neglect to perform the duties assigned you by your commanding officer, and complain when some rather hard order is given you, and fail to understand to what a state you are bringing the army, as far as in you lies; because, if they all imitate you, no one will dig a trench, no one construct a palisade, or watch through the night, or risk his life in fighting, but they will seem useless soldiers. Again, if you take ship as a sailor, take up one place and stick to that! and if you have to climb the mast, be unwilling; if you have to run to the bow, be unwilling! And what ship's captain will put up with you? Won't he throw you overboard like a piece of junk, nothing but a nuisance, and a bad example to the other sailors? So also in this world; each man's life is a kind of campaign, and a long and complicated one at that. You have to maintain the character of a soldier, and do each separate act at the bidding of the General, if possible divining what He wishes. For there is no comparison between this General and an ordinary one, either in His power, or in the pre-eminence of His character. You have been given a post in an imperial city, and not in some mean place; not for a

---

³ C. Schenkl; ἡγεμονίᾳ S.

εἰς¹ ἀεὶ βουλευτής. οὐκ οἶσθ', ὅτι τὸν τοιοῦτον
ὀλίγα μὲν δεῖ οἰκονομεῖν, τὰ πολλὰ δ' ἀποδημεῖν
ἄρχοντα ἢ ἀρχόμενον ἢ ὑπηρετοῦντά τινι ἀρχῇ ἢ
στρατευόμενον ἢ δικάζοντα; εἶτά μοι θέλεις ὡς
φυτὸν προσηρτῆσθαι τοῖς αὐτοῖς τόποις καὶ
37 προσερριζῶσθαι; — Ἡδὺ γάρ ἐστιν. — Τίς οὔ
φησιν; ἀλλὰ καὶ ζωμὸς ἡδύς ἐστι καὶ γυνὴ καλὴ
ἡδύ ἐστιν. τί ἄλλο λέγουσιν οἱ τέλος ποιούμενοι
τὴν ἡδονήν;
38   Οὐκ αἰσθάνῃ, τίνων ἀνθρώπων φωνὴν ἀφῆκας;
ὅτι Ἐπικουρείων καὶ κιναίδων; εἶτα τὰ ἐκείνων
ἔργα πράσσων καὶ τὰ δόγματα ἔχων τοὺς λόγους
ἡμῖν λέγεις τοὺς Ζήνωνος καὶ Σωκράτους; οὐκ
39 ἀπορρίψεις ὡς μακροτάτω τἀλλότρια, οἷς κοσμῇ
μηδέν σοι προσήκουσιν; ἢ τί ἄλλο θέλουσιν
ἐκεῖνοι ἢ καθεύδειν ἀπαραποδίστως καὶ ἀναναγ-
κάστως καὶ ἀναστάντες ἐφ' ἡσυχίας χασμή-
σασθαι καὶ τὸ πρόσωπον ἀποπλῦναι, εἶτα
γράψαι καὶ ἀναγνῶναι ἃ θέλουσιν, εἶτα φλυα-
ρῆσαί τί ποτ' ἐπαινούμενοι ὑπὸ τῶν φίλων, ὅ τι
ἂν λέγωσιν, εἶτα εἰς περίπατον προελθόντες καὶ
ὀλίγα περιπατήσαντες λούσασθαι, εἶτα φαγεῖν,
εἶτα κοιμηθῆναι, οἵαν δὴ κοίτην καθεύδειν τοὺς
τοιούτους εἰκός—τί ἄν τις λέγοι; ἔξεστιν γὰρ
τεκμαίρεσθαι.
40   Ἄγε, φέρε μοι καὶ σὺ τὴν σαυτοῦ διατριβήν,
ἣν ποθεῖς, ζηλωτὰ τῆς ἀληθείας καὶ Σωκράτους
καὶ Διογένους. τί θέλεις ἐν Ἀθήναις ποιεῖν;

---

¹ εἰς added by Capps: χώρᾳ ἀλλάεί S. The senators at
Athens, for example, served only one year.

short time either, but you are a senator for life. Do
you not know that a man in such a post has to give
only a little attention to the affairs of his own
household, but for most of the time has to be away,
in command, or under command, or serving some
official, or in the field, or on the judge's bench? And
then you want to be attached to the same spot and
rooted in it like a plant?—Yes, it is pleasant.—Why
deny it? But soup is pleasant too, and a pretty
woman is a pleasant thing. What else do those say
who make pleasure their end?

Do you not realize the kind of men they are
whose language you have just uttered? That they
are Epicureans and blackguards? And yet, while
doing their deeds and holding their opinions, you
recite to us the words of Zeno and Socrates? Will
you not cast away from you, as far as you can fling
them, these alien trappings with which you adorn
yourself, although they do not at all become you?
Or what else do these fellows want but to sleep
without hindrance or compulsion, and after they
have arisen, to yawn at their ease, and wash their
faces; then to write and read what they please,
then to babble something or other, to the applause
of their friends, no matter what they say; then to go
out for a stroll, and after a short walk to take a bath;
then to eat, then to seek their rest, and sleep in such
a bed as you might expect such persons to enjoy—
why should I say the word? For you can infer what
it is like.

Come now, do you also tell me your style of life,
the one on which you have set your heart, you eager
follower of the truth, and of Socrates, and of Diogenes!
What do *you* want to do in Athens? Just what I

41 ταῦτα αὐτά; μή τι ἕτερα; τί οὖν Στωικὸν σαυτὸν
εἶναι λέγεις; εἶτα οἱ μὲν τῆς Ῥωμαίων πολιτείας
καταψευδόμενοι κολάζονται πικρῶς, τοὺς δ'
οὕτως μεγάλου καὶ σεμνοῦ καταψευδομένους
πράγματος καὶ ὀνόματος ἀθώους ἀπαλλάττεσθαι
42 δεῖ; ἢ τοῦτό γε οὐ δυνατόν, ἀλλ' ὁ νόμος θεῖος
καὶ ἰσχυρὸς καὶ ἀναπόδραστος οὗτός ἐστιν ὁ τὰς
μεγίστας εἰσπρασσόμενος κολάσεις παρὰ τῶν τὰ
43 μέγιστα ἁμαρτανόντων; τί γὰρ λέγει; " ὁ
προσποιούμενος τὰ μηδὲν πρὸς αὑτὸν ἔστω
ἀλαζών, ἔστω κενόδοξος· ὁ ἀπειθῶν τῇ θείᾳ
διοικήσει ἔστω ταπεινός, ἔστω δοῦλος, λυπείσθω,
φθονείτω, ἐλεείτω, τὸ κεφάλαιον πάντων, δυστυχείτω, θρηνείτω."

44 Τί οὖν; θέλεις με τὸν δεῖνα θεραπεύειν;
ἐπὶ θύρας¹ αὐτοῦ πορεύεσθαι;—Εἰ τοῦτο αἱρεῖ
λόγος, ὑπὲρ τῆς πατρίδος, ὑπὲρ τῶν συγγενῶν,
ὑπὲρ ἀνθρώπων, διὰ τί μὴ ἀπέλθῃς; ἀλλ' ἐπὶ
μὲν τὰς τοῦ σκυτέως οὐκ αἰσχύνῃ πορευόμενος,
ὅταν δέῃ ὑποδημάτων, οὐδ' ἐπὶ τὰς τοῦ κηπουροῦ,
ὅταν θιδράκων, ἐπὶ δὲ τὰς τῶν πλουσίων, ὅταν
45 τινὸς ὁμοίου δέῃ;—Ναί· τὸν σκυτέα γὰρ οὐ
θαυμάζω.—Μηδὲ τὸν πλούσιον.—Οὐδὲ τὸν
κηπουρὸν κολακεύσω.—Μηδὲ τὸν πλούσιον.
46 Πῶς οὖν τύχω οὗ δέομαι;—Ἐγὼ δέ σοι λέγω
ὅτι " ὡς τευξόμενος ἀπέρχου"; οὐχὶ δὲ μόνον,
47 ἵνα πράξῃς τὸ σαυτῷ πρέπον;—Τί οὖν ἔτι
πορεύομαι;—Ἵν' ἀπέλθῃς, ἵνα ἀποδεδωκὼς ᾖς

¹ Wolf: θύραις S.

---

¹ Because it was a disturbing passion which interfered
with serenity.

have described? Nothing at all different? Why, then, do you call yourself a Stoic? Well, but those who falsely claim Roman citizenship are severely punished, and ought those who falsely claim so great and so dignified a calling and title to get off scot-free? Or is that impossible? whereas the divine and mighty and inescapable law is the law which exacts the greatest penalties from those who are guilty of the greatest offences. Now what are its terms? "Let him who makes pretence to things which in no wise concern him be a braggart, let him be a vainglorious man; let him who disobeys the divine governance be abject, be a slave, suffer grief, envy, pity,[1]—in a word, be miserable, and lament."

Well, what then? Do you want me to pay court to So-and-so? go to his front-door?[2]—If reason so decides, for the sake of your country, your kinsmen, mankind in general, why not go? Why, you are not ashamed to go to the door of the cobbler when you need shoes, nor to that of the market-gardener when you need lettuce; and are you ashamed to go to the door of the rich when you want something that rich men have?— Very true, for as to the cobbler, I do not have to admire him.—Don't admire the rich man, either.—And I shall not have to flatter the market-gardener.—Don't flatter the rich man either.—How, then, shall I get what I need?—Am I telling you, "Go like a man who is certain to get what he wants," and not simply, " Go in order to do what becomes you"? —Why, then, do I go at all?—So as to have gone, so as to have performed the function of the citizen that

---

[2] The transition is most abrupt, but obviously the interlocutor has been expected by his friends to pay court to some rich and influential man.

τὰ τοῦ πολίτου ἔργα, τὰ ἀδελφοῦ, τὰ φίλου.

48 καὶ λοιπὸν μέμνησο, ὅτι πρὸς σκυτέα ἀφῖξαι, πρὸς λαχανοπώλην, οὐδενὸς μεγάλου ἢ σεμνοῦ ἔχοντα τὴν ἐξουσίαν, κἂν αὐτὸ πολλοῦ πωλῇ. ὡς ἐπὶ τὰς θίδρακας[1] ἀπέρχῃ· ὀβολοῦ γάρ εἰσιν,

49 ταλάντου δ' οὐκ εἰσίν. οὕτως κἀνταῦθα. τοῦ ἐπὶ θύρας ἐλθεῖν ἄξιον τὸ πρᾶγμα· ἔστω, ἀφίξομαι. τοῦ διαλεχθῆναι οὕτως· ἔστω, διαλεχθήσομαι. ἀλλὰ καὶ τὴν χεῖρα δεῖ καταφιλῆσαι καὶ θωπεῦσαι δι' ἐπαίνου. ἄπαγε, ταλάντου ἐστίν· οὐ λυσιτελεῖ μοι οὐδὲ τῇ πόλει οὐδὲ τοῖς φίλοις ἀπολέσαι καὶ πολίτην ἀγαθὸν καὶ φίλον.

50 Ἀλλὰ δόξεις μὴ προτεθυμῆσθαι μὴ ἀνύσας. πάλιν ἐπελάθου, τίνος ἕνεκα ἐλήλυθας ; οὐκ οἶσθ', ὅτι ἀνὴρ καλὸς καὶ ἀγαθὸς οὐδὲν ποιεῖ τοῦ δόξαι ἕνεκα, ἀλλὰ τοῦ πεπρᾶχθαι καλῶς ;—

51 Τί οὖν ὄφελος αὐτῷ τοῦ πρᾶξαι καλῶς ;—Τί δ' ὄφελος τῷ γράφοντι τὸ Δίωνος ὄνομα, ὡς χρὴ γράφειν ; αὐτὸ τὸ γράψαι.—Ἔπαθλον οὖν οὐδέν ; —Σὺ δὲ ζητεῖς ἔπαθλον ἀνδρὶ ἀγαθῷ μεῖζον τοῦ

52 τὰ καλὰ καὶ δίκαια πράττειν ; ἐν Ὀλυμπίᾳ δ' οὐδεὶς ἄλλο οὐδέν, ἀλλ' ἀρκεῖν σοι δοκεῖ τὸ ἐστεφανῶσθαι Ὀλύμπια. οὕτως σοι μικρὸν καὶ οὐδενὸς ἄξιον εἶναι φαίνεται τὸ εἶναι καλὸν καὶ ἀγαθὸν καὶ εὐδαίμονα ; πρὸς ταῦτα ὑπὸ

53 θεῶν εἰς τὴν πόλιν ταύτην εἰσηγμένος καὶ ἤδη τῶν ἀνδρὸς ἔργων[2] ὀφείλων ἅπτεσθαι τιτθὰς

---

[1] Schenkl: θρίδακας S.
[2] Wolf, after Schegk : ἀνδροέργων S.

---

[1] i.e. the world.

you are, of a brother, of a friend. And furthermore, remember that you have come to see a cobbler, a vegetable-dealer, a man who has authority over nothing great or important, even if he sell it for a high price. You are going, as it were, for heads of lettuce; they are worth an obol, not a talent. So it is in our life also. The matter in hand is worth going to a person's door about; very well, I will go. It is also worth an interview; very well, I will interview him about it. Yes, but I will have to kiss his hand also, and flatter him with words of praise. Go to! that is paying a talent for a head of lettuce! It is not profitable to me, nor to the State, nor to my friends, to ruin by so acting a good citizen and friend.

Yes, but if you fail, people will think that you didn't try hard. Have you gone and forgotten again why you went? Don't you know that a good and excellent man does nothing for the sake of appearances, but only for the sake of having acted right?—What good does he get, then, from acting right?—And what good does the person get for writing the name " Dio " as it ought to be written ? The mere fact of writing it that way.—Is there, then, no further reward ?—And are you looking for some further reward in the case of a good man, a reward which is greater than the doing of what is fine and right? At Olympia nobody wants anything else, but you feel content with having received an Olympic crown. Does it seem to you so small and worthless a thing to be good, and excellent, and happy? Therefore, when you have been introduced into this city-state [1] by the gods, and find it now your duty to lay hand to the work of a man, do you

ἐπιποθεῖς [1] καὶ μάμμην καὶ κάμπτει σε καὶ ἀπο-
θηλύνει κλαίοντα γύναια μωρά; οὕτως οὐδέποτε
παύσει παιδίον ὢν νήπιον; οὐκ οἶσθ', ὅτι ὁ τὰ
παιδίου ποιῶν ὅσῳ πρεσβύτερος τοσούτῳ γελοιό-
τερος;

54 Ἐν Ἀθήναις δ' οὐδένα ἑώρας εἰς οἶκον αὐτοῦ
φοιτῶν;—Ὃν ἐβουλόμην.—Καὶ ἐνθάδε τοῦτον
θέλε ὁρᾶν καὶ ὃν βούλει ὄψει· μόνον μὴ ταπεινῶς,
μὴ μετ' ὀρέξεως ἢ ἐκκλίσεως καὶ ἔσται τὰ σὰ
55 καλῶς. τοῦτο δ' οὐκ ἐν τῷ ἐλθεῖν ἐστιν οὐδ'
ἐν τῷ ἐπὶ θύραις στῆναι, ἀλλ' ἔνδον ἐν τοῖς
56 δόγμασιν. ὅταν τὰ ἐκτὸς καὶ ἀπροαίρετα ἠτι-
μακὼς ᾖς καὶ μηδὲν αὐτῶν σὸν ἡγημένος, μόνα
δ' ἐκεῖνα σά, τὸ κρῖναι καλῶς, τὸ ὑπολαβεῖν, τὸ
ὁρμῆσαι, τὸ ὀρεχθῆναι, τὸ ἐκκλῖναι, ποῦ ἔτι
κολακείας τόπος, ποῦ ταπεινοφροσύνης; τί ἔτι
57 ποθεῖς τὴν ἡσυχίαν τὴν ἐκεῖ, τί τοὺς συνήθεις
τόπους; ἔκδεξαι βραχὺ καὶ τούτους πάλιν ἕξεις
συνήθεις. εἶτα ἂν οὕτως ἀγεννῶς ἔχῃς, πάλιν
καὶ τούτων ἀπαλλαττόμενος κλαῖε καὶ στένε.

58 Πῶς οὖν γένωμαι φιλόστοργος;—Ὡς γενναῖος,
ὡς εὐτυχής· οὐδέποτε γὰρ αἱρεῖ [2] ὁ λόγος ταπεινὸν εἶναι οὐδὲ κατακλᾶσθαι οὐδ' ἐξ ἄλλου
κρέμασθαι οὐδὲ μέμψασθαί ποτε θεὸν ἢ ἄνθρω-
59 πον. οὕτως μοι γίνου φιλόστοργος ὡς ταῦτα
τηρήσων· εἰ δὲ διὰ τὴν φιλοστοργίαν ταύτην,
ἥντινά [3] ποτε καὶ καλεῖς φιλοστοργίαν, δοῦλος

[1] Salmasius suggests ἔτι ποθεῖς. [2] Upton: ἐρεῖ S.
[3] Upton's "codex": ταῦτα· τὴν τινά S.

yearn for nurses and the breast, and does the weeping of poor silly women move you and make you
effeminate? And so will you never get over being
an infant? Don't you know that, when a person
acts like a child, the older he is the more ridiculous
he is?

In Athens did you see nobody when you went to
his house?—Yes, the man I wanted to see.—Here also
make up your mind to see this man, and you will
see the man you want; only do not go humbly, not
with desire or aversion, and all will be well with
you. But this result is not to be found by mere
going, nor by standing at gates, but in one's
judgements within. When you have contemned
things external and outside the province of your
moral purpose, and have come to regard none of
them as your own, but only the being right in
judgement, in thinking, in choosing, in desiring,
in avoiding,—where is there any longer room for
flattery, where for an abject spirit? Why any
longer yearn for the quiet you enjoyed there, or
your familiar haunts? Wait a little while and you
will find the places here familiar in their turn. And
then, if you are so ignoble in spirit, weep and wail
again when you leave these too!

How, then, shall I become affectionate?—As a
man of noble spirit, as one who is fortunate; for
it is against all reason to be abject, or broken in
spirit, or to depend on something other than yourself, or even to blame either God or man. I would
have you become affectionate in such a way as to
maintain at the same time all these rules; if, however, by virtue of this natural affection, whatever it
is you call by that name, you are going to be a

μέλλεις εἶναι καὶ ἄθλιος, οὐ λυσιτελεῖ φιλό-
60 στοργον εἶναι. καὶ τί κωλύει φιλεῖν τινὰ ὡς
θνητόν, ὡς ἀποδημητικόν; ἢ Σωκράτης οὐκ
ἐφίλει τοὺς παῖδας τοὺς ἑαυτοῦ; ἀλλ' ὡς ἐλεύθερος, ὡς μεμνημένος, ὅτι πρῶτον δεῖ θεοῖς εἶναι
61 φίλον. διὰ τοῦτο οὐδὲν παρέβη τῶν πρεπόντων
ἀνδρὶ ἀγαθῷ οὔτ' ἀπολογούμενος οὔθ' ὑποτι-
μώμενος οὔτ' ἔτι πρόσθεν βουλεύων ἢ στρατευό-
62 μενος. ἡμεῖς δὲ πάσης προφάσεως πρὸς τὸ
ἀγεννεῖς εἶναι εὐποροῦμεν, οἱ μὲν διὰ παῖδα,
63 οἱ δὲ διὰ μητέρα, ἄλλοι δὲ δι' ἀδελφούς. δι'
οὐδένα δὲ προσήκει δυστυχεῖν, ἀλλὰ εὐτυχεῖν
διὰ πάντας, μάλιστα δὲ διὰ τὸν θεὸν τὸν ἐπὶ
64 τοῦτο ἡμᾶς κατασκευάσαντα. ἄγε, Διογένης δ'
οὐκ ἐφίλει οὐδένα, ὃς οὕτως ἥμερος ἦν καὶ
φιλάνθρωπος, ὥστε ὑπὲρ τοῦ κοινοῦ τῶν ἀνθρώπων τοσούτους πόνους καὶ ταλαιπωρίας τοῦ
σώματος ἄσμενος ἀναδέχεσθαι; ἀλλ' ἐφίλει
65 πῶς; ὡς τοῦ Διὸς διάκονον ἔδει, ἅμα μὲν κηδόμενος, ἅμα δ' ὡς τῷ θεῷ ὑποτεταγμένος. διὰ
66 τοῦτο πᾶσα γῆ πατρὶς ἦν ἐκείνῳ μόνῳ, ἐξαίρετος
δ' οὐδεμία· καὶ ἁλοὺς οὐκ ἐπόθει τὰς Ἀθήνας
οὐδὲ τοὺς ἐκεῖ συνήθεις καὶ φίλους, ἀλλ' αὐτοῖς
τοῖς πειραταῖς συνήθης ἐγίνετο καὶ ἐπανορθοῦν
ἐπειρᾶτο. καὶ πραθεὶς ὕστερον ἐν Κορίνθῳ
διῆγεν οὕτως ὡς πρόσθεν ἐν Ἀθήναις καὶ εἰς
Περραιβοὺς δ' ἂν ἀπελθὼν ὡσαύτως εἶχεν.

slave and miserable, it does not profit you to be
affectionate.   And what keeps you from loving a
person as one subject to death, as one who may leave
you?   Did not Socrates love his own children?   But
in a free spirit, as one who remembers that it was his
first duty to be a friend to the gods.   That is why
he succeeded in everything that becomes a good
man, both in making his defence, and in assessing
his own penalty, and before that time in his services
as senator or soldier.   But *we* abound in all manner
of excuses for being ignoble; with some it is a
child, with others a mother, and then again it is
brothers.   But it is not becoming for us to be unhappy on any person's account, but to be happy
because of all, and above all others because of God,
who has made us for this end.   Come, was there
anybody that Diogenes did not love, a man who was
so gentle and kind-hearted that he gladly took upon
himself all those troubles and physical hardships for
the sake of the common weal?   But what was the
manner of his loving?   As became a servant of Zeus,
caring for men indeed, but at the same time subject
unto God.   That is why for him alone the whole
world, and no special place, was his fatherland;
and when he had been taken prisoner he did not
hanker for Athens nor his acquaintances and friends
there, but he got on good terms with the pirates
and tried [1] to reform them.   And later, when he was
sold into slavery at Corinth he kept on living there
just as he had formerly lived at Athens; yes, and
if he had gone off to the Perrhaebians he would
have acted in quite the same way.   That is how

---

[1] The humorous touch here in the word-jingle πειραταῖς
and ἐπειρᾶτο is worthy of note, but hard to reproduce.   For
the incident in question see IV. 1, 115 f.

67 οὕτως ἐλευθερία γίνεται. διὰ τοῦτο ἔλεγεν ὅτι
"ἐξ οὗ μ' Ἀντισθένης ἠλευθέρωσεν, οὐκέτι ἐδού-
68 λευσα." πῶς ἠλευθέρωσεν ; ἄκουε, τί λέγει· "ἐδί-
δαξέν με τὰ ἐμὰ καὶ τὰ οὐκ ἐμά. κτῆσις οὐκ ἐμή·
συγγενεῖς, οἰκεῖοι, φίλοι, φήμη, συνήθεις τόποι,
69 διατριβή, πάντα ταῦτα ὅτι ἀλλότρια. ʿ σὸν οὖν
τί ; χρῆσις φαντασιῶν.ʾ ταύτην ἔδειξέν μοι ὅτι
ἀκώλυτον ἔχω, ἀνανάγκαστον· οὐδεὶς ἐμποδίσαι
δύναται, οὐδεὶς βιάσασθαι ἄλλως χρήσασθαι ἢ ὡς
70 θέλω. τίς οὖν ἔτι ἔχει μου ἐξουσίαν ; Φίλιππος
ἢ Ἀλέξανδρος ἢ Περδίκκας ἢ ὁ μέγας βασιλεύς ;
πόθεν αὐτοῖς ; τὸν γὰρ ὑπ' ἀνθρώπου μέλλοντα
ἡττᾶσθαι πολὺ πρότερον ὑπὸ τῶν πραγμάτων
71 δεῖ ἡττᾶσθαι." οὗτινος οὖν οὐχ ἡδονὴ κρείττων
ἐστίν, οὐ πόνος, οὐ δόξα, οὐ πλοῦτος, δύναται δ',
ὅταν αὐτῷ δόξῃ, τὸ σωμάτιον ὅλον προσπτύσας
τινὶ ἀπελθεῖν, τίνος ἔτι οὗτος δοῦλός ἐστιν, τίνι
72 ὑποτέτακται ; εἰ δ' ἡδέως ἐν Ἀθήναις διῆγεν καὶ
ἥττητο ταύτης τῆς διατριβῆς, ἐπὶ παντὶ ἂν ἦν
τὰ ἐκείνου πράγματα, ὁ ἰσχυρότερος κύριος ἂν
73 ἦν λυπῆσαι αὐτόν. πῶς ἂν δοκεῖς τοὺς πειρατὰς
ἐκολάκευεν, ἵν' αὐτὸν Ἀθηναίων τινὶ πωλήσωσιν,
ἵν' ἴδῃ ποτὲ τὸν Πειραιᾶ τὸν καλὸν καὶ τὰ μακρὰ
74 τείχη καὶ τὴν ἀκρόπολιν ; τίς ὢν ἴδῃς, ἀνδρά-
75 ποδον ; δοῦλος καὶ ταπεινός· καὶ τί σοι ὄφελος ;
—Οὔ· ἀλλ' ἐλεύθερος.—Δεῖξον, πῶς ἐλεύθερος.

---

[1] His teacher, the famous philosopher.
[2] Of Persia.
[3] Perhaps a reference to the story that Anaxarchus, when
Nicocreon ordered that his tongue be cut out, bit it off and
spat it in the other's face. Diogenes Laertius, 9, 59.

freedom is achieved. That is why he used to say, "From the time that Antisthenes[1] set me free, I have ceased to be a slave." How did Antisthenes set him free? Listen to what Diogenes says. "He taught me what was mine, and what was not mine. Property is not mine; kinsmen, members of my household, friends, reputation, familiar places, converse with men—all these are not my own. 'What, then, *is* yours? Power to deal with external impressions.' He showed me that I possess this beyond all hindrance and constraint; no one can hamper me; no one can force me to deal with them otherwise than as I will. Who, then, has authority over me? Philip, or Alexander, or Perdiccas, or the Great King?[2] Where can they get it? For the man who is destined to be overpowered by a man must long before that have been overpowered by things." Therefore, the man over whom pleasure has no power, nor evil, nor fame, nor wealth, and who, whenever it seems good to him, can spit his whole paltry body into some oppressor's face[3] and depart from this life—whose slave can he any longer be, whose subject? But if he had gone on living pleasantly in Athens, and had been enamoured of his life there, his fortune would have been in every man's control, and the man who was stronger than he would have had power to cause him grief. How do you imagine he would have wheedled the pirates to sell him to some Athenian, so that he might some time see the beautiful Piraeus, and the Long Walls and the Acropolis! Who are you that you should see them, slave? A thrall and a person of abject spirit; and what good are they to you?—No, not a slave, but a free man.—Show me how you are free.

ἰδοὺ ἐπείληπταί σου τίς ποτε οὗτος, ὁ ἐξάγων σε
ἀπὸ τῆς συνήθους σοι διατριβῆς καὶ λέγει
"δοῦλος ἐμὸς εἶ· ἐπ' ἐμοὶ γάρ ἐστι κωλῦσαί σε
διάγειν ὡς θέλεις, ἐπ' ἐμοὶ τὸ ἀνεῖναί σε, τὸ
ταπεινοῦν· ὅταν θέλω, πάλιν εὐφραίνῃ καὶ
76 μετέωρος πορεύῃ εἰς 'Αθήνας." τί λέγεις πρὸς
τοῦτον τὸν δουλαγωγοῦντά σε; ποῖον αὐτῷ
καρπιστὴν δίδως; ἢ οὐδ' ὅλως ἀντιβλέπεις, ἀλλ'
77 ἀφεὶς τοὺς πολλοὺς λόγους ἱκετεύεις, ἵνα ἀφεθῇς;
ἄνθρωπε, εἰς φυλακήν σε δεῖ χαίροντα ἀπιέναι,
σπεύδοντα, φθάνοντα τοὺς ἀπάγοντας. εἶτά μοι
σὺ μὲν ἐν 'Ρώμῃ διάγειν ὀκνεῖς, τὴν 'Ελλάδα
ποθεῖς; ὅταν δ' ἀποθνήσκειν δέῃ, καὶ τότε μέλλεις ἡμῶν κατακλαίειν, ὅτι τὰς 'Αθήνας οὐ
μέλλεις βλέπειν καὶ ἐν Λυκείῳ οὐ περιπατήσεις;
78 'Επὶ τοῦτο ἀπεδήμησας; τούτου ἕνεκα ἐζήτη-
σάς τινι συμβαλεῖν, ἵν' ὠφεληθῇς ὑπ' αὐτοῦ;
ποίαν ὠφέλειαν; συλλογισμοὺς ἵν' ἀναλύσῃς
ἐκτικώτερον ἢ ἐφοδεύσῃς ὑποθετικούς; καὶ διὰ
ταύτην τὴν αἰτίαν ἀδελφὸν ἀπέλιπες, πατρίδα,
φίλους, οἰκείους, ἵνα ταῦτα μαθὼν ἐπανέλθῃς;
79 ὥστ' οὐχ ὑπὲρ εὐσταθείας ἀπεδήμεις, οὐχ ὑπὲρ
ἀταραξίας, οὐχ ἵν' ἀβλαβὴς γενόμενος μηκέτι
μηδένα μέμφῃ, μηδενὶ ἐγκαλῇς, μηδείς σε ἀδικῇ
καὶ οὕτως τὰς σχέσεις ἀποσῴζῃς ἀπαραποδίσ-
80 τως; καλὴν ἐστείλω ταύτην τὴν ἐμπορίαν,
συλλογισμοὺς καὶ μεταπίπτοντας καὶ ὑποθε-

See, some person or other has laid hands on you—
the man who takes you away from your accustomed
way of life, and says, "You are my slave; for it is
in my power to prevent you from living as you will,
it is in my power to lighten your servitude, or to
humble you; whenever I wish, you can be happy
again, and go off to Athens in high spirits." What
do you say to this man who makes you his
slave? Whom have you to offer him as your
emancipator? Or do you not even look him in the
face at all, but cutting all argument short do you
implore him to set you free? Man, you ought to
go gladly to prison, in haste, outstripping those
who lead you away. And then, I do beseech you,
are you loath to live in Rome, and do you yearn
for Greece? And when you have to die, then also,
I suppose, will you weep all over us, because you are
never going to see Athens again or stroll in the
Lyceum?

Was that what you went abroad for? Was it for this
that you sought to meet someone—that he might do
you good? Good indeed! That you might analyse
syllogisms more readily, or run down hypothetical
arguments? It was for *this* reason, was it, you left
brother, country, friends, and those of your own
household—so as to return with *this* kind of learning?
And so you did not go abroad to acquire constancy
of character, or peace of mind; not to become secure
yourself and thenceforward blame and find fault
with no man; not to make it impossible for another
to do you wrong, and so maintain without hindrance
your relations in society? A fine exchange of goods
this which you have achieved, syllogisms, and arguments with equivocal and hypothetical premisses!

τικούς· κἂν σοι φανῇ, ἐν τῇ ἀγορᾷ καθίσας
81 πρόγραψον ὡς οἱ φαρμακοπῶλαι. οὐκ ἀρνήσῃ
καὶ ὅσα ἔμαθες εἰδέναι, ἵνα μὴ διαβάλῃς τὰ
θεωρήματα ὡς ἄχρηστα; τί σοι κακὸν ἐποίησεν
φιλοσοφία; τί σε ἠδίκησε Χρύσιππος, ἵν' αὐτοῦ
τοὺς πόνους ἔργῳ αὐτὸς ἀχρήστους ἐξελέγχῃς;
οὐκ ἤρκει σοι τὰ ἐκεῖ κακά, ὅσα εἶχες αἴτια τοῦ
λυπεῖσθαι καὶ πενθεῖν, εἰ καὶ μὴ ἀπεδήμησας,
82 ἀλλὰ πλείω προσέλαβες; κἂν ἄλλους πάλιν
ἔχῃς συνήθεις καὶ φίλους, ἕξεις πλείονα τοῦ
οἰμώζειν αἴτια, κἂν πρὸς ἄλλην χώραν προσπαθῇς. τί οὖν ζῇς; ἵνα λύπας ἄλλας ἐπ' ἄλλαις
83 περιβάλῃ, δι' ἃς ἀτυχεῖς; εἶτά μοι καλεῖς τοῦτο
φιλοστοργίαν; ποίαν, ἄνθρωπε, φιλοστοργίαν;
εἰ ἀγαθόν ἐστιν, οὐδενὸς κακοῦ αἴτιον γίνεται· εἰ
κακόν ἐστιν, οὐδέν μοι καὶ αὐτῇ. ἐγὼ πρὸς τὰ
ἀγαθὰ τὰ ἐμαυτοῦ πέφυκα, πρὸς κακὰ οὐ πέφυκα.

84 Τίς οὖν ἡ πρὸς τοῦτο ἄσκησις; πρῶτον μὲν ἡ
ἀνωτάτω καὶ κυριωτάτη καὶ εὐθὺς ὥσπερ ἐν
πύλαις, ὅταν τινὶ προσπάσχῃς, ὡς[1] οὐδενὶ τῶν
ἀναφαιρέτων, ἀλλά τινι τοιούτῳ γένει, οἷόν ἐστι
χύτρα, οἷον ὑάλινον ποτήριον, ἵν' ὅταν καταγῇ,
85 μεμνημένος μὴ ταραχθῇς. οὕτως καὶ ἐνθάδ', ἐὰν
παιδίον σαυτοῦ καταφιλῇς, ἐὰν ἀδελφόν, ἐὰν
φίλον, μηδέποτε ἐπιδῷς τὴν φαντασίαν εἰς ἅπαν
μηδὲ τὴν διάχυσιν ἐάσῃς προελθεῖν ἐφ' ὅσον αὐτὴ
θέλει, ἀλλ' ἀντίσπασον, κώλυσον, οἷον οἱ τοῖς

[1] ὡς added by Sb.

Yes, and if you see fit, seat yourself in the market-place, and hang out a sign, as the drug-peddlers do. Ought you not rather to deny that you know even all you have learned, so as not to bring your philosophical precepts into ill repute as being useless? What harm has philosophy done you? How has Chrysippus wronged you that you should prove by your own conduct his labours to be useless? Were not the ills at home enough for you, all that you had to cause you grief and sorrow, even if you had not gone abroad, but did you add yet others in addition to them? And if you get other intimates and friends again, you will have more reasons for lamentation, yes, and if you get attached to another land. Why, then, live? Is it to involve yourself in one grief after another that makes you miserable? And then, I ask you, do you call this natural affection? Natural affection forsooth, man! If it is good, it is the source of no evil; if it is evil, I have nothing to do with it. I am born for the things that are good and belong to me, not for things evil.

What, then, is the proper discipline for this? In the first place, the highest and principal discipline, and one that stands at the very gates of the subject, is this: Whenever you grow attached to something, do not act as though it were one of those things that cannot be taken away, but as though it were something like a jar or a crystal goblet, so that when it breaks you will remember what it was like, and not be troubled. So too in life; if you kiss your child, your brother, your friend, never allow your fancy free rein, nor your exuberant spirits to go as far as they like, but hold them back, stop them, just like those who

θριαμβεύουσιν ἐφεστῶτες ὄπισθεν καὶ ὑπομιμνή-
86 σκοντες, ὅτι ἄνθρωποί εἰσιν. τοιοῦτόν τι καὶ
σὺ ὑπομίμνησκε σεαυτόν, ὅτι θνητὸν φιλεῖς,
οὐδὲν τῶν σεαυτοῦ φιλεῖς· ἐπὶ τοῦ παρόντος σοι
δέδοται, οὐκ ἀναφαίρετον οὐδ᾽ εἰς ἅπαν, ἀλλ᾽ ὡς
σῦκον, ὡς σταφυλή, τῇ τεταγμένῃ ὥρᾳ τοῦ ἔτους·
87 ἂν δὲ χειμῶνος ἐπιποθῇς, μωρὸς εἶ. οὕτως κἂν
τὸν υἱὸν ἢ τὸν φίλον τότε ποθῇς, ὅτε οὐ δέδοταί
σοι, ἴσθι, ὅτι χειμῶνος σῦκον ἐπιποθεῖς. οἷον
γάρ ἐστι χειμὼν πρὸς σῦκον, τοιοῦτόν ἐστι πᾶσα
ἡ ἀπὸ τῶν ὅλων περίστασις πρὸς τὰ κατ᾽ αὐτὴν
ἀναιρούμενα.

88 Καὶ λοιπὸν ἐν αὐτοῖς οἷς χαίρεις τινί, τὰς
ἐναντίας φαντασίας σαυτῷ πρόβαλε.[1] τί κακόν ἐστι μεταξὺ καταφιλοῦντα τὸ παιδίον
ἐπιψελλίζοντα λέγειν "αὔριον ἀποθανῇ," τῷ
φίλῳ ὡσαύτως "αὔριον ἀποδημήσεις ἢ σὺ ἢ
89 ἐγὼ καὶ οὐκέτι ὀψόμεθα ἀλλήλους";—Ἀλλὰ
δύσφημά ἐστι ταῦτα.—Καὶ γὰρ τῶν ἐπαοιδῶν
ἔνιαι, ἀλλ᾽ ὅτι ὠφελοῦσιν, οὐκ ἐπιστρέφομαι,
μόνον ὠφελείτω. σὺ δὲ δύσφημα καλεῖς ἄλλα ἢ
τὰ κακοῦ τινὸς σημαντικά; δύσφημόν ἐστι δειλία,
90 δύσφημον ἀγέννεια, πένθος, λύπη, ἀναισχυντία·
ταῦτα τὰ ὀνόματα δύσφημά ἐστιν. καίτοι γε
οὐδὲ ταῦτα ὀκνεῖν δεῖ φθέγγεσθαι ὑπὲρ φυλακῆς

---

[1] Schenkl: πρόσβαλε S.

---

[1] Among the means of warding off the evil eye from the
triumphator was this, that a slave rode behind him in his
triumphal car, and in the midst of the acclamations of the

stand behind generals when they ride in triumph, and keep reminding them that they are mortal.[1] In such fashion do you too remind yourself that the object of your love is mortal; it is not one of your own possessions; it has been given you for the present, not inseparably nor for ever, but like a fig, or a cluster of grapes, at a fixed season of the year, and that if you hanker for it in the winter, you are a fool. If in this way you long for your son, or your friend, at a time when he is not given to you, rest assured that you are hankering for a fig in winter-time. For as winter-time is to a fig, so is every state of affairs, which arises out of the universe, in relation to the things which are destroyed in accordance with that same state of affairs.

Furthermore, at the very moment when you are taking delight in something, call to mind the opposite impressions. What harm is there if you whisper to yourself, at the very moment you are kissing your child, and say, "To-morrow you will die"? So likewise to your friend, "To-morrow you will go abroad, or I shall, and we shall never see each other again"?—Nay, but these are words of bad omen.—Yes, and so are certain incantations, but because they do good, I do not care about that, only let the incantation do us good. But do you call any things ill-omened except those which signify some evil for us? Cowardice is ill-omened, a mean spirit, grief, sorrow, shamelessness; these are words of ill-omen. And yet we ought not to hesitate to utter even these words, in order to guard

people kept saying: "Look behind you, and remember that you are a mortal." For the evidence and literature, see J. Marquardt: *Römische Staatsverwaltung*, II. 568-9.

91 τῶν πραγμάτων. δύσφημον δέ μοι λέγεις ὄνομα
φυσικοῦ τινὸς πράγματος σημαντικόν; λέγε
δύσφημον εἶναι καὶ τὸ θερισθῆναι τοὺς στάχυας·
ἀπώλειαν γὰρ σημαίνει τῶν σταχύων· ἀλλ'
οὐχὶ τοῦ κόσμου. λέγε δύσφημον καὶ τὸ φυλ-
λορροεῖν καὶ τὸ ἰσχάδα γίνεσθαι ἀντὶ σύκου καὶ
92 ἀσταφίδας ἐκ σταφυλῆς. πάντα γὰρ ταῦτα τῶν
προτέρων εἰσὶν εἰς ἕτερα μεταβολαί· οὐκ ἀπώλεια, ἀλλὰ τεταγμένη τις οἰκονομία καὶ διοίκησις.
93 τοῦτ' ἔστιν ἀποδημία, μεταβολὴ[1] μικρά· τοῦτο
θάνατος, μεταβολὴ μείζων ἐκ τοῦ νῦν ὄντος οὐκ[2]
94 εἰς τὸ μὴ ὄν, ἀλλ' εἰς τὸ νῦν μὴ ὄν.—Οὐκέτι οὖν
ἔσομαι;—Οὐκ ἔσει· ἀλλ' ἄλλο τι οὗ νῦν ὁ
κόσμος χρείαν ἔχει. καὶ γὰρ σὺ ἐγένου οὐχ ὅτε
σὺ ἠθέλησας, ἀλλ' ὅτε ὁ κόσμος χρείαν ἔσχεν.

95 Διὰ τοῦτο ὁ καλὸς καὶ ἀγαθὸς μεμνημένος, τίς
τ' ἐστὶ καὶ πόθεν ἐλήλυθεν καὶ ὑπὸ τίνος γέγονεν,
πρὸς μόνῳ τούτῳ ἐστίν, πῶς τὴν αὑτοῦ χώραν
ἐκπληρώσῃ εὐτάκτως καὶ εὐπειθῶς τῷ θεῷ.
96 "ἔτι με μεῖναι[3] θέλεις; ὡς ἐλεύθερος, ὡς
γενναῖος, ὡς σὺ ἠθέλησας· σὺ γάρ με ἀκώ-
97 λυτον ἐποίησας ἐν τοῖς ἐμοῖς. ἀλλ' οὐκέτι μου
χρείαν ἔχεις; καλῶς σοι γένοιτο· καὶ μέχρι νῦν
διὰ σὲ ἔμενον, δι' ἄλλον οὐδένα, καὶ νῦν σοι πει-

---

[1] καί before this word was deleted by Upton.
[2] οὐκ added by *Sb*, a correction supported by the paraphrase of this passage in Marcus Aurelius, 11, 35.
[3] Reiske : μ' εἶναι *S*.

---

[1] This seems to me to be the most probable meaning of a
vexed passage. If any change is needed, which I doubt
(for ἄλλος with the simple genitive is abundantly attested,
at least in other authors), I should prefer to read ἄλλο τι ἢ

214

against the things themselves. Do you tell me
that any word is ill-omened which signifies some
process of nature? Say that also the harvesting of
ears of grain is ill-omened, for it signifies the
destruction of the ears; but not of the universe.
Say that also for leaves to fall is ill-omened, and
for the fresh fig to turn into a dried fig, and a
cluster of grapes to turn into raisins. For all these
things are changes of a preliminary state into
something else; it is not a case of destruction, but
a certain ordered dispensation and management.
This is what going abroad means, a slight change;
this is the meaning of death, a greater change of that
which now is, not into what is not, but into what is
not *now*.—Shall I, then, be no more?—No, you
will not be, but something else will be, something
different from that of which the universe now has
need.[1] And this is but reasonable, for you came
into being, not when *you* wanted, but when the
universe had need of you.

For this reason the good and excellent man,
bearing in mind who he is, and whence he has
come, and by whom he was created, centres his
attention on this and this only, how he may fill his
place in an orderly fashion, and with due obedience
to God. " Is it Thy will that I should still remain ?
I will remain as a free man, as a noble man, as Thou
didst wish it; for Thou hast made me free from
hindrance in what was mine own. And now hast
Thou no further need of me ? Be it well with Thee.
I have been waiting here until now because of Thee
and of none other, and now I obey Thee and depart."

οὗ, rather than to change οὐκ into οὖ, delete or transpose it,
or take νῦν in the sense of τότε.

98 θόμενος ἀπέρχομαι." "πῶς ἀπέρχῃ ; " "πάλιν
ὡς σὺ ἠθέλησας, ὡς ἐλεύθερος, ὡς ὑπηρέτης σός,
ὡς ᾐσθημένος σου τῶν προσταγμάτων καὶ ἀπαγο-
99 ρευμάτων. μέχρι δ᾽ ἂν οὗ διατρίβω ἐν τοῖς σοῖς, τίνα
με θέλεις εἶναι ; ἄρχοντα ἢ ἰδιώτην, βουλευτὴν ἢ
δημότην, στρατιώτην ἢ στρατηγόν, παιδευτὴν ἢ
οἰκοδεσπότην ; ἣν ἂν χώραν καὶ τάξιν ἐγχει-
ρίσῃς, ὡς λέγει ὁ Σωκράτης, μυριάκις ἀπο-
θανοῦμαι πρότερον ἢ ταύτην ἐγκαταλείψω.
100 ποῦ δέ μ᾽ εἶναι θέλεις ; ἐν Ῥώμῃ ἢ ἐν Ἀθήναις
ἢ ἐν Θήβαις ἢ ἐν Γυάροις ; μόνον ἐκεῖ μου
101 μέμνησο. ἄν μ᾽ ἐκεῖ πέμψῃς, ὅπου κατὰ φύσιν
διεξαγωγὴ οὐκ ἔστιν ἀνθρώπων, οὐ σοὶ ἀπειθῶν
ἔξειμι, ἀλλ᾽ ὡς σοῦ μοι σημαίνοντος τὸ ἀνακλητι-
κόν· οὐκ ἀπολείπω σε· μὴ γένοιτο· ἀλλ᾽ αἰσ-
102 θάνομαι, ὅτι μου χρείαν οὐκ ἔχεις. ἂν δὲ διδῶται
κατὰ φύσιν διεξαγωγή, οὐ ζητήσω ἄλλον τόπον[1]
ἢ ἐν ᾧ εἰμὶ ἢ ἄλλους ἀνθρώπους ἢ μεθ᾽ ὧν
εἰμί."

103 Ταῦτα νυκτός, ταῦτα ἡμέρας πρόχειρα ἔστω·
ταῦτα γράφειν, ταῦτα ἀναγιγνώσκειν· περὶ
τούτων τοὺς λόγους ποιεῖσθαι, αὐτὸν πρὸς αὑτόν,
πρὸς ἕτερον "μή τι ἔχεις μοι πρὸς τοῦτο βοηθῆσαι ; " καὶ πάλιν ἄλλῳ προσελθεῖν[2] καὶ ἄλλῳ.
104 εἶτα ἄν τι γένηται τῶν λεγομένων ἀβουλήτων,
εὐθὺς ἐκεῖνο πρῶτον ἐπικουφίσει σε, ὅτι οὐκ
105 ἀπροσδόκητον. μέγα γὰρ ἐπὶ πάντων τὸ "ᾔδειν

---

[1] τόπον added by Schweighäuser, after Schegk.
[2] Wolf, after Schegk : ἐλθεῖν S.

---

[1] A very free paraphrase of Plato, *Apology*, 28 D–29 A.

"How do you depart?" "Again, as Thou didst
wish it, as a free man, as Thy servant, as one who
has perceived Thy commands and Thy prohibitions.
But so long as I continue to live in Thy service,
what manner of man wouldst Thou have me be?
An official or a private citizen, a senator or one of
the common people, a soldier or a general, a teacher
or the head of a household? Whatsoever station
and post Thou assign me, I will die ten thousand
times, as Socrates says, or ever I abandon it.[1] And
where wouldst Thou have me be? In Rome, or in
Athens, or in Thebes, or in Gyara?[2] Only remember
me there. If Thou sendest me to a place where men
have no means of living in accordance with nature,
I shall depart this life, not in disobedience to Thee,
but as though Thou wert sounding for me the recall.
I do not abandon Thee—far be that from me! but
I perceive that Thou hast no need of me. Yet if
there be vouchsafed a means of living in accordance
with nature, I will seek no other place than that in
which I am, or other men than those who are now
my associates."

Have thoughts like these ready at hand by night
and by day; write them, read them, make your
conversation about them, communing with yourself,
or saying to another, "Can you give me some help
in this matter?" And again, go now to one man
and now to another. Then, if some one of those
things happens which are called undesirable, immediately the thought that it was not unexpected
will be the first thing to lighten the burden. For
in every case it is a great help to be able to say,
"I knew that the son whom I had begotten was

<hr>

[2] See on I. 24, 19.

θνητὸν γεγεννηκώς." οὕτως γὰρ ἐρεῖς καὶ ὅτι
"ᾔδειν θνητὸς ὤν," "ᾔδειν ἀποδημητικὸς ὤν,"
"ᾔδειν ἔκβλητος ὤν," "ᾔδειν εἰς φυλακὴν ἀπό-
106 τακτος ὤν." εἶτ' ἂν ἐπιστρέφῃς κατὰ σαυτὸν
καὶ ζητήσῃς τὴν χώραν, ἐξ ἧς ἐστὶ τὸ συμβεβη-
κός, εὐθὺς ἀναμνησθήσῃ, ὅτι "ἐκ τῆς τῶν
ἀπροαιρέτων, τῶν οὐκ ἐμῶν· τί οὖν πρὸς ἐμέ;"
107 εἶτα τὸ κυριώτατον "τίς δ' αὐτὸ καὶ ἐπιπέ-
πομφεν;" ὁ ἡγεμὼν ἢ ὁ στρατηγός, ἡ
πόλις, ὁ τῆς πόλεως νόμος. "δὸς οὖν αὐτό·
δεῖ γάρ με ἀεὶ τῷ νόμῳ πείθεσθαι ἐν παντί."
108 εἶθ' ὅταν σε ἡ φαντασία δάκνῃ (τοῦτο γὰρ
οὐκ ἐπὶ σοί), ἀναμάχου τῷ λόγῳ, καταγωνίζου
αὐτήν, μὴ ἐάσῃς ἐνισχύειν μηδὲ προάγειν ἐπὶ τὰ
ἑξῆς ἀναπλάσσουσαν ὅσα θέλει καὶ ὡς θέλει.
109 ἂν ἐν Γυάροις ᾖς, μὴ ἀνάπλασσε τὴν ἐν Ῥώμῃ
διατριβὴν καὶ ὅσαι διαχύσεις ἦσαν ἐκεῖ διάγοντι,
ὅσαι γένοιντ' ἂν ἐπανελθόντι· ἀλλ' ἐκεῖ τέτασο,
ὅπως δεῖ τὸν ἐν Γυάροις διάγοντα, ἐν Γυάροις
ἐρρωμένως διάγειν. κἂν ἐν Ῥώμῃ ᾖς, μὴ ἀνάπλασσε τὴν ἐν Ἀθήναις διατριβήν, ἀλλὰ περὶ
μόνης τῆς ἐκεῖ μελέτα.
110   Εἶτ' ἀντὶ τῶν ἄλλων ἁπασῶν διαχύσεων ἐκείνην
ἀντείσαγε, τὴν ἀπὸ τοῦ παρακολουθεῖν, ὅτι πείθῃ
τῷ θεῷ, ὅτι οὐ λόγῳ, ἀλλ' ἔργῳ τὰ τοῦ καλοῦ καὶ
111 ἀγαθοῦ ἐκτελεῖς. οἷον γάρ ἐστιν αὐτὸν αὑτῷ

---

¹ Variously attributed to Solon (Diogenes Laertius, 2, 13),
Anaxagoras (Cicero, *Tusc.* 3, 30 ; Diogenes Laertius, 2, 13),
or Xenophon (Diogenes Laertius, 2. 13 and 55). Compare
also Seneca, *De Consol. ad Polyb.* 11, 2, and Hierocles on the
Golden Verses of Pythagoras, chap. 11 (p. 439 *a*, Mullach).

mortal." [1] For that is what you will say, and again,
" I knew that I was mortal," " I knew that I was
likely to leave home," " I knew that I was liable to
banishment," " I knew that I might be sent off to
prison." And in the next place, if you reflect with
yourself and look for the quarter from which the
happening comes, immediately you will be reminded
of the principle : " It comes from the quarter of the
things that are outside the sphere of the moral
purpose, that are not mine own ; what, then, is it
to me ? " Then comes the most decisive consideration : " Who was it that has sent the order ? " Our
Prince, or our General, the State, or the law of the
State ? " Give it to me, then, for I must always
obey the law in every particular." Later on, when
your imagination bites you (for this is something
you cannot control), fight against it with your reason,
beat it down, do not allow it to grow strong, or to
take the next step and draw all the pictures it
wants, in the way it wants to do. If you are at Gyara,
don't picture the style of life at Rome, and all the
relaxations a man had who was living there, as well
as all that he might have upon his return ; but since
you have been stationed there, you ought to strive to
live manfully at Gyara, as beseems the man whose life
is spent in Gyara. And again, if you are in Rome,
don't picture the style of life at Athens, but make
your life in Rome the one object of your study and
practice.

Then, in the place of all the other relaxations,
introduce that which comes from the consciousness
that you are obedient to God, and that you are
playing the part of the good and excellent man, not
ostensibly but in reality. For what a fine thing it

ARRIAN'S DISCOURSES OF EPICTETUS

δύνασθαι εἰπεῖν " νῦν ἃ οἱ ἄλλοι ἐν ταῖς σχολαῖς
σεμνολογοῦσιν καὶ παραδοξολογεῖν δοκοῦσι, ταῦτα
ἐγὼ ἐπιτελῶ· κἀκεῖνοι καθήμενοι τὰς ἐμὰς ἀρετὰς
ἐξηγοῦνται καὶ περὶ ἐμοῦ ζητοῦσιν καὶ ἐμὲ
112 ὑμνοῦσιν· καὶ τούτου με ὁ Ζεὺς αὐτὸν παρ'
ἐμαυτοῦ λαβεῖν ἀπόδειξιν ἠθέλησεν καὶ αὐτὸς δὲ
γνῶναι, εἰ ἔχει στρατιώτην οἷον δεῖ, πολίτην οἷον
δεῖ, καὶ τοῖς ἄλλοις ἀνθρώποις προάγειν με
μάρτυρα τῶν ἀπροαιρέτων.   ' ἴδετε, ὅτι εἰκῆ
φοβεῖσθε, μάτην ἐπιθυμεῖτε ὧν ἐπιθυμεῖτε. τὰ
ἀγαθὰ ἔξω μὴ ζητεῖτε, ἐν ἑαυτοῖς ζητεῖτε· εἰ δὲ
113 μή, οὐχ εὑρήσετε.' ἐπὶ τούτοις με νῦν μὲν
ἐνταῦθα ἄγει, νῦν δ' ἐκεῖ πέμπει, πένητα δείκνυσι
τοῖς ἀνθρώποις, δίχα ἀρχῆς, νοσοῦντα· εἰς Γύαρα
ἀποστέλλει, εἰς δεσμωτήριον εἰσάγει. οὐ μισῶν·
μὴ γένοιτο· τίς δὲ μισεῖ τὸν ἄριστον τῶν ὑπηρε-
τῶν τῶν ἑαυτοῦ ; οὐδ' ἀμελῶν, ὅς γε οὐδὲ τῶν
μικροτάτων τινὸς ἀμελεῖ, ἀλλὰ γυμνάζων καὶ
114 μάρτυρι πρὸς τοὺς ἄλλους χρώμενος. εἰς τοιαύτην ὑπηρεσίαν κατατεταγμένος ἔτι φροντίζω,
ποῦ εἰμὶ ἢ μετὰ τίνων ἢ τί περὶ ἐμοῦ λέγουσιν ;
οὐχὶ δ' ὅλος πρὸς τὸν θεὸν τέταμαι καὶ τὰς
ἐκείνου ἐντολὰς καὶ τὰ προστάγματα ; "
115   Ταῦτα ἔχων ἀεὶ ἐν χερσὶ καὶ τρίβων αὐτὸς
παρὰ σαυτῷ καὶ πρόχειρα ποιῶν οὐδέποτε δεήσῃ
116 τοῦ παραμυθουμένου, τοῦ ἐπιρρωννύντος. καὶ
γὰρ αἰσχρὸν οὐ τὸ φαγεῖν μὴ ἔχειν, ἀλλὰ τὸ

is to be able to say to oneself, " Now I am actually performing what the rest talk solemnly about in their lectures, and are thought to be uttering paradoxes. Yes, they sit and expound my virtues, and study about me, and sing my praise. And of this Zeus wished me to get a demonstration in my own person, while at the same time He wished to know whether He has the right kind of soldier, the right kind of citizen, and to present me before all other men as a witness about the things which lie outside the sphere of the moral purpose. 'Behold,' says He, 'your fears are at haphazard, it is in vain that you desire what you desire. Do not look for your blessings outside, but look for them within yourselves; otherwise you will not find them.' These are the terms upon which now He brings me here, and again He sends me there; to mankind exhibits me in poverty, without office, in sickness; sends me away to Gyara, brings me into prison. Not because He hates me—perish the thought! And who hates the best of his servants? Nor because He neglects me, for He does not neglect any of even the least of His creatures; but because He is training me, and making use of me as a witness to the rest of men. When I have been appointed to such a service, am I any longer to take thought as to where I am, or with whom, or what men say about me? Am I not wholly intent upon God, and His commands and ordinances?"

If you have these thoughts always at hand and go over them again and again in your own mind, and keep them in readiness, you will never need a person to console you, or strengthen you. For disgrace does not consist in not having anything to

λόγον μὴ ἔχειν ἀρκοῦντα πρὸς ἀφοβίαν, πρὸς
117 ἀλυπίαν. ἂν δ' ἅπαξ περιποιήσῃ τὸ ἄλυπον καὶ
ἄφοβον, ἔτι σοι τύραννος ἔσται τις ἢ δορυφόρος ἢ
Καισαριανοὶ ἢ ὀρδινατίων¹ δήξεταί σε ἢ οἱ ἐπι-
θύοντες ἐν τῷ Καπιτωλίῳ ἐπὶ τοῖς ὀπτικίοις τὸν
τηλικαύτην ἀρχὴν παρὰ τοῦ Διὸς εἰληφότα;
118 μόνον μὴ πόμπευε αὐτὴν μηδ' ἀλαζονεύου ἐπ'
αὐτῇ, ἀλλ' ἔργῳ δείκνυε· κἂν μηδεὶς αἰσθάνηται,
ἀρκοῦ αὐτὸς ὑγιαίνων καὶ εὐδαιμονῶν.

κεʹ. Πρὸς τοὺς ἀποπίπτοντας ὧν προέθεντο.

1 Σκέψαι, ὧν προέθου ἀρχόμενος, τίνων μὲν
ἐκράτησας, τίνων δ' οὔ, καὶ πῶς ἐφ' οἷς μὲν
εὐφραίνῃ ἀναμιμνῃσκόμενος, ἐφ' οἷς δ' ἄχθῃ, καὶ εἰ
2 δυνατόν, ἀνάλαβε κἀκεῖνα ὧν ἀπώλισθες. οὐ
γὰρ ἀποκνητέον τὸν ἀγῶνα τὸν μέγιστον ἀγωνιζο-
3 μένοις, ἀλλὰ καὶ πληγὰς ληπτέον· οὐ γὰρ ὑπὲρ
πάλης καὶ παγκρατίου ὁ ἀγὼν πρόκειται, οὗ καὶ
τυχόντι καὶ μὴ τυχόντι ἔξεστιν μὲν πλείστου
ἀξίῳ, ἔξεστι δὲ ὀλίγου εἶναι καὶ νὴ Δία ἔξεστιν
μὲν εὐτυχεστάτῳ, ἔξεστι δὲ κακοδαιμονεστάτῳ
εἶναι, ἀλλ' ὑπὲρ αὐτῆς εὐτυχίας καὶ εὐδαιμονίας.
4 τί οὖν; οὐδ' ἂν ἀπαυδήσωμεν ἐνταῦθα, κωλύει

---

¹ In this passage the words *Caesariani* and *ordinatio* have
been taken over direct from the Latin. In ὀπτικίοις, a word
which seems to occur nowhere else in Greek or in Latin, it
may be that the Latin *auspicia* (sacrifices at the inauguration
of some official enterprise) are meant, as Wolf suggested,
and so the passage is translated; but the word is very un-

eat, but in not having reason sufficient to secure you
against fear and against grief.   But if once you win
for yourself security against grief and fear, will
there any longer exist for you a tyrant, or a guards-
man, or members of Caesar's household; or will some
appointment to office sting you with envy, or those
who perform sacrifices on the Capitol in taking the
auspices,[1] you who have received so important an office
from Zeus?   Only make no display of your office,
and do not boast about it; but prove it by your
conduct; and if no one perceives that you have it,
be content to live in health and happiness yourself.

CHAPTER XXV

To those who fail to achieve their purposes

CONSIDER which of the things that you purposed
at the start you have achieved, and which you have
not; likewise, how it gives you pleasure to recall
some of them, and pain to recall others, and, if
possible, recover also those things which have slipped
out of your grasp.   For men who are engaged in the
greatest of contests ought not to flinch, but to take
also the blows; for the contest before us is not in
wrestling or the pancratium, in which, whether a
man succeeds or fails, he may be worth a great deal,
or only a little,—yes, by Zeus, he may even be
extremely happy or extremely miserable, – but it is
a contest for good fortune and happiness itself.
What follows?   Why here, even if we give in for

certain (Chinnock, *Class. Rev.* 3 (1889), 70, thinks it stands
for *officia*), and several emendations have been proposed, of
which ὀπφικίοις (*officia*, Koraes) is perhaps the most plausible.

τις πάλιν ἀγωνίζεσθαι οὐδὲ δεῖ περιμεῖναι τετραε-
τίαν ἄλλην, ἵν᾽ ἔλθῃ ἄλλα Ὀλύμπια, ἀλλ᾽ εὐθὺς
ἀναλαβόντι καὶ ἀνακτησαμένῳ ἑαυτὸν καὶ τὴν
αὐτὴν εἰσφέροντι προθυμίαν ἔξεστιν ἀγωνίζεσθαι·
κἂν πάλιν ἀπείπῃς, πάλιν ἔξεστιν, κἂν ἅπαξ
νικήσῃς, ὅμοιος εἶ τῷ μηδέποτε ἀπειπόντι.
5 μόνον μὴ ὑπὸ ἔθους τοῦ αὐτοῦ ἡδέως αὐτὸ ἄρξῃ
ποιεῖν· καὶ λοιπὸν ὡς κακὸς ἀθλητὴς περιέρχῃ
νικώμενος τὴν περίοδον ὅμοιος τοῖς ἀποφυγοῦσιν
6 ὄρτυξιν. "ἡττᾷ με φαντασία παιδισκαρίου
καλοῦ. τί γάρ; πρώην οὐχ ἡττήθην;" "προ-
θυμία μοι γίνεται ψέξαι τινά. πρώην γὰρ οὐκ
7 ἔψεξα;" οὕτως ἡμῖν λαλεῖς ὡς ἀζήμιος ἐξελη-
λυθώς, οἱονεί τις τῷ ἰατρῷ κωλύοντι λούσασθαι
λέγοι "πρώην γὰρ οὐκ ἐλουσάμην;" ἂν οὖν ὁ
ἰατρὸς αὐτῷ ἔχῃ λέγειν "ἄγε, λουσάμενος οὖν τί
ἔπαθες; οὐκ ἐπύρεξας; οὐκ ἐκεφαλάλγησας;"
8 καὶ σὺ ψέξας πρώην τινὰ οὐ κακοήθους ἔργον
ἔπραξας; οὐ φλυάρου; οὐκ ἔθρεψάς σου τὴν
ἕξιν ταύτην παραβάλλων αὐτῇ τὰ οἰκεῖα ἔργα;
ἡττηθεὶς δὲ τοῦ παιδισκαρίου ἀπῆλθες ἀζήμιος;
9 τί οὖν τὰ πρώην λέγεις; ἔδει δ᾽ οἶμαι μεμνημένον,
ὡς οἱ δοῦλοι τῶν πληγῶν, ἀπέχεσθαι τῶν αὐτῶν
10 ἁμαρτημάτων. ἀλλ᾽ οὐχ ὅμοιον· ἐνταῦθα μὲν

---

[1] The comparison is brief, but I presume that a fighting
quail, on once having submitted to defeat, became very
ready to do so again, as is the case among ordinary chickens.
One shouted into his ear in order to make him forget, as they
said, the voice of the victor, and to restore his courage.
Pollux, 9, 109.

the time being, no one prevents us from struggling
again, and we do not have to wait another four-year
period for another Olympic festival to come around,
but the moment a man has picked himself up, and
recovered himself, and exhibits the same eagerness,
he is allowed to contest; and if you give in again,
you can enter again; and if once you win a victory,
you are as though you had never given in at all.
Only don't begin cheerfully to do the same thing
over again out of sheer habit, and end up as a bad
athlete, going the whole circuit of the games, and
getting beaten all the time, like quails that have
once run away.[1] "I am overcome by the impression
of a pretty maid. Well, what of it? Wasn't I
overcome just the other day?" "I feel strongly
inclined to censure somebody, for didn't I censure
somebody just the other day?" You talk thus to
us as though you had come off scot-free; just as if
a man should say to his physician who was for-
bidding him to bathe, "Why, but didn't I bathe
just the other day?" If, then, the physician is
able to say to him, "Very well, after you had
bathed, then, how did you feel? Didn't you have
a fever? Didn't your head ache?" So, too, when
you censured somebody the other day, didn't you
act like an ugly-spirited man, like a silly babbler?
Didn't you feed this habit by citing the example of
your own previous acts? And when you were overcome by the maid, did you escape scot-free? Why,
then, do you talk about what you were doing just
the other day? In my opinion, you ought to have
remembered, as slaves remember their blows, and
to have kept away from the same mistakes. But
one case is not like the other; for with slaves it is

γὰρ ὁ πόνος τὴν μνήμην ποιεῖ, ἐπὶ δὲ τῶν ἁμαρτημάτων ποῖος πόνος, ποία ζημία; πότε γὰρ
εἰθίσθης φεύγειν τὸ κακῶς ἐνεργῆσαι;

κϛ'. Πρὸς τοὺς τὴν ἀπορίαν δεδοικότας.

1 Οὐκ αἰσχύνῃ δειλότερος ὢν καὶ ἀγεννέστερος τῶν
δραπετῶν; πῶς ἐκεῖνοι φεύγοντες ἀπολείπουσι
τοὺς δεσπότας, ποίοις ἀγροῖς πεποιθότες, ποίοις
οἰκέταις; οὐχὶ δ' ὀλίγον ὅσον πρὸς τὰς πρώτας
ἡμέρας ὑφελόμενοι εἶθ' ὕστερον διὰ γῆς ἢ καὶ
θαλάττης φέρονται ἄλλην ἐξ ἄλλης ἀφορμὴν πρὸς
2 τὸ διατρέφεσθαι φιλοτεχνοῦντες; καὶ τίς πώποτε
δραπέτης λιμῷ ἀπέθανεν; σὺ δὲ τρέμεις, μή σοι
λείπῃ τὰ ἀναγκαῖα, καὶ τὰς νύκτας ἀγρυπνεῖς.
3 ταλαίπωρε, οὕτως τυφλὸς εἶ καὶ τὴν ὁδὸν οὐχ
ὁρᾷς, ὅποι φέρει ἡ τῶν ἀναγκαίων ἔνδεια; ποῦ
γὰρ φέρει; ὅπου καὶ ὁ πυρετός, ὅπου καὶ
λίθος ἐπιπεσών, εἰς θάνατον. τοῦτο[1] οὖν οὐ
πολλάκις σὺ αὐτὸς[2] εἶπες πρὸς τοὺς ἑταίρους,
πολλὰ δ' ἀνέγνως τοιαῦτα, πολλὰ δ' ἔγραφες;
ποσάκις δ' ἠλαζονεύσω, ὅτι πρός γε τὸ ἀπο-
4 θανεῖν μετρίως ἔχεις;—Ναί· ἀλλὰ καὶ οἱ ἐμοὶ
πεινήσουσιν.—Τί οὖν; μή τι καὶ ὁ ἐκείνων
λιμὸς ἀλλαχοῦ που φέρει; οὐχὶ καὶ ἡ αὐτή που
5 κάθοδος; τὰ κάτω τὰ αὐτά; οὐ θέλεις οὖν ἐκεῖ
βλέπειν θαρρῶν πρὸς πᾶσαν ἀπορίαν καὶ ἔνδειαν,
ὅπου καὶ τοὺς πλουσιωτάτους καὶ τὰς ἀρχὰς τὰς

---

[1] Meibom, after Wolf : τοῦτον S.
[2] Reiske : δαυτός S.

the suffering which produces the memory, but in the case of your mistakes, what suffering is there, what penalty do you feel? Why, when did *you* ever acquire the habit of avoiding evil activities?

CHAPTER XXVI

To those who fear want

Aren't you ashamed to be more cowardly and ignoble than a runaway slave? How do they, when they run off, leave their masters? in what estates or slaves do they put their confidence? Don't they steal just a little bit to last them for the first few days, and then afterwards drift along over land or sea, contriving one scheme after another to keep themselves fed? And what runaway slave ever died of hunger? But you tremble, and lie awake at night, for fear the necessities of life will fail you. Wretch, are you so blind, and do you so fail to see the road to which lack of the necessities of life leads? Where, indeed, does it lead? Where also fever, or a stone that drops on your head, lead,—to death. Have you not, then, often said this same thing yourself to your companions, read much of the same sort, and written much? How many times have you boasted that, as far as death at least was concerned, you are in a fairly good state?—Yes, but my family too will starve.—What then? Their starvation does not lead to some other end than yours, does it? Have they not also much the same descent thereto, and the same world below? Are you not willing, then, to look with courage sufficient to face every necessity and want, at that place to which the

μεγίστας ἄρξαντας καὶ αὐτοὺς τοὺς βασιλεῖς καὶ
τυράννους δεῖ κατελθεῖν, καὶ [1] σὲ πεινῶντα, ἂν
οὕτως τύχῃ, ἐκείνους δὲ διαρραγέντας ὑπὸ ἀπε-
6 ψιῶν καὶ μέθης ; τίνα πώποτ' ἐπαίτην ῥᾳδίως
εἶδες μὴ γέροντα ; τίνα δ' οὐκ ἐσχατόγηρων ;
ἀλλὰ ῥιγῶντες τὰς νύκτας καὶ τὰς ἡμέρας καὶ
χαμαὶ ἐρριμμένοι καὶ ὅσον αὐτὸ τὸ ἀναγκαῖον
σιτούμενοι ἐγγὺς ἥκουσιν τῷ μηδ' ἀποθανεῖν
7 δύνασθαι, σὺ [2] δ' ὁλόκληρος ἄνθρωπος χεῖρας
ἔχων καὶ πόδας περὶ λιμοῦ δέδοικας οὕτως ; οὐκ
ἀντλεῖν δύνασαι, οὐ γράφειν, οὐ παιδαγωγεῖν, οὐ
θύραν ἀλλοτρίαν φυλάττειν ;—Ἀλλ' αἰσχρὸν εἰς
ταύτην ἐλθεῖν τὴν ἀνάγκην.—Μάθε οὖν πρῶτον,
τίνα τὰ αἰσχρά ἐστιν, καὶ οὕτως ἡμῖν λέγε
σαυτὸν φιλόσοφον. τὸ νῦν δὲ μηδ' ἂν ἄλλος τις
εἴπῃ σε, ἀνέχου.

8   Αἰσχρόν ἐστί σοι τὸ μὴ σὸν ἔργον, οὗ σὺ αἴτιος
οὐκ εἶ, ὃ ἄλλως ἀπήντησέν σοι, ὡς κεφαλαλγία,
ὡς πυρετός ; εἴ σου οἱ γονεῖς πένητες ἦσαν, ἢ
πλούσιοι μὲν ἦσαν [3] ἄλλους δὲ κληρονόμους
ἀπέλιπον, καὶ ζῶντες οὐκ ἐπαρκοῦσιν οὐδέν, σοὶ
9 ταῦτα αἰσχρά ἐστιν ; ταῦτα ἐμάνθανες παρὰ τοῖς
φιλοσόφοις ; οὐδέποτε ἤκουσας, ὅτι τὸ αἰσχρὸν
ψεκτόν ἐστιν, τὸ δὲ ψεκτὸν ἄξιόν ἐστι τοῦ
ψέγεσθαι ; τίνα δ' [4] ἐπὶ τῷ μὴ αὐτοῦ ἔργῳ, ὃ
10 αὐτὸς οὐκ ἐποίησεν ; σὺ οὖν ἐποίησας τοῦτο, τὸν

---

[1] Meibom, after Wolf: εἰ S.
[2] From here through δύνασαι the passage is written in the margin by the first hand of S.
[3] ἢ πλούσιοι μέν supplied by Schweighäuser, ἦσαν by C. Schenkl.
[4] δ' added by Schweighäuser.

wealthiest needs must go, and those who have held
the highest offices, and very kings and tyrants?
Only you will descend hungry, if it so happen, and
they bursting with indigestion and drunkenness. Did
you ever easily find a beggar who was not an old man?
Wasn't he extremely old? But though they are cold
night and day, and lie forlorn on the ground, and have
to eat only what is absolutely necessary, they approach
a state where it is almost impossible for them to
die;[1] yet you who are physically perfect, and have
hands and feet, are you so alarmed about starving?
Can't you draw water, or write, or escort boys to and
from school, or be another's doorkeeper?—But it is
disgraceful to come to such a necessity.—Learn,
therefore, first of all, what the disgraceful things are,
and after you have done that, come into our
presence and call yourself a philosopher. But as
the case stands now, do not even allow anyone else
to call you one!

Is anything disgraceful to you which is not your
own doing, for which you are not responsible, which
has befallen you accidentally, as a headache or a
fever? If your parents were poor, or if they were
rich but left others as their heirs, and if they give
you no help though they are living, is all this disgraceful to you? Is that what you learned at the
feet of the philosophers? Have you never heard
that the disgraceful thing is censurable, and the
censurable is that which deserves censure? And
whom do you censure for what is not his own doing,
which he didn't produce himself? Well, did you
produce this situation? did you make your father

---

[1] The argument is, one need hardly remark, quite
unsound, for the death-rate among the poor is unquestion-
ably much higher than among the wealthy.

πατέρα τοιοῦτον; ἢ ἔξεστίν σοι ἐπανορθῶσαι
αὐτόν; δίδοταί σοι τοῦτο; τί οὖν; δεῖ σε θέλειν
τὰ μὴ διδόμενα ἢ μὴ τυγχάνοντα αὐτῶν αἰσχύνε-
11 σθαι; οὕτως δὲ καὶ εἰθίζου φιλοσοφῶν ἀφορᾶν
εἰς ἄλλους καὶ μηδὲν αὐτὸς ἐλπίζειν ἐκ σεαυτοῦ;
12 τοιγαροῦν οἴμωζε καὶ στένε καὶ ἔσθιε δεδοικώς, μὴ
οὐ σχῇς τροφὰς αὔριον· περὶ τῶν δουλαρίων
τρέμε, μὴ κλέψῃ τι, μὴ φύγῃ, μὴ ἀποθάνῃ.
13 οὕτως σὺ ζῆθι καὶ μὴ παύσῃ μηδέποτε, ὅστις
ὀνόματι μόνον πρὸς φιλοσοφίαν προσῆλθες καὶ τὰ
θεωρήματα αὐτῆς ὅσον ἐπὶ σοὶ κατῄσχυνας
ἄχρηστα ἐπιδείξας καὶ ἀνωφελῆ τοῖς ἀναλαμβά-
νουσιν· οὐδέποτε δ' εὐσταθείας ὠρέχθης, ἀταραξίας, ἀπαθείας· οὐδένα τούτου ἕνεκα ἐθεράπευσας,
συλλογισμῶν δ' ἕνεκα πολλούς· οὐδέποτε τούτων
τινὰ τῶν φαντασιῶν διεβασάνισας αὐτὸς ἐπὶ
14 σεαυτοῦ " δύναμαι φέρειν ἢ οὐ δύναμαι; τί μοι τὸ
λοιπόν ἐστιν;", ἀλλ' ὡς πάντων ἐχόντων σοι
καλῶς καὶ ἀσφαλῶς περὶ τὸν τελευταῖον κατε-
γίνου τόπον, τὸν τῆς ἀμεταπτωσίας, ἵν' ἀμε-
τάπτωτα σχῇς τίνα; τὴν δειλίαν, τὴν ἀγέννειαν,
τὸν θαυμασμὸν τῶν πλουσίων, τὴν ἀτελῆ ὄρεξιν,
τὴν ἀποτευκτικὴν[1] ἔκκλισιν· περὶ τῆς τούτων
ἀσφαλείας ἐφρόντιζες.
15 Οὐκ ἔδει προσκτήσασθαι πρῶτον ἐκ τοῦ λόγου,

[1] See explanatory note.

---

[1] So the text as it stands in S, but the singular mixture of
technical terms in ἀποτευκτικὴ ἔκκλισις is incredible. Elsewhere, and quite properly, it is desire that fails to get what
it wills (ἀποτευκτικὴ), and aversion that falls into what it
would avoid (see III. 6, 6 and especially IV. 10, 4). Hence
there is great plausibility in Schenkl's suggestion (partly

what he is? Or is it in your power to reform him?
Is that vouchsafed you? What follows? Ought
you to wish for what is not given you, or to be
ashamed when you fail to get it? And did you
really, while studying philosophy, acquire the
habit of looking to other persons, and of hoping
for nothing yourself from yourself? Very well then,
lament and groan, and eat in fear of not having food
to-morrow; tremble about your paltry slaves, for fear
they will steal something, or run away, or die! Live
in this spirit and never cease to live so, you who in
name only have approached philosophy, and, as far
as in you lay, have discredited its principles by
showing them to be useless and good for nothing to
those who receive them! But you never desired
stability, serenity, peace of mind; you never culti-
vated anybody's acquaintance for that purpose, but
many persons' acquaintance for the sake of syllogisms; you never thoroughly tested for yourself any
one of these external impressions, asking the questions: "Am I able to bear it, or am I not? What
may I expect next?" but just as though everything
about you were in an excellent and safe condition,
you have been devoting your attention to the last of all
topics, that which deals with immutability, in order
that you may have immutable—what? your cowardice,
your ignoble character, your admiration of the rich,
your ineffectual desire, your aversion that fails of its
mark![1] These are the things about whose security
you have been anxious!

Ought you not, first, to have acquired something

after Reiske), ὄρεξιν, τὴν ἀποτευκτικήν, <τὴν περιπτωτικὴν>
ἔκκλισιν: "desire, that fails to get what it wills, and
aversion that falls into what it would avoid."

εἶτα τούτῳ περιποιεῖν τὴν ἀσφάλειαν ; καὶ τίνα
πώποτ' εἶδες τριγχὸν περιοικοδομοῦντα μηδενὶ
τειχίῳ περιβαλόμενον αὐτόν ;[1] ποῖος δὲ θυρωρὸς
16 καθίσταται ἐπὶ οὐδεμιᾷ θύρᾳ ; ἀλλὰ σὺ μελετᾷς ἀποδεικνύειν δύνασθαι· τίνα ; μελετᾷς μὴ
ἀποσαλεύεσθαι διὰ σοφισμάτων· ἀπὸ τίνων ;
17 δεῖξόν μοι πρῶτον, τί τηρεῖς, τί μετρεῖς ἢ τί
ἱστάνεις· εἶθ' οὕτως ἐπιδείκνυε τὸν ζυγὸν ἢ τὸν
18 μέδιμνον. ἢ μέχρι τίνος μετρήσεις τὴν σποδόν ;
οὐ ταῦτά σε ἀποδεικνύειν δεῖ, ἃ ποιεῖ τοὺς
ἀνθρώπους εὐδαίμονας, ἃ ποιεῖ προχωρεῖν αὐτοῖς
τὰ πράγματα ὡς θέλουσιν, δι' ἃ οὐ δεῖ μέμφεσθαι
οὐδενί, ἐγκαλεῖν οὐδενί, πείθεσθαι τῇ διοικήσει
19 τῶν ὅλων ; ταῦτά μοι δείκνυε. " ἰδοὺ δεικνύω,"
φησίν, "ἀναλύσω σοι συλλογισμούς." τοῦτο
τὸ μετροῦν ἐστιν, ἀνδράποδον· τὸ μετρούμενον
20 δ' οὐκ ἔστιν. διὰ ταῦτα νῦν τίνεις δίκας ὧν
ἠμέλησας·[2] τρέμεις, ἀγρυπνεῖς, μετὰ πάντων
βουλεύῃ· κἂν μὴ πᾶσιν ἀρέσκειν μέλλῃ τὰ
βουλεύματα, κακῶς οἴει βεβουλεῦσθαι.
21 Εἶτα φοβῇ λιμόν, ὡς δοκεῖς. σὺ δ' οὐ λιμὸν
φοβῇ, ἀλλὰ δέδοικας μὴ οὐ σχῇς μάγειρον, μὴ
οὐ σχῇς ἄλλον ὀψωνητήν, ἄλλον τὸν ὑποδή-
σοντα, ἄλλον τὸν ἐνδύσοντα, ἄλλους τοὺς
22 τρίψοντας, ἄλλους τοὺς ἀκολουθήσοντας, ἵν' ἐν

---

[1] *Sb* (περιβαλόμενον Schenkl): μηδενὶ τειχίον περιβαλλό-
μενον αὐτὸ αὐτοῦ *S*. The correct form of the text is highly
uncertain, and the version in *Sb* is acceptable only as meeting
in a general way the requirement of the context.
[2] φιλοσοφίας after ἠμέλησας deleted by Schenkl.

from reason, and then to have made that something secure? Why, did you ever see anyone building a cornice all around without first having a wall about which to build it?[1] And what kind of doorkeeper is placed on guard where there isn't any door? But you practise to get the power to demonstrate; demonstrate what? You practise to avoid being shaken by sophisms; shaken from what? Show me first what you are maintaining, what you are measuring, or what you are weighing; and after that, under those conditions, show me your scales or your bushel-measure. Or how long will you keep measuring ashes? Are not these what you ought to be demonstrating, the things, namely, that make men happy, that make their affairs prosper for them as they desire, that make it unnecessary for them to blame anybody, and to find fault with anybody, but to acquiesce in the government of the universe? Show me these. "See, I do show you," a man says; "I will analyse syllogisms for you." Slave, this is a mere measuring instrument, it is not the thing measured. That is why you are now being punished for what you neglected; you tremble, lie awake, take counsel with everyone, and, if your plans are not likely to win the approval of all men, you think that your deliberations have been faulty.

And then you fear hunger, as you fancy. Yet it is not hunger that you fear, but you are afraid that you will not have a professional cook, you will not have another servant to buy the delicacies, another to put on your shoes for you, another to dress you, others to give you your massage, others to follow at your heels, in order that when you have undressed

---

[1] The figure is reminiscent of Plato, *Rep.* VII, 534 E.

τῷ βαλανείῳ ἐκδυσάμενος καὶ ἐκτείνας σεαυτὸν
ὡς οἱ ἐσταυρωμένοι τρίβῃ ἔνθεν καὶ ἔνθεν, εἶθ'
ὁ ἀλείπτης ἐπιστὰς λέγῃ " μετάβηθι, δὸς
πλευρόν, κεφαλὴν αὐτοῦ λάβε, παράθες τὸν
ὦμον," εἶτ' ἐλθὼν ἐκ τοῦ βαλανείου εἰς οἶκον
κραυγάσῃς " οὐδεὶς φέρει φαγεῖν ; " εἶτ' "ἆρον
23 τὰς τραπέζας· σπόγγισον." τοῦτο φοβῇ, μὴ
οὐ δύνῃ ζῆν ἀρρώστου βίον, ἐπεί τοι τὸν τῶν
ὑγιαινόντων μάθε, πῶς οἱ δοῦλοι ζῶσιν, πῶς οἱ
ἐργάται, πῶς οἱ γνησίως φιλοσοφοῦντες, πῶς
Σωκράτης ἔζησεν, ἐκεῖνος μὲν καὶ μετὰ γυναικὸς
καὶ παίδων, πῶς Διογένης, πῶς Κλεάνθης ἅμα
24 σχολάζων καὶ ἀντλῶν. ταῦτα ἂν θέλῃς ἔχειν,
ἕξεις πανταχοῦ καὶ ζήσεις θαρρῶν, τίνι ; ᾧ
μόνῳ θαρρεῖν ἐνδέχεται, τῷ πιστῷ, τῷ ἀκωλύτῳ,
τῷ ἀναφαιρέτῳ, τοῦτ' ἔστι τῇ προαιρέσει τῇ
25 σεαυτοῦ. διὰ τί δ' οὕτως ἄχρηστον καὶ ἀνωφελῆ
σαυτὸν παρεσκεύακας, ἵνα μηδείς σε εἰς οἰκίαν
θέλῃ δέξασθαι, μηδεὶς ἐπιμεληθῆναι ; ἀλλὰ
σκεῦος μὲν ὁλόκληρον καὶ χρήσιμον ἔξω ἐρριμμέ-
νον πᾶς τις εὑρὼν ἀναιρήσεται καὶ κέρδος
ἡγήσεται, σὲ δ' οὐδείς, ἀλλὰ πᾶς ζημίαν.
26 οὕτως οὐδὲ κυνὸς δύνασαι χρείαν παρασχεῖν
οὐδ' ἀλεκτρυόνος. τί οὖν ἔτι ζῆν θέλεις τοιοῦτος
ὤν ;
27 Φοβεῖταί τις ἀνὴρ ἀγαθός, μὴ λείπωσιν αὐτῷ
τροφαί ; τοῖς τυφλοῖς οὐ λείπουσι, τοῖς χωλοῖς
οὐ λείπουσι· λείψουσιν ἀνδρὶ ἀγαθῷ ; καὶ
στρατιώτῃ μὲν ἀγαθῷ οὐ λείπει ὁ μισθοδοτῶν

---

[1] Diogenes Laertius, 7, 168.

in a bath, and stretched yourself out like men who
have been crucified, you may be massaged on this side
and on that; and that then the masseur may stand
over you and say, "Move over, give me his side, you
take his head, hand me his shoulder"; and then, when
you have left the bath and gone home, that you may
shout out, "Is no one bringing me something to
eat?" and after that, "Clear away the tables; wipe
them off with a sponge." What *you* are afraid of is
this—that you may not be able to live the life of an
invalid, since, I tell you, you have only to learn the
life of healthy men—how the slaves live, the workmen,
the genuine philosophers, how Socrates lived—he too
with a wife and children—how Diogenes lived, how
Cleanthes, who combined going to school and pump-
ing water.[1] If this is what you want, you will have
it everywhere, and will live with full confidence.
Confidence in what? In the only thing in which
one can have confidence—in what is faithful, free
from hindrance, cannot be taken away, that is, in your
own moral purpose. And why have you made yourself so useless and unprofitable, that no one is willing
to take you into his house, no one willing to
take care of you? But when a whole and useful
implement has been thrown out, anyone who finds
it will pick it up and count it gain; yet not when he
picks up *you*, but everyone will count *you* a loss.
You are so unable to serve the purpose of even a
dog or a cock. Why, then, do you care to keep on
living, if that is the sort of person you are?

Does a good man fear that food will fail him? It
does not fail the blind, it does not fail the lame;
will it fail a good man? A good soldier does not
lack someone to give him pay, or a workman, or a

235

οὐδ' ἐργάτῃ οὐδὲ σκυτεῖ· τῷ δ' ἀγαθῷ λείψει ;
28 οὕτως ὁ θεὸς ἀμελεῖ τῶν αὑτοῦ ἐπιτευγμάτων,
τῶν διακόνων, τῶν μαρτύρων, οἷς μόνοις χρῆται
παραδείγμασιν πρὸς τοὺς ἀπαιδεύτους, ὅτι καὶ
ἔστι καὶ καλῶς διοικεῖ τὰ ὅλα καὶ οὐκ ἀμελεῖ
τῶν ἀνθρωπίνων πραγμάτων καὶ ὅτι ἀνδρὶ ἀγαθῷ οὐδέν ἐστι κακὸν οὔτε ζῶντι οὔτ' ἀποθανόντι ;
29 —Τί οὖν, ὅταν μὴ παρέχῃ τροφάς ;—Τί γὰρ
ἄλλο ἢ ὡς ἀγαθὸς στρατηγὸς τὸ ἀνακλητικόν
μοι σεσήμαγκεν ; πείθομαι, ἀκολουθῶ, ἐπευφη-
μῶν τὸν ἡγεμόνα, ὑμνῶν αὐτοῦ τὰ ἔργα. καὶ
30 γὰρ ἦλθον, ὅτ' ἐκείνῳ ἔδοξεν, καὶ ἄπειμι πάλιν
ἐκείνῳ δοκοῦν καὶ ζῶντός μου τοῦτο τὸ ἔργον
ἦν, ὑμνεῖν τὸν θεὸν καὶ αὐτὸν ἐπ' ἐμαυτοῦ καὶ
31 πρὸς ἕνα καὶ πρὸς πολλούς. οὐ παρέχει μοι
πολλά, οὐκ ἄφθονα, τρυφᾶν με οὐ θέλει· οὐδὲ
γὰρ τῷ Ἡρακλεῖ παρεῖχεν, τῷ υἱεῖ τῷ ἑαυτοῦ,
ἀλλ' ἄλλος ἐβασίλευεν Ἄργους καὶ Μυκηνῶν,
32 ὁ δ' ἐπετάσσετο καὶ ἐπόνει καὶ ἐγυμνάζετο. καὶ
ἦν Εὐρυσθεὺς μέν, ὃς ἦν, οὔτε Ἄργους οὔτε
Μυκηνῶν βασιλεύς, ὅς γ' οὐδ' αὐτὸς ἑαυτοῦ, ὁ
δ' Ἡρακλῆς ἁπάσης γῆς καὶ θαλάττης ἄρχων
καὶ ἡγεμὼν ἦν, καθαρτὴς ἀδικίας καὶ ἀνομίας,
εἰσαγωγεὺς δὲ δικαιοσύνης καὶ ὁσιότητος· καὶ
33 ταῦτα ἐποίει καὶ γυμνὸς καὶ μόνος. ὁ δ'
Ὀδυσσεὺς ὅτε ναυαγὸς ἐξερρίφη, μή τι ἐτα-
πείνωσεν αὐτὸν ἡ ἀπορία, μή τι ἐπέκλασεν ;
ἀλλὰ πῶς ἀπῄει πρὸς τὰς παρθένους αἰτήσων
236

cobbler; and shall a good man?[1] Does God so
neglect His own creatures, His servants, His witnesses, whom alone He uses as examples to the
uninstructed, to prove that He both is, and governs
the universe well, and does not neglect the affairs of
men, and that no evil befalls a good man either in
life or in death?[2]—Yes, but what if He does not
provide food?—Why, what else but that as a good
general He has sounded the recall? I obey, I follow,
lauding my commander, and singing hymns of praise
about His deeds. For I came into the world when
it so pleased Him, and I leave it again at His
pleasure, and while I live this was my function—to
sing hymns of praise unto God, to myself and to
others, be it to one or to many. God does not give
me much, no abundance, He does not want me to
live luxuriously; He did not give much to Heracles,
either, though he was His own son, but someone
else was king over Argos and Mycenae, while he was
subject, and suffered labours and discipline. And
Eurystheus, such as he was, was not king over either
Argos or Mycenae, for *he* was not king even over
himself; but Heracles was ruler and leader of all the
land and sea, purging them of injustice and lawless-
ness, and introducing justice and righteousness; and
all this he did naked and by himself. And when
Odysseus was shipwrecked and cast ashore, did his
necessity make abject his spirit, or break it? Nay,
but how did he advance upon the maidens to ask for

[1] The scholiast appropriately compares Matt. vi. 31
and 33 : "Take no thought," and "Seek ye first the kingdom of God, and all these things shall be added unto you."
[2] This last clause is slightly modified from Plato, *Apol.*
41 D.

τὰ ἀναγκαῖα, ὧν αἴσχιστον εἶναι δοκεῖ δεῖσθαι
παρ' ἄλλου ;

ὥς τε λέων ὀρεσίτροφος.

34 τίνι πεποιθώς ; οὐ δόξῃ οὐδὲ χρήμασιν οὐδ'
ἀρχαῖς, ἀλλ' ἀλκῇ τῇ ἑαυτοῦ, τοῦτ' ἔστι δόγμασι
35 περὶ[1] τῶν ἐφ' ἡμῖν καὶ οὐκ ἐφ' ἡμῖν. ταῦτα
γάρ ἐστι μόνα τὰ τοὺς ἐλευθέρους ποιοῦντα, τὰ
τοὺς ἀκωλύτους, τὰ τὸν τράχηλον ἐπαίροντα
τῶν τεταπεινομένων, τὰ ἀντιβλέπειν ποιοῦντα
ὀρθοῖς τοῖς ὀφθαλμοῖς πρὸς τοὺς πλουσίους,
36 πρὸς τοὺς τυράννους. καὶ τὸ τοῦ φιλοσόφου
δῶρον τοῦτο ἦν, σὺ δ' οὐκ ἐξελεύσῃ θαρρῶν,
ἀλλὰ περιτρέμων τοῖς ἱματιδίοις καὶ τοῖς ἀργυ-
ρωματίοις ; δύστηνε, οὕτως ἀπώλεσας τὸν μέχρι
νῦν χρόνον ;

37   Τί οὖν, ἂν νοσήσω ;—Νοσήσεις καλῶς.—Τίς
με θεραπεύσει ;—Ὁ θεός, οἱ φίλοι.—Σκληρῶς
κατακείσομαι.—Ἀλλ' ὡς ἀνήρ.—Οἴκημα ἐπιτήδειον οὐχ ἕξω.—Ἐν ἀνεπιτηδείῳ οὖν[2] νοσήσεις.—
Τίς μοι ποιήσει τὰ τροφεῖα ;—Οἱ καὶ τοῖς ἄλλοις
ποιοῦντες· ὡς Μάνης νοσήσεις.—Τί δὲ καὶ τὸ
38 πέρας τῆς νόσου.—Ἄλλο τι ἢ θάνατος ; ἆρ' οὖν
ἐνθυμῇ, ὅτι κεφάλαιον τοῦτο πάντων τῶν κακῶν
τῷ ἀνθρώπῳ καὶ ἀγεννείας καὶ δειλίας οὐ

---

[1] περί supplied by Schenkl.
[2] ἀνεπιτηδείῳ the Cambridge ed., after Wolf ; οὖν supplied
by Oldfather : ἐνεπιτηδείῳ νοσήσεις S.

---

[1] Homer, *Odyssey*, VI. 130.
[2] The text is very uncertain. Schenkl reads Ἐν ἐπιτηδείῳ
οὐ νοσήσεις ; which would appear to mean something like :

food, which is regarded as being the most disgraceful thing for one person to ask of another?

As a lion reared in the mountains.[1]

In what did he trust? Not in reputation, or money, or office, but in his own might, that means, his judgements about the things which are under our control, and those which are not under our control. For these are the only things that make men free, that make men unhampered, that lift up the neck of those who have become abject, that make them look with level eyes into the faces of the rich, and the faces of tyrants. And all this was what the philosopher had to give, yet will you not come forth bold, instead of trembling for your paltry clothes and silver plate? Miserable man, have you so wasted your time down to the present?

Yes, but what if I fall ill?—You will bear illness well.—Who will nurse me?—God and your friends. —I shall have a hard bed to lie on.—But like a man. —I shall not have a suitable house.—Then you will fall ill in an unsuitable house.[2]—Who will prepare my food for me?—Those who prepare it for others also. You will be ill like Manes.[3]—And what is also the end of the illness?—Anything but death? Will you, then, realize that this epitome of all the ills that befall man, of his ignoble spirit, and his

"Will you not choose a suitable house in which to fall ill?" But that sort of reply seems scarcely to fit the context.

[3] That is, like a slave, for this was a typical slave name, like "Sambo" among American negroes. In particular the reference seems to be to Zeno, who, when his physicians ordered him to eat young pigeons, insisted, "Cure me as you do Manes." Musonius, frag. 18 A (p. 98, 4 ff., Hense).

θάνατός ἐστιν, μᾶλλον δ' ὁ τοῦ θανάτου φόβος;
39 ἐπὶ τοῦτον οὖν μοι γυμνάζου, ἐνταῦθα νευέ-
τωσαν οἱ λόγοι πάντες, τὰ ἀσκήματα, τὰ
ἀναγνώσματα, καὶ εἴσῃ, ὅτι οὕτως μόνως ἐλευθε-
ροῦνται ἄνθρωποι.

cowardice, is not death, but it is rather the fear
of death ?   Against this fear, then, I would have
you discipline yourself, toward this let all your
reasoning tend, your exercises, your reading; and
then you will know that this is the only way in
which men achieve freedom.

BOOK IV

$$\bar{\Delta}$$

α΄. Περὶ ἐλευθερίας.

1 Ἐλεύθερός ἐστιν ὁ ζῶν ὡς βούλεται, ὃν οὔτ᾽
ἀναγκάσαι ἔστιν οὔτε κωλῦσαι οὔτε βιάσασθαι,
οὗ αἱ ὁρμαὶ ἀνεμπόδιστοι, αἱ ὀρέξεις ἐπιτευκτι-
καί, αἱ ἐκκλίσεις ἀπερίπτωτοι. τίς οὖν θέλει
2 ζῆν ἁμαρτάνων ;—Οὐδείς.—Τίς θέλει ζῆν ἐξαπα-
τώμενος, προπίπτων, ἄδικος ὤν, ἀκόλαστος,
3 μεμψίμοιρος, ταπεινός ;—Οὐδείς.—Οὐδεὶς ἄρα
τῶν φαύλων ζῇ ὡς βούλεται· οὐ τοίνυν οὐδ᾽

244

BOOK IV

Chapters of the Fourth Book

CHAPTER I

Of freedom

He is free who lives as he wills, who is subject neither to compulsion, nor hindrance, nor force, whose choices are unhampered, whose desires attain their end, whose aversions do not fall into what they would avoid. Who, then, wishes to live in error?—No one.—Who wishes to live deceived, impetuous, unjust, unrestrained, peevish, abject?—No one.—Therefore, there is no bad man who lives as

245

4 ἐλεύθερός ἐστιν. τίς δὲ θέλει λυπούμενος ζῆν, φοβούμενος, φθονῶν, ἐλεῶν, ὀρεγόμενος καὶ ἀποτυγχάνων, ἐκκλίνων καὶ περιπίπτων ;—Οὐδὲ 5 εἷς.—Ἔχομεν οὖν τινὰ τῶν φαύλων ἄλυπον, ἄφοβον, ἀπερίπτωτον, ἀναπότευκτον ;—Οὐδένα. —Οὐκ ἄρα οὐδὲ ἐλεύθερον.

6 Ταῦτα ἄν τις ἀκούσῃ δισύπατος, ἂν μὲν προσθῇς ὅτι "ἀλλὰ σύ γε σοφὸς εἶ, οὐδὲν πρὸς σὲ ταῦτα," συγγνώσεταί σοι. ἂν δ᾽ αὐτῷ τὰς 7 ἀληθείας εἴπῃς ὅτι "τῶν τρὶς πεπραμένων οὐδὲν διαφέρεις πρὸς τὸ μὴ καὶ αὐτὸς δοῦλος εἶναι," τί ἄλλο ἢ πληγάς σε δεῖ προσδοκᾶν ; 8 "πῶς γάρ," φησίν, "ἐγὼ δοῦλός εἰμι ; ὁ πατὴρ ἐλεύθερος, ἡ μήτηρ ἐλευθέρα, οὗ ὠνὴν οὐδεὶς ἔχει· ἀλλὰ καὶ συγκλητικός εἰμι καὶ Καίσαρος φίλος καὶ ὑπάτευκα καὶ δούλους πολλοὺς ἔχω." 9 πρῶτον μέν, ὦ βέλτιστε συγκλητικέ, τάχα σου καὶ ὁ πατὴρ τὴν αὐτὴν δουλείαν δοῦλος ἦν καὶ ἡ μήτηρ καὶ ὁ πάππος καὶ ἐφεξῆς πάντες οἱ 10 πρόγονοι. εἰ δὲ δὴ καὶ τὰ μάλιστα ἦσαν ἐλεύθεροι, τί τοῦτο πρὸς σέ ; τί γάρ, εἰ ἐκεῖνοι μὲν γενναῖοι ἦσαν, σὺ δ᾽ ἀγεννής ; ἐκεῖνοι μὲν ἄφοβοι, σὺ δὲ δειλός ; ἐκεῖνοι μὲν ἐγκρατεῖς, σὺ δ᾽ ἀκόλαστος ;

11 Καὶ τί, φησί, τοῦτο πρὸς τὸ δοῦλον εἶναι ;— Οὐδέν σοι φαίνεται εἶναι τὸ ἄκοντά τι ποιεῖν, τὸ ἀναγκαζόμενον, τὸ στένοντα πρὸς τὸ δοῦλον 12 εἶναι ;—Τοῦτο μὲν ἔστω, φησίν. ἀλλὰ τίς με δύναται ἀναγκάσαι, εἰ μὴ ὁ πάντων κύριος

he wills, and accordingly no bad man is free. And who wishes to live in grief, fear, envy, pity, desiring things and failing to get them, avoiding things and falling into them?—No one at all.—Do we find, then, any bad man free from grief or fear, not falling into what he would avoid, nor failing to achieve what he desires?—No one.—Then we find no bad man free, either.

Now if some man who has been consul twice hear this, he will forgive you, if you add, " But *you* are a wise man; this does not apply to you." Yet if you tell him the truth, to wit: " In point of being a slave you are not a whit better than those who have been thrice sold," what else can you expect but a flogging? " Why, how am I a slave?" says he. " My father was free, my mother free; no one has a deed of sale for me. More than that, I am a member of the senate, and a friend of Caesar, and I have been consul, and I own many slaves." Now in the first place, most worthy senator, it is very likely that your father was the same kind of slave that you are, and your mother, and your grandfather, and all your ancestors from first to last. But even if they were free to the limit, what does that prove in your case? Why, what does it prove if they were noble, and you are mean-spirited? If they were brave, and you a coward? If they were self-controlled, and you unrestrained?

And what, says someone, has this to do with being a slave?—Doesn't it strike you as " having to do with being a slave " for a man to do something against his will, under compulsion?—Granted the point, he replies. But who can put me under compulsion, except Caesar, the lord of all?—There,

ARRIAN'S DISCOURSES OF EPICTETUS

13 Καῖσαρ;—Οὐκοῦν ἕνα μὲν δεσπότην σαυτοῦ καὶ
σὺ αὐτὸς ὡμολόγησας. ὅτι δὲ πάντων, ὡς
λέγεις, κοινός ἐστιν, μηδέν σε τοῦτο παραμυ-
θείσθω, ἀλλὰ γίγνωσκε, ὅτι ἐκ μεγάλης οἰκίας
14 δοῦλος εἶ. οὕτως καὶ Νικοπολῖται ἐπιβοᾶν
εἰώθασι "νὴ τὴν Καίσαρος τύχην, ἐλεύθεροί
ἐσμεν."

15 Ὅμως δ', ἐάν σοι δοκῇ, τὸν μὲν Καίσαρα
πρὸς τὸ παρὸν ἀφῶμεν, ἐκεῖνο δέ μοι εἰπέ·
οὐδέποτ' ἠράσθης τινός; οὐ παιδισκαρίου, οὐ
16 παιδαρίου, οὐ δούλου, οὐκ ἐλευθέρου;—Τί οὖν
τοῦτο πρὸς τὸ δοῦλον εἶναι ἢ ἐλεύθερον;—
17 Οὐδέποθ' ὑπὸ τῆς ἐρωμένης ἐπετάγης οὐδὲν ὧν
οὐκ ἤθελες; οὐδέποτέ σου τὸ δουλάριον ἐκο-
λάκευσας; οὐδέποτ' αὐτοῦ τοὺς πόδας κατε-
φίλησας; καίτοι τοῦ Καίσαρος ἄν σέ τις
ἀναγκάσῃ, ὕβριν αὐτὸ ἡγῇ καὶ ὑπερβολὴν
18 τυραννίδος. τί οὖν ἄλλο ἐστὶ δουλεία; νυκτὸς
οὐδέποτ' ἀπῆλθες, ὅπου οὐκ ἤθελες; ἀνάλωσας,
ὅσα οὐκ ἤθελες; εἰπάς τινα οἰμώζων καὶ
στένων, ἠνέσχου λοιδορούμενος, ἀποκλειόμενος;
19 ἀλλ' εἰ σὺ αἰσχύνῃ τὰ σαυτοῦ ὁμολογεῖν,
ὅρα ἃ λέγει καὶ ποιεῖ ὁ Θρασωνίδης, ὃς
τοσαῦτα στρατευσάμενος, ὅσα τάχα οὐδὲ σύ,
πρῶτον μὲν ἐξελήλυθε νυκτός, ὅτε ὁ Γέτας οὐ
τολμᾷ ἐξελθεῖν, ἀλλ' εἰ προσηναγκάζετο ὑπ'
αὐτοῦ, πόλλ' ἂν ἐπικραυγάσας καὶ τὴν πικρὰν
20 δουλείαν ἀπολοφυράμενος ἐξῆλθεν. εἶτα, τί
λέγει;
248

you have yourself admitted that you have one master. And let it not comfort you that he is, as you say, the common master of all men, but realize that you are a slave in a great house. So also the men of Nicopolis[1] are wont to shout: "Yea, by the fortune of Caesar, we are free men!"

However, let us leave Caesar out of account, if you please, for the present, but answer me this: Were you never in love with anyone, a pretty girl, or pretty boy, a slave, a freedman?—What, then, has that to do with being either slave or free?—Were you never commanded by your sweetheart to do something you didn't wish to do? Did you never cozen your pet slave? Did you never kiss his feet? Yet if someone should compel you to kiss the feet of Caesar, you would regard that as insolence and most extravagant tyranny. What else, then, is slavery? Did you never go out at night where you didn't want to go? Did you never spend more than you wanted to spend? Did you never utter words with groaning and lamentation, endure to be reviled, to have the door shut in your face? Well, if you are ashamed to admit such things about yourself, observe what Thrasonides says and does, a man who had served on so many campaigns—perhaps more even than you have. First, he went out at night when Geta hasn't the courage to go abroad, but, if the latter had been compelled by him to do so, he would have gone out crying aloud and bewailing his bitter slavery. And then what does Thrasonides say? Says he,

---

[1] Where he was teaching. The very form of the oath contradicts the statement made.

παιδισκάριόν με,

φησίν,

καταδεδούλωκ᾽ εὐτελές,
ὃν οὐδὲ εἷς ¹ τῶν πολεμίων οὐπώποτε.²

21 τάλας, ὅς γε καὶ παιδισκαρίου δοῦλος εἶ καὶ
παιδισκαρίου εὐτελοῦς. τί οὖν ἔτι σαυτὸν
ἐλεύθερον λέγεις ; τί δὲ προφέρεις σου τὰς
22 στρατείας ; εἶτα ξίφος αἰτεῖ καὶ πρὸς τὸν ὑπ᾽
εὐνοίας μὴ διδόντα χαλεπαίνει καὶ δῶρα τῇ
μισούσῃ πέμπει καὶ δεῖται καὶ κλαίει, πάλιν
23 δὲ μικρὰ εὐημερήσας ἐπαίρεται· πλὴν καὶ τότε
πῶς μηδ᾽ ἐπιθυμεῖν ἢ φοβεῖσθαι ἀπομαθὼν
οὗτος ἐλευθερίαν ἂν εἶχε ; ³

24 Σκέψαι δ᾽ ἐπὶ τῶν ζῴων, πῶς χρώμεθα τῇ
25 ἐννοίᾳ τῆς ἐλευθερίας. λέοντας τρέφουσιν ἡμέ-
ρους ἐγκλείσαντες καὶ σιτίζουσι καὶ κομίζουσιν
ἔνιοι μεθ᾽ αὑτῶν. καὶ τίς ἐρεῖ τοῦτον τὸν
λέοντα ἐλεύθερον ; οὐχὶ δ᾽ ὅσῳ μαλακώτερον
διεξάγει, τοσούτῳ δουλικώτερον ; τίς δ᾽ ἂν λέων
αἴσθησιν καὶ λογισμὸν λαβὼν βούλοιτο τού-
26 των τις εἶναι τῶν λεόντων ; ἄγε, τὰ δὲ πτηνὰ
ταῦτα ὅταν ληφθῇ καὶ ἐγκεκλειμένα τρέφηται,
οἷα πάσχει ζητοῦντα ἐκφυγεῖν ; καὶ ἔνιά γε
αὐτῶν λιμῷ διαφθείρεται μᾶλλον ἢ ὑπομένει τὴν
27 τοιαύτην διεξαγωγήν, ὅσα δ᾽ οὖν διασώζεται,
μόγις καὶ χαλεπῶς καὶ φθίνοντα, κἂν ὅλως

¹ Koraes : οὐδείς S.   ² Meineke : πώποτε S.
³ Carl Schenkl's rewriting, based in part upon some old
corrections in S, which is clearly right in the general sense:

A cheap little wench has made of me a perfect
  slave,
Of me, though never a one among all my
  foemen might.[1]

Sad wretch, to be the slave of a wench, and a cheap
one at that ! Why, then, do you call yourself free
any longer? And why do you talk of your campaigns ? Then he calls for a sword, and gets angry
at the man who refuses out of good-will to give it
to him, and sends presents to the girl who hates
him, and begs, and weeps, and again, when he
has had a little success, he is elated. And yet even
then, so long as he had not learned to give up
passionate desire or fear, could this man have been
in possession of freedom?

Consider now, in the case of the animals, how we
employ the concept of freedom. Men shut up tame
lions in a cage, and bring them up, and feed them,
and some take them around with them. And yet
who will call such a lion free ? Is it not true that
the more softly the lion lives the more slavishly he
lives ? And what lion, were he to get sense and
reason, would care to be one of these lions ? Why,
yes, and the birds yonder, when they are caught
and brought up in cages, what do they suffer in
their efforts to escape ? And some of them starve
to death rather than endure such a life, while even
such as live, barely do so, and suffer and pine away,

[1] From the *Misoumenos* of Menander : Koch 338 ; Körte²,
p. 129 ; Allinson, p. 412 (Loeb Classical Library).

φοβεῖσθαι οὔτ' ἐλευθερίαν *S* apparently at first ; that is,
ἀπομαθών and ἂν εἶχε are additions.

εὕρῃ τι παρεῳγμένον, ἐξεπήδησεν. οὕτως ὀρέ-
γεται τῆς φυσικῆς ἐλευθερίας καὶ τοῦ αὐτόνομα
28 καὶ ἀκώλυτα εἶναι. καὶ τί σοι κακόν ἐστιν
ἐνταῦθα · "οἷα λέγεις; πέτεσθαι πέφυκα ὅπου
θέλω, ὕπαιθρον διάγειν, ᾄδειν ὅταν θέλω· σύ
με πάντων τούτων ἀφαιρῇ καὶ λέγεις 'τί σοι
κακόν ἐστιν;'"

29   Διὰ τοῦτο ἐκεῖνα μόνα ἐροῦμεν ἐλεύθερα, ὅσα
τὴν ἅλωσιν οὐ φέρει, ἀλλ᾽ ἅμα τε ἑάλω καὶ
30 ἀποθανόντα διέφυγεν. οὕτως καὶ Διογένης που
λέγει μίαν εἶναι μηχανὴν πρὸς ἐλευθερίαν τὸ
εὐκόλως ἀποθνήσκειν, καὶ τῷ Περσῶν βασιλεῖ
γράφει ὅτι "τὴν Ἀθηναίων πόλιν κατα-
δουλώσασθαι οὐ δύνασαι· οὐ μᾶλλον," φησίν,
31 "ἢ τοὺς ἰχθύας." "πῶς; οὐ γὰρ λήψομαι
αὐτούς;" "ἂν λάβῃς," φησίν, "εὐθὺς ἀπο-
λιπόντες σε οἰχήσονται, καθάπερ οἱ ἰχθύες.
καὶ γὰρ ἐκείνων ὃν ἂν λάβῃς, ἀπέθανεν· καὶ
οὗτοι ληφθέντες ἐὰν ἀποθνήσκωσιν, τί σοί ἐστι
32 τῆς παρασκευῆς ὄφελος;"[1] τοῦτ᾽ ἔστιν ἐλευθέρου
ἀνδρὸς φωνὴ σπουδῇ ἐξητακότος τὸ πρᾶγμα καὶ
ὥσπερ εἰκὸς εὑρηκότος. ἂν δ᾽ ἀλλαχοῦ ζητῇς
ἢ ὅπου ἐστίν, τί θαυμαστόν, εἰ οὐδέποτε αὐτὸ
εὑρίσκεις;

33   Ὁ δοῦλος εὐθὺς εὔχεται ἀφεθῆναι ἐλεύθερος.
διὰ τί; δοκεῖτε, ὅτι τοῖς εἰκοστώναις ἐπιθυμεῖ

___

[1] There is some uncertainty about the extent of the
quotation from Diogenes. Capps extends it as far as this
point, while Schenkl thought it stopped with ἰχθύες, three
lines above.

[1] Here as in II. 3 and in § 156 of this same chapter
Epictetus seems to have used a larger collection of letters

and if ever they find any opening, make their
escape. Such is their desire for physical freedom,
and a life of independence and freedom from restraint. And what is wrong with you here in your
cage? "What a question! My nature is to fly
where I please, to live in the open air, to sing when
I please. You rob me of all this, and then ask,
' What is wrong with you?' "

That is why we shall call free only those animals
which do not submit to captivity, but escape by
dying as soon as they are captured. So also Diogenes
says somewhere:[1] "The one sure way to secure
freedom is to die cheerfully"; and to the Persian[2]
king he writes: "You cannot enslave the Athenian
State any more than you can enslave the fish."
"How so? Shall I not lay hold of them?" "If you
do," he replies, "they will forthwith leave you and
escape, like the fish. And that is true, for if you
lay hold of one of them, it dies; and if these
Athenians die when you lay hold of them, what
good will you get from your armament?" That is
the word of a free man who has seriously examined
the matter, and, as you might expect, had discovered
truth about it. But if you look for it where it does
not exist, why be surprised if you never find it?

It is the slave's prayer that he be set free
immediately. Why? Do you think it is because
he is eager to pay his money to the men who collect

ascribed to Diogenes than that which has survived to our
time. See Schenkl's note on § 156 below.

[2] Schenkl deletes the word, and Orelli conjectures Μακε-
δόνων, making the reference to Philip or Alexander; but
about 355 Artaxerxes Ochus seems actually to have threatened
war against Athens. See Judeich in the *Real-Encyclopädie*[2],
2, 1319, 25 ff.

δοῦναι ἀργύριον; οὔ· ἀλλ' ὅτι φαντάζεται μέχρι
νῦν διὰ τὸ μὴ τετυχηκέναι τούτου ἐμποδίζεσθαι
34 καὶ δυσροεῖν. "ἂν ἀφεθῶ," φησίν, "εὐθὺς πᾶσα
εὔροια, οὐδενὸς ἐπιστρέφομαι, πᾶσιν ὡς ἴσος καὶ
ὅμοιος λαλῶ, πορεύομαι ὅπου θέλω, ἔρχομαι
35 ὅθεν θέλω καὶ ὅπου θέλω." εἶτα ἀπηλευθέρω-
ται καὶ εὐθὺς μὲν οὐχ ἔχων, ποῖ φάγῃ, ζητεῖ,
τίνα κολακεύσῃ, παρὰ τίνι δειπνήσῃ· εἶτα ἢ
ἐργάζεται τῷ σώματι καὶ πάσχει τὰ δεινότατα
κἂν σχῇ τινὰ φάτνην, ἐμπέπτωκεν εἰς δουλείαν
36 πολὺ τῆς προτέρας χαλεπωτέραν ἢ καὶ εὐ-
πορήσας ἄνθρωπος ἀπειρόκαλος πεφίληκε παιδισκάριον καὶ δυστυχῶν ἀνακλαίεται καὶ τὴν
37 δουλείαν ποθεῖ. "τί γάρ μοι κακὸν ἦν; ἄλλος
μ' ἐνέδυεν, ἄλλος μ' ὑπέδει, ἄλλος ἔτρεφεν,
ἄλλος ἐνοσοκόμει, ὀλίγα αὐτῷ ὑπηρέτουν. νῦν
δὲ τάλας οἷα πάσχω πλείοσι δουλεύων ἀνθ'
38 ἑνός; ὅμως δ' ἐὰν δακτυλίους," φησίν, "λάβω,
τότε γ' εὐρούστατα διάξω καὶ εὐδαιμονέστατα."
πρῶτον μὲν ἵνα λάβῃ, πάσχει ὧν ἐστὶν ἄξιος·
39 εἶτα λαβὼν πάλιν ταὐτά. εἶτά φησιν "ἂν μὲν
στρατεύσωμαι, ἀπηλλάγην πάντων τῶν κακῶν."
στρατεύεται, πάσχει ὅσα μαστιγίας καὶ οὐδὲν
ἧττον δευτέραν αἰτεῖ στρατείαν καὶ τρίτην.

---

[1] See note on II. 1, 26.
[2] For the euphemistic phrase used in the Greek see
Demosthenes, 59, 20.
[3] The members of the Equestrian order at Rome had the
right to wear a gold ring.

the five per cent. tax?[1]   No, it is because he fancies
that up till now he is hampered and uncomfortable,
because he has not obtained his freedom from
slavery.   "If I am set free," he says, "immediately
it is all happiness, I shall pay no attention to
anybody, I talk to everybody as an equal and as
one in the same station in life, I go where I please,
I come whence I please, and where I please."
Then he is emancipated, and forthwith, having no
place to which to go and eat, he looks for someone
to flatter, for someone at whose house to dine.
Next he either earns a living by prostitution,[2] and
so endures the most dreadful things, and if he gets
a manger at which to eat he has fallen into a slavery
much more severe than the first; or even if he
grows rich, being a vulgarian he has fallen in love
with a chit of a girl, and is miserable, and laments,
and yearns for his slavery again.   "Why, what was
wrong with me?   Someone else kept me in clothes,
and shoes, and supplied me with food, and nursed
me when I was sick; I served him in only a few
matters.   But now, miserable man that I am, what
suffering is mine, who am a slave to several instead
of one!   However, if I get rings on my fingers,"[3]
he says, "then indeed I shall live most prosperously
and happily."   And so, first, in order to get them
he submits to—what he deserves!   Then when he
has got them, you have the same thing over again.
Next he says, "If I serve in a campaign, I am rid of
all my troubles."   He serves in a campaign, he
submits to all that a jail-bird suffers, but none the
less he demands a second campaign and a third.[4]

[4] Required of those who held the higher offices.   See note
on II. 14, 17.

40 εἶθ' ὅταν αὐτὸν τὸν κολοφῶνα ἐπιθῇ καὶ γένηται συγκλητικός, τότε γίνεται δοῦλος εἰς
σύλλογον ἐρχόμενος, τότε τὴν καλλίστην¹ καὶ
λιπαρωτάτην δουλείαν δουλεύει.

41 "Ἵνα μὴ μωρὸς ᾖ, ἄγ',² ἵνα μάθῃ, ἃ ἔλεγεν ὁ
Σωκράτης, "τί ἐστὶ τῶν ὄντων ἕκαστον," καὶ
μὴ εἰκῆ τὰς προλήψεις ἐφαρμόζῃ ταῖς ἐπὶ
42 μέρους οὐσίαις. τοῦτο γάρ ἐστι τὸ αἴτιον τοῖς
ἀνθρώποις πάντων τῶν κακῶν, τὸ τὰς προλήψεις
τὰς κοινὰς μὴ δύνασθαι ἐφαρμόζειν τοῖς³ ἐπὶ
43 μέρους. ἡμεῖς δ' ἄλλοι ἄλλο οἰόμεθα. ὁ μὲν
ὅτι νοσεῖ. οὐδαμῶς, ἀλλ' ὅτι τὰς προλήψεις
οὐκ ἐφαρμόζει. ὁ δ' ὅτι πτωχός ἐστιν, ὁ δ'
ὅτι πατέρα χαλεπὸν ἔχει ἢ μητέρα, τῷ δ' ὅτι
ὁ Καῖσαρ οὐχ ἵλεώς ἐστιν. τοῦτο δ' ἐστὶν ἓν
καὶ μόνον τὸ τὰς προλήψεις ἐφαρμόζειν μὴ
44 εἰδέναι. ἐπεὶ τίς οὐκ ἔχει κακοῦ πρόληψιν, ὅτι
βλαβερόν ἐστιν, ὅτι φευκτόν ἐστιν, ὅτι παντὶ
τρόπῳ ἀποικονόμητόν ἐστιν; πρόληψις προλήψει
45 οὐ μάχεται, ἀλλ' ὅταν ἔλθῃ ἐπὶ τὸ ἐφαρμόζειν.
τί οὖν τὸ κακόν ἐστι τοῦτο καὶ βλαβερὸν καὶ
φευκτόν; λέγει τὸ Καίσαρος μὴ εἶναι φίλον·
ἀπῆλθεν, ἀπέπεσεν τῆς ἐφαρμογῆς, θλίβεται,
ζητεῖ τὰ μηδὲν πρὸς τὸ προκείμενον· ὅτι τυχὼν
τοῦ φίλος εἶναι Καίσαρος οὐδὲν ἧττον τοῦ
46 ζητουμένου οὐ τέτευχεν. τί γάρ ἐστιν, ὃ ζητεῖ
πᾶς ἄνθρωπος; εὐσταθῆσαι, εὐδαιμονῆσαι, πάντα

---

¹ Schweighäuser: καλλί (?) S.   ² Elter: ἀλλ' S.
³ Wolf: ταῖς S.

---

¹ i.e. the finishing touch. See note on II. 14, 19.

After that, when he adds the very colophon,[1] and becomes a senator, then he becomes a slave as he enters the senate, then he serves in the handsomest and sleekest slavery.

Come, let him not be a fool, let him learn, as Socrates used to say, " What each several thing means,"[2] and not apply his preconceptions at random to the particular cases. For this is the cause to men of all their evils, namely, their inability to apply their general preconceptions to the particular instances. But some of us think one thing and some another. One man fancies he is ill. Not at all; the fact is that he is not applying his preconceptions. Another fancies he is a beggar; another that he has a hard-hearted father or mother; still another that Caesar is not gracious to him. But this means one thing and one thing only—ignorance of how to apply their preconceptions. Why, who does not have a preconception of evil, that it is harmful, that it is to be avoided, that it is something to get rid of in every way? One preconception does not conflict with another, but conflict arises when one proceeds to apply them. What, then, is this evil that is harmful and is to be avoided? One person says it is not to be Caesar's friend;[3] he is off the course, he has missed the proper application, he is in a bad way, he is looking for what is not pertinent to the case in hand; because, when he has succeeded in being Caesar's friend, he has none the less failed to get what he was seeking. For what is it that every man is seeking? To live securely, to be happy, to do everything as he wishes to do,

[2] Xenophon, *Mem.* IV. 6, 1.
[3] That is, *persona grata* at court.

ARRIAN'S DISCOURSES OF EPICTETUS

ὡς θέλει ποιεῖν, μὴ κωλύεσθαι, μὴ ἀναγκάζεσθαι.
ὅταν οὖν γένηται Καίσαρος φίλος, πέπαυται
κωλυόμενος, πέπαυται ἀναγκαζόμενος, εὐσταθεῖ,
εὐροεῖ; τίνος πυθώμεθα; τίνα ἔχομεν ἀξιο-
πιστότερον ἢ αὐτὸν τοῦτον τὸν γεγονότα φίλον;
47 ἐλθὲ εἰς τὸ μέσον καὶ εἰπὲ ἡμῖν, πότε ἀταραχώτερον ἐκάθευδες, νῦν ἢ πρὶν γενέσθαι φίλος τοῦ
Καίσαρος; εὐθὺς ἀκούεις ὅτι " παῦσαι, τοὺς
θεούς σοι, ἐμπαίζων μου τῇ τύχῃ[1] οὐκ οἶδας,
οἷα πάσχω τάλας· οὐδ' ὕπνος ἐπέρχεταί μοι,
ἀλλ' ἄλλος ἐπ' ἄλλῳ[2] ἐλθὼν λέγει, ὅτι ἤδη
ἐγρηγορεῖ, ἤδη πρόεισιν· εἶτα ταραχαί, εἶτα
48 φροντίδες." ἄγε, ἐδείπνεις δὲ πότε εὐαρεστό-
τερον, νῦν ἢ πρότερον; ἄκουσον αὐτοῦ καὶ περὶ
τούτων τί λέγει· ὅτι, ἂν μὲν μὴ κληθῇ,[3] ὀδυνᾶται,
ἂν δὲ κληθῇ, ὡς δοῦλος παρὰ κυρίῳ δειπνεῖ
μεταξὺ προσέχων, μή τι μωρὸν εἴπῃ ἢ ποιήσῃ. καὶ
τί δοκεῖς φοβεῖται; μὴ μαστιγωθῇ ὡς δοῦλος;
πόθεν αὐτῷ οὕτως καλῶς; ἀλλ' ὡς πρέπει
τηλικοῦτον ἄνδρα, Καίσαρος φίλον, μὴ ἀπο-
49 λέσῃ τὸν τράχηλον. ἐλούου δὲ πότ' ἀταραχώτερον; ἐγυμνάζου δὲ πότε σχολαίτερον; τὸ
σύνολον ποῖον μᾶλλον ἤθελες βίον βιοῦν, τὸν νῦν
50 ἢ τὸν τότε; ὀμόσαι δύναμαι, ὅτι οὐδεὶς οὕτως
ἐστὶν ἀναίσθητος ἢ ἀναλθής,[4] μὴ ἀποδύρασθαι
τὰς αὑτοῦ συμφοράς, ὅσῳ ἂν ᾖ φίλτερος.

[1] Schweighäuser: ψυχῆι S.
[2] ἐπ' ἄλλῳ added by Reiske.   [3] κληθῇ repeated in S.
[4] Oldfather: ἀναληθής S (and Scholiast).

[1] Compare with this section the grave words of Francis
Bacon : "Men in great place are thrice servants, servants to
the sovereign or state, servants of fame, and servants of

258

not to be hindered, not to be subject to compulsion.
When, therefore, he becomes a friend of Caesar,
has he been relieved of hindrance, relieved of compulsion, does he live securely, does he live serenely?
From whom shall we inquire? What better witness
have we than this very man who has become
Caesar's friend? Come into the midst and tell us.
When did you sleep more peacefully, now or before
you became Caesar's friend? Immediately the
answer comes: "Stop, I implore you by the gods,
and do not jest at my lot; you don't know what I
suffer, miserable man that I am; no sleep visits me,
but first one person comes in and then another and
reports that Caesar is already awake, and is already
coming out; then troubles, then worries!" Come,
when did you dine more pleasantly, now or formerly?
Listen to him and to what he has to say on this topic.
If he is not invited, he is hurt, and if he is invited,
he dines like a slave at a master's table, all the time
careful not to say or do something foolish. And what
do you suppose he is afraid of? That he be scourged
like a slave? How can he expect to get off as well
as that? But as befits so great a man, a friend
of Caesar, he is afraid he will lose his head. When
did you take your bath in greater peace? And
when did you take your exercise at greater leisure?
In a word, which life would you rather live, your
present life or the old one? I can take oath that
no one is so insensate or so incurable as not to
lament his misfortunes the more he is a friend of
Caesar.[1]

business, so as they have no freedom, neither in their persons,
nor in their actions, nor in their times." *Essays*, " Of Great
Place."

51 Ὅταν οὖν μήτε οἱ βασιλεῖς λεγόμενοι ζῶσιν
ὡς θέλουσι μήθ᾽ οἱ φίλοι τῶν βασιλέων, τίνες
ἔτι εἰσὶν ἐλεύθεροι ;—Ζήτει καὶ εὑρήσεις. ἔχεις
γὰρ ἀφορμὰς παρὰ τῆς φύσεως πρὸς εὕρεσιν τῆς
ἀληθείας. εἰ δ᾽ αὐτὸς οὐχ οἷός τε εἶ κατὰ ταύτας
52 ψιλὰς πορευόμενος εὑρεῖν τὸ ἑξῆς, ἄκουσον παρὰ
τῶν ἐζητηκότων. τί λέγουσιν ; ἀγαθόν σοι
δοκεῖ ἡ ἐλευθερία ;—Τὸ μέγιστον.—Δύναται οὖν
τις τοῦ μεγίστου ἀγαθοῦ τυγχάνων κακοδαι-
μονεῖν ἢ κακῶς πράσσειν ;—Οὔ.—Ὅσους οὖν
ἂν ἴδῃς κακοδαιμονοῦντας, δυσροοῦντας, πεν-
θοῦντας, ἀποφαίνου θαρρῶν μὴ εἶναι ἐλευ-
53 θέρους.—Ἀποφαίνομαι.—Οὐκοῦν ἀπὸ μὲν ὠνῆς
καὶ πράσεως καὶ τῆς τοιαύτης ἐν κτήσει κατα-
τάξεως ἤδη ἀποκεχωρήκαμεν. εἰ γὰρ ὀρθῶς
ὡμολόγησας ταῦτα, ἄν τε μέγας βασιλεὺς κακο-
δαιμονῇ, οὐκ ἂν ἐλεύθερος, ἄν τε μικρός, ἄν θ᾽
ὑπατικός, ἄν τε δισύπατος.—Ἔστω.
54 Ἔτι οὖν ἀπόκριναί μοι κἀκεῖνο· δοκεῖ σοι μέγα
τι εἶναι καὶ γενναῖον ἡ ἐλευθερία καὶ ἀξιόλογον ;
—Πῶς γὰρ οὔ ;—Ἔστιν οὖν τυγχάνοντά τινος
οὕτως μεγάλου καὶ ἀξιολόγου καὶ γενναίου τα-
55 πεινὸν εἶναι ;—Οὐκ ἔστιν.—Ὅταν οὖν ἴδῃς τινὰ
ὑποπεπτωκότα ἑτέρῳ ἢ κολακεύοντα παρὰ τὸ
φαινόμενον αὐτῷ, λέγε καὶ τοῦτον θαρρῶν μὴ
εἶναι ἐλεύθερον· καὶ μὴ μόνον, ἂν δειπναρίου
ἕνεκα αὐτὸ ποιῇ, ἀλλὰ κἂν ἐπαρχίας ἕνεκα κἂν
ὑπατείας. ἀλλ᾽ ἐκείνους μὲν μικροδούλους λέγε
τοὺς μικρῶν τινων ἕνεκα ταῦτα ποιοῦντας, τού-

---

[1] The reference is to the ordinary method of acquiring
slaves, since relatively few were ever bred.

When, therefore, neither those who are styled kings live as they will, nor the friends of these kings, what free men are left?—Seek and you will find. For nature has given you resources to find the truth. But if you are unable of yourself, by employing these resources alone, to find the next step, listen to those who have already made the search. What do they say? Does freedom seem to you to be a good? —Yes, the greatest.—Is it possible, then, for a man who has this greatest good to be unhappy, or to fare ill?—No.—When, therefore, you see men unhappy, miserable, grieving, declare confidently that they are not free.—I do so declare.—Very well, then, we have now got away from buying and selling[1] and arrangements of that kind in the acquisition of property. For if you are right in agreeing to these propositions, whether it be the Great King[2] who is unhappy, or a little king, whether it be a man of consular rank, or one who has been a consul twice, he could not be free.—Granted.

Answer me, then, this further question: Does freedom seem to you to be a great and noble thing, and precious?—Of course.—Is it possible, then, for a man who achieves a thing so great and precious and noble, to be of abject spirit?—It is not.—When, therefore, you see one man cringing before another, or flattering him contrary to his own opinion, say confidently of this man also that he is not free; and that not merely if he be doing so for the sake of a paltry meal, but even if it be for a governorship or a consulship. Call rather those who do these things for certain small ends slaves on a small scale, and

[2] That is, of Persia.

56 τους δ', ὡς εἰσὶν ἄξιοι, μεγαλοδούλους.—Ἔστω
καὶ ταῦτα.—Δοκεῖ δέ σοι ἡ ἐλευθερία αὐτεξού-
σιόν τι εἶναι καὶ αὐτόνομον ;—Πῶς γὰρ οὔ ;—
Ὅντινα οὖν ἐπ' ἄλλῳ κωλῦσαι ἔστι καὶ ἀναγ-
57 κάσαι, θαρρῶν λέγε μὴ εἶναι ἐλεύθερον. καὶ
μή μοι πάππους αὐτοῦ καὶ προπάππους βλέπε
καὶ ὠνὴν ζήτει καὶ πρᾶσιν, ἀλλ' ἂν ἀκούσῃς
λέγοντος ἔσωθεν καὶ ἐκ πάθους "κύριε," κἂν
δώδεκα ῥάβδοι προάγωσιν, λέγε δοῦλον· κἂν
ἀκούσῃς λέγοντος "τάλας ἐγώ, οἷα πάσχω," λέγε
δοῦλον· ἂν ἁπλῶς ἀποκλαιόμενον ἴδῃς, μεμφόμενον, δυσροοῦντα, λέγε δοῦλον περιπόρφυρον
58 ἔχοντα. ἂν οὖν μηδὲν τούτων ποιῇ, μήπω εἴπῃς
ἐλεύθερον, ἀλλὰ τὰ δόγματα αὐτοῦ κατάμαθε,
μή τι ἀναγκαστά, μή τι κωλυτικά, μή τι δυσροη-
τικά· κἂν εὕρῃς τοιοῦτον, λέγε δοῦλον ἀνοχὰς
ἔχοντα ἐν Σατουρναλίοις· λέγε, ὅτι ὁ κύριος
αὐτοῦ ἀποδημεῖ· εἶθ' ἥξει καὶ γνώσῃ οἷα πάσχει.
59 —Τίς ἥξει ;—Πᾶς ὃς ἂν ἐξουσίαν ἔχῃ τῶν ὑπ'
αὐτοῦ τινὸς θελομένων πρὸς τὸ περιποιῆσαι
ταῦτα ἢ ἀφελέσθαι.—Οὕτως οὖν πολλοὺς κυρίους
ἔχομεν ;—Οὕτως. τὰ γὰρ πράγματα προτέρους
τούτων κυρίους ἔχομεν· ἐκεῖνα δὲ πολλά ἐστιν.
διὰ ταῦτα ἀνάγκη καὶ τοὺς τούτων τινὸς ἔχοντας
60 ἐξουσίαν κυρίους εἶναι· ἐπεί τοι οὐδεὶς αὐτὸν τὸν
Καίσαρα φοβεῖται, ἀλλὰ θάνατον, φυγήν, ἀφαί-
ρεσιν τῶν ὄντων, φυλακήν, ἀτιμίαν. οὐδὲ φιλεῖ
τις τὸν Καίσαρα, ἂν μή τι ᾖ πολλοῦ ἄξιος, ἀλλὰ

---

[1] The number for a consul.
[2] The robe worn by high officials at Rome. Cf. I. 2, 18.
[3] When slaves had special liberties.

the others, as they deserve, slaves on a grand scale.
—This also I grant.—And does freedom seem to you
to be something independent and self-governing?—
Of course.—When, therefore, it is in another's power
to put hindrances in a man's way and subject him to
compulsion, say confidently that this man is not free.
And please don't look at his grandfathers and great-
grandfathers, or look for a deed of sale or purchase,
but if you hear him say "Master," in the centre of his
being and with deep emotion, call him a slave, even if
twelve fasces [1] precede him; and if you hear him say,
"Alas! What I must suffer!" call him a slave; and, in
short, if you see him wailing, complaining, in misery,
call him a slave in a *toga praetexta*.[2] However, if he
does none of these things, do not call him free yet,
but find out what his judgements are, whether they
are in any respect subject to compulsion, to hindrance,
to unhappiness; and if you find him to be that kind
of a person, call him a slave on holiday at the
Saturnalia; [3] say that his master is out of town;
later on he will return, and then you will learn what
the fellow suffers.—Who will return?—Anyone
who has control over the things which some man
desires, to get these for him or to take them away.—
Have we, then, so many masters?—Yes, so many. For
even before these personal masters we have masters
in the form of circumstances, and these are many.
Hence, it needs must follow that those too who
have authority over some one of these circumstances
are our masters. Why, look you, no one is afraid of
Caesar himself, but he is afraid of death, exile, loss of
property, prison, disfranchisement. Nor does anyone
love Caesar himself, unless in some way Caesar
is a person of great merit; but we love wealth, a

πλοῦτον φιλοῦμεν, δημαρχίαν, στρατηγίαν, ὑπατείαν. ὅταν ταῦτα φιλῶμεν καὶ μισῶμεν καὶ
φοβώμεθα, ἀνάγκη τοὺς ἐξουσίαν αὐτῶν ἔχοντας
κυρίους ἡμῶν εἶναι. διὰ τοῦτο καὶ ὡς θεοὺς

61 αὐτοὺς προσκυνοῦμεν· ἐννοοῦμεν γάρ, ὅτι τὸ
ἔχον ἐξουσίαν τῆς μεγίστης ὠφελείας θεῖόν ἐστιν.
εἶθ᾽ ὑποτάσσομεν κακῶς "οὗτος δ᾽ ἔχει τῆς
μεγίστης ὠφελείας¹ ἐξουσίαν." ἀνάγκη καὶ τὸ
γενόμενον ἐξ αὐτῶν ἐπενεχθῆναι κακῶς.

62 Τί οὖν ἐστι τὸ ποιοῦν ἀκώλυτον τὸν ἄνθρωπον
καὶ αὐτεξούσιον; πλοῦτος γὰρ οὐ ποιεῖ οὐδ᾽

63 ὑπατεία οὐδ᾽ ἐπαρχία οὐδὲ βασιλεία, ἀλλὰ δεῖ
τι ἄλλο εὑρεθῆναι. τί οὖν ἐστι τὸ ἐν τῷ γράφειν
ἀκώλυτον ποιοῦν καὶ ἀπαραπόδιστον;—Ἡ ἐπιστήμη τοῦ γράφειν.—Τί δ᾽ ἐν τῷ κιθαρίζειν;—
Ἡ ἐπιστήμη τοῦ κιθαρίζειν.—Οὐκοῦν καὶ ἐν τῷ

64 βιοῦν ἡ ἐπιστήμη τοῦ βιοῦν. ὡς μὲν οὖν ἁπλῶς,
ἀκήκοας· σκέψαι δ᾽ αὐτὸ καὶ ἐκ τῶν ἐπὶ²
μέρους. τὸν ἐφιέμενόν τινος τῶν ἐπ᾽ ἄλλοις
ὄντων ἐνδέχεται ἀκώλυτον εἶναι;—Οὔ.—Ἐνδέ-

65 χεται ἀπαραπόδιστον;—Οὔ.—Οὐκοῦν οὐδ᾽ ἐλεύθερον. ὅρα οὖν· πότερον οὐδὲν ἔχομεν, ὃ ἐφ᾽
ἡμῖν μόνοις ἐστίν, ἢ πάντα, ἢ τὰ μὲν ἐφ᾽ ἡμῖν

66 ἐστίν, τὰ δ᾽ ἐπ᾽ ἄλλοις;—Πῶς λέγεις;—Τὸ
σῶμα ὅταν θέλῃς ὁλόκληρον εἶναι, ἐπὶ σοί ἐστιν

---

¹ The last eleven words are here wrongly repeated in S,
as Schenkl observed; but he was mistaken in assuming that
the repetition began immediately after ἔχει, whereas it
probably was due to the eye going back to the wrong
ὠφελείας.
² ἐπί added by Sb.

---

¹ The major premiss is: "What has power to confer the
greatest advantage is divine"; the minor premiss, as in the

tribuneship, a praetorship, a consulship. When we love and hate and fear these things, it needs must be that those who control them are masters over us. That is why we even worship those persons as gods; for we consider that what has power to confer the greatest advantage is divine. And then we lay down the wrong minor premiss: "This man has power to confer the greatest advantage." It needs must be that the conclusion from these premisses is wrong too.[1]

What, then, is it which makes a man free from hindrance and his own master? For wealth does not do it, nor a consulship, nor a province, nor a kingdom, but something else has to be found. What, therefore, is it which makes a man free from hindrance and restraint in writing?—The knowledge of how to write.—And what in playing on the harp?—The knowledge of how to play on the harp.—So also in living, it is the knowledge of how to live. Now you have already heard this, as a general principle, but consider it also in its particular applications. Is it possible for the man who is aiming at some one of these things which are under the control of others to be free from hindrance?—No.—Is it possible for him to be free from restraint?—No.—Therefore, it is not possible for him to be free, either. Consider then: Have we nothing which is under our own exclusive control, or is everything in that state; or are some things under our control and others under the control of others?—How do you mean?—When you want your body to be whole, is the matter under

text; from which follows the conclusion: "Therefore, this man is divine," which is wrong because of the false minor premiss.

ἢ οὔ;—Οὐκ ἐπ᾽ ἐμοί.—Ὅταν δ᾽ ὑγιαίνειν;—
Οὐδὲ τοῦτο.—Ὅταν δὲ καλὸν εἶναι;—Οὐδὲ
τοῦτο.—Ζῆν δὲ καὶ ἀποθανεῖν;—Οὐδὲ τοῦτο.—
Οὐκοῦν τὸ μὲν σῶμα ἀλλότριον, ὑπεύθυνον παν-
67 τὸς τοῦ ἰσχυροτέρου.—Ἔστω.—Τὸν ἀγρὸν δ᾽ ἐπὶ
σοί ἐστιν ἔχειν, ὅταν θέλῃς καὶ ἐφ᾽ ὅσον θέλεις
καὶ οἷον θέλεις;—Οὔ.—Τὰ δὲ δουλάρια;—Οὔ.—
Τὰ δ᾽ ἱμάτια;—Οὔ.—Τὸ δὲ οἰκίδιον;—Οὔ.—
Τοὺς δ᾽ ἵππους;—Τούτων μὲν οὐδέν.—Ἂν δὲ τὰ
τέκνα σου ζῆν θέλῃς ἐξ ἅπαντος ἢ τὴν γυναῖκα
ἢ τὸν ἀδελφὸν ἢ τοὺς φίλους, ἐπὶ σοί ἐστιν;—
Οὐδὲ ταῦτα.

68 Πότερον οὖν οὐδὲν ἔχεις αὐτεξούσιον, ὃ ἐπὶ
μόνῳ ἐστὶ σοί, ἢ ἔχεις τι τοιοῦτον;—Οὐκ οἶδα.
69 —Ὅρα οὖν οὕτως καὶ σκέψαι αὐτό. μή τις
δύναταί σε ποιῆσαι συγκαταθέσθαι τῷ ψεύδει;
—Οὐδείς.—Οὐκοῦν ἐν μὲν τῷ συγκαταθετικῷ
τόπῳ ἀκώλυτος εἶ καὶ ἀνεμπόδιστος.—Ἔστω.—
70 Ἄγε, ὁρμῆσαι δέ σε ἐφ᾽ ὃ μὴ θέλεις τις δύναται
ἀναγκάσαι;—Δύναται. ὅταν γάρ μοι θάνατον
ἢ δεσμὰ ἀπειλῇ, ἀναγκάζει μ᾽ ὁρμῆσαι.—Ἂν
οὖν καταφρονῇς τοῦ ἀποθανεῖν καὶ τοῦ δεδέσθαι,
71 ἔτι αὐτοῦ ἐπιστρέφῃ;—Οὔ.—Σὸν οὖν ἐστιν
ἔργον τὸ καταφρονεῖν θανάτου ἢ οὐ σόν;—Ἐμόν.
—Σὸν ἄρα ἐστὶ καὶ τὸ ὁρμῆσαι ἢ οὔ;—Ἔστω
ἐμόν.—Τὸ δ᾽ ἀφορμῆσαι τίνος; σὸν καὶ τοῦτο.—
72 Τί οὖν, ἂν ἐμοῦ ὁρμήσαντος περιπατῆσαι ἐκεῖνός
με κωλύσῃ;—Τί σου κωλύσει; μή τι τὴν
συγκατάθεσιν;—Οὔ· ἀλλὰ τὸ σωμάτιον.—Ναί,
ὡς λίθον.—Ἔστω· ἀλλ᾽ οὐκέτι ἐγὼ περιπατῶ.—

your control, or not?—It is not.—And when you want it to be well?—Nor that, either.—And to live or to die?—Nor that, either.—Therefore, your body is not your own possession, it is subject to everyone who is stronger than you are.—Granted.—And your farm, is it under your control to have it when you want, and as long as you want, and in the condition that you want?—No.—And your paltry slaves?—No. —And your clothes?—No.—And your paltry house? —No.—And your horses?—None of these things.— And if you wish by all means your children to live, or your wife, or your brother, or your friends, is the matter under your control?—No, nor that, either.

Have you, then, nothing subject to your authority, which is under your control and yours only, or do you have something of that sort?—I do not know.— Look, then, at the matter this way, and consider it. No one can make you assent to what is false, can he? —No one.—Well, then, in the region of assent you are free from hindrance and restraint.—Granted.— Come, can anyone force you to choose something that you do not want?—He can; for when he threatens me with death or bonds, he compels me to choose.—If, however, you despise death and bonds, do you pay any further heed to him?—No.—Is it, then, an act of your own to despise death, or is it not your own act?—It is mine.—So it is your own act to choose, or is it not?—Granted that it is mine. —And to refuse something? This also is yours.— Yes, but suppose I choose to go for a walk and the other person hinders me?—What part of you will he hinder? Surely not your assent?—No; but my poor body.—Yes, as he would a stone.—Granted that, but I do not proceed to take my walk.—But

73 Τίς δέ σοι εἶπεν "τὸ περιπατῆσαι σὸν ἔργον
ἐστὶν ἀκώλυτον"; ἐγὼ γὰρ ἐκεῖνο ἔλεγον ἀκώλυτον μόνον τὸ ὁρμῆσαι· ὅπου δὲ σώματος χρεία
καὶ τῆς ἐκ τούτου συνεργείας, πάλαι ἀκήκοας,
74 ὅτι οὐδέν ἐστι σόν.—Ἔστω καὶ ταῦτα.—Ὀρέγεσθαι δέ σε οὗ μὴ θέλεις τις ἀναγκάσαι δύναται;—Οὐδείς.—Προθέσθαι δ' ἢ ἐπιβαλέσθαι τις
ἢ ἁπλῶς χρῆσθαι ταῖς προσπιπτούσαις φαν-
75 τασίαις;—Οὐδὲ τοῦτο· ἀλλὰ ὀρεγόμενόν με
κωλύσει τυχεῖν οὗ ὀρέγομαι.—Ἂν τῶν σῶν τινὸς
ὀρέγῃ καὶ τῶν ἀκωλύτων, πῶς σε κωλύσει;—
Οὐδαμῶς.—Τίς οὖν σοι λέγει, ὅτι ὁ τῶν ἀλλοτρίων ὀρεγόμενος ἀκώλυτός ἐστιν;

76 Ὑγείας οὖν μὴ ὀρέγωμαι;—Μηδαμῶς, μηδ'
77 ἄλλου ἀλλοτρίου μηδενός. ὃ γὰρ οὐκ ἔστιν ἐπὶ
σοὶ παρασκευάσαι ἢ τηρῆσαι ὅτε θέλεις, τοῦτο
ἀλλότριόν ἐστιν. μακρὰν ἀπ' αὐτοῦ οὐ μόνον
τὰς χεῖρας, ἀλλὰ πολὺ πρότερον τὴν ὄρεξιν· εἰ
δὲ μή, παρέδωκας σαυτὸν δοῦλον, ὑπέθηκας τὸν
τράχηλον, ὅ τι[1] ἂν θαυμάσῃς τῶν μὴ σῶν, ᾧ τινι
78 ἂν τῶν ὑπευθύνων καὶ θνητῶν προσπαθῇς.—Ἡ
χεὶρ οὐκ ἔστιν ἐμή;—Μέρος ἐστὶ σόν, φύσει δὲ
πηλός, κωλυτόν, ἀναγκαστόν, δοῦλον παντὸς τοῦ
79 ἰσχυροτέρου. καὶ τί σοι λέγω χεῖρα; ὅλον τὸ
σῶμα οὕτως ἔχειν σε δεῖ ὡς ὀνάριον ἐπισεσαγ-
μένον, ἐφ' ὅσον ἂν οἷόν τε ᾖ, ἐφ' ὅσον ἂν διδῶται·
ἂν δ' ἀγγαρεία ᾖ καὶ στρατιώτης ἐπιλάβηται,
ἄφες, μὴ ἀντίτεινε μηδὲ γόγγυζε. εἰ δὲ μή,
πληγὰς λαβὼν οὐδὲν ἧττον ἀπολεῖς καὶ τὸ ὀνά-

---

[1] ὅ τι added by Elter: τράχηλον, ἂν θαυμάσῃς τῶν τϊ (later erased) μή S.

who told you, "It is your own act to take a walk
unhindered"? As for me, I told you that the only
unhindered thing was the desire; but where there is
a use of the body and its co-operation, you have heard
long ago that nothing is your own.—Granted that
also.—Can anyone force you to desire what you do
not want?—No one.—Or to purpose or plan, or, in a
word, to deal with the impressions that come to
you?—No, nor that, either; but he will hinder me,
when I set my desire upon something, from achieving
what I desire.—If you desire something which is your
own and not subject to hindrance, how will he hinder
you?—Not at all.—Who, then, tells you that the
man who sets his desire upon what is not his own is
free from hindrance?

Shall I not, then, set my desire on health?—No,
not at all, nor on anything else which is not your
own. For that which is not in your power to
acquire or to keep is none of yours. Keep far away
from it not merely your hands, but above all your
desire; otherwise, you have delivered yourself into
slavery, you have bowed your neck to the burden, if
you admire anything that is not your own, if you
conceive a violent passion for anything that is in
subjection to another and mortal.—Is not my hand
my own?—It is a part of you, but by nature it is
clay, subject to hindrance and compulsion, a slave to
everything that is stronger than you are. And why
do I name you the hand? You ought to treat your
whole body like a poor loaded-down donkey, as long
as it is possible, as long as it is allowed; and if it be
commandeered and a soldier lay hold of it, let it go,
do not resist nor grumble. If you do, you will get
a beating and lose your little donkey just the same.

80 ριον. ὅταν δὲ πρὸς τὸ σῶμα οὕτως ἔχειν σε δέῃ,
ὅρα, τί ἀπολείπεται περὶ τὰ ἄλλα, ὅσα τοῦ
σώματος ἕνεκα παρασκευάζεται. ὅταν ἐκεῖνο
ὀνάριον ᾖ, τἆλλα γίνεται χαλινάρια τοῦ ὀναρίου,
σαγμάτια, ὑποδημάτια, κριθαί, χόρτος. ἄφες
κἀκεῖνα, ἀπόλυε θᾶττον καὶ εὐκολώτερον ἢ τὸ
ὀνάριον.

81 Καὶ ταύτην τὴν παρασκευὴν παρασκευασάμενος
καὶ τὴν ἄσκησιν ἀσκήσας τὰ ἀλλότρια ἀπὸ τῶν
ἰδίων διακρίνειν, τὰ κωλυτὰ ἀπὸ τῶν ἀκωλύτων,
ταῦτα πρὸς σαυτὸν ἡγεῖσθαι, ἐκεῖνα μὴ πρὸς
σαυτόν, ἐνταῦθα ἐπιστρόφως ἔχειν τὴν ὄρεξιν,
ἐνταῦθα τὴν ἔκκλισιν, μή τι ἔτι φοβῇ τινά;—

82 Οὐδένα.—Περὶ τίνος γὰρ φοβήσῃ; περὶ τῶν
σεαυτοῦ, ὅπου σοι ἡ οὐσία τοῦ ἀγαθοῦ καὶ τοῦ
κακοῦ; καὶ τίς τούτων ἐξουσίαν ἔχει; τίς ἀφελέσθαι αὐτὰ δύναται, τίς ἐμποδίσαι; οὐ μᾶλλον

83 ἢ τὸν θεόν. ἀλλ' ὑπὲρ τοῦ σώματος καὶ τῆς
κτήσεως; ὑπὲρ τῶν ἀλλοτρίων; ὑπὲρ τῶν οὐδὲν
πρὸς σέ; καὶ τί ἄλλο ἐξ ἀρχῆς ἐμελέτας ἢ διακρίνειν τὰ σὰ καὶ οὐ σά, τὰ ἐπὶ σοὶ καὶ οὐκ ἐπὶ
σοί, τὰ κωλυτὰ καὶ ἀκώλυτα; τίνος δὲ ἕνεκα
προσῆλθες τοῖς φιλοσόφοις; ἵνα μηδὲν ἧττον

84 ἀτυχῆς καὶ δυστυχῆς; οὐκ οὖν[1] ἄφοβος μὲν οὕτως
ἔσει καὶ ἀτάραχος. λύπη δὲ τί πρὸς σέ; ὧν

---

[1] Elter : οὐκοῦν S.

But when this is the way in which you should act as regards the body, consider what is left for you to do about all the other things that are provided for the sake of the body. Since the body is a little donkey, the other things become little bridles for a little donkey, little pack-saddles, little shoes, and barley, and fodder. Let them go too, get rid of them more quickly and cheerfully than of the little donkey itself.

Once prepared and trained in this fashion to distinguish what is not your own from what is your own possession, the things which are subject to hindrance from those which are free from it, to regard these latter as your concern, and the former as no concern of yours, diligently to keep your desire fixed on the latter, and your aversion directed toward the former, then have you any longer anyone to fear?—No one.—Of course; what is there to be fearful about? About the things that are your own, wherein is the true nature of good and evil for you? And who has authority over these? Who can take them away, who can hinder them, any more than one can hinder God? But shall you be fearful about your body and your property? About the things that are not your own? About the things that are nothing to you? And what else have you been studying, from the very outset, but how to discriminate between what is your own and what is not your own, what is under your control and what is not under your control, what is subject to hindrance and what is free from it? For what purpose did you go to the philosophers? That you might no less than before be unfortunate and miserable? You will not, then, in that case, be free from fear and perturbation. And what has pain to

γὰρ προσδοκωμένων φόβος, γίνεται[1] καὶ λύπη
παρόντων. ἐπιθυμήσεις δὲ τίνος ἔτι; τῶν μὲν
γὰρ προαιρετικῶν ἅτε καλῶν ὄντων καὶ παρόντων
σύμμετρον ἔχεις καὶ καθισταμένην τὴν ὄρεξιν,
τῶν δ' ἀπροαιρέτων οὐδενὸς ὀρέγῃ, ἵνα καὶ τόπον
σχῇ τὸ ἄλογον ἐκεῖνο καὶ ὠστικὸν καὶ παρὰ τὰ
μέτρα ἠπειγμένον.

85 Ὅταν οὖν πρὸς τὰ πράγματα οὕτως ἔχῃς, τίς ἔτι
ἄνθρωπος δύναται φοβερὸς εἶναι; τί γὰρ ἔχει
ἄνθρωπος ἀνθρώπῳ φοβερὸν ἢ ὀφθεὶς ἢ λαλήσας
ἢ ὅλως συναναστραφείς; οὐ μᾶλλον ἢ ἵππος
ἵππῳ ἢ κύων κυνὶ ἢ μέλισσα μελίσσῃ. ἀλλὰ τὰ
πράγματα ἑκάστῳ φοβερά ἐστιν· ταῦτα δ' ὅταν
περιποιεῖν τις δύνηταί τινι ἢ ἀφελέσθαι, τότε καὶ
αὐτὸς φοβερὸς γίνεται.

86 Πῶς οὖν ἀκρόπολις καταλύεται; οὐ σιδήρῳ
οὐδὲ πυρί, ἀλλὰ δόγμασιν. ἂν γὰρ τὴν οὖσαν ἐν
τῇ πόλει καθέλωμεν, μή τι καὶ τὴν τοῦ πυρετοῦ,
μή τι καὶ τὴν τῶν καλῶν γυναικαρίων, μή τι
ἁπλῶς τὴν ἐν ἡμῖν ἀκρόπολιν καὶ τοὺς ἐν ἡμῖν
τυράννους ἀποβεβλήκαμεν, οὓς ἐφ' ἑκάστοις καθ'
ἡμέραν ἔχομεν, ποτὲ μὲν τοὺς αὐτούς, ποτὲ δ'
87 ἄλλους; ἀλλ' ἔνθεν ἄρξασθαι δεῖ καὶ ἔνθεν
καθελεῖν τὴν ἀκρόπολιν, ἐκβάλλειν τοὺς τυράν-
νους· τὸ σωμάτιον ἀφεῖναι, τὰ μέρη αὐτοῦ, τὰς

---

[1] The punctuation is by Capps; φόβος γίνεται, καί is
the ordinary reading.

---

[1] Probably a reference to some proverb, or well-known
saying, like that of Alcaeus, "Valiant men are the tower of
a city" (Smyth, *Greek Melic Poets*, frag. 15).—The citadel
is the keep, or tower, from which a tyrant is represented as
overawing a city.

do with you? For fear of things anticipated becomes pain when these things are present. And
what will you any longer passionately seek? For
you possess a harmonious and regulated desire for
the things that are within the sphere of the moral
purpose, as being excellent, and as being within your
reach; and you desire nothing outside the sphere
of the moral purpose, so as to give place to that
other element of unreason, which pushes you along
and is impetuous beyond all measure.

Now when you face things in this fashion, what
man can inspire fear in you any longer? For what
has one human being about him that is calculated to
inspire fear in another human being, in either his
appearance, or conversation, or intercourse in general,
any more than one horse, or dog, or bee inspires fear
in another horse, or dog, or bee? Nay, it is *things*
that inspire man with fear; and when one person
is able to secure them for another, or to take them
away, then he becomes capable of inspiring fear.

How, then, is a citadel destroyed?[1] Not by iron,
nor by fire, but by judgements. For if we capture
the citadel in the city, have we captured the citadel
of fever also, have we captured that of pretty wenches
also, in a word, the acropolis within us, and have we
cast out the tyrants within us, whom we have lord-
ing it over each of us[2] every day, sometimes the
same tyrants, and sometimes others? But here is
where we must begin, and it is from this side that we
must seize the acropolis and cast out the tyrants; we
must yield up the paltry body, its members, the

---

[2] So Schweighäuser; but there is some uncertainty about
the meaning of ἐφ' ἑκάστοις, which Schegk, Wolf, and Upton
take to refer to matters, or affairs (πράγματα, as in § 85).

δυνάμεις, τὴν κτῆσιν, τὴν φήμην, ἀρχάς, τιμάς,
τέκνα, ἀδελφούς, φίλους, πάντα ταῦτα ἡγήσασθαι
88 ἀλλότρια.   κἂν ἔνθεν ἐκβληθῶσιν οἱ τύραννοι, τί
ἔτι ἀποτειχίζω τὴν ἀκρόπολιν ἐμοῦ γε ἕνεκα;
ἑστῶσα γὰρ τί μοι ποιεῖ; τί ἔτι ἐκβάλλω τοὺς
δορυφόρους ; ποῦ γὰρ αὐτῶν αἰσθάνομαι; ἐπ᾿
ἄλλους ἔχουσιν τὰς ῥάβδους καὶ τοὺς κοντοὺς καὶ
89 τὰς μαχαίρας.   ἐγὼ δ᾿ οὐπώποτ᾿ οὔτε θέλων
ἐκωλύθην οὔτ᾿ ἠναγκάσθην μὴ θέλων.   καὶ πῶς
τοῦτο δυνατόν; προσκατατέταχά μου τὴν ὁρμὴν
τῷ θεῷ.   θέλει μ᾿ ἐκεῖνος πυρέσσειν· κἀγὼ
θέλω.   θέλει ὁρμᾶν ἐπί τι· κἀγὼ θέλω.   θέλει
ὀρέγεσθαι· κἀγὼ θέλω.   θέλει με τυχεῖν τινός·
90 κἀγὼ βούλομαι.   οὐ θέλει· οὐ βούλομαι.   ἀποθανεῖν οὖν θέλω· στρεβλωθῆναι οὖν θέλω.   τίς
ἔτι με κωλῦσαι δύναται παρὰ τὸ ἐμοὶ φαινόμενον
ἢ ἀναγκάσαι; οὐ μᾶλλον ἢ τὸν Δία.

91   Οὕτως ποιοῦσι καὶ τῶν ὁδοιπόρων οἱ ἀσφα-
λέστεροι.   ἀκήκοεν ὅτι λῃστεύεται ἡ ὁδός· μόνος
οὐ τολμᾷ καθεῖναι, ἀλλὰ περιέμεινεν συνοδίαν ἢ
πρεσβευτοῦ ἢ ταμίου ἢ ἀνθυπάτου καὶ προσ-

---

[1] The metaphor in this passage is complicated.   I take it
to mean, using wealth as a convenient example, something
like this : The tyrant is a false judgement (δόγμα) about
wealth ; the acropolis and the bodyguard are wealth itself,
which is dangerous only so long as the false judgement pre-
vails.   Once that is overthrown, actual wealth itself need
not be destroyed, at least for the man who is freed from the
false judgement about it, because wealth as such has no
longer any power over him.   Other people may be menaced
by it, but every man has a ready means of defence, which is
to secure a correct judgement about the thing itself.   Many
matters or affairs (πράγματα) like death and disease cannot,

faculties, property, reputation, offices, honours, children, brothers, friends—count all these things as alien to us. And if the tyrants be thrown out of the spot, why should I any longer raze the fortifications of the citadel, on my own account, at least? For what harm does it do me by standing? Why should I go on and throw out the tyrant's body-guard? For where do I feel them? Their rods, their spears, and their swords they are directing against others. But I have never been hindered in the exercise of my will, nor have I ever been subjected to compulsion against my will.[1] And how is this possible? I have submitted my freedom of choice unto God. He wills that I shall have fever; it is my will too. He wills that I should choose something; it is my will too. He wills that I should desire something; it is my will too. He wills that I should get something; it is my wish too. He does not will it; I do not wish it. Therefore, it is my will to die; therefore, it is my will to be tortured on the rack. Who can hinder me any longer against my own views, or put compulsion upon me? That is no more possible in my case than it would be with Zeus.

This is the way also with the more cautious among travellers. A man has heard that the road which he is taking is infested with robbers; he does not venture to set forth alone, but he waits for a company, either that of an ambassador, or of a quaestor, or of a proconsul, and when he has attached

in any event, be destroyed. It is vain labour to try to destroy the things themselves, when it is only the false judgements that are dangerous, and these any man can himself overcome.

92 κατατάξας ἑαυτὸν παρέρχεται ἀσφαλῶς. οὕτως
καὶ ἐν τῷ κόσμῳ ποιεῖ ὁ φρόνιμος. "πολλὰ
λῃστήρια, τύραννοι, χειμῶνες, ἀπορίαι, ἀποβολαὶ
93 τῶν φιλτάτων. ποῦ τις καταφύγῃ; πῶς ἀλῄστευ-
τος παρέλθῃ; ποίαν συνοδίαν περιμείνας ἀσφα-
94 λῶς διέλθῃ; τίνι προσκατατάξας ἑαυτόν; τῷ
δεῖνι, τῷ πλουσίῳ, τῷ ὑπατικῷ; καὶ τί μοι
ὄφελος; αὐτὸς ἐκδύεται, οἰμώζει, πενθεῖ. τί δ',
ἂν ὁ συνοδοιπόρος αὐτὸς ἐπ' ἐμὲ στραφεὶς λῃστής
95 μου γένηται; τί ποιήσω; φίλος ἔσομαι Καίσα-
ρος· ἐκείνου με ὄντα ἑταῖρον οὐδεὶς ἀδικήσει.
πρῶτον μέν, ἵνα γένωμαι, πόσα[1] με δεῖ τλῆναι
καὶ παθεῖν, ποσάκις καὶ ὑπὸ πόσων λῃστευθῆναι·
96 εἶτα ἐὰν γένωμαι, καὶ οὗτος θνητός ἐστιν.[2] ἂν
δ' αὐτὸς ἔκ τινος περιστάσεως ἐχθρός μου γένηται,
ἀναχωρῆσαί πού ποτε κρεῖσσον; εἰς ἐρημίαν;
97 ἄγε, ἐκεῖ πυρετὸς οὐκ ἔρχεται; τί οὖν γένηται;
οὐκ ἔστιν εὑρεῖν ἀσφαλῆ σύνοδον, πιστόν, ἰσχυ-
98 ρόν, ἀνεπιβούλευτον;" οὕτως ἐφίστησιν καὶ
ἐννοεῖ, ὅτι, ἐὰν τῷ θεῷ προσκατατάξῃ ἑαυτόν,
διελεύσεται ἀσφαλῶς.

99   Πῶς λέγεις προσκατατάξαι;—῏Ιν', ὃ ἂν
ἐκεῖνος θέλῃ, καὶ αὐτὸς θέλῃ, καὶ ὃ ἂν ἐκεῖνος μὴ
100 θέλῃ, τοῦτο μηδ' αὐτὸς θέλῃ.—Πῶς οὖν τοῦτο
γένηται;—Πῶς γὰρ ἄλλως ἢ ἐπισκεψαμένῳ τὰς
ὁρμὰς τοῦ θεοῦ καὶ τὴν διοίκησιν; τί μοι δέδωκεν
ἐμὸν καὶ αὐτεξούσιον, τί αὐτῷ κατέλιπεν; τὰ

---

[1] Schenkl: πρόσα S.
[2] After this word S repeats καὶ οὗτος θνητός.

himself to them he travels along the road in safety.
So in this world the wise man acts. Says he to
himself: "There are many robber-bands, tyrants,
storms, difficulties, losses of what is most dear.
Where shall a man flee for refuge? How shall he
travel secure against robbery? What company shall
he wait for that he may pass through in safety? To
whom shall he attach himself? To So-and-so, the
rich man, or the proconsul? And what is the good
of that? He himself is stripped, groans, sorrows.
Yes, and what if my fellow-traveller himself turn
upon me and rob me? What shall I do? I will
become a friend of Caesar; no one will wrong me if
I am a companion of his. But, in the first place,
the number of things I must suffer and endure in
order to become his friend! and the number of
times, and the number of persons by whom I must
first be robbed! And then, even if I do become his
friend, he too is mortal. And if some circumstance
lead him to become my enemy, where indeed had I
better retire? To a wilderness? What, does not
fever go there? What, then, is to become of me?
Is it impossible to find a fellow-traveller who is safe,
faithful, strong, free from the suspicion of treachery?"
Thus he reflects and comes to the thought that, if
he attach himself to God, he will pass through the
world in safety.

How do you mean "attach himself"?—Why, so that
whatever God wills, he also wills, and whatever God
does not will, this he also does not will.—How, then,
can this be done?—Why, how else than by observing
the choices of God and His governance? What has
He given me for my own and subject to my authority,
and what has He left for Himself? Everything

προαιρετικά μοι δέδωκεν, ἐπ᾿ ἐμοὶ πεποίηκεν,
ἀνεμπόδιστα, ἀκώλυτα. τὸ σῶμα τὸ πήλινον
πῶς ἐδύνατο ἀκώλυτον ποιῆσαι; ὑπέταξεν οὖν τῇ
τῶν ὅλων περιόδῳ, τὴν κτῆσιν, τὰ σκεύη, τὴν
101 οἰκίαν, τὰ τέκνα, τὴν γυναῖκα. τί οὖν θεομα-
χῶ; τί θέλω τὰ μὴ θελητά, τὰ μὴ δοθέντα μοι
ἐξ ἅπαντος ἔχειν; ἀλλὰ πῶς; ὡς δέδοται
καὶ ἐφ᾿ ὅσον δύναται.[1] ἀλλ᾿ ὁ δοὺς ἀφαιρεῖται.
τί οὖν ἀντιτείνω; οὐ λέγω, ὅτι ἠλίθιος ἔσομαι
τὸν ἰσχυρότερον βιαζόμενος, ἀλλ᾿ ἔτι πρότερον
102 ἄδικος. πόθεν γὰρ ἔχων αὐτὰ ἦλθον; ὁ πατήρ
μου αὐτὰ ἔδωκεν. ἐκείνῳ δὲ τίς; τὸν ἥλιον δὲ
τίς πεποίηκε, τοὺς καρποὺς δὲ τίς, τὰς δ᾿ ὥρας
τίς, τὴν δὲ πρὸς ἀλλήλους συμπλοκὴν καὶ κοινωνίαν τίς;
103 Εἶτα σύμπαντα εἰληφὼς παρ᾿ ἄλλου καὶ αὐτὸν
σεαυτόν, ἀγανακτεῖς καὶ μέμφῃ τὸν δόντα, ἄν σού
104 τι ἀφέληται; τίς ὢν καὶ ἐπὶ τί ἐληλυθώς; οὐχὶ
ἐκεῖνός σε εἰσήγαγεν; οὐχὶ τὸ φῶς ἐκεῖνός σοι
ἔδειξεν; οὐ συνεργοὺς δέδωκεν; οὐ καὶ αἰσθήσεις;
οὐ λόγον; ὡς τίνα δὲ εἰσήγαγεν; οὐχ ὡς θνητόν;
οὐχ ὡς μετὰ ὀλίγου σαρκιδίου ζήσοντα ἐπὶ γῆς
καὶ θεασόμενον τὴν διοίκησιν αὐτοῦ καὶ συμπομ-
πεύσοντα αὐτῷ καὶ συνεορτάσοντα πρὸς ὀλίγον;

---

[1] δέδοται s. But cf. explanatory note.

---

[1] Very similar is the phrase ἐφ᾿ ὅσον ἂν οἷόν τε ᾖ in § 79
above.
[2] As Job i. 21: "The Lord gave, and the Lord hath taken
away."
[3] That is, God.

within the sphere of the moral purpose He has given me, subjected them to my control, unhampered and unhindered. My body that is made of clay, how could He make that unhindered? Accordingly He has made it subject to the revolution of the universe— my property, my furniture, my house, my children, my wife. Why, then, shall I strive against God? Why shall I will what is not in the province of the will, to keep under all circumstances what has not been given me outright? But how should I keep them? In accordance with the terms upon which they have been given, and for as long as they can be given.[1] But He who gave also takes away.[2] Why, then, shall I resist? I do not say that I shall be a fool for trying to use force upon one who is stronger than I am, but before that I shall be wicked. For where did I get these things when I came into the world? My father gave them to me. And who gave them to him? Who has made the sun, who the fruits, who the seasons, who the union and fellowship of men one with another?

And so, when you have received everything, and your very self, from Another,[3] do you yet complain and blame the Giver, if He take something away from you? Who are you, and for what purpose have you come? Did not He bring you into the world? Did not He show you the light? Did not He give you fellow-workers? Did not He give you senses also and reason? And as what did He bring you into the world? Was it not as a mortal being? Was it not as one destined to live upon earth with a little portion of paltry flesh, and for a little while to be a spectator of His governance, and to join with Him in His pageant and holiday? Are

279

105 οὐ θέλεις οὖν, ἕως δέδοταί σοι, θεασάμενος τὴν
πομπὴν καὶ τὴν πανήγυριν εἶτα, ὅταν σ' ἐξάγῃ,
πορεύεσθαι προσκυνήσας καὶ εὐχαριστήσας ὑπὲρ
ὧν ἤκουσας καὶ εἶδες ; "οὔ· ἀλλ' ἔτι ἑορτάζειν
106 ἤθελον." καὶ γὰρ οἱ μύσται μυεῖσθαι, τάχα καὶ
οἱ ἐν Ὀλυμπίᾳ ἄλλους ἀθλητὰς βλέπειν· ἀλλὰ ἡ
πανήγυρις πέρας ἔχει· ἔξελθε, ἀπαλλάγηθι ὡς
εὐχάριστος, ὡς αἰδήμων· δὸς ἄλλοις τόπον· δεῖ
γενέσθαι καὶ ἄλλους, καθάπερ καὶ σὺ ἐγένου, καὶ
γενομένους ἔχειν χώραν καὶ οἰκήσεις, τὰ ἐπιτήδεια.
ἂν δ' οἱ πρῶτοι μὴ ὑπεξάγωσιν, τί ὑπολείπεται ;
τί ἄπληστος εἶ ; τί ἀνίκανος ; τί στενοχωρεῖς
τὸν κόσμον ;
107 Ναί· ἀλλὰ τὰ τεκνία μετ' ἐμαυτοῦ εἶναι θέλω καὶ
τὴν γυναῖκα.—Σὰ γάρ ἐστιν ; οὐχὶ τοῦ δόντος ;
οὐχὶ καὶ τοῦ σὲ πεποιηκότος ; εἶτα οὐκ ἐκστήσῃ
τῶν ἀλλοτρίων ; οὐ παραχωρήσεις τῷ κρείσσονι ;
108 —Τί οὖν μ' εἰσῆγεν ἐπὶ τούτοις ;—Καὶ εἰ μὴ
ποιεῖ σοι, ἔξελθε· οὐκ ἔχει χρείαν θεατοῦ μεμψι-
μοίρου. τῶν συνεορταζόντων δεῖται, τῶν συγχο-
ρευόντων, ἵν' ἐπικροτῶσι μᾶλλον, ἐπιθειάζωσιν,
109 ὑμνῶσι δὲ τὴν πανήγυριν. τοὺς ἀταλαιπώρους [1]
δὲ καὶ δειλοὺς οὐκ ἀηδῶς ὄψεται ἀπολελειμμένους
τῆς πανηγύρεως· οὐδὲ γὰρ παρόντες ὡς ἐν ἑορτῇ
διῆγον οὐδ' ἐξεπλήρουν τὴν χώραν τὴν πρέπουσαν,
ἀλλ' ὠδυνῶντο, ἐμέμφοντο τὸν δαίμονα, τὴν
τύχην, τοὺς συνόντας· ἀναίσθητοι καὶ ὧν ἔτυχον

---

[1] Schweighäuser : ταλαιπώρους S.

---

[1] Or possibly, "He does not suit you," as Capps suggests.

you not willing, then, for so long as has been given you, to be a spectator of His pageant and His festival, and then when He leads you forth, to go, after you have made obeisance and returned thanks for what you have heard and seen ? " No," you say, " but I wanted to go on with the holiday." Yes, and so do the initiates in the mysteries want to go on with the initiation, and no doubt the spectators at Olympia want to see still other athletes ; but the festival has come to an end ; leave, depart as a grateful and reverent spectator departs ; make room for others ; yet others must be born, even as you were born, and once born they must have land, and houses, and provisions. But if the first-comers do not move along, what is left for those who follow after ? Why are you insatiate ? Why never satisfied ? Why do you crowd the world ?

Yes, but I want my little children and my wife to be with me.—Are they yours ? Do they not belong to Him who gave them ? To Him who made you ? Will you not, therefore, give up what is not your own ? Will you not yield to your superior ?—Why, then, did He bring me into the world on these conditions ?—And if they do[1] not suit you, leave ; God has no need of a fault-finding spectator. He needs those who join in the holiday and the dance, that they may applaud rather, and glorify, and sing hymns of praise about the festival. But the peevish and the cowardly He will not be distressed to see left out of the festival ; for when they were present they did not act as though they were on a holiday, nor did they fill the proper rôle ; but they were distressed, found fault with the Deity, with fate, and with the company ; insensible to what had been

καὶ τῶν ἑαυτῶν δυνάμεων, ἃς εἰλήφασι πρὸς τὰ
ἐναντία, μεγαλοψυχίας, γενναιότητος, ἀνδρείας,
110 αὐτῆς τῆς νῦν ζητουμένης ἐλευθερίας.—Ἐπὶ τί
οὖν εἴληφα ταῦτα ;—Χρησόμενος.—Μέχρι τίνος ;
—Μέχρις ἂν ὁ χρήσας θέλῃ.—Ἂν οὖν ἀναγκαῖα
μοι ᾖ ;—Μὴ πρόσπασχε αὐτοῖς καὶ οὐκ ἔσται.
σὺ αὐτὰ αὑτῷ μὴ εἴπῃς ἀναγκαῖα καὶ οὐκ ἔστιν.
111 Ταύτην τὴν μελέτην ἕωθεν εἰς ἑσπέραν μελετᾶν
ἔδει. ἀπὸ τῶν μικροτάτων, ἀπὸ τῶν εὐεπηρεασ-
τοτάτων ἀρξάμενος, ἀπὸ χύτρας, ἀπὸ ποτη-
ρίου, εἶθ' οὕτως ἐπὶ χιτωνάριον πρόσελθε, ἐπὶ
κυνάριον, ἐπὶ ἱππάριον, ἐπὶ ἀγρίδιον· ἔνθεν ἐπὶ
σαυτόν, τὸ σῶμα, τὰ μέρη τοῦ σώματος, τὰ τέκνα,
112 τὴν γυναῖκα, τοὺς ἀδελφούς. πανταχοῦ περι-
βλέψας ἀπόρριψον ἀπὸ σεαυτοῦ· κάθηρον τὰ
δόγματα, μή τι προσήρτηταί σοι τῶν οὐ σῶν, μή
τι συμπέφυκεν, μή τι ὀδυνήσει σ' ἀποσπώμενον.
113 καὶ λέγε γυμναζόμενος καθ' ἡμέραν, ὡς ἐκεῖ, μὴ
ὅτι φιλοσοφεῖς (ἔστω φορτικὸν τὸ ὄνομα), ἀλλ'
ὅτι καρπιστὴν¹ δίδως· τοῦτο γάρ ἐστιν ἡ ταῖς
114 ἀληθείαις ἐλευθερία. ταύτην ἠλευθερώθη Διογένης παρ' Ἀντισθένους καὶ οὐκέτι ἔφη καταδου-
115 λωθῆναι δύνασθαι ὑπ' οὐδενός. διὰ τοῦτο πῶς
ἑάλω, πῶς τοῖς πειραταῖς ἐχρῆτο· μή τι κύριον

---

¹ It is tempting to conjecture καρπιστείαν, "making provision for your emancipation," since every man must win his
own freedom for himself. But Epictetus probably is thinking here of a man being won to freedom by following some
great philosopher, who is his emancipator, as in the famous
illustration in the next sentence. It is interesting to observe
how, with all its insistence upon individual responsibility,
even Stoicism at this time was becoming a religion of books,
examples, and saviours.

vouchsafed them, and to their own powers which
they had received for the very opposite use—high-
mindedness, nobility of character, courage, and the
very freedom for which we are now seeking.—For
what purpose, then, did I receive these gifts?—To
use them.—How long?—For as long as He who lent
them to you wills.—But what if they are necessary
to me?—Do not set your heart upon them, and they
will not be necessary to you. Do not say to yourself
that they are necessary, and they will not be.

This is what you ought to practise from morning
till evening. Begin with the most trifling things,
the ones most exposed to injury, like a pot, or a cup,
and then advance to a tunic, a paltry dog, a mere
horse, a bit of land; thence to yourself, your body,
and its members, your children, wife, brothers. Look
about on every side and cast these things away from
you. Purify your judgements, for fear lest something
of what is not your own may be fastened to them, or
grown together with them, and may give you pain
when it is torn loose. And every day while you are
training yourself, as you do in the gymnasium, do
not say that you are "pursuing philosophy" (indeed
an arrogant phrase!), but that you are a slave
presenting your emancipator in court;[1] for this is
the true freedom. This is the way in which Diogenes
was set free by Antisthenes,[2] and afterwards said
that he could never be enslaved again by any
man. How, in consequence, did he behave when
he was captured![3] How he treated the pirates!

---

[2] See III. 24, 67.
[3] A very famous incident in the life of the philosopher.
See especially, Musonius frag. 9 (p. 49, 8 ff., Hense): Gellius,
II, 18, 9–10 ; Lucian, *Vit. Auct.* 7 ; Diogenes Laertius, 6, 30 ;
36 ; 74 ; Ps.-Crates, *Epist.* 34 ; and above, III. 24, 66.

εἰπέν τινα αὐτῶν; καὶ οὐ λέγω τὸ ὄνομα· οὐ γὰρ
τὴν φωνὴν φοβοῦμαι, ἀλλὰ τὸ πάθος, ἀφ' οὗ ἡ
116 φωνὴ ἐκπέμπεται. πῶς ἐπιτιμᾷ αὐτοῖς, ὅτι
κακῶς ἔτρεφον τοὺς ἑαλωκότας· πῶς ἐπράθη·
μή τι κύριον ἐζήτει; ἀλλὰ δοῦλον. πῶς δὲ
πραθεὶς ἀνεστρέφετο πρὸς τὸν δεσπότην· εὐθὺς
διελέγετο πρὸς αὐτόν, ὅτι οὐχ οὕτως ἐστολίσθαι
δεῖ αὐτόν, οὐχ οὕτως κεκάρθαι, περὶ τῶν υἱῶν,
117 πῶς δεῖ αὐτοὺς διάγειν. καὶ τί θαυμαστόν; εἰ
γὰρ παιδοτρίβην ἐώνητο, ἐν τοῖς παλαιστρικοῖς
ὑπηρέτῃ ἂν αὐτῷ ἐχρῆτο ἢ κυρίῳ; εἰ δ' ἰατρόν,
ὡσαύτως, εἰ δ' ἀρχιτέκτονα. καὶ οὕτως ἐφ'
ἑκάστης ὕλης τὸν ἔμπειρον τοῦ ἀπείρου κρατεῖν
118 πᾶσα ἀνάγκη. ὅστις οὖν καθόλου τὴν περὶ βίον
ἐπιστήμην κέκτηται, τί ἄλλο ἢ τοῦτον εἶναι δεῖ
τὸν δεσπότην; τίς γάρ ἐστιν ἐν νηὶ κύριος;—Ὁ
κυβερνήτης.—Διὰ τί; ὅτι ὁ ἀπειθῶν αὐτῷ ζη-
119 μιοῦται.—Ἀλλὰ δεῖραί με δύναται.—Μή τι οὖν
ἀζημίως;—Οὕτως μὲν κἀγὼ ἔκρινον.—Ἀλλ' ὅτι
οὐκ ἀζημίως, διὰ τοῦτο οὐκ ἔξεστιν· οὐδενὶ δ'
120 ἀζήμιόν ἐστι τὸ ποιεῖν τὰ ἄδικα.—Καὶ τίς ἡ
ζημία τῷ δήσαντι τὸν αὐτοῦ δοῦλον, ἢν δοκῇ ; [1]
—Τὸ δῆσαι· τοῦτο ὃ καὶ σὺ ὁμολογήσεις, ἂν
θέλῃς σώζειν, ὅτι ἄνθρωπος οὐκ ἔστι θηρίον, ἀλλ'
121 ἥμερον ζῷον. ἐπεὶ πότ' ἄμπελος πράσσει κακῶς;
ὅταν παρὰ τὴν ἑαυτῆς φύσιν πράσσῃ. πότ'

---

[1] Matheson : ἢν δοκεῖς S.

---

[1] The phrase is from Plato, *Sophistes*, 222 B.   See also IV.
5, 10.

He called none of them master, did he? And I am
not referring to the name! it is not the word that I
fear, but the emotion, which produces the word.
How he censures them because they gave bad food
to their captives! How he behaved when he was
sold! Did he look for a master? No, but for a
slave. And how he behaved toward his master after
he had been sold! He began immediately to argue
with him, telling him that he ought not to dress
that way, or have his hair cut that way, and about
his sons, how they ought to live. And what is there
strange about that? Why, if he had bought a
gymnastic trainer, would he have employed him as a
servant, or as a master, in the exercises of the
palaestra? And if he had bought a physician, or a
master-builder, the same would have been true.
And thus in every subject-matter, it is quite un-
avoidable that the man of skill should be superior to
the man without skill. In general, therefore, whoever possesses the science of how to live, how can
he help but be the master? For who is master in a
ship?—The helmsman.—Why? Because the man
who disobeys him is punished.—But my master is
able to give me a sound flogging.—He cannot do so
with impunity, can he?—So I thought.—But because
he cannot do so with impunity, therefore he has no
authority to do it; no man can do wrong with impunity.—And what is the punishment that befalls
the man who has put his own slave in chains, when
he felt like it?—The putting of him in chains; this
is something which you will admit yourself, if you
wish to maintain the proposition that man is not a
wild beast but a tame animal.[1] For when is a vine
faring badly? When it is acting contrary to its own

285

122 ἀλεκτρυών; ὡσαύτως. οὐκοῦν καὶ ἄνθρωπος.
τίς οὖν αὐτοῦ ἡ φύσις; δάκνειν καὶ λακτίζειν καὶ
εἰς φυλακὴν βάλλειν καὶ ἀποκεφαλίζειν; οὔ·
ἀλλ᾽ εὖ ποιεῖν, συνεργεῖν, ἐπεύχεσθαι. τότ᾽ οὖν
κακῶς πράσσει, ἄν τε θέλῃς ἄν τε μή, ὅταν
ἀγνωμονῇ.

123 Ὥστε Σωκράτης οὐκ ἔπραξε κακῶς;—Οὔ,
ἀλλ᾽ οἱ δικασταὶ καὶ οἱ κατήγοροι.—Οὐδ᾽ ἐν
Ῥώμῃ Ἑλουίδιος ;— Οὔ, ἀλλ᾽ ὁ ἀποκτείνας

124 αὐτόν.—Πῶς λέγεις ;—Ὡς καὶ σὺ ἀλεκτρυόνα
οὐ λέγεις κακῶς πρᾶξαι τὸν νικήσαντα καὶ
κατακοπέντα, ἀλλὰ τὸν ἀπλῆγα ἡττηθέντα·
οὐδὲ κύνα εὐδαιμονίζεις τὸν μήτε διώκοντα μήτε
πονοῦντα, ἀλλ᾽ ὅταν ἱδρῶντα ἴδῃς, ὅταν ὀδυνώ-

125 μενον, ὅταν ῥηγνύμενον ὑπὸ τοῦ δρόμου. τί
παραδοξολογοῦμεν, εἰ λέγομεν παντὸς κακὸν
εἶναι τὸ παρὰ τὴν ἐκείνου φύσιν; τοῦτο παρά-
δοξόν ἐστιν; σὺ γὰρ αὐτὸ ἐπὶ πάντων τῶν
ἄλλων οὐ λέγεις; διὰ τί ἐπὶ μόνου οὖν τοῦ

126 ἀνθρώπου ἄλλως φέρῃ; ἀλλ᾽ ὅτι λέγομεν
ἥμερον εἶναι τοῦ ἀνθρώπου τὴν φύσιν καὶ
φιλάλληλον καὶ πιστήν, τοῦτο παράδοξον οὐκ

127 ἔστιν ;—Οὐδὲ τοῦτο.—Πῶς οὖν ἔτι οὐ δερόμενος
βλάπτεται ἢ δεσμευόμενος ἢ ἀποκεφαλιζόμενος ;
οὐχὶ οὕτως μέν· εἰ[1] γενναίως πάσχει, καὶ
προσκερδαίνων καὶ προσωφελούμενος ἀπέρχεται,
ἐκεῖνος δὲ ὁ[2] βλαπτόμενός ἐστιν ὁ τὰ οἰκτρότατα
πάσχων καὶ αἴσχιστα, ὁ ἀντὶ ἀνθρώπου λύκος
γινόμενος ἢ ἔχις ἢ σφήξ;

---

[1] εἰ added by Schenkl (after Upton).   [2] ὁ added by Blass.

---

[1] A prominent Stoic senator at Rome. See I. 2, 19 ff.

nature. When is a cock faring badly? Under the
same conditions. So also man. What, then, is his
nature? To bite, and kick, and throw into prison,
and behead? No, but to do good, to work together,
and to pray for the success of others. Therefore, he
is faring badly, whether you will or no, when he acts
unfeelingly.

You imply, then, that Socrates did not fare badly?
—He did not; it was his judges and accusers who
fared badly.—Nor Helvidius [1] at Rome?—No, but the
man who put him to death.—How so?—Just as you
too do not say that the cock which has won a victory,
even though he be severely cut up, has fared badly,
but rather the one who has been beaten without
suffering a blow. Nor do you call a dog happy
when he is neither in pursuit nor toiling hard, but
when you see him sweating, suffering, bursting from
the chase. What is there paradoxical in the statement, if we say that everything's evil is what is
contrary to its own nature? Is that paradoxical?
Do you not say it yourself in the case of everything
else? Why, then, do you take a different course in
the case of man alone? But our statement that the
nature of man is gentle, and affectionate, and faithful,
is this not paradoxical?—No, that is not paradoxical,
either.—How, then, does it come about that he
suffers no harm, even though he is soundly flogged,
or imprisoned, or beheaded? Is it not thus—if he
bears it all in a noble spirit, and comes off with increased profit and advantage, while the other man is
the one who suffers harm, the man who is subjected
to the most pitiful and disgraceful experience, who
becomes a wolf, or a snake, or a wasp, instead of a
human being?

128 Ἄγε οὖν ἐπέλθωμεν τὰ ὡμολογημένα. ὁ
ἀκώλυτος ἄνθρωπος ἐλεύθερος, ᾧ πρόχειρα τὰ
πράγματα ὡς βούλεται. ὃν δ᾽ ἔστιν ἢ κωλῦσαι ἢ
ἀναγκάσαι ἢ ἐμποδίσαι ἢ ἄκοντα εἴς τι ἐμβαλεῖν,
129 δοῦλός ἐστιν. τίς δ᾽ ἀκώλυτος ; ὁ μηδενὸς τῶν
ἀλλοτρίων ἐφιέμενος. τίνα δ᾽ ἀλλότρια ; ἃ οὐκ
ἔστιν ἐφ᾽ ἡμῖν οὔτ᾽ ἔχειν οὔτε μὴ ἔχειν οὔτε
130 ποιὰ ἔχειν ἢ πῶς ἔχοντα. οὐκοῦν τὸ σῶμα
ἀλλότριον, τὰ μέρη αὐτοῦ ἀλλότρια, ἡ κτῆσις
ἀλλοτρία. ἂν οὖν τινὶ τούτων ὡς ἰδίῳ προσπαθῇς, δώσεις δίκας ἃς ἄξιον τὸν τῶν ἀλλοτρίων
131 ἐφιέμενον. αὕτη ἡ ὁδὸς ἐπ᾽ ἐλευθερίαν ἄγει,
αὕτη μόνη ἀπαλλαγὴ δουλείας, τὸ δυνηθῆναί
ποτ᾽ εἰπεῖν ἐξ ὅλης ψυχῆς τὸ

ἄγου δέ μ᾽, ὦ Ζεῦ, καὶ σύ γ᾽ ἡ Πεπρωμένη,
ὅποι ποθ᾽ ὑμῖν εἰμὶ διατεταγμένος.

132 Ἀλλὰ τί λέγεις, φιλόσοφε ; καλεῖ σε ὁ
τύραννος ἐροῦντά τι ὧν οὐ πρέπει σοι. λέγεις
ἢ οὐ λέγεις ; εἰπέ μοι.—Ἄφες σκέψωμαι.—
Νῦν σκέψῃ ; ὅτε δ᾽ ἐν τῇ σχολῇ ἦς, τί ἐσκέπτου ;
οὐκ ἐμελέτας, τίνα ἐστὶ τὰ ἀγαθὰ καὶ τὰ κακὰ
133 καὶ τίνα οὐδέτερα ;—Ἐσκεπτόμην.—Τίνα οὖν
ἤρεσκεν ὑμῖν ;—Τὰ δίκαια καὶ καλὰ ἀγαθὰ
εἶναι, τὰ ἄδικα καὶ αἰσχρὰ κακά.—Μή τι τὸ
ζῆν ἀγαθόν ;—Οὔ.—Μή τι τὸ ἀποθανεῖν κακόν ;

---

[1] From the *Hymn* of Cleanthes. See on II. 23, 42.

Come, now, and let us review the points on which we have reached agreement. The unhampered man, who finds things ready to hand as he wants them, is free. But the man who can be hampered, or subjected to compulsion, or hindered, or thrown into something against his will, is a slave. And who is unhampered? The man who fixes his aim on nothing that is not his own. And what are the things which are not our own? All that are not under our control, either to have, or not to have, or to have of a certain quality, or under certain conditions. Therefore, the body is not our own, its members are not our own, property is not our own. If, then, you conceive a strong passion for some one of these things, as though it were your immediate possession, you will be punished as he should be who fixes his aim upon what is not his own. This is the road which leads to freedom, this is the only surcease of slavery, to be able to say at any time with your whole heart,

> Lead thou me on, O Zeus, and Destiny,
> To that goal long ago to me assigned.[1]

But what say you, philosopher? The tyrant calls upon you to say something that is unworthy of you. Do you say it, or not say it? Tell me.—Let me think about it.—Think about it *now*? But what were you thinking about when you were attending lectures? Did you not study the questions, what things are good, and what bad, and what are neither good nor bad?—I did.—What conclusions were approved, then, by you and your fellows? —That things righteous and excellent were good, things unrighteous and disgraceful bad.—Life is not a good thing, is it?—No.—Nor death a bad thing?

289

Οὔ.—Μή τι φυλακή;—Οὔ.—Λόγος δ' ἀγεννὴς
καὶ ἄπιστος καὶ φίλου προδοσία καὶ κολακεία
134 τυράννου τί ὑμῖν ἐφαίνετο;—Κακά.—Τί οὖν;
οὐχὶ σκέπτῃ, οὐχὶ δ' ἔσκεψαι καὶ βεβούλευσαι.
ποία γὰρ σκέψις, εἰ καθήκει μοι δυναμένῳ τὰ
μέγιστα ἀγαθὰ ἐμαυτῷ περιποιῆσαι, τὰ μέγιστα
κακὰ μὴ περιποιῆσαι; καλὴ σκέψις καὶ ἀναγ-
καία, πολλῆς βουλῆς δεομένη. τί ἡμῖν ἐμπαί-
ζεις, ἄνθρωπε; οὐδέποτε τοιαύτη σκέψις γίνεται.
135 οὐδ' εἰ ταῖς ἀληθείαις κακὰ μὲν ἐφαντάζου τὰ
αἰσχρά, τὰ δ' ἄλλα οὐδέτερα, ἦλθες ἂν ἐπὶ
ταύτην τὴν ἐπίστασιν, οὐδ' ἐγγύς· ἀλλ' αὐτόθεν
136 διακρίνειν εἶχες, ὥσπερ ὄψει, τῇ διανοίᾳ. πότε
γὰρ σκέπτῃ, εἰ τὰ μέλανα λευκά ἐστιν, εἰ τὰ
βαρέα κοῦφα; οὐχὶ δὲ τοῖς ἐναργῶς φαινομένοις
ἐπακολουθεῖς; πῶς οὖν νῦν σκέπτεσθαι λέγεις,
137 εἰ[1] τὰ οὐδέτερα τῶν κακῶν φευκτότερα; ἀλλ'
οὐκ ἔχεις τὰ δόγματα ταῦτα, ἀλλὰ φαίνεταί σοι
οὔτε ταῦτα οὐδέτερα, ἀλλὰ τὰ μέγιστα κακά,
138 οὔτ' ἐκεῖνα κακά,[2] ἀλλ' οὐδὲν πρὸς ἡμᾶς. οὕτως
γὰρ ἐξ ἀρχῆς εἴθισας σεαυτόν· "ποῦ εἰμί; ἐν
σχολῇ. καὶ ἀκούουσί μου τίνες; λέγω μετὰ τῶν
φιλοσόφων. ἀλλ' ἐξελήλυθα τῆς σχολῆς· ἆρον

---

[1] εἰ added by Wolf.   [2] κακά added by Upton.

— No. — Nor imprisonment? — No. — But ignoble speech and faithless, and betrayal of a friend, and flattery of a tyrant, what did you and your fellows think of these?—We thought them evil.—What then? You are not thinking about the question now, nor have you thought about it and considered it hitherto. Why, what kind of inquiry is it, to raise the question whether it is fitting, when it is in my power to get for myself the greatest goods, not to get for myself the greatest evils! A fine and necessary question, forsooth, that requires a great deal of deliberation. Why are you making fun of us, man? Such an inquiry is never made. Besides, if you had honestly imagined that disgraceful things were bad, and all else indifferent, you would never have approached this inquiry, no, nor anything near it; but you would have been able to settle the question on the spot, by intuition, just as in a case involving sight. Why, when do you stop to "think about it," if the question is, Are black things white, or, Are heavy things light? Do you not follow the clear evidence of your senses? How comes it, then, that now you say you are thinking it over, whether things indifferent are more to be avoided than things bad? But you do not have these judgements; on the contrary, imprisonment and death do not appear to you to be indifferent, but rather the greatest evils, and dishonourable words and deeds are not bad in your sight, but rather things that do not concern us. For that is the habit which you developed from the start. "Where am I?" you say. "In school. And who are listening to me? I am talking in the company of philosophers. But now I have left the

ἐκεῖνα τὰ τῶν σχολαστικῶν καὶ τῶν μωρῶν."
οὕτως καταμαρτυρεῖται φίλος ὑπὸ φιλοσόφου,
139 οὕτως παρασιτεῖ φιλόσοφος, οὕτως ἐπ᾽ ἀργυρίῳ
ἐκμισθοῖ ἑαυτόν, οὕτως ἐν συγκλήτῳ τις οὐ
λέγει τὰ φαινόμενα· ἔνδοθεν τὸ δόγμα αὐτοῦ
140 βοᾷ, οὐ¹ ψυχρὸν καὶ ταλαίπωρον ὑπολη-
ψείδιον ἐκ λόγων εἰκαίων² ὡς ἐκ τριχὸς ἠρτη-
μένον, ἀλλὰ ἰσχυρὸν καὶ χρηστικὸν καὶ ὑπὸ
τοῦ διὰ τῶν ἔργων γεγυμνάσθαι μεμυημένον.
141 παραφύλαξον σαυτόν, πῶς ἀκούεις—οὐ λέγω,
ὅτι τὸ παιδίον σου ἀπέθανεν· πόθεν σοι; ἀλλ᾽
ὅτι σου τὸ ἔλαιον ἐξεχέθη, ὁ οἶνος ἐξεπόθη,
142 ἵνα τις ἐπιστὰς διατεινομένῳ σοι τοῦτ᾽ αὐτὸ
μόνον εἴπῃ "φιλόσοφε, ἄλλα λέγεις ἐν τῇ
σχολῇ· τί ἡμᾶς ἐξαπατᾷς; τί σκώληξ ὢν
143 λέγεις, ὅτι ἄνθρωπος εἶ;᾽᾽ ἤθελον ἐπιστῆναί
τινι αὐτῶν συνουσιάζοντι, ἵνα ἴδω, πῶς τείνεται
καὶ ποίας φωνὰς ἀφίησιν, εἰ μέμνηται τοῦ
ὀνόματος αὐτοῦ, τῶν λόγων οὓς ἀκούει ἢ λέγει
ἢ ἀναγιγνώσκει.

144   Καὶ τί ταῦτα πρὸς ἐλευθερίαν ;—Οὐκ ἄλλα
μὲν οὖν ἢ ταῦτ᾽, ἄν τε θέλητε ὑμεῖς οἱ πλούσιοι
145 ἄν τε μή.—Καὶ τί³ σοι μαρτυρεῖ ταῦτα ;—Τί
γὰρ ἄλλο ἢ αὐτοὶ ὑμεῖς οἱ τὸν κύριον τὸν μέγαν
ἔχοντες καὶ πρὸς τὸ ἐκείνου νεῦμα καὶ κίνημα
ζῶντες, κἄν τινα ὑμῶν ἴδῃ μόνον συνεστραμμένῳ
βλέμματι, ἀποψυχόμενοι, τὰς γραίας θεραπεύον-

---

¹ Schweighäuser : σύ S.   ² Reiske : εἰ καὶ ὢν S.
³ Schenkl : τίς S.

---

¹ Possibly an allusion to Egnatius Celer, who accused his
friend, Barea Soranus, in the reign of Nero, A.D. 66, when

school; away with those sayings of pedants and fools!" That is how a friend is condemned on the testimony of a philosopher,[1] that is how a philosopher turns parasite, that is how he hires himself out for money, that is how at a meeting of the senate a man does not say what he thinks, while within his breast his judgement shouts loudly, no cold and miserable remnant suspended from idle argumentations as by a hair, but a strong and serviceable judgement, and familiar with its business by having been trained in action. Watch yourself, and see how you take the word—I do not say the word that your child is dead; how could you possibly bear that?—but the word that your oil is spilled, or your wine drunk up. Well might someone stand over you, when you are in this excited condition, and say simply, "Philosopher, you talk differently in the school; why are you deceiving us? Why, when you are a worm, do you claim that you are a man?" I should like to stand over one of these philosophers when he is engaged in sexual intercourse, so as to see how he exerts himself, what manner of words he utters, whether he remembers his own name, or the arguments that he hears, or repeats, or reads!

And what has all this to do with freedom?—Nay, nothing but all this has to do with freedom, whether you rich people so wish or not.—And what is your witness to this?—Why, what else but you yourselves who have this mighty master,[2] and live at his nod and gesture, who faint away if he but look at one of you with a scowl on his face, paying court to the

Epictetus was a boy. See Tacitus, *Annals*, 16, 32, and Juvenal, 3, 116 f.

  [2] *i.e.*, the Emperor.

τες καὶ τοὺς γέροντας καὶ λέγοντες ὅτι " οὐ
146 δύναμαι τοῦτο ποιῆσαι· οὐκ ἔξεστί μοι " ; διὰ
τί οὐκ ἔξεστίν σοι ; οὐκ ἄρτι ἐμάχου μοι λέγων
ἐλεύθερος εἶναι ; " ἀλλὰ ᾿Απρυλλά¹ με κεκώλυ-
κεν." λέγε οὖν τὰς ἀληθείας, δοῦλε, καὶ μὴ
δραπέτευέ σου τοὺς κυρίους μηδ᾿ ἀπαρνοῦ μηδὲ
τόλμα καρπιστὴν² διδόναι τοσούτους ἔχων τῆς
147 δουλείας ἐλέγχους. καίτοι τὸν μὲν ὑπ᾿ ἔρωτος
ἀναγκαζόμενόν τι ποιεῖν παρὰ τὸ φαινόμενον
καὶ ἅμα μὲν ὁρῶντα τὸ ἄμεινον, ἅμα δ᾿ οὐκ
ἐξευτονοῦντα ἀκολουθῆσαι αὐτῷ ἔτι μᾶλλον ἄν
τις συγγνώμης ἄξιον ὑπολάβοι, ἄθ᾿ ὑπό τινος
βιαίου καὶ τρόπον τινὰ θείου κατεσχημένον.
148 σοῦ δὲ τίς ἀνάσχοιτο τῶν γραῶν ἐρῶντος καὶ
τῶν γερόντων καὶ ἐκείνας ἀπομύσσοντος καὶ
ἀποπλύνοντος καὶ δωροδοκοῦντος καὶ ἅμα μὲν
νοσούσας θεραπεύοντος ὡς δούλου, ἅμα δ᾿ ἀποθανεῖν εὐχομένου καὶ τοὺς ἰατροὺς διακρίνοντος,
εἰ ἤδη θανασίμως ἔχουσιν ; ἢ πάλιν ὅταν ὑπὲρ
τῶν μεγάλων τούτων καὶ σεμνῶν ἀρχῶν καὶ
τιμῶν τὰς χεῖρας τῶν ἀλλοτρίων δούλων κατα-
149 φιλῇς, ἵνα μηδ᾿ ἐλευθέρων δοῦλος ᾖς ; εἶτά μοι
σεμνὸς περιπατεῖς στρατηγῶν, ὑπατεύων. οὐκ
οἶδα, πῶς ἐστρατήγησας, πόθεν τὴν ὑπατείαν
150 ἔλαβες, τίς σοι αὐτὴν ἔδωκεν ; ἐγὼ μὲν οὐδὲ
ζῆν ἤθελον, εἰ διὰ Φηλικίωνα³ ἔδει ζῆσαι τῆς
ὀφρύος αὐτοῦ καὶ τοῦ δουλικοῦ φρυάγματος
ἀνασχόμενον· οἶδα γάρ, τί ἐστὶ δοῦλος εὐτυχῶν
ὡς δοκεῖ καὶ τετυφωμένος.

---

¹ Obviously some rich old woman.
² See § 113 and note.
³ A freedman of Nero's. See I. 17, 19, 20 and 21.

old women and the old men, and saying, "I cannot do this; I am not allowed"? Why are you not allowed? Were you not just now arguing with me and claiming that you were free? "But Aprulla[1] has prevented me." Tell the truth, then, slave, and do not run away from your masters, nor make denial, nor dare to present your emancipator,[2] when you have so many proofs to convict you of slavery. And, indeed, when a man out of passionate love is under the compulsion to do something contrary to his opinion, all the time seeing the better thing but lacking the strength to follow, one might be all the more inclined to regard him as deserving pity, because he is in the grip of something violent, and, in a manner of speaking, divine. But who could endure you with your passion for old women and old men, wiping the noses and washing the faces of old women, corrupting them with presents, and all the while you are nursing them, like a slave, in some illness, praying for them to die, and asking the physicians if they are finally on their deathbed? Or again, when for the sake of these mighty and dignified offices and honours you kiss the hands of other men's slaves, so as to be the slave of men who are not even free? And then, God save the mark, you walk around in your dignity as a praetor or a consul! Don't I know how you came to be praetor, how you got your consulship, who gave it to you? As for me, I should not care even to live, if I had to owe my life to Felicio,[3] putting up with his insolence and slavish arrogance; for I know what a slave is, who is prosperous as the world goes, and puffed up with pride.[4]

[4] A pretty clear reference to his experiences with his master, Epaphroditus, who had been a slave of Nero.

151 Σὺ οὖν, φησίν, ἐλεύθερος εἶ ;—Θέλω νὴ τοὺς
θεοὺς καὶ εὔχομαι, ἀλλ' οὔπω δύναμαι ἀντι-
βλέψαι τοῖς κυρίοις, ἔτι τιμῶ τὸ σωμάτιον,
ὁλόκληρον αὐτὸ ἔχειν ἀντὶ πολλοῦ ποιοῦμαι

152 καίτοι μηδ' ὁλόκληρον ἔχων. ἀλλὰ δύναμαί σοι
δεῖξαι ἐλεύθερον, ἵνα μηκέτι ζητῇς τὸ παράδειγμα. Διογένης ἦν ἐλεύθερος. πόθεν τοῦτο ;
οὐχ ὅτι ἐξ ἐλευθέρων ἦν, οὐ γὰρ ἦν, ἀλλ' ὅτι
αὐτὸς ἦν, ὅτι ἀποβεβλήκει πάσας τὰς τῆς
δουλείας λαβὰς[1] οὐδ' ἦν, ὅπως τις προσέλθῃ
πρὸς αὐτὸν οὐδ' ὅθεν λάβηται πρὸς τὸ κατα-

153 δουλώσασθαι. πάντα εὔλυτα εἶχεν, πάντα
μόνον προσηρτημένα. εἰ τῆς κτήσεως ἐπελάβου,
αὐτὴν ἀφῆκεν ἄν σοι μᾶλλον ἢ ἠκολούθησεν
δι' αὐτήν· εἰ τοῦ σκέλους, τὸ σκέλος· εἰ ὅλου
τοῦ σωματίου, ὅλον τὸ σωμάτιον· οἰκείους,
φίλους, πατρίδα ὡσαύτως. ᾔδει, πόθεν ἔχει καὶ

154 παρὰ τίνος καὶ ἐπὶ τίσιν λαβών. τοὺς μέν γ'
ἀληθινοὺς προγόνους, τοὺς θεούς, καὶ τὴν τῷ
ὄντι πατρίδα οὐδέπωποτ' ἂν ἐγκατέλιπεν, οὐδὲ
παρεχώρησεν ἄλλῳ μᾶλλον πείθεσθαι αὐτοῖς
καὶ ὑπακούειν, οὐδ' ὑπεραπέθανεν ἂν εὐκολώτερον

155 τῆς πατρίδος ἄλλος. οὐ γὰρ ἐζήτει ποτὲ δόξαι[2]
τι ποιεῖν ὑπὲρ τῶν ὅλων, ἀλλ' ἐμέμνητο, ὅτι
πᾶν τὸ γενόμενον ἐκεῖθέν ἐστιν καὶ ὑπὲρ[3]
ἐκείνης πράττεται καὶ ὑπὸ τοῦ διοικοῦντος

---

[1] Sb : βλαβάς S. [2] Meibom: δόξει S.
[3] Schweighäuser: ὑπ' S.

---

[1] Alluding to his lameness, as the Scholiast observes. See
Vol. I, Introd., pp. ix–x.
[2] That is, not grown to him so as to cause pain when torn
loose, as in § 112.

Are *you*, then, free, says someone?—By the gods I wish to be, and pray to be, but I am not yet able to look into the face of my masters, I still honour my paltry body, I take great pains to keep it sound, although it is not sound in any case.[1] But I can show you a free man, so that you will never again have to look for an example. Diogenes was free. How did that come? It was not because he was born of free parents, for he was not, but because he himself was free, because he had cast off all the handles of slavery, and there was no way in which a person could get close and lay hold of him to enslave him. Everything he had was easily loosed, everything was merely tied on.[2] If you had laid hold of his property, he would have let it go rather than followed you for its sake; if you had laid hold of his leg, he would have let his leg go; if of his whole paltry body, his whole paltry body; and so also his kindred, friends, and country. He knew the source from which he had received them, and from whom, and upon what conditions. His true ancestors, indeed, the gods, and his real Country[3] he would never have abandoned, nor would he have suffered another to yield them more obedience and submission, nor could any other man have died more cheerfully for his Country. For it was never his wont to seek to *appear* to do anything in behalf of the Universe,[4] but he bore in mind that everything which has come into being has its source there, and is done on behalf of that Country, and is entrusted

---

[3] Clearly, from what follows, the Universe.
[4] Compare Marcus Aurelius, 7, 73: "When thou hast done well to another . . . why go on like the foolish to look for . . . the credit of having done well?" (Haines).

αὐτὴν παρεγγυᾶται. τοιγαροῦν ὅρα, τί λέγει
156 αὐτὸς καὶ γράφει· "διὰ τοῦτό σοι," φησίν,
"ἔξεστιν, ὦ Διόγενες, καὶ τῷ Περσῶν βασιλεῖ
καὶ Ἀρχιδάμῳ τῷ Λακεδαιμονίων ὡς βούλει
157 διαλέγεσθαι." ἀρά γ' ὅτι ἐξ ἐλευθέρων ἦν;
πάντες γὰρ Ἀθηναῖοι καὶ πάντες Λακεδαιμόνιοι
καὶ Κορίνθιοι διὰ τὸ ἐκ δούλων εἶναι οὐκ
ἠδύναντο αὐτοῖς ὡς ἠβούλοντο διαλέγεσθαι,
158 ἀλλ' ἐδεδοίκεσαν καὶ ἐθεράπευον; διὰ τί οὖν,
φησίν, ἔξεστιν; "ὅτι τὸ σωμάτιον ἐμὸν οὐχ
ἡγοῦμαι, ὅτι οὐδενὸς δέομαι, ὅτι ὁ νόμος μοι
πάντα ἐστὶ καὶ ἄλλο οὐδέν." ταῦτα ἦν τὰ
ἐλεύθερον ἐκεῖνον ἐάσαντα.

159 Καὶ ἵνα μὴ δόξῃς, ὅτι παράδειγμα δείκνυμι
ἀνδρὸς ἀπεριστάτου μήτε γυναῖκα ἔχοντος μήτε
τέκνα μήτε πατρίδα ἢ φίλους ἢ συγγενεῖς, ὑφ'
ὧν κάμπτεσθαι καὶ περισπᾶσθαι ἠδύνατο, λάβε
Σωκράτη καὶ θέασαι γυναῖκα καὶ παιδία ἔχοντα,
ἀλλὰ ὡς ἀλλότρια,[1] πατρίδα, ἐφ' ὅσον ἔδει καὶ
ὡς ἔδει, φίλους, συγγενεῖς, πάντα ταῦτα ὑποτεταχότα τῷ νόμῳ καὶ τῇ πρὸς ἐκεῖνον εὐπειθείᾳ.
160 διὰ τοῦτο, στρατεύεσθαι μὲν ὁπότ' ἔδει, πρῶτος
ἀπῄει κἀκεῖ ἐκινδύνευεν ἀφειδέστατα· ἐπὶ Λέοντα
δ' ὑπὸ τῶν τυράννων πεμφθείς, ὅτι αἰσχρὸν
ἡγεῖτο, οὐδ' ἐπεβουλεύσατο εἰδώς, ὅτι ἀποθανεῖν
161 δεήσει, ἂν οὕτως τύχῃ. καὶ τί αὐτῷ διέφερεν;

---

[1] Salmasius: ἀλλοτρίαν S.

---

[1] A leader of the opposition, whom the Thirty Tyrants
wished to murder. See Plato, *Apology*, 32 C.

to us by Him who governs it. Therefore, see what he himself says and writes: "For this reason," he says, "you are permitted, O Diogenes, to converse as you please with the king of the Persians and with Archidamus, the king of the Lacedaemonians." Was it, indeed, because he was born of free parents? No doubt it was because they were all the children of slaves that the Athenians, and Lacedaemonians, and Corinthians were unable to converse with these monarchs as they pleased, but were afraid of them and paid court to them! Why, then, someone asks, are you permitted? "Because I do not regard my paltry body as my own; because I need nothing; because the law, and nothing else, is everything to me." This it was which allowed him to be a free man.

And that you may not think I am showing you an example of a man who was solitary, and had neither wife, nor children, nor country, nor friends, nor kinsmen, who might have bent him and diverted him from his purpose, take Socrates and observe a man who had a wife and little children, but regarded them as not his own, who had a country, as far as it was his duty, and in the way in which it was his duty, and friends, and kinsmen, one and all subject to the law and to obedience to the law. That is why, when it was his duty to serve as a soldier, he was the first to leave home, and ran the risks of battle most ungrudgingly; and when he was sent by the Tyrants to fetch Leon,[1] because he regarded it as disgraceful, he never deliberated about the matter at all, although he knew that he would have to die, if it so chanced. And what difference did it make to him? For there was

ἄλλο γάρ τι σῴζειν ἤθελεν· οὐ τὸ σαρκίδιον,
ἀλλὰ τὸν πιστόν, τὸν αἰδήμονα. ταῦτα ἀπαρεγ-
162 χείρητα, ἀνυπότακτα. εἶθ᾽ ὅτ᾽ ἀπολογεῖσθαι
ἔδει ὑπὲρ τοῦ ζῆν, μή τι ὡς τέκνα ἔχων ἀναστρέφεται, μή τι ὡς γυναῖκα; ἀλλ᾽ ὡς μόνος. τί δ᾽,
ὅτε πιεῖν ἔδει τὸ φάρμακον, πῶς ἀναστρέφεται ;
163 δυνάμενος διασωθῆναι καὶ τοῦ Κρίτωνος αὐτῷ
λέγοντος ὅτι "ἔξελθε διὰ τὰ παιδία" τί λέγει ;
ἕρμαιον ἡγεῖτο αὐτό ; πόθεν ; ἀλλὰ τὸ εὔσχημον
σκοπεῖ, τἆλλα δ᾽ οὐδ᾽ ὁρᾷ, οὐδ᾽ ἐπιλογίζεται. οὐ
γὰρ ἤθελεν, φησίν, σῶσαι τὸ σωμάτιον, ἀλλ᾽
ἐκεῖνο, ὃ τῷ δικαίῳ μὲν αὔξεται καὶ σῴζεται, τῷ
164 δ᾽ ἀδίκῳ μειοῦται καὶ ἀπόλλυται. Σωκράτης δ᾽
αἰσχρῶς οὐ σῴζεται, ὁ μὴ ἐπιψηφίσας Ἀθηναίων
κελευόντων, ὁ τοὺς τυράννους ὑπεριδών, ὁ τοιαῦτα
περὶ ἀρετῆς καὶ καλοκἀγαθίας διαλεγόμενος·
165 τοῦτον οὐκ ἔστι σῶσαι αἰσχρῶς, ἀλλ᾽ ἀποθνήσκων
σῴζεται, οὐ φεύγων. καὶ γὰρ ὁ ἀγαθὸς ὑποκριτὴς
παυόμενος ὅτε δεῖ σῴζεται μᾶλλον ἢ ὑποκρινό-
166 μενος παρὰ καιρόν. τί οὖν ποιήσει τὰ παιδία ;
"εἰ μὲν εἰς Θετταλίαν ἀπῄειν, ἐπεμελήθητε
αὐτῶν· εἰς Ἅιδου δέ μου ἀποδημήσαντος οὐδεὶς
ἔσται ὁ ἐπιμελησόμενος ;" ὅρα, πῶς ὑποκορίζεται
167 καὶ σκώπτει τὸν θάνατον. εἰ δ᾽ ἐγὼ καὶ σὺ

---

[1] A free paraphrase of Plato, *Crito*, 47 D.

[2] In the illegal action of the assembly after the battle of
Arginusae. See Xenophon, *Memorabilia*, I. 1, 18; Plato,
Apology, 32 B.

[3] A singular parallel to "He that loseth his life for my
sake shall find it" (Matt. x. 39).

[4] A paraphrase of Plato, *Crito*, 54 A.

something else that he wished to preserve; not his paltry flesh, but the man of honour, the man of reverence, that he was. These are things which are not to be entrusted to another, not to be made subject. Later on, when he had to speak in defence of his life, he did not behave as one who had children, or a wife, did he? Nay, but as one who was alone in the world. Yes, and when he had to drink the poison, how does he act? When he might have saved his life, and when Crito said to him, "Leave the prison for the sake of your children," what is his reply? Did he think it a bit of good luck? Impossible! No, he regards what is fitting, and as for other considerations, he does not so much as look at or consider them. For he did not care, he says, to save his paltry body, but only that which is increased and preserved by right conduct, and is diminished and destroyed by evil conduct.[1] Socrates does not save his life with dishonour, the man who refused to put the vote when the Athenians demanded it of him,[2] the man who despised the Tyrants, the man who held such noble discourse about virtue and moral excellence; this man it is impossible to save by dishonour, but he is saved by death,[3] and not by flight. Yes, and the good actor, too, is saved when he stops at the right time, rather than the one who acts out of season. What, then, will the children do? "If I had gone to Thessaly, you would have looked after them; but when I have gone down to the house of Hades, will there be no one to look after them?"[4] See how he calls death soft names,[5] and jests at it. But if it

[5] "I have been half in love with easeful Death,
    Call'd him soft names in many a musèd rime."
                                   Keats, *Ode to a Nightingale.*

ἦμεν, εὐθὺς ἂν καταφιλοσοφήσαντες ὅτι " τοὺς
ἀδικοῦντας δεῖ τοῖς ἴσοις ἀμύνεσθαι" καὶ προσ-
θέντες ὅτι "ὄφελος ἔσομαι πολλοῖς ἀνθρώποις
σωθείς, ἀποθανὼν δ' οὐδενί," εἰ ἄρ'¹ ἔδει διὰ
168 τρώγλης ἐκδύντας, ἐξήλθομεν ἄν. καὶ πῶς ἂν
ὠφελήσαμέν τινα ; ποῦ γὰρ ἄν, εἰ ἔτι ἔμενον ἐκεῖ ; ²
ἢ εἰ³ ὄντες ἦμεν ὠφέλιμοι, οὐχὶ πολὺ μᾶλλον
ἀποθανόντες ἂν ὅτε ἔδει καὶ ὡς ἔδει ὠφελήσαμεν
169 ἀνθρώπους ; καὶ νῦν Σωκράτους ἀποθανόντος
οὐθὲν ἧττον ἢ καὶ πλεῖον ὠφέλιμός ἐστιν ἀνθρώποις ἡ μνήμη ὧν ἔτι ζῶν ἔπραξεν ἢ εἶπεν.

170   Ταῦτα μελέτα, ταῦτα τὰ δόγματα, τούτους
τοὺς λόγους, εἰς ταῦτα ἀφόρα τὰ παραδείγματα,
εἰ θέλεις ἐλεύθερος εἶναι, εἰ ἐπιθυμεῖς κατ' ἀξίαν
171 τοῦ πράγματος. καὶ τί θαυμαστόν, εἰ τηλικοῦτο
πρᾶγμα τοσούτων καὶ τηλικούτων ὠνῇ ; ὑπὲρ
τῆς νομιζομένης ἐλευθερίας ταύτης οἱ μὲν ἀπάγ-
χονται, οἱ δὲ κατακρημνίζουσιν αὑτούς, ἔστι δ'
172 ὅτε καὶ πόλεις ὅλαι ἀπώλοντο· ὑπὲρ τῆς ἀ-
ληθινῆς καὶ ἀνεπιβουλεύτου καὶ ἀσφαλοῦς
ἐλευθερίας ἀπαιτοῦντι τῷ θεῷ ἃ δέδωκεν οὐκ
ἐκστήσῃ ; ⁴ οὐχ, ὡς Πλάτων λέγει, μελετήσεις
οὐχὶ ἀποθνήσκειν μόνον, ἀλλὰ καὶ στρεβλοῦσθαι
καὶ φεύγειν καὶ δέρεσθαι καὶ πάνθ' ἁπλῶς
173 ἀποδιδόναι τἀλλότρια ; ἔσει τοίνυν δοῦλος ἐν
δούλοις, κἂν μυριάκις ὑπατεύσῃς, κἂν εἰς τὸ

---

¹ Schenkl : γάρ S.   ² Capps : ἂν ἔτι ἔμενον ἐκεῖνοι S.
³ Salmasius : **οἱ S.
Schenkl (apparently) : οὐκ*στήσηι S.

---

¹ This is probably the best emendation that has been
suggested for a corrupt passage, but I do not feel certain
that it is what Epictetus actually said.

had been you or I, we should forthwith have fallen into the philosophic vein, and said, "One ought to repay evil-doers in kind," and added, " If I save my life I shall be useful to many persons, but if I die I shall be useful to no one"; yes, indeed, and if we had had to crawl out through a hole to escape, we should have done so! And how should we have been of use to anybody? For where could we have been of use, if the others still remained in Athens?[1] Or if we were useful to men by living, should we not have done much more good to men by dying when we ought, and as we ought? And now that Socrates is dead the memory of him is no less useful to men, nay, is perhaps even more useful, than what he did or said while he still lived.

Study these things, these judgements, these arguments, look at these examples, if you wish to be free, if you desire the thing itself in proportion to its value. And what wonder is there if you buy something so great at the price of things so many and so great? For the sake of what is called freedom some men hang themselves, others leap over precipices, sometimes whole cities perish; for true freedom, which cannot be plotted against and is secure, will you not yield up to God, at His demand, what He has given? Will you not, as Plato[2] says, study not merely to die, but even to be tortured on the rack, and to go into exile, and to be severely flogged, and, in a word, to give up everything that is not your own? If not, you will be a slave among slaves; even if you are consul ten thousand times, even if you go up to the

---

[2] *Phaedo*, 64 A, and *Republic*, II. 361 E.

παλάτιον ἀναβῇς, οὐδὲν ἧττον· καὶ αἰσθήσει,
ὅτι παράδοξα μὲν ἴσως φασὶν οἱ φιλόσοφοι,
καθάπερ καὶ ὁ Κλεάνθης ἔλεγεν, οὐ μὴν παρά-
174 λογα. ἔργῳ γὰρ εἴσῃ, ὅτι ἀληθῆ ἐστὶ καὶ τούτων τῶν θαυμαζομένων καὶ σπουδαζομένων
ὄφελος οὐδέν ἐστι τοῖς τυχοῦσι· τοῖς δὲ μηδέπω
τετευχόσι φαντασία γίνεται, ὅτι παραγενομένων
αὐτῶν ἄπαντα παρέσται αὐτοῖς τὰ ἀγαθά· εἶθ'
ὅταν παραγένηται, τὸ καῦμα ἴσον, ὁ ῥιπτασμὸς
ὁ αὐτός, ἡ ἄση, ἡ¹ τῶν οὐ παρόντων ἐπιθυμία.
175 οὐ γὰρ ἐκπληρώσει τῶν ἐπιθυμουμένων ἐλευθερία
παρασκευάζεται, ἀλλὰ ἀνασκευῇ τῆς ἐπιθυμίας.
176 καὶ ἵν' εἰδῇς, ὅτι ἀληθῆ ταῦτά ἐστιν, ὡς ἐκείνων
ἕνεκα πεπόνηκας, οὕτως καὶ ἐπὶ ταῦτα μετάθες
τὸν πόνον· ἀγρύπνησον ἕνεκα τοῦ δόγμα περι-
177 ποιήσασθαι ἐλευθεροποιόν, θεράπευσον ἀντὶ
γέροντος πλουσίου φιλόσοφον, περὶ θύρας
ὄφθητι τὰς τούτου· οὐκ ἀσχημονήσεις ὀφθείς,
οὐκ ἀπελεύσῃ κενὸς οὐδ' ἀκερδής, ἂν ὡς δεῖ
προσέλθῃς. εἰ δὲ μή, πείρασόν γ'· οὐκ ἔστιν
αἰσχρὰ ἡ πεῖρα.

β'. Περὶ συμπεριφορᾶς.²

1 Τούτῳ τῷ τόπῳ πρὸ πάντων σε δεῖ προσέχειν,
μή ποτε ἄρα τῶν προτέρων συνήθων ἢ φίλων

---

¹ ἡ added by Wolf.
² Bentley (and the index of chapters): συμφορᾶς S here.

---

¹ A somewhat similar remark ascribed to Zeno (*Gnomol.
Vat.*, ed. Sternbach, 295) has in the second clause "contrary
to law," a much less pointed remark, and true only with
important qualifications.

Palace—a slave none the less; and you will perceive that, as Cleanthes[1] used to say, "Possibly the philosophers say what is contrary to opinion, but assuredly not what is contrary to reason." For you will learn by experience that what they say is true, and that none of these things which are admired and sought after are of any good to those who attain them; while those who have not yet attained them get an impression that, if once these things come to them, they will be possessed of all things good, and then, when they do come, the burning heat is just as bad, there is the same tossing about on the sea, the same sense of surfeit, the same desire for what they do not have. For freedom is not acquired by satisfying yourself with what you desire, but by destroying your desire. And that you may learn the truth of all this, as you have toiled for those other things, so also transfer your toil to these; keep vigils for the sake of acquiring a judgement which will make you free, devote yourself to a philosopher instead of to a rich old man, be seen about *his* doors; it will be no disgrace to be so seen, you will not retire thence empty and without profit, if you approach him in the right fashion. Anyway, try it at least; there is no disgrace in making the attempt.

CHAPTER II

Of social intercourse

To this topic you ought to devote yourself before every other, how, namely, you may avoid ever being so intimately associated with some one of your

ἀνακραθῇς τινὶ οὕτως, ὥστ' εἰς τὰ αὐτὰ συγκατα-
2 βῆναι αὐτῷ· εἰ δὲ μή, ἀπολεῖς σεαυτόν. ἂν δέ σ'
ὑποτρέχῃ ὅτι " ἀδέξιος αὐτῷ φανοῦμαι καὶ οὐχ
ὁμοίως ἕξει ὡς πρότερον," μέμνησο, ὅτι προῖκα
οὐδὲν γίνεται οὐδ' ἔστι δυνατὸν μὴ τὰ αὐτὰ
3 ποιοῦντα τὸν αὐτὸν εἶναι τῷ ποτέ. ἑλοῦ οὖν
πότερον θέλεις, ὁμοίως φιλεῖσθαι ὑφ' ὧν πρότερον
ὅμοιος ὢν τῷ πρότερον σεαυτῷ ἢ κρείσσων ὢν
4 μὴ τυγχάνειν τῶν ἴσων. εἰ γὰρ τοῦτο κρεῖσσον,
αὐτόθεν ἀπόνευσον ἐπὶ τοῦτο μηδέ σε περι-
σπάτωσαν οἱ ἕτεροι διαλογισμοί· οὐδεὶς γὰρ
ἐπαμφοτερίζων δύναται προκόψαι, ἀλλ' εἰ τοῦτο
πάντων προκέκρικας, εἰ πρὸς τούτῳ μόνῳ θέλεις
εἶναι, εἰ τοῦτο ἐκπονῆσαι, ἄφες ἅπαντα τἆλλα·
5 εἰ δὲ μή, οὗτος ὁ ἐπαμφοτερισμὸς ἀμφότερόν[1] σοι
ποιήσει, οὔτε προκόψεις κατ' ἀξίαν οὔτ' ἐκείνων
6 τεύξῃ, ὧν πρότερον ἐτύγχανες. πρότερον γὰρ
εἰλικρινῶς ἐφιέμενος τῶν οὐδενὸς ἀξίων ἡδὺς
7 ἦς τοῖς συνοῦσιν. οὐ δύνασαι δ' ἐν ἀμφοτέρῳ τῷ
εἴδει διενεγκεῖν ἀλλ' ἀνάγκη, καθόσον ἂν τοῦ
ἑτέρου κοινωνῇς, ἀπολείπεσθαί σ' ἐν θατέρῳ. οὐ
δύνασαι μὴ πίνων μεθ' ὧν ἔπινες ὁμοίως ἡδὺς
αὐτοῖς φαίνεσθαι· ἑλοῦ οὖν, πότερον μεθυστὴς
εἶναι θέλεις καὶ ἡδὺς ἐκείνοις ἢ νήφων ἀηδής. οὐ
δύνασαι μὴ ᾄδων μεθ' ὧν ᾖδες ὁμοίως φιλεῖσθαι

[1] Oldfather : ἑκάτερον S. Cf. IV. 10, 25; Ench. 1, 4.

acquaintances or friends as to descend to the same
level with him; otherwise you will ruin yourself.
But if there slips into your mind the thought, " He
will think me unmannerly and will not be as friendly
as he used to be," remember that nothing is done
without paying for it, and that it is impossible for
a man to remain the same person that he used to
be, if he does not do the same things. Choose,
therefore, which you prefer; either to be loved just
as much as you used to be by the same persons,
remaining like your former self, or else, by being
superior to your former self, to lose the same
affection. Because if this latter alternative is the
better choice, turn forthwith in that direction, and
let not the other considerations draw you away; for
no man is able to make progress when he is facing
both ways. But if you have preferred this course
to every other, if you wish to devote yourself to
this alone, and labour to perfect it, give up everything else. Otherwise this facing both ways will
bring about a double result: You will neither make
progress as you ought, nor will you get what you
used to get before. For before, when you frankly
aimed at nothing worth while, you made a pleasant
companion. You cannot achieve distinction along
both lines, but you must needs fall short in the one
to the degree in which you take part in the other.
If you do not drink with those you used to drink
with, you cannot in their eyes be as pleasant a companion as you used to be; choose, therefore, whether
you wish to be a hard drinker and pleasant to those
persons, or a sober man and unpleasant. If you do
not sing with those you used to sing with, you cannot be loved by them as you used to be; choose,

ὑπ᾽ αὐτῶν· ἑλοῦ οὖν καὶ ἐνταῦθα, πότερον θέλεις.
8 εἰ γὰρ κρεῖσσον τὸ αἰδήμονα εἶναι καὶ κόσμιον
τοῦ εἰπεῖν τινα " ἡδὺς ἄνθρωπος," ἄφες τὰ ἕτερα,
ἀπόγνωθι, ἀποστράφηθι, μηδὲν σοὶ καὶ αὐτοῖς.
9 εἰ δὲ μὴ ἀρέσει ταῦτα, ὅλος ἀπόκλινον ἐπὶ
τἀναντία· γενοῦ εἷς τῶν κιναίδων, εἷς τῶν μοιχῶν,
καὶ ποίει τὰ ἑξῆς καὶ τεύξῃ ὧν θέλεις. καὶ
10 ἀναπηδῶν ἐπικραύγαζε τῷ ὀρχηστῇ. διάφορα δ᾽
οὕτως πρόσωπα οὐ μίγνυται· οὐ δύνασαι καὶ
Θερσίτην ὑποκρίνασθαι καὶ Ἀγαμέμνονα. ἂν
Θερσίτης εἶναι θέλῃς, κυρτόν σε εἶναι δεῖ,
φαλακρόν· ἂν Ἀγαμέμνων, μέγαν καὶ καλὸν καὶ
τοὺς ὑποτεταγμένους φιλοῦντα.

γ. Τίνα τίνων ἀντικαταλλακτέον;

1   Ἐκεῖνο πρόχειρον ἔχε, ὅταν τινὸς ἀπολείπῃ
τῶν ἐκτός, τί ἀντ᾽ αὐτοῦ περιποιῇ· κἂν ᾖ πλείονος
2 ἄξιον, μηδέποτ᾽ εἴπῃς ὅτι " ἐζημίωμαι"· οὐδ᾽ ἂν[1]
ἀντὶ ὄνου ἵππον, οὐδ᾽ ἀντὶ προβάτου βοῦν οὐδ᾽
ἀντὶ κέρματος πρᾶξιν καλήν, οὐδ᾽ ἀντὶ ψυχρο-
λογίας ἡσυχίαν οἵαν δεῖ, οὐδ᾽ ἀντὶ αἰσχρολογίας
3 αἰδῶ. τούτων μεμνημένος πανταχοῦ διασώσεις
τὸ σαυτοῦ πρόσωπον οἷον ἔχειν σε δεῖ. εἰ δὲ
μή, σκόπει, ὅτι ἀπόλλυνται οἱ χρόνοι εἰκῇ καὶ

---

[1] ἄν added by Schweighäuser.

therefore, here also, which you wish. For if it is
better to be a man of respectful and modest behaviour than for someone to say of you, "He is a
pleasant fellow," give up all other considerations,
renounce them, turn your back upon them, have
nothing to do with them. But if that does not
please you, turn about, the whole of you, to
the opposite; become one of the addicts to unnatural vice, one of the adulterers, and act in the
corresponding fashion, and you will get what you
wish. Yes, and jump up and shout your applause
to the dancer. But different characters do not mix
in this fashion; you cannot act the part of Thersites
and that of Agamemnon too. If you wish to be a
Thersites, you ought to be humpbacked and bald;
if an Agamemnon, you ought to be tall and handsome, and to love those who have been made subject
to you.

CHAPTER III

What things should be exchanged for what things?

HERE is a thought to keep ready at hand
whenever you lose some external thing: What are
you acquiring in its place? and if this be more
valuable than the other, never say, "I have suffered
a loss." You have lost nothing if you get a horse
for an ass, an ox for a sheep, a noble action for
a small piece of money, the proper kind of peace
for futile discourse, and self-respect for smutty talk.
If you bear this in mind you will everywhere maintain your character as it ought to be. If not, I
would have you observe that your time is being

ὅσα νῦν προσέχεις σεαυτῷ, μέλλεις ἐκχεῖν
4 ἅπαντα ταῦτα καὶ ἀνατρέπειν. ὀλίγου δὲ χρεία
ἐστὶ πρὸς τὴν ἀπώλειαν τὴν πάντων καὶ ἀνατρο-
5 πήν, μικρᾶς ἀποστροφῆς τοῦ λόγου. ἵνα ὁ
κυβερνήτης ἀνατρέψῃ τὸ πλοῖον, οὐ χρείαν ἔχει
τῆς αὐτῆς παρασκευῆς, ὅσης εἰς τὸ σῶσαι· ἀλλὰ
μικρὸν πρὸς τὸν ἄνεμον ἂν ἐπιστρέψῃ, ἀπώλετο.
κἂν μὴ αὐτὸς ἑκών, ὑποπαρενθυμηθῇ δ᾽, ἀπώλετο.
6 τοιοῦτόν ἐστί τι καὶ ἐνθάδε· μικρὸν ἂν ἀπονυσ-
τάξῃς, ἀπῆλθεν πάντα τὰ μέχρι νῦν συνειλεγ-
7 μένα. πρόσεχε οὖν ταῖς φαντασίαις, ἐπαγρύπνει.
οὐ γὰρ μικρὸν τὸ τηρούμενον, ἀλλ᾽ αἰδὼς καὶ
πίστις καὶ εὐστάθεια, ἀπάθεια, ἀλυπία, ἀφοβία,
8 ἀταραξία, ἁπλῶς ἐλευθερία. τίνων μέλλεις
ταῦτα πωλεῖν; βλέπε, πόσου ἀξίων.—'Αλλ᾽ οὐ
τεύξομαι τοιούτου τινὸς ἀντ᾽ αὐτοῦ.—Βλέπε καὶ
τυγχάνων¹ πάλιν ἐκείνου, τί ἀντ᾽ αὐτοῦ λαμβά-
9 νεις.² "ἐγὼ εὐκοσμίαν, ἐκεῖνος δημαρχίαν· ἐκεῖνος
στρατηγίαν, ἐγὼ αἰδῶ. ἀλλ᾽ οὐ κραυγάζω, ὅπου
ἀπρεπές· ἀλλ᾽ οὐκ ἀναστήσομαι, ὅπου μὴ δεῖ.
ἐλεύθερος γάρ εἰμι καὶ φίλος τοῦ θεοῦ, ἵν᾽ ἑκὼν
10 πείθωμαι αὐτῷ. τῶν δ᾽ ἄλλων οὐδενὸς ἀντι-
ποιεῖσθαί με δεῖ, οὐ σώματος, οὐ κτήσεως, οὐκ
ἀρχῆς, οὐ φήμης, ἁπλῶς οὐδενός· οὐδὲ γὰρ

¹ ἀποτυγχάνων Reiske : τυγχάνοντος Elter.
² λαμβάνει Schweighäuser.

¹ This sense may conceivably be contained in the MS.
reading, but it seems more probable that the text is corrupt,
although no convincing correction has yet been made.—Capps
regards ἐκείνου and ἐκεῖνος (§ 9) as referring to the same
person.—The quotation following is what Epictetus suggests as appropriate comment for the man who has made a
wise choice.

spent to no purpose, and all the pains you are now
taking with yourself you are sure to spill out utterly
and upset.   Little is needed to ruin and upset
everything, only a slight aberration from reason.
For the helmsman to upset his ship he does not need
the same amount of preparation that he does to
keep it safe ; but if he heads it a little too much
into the wind, he is lost ; yes, even if he does nothing
by his own deliberate choice, but merely falls to
thinking about something else for a moment, he is
lost.   In life also it is very much the same ; if you
doze but for a moment, all that you have amassed
hitherto is gone.   Pay attention, therefore, to your
sense-impressions, and watch over them sleeplessly.
For it is no small matter that you are guarding, but
self-respect, and fidelity, and constancy, a state of
mind undisturbed by passion, pain, fear, or confusion—in a word, freedom.   What are the things
for which you are about to sell *these* things ?   Look,
how valuable are they ?—But, you say, I shall
not get anything of that kind in return for what
I am giving up.—Observe also, when you do get
something in the exchange, just what it is you
are getting for what you give up.[1]   "I have a
modest behaviour, he has a tribuneship ; he has a
praetorship, I have self-respect.   But I do not shout
where it is unseemly ; I shall not stand up where I
ought not ; for I am a free man and a friend of God,[2]
so as to obey Him of my own free will.   No other
thing ought I to claim, not body, or property, or
office, or reputation—nothing, in short ; nor does

---

[2] Probably this was the phrase which suggested the point
of the famous epigram : ". . . I, Epictetus, was the friend
of God " (quoted Vol. I, Introd. p. vii).

ἐκεῖνος βούλεταί μ' ἀντιποιεῖσθαι αὐτῶν. εἰ γὰρ
ἤθελεν, ἀγαθὰ πεποιήκει αὐτὰ ἂν ἐμοί. νῦν δ'
οὐ πεποίηκεν· διὰ τοῦτο οὐδὲν δύναμαι παρα-
11 βῆναι τῶν ἐντολῶν." τήρει τὸ ἀγαθὸν τὸ σαυτοῦ
ἐν παντί, τῶν δ' ἄλλων κατὰ τὸ διδόμενον μέχρι
τοῦ εὐλογιστεῖν ἐν αὐτοῖς, τούτῳ μόνῳ ἀρκούμενος. εἰ δὲ μή, δυστυχήσεις, ἀτυχήσεις, κωλυ-
12 θήσῃ, ἐμποδισθήσῃ. οὗτοί εἰσιν οἱ ἐκεῖθεν
ἀπεσταλμένοι νόμοι, ταῦτα τὰ διατάγματα·
τούτων ἐξηγητὴν δεῖ γενέσθαι, τούτοις ὑποτεταγ-
μένον, οὐ τοῖς Μασουρίου καὶ Κασσίου.

δ'. Πρὸς τοὺς περὶ τὸ ἐν ἡσυχίᾳ διάγειν
ἐσπουδακότας.

1 Μέμνησο, ὅτι οὐ μόνον ἐπιθυμία ἀρχῆς καὶ
πλούτου ταπεινοὺς ποιεῖ καὶ ἄλλοις ὑποτεταγμένους, ἀλλὰ καὶ ἡσυχίας καὶ σχολῆς καὶ ἀπο-
δημίας καὶ φιλολογίας. ἁπλῶς γὰρ οἷον ἂν[1] ᾖ
2 τὸ ἐκτός, ἡ τιμὴ αὐτοῦ ὑποτάσσει ἄλλῳ. τί οὖν
διαφέρει συγκλήτου ἐπιθυμεῖν ἢ τοῦ μὴ εἶναι
συγκλητικόν; τί διαφέρει ἀρχῆς ἐπιθυμεῖν ἢ
ἀναρχίας; τί διαφέρει λέγειν ὅτι " κακῶς μοί
ἐστιν, οὐδὲν ἔχω τί πράξω, ἀλλὰ τοῖς βιβλίοις
προσδέδεμαι ὡς νεκρός," ἢ λέγειν " κακῶς μοί
3 ἐστιν, οὐκ εὐσχολῶ ἀναγνῶναι" ; ὡς γὰρ ἀσπασ-

---

[1] Upton from his "codex" (after Schegk and Meibom):
ἐάν S.

He wish me to claim them. Had He so desired
He would have made them good for me. But as it
is, He has not so made them; therefore I cannot
transgress any of His commands." Guard your own
good in everything you do; and for the rest be
content to take simply what has been given you,
in so far as you can make a rational use of it. If
you do not, you will have bad luck and no good
luck, you will be hampered and hindered. These
are the laws that have been sent you from God,
these are His ordinances; it is of these you ought
to become an interpreter, to these you ought to
subject yourself, not the laws of Masurius and
Cassius.[1]

CHAPTER IV

To those who have set their hearts upon living in peace

REMEMBER that it is not merely desire for office
and wealth which makes men abject and subservient
to others, but desire also for peace, and leisure, and
travel, and scholarship. For it makes no difference
what the external object be, the value you set
upon it makes you subservient to another. What
difference, then, does it make for you to set your
heart on the senate, or on not becoming a senator?
What difference does it make to desire office or to
desire not to hold office? What difference does it
make to say, " I am in a bad way, I have nothing to
do, but am tied to my books as though I were a
corpse," or to say, " I am in a bad way, I have no
leisure to read " ? For just as salutations and office-

[1] Two distinguished jurists of the first half of the first
century after Christ.

4 μοὶ καὶ ἀρχὴ τῶν ἐκτός ἐστι καὶ ἀπροαιρέτων,
οὕτως καὶ βιβλίον. ἢ τίνος ἕνεκα θέλεις ἀναγνῶναι; εἰπέ μοι. εἰ μὲν γὰρ ἐπ᾽ αὐτὸ¹ καταστρέ-
φεις² τὸ ψυχαγωγηθῆναι ἢ μαθεῖν τι, ψυχρὸς
εἶ καὶ ἀταλαίπωρος.³ εἰ δ᾽ ἐφ᾽ ὃ δεῖ ἀναφέρεις, τί τοῦτ᾽ ἔστιν ἄλλο ἢ εὔροια; εἰ δέ σοι τὸ
ἀναγιγνώσκειν εὔροιαν μὴ περιποιῇ, τί ὄφελος
5 αὐτοῦ;—Ἀλλὰ περιποιεῖ, φησίν, καὶ διὰ τοῦτο
ἀγανακτῶ ὡς ἀπολειπόμενος αὐτοῦ.—Καὶ τίς αὕτη
ἡ εὔροια, ἣν ὁ τυχὼν ἐμποδίσαι δύναται, οὐ λέγω
Καῖσαρ ἢ Καίσαρος φίλος, ἀλλὰ κόραξ, αὐλητής,
πυρετός, ἄλλα τρισμύρια; ἡ δ᾽ εὔροια οὐδὲν οὕτως
ἔχει ὡς τὸ διηνεκὲς καὶ ἀνεμπόδιστον.
6 Νῦν καλοῦμαι πράξων τι, ἄπειμι νῦν προσ-
έξων τοῖς μέτροις ἃ δεῖ τηρεῖν, ὅτι αἰδημόνως,
ὅτι ἀσφαλῶς, ὅτι δίχα ὀρέξεως καὶ ἐκκλίσεως
7 τῆς πρὸς τὰ ἐκτός, καὶ λοιπὸν προσέχω τοῖς
ἀνθρώποις, τίνα φασί, πῶς κινοῦνται, καὶ τοῦτο
οὐ κακοήθως οὐδ᾽ ἵνα ἔχω ψέγειν ἢ καταγελῶ,
ἀλλ᾽ ἐπ᾽ ἐμαυτὸν ἐπιστρέφω, εἰ ταὐτὰ κἀγὼ
ἁμαρτάνω. "πῶς οὖν παύσωμαι;" τότε καὶ ἐγὼ
ἡμάρτανον· νῦν δ᾽ οὐκέτι, χάρις τῷ θεῷ. . . .⁴

¹ Reiske: αὐτοῦ S.
² The words ἐπ᾽ αὐτό after this were deleted by Schweighäuser.
³ Schweighäuser: ταλαίπωρος S.
⁴ The lacuna marked by Oldfather. An answer to the
question asked is obviously required.

¹ Answering the man who complains because he has
"nothing to do" (§ 2).
² So Horace, Sat. I. 4, 136 f.: . . . numquid ego illi
imprudens olim faciam simile? Both were following the
custom of Plato as recorded by Plutarch, De capienda ex
inimicis utilitate, 5.

holding are among things external and those which lie outside the province of the moral purpose, so also is a book. Or for what purpose do you wish to read? Tell me. If you turn to reading merely for entertainment, or in order to learn something, you are futile and lazy. But if you refer reading to the proper standard, what else is this but a life of serenity? However, if reading does not secure for you a life of serenity, of what good is it?—Nay, it does secure me serenity, one says, and that is why I am discontented because I am deprived of it.— And what kind of serenity is this which any chance comer can impede, not merely Caesar, or a friend of Caesar, but a crow, a flutist, fever, thirty thousand other things? But no feature of serenity is so characteristic as continuity and freedom from hindrance.

At this instant I *am* being called to do something;[1] at this instant I shall go home with the purpose of observing the due measure which I ought to maintain, acting with self-respect, with security, apart from desire and avoidance of things external; and in the second place I observe men, what they say, how they move, and this in no malignant spirit, nor in order to have something to censure or ridicule, but I look at myself the while, to see if I too am making the same mistakes.[2] "How, then, shall I cease to make mistakes?" There was a time when I too made mistakes, but now no longer, thanks be to God. . . .[3]

[3] The exact connection of these two sentences is obscure. Matheson, with a certain degree of plausibility, divides them between the interlocutor and Epictetus, but they are generally assigned to one person. – See also the crit. note.

8 Ἄγε, ταῦτα ποιήσας καὶ πρὸς τούτοις γενόμενος χεῖρον ἔργον πεποίηκας ἢ χιλίους στίχους
ἀναγνοὺς ἢ γράψας ἄλλους τοσούτους; ὅταν
γὰρ ἐσθίῃς, ἄχθῃ, ὅτι μὴ ἀναγιγνώσκεις; οὐκ
ἀρκῇ τῷ καθ' ἃ ἀνέγνωκας ἐσθίειν; ὅταν λούῃ;
9 ὅταν γυμνάζῃ; διὰ τί οὖν ἐπὶ πάντων οὐχ ὁμα-
λίζεις, καὶ ὅταν Καίσαρι προσίῃς καὶ ὅταν τῷ
δεῖνι; εἰ τὸν ἀπαθῆ τηρεῖς, εἰ τὸν ἀκατάπληκτον,
10 εἰ τὸν κατεσταλμένον, εἰ βλέπεις μᾶλλον τὰ
γινόμενα ἢ βλέπῃ, εἰ μὴ φθονεῖς τοῖς προτιμω-
μένοις, εἰ μὴ ἐκπλήσσουσίν σε αἱ ὗλαι, τί σοι
11 λείπει; βιβλία; πῶς ἢ ἐπὶ τί; οὐχὶ γὰρ ἐπὶ
τὸ βιοῦν παρασκευή τίς ἐστιν αὕτη; τὸ βιοῦν
δ' ἐξ ἄλλων τινῶν ἢ τούτων συμπληροῦται.
οἷον ἂν εἰ ὁ ἀθλητὴς κλαίη εἰς τὸ στάδιον εἰσιών,
12 ὅτι μὴ ἔξω γυμνάζεται. τούτων ἕνεκα ἐγυμνάζου,
ἐπὶ τοῦτο οἱ ἁλτῆρες, ἡ ἁφή, οἱ νεανίσκοι. καὶ
νῦν ἐκεῖνα ζητεῖς, ὅτε τοῦ ἔργου καιρός ἐστιν;
13 οἷον εἰ ἐπὶ τοῦ συγκαταθετικοῦ τόπου παριστα-
μένων φαντασιῶν τῶν μὲν καταληπτικῶν, τῶν
δ' ἀκαταλήπτων μὴ ταύτας διακρίνειν θέλοιμεν,
ἀλλ' ἀναγιγνώσκειν τὰ Περὶ καταλήψεως.
14 Τί οὖν τὸ αἴτιον; ὅτι οὐδέποτε τούτου ἕνεκα
ἀνέγνωμεν, οὐδέποτε τούτου ἕνεκα ἐγράψαμεν,

---

[1] In the absence of pages, as in the case of the papyrus
roll, prose as well as poetry was counted by lines.
[2] See III. 15, 4.

Come, if you have acted like this and devoted yourself to these things, have you done anything worse than reading a thousand lines, or writing a thousand?[1] For when you eat, are you annoyed because you are not reading? Are you not satisfied to be eating in accordance with the principles you learned by reading? And when you bathe and take exercise? Why, then, are you not consistent in everything, both when you approach Caesar, and when you approach So-and-so? If you are maintaining the character of a man of tranquillity, of imperturbability, of sedateness, if you are observing what happens rather than being yourself observed, if you are not envying those who are preferred in honour above you, if the mere subject-matter of actions does not dazzle you, what do you lack? Books? How, or for what end? What, is not the reading of books a kind of preparation for the act of living? But the full measure of the act of living is made up of things other than books. It is as though the athlete on entering the stadium were to fall a-wailing because he is not exercising outside. This was what you exercised for, this is the purpose of your jumping-weights, your wrestler's sand,[2] your young training partners. And are you now asking for these things, when the time for action is come? It is as if, when in the sphere of assent we were surrounded with sense-impressions, some of them convincing, and others not convincing, we should not wish to distinguish between them, but to read a treatise *On Comprehension*!

What, then, is the reason for this? It is because we have never read for this purpose, we have never written for this purpose—in our actions, to treat in

ἵν' ἐπὶ τῶν ἔργων κατὰ φύσιν χρώμεθα ταῖς
προσπιπτούσαις φαντασίαις, ἀλλ' αὐτοῦ κατα-
λήγομεν ἐν τῷ¹ μαθεῖν, τί λέγεται, καὶ ἄλλῳ
δύνασθαι ἐξηγήσασθαι, τὸν συλλογισμὸν ἀνα-
15 λῦσαι καὶ τὸν ὑποθετικὸν ἐφοδεῦσαι. διὰ τοῦτο
ὅπου ἡ σπουδή, ἐκεῖ καὶ ὁ ἐμποδισμός. θέλεις
τὰ μὴ ἐπὶ σοὶ ἐξ ἅπαντος; κωλύου τοίνυν, ἐμπο-
16 δίζου, ἀποτύγχανε. εἰ δὲ τὰ Περὶ ὁρμῆς τούτου
ἕνεκα ἀναγιγνώσκοιμεν, οὐχ ἵνα ἴδωμεν, τί λέγεται περὶ ὁρμῆς, ἀλλ' ἵνα εὖ ὁρμῶμεν·² τὰ Περὶ
ὀρέξεως δὲ καὶ ἐκκλίσεως, ἵνα μήποτ' ὀρεγόμενοι
ἀποτυγχάνωμεν μήτ' ἐκκλίνοντες περιπίπτωμεν·
τὰ Περὶ καθήκοντος δ', ἵνα μεμνημένοι τῶν
σχέσεων μηδὲν ἀλογίστως μηδὲ παρ' αὐτὰ ποιῶ-
17 μεν· οὐκ ἂν ἠγανακτοῦμεν πρὸς τὰ ἀναγνώσματα
ἐμποδιζόμενοι, ἀλλὰ τῷ τὰ ἔργα ἀποδιδόναι τὰ
κατάλληλα ἠρκούμεθα καὶ ἠριθμοῦμεν ἂν οὐ
ταῦτα, ἃ μέχρι νῦν ἀριθμεῖν εἰθίσμεθα, "σήμερον
18 ἀνέγνων στίχους τοσούσδε, ἔγραψα τοσούσδε,"
ἀλλὰ "σήμερον ὁρμῇ ἐχρησάμην, ὡς παραγγέλ-
λεται ὑπὸ τῶν φιλοσόφων, ὀρέξει οὐκ ἐχρησάμην,
ἐκκλίσει πρὸς μόνα τὰ προαιρετικά, οὐ κατε-
πλάγην τὸν δεῖνα, οὐκ ἐδυσωπήθην ὑπὸ τοῦ
δεῖνος, τὸ ἀνεκτικὸν ἐγύμνασα, τὸ ἀφεκτικόν, τὸ
συνεργητικόν," καὶ οὕτως ἂν ηὐχαριστοῦμεν τῷ
θεῷ ἐφ' οἷς δεῖ εὐχαριστεῖν.
19   Νῦν δ' ἡμεῖς οὐκ ἴσμεν, ὅτι καὶ αὐτοὶ ἄλλον
τρόπον ὅμοιοι τοῖς πολλοῖς γινόμεθα. ἄλλος
φοβεῖται, μὴ οὐκ ἄρξῃ σύ, μὴ³ ἄρξῃς. μηδα-

---

¹ ἐν τῷ added by Richards.
² A late hand in S: ἵνα ὁ*ῶμεν S.
³ Wolf: μήσυ S.

318

accordance with nature the sense-impressions which come to us; but we stop with having learned what is said, and with the ability to explain it to someone else, and with analysing the syllogism, and examining the hypothetical argument. That is why, where our heart is set, there also our impediment lies. Do you wish at any cost to have the things that are not under your control? Very well then, be hindered, be obstructed, fail. If we should read a treatise *On Choice*, not in order to know about the subject, but in order to make correct choices; a treatise *On Desire and Aversion*, in order that we may never fail in our desire nor fall into that which we are trying to avoid; a treatise *On Duty*, in order that we may remember our relations in society and do nothing irrationally or contrary to the principles of duty; we should not be vexed by being hindered in regard to what we have read, but we should find satisfaction in doing the deeds required by our mutual relations, and we should be reckoning, not the things which we have been accustomed hitherto to reckon: "To-day I have read so many lines, I have written so many," but, "To-day I made a choice in the way that the philosophers teach, I did not entertain desire, I avoided only those things that are in the sphere of the moral purpose, I was not overawed by So-and-so, I was not put out of countenance by So-and-so, I exercised my patience, my abstinence, my co-operation," and thus we should be giving thanks to God for those things for which we ought to give Him thanks.

But as it is, we do not realize that we ourselves, though in a different fashion, grow like the multitude. Another man is afraid that he will not have an office; you are afraid that you will. Do not so,

20 μῶς, ἄνθρωπε. ἀλλ' ὡς καταγελᾷς τοῦ φοβου-
μένου μὴ οὐκ¹ ἄρξαι, οὕτως καὶ σαυτοῦ καταγέλα.
οὐδὲν γὰρ διαφέρει ἢ διψῆν πυρέσσοντα ἢ ὡς
21 λυσσώδη ὑδροφόβον εἶναι. ἢ πῶς ἔτι δυνήσῃ
εἰπεῖν τὸ τοῦ Σωκράτους "εἰ ταύτῃ φίλον τῷ
θεῷ, ταύτῃ γινέσθω"; δοκεῖς, Σωκράτης εἰ
ἐπεθύμει ἐν Λυκείῳ ἢ ἐν Ἀκαδημείᾳ σχολάζειν
καὶ διαλέγεσθαι καθ' ἡμέραν τοῖς νέοις, εὐκόλως
ἂν ἐστρατεύσατο ὁσάκις ἐστρατεύσατο; οὐχὶ δ'
ὠδύρετ' ἂν καὶ ἔστενεν "τάλας ἐγώ, νῦν ἐνθάδ'
ἀτυχῶ ἄθλιος δυνάμενος ἐν Λυκείῳ ἡλιάζεσθαι";
22 τοῦτο γάρ σου τὸ ἔργον ἦν, ἡλιάζεσθαι; οὐχὶ
δὲ τὸ εὑροεῖν, τὸ ἀκώλυτον εἶναι, τὸ ἀπαραπόδιστον; καὶ πῶς ἂν ἔτι ἦν Σωκράτης, εἰ ταῦτα
ὠδύρετο; πῶς ἂν ἔτι ἐν τῇ φυλακῇ παιᾶνας
ἔγραφεν;
23 Ἁπλῶς οὖν ἐκείνου μέμνησο, ὅτι, πᾶν ὃ ἔξω
τῆς προαιρέσεως τῆς σαυτοῦ τιμήσεις, ἀπώλεσας
τὴν προαίρεσιν. ἔξω δ' ἐστὶν οὐ μόνον ἀρχή,
ἀλλὰ καὶ ἀναρχία, οὐ μόνον ἀσχολία, ἀλλὰ καὶ
24 σχολή. "νῦν οὖν ἐμὲ ἐν τῷ θορύβῳ τούτῳ
διεξάγειν;" τί λέγεις θορύβῳ; ἐν πολλοῖς
ἀνθρώποις; καὶ τί χαλεπόν; δόξον ἐν Ὀλυμπίᾳ
εἶναι, πανήγυριν αὐτὸν ἤγησαι. κἀκεῖ ἄλλος
ἄλλο τι κέκραγεν, ἄλλος ἄλλο τι πράσσει, ἄλλος

---

¹ οὐκ added by Schweighäuser.

---

¹ Plato, *Crito*, 43 D (slightly modified). Compare I. 4, 24,
where the quotation is exact.

² Referring to the famous gymnasia in these places.

³ Plato, *Phaedo*, 60 D, says that he translated some fables
of Aesop into verse and composed a hymn (προοίμιον) to
Apollo. This latter composition is called a paean by

man! But just as you laugh at the man who is afraid he will not have an office, so also laugh at yourself. For it makes no difference whether a person is thirsty with fever, or is afraid of water like a man with the rabies. Or how can you any longer say with Socrates, " If so it please God, so be it "? [1] Do you suppose that, if Socrates had yearned to spend his leisure in the Lyceum or the Academy, [2] and to converse daily with the young men, he would have gone forth cheerfully on all the military expeditions in which he served? Would he not have wailed and groaned, " Wretched man that I am! here I am now in misery and misfortune, when I might be sunning myself in the Lyceum"? What, was this your function in life, to sun yourself? Was it not rather to be serene, to be unhampered, to be unhindered? And how would he have been Socrates any longer, if he had wailed like this? How would he have gone on to write paeans in prison? [3]

In a word, then, remember this—that if you are going to honour anything at all outside the sphere of the moral purpose, you have destroyed your moral purpose. And outside the sphere of your moral purpose lie not merely office, but also freedom from office; not merely business, but also leisure. " Am I now, therefore, to pass my life in this turmoil?" What do you mean by " turmoil "? Among many people? And what is there hard about that? Imagine that you are in Olympia, regard the turmoil as a festival. There, too, one man shouts this and another that; one man does this and another

Diogenes Laertius, 2, 42, who professes to give the first line of it.

τῷ ἄλλῳ ἐνσείεται· ἐν τοῖς βαλανείοις ὄχλος.
καὶ τίς ἡμῶν οὐ χαίρει τῇ πανηγύρει ταύτῃ καὶ
25 ὀδυνώμενος αὐτῆς ἀπαλλάσσεται; μὴ γίνου
δυσάρεστος μηδὲ κακοστόμαχος πρὸς τὰ γινόμενα. "τὸ ὄξος σαπρόν, δριμὺ γάρ"· "τὸ μέλι
σαπρόν, ἀνατρέπει γάρ μου τὴν ἕξιν"· "λάχανα
οὐ θέλω." οὕτως καὶ "σχολὴν οὐ θέλω, ἐρημία
26 ἐστίν," "ὄχλον οὐ θέλω, θόρυβός ἐστιν." ἀλλ'
ἂν μὲν οὕτως φέρῃ τὰ πράγματα, ὥστε μόνον ἢ
μετ' ὀλίγων διεξαγαγεῖν, ἡσυχίαν αὐτὸ κάλει καὶ
χρῶ τῷ πράγματι εἰς ὃ δεῖ· λάλει σεαυτῷ,
γύμναζε τὰς φαντασίας, ἐξεργάζου τὰς προλήψεις. ἂν δ' εἰς ὄχλον ἐμπέσῃς, ἀγῶνα αὐτὸ λέγε,
27 πανήγυριν, ἑορτήν, συνεορτάζειν πειρῶ τοῖς
ἀνθρώποις. τί γάρ ἐστιν ἥδιον θέαμα τῷ φιλαν-
θρώπῳ ἢ ἄνθρωποι πολλοί; ἵππων ἀγέλας ἢ
βοῶν ἡδέως ὁρῶμεν, πλοῖα πολλὰ ὅταν ἴδωμεν,
διαχεόμεθα· ἀνθρώπους πολλοὺς βλέπων τις
28 ἀνιᾶται; "ἀλλὰ κατακραυγάζουσί μου." οὐκοῦν
ἡ ἀκοή σου ἐμποδίζεται. τί οὖν πρὸς σέ; μή τι
καὶ δύναμις ἡ ταῖς φαντασίαις χρηστική; καὶ
τίς σε κωλύει ὀρέξει καὶ ἐκκλίσει χρῆσθαι κατὰ
φύσιν, ὁρμῇ καὶ ἀφορμῇ; ποῖος θόρυβος πρὸς
τοῦτο ἱκανός;

---

[1] Referring clearly, I believe, to the baths at Olympia,
where the accommodation seems to have been inadequate.
See I. 6, 26.

[2] Cf. "But when he saw the multitudes, he was moved
with compassion on them" (Matt. ix. 36); and the remark
attributed to Abraham Lincoln: "God must have loved
the common people; He made so many of them." The
characteristic emotions here indicated as arising at the con-

that; one man jostles another; there is a crowd in the baths.[1]   And yet who of us does not take delight in the Olympic festival and leave it with sorrow? Do not become peevish or fastidious towards events. "The vinegar is rotten, for it is sour." "The honey is rotten, for it upsets my digestion." "I don't like vegetables."   In the same fashion you say, " I don't like leisure, it is a solitude."   "I don't like a crowd, it is turmoil."   Say not so, but if circumstances bring you to spend your life alone or in the company of a few, call it peace, and utilize the condition for its proper end; converse with yourself, exercise your sense-impressions, develop your preconceptions. If, however, you fall in with a crowd, call it games, a festival, a holiday, try to keep holiday with the people.   For what is pleasanter to a man who loves his fellow-men than the sight of large numbers of them?[2]   We are glad to see herds of horses or cattle; when we see many ships we are delighted; is a person annoyed at the sight of many human beings? "Yes, but they deafen me with their shouting." Oh, well, it is your hearing that is interfered with! What, then, is that to you? Your faculty of employing external impressions is not interfered with, is it?   And who prevents you from making natural use of desire and aversion, of choice and refusal?   What manner of turmoil avails to do that?

templation of large numbers of one's fellow-men, though somewhat different in tone from that in Epictetus, as well as from one another, are still essentially at one with the Stoic ideal of sympathetic fellowship, and are fundamentally opposed to that selfish or snobbish aversion towards mankind, which became so prevalent, even in religious circles, during the great decadence of ancient civilization.

29   Σὺ μόνον μέμνησο τῶν καθολικῶν· "τί ἐμόν,
τί οὐκ ἐμόν; τί μοι δίδοται; τί θέλει με ποιεῖν
30 ὁ θεὸς νῦν, τί οὐ θέλει;" πρὸ ὀλίγου χρόνου
ἤθελέν σε σχολάζειν, σαυτῷ λαλεῖν, γράφειν
περὶ τούτων, ἀναγιγνώσκειν, ἀκούειν, παρα-
σκευάζεσθαι· ἔσχες εἰς τοῦτο ἱκανὸν χρόνον. νῦν
σοι λέγει "ἐλθὲ ἤδη ἐπὶ τὸν ἀγῶνα, δεῖξον ἡμῖν,
τί ἔμαθες, πῶς ἤθλησας. μέχρι τίνος γυμνασ-
θήσῃ μόνος; ἤδη καιρὸς γνῶναί σε, πότερον τῶν
ἀξιονίκων εἶ τις ἀθλητῶν ἢ ἐκείνων, οἳ τὴν οἰκου-
31 μένην περιέρχονται νικώμενοι." τί οὖν ἀγανακτεῖς; οὐδεὶς ἀγὼν δίχα[1] θορύβου γίνεται.
πολλοὺς δεῖ προγυμναστὰς εἶναι, πολλοὺς τοὺς
ἐπικραυγάζοντας, πολλοὺς ἐπιστάτας, πολλοὺς
32 θεατάς.—'Αλλ' ἐγὼ ἤθελον ἐφ' ἡσυχίας διάγειν.
—Οἴμωζε τοίνυν καὶ στένε, ὥσπερ ἄξιος εἶ. τίς
γὰρ ἄλλη μείζων ταύτης ζημία τῷ ἀπαιδεύτῳ
καὶ ἀπειθοῦντι τοῖς θείοις διατάγμασιν ἢ τὸ
λυπεῖσθαι, τὸ πενθεῖν, τὸ φθονεῖν, ἁπλῶς τὸ
ἀτυχεῖν καὶ δυστυχεῖν; τούτων οὐ θέλεις ἀπαλ-
λάξαι σεαυτόν;
33   Καὶ πῶς ἀπαλλάξω;—Οὐ πολλάκις ἤκουσας,
ὅτι ὄρεξιν ἆραί σε δεῖ παντελῶς, τὴν ἔκκλισιν
ἐπὶ μόνα τρέψαι τὰ προαιρετικά, ἀφεῖναί σε δεῖ
πάντα, τὸ σῶμα, τὴν κτῆσιν, τὴν φήμην, τὰ
βιβλία, θόρυβον, ἀρχάς, ἀναρχίαν; ὅπου γὰρ ἂν
κλίνῃς, ἐδούλευσας, ὑπετάγης, κωλυτὸς ἐγένου,

---

[1] Ed. of Salamanca, Bentley, and Upton's "codex" (after
Schegk): διά S.

324

Do but keep in remembrance your general principles: "What is mine? What is not mine? What has been given me? What does God will that I do now, what does He not will?" A little while ago it was His will for you to be at leisure, to converse with yourself, to write about these things, to read, to listen, to prepare yourself; you had time sufficient for that. Now God says to you, "Come at length to the contest, show us what you have learned, how you have trained yourself. How long will you exercise alone? Now the time has come for you to discover whether you are one of the athletes who deserve victory, or belong to the number of those who travel about the world and are everywhere defeated." Why, then, are you discontented? No contest is held without turmoil. There must be many training-partners, many to shout applause, many officials, many spectators.—But I wanted to live a life of peace.—Wail, then, and groan, as you deserve to do. For what greater penalty can befall the man who is uninstructed and disobedient to the divine injunctions than to grieve, to sorrow, to envy, in a word to have no good fortune but only misfortune? Do you not wish to free yourself from all this?

And how shall I free myself?—Have you not heard over and over again that you ought to eradicate desire utterly, direct your aversion towards the things that lie within the sphere of the moral purpose, and these things only, that you ought to give up everything, your body, your property, your reputation, your books, turmoil, office, freedom from office? For if once you swerve aside from this course, you are a slave, you are a subject, you have become liable to hindrance and to compulsion, you

34 ἀναγκαστός, ὅλος ἐπ' ἄλλοις. ἀλλὰ τὸ Κλεάν-
θους πρόχειρον

ἄγου δέ μ', ὦ Ζεῦ, καὶ συ γ' ἡ Πεπρωμένη.

θέλετ' εἰς Ῥώμην ; εἰς Ῥώμην.[1] εἰς Γύαρα ; εἰς
Γύαρα. εἰς Ἀθήνας ; εἰς Ἀθήνας. εἰς φυλα-
35 κήν ; εἰς φυλακήν. ἂν ἅπαξ εἴπῃς " πότε τις
εἰς Ἀθήνας ἀπέλθῃ ; " ἀπώλου. ἀνάγκη γε ταύτην τὴν ὄρεξιν ἀτελῆ μὲν οὖσαν ἀτυχῆ σε ποιεῖν,
τελειωθεῖσαν δὲ κενόν, ἐφ' οἷς οὐ δεῖ ἐπαιρό-
μενον· πάλιν ἂν ἐμποδισθῇς, δυστυχῆ, περι-
36 πίπτοντα οἷς οὐ θέλεις. ἄφες οὖν ταῦτα πάντα.
" καλαὶ αἱ Ἀθῆναι." ἀλλὰ τὸ εὐδαιμονεῖν κάλλιον πολύ, τὸ ἀπαθῆ εἶναι, τὸ ἀτάραχον, τὸ ἐπὶ
37 μηδενὶ κεῖσθαι τὰ σὰ πράγματα. " θόρυβος ἐν
Ῥώμῃ καὶ ἀσπασμοί." ἀλλὰ τὸ εὐροεῖν ἀντὶ
πάντων τῶν δυσκόλων. εἰ οὖν τούτων καιρός
ἐστιν, διὰ τί οὐκ αἴρεις αὐτῶν τὴν ἔκκλισιν ; τίς
38 ἀνάγκη ὡς ὄνον ξυλοκοπούμενον ἀχθοφορεῖν ; εἰ
δὲ μή, ὅρα ὅτι[2] δεῖ σε δουλεύειν ἀεὶ τῷ δυναμένῳ σοι διαπράξασθαι τὴν ἔξοδον, τῷ πᾶν
ἐμποδίσαι δυναμένῳ, κἀκεῖνον θεραπεύειν ὡς
Κακοδαίμονα.

39 Μία ὁδὸς ἐπὶ εὔροιαν (τοῦτο καὶ ὄρθρου καὶ

---

[1] The second εἰς Ῥώμην is supplied in the margin by *Sb*.
[2] Wolf (and Upton's "codex"): τί *S*.

---

[1] From a celebrated hymn. See on II. 23, 42.
[2] An island used as a place of exile. See on I. 25, 19.
[3] There may be here an allusion (before Lucian and
Apuleius) to the theme of a (bewitched) ass trying to escape
from being an ass, and constantly being hindered. In the
famous romance the ass is certainly often enough overloaded
and soundly cudgelled.

are entirely under the control of others. Nay, the word of Cleanthes is ready at hand,

Lead thou me on, O Zeus, and Destiny. [1]

Will ye have me go to Rome? I go to Rome. To Gyara? I go to Gyara.[2] To Athens? I go to Athens. To prison? I go to prison. If but once you say, "Oh, when may a man go to Athens?" you are lost. This wish, if unfulfilled, must necessarily make you unfortunate; if fulfilled, vain and puffed up over the wrong kind of thing; again, if you are hindered, you suffer a misfortune, falling into what you do not wish. Give up, then, all these things. "Athens is beautiful." But happiness is much more beautiful, tranquillity, freedom from turmoil, having your own affairs under no man's control. "There is turmoil in Rome, and salutations." But serenity is worth all the annoyances. If, then, the time for these things has come, why not get rid of your aversion for them? Why must you needs bear burdens like a belaboured donkey? Otherwise, I would have you see that you must be ever the slave of the man who is able to secure your release, to the man who is able to hinder you in everything,[3] and you must serve him as an Evil Genius.[4]

There is but one way to serenity (keep this

[4] For this rare spirit of folk-lore, see Aristophanes, *Equites*, 111-12, where he is called the Δαίμων Κακοδαίμων. His counterpart is the much commoner Ἀγαθὸς Δαίμων. The Evil Genius, though seldom referred to (and in fact ignored by many, if not all the standard works of reference, I believe), is presupposed by the association of the Κακοδαιμονισταί (Lysias, frag. 53, 2, Thalheim), and by the very word κακοδαίμων itself. For similar devil-worship, cf. I. 19, 6, of the God Fever.

μεθ' ἡμέραν καὶ νύκτωρ ἔστω πρόχειρον),
ἀπόστασις τῶν ἀπροαιρέτων, τὸ μηδὲν ἴδιον
ἡγεῖσθαι, τὸ παραδοῦναι πάντα τῷ δαιμονίῳ,
τῇ τύχῃ, ἐκείνους ἐπιτρόπους αὐτῶν ποιήσασθαι,
40 οὓς καὶ ὁ Ζεὺς πεποίηκεν, αὐτὸν δὲ πρὸς ἑνὶ
εἶναι μόνῳ, τῷ ἰδίῳ, τῷ ἀκωλύτῳ, καὶ ἀναγιγνώσκειν ἐπὶ τοῦτο ἀναφέροντα τὴν ἀνάγνωσιν
41 καὶ γράφειν καὶ ἀκούειν. διὰ τοῦτο οὐ δύναμαι
εἰπεῖν φιλόπονον, ἂν ἀκούσω τοῦτο μόνον, ὅτι
ἀναγιγνώσκει ἢ γράφει, κἂν προσθῇ τις, ὅτι
ὅλας τὰς νύκτας, οὔπω λέγω, ἂν μὴ γνῶ τὴν
ἀναφοράν. οὐδὲ γὰρ σὺ λέγεις φιλόπονον τὸν
διὰ παιδισκάριον ἀγρυπνοῦντα· οὐ τοίνυν οὐδ'
42 ἐγώ. ἀλλ' ἐὰν μὲν ἕνεκα δόξης αὐτὸ ποιῇ, λέγω
φιλόδοξον, ἂν δ' ἕνεκα ἀργυρίου, φιλάργυρον, οὐ
43 φιλόπονον. ἂν δ' ἐπὶ τὸ ἴδιον ἡγεμονικὸν ἀνα-
φέρῃ τὸν πόνον, ἵν' ἐκεῖνο κατὰ φύσιν ἔχῃ καὶ
44 διεξάγῃ, τότε λέγω μόνον φιλόπονον. μηδέποτε
γὰρ ἀπὸ τῶν κοινῶν μήτ' ἐπαινεῖτε μήτε ψέγετε,
ἀλλὰ ἀπὸ δογμάτων. ταῦτα γάρ ἐστι τὰ ἴδια
ἑκάστου, τὰ καὶ τὰς πράξεις αἰσχρὰς ἢ καλὰς
45 ποιοῦντα· τούτων μεμνημένος χαῖρε τοῖς πα-
46 ροῦσιν καὶ ἀγάπα ταῦτα, ὧν καιρός ἐστιν. εἴ
τινα ὁρᾷς, ὧν ἔμαθες καὶ διεσκέψω, ἀπαντῶντά
σοι εἰς τὰ ἔργα, εὐφραίνου ἐπ' αὐτοῖς. εἰ τὸ
κακόηθες καὶ λοίδορον ἀποτέθεισαι, μεμείωκας,

thought ready for use at dawn, and by day, and at
night), and that is to yield up all claim to the things
that lie outside the sphere of the moral purpose, to
regard nothing as your own possession; to surrender
everything to the Deity, to Fortune; to yield everything to the supervision of those persons whom
even Zeus has made supervisors; and to devote yourself to one thing only, that which is your own, that
which is free from hindrance, and to read referring
your reading to this end, and so to write and
so to listen. That is why I cannot call a man
industrious, if I hear merely that he reads or writes,
and even if one adds that he sits up all night, I cannot
yet say that the man is industrious, until I know
for what end he does so. For neither do you call
a man industrious who loses sleep for the sake of a
wench; no more do I. But if he acts this way for
the sake of reputation, I call him ambitious; if for
the sake of money, I call him fond of money, not fond
of toil. If, however, the end for which he toils is
his own governing principle, to have it be, and live
continually, in accordance with nature, then and
then only I call him industrious. For I would not
have you men ever either praise or blame a man for
things that may be either good or bad, but only for
judgements. Because these are each man's own
possessions, which make his actions either base or
noble. Bearing all this in mind, rejoice in what
you have and be satisfied with what the moment
brings. If you see any of the things that you have
learned and studied thoroughly coming to fruition
for you in action, rejoice in these things. If you
have put away or reduced a malignant disposition,
and reviling, or impertinence, or foul language, or

εἰ τὸ προπετές, εἰ τὸ αἰσχρολόγον, εἰ τὸ εἰκαῖον,
εἰ τὸ ἐπισεσυρμένον, εἰ οὐ κινῇ ἐφ' οἷς πρότερον,
εἰ οὐχ ὁμοίως γ' ὡς πρότερον, ἑορτὴν ἄγειν
δύνασαι καθ' ἡμέραν, σήμερον, ὅτι καλῶς ἀνε-
στράφης ἐν τῷδε τῷ ἔργῳ, αὔριον, ὅτι ἐν ἑτέρῳ.
47 πόσῳ μείζων αἰτία θυσίας ἢ ὑπατεία ἢ ἐπαρχία.
ταῦτα ἐκ σοῦ αὐτοῦ γίνεταί σοι καὶ ἀπὸ τῶν
θεῶν. ἐκεῖνο μέμνησο, τίς ὁ διδούς ἐστι καὶ
48 τίσιν καὶ διὰ τίνα. τούτοις τοῖς διαλογισμοῖς
ἐντρεφόμενος ἔτι διαφέρῃ, ποῦ ὢν εὐδαιμονήσεις,
ποῦ ὢν ἀρέσεις τῷ θεῷ; οὐ πανταχόθεν τὸ
ἴσον ἀπέχουσιν; οὐ πανταχόθεν ὁμοίως ὁρῶσιν
τὰ γινόμενα;

ε'. Πρὸς τοὺς μαχίμους καὶ θηριώδεις.

1 Ὁ καλὸς καὶ ἀγαθὸς οὔτ' αὐτὸς μάχεταί τινι
2 οὔτ' ἄλλον ἐᾷ κατὰ δύναμιν. παράδειγμα δὲ καὶ
τούτου καθάπερ καὶ τῶν ἄλλων ἔκκειται ἡμῖν ὁ
βίος ὁ Σωκράτους, ὃς οὐ μόνον αὐτὸς πανταχοῦ
ἐξέφυγεν μάχην, ἀλλ' οὐδ' ἄλλους μάχεσθαι εἴα.
3 ὅρα παρὰ Ξενοφῶντι ἐν τῷ Συμποσίῳ πόσας
μάχας λέλυκεν, πῶς πάλιν ἠνέσχετο Θρασυ-
μάχου, πῶς Πώλου, πῶς Καλλικλέους, πῶς τῆς
γυναικὸς ἠνείχετο, πῶς τοῦ υἱοῦ ἐξελεγχόμενος

---

[1] The first in Plato's *Republic*, Book I ; the other two in
his *Gorgias*.

recklessness, or negligence; if you are not moved
by the things that once moved you, or at least not
to the same degree, then you can keep festival day
after day; to-day because you behaved well in this
action, to-morrow because you behaved well in
another. How much greater cause for thanksgiving
is this than a consulship or a governorship! These
things come to you from your own self and from
the gods. Remember who the Giver is, and to
whom He gives, and for what end. If you are
brought up in reasonings such as these, can you any
longer raise the questions where you are going to be
happy, and where you will please God? Are not
men everywhere equally distant from God? Do
they not everywhere have the same view of what
comes to pass?

CHAPTER V

Against the contentious and brutal

The good and excellent man neither contends
with anyone, nor, as far as he has the power, does
he allow others to contend. We have an example
before us of this also, as well as of everything else,
in the life of Socrates, who did not merely himself
avoid contention upon every occasion, but tried to
prevent others as well from contending. See in
Xenophon's *Symposium* how many contentions he
has resolved, and again how patient he was with
Thrasymachus, Polus, and Callicles,[1] and habitually
so with his wife, and also with his son when the
latter tried to confute him with sophistical argu-

4 ὑπ' αὐτοῦ, σοφιζόμενος. λίαν γὰρ ἀσφαλῶς
ἐμέμνητο, ὅτι οὐδεὶς ἀλλοτρίου ἡγεμονικοῦ κυ-
5 ριεύει. οὐδὲν οὖν ἄλλο ἤθελεν ἢ τὸ ἴδιον. τί
δ' ἐστὶ τοῦτο; οὐχ ἱκ .. ος οὗτος ...¹ κατὰ
φύσιν· τοῦτο γὰρ ἀλλότριον· ἀλλ' ὅπως ἐκείνων
τὰ ἴδια ποιούντων, ὡς αὐτοῖς δοκεῖ, αὐτὸς μηδὲν
ἧττον κατὰ φύσιν ἕξει καὶ διεξάξει² μόνον τὰ
αὐτοῦ ποιῶν πρὸς τὸ κἀκείνους ἔχειν κατὰ φύσιν.
6 τοῦτο γάρ ἐστιν, ὃ ἀεὶ πρόκειται τῷ καλῷ καὶ
ἀγαθῷ. στρατηγῆσαι; οὔ· ἀλλ', ἂν διδῶται,
ἐπὶ ταύτης τῆς ὕλης τὸ ἴδιον ἡγεμονικὸν τηρῆσαι.
γῆμαι; οὔ· ἀλλ', ἂν διδῶται γάμος, ἐν ταύτῃ
7 τῇ ὕλῃ κατὰ φύσιν ἔχοντα αὐτὸν τηρῆσαι. ἂν
δὲ θέλῃ τὸν υἱὸν μὴ ἁμαρτάνειν ἢ τὴν γυναῖκα,
θέλει τὰ ἀλλότρια μὴ εἶναι ἀλλότρια. καὶ τὸ
παιδεύεσθαι τοῦτ' ἔστιν, μανθάνειν τὰ ἴδια καὶ
τὰ ἀλλότρια.
8 Ποῦ οὖν ἔτι μάχης τόπος τῷ οὕτως ἔχοντι;
μὴ γὰρ θαυμάζει τι τῶν γινομένων; μὴ γὰρ
καινὸν αὐτῷ φαίνεται; μὴ γὰρ οὐ χείρονα καὶ
χαλεπώτερα προσδέχεται τὰ παρὰ τῶν φαύλων
ἢ ἀποβαίνει αὐτῷ; μὴ γὰρ οὐ κέρδος λογίζεται
πᾶν ὅ τι ἀπολείπουσιν³ τοῦ ἐσχάτου; "ἐλοι-
9 δόρησέν σε ὁ δεῖνα." πολλὴ χάρις αὐτῷ, ὅτι

---

¹ Schenkl places a lacuna here: ἱκ .. ος οὗτος κατά S.
² Salmasius: ἐξάξει S.
³ Schenkl: ἀπολείπωσιν S.

---

¹ This may be a reference to Xenophon, *Memorabilia*, II.
2, as is commonly supposed, but if so, it is a highly inadequate presentation of the case there described, where
Socrates is the "confuter," and the son merely makes a few
natural and quite conventional attempts to defend himself. I

ments.[1]   For Socrates bore very firmly in mind that
no one is master over another's governing principle.
He willed, accordingly, nothing but what was his
own.   And what is that?   [Not to try to make
other people act[2]] in accordance with nature, for
that does not belong to one; but, while they are
attending to their own business as they think best,
himself none the less to be and to remain in a state
of harmony with nature, attending only to his own
business, to the end that they also may be in
harmony with nature.   For this is the object which
the good and excellent man has ever before him.
To become praetor?   No; but if this be given him,
to maintain his own governing principle in these
circumstances.   To marry?   No; but if marriage be
given him, to maintain himself as one who in these
circumstances is in harmony with nature.   But if he
wills that his son or his wife make no mistake, he
wills that what is not his own should cease to be
not his own.   And to be getting an education means
this : To be learning what *is* your own, and what is
not your own.

Where, then, is there any longer room for contention, if a man is in such a state?   Why, he is
not filled with wonder at anything that happens, is
he?   Does anything seem strange to him?   Does
he not expect worse and harsher treatment from
the wicked than actually befalls him?   Does he not
count it as gain whenever they fail to go to the limit?
" So-and-so reviled you."   I am greatly obliged to

suspect that Epictetus was referring (following Chrysippus,
probably) to some other incident recorded in the very large
body of Socratic dialogues that once existed.
    [2] This is probably the general sense of a passage where
something has evidently been lost.

μὴ ἔπληξεν. "ἀλλὰ καὶ ἔπληξεν." πολλὴ
χάρις, ὅτι μὴ ἔτρωσεν. "ἀλλὰ καὶ ἔτρωσεν."
10 πολλὴ χάρις, ὅτι μὴ ἀπέκτεινεν. πότε γὰρ
ἔμαθεν ἢ παρὰ τίνι, ὅτι ἥμερόν ἐστι ζῷον, ὅτι
φιλάλληλον, ὅτι μεγάλη βλάβη τῷ ἀδικοῦντι
αὐτὴ ἡ ἀδικία; ταῦτα οὖν μὴ μεμαθηκὼς μηδὲ
πεπεισμένος, διὰ τί μὴ ἀκολουθήσῃ τῷ φαινο-
11 μένῳ συμφέροντι; "βέβληκεν ὁ γείτων λίθους."
μή τι οὖν σὺ ἡμάρτηκας; "ἀλλὰ τὰ ἐν οἴκῳ
12 κατεάγη." σὺ οὖν σκευάριον εἶ; οὔ, ἀλλὰ
προαίρεσις. τί οὖν σοι δίδοται πρὸς τοῦτο; ὡς
μὲν λύκῳ ἀντιδάκνειν καὶ ἄλλους πλείονας
λίθους βάλλειν· ἀνθρώπῳ δ' ἐὰν ζητῇς, ἐπί-
σκεψαί σου τὸ ταμιεῖον, ἴδε τίνας δυνάμεις ἔχων
ἐλήλυθας· μή τι τὴν θηριώδη; μή τι τὴν μνησι-
13 κακητικήν; ἵππος οὖν πότ' ἄθλιός ἐστιν; ὅταν
τῶν φυσικῶν δυνάμεων στέρηται· οὐχ ὅταν μὴ
δύνηται κοκκύζειν, ἀλλ' ὅταν μὴ τρέχειν·
14 ὁ δὲ κύων; ὅταν πέτεσθαι μὴ δύνηται; ἀλλ'
ὅταν μὴ ἰχνεύειν. μή ποτ' οὖν οὕτως καὶ
ἄνθρωπος δυστυχής ἐστιν οὐχ ὁ μὴ δυνάμενος
λέοντας πνίγειν ἢ ἀνδριάντας περιλαμβάνειν (οὐ
γὰρ πρὸς τοῦτο δυνάμεις τινὰς ἔχων ἐλήλυθεν
παρὰ τῆς φύσεως), ἀλλ' ὁ ἀπολωλεκὼς τὸ

---

[1] See IV. 1, 120.

[2] A familiar idea in Plato, especially in the *Crito*, *Gorgias*,
and *Republic*, but nowhere, as I recall, in exactly these words,
though *Crito* 49 B and *Republic* 366 E and 367 D bear a close
resemblance.

him for not striking me. "Yes, but he struck you too." I am greatly obliged to him for not wounding me. "Yes, but he wounded you too." I am greatly obliged to him for not killing me. For when, or from what teacher, did he learn that man is a tame animal,[1] that he manifests mutual affection, that injustice in itself is a great injury to the unjust man?[2] If, therefore, he has never learned this, or become persuaded of this, why shall he not follow what appears to him to be his advantage? "My neighbour has thrown stones." *You* have not made a mistake, have you? "No, but my crockery is broken." Are *you* a piece of crockery, then? No, but *you* are moral purpose. What, then, has been given you with which to meet this attack? If you seek to act like a wolf, you can bite back and throw more stones than your neighbour did; but if you seek to act like a man, examine your store, see what faculties you brought with you into the world. You brought no faculty of brutality, did you? No faculty of bearing grudges, did you? When, then, is a horse miserable? When he is deprived of his natural faculties. Not when he can't sing "cuckoo!" but when he can't run. And a dog? Is it when he can't fly? No, but when he can't keep the scent. Does it not follow, then, that on the same principles a man is wretched, not when he is unable to choke lions,[3] or throw his arms about statues[4] (for no man has brought with him from nature into this world faculties for this), but when he has lost his kind-

---

[3] That is, accomplish something almost superhuman, like Heracles.

[4] That is, in cold weather, as Diogenes was able to do. See III. 12, 2.

15 εὔγνωμον, ὁ τὸ πιστόν; τοῦτον ἔδει συνελθόντας
θρηνεῖν, εἰς ὅσα κακὰ ἐλήλυθεν· οὐχὶ μὰ Δία
τὸν φύντα ἢ τὸν ἀποθανόντα, ἀλλ' ᾧ ζῶντι
συμβεβήκει ἀπολέσαι τὰ ἴδια, οὐ τὰ πατρῷα,
τὸ ἀγρίδιον καὶ τὸ οἰκίδιον καὶ τὸ πανδοκεῖον
καὶ τὰ δουλάρια (τούτων γὰρ οὐδὲν ἴδιον τῷ
ἀνθρώπῳ ἐστίν, ἀλλὰ πάντα ἀλλότρια, δοῦλα,
ὑπεύθυνα ἄλλοτε ἄλλοις διδόμενα ὑπὸ τῶν κυ-
ρίων), ἀλλὰ τὰ ἀνθρωπικά, τοὺς χαρακτῆρας,
16 οὓς ἔχων ἐν τῇ διανοίᾳ ἐλήλυθεν, οἵους καὶ ἐπὶ
τῶν νομισμάτων ζητοῦντες, ἂν μὲν εὕρωμεν, δοκι-
μάζομεν, ἂν δὲ μὴ εὕρωμεν, ῥιπτοῦμεν. " τίνος
17 ἔχει τὸν χαρακτῆρα τοῦτο τὸ τετράσσαρον ;
Τραιανοῦ ; φέρε. Νέρωνος ; ῥῖψον ἔξω, ἀδό-
κιμόν ἐστιν, σαπρόν." οὕτως καὶ ἐνθάδε. τίνα

---

[1] The quotations (slightly modified) are from a famous
passage in Euripides, *Cresphontes*, frag. 449, Nauck[2]: "For
we ought rather to come together to mourn for the one who
is born, because of all the evils into which he is coming;
but, on the other hand, the one who has died, we ought with
joy and words of gladness to send forth from his former
abode."

[2] The gods.

[3] This reference is most obscure, for the coins of Nero still
preserved are numerous and excellent, and there was a great
systematic reform of coinage in A.D. 64, which became "the
most complete monetary system of ancient times" (Mattingly
and Sydenham, *The Roman Imperial Coinage* (1923), I, 138).
After the death of Caligula, indeed, the senate ordered all
his bronze coinage to be melted down (Dio, LX. 22, 3), but
nothing of the sort is recorded, so far as I know, for Nero.
There was, of course, a slight reduction in weight for the
aureus and the denarius, and "the amount of alloy in the
silver was increased from 5 to about 10 per cent.," changes
which have been regarded as the first step in the process
of debasement that reached its climax in the third century.

ness, and his faithfulness? This is the kind of
person for whom "men should come together and
mourn, because of all the evils into which he has
come"; not, by Zeus, "the one who is born," or
"the one who has died,"[1] but the man whose
misfortune it has been while he still lives to lose
what is his own; not his patrimony, his paltry farm,
and paltry dwelling, and his tavern, and his poor
slaves (for none of these things is a man's own
possession, but they all belong to others, are subservient and subject, given by their masters[2] now to
one person and now to another); but the qualities
which make him a human being, the imprints
which he brought with him in his mind, such as
we look for also upon coins, and, if we find them,
we accept the coins, but if we do not find them,
we throw the coins away. "Whose imprint does
this sestertius bear? Trajan's? Give it to me.
Nero's? Throw it out, it will not pass, it is rotten."[3]
So also in the moral life. What imprint do his

See E. A. Sydenham, *Num. Chron.*, ser. 4, vol. 16 (1916), 19.
Nero's particular system of brass and copper coinage was
also discontinued after his death (*ibid.* p. 28). Yet it is
scarcely credible that Epictetus can have had any trifles
like these in mind.—Of course the *moral* point here, which
Dr. Page wishes to have emphasized, is that Trajan was the
typically good man (*felicior Augusto, melior Traiano* was
an acclamation in the Roman Senate for centuries after his
death – Eutropius, 8, 5), and Nero the opposite. But the
difficulty in the passage is to understand how it ever
occurred to Epictetus to imply that people actually refused
to take coins of Nero, simply because they bore the imprint
of a morally bad man, when, as a matter of fact, it is
extremely doubtful if any human being, except perhaps
some hopeless fanatic, ever really did so refuse. A note by
T. O. Mabbott, "Epictetus and Nero's Coinage", *CP* 36 (1941)
398-9, explains this perfectly.

ἔχει χαρακτῆρα τὰ δόγματα αὐτοῦ; "ἥμερον,
κοινωνικόν, ἀνεκτικόν, φιλάλληλον." φέρε, παραδέχομαι, ποιῶ πολίτην τοῦτον, παραδέχομαι
18 γείτονα, σύμπλουν. ὅρα μόνον, μὴ Νερωνιανὸν
ἔχει χαρακτῆρα. μή τι ὀργίλος ἐστίν, μή τι
μηνιτής, μή τι μεμψίμοιρος; "ἂν αὐτῷ φανῇ,
19 πατάσσει τὰς κεφαλὰς τῶν ἀπαντώντων." τί
οὖν ἔλεγες, ὅτι ἄνθρωπός ἐστιν; μὴ γὰρ ἐκ
ψιλῆς μορφῆς κρίνεται τῶν ὄντων ἕκαστον; ἐπεὶ
20 οὕτως λέγε καὶ τὸ κήρινον μῆλον εἶναι. καὶ
ὀδμὴν ἔχειν αὐτὸ δεῖ καὶ γεῦσιν· οὐκ ἀρκεῖ ἡ
ἐκτὸς περιγραφή. οὐκοῦν οὐδὲ πρὸς τὸν ἄνθρωπον ἡ ῥὶς ἐξαρκεῖ καὶ οἱ ὀφθαλμοί, ἀλλ' ἂν τὰ
21 δόγματα ἔχῃ ἀνθρωπικά. οὗτος οὐκ ἀκούει
λόγου, οὐ παρακολουθεῖ ἐλεγχόμενος· ὄνος ἐστίν.
τούτου τὸ αἰδῆμον ἀπονενέκρωται· ἄχρηστός
ἐστιν, πρόβατον,[1] πάντα μᾶλλον ἢ ἄνθρωπος.
οὗτος ζητεῖ, τίνα ἀπαντήσας λακτίσῃ ἢ δάκῃ·
ὥστε οὐδὲ πρόβατον ἢ ὄνος, ἀλλά τί ποτε ἄγριον
θηρίον.
22 Τί οὖν; θέλεις με καταφρονεῖσθαι;—Ὑπὸ
τίνων; ὑπὸ εἰδότων; καὶ πῶς καταφρονήσουσιν
εἰδότες τοῦ πράου, τοῦ αἰδήμονος; ἀλλ' ὑπὸ τῶν
ἀγνοούντων; τί σοι μέλει; οὐ τινι γὰρ ἄλλῳ
23 τεχνίτῃ τῶν ἀτέχνων.—Ἀλλὰ πολὺ μᾶλλον

---

[1] πρόβατον added by C. Schenkl (after Salmasius).

---

[1] Suetonius, *Nero*, 26.
[2] It would seem that the beeswax used in leather sewing
was familiarly called "the cobbler's apple," and when on sale
may have been moulded in that shape. Such metaphors are
common enough, as is also the habit of making things like

judgements bear? "He is gentle, generous, patient, affectionate." Give him to me, I accept him, I make this man a citizen, I accept him as a neighbour and a fellow-voyager. Only see that he does not have the imprint of Nero. Is he choleric, furious, querulous? "If he feels like it, he punches the heads of the people he meets."[1] Why, then, did you call him a human being? For surely everything is not judged by its outward appearance only, is it? Why, if that is so, you will have to call the lump of beeswax an apple.[2] No, it must have the smell of an apple and the taste of an apple; its external outline is not enough. Therefore, neither are the nose and the eyes sufficient to prove that one is a human being, but you must see whether one has the judgements that belong to a human being. Here is a man who does not listen to reason, he does not understand when he is confuted; he is an ass. Here is one whose sense of self-respect has grown numb; he is useless, a sheep, anything but a human being. Here is a man who is looking for someone whom he can kick or bite when he meets him; so that *he* is not even a sheep or an ass, but some wild beast.

What then? Do you want me to be despised?— By whom? By men of understanding? And how will men of understanding despise the gentle and the self-respecting person? No, but by men without understanding? What difference is that to you? Neither you nor any other craftsman cares about those who are not skilled in his art.—Yes, but they will fasten themselves upon me all the more.—What

vases, cakes, candy, pincushions, soap, etc., in the shape of fruits or animals.

ἐπιφυήσονταί μοι.—Τί λέγεις τὸ ἐμοί ; δύναταί
τις τὴν προαίρεσιν τὴν σὴν βλάψαι ἢ κωλῦσαι
ταῖς προσπιπτούσαις φαντασίαις χρῆσθαι ὡς
24 πέφυκεν ;—Οὔ.—Τί οὖν ἔτι ταράσσῃ καὶ φοβερὸν σαυτὸν θέλεις ἐπιδεικνύειν ; οὐχὶ δὲ παρελθὼν εἰς μέσον κηρύσσεις, ὅτι εἰρήνην ἄγεις
πρὸς πάντας ἀνθρώπους, ὅ τι ἂν ἐκεῖνοι ποιῶσι,
καὶ μάλιστ' ἐκείνων καταγελᾷς, ὅσοι σε βλάπτειν
δοκοῦσιν ; "ἀνδράποδα ταῦτα οὐκ οἶδεν οὐδὲ τίς
εἰμὶ οὐδὲ ποῦ μου τὸ ἀγαθὸν καὶ τὸ κακόν· οὐ¹
πρόσοδος αὐτοῖς πρὸς τὰ ἐμά."
25   Οὕτως καὶ ἐχυρὰν πόλιν οἱ² οἰκοῦντες κατα-
γελῶσι τῶν πολιορκούντων· "νῦν οὗτοι τί
πρᾶγμα ἔχουσιν ἐπὶ τῷ μηδενί ; ἀσφαλές ἐστιν
ἡμῶν τὸ τεῖχος, τροφὰς ἔχομεν ἐπὶ πάμπολυν
26 χρόνον, τὴν ἄλλην ἅπασαν παρασκευήν." ταῦτά
ἐστι τὰ πόλιν ἐχυρὰν καὶ ἀνάλωτον ποιοῦντα,
ἀνθρώπου δὲ ψυχὴν οὐδὲν ἄλλο ἢ δόγματα.
ποῖον γὰρ τεῖχος οὕτως ἰσχυρὸν ἢ ποῖον σῶμα
οὕτως ἀδαμάντινον ἢ ποία κτῆσις ἀναφαίρετος ἢ
27 ποῖον ἀξίωμα οὕτως ἀνεπιβούλευτον ; πάντα
πανταχοῦ θνητά, εὐάλωτα, οἷς τισιν τὸν ὁπωσοῦν
προσέχοντα πᾶσα ἀνάγκη ταράσσεσθαι, κακελ-
πιστεῖν, φοβεῖσθαι, πενθεῖν, ἀτελεῖς ἔχειν τὰς
28 ὀρέξεις, περιπτωτικὰς ἔχειν τὰς ἐκκλίσεις. εἶτα
οὐ θέλομεν τὴν μόνην δεδομένην ἡμῖν ἀσφάλειαν
ἐχυρὰν ποιεῖν ; οὐδ' ἀποστάντες τῶν θνητῶν καὶ
δούλων τὰ ἀθάνατα καὶ φύσει ἐλεύθερα ἐκπο-

---

¹ Schenkl : ὅτι S.   ² οἱ added by Schenkl.

¹ Perhaps a reference to Xenophon, *Cyropaedeia*, VII.
5, 13.

do you mean by the word "me"? Can anyone hurt your moral purpose, or prevent you from employing in a natural way the sense-impressions which come to you?—No.—Why, then, are you any longer disturbed, and why do you want to show that you are a timid person? Why do you not come forth and make the announcement that you are at peace with all men, no matter what they do, and that you are especially amused at those who think that they are hurting you? "These slaves do not know either who I am, or where my good and my evil are; they cannot get at the things that are mine."

In this way also those who inhabit a strong city laugh at the besiegers:[1] "Why are these men taking trouble now to no end? Our wall is safe, we have food for ever so long a time, and all other supplies." These are the things which make a city strong and secure against capture; and nothing but judgements make similarly secure the soul of man. For what manner of wall is so strong, or what manner of body so invincible, or what manner of possession so secure against theft, or what manner of reputation so unassailable? For all things everywhere are perishable, and easy to capture by assault, and the man who in any fashion sets his mind upon any of them must needs be troubled in mind, be discouraged, suffer fear and sorrow, have his desires fail, and his aversions fall into what they would avoid. If this be so, are we not willing to make secure the one means of safety which has been vouchsafed us? And are we not willing to give up these perishable and slavish things, and devote our labours to those which are imperishable and by

νεῖν; οὐδὲ μεμνήμεθα, ὅτι οὔτε βλάπτει ἄλλος
ἄλλον οὔτε ὠφελεῖ, ἀλλὰ τὸ περὶ ἑκάστου τούτων δόγμα, τοῦτό ἐστι τὸ βλάπτον, τοῦτο τὸ
ἀνατρέπον, τοῦτο μάχη, τοῦτο στάσις, τοῦτο
29 πόλεμος; Ἐτεοκλέα καὶ Πολυνείκη τὸ πεποιηκὸς
οὐκ ἄλλο ἢ τοῦτο, τὸ δόγμα τὸ περὶ τυραννίδος,
τὸ δόγμα τὸ περὶ φυγῆς, ὅτι τὸ μὲν ἔσχατον
30 τῶν κακῶν, τὸ δὲ μέγιστον τῶν ἀγαθῶν. φύσις
δ' αὕτη παντός, τὸ διώκειν τὸ ἀγαθόν, φεύγειν τὸ
κακόν· τὸν ἀφαιρούμενον θατέρου καὶ περι-
βάλλοντα τῷ ἐναντίῳ, τοῦτον ἡγεῖσθαι πολέμιον,
ἐπίβουλον, κἂν ἀδελφὸς ᾖ, κἂν υἱός, κἂν πατήρ·
31 τοῦ γὰρ ἀγαθοῦ συγγενέστερον οὐδέν. λοιπὸν εἰ
ταῦτα ἀγαθὰ καὶ κακά, οὔτε πατὴρ υἱοῖς φίλος
οὔτ' ἀδελφὸς ἀδελφῷ, πάντα δὲ πανταχοῦ μεστὰ
32 πολεμίων, ἐπιβούλων, συκοφαντῶν. εἰ δ' οἵα
δεῖ προαίρεσις, τοῦτο μόνον ἀγαθόν ἐστιν, καὶ οἵα
μὴ δεῖ, τοῦτο μόνον κακόν, ποῦ ἔτι μάχη, ποῦ
λοιδορία; περὶ τίνων; περὶ τῶν οὐδὲν πρὸς
ἡμᾶς; πρὸς τίνας; πρὸς τοὺς ἀγνοοῦντας, πρὸς
τοὺς δυστυχοῦντας, πρὸς τοὺς ἠπατημένους περὶ
τῶν μεγίστων;
33 Τούτων Σωκράτης μεμνημένος τὴν οἰκίαν τὴν
αὑτοῦ ᾤκει γυναικὸς ἀνεχόμενος τραχυτάτης,
υἱοῦ ἀγνώμονος. τραχεῖα γὰρ πρὸς τί ἦν; ἵν'

---

[1] Famous enemy brothers : cf. II. 22, 13–14.

nature free? And do we not remember that no
man either hurts or helps another, but that it is his
judgement about each of these things which is the
thing that hurts him, that overturns him; this **is**
contention, and civil strife, and war? That which
made Eteocles and Polyneices[1] what they were was
nothing else but this—their judgement about a throne,
and their judgement about exile, namely, that one
was the greatest of evils, the other the greatest
of goods. And this is the nature of every being,
to pursue the good and to flee from the evil;
and to consider the man who robs us of the one
and invests us with the other as an enemy and
an aggressor, even though he be a brother, even
though he be a son, even though he be a father;
for nothing is closer kin to us than our good. It
follows, then, that if these externals are good or
evil, neither is a father dear to his sons, nor a brother
dear to a brother, but everything on all sides is full
of enemies, aggressors, slanderers. But if the right
kind of moral purpose and that alone is good, and
if the wrong kind of moral purpose and that alone
is bad, where is there any longer room for contention,
where for reviling? About what? About the
things that mean nothing to us? Against whom?
Against the ignorant, against the unfortunate, against
those who have been deceived in the most important
values?

All this is what Socrates bore in mind as he
managed his house, putting up with a shrewish wife
and an unkindly son.[2] For to what end was she

---

[2] Perhaps referring to Xenophon, *Memorabilia*, II. 2, where
his son Lamprocles is represented as having lost his temper
at the constant scolding of Xanthippe.

ὕδωρ καταχέῃ τῆς κεφαλῆς ὅσον καὶ θέλει, ἵνα
καταπατήσῃ τὸν πλακοῦντα· καὶ τί πρὸς ἐμέ, ἂν
34 ὑπολάβω, ὅτι ταῦτα οὐκ ἔστι πρὸς ἐμέ; τοῦτο δ'
ἐμὸν ἔργον ἐστὶ καὶ οὔτε τύραννος κωλύσει με
θέλοντα οὔτε δεσπότης οὔτε οἱ πολλοὶ τὸν ἕνα
οὔθ' ὁ ἰσχυρότερος τὸν ἀσθενέστερον· τοῦτο γὰρ
35 ἀκώλυτον δέδοται ὑπὸ τοῦ θεοῦ ἑκάστῳ. ταῦτα
τὰ δόγματα ἐν οἰκίᾳ φιλίαν ποιεῖ, ἐν πόλει
ὁμόνοιαν, ἐν ἔθνεσιν εἰρήνην, πρὸς θεὸν εὐχάρισ-
τον, πανταχοῦ θαρροῦντα, ὡς περὶ τῶν ἀλλο-
36 τρίων, ὡς περὶ οὐδενὸς ἀξίων. ἀλλ' ἡμεῖς
γράψαι μὲν καὶ ἀναγνῶναι ταῦτα καὶ ἀναγιγνω-
σκόμενα ἐπαινέσαι ἱκανοί, πεισθῆναι δ' οὐδ'
37 ἐγγύς. τοιγαροῦν τὸ περὶ τῶν Λακεδαιμονίων
λεγόμενον

οἴκοι λέοντες, ἐν Ἐφέσῳ δ' ἀλώπεκες

καὶ ἐφ' ἡμῶν ἁρμόσει· ἐν σχολῇ λέοντες, ἔξω δ'
ἀλώπεκες.

ϛ'. Πρὸς τοὺς ἐπὶ τῷ ἐλεεῖσθαι ὀδυνωμένους.

1 Ἀνιῶμαι, φησίν, ἐλεούμενος.—Πότερον οὖν σὸν
ἔργον ἐστὶ τὸ ἐλεεῖσθαί σε ἢ τῶν ἐλεούντων; τί
δ'; ἐπὶ σοί ἐστι τὸ παῦσαι αὐτό;—Ἐπ' ἐμοί, ἂν

---

[1] It was a present from Alcibiades. For the incidents
here referred to see Seneca, *De Constantia*, 18, 5; Diogenes
Laertius, 2, 36; Athenaeus, 5, 219 B and 14, 643 F; Aelian,
Varia Historia, 11, 12.

shrewish? To the end that she might pour all the water she pleased over his head, and might trample underfoot the cake.[1] Yet what is that to me, if I regard these things as meaning nothing to me? But this control over the moral purpose is my true business, and in it neither shall a tyrant hinder me against my will, nor the multitude the single individual, nor the stronger man the weaker; for this has been given by God to each man as something that cannot be hindered. These are the judgements which produce love in the household, concord in the State, peace among the nations, make a man thankful toward God, confident at all times, on the ground that he is dealing with things not his own, with worthless things. We, however, although we are capable of writing and reading these things, and praising them when read, are nowhere near capable of being persuaded of them. Wherefore, the proverb about the Lacedaemonians,

Lions at home, but at Ephesus foxes,[2]

will fit us too: Lions in the school-room, foxes outside.

CHAPTER VI

To those who are vexed at being pitied

I am annoyed, says one, at being pitied.—Is it, then, some doing of yours that you are pitied, or the doing of those who show the pity? Or again; is it in your power to stop it?—It is, if I can show

[2] Because of their ill-success in Asia Minor. See also the scholium on Aristophanes, *Pax*, 1189.

δεικνύω αὐτοῖς μὴ ἄξιον ἐλέου ὄντα ἐμαυτόν.—
2 Πότερον δ' ἤδη σοι ὑπάρχει τοῦτο, τὸ μὴ εἶναι
ἐλέου ἄξιον ἢ οὐχ ὑπάρχει ;—Δοκῶ ἔγωγε, ὅτι
ὑπάρχει. ἀλλ' οὑτοί γ' οὐκ ἐπὶ τούτοις ἐλεοῦσιν,
ἐφ' οἷς, εἴπερ ἄρα, ἦν ἄξιον, ἐπὶ τοῖς ἁμαρτανο-
μένοις, ἀλλ' ἐπὶ πενίᾳ καὶ ἀναρχίᾳ καὶ νόσοις
3 καὶ θανάτοις καὶ ἄλλοις τοιούτοις.—Πότερον οὖν
πείθειν παρεσκεύασαι τοὺς πολλούς, ὡς ἄρα
οὐδὲν τούτων κακόν ἐστιν, ἀλλ' οἷόν τε καὶ πένητι
καὶ ἀνάρχοντι[1] καὶ ἀτίμῳ εὐδαιμονεῖν, ἢ σαυτὸν
ἐπιδεικνύειν αὐτοῖς πλουτοῦντα καὶ ἄρχοντα ;
4 τούτων γὰρ τὰ μὲν δεύτερα ἀλαζόνος καὶ ψυχροῦ
καὶ οὐδενὸς ἀξίου. καὶ ἡ προσποίησις ὅρα δι'
οἵων ἂν γένοιτο· δουλάρια σε χρήσασθαι δεήσει
καὶ ἀργυρωμάτια ὀλίγα κεκτῆσθαι καὶ ταῦτα ἐν
φανερῷ δεικνύειν, εἰ οἷόν τε, ταὐτὰ πολλάκις καὶ
λανθάνειν πειρᾶσθαι ὅτι ταὐτά ἐστιν, καὶ ἱματίδια στιλπνὰ καὶ τὴν ἄλλην πομπὴν καὶ τὸν
τιμώμενον ἐπιφαίνειν ὑπὸ τῶν ἐπιφανεστάτων[2]
καὶ δειπνεῖν πειρᾶσθαι παρ' αὐτοῖς ἢ δοκεῖν γε,
ὅτι δειπνεῖς, καὶ περὶ τὸ σῶμα δέ τινα κακοτεχ-
νεῖν, ὡς εὐμορφότερον φαίνεσθαι καὶ γενναιότε-
5 ρον τοῦ ὄντος· ταῦτά σε δεῖ μηχανᾶσθαι, εἰ τὴν
δευτέραν ὁδὸν ἀπιέναι θέλεις ὥστε μὴ ἐλεεῖσθαι.

Ἡ πρώτη δὲ καὶ ἀνήνυτος καὶ μακρά, ὃ ὁ Ζεὺς
οὐκ ἠδυνήθη ποιῆσαι, τοῦτο αὐτὸ ἐπιχειρεῖν,
πάντας ἀνθρώπους πεῖσαι, τίνα ἐστὶν ἀγαθὰ καὶ

---

[1] Upton's "codex": ἄρχοντι S.
[2] Elter: ἐπιφανῶν τούτων S.

them that I do not deserve their pity.—And do you now possess the power of not being deserving of pity, or do you not possess it?—It seems to me, indeed, that I possess it. Yet these people do not pity me for what would deserve pity, if anything does, that is, my mistakes; but for poverty, and for not holding office, and for things like disease, and death, and the like.—Are you, then, prepared to convince the multitude that none of these things is bad, but that it is possible for a poor man, and one who holds no office or position of honour, to be happy; or are you prepared to show yourself off to them as a rich man and an official? Of these alternatives the second is the part of a braggart, and a tasteless and worthless person. Besides, observe the means by which you must achieve your pretence: You will have to borrow some paltry slaves; and possess a few pieces of silver plate, and exhibit these same pieces conspicuously and frequently, if you can, and try not to let people know that they are the same; and possess contemptible bright clothes, and all other kinds of finery, and show yourself off as the one who is honoured by the most distinguished persons; and try to dine with them, or at least make people think that you dine with them; and resort to base arts in the treatment of your person, so as to appear more shapely and of gentler birth than you actually are. All these contrivances you must adopt, if you wish to take the way of the second alternative and avoid pity.

But the first way is ineffectual and tedious—to attempt the very thing which Zeus himself has been unable to accomplish, that is, to convince all men of what things are good, and what evil. Why, that

6 κακά. μὴ γὰρ δέδοταί σοι τοῦτο; ἐκεῖνο μόνον
σοι δέδοται, σαυτὸν πεῖσαι. καὶ οὔπω πέπεικας·
7 εἶτά μοι νῦν ἐπιχειρεῖς πείθειν τοὺς ἄλλους; καὶ
τίς σοι τοσούτῳ χρόνῳ σύνεστιν ὡς σὺ σαυτῷ; τίς
δὲ οὕτως πιθανός ἐστί σοι πρὸς τὸ πεῖσαι ὡς σὺ
σαυτῷ; τίς δ' εὐνούστερον καὶ οἰκειότερον ἔχων ἢ
8 σὺ σαυτῷ; πῶς οὖν οὔπω πέπεικας σαυτὸν μαθεῖν;
νῦν οὐχὶ ἄνω κάτω; τοῦτ' ἔστι περὶ ὃ ἐσπούδακας; οὐ¹ μανθάνειν, ὥστε ἄλυπος εἶναι καὶ
9 ἀτάραχος καὶ ἀταπείνωτος καὶ ἐλεύθερος; πρὸς
ταῦτα οὖν οὐκ ἀκήκοας, ὅτι μία ἐστὶν ἡ ὁδὸς ἡ
φέρουσα, ἀφεῖναι τὰ ἀπροαίρετα καὶ ἐκστῆναι
10 αὐτῶν καὶ ὁμολογῆσαι αὐτὰ ἀλλότρια; τὸ οὖν
ἄλλον τι ὑπολαβεῖν περὶ σοῦ ποίου εἴδους ἐστίν;
—Τοῦ ἀπροαιρέτου.—Οὐκοῦν οὐδὲν πρὸς σέ;—
Οὐδέν.—Ἔτι οὖν δακνόμενος ἐπὶ τούτῳ καὶ
ταρασσόμενος οἴει πεπεῖσθαι περὶ ἀγαθῶν καὶ
κακῶν;

11 Οὐ θέλεις οὖν ἀφεὶς τοὺς ἄλλους αὐτὸς σαυτῷ
γενέσθαι καὶ μαθητὴς καὶ διδάσκαλος; "ὄψονται
οἱ ἄλλοι, εἰ λυσιτελεῖ αὐτοῖς παρὰ φύσιν ἔχειν
καὶ διεξάγειν, ἐμοὶ δ' οὐδείς ἐστιν ἐγγίων ἐμοῦ.
12 τί οὖν τοῦτό ἐστιν, ὅτι τοὺς μὲν λόγους ἀκήκοα
τοὺς τῶν φιλοσόφων καὶ συγκατατίθεμαι αὐτοῖς,

¹ οὐ added by Schenkl.

has not been vouchsafed to you, has it? Nay, this
only has been vouchsafed—to convince yourself.
And you have not convinced yourself yet! And
despite that, bless me! are you now trying to
convince all other men? Yet who has been living
with you so long as you have been living with
yourself? And who is so gifted with powers of
persuasion to convince you, as you are to convince
yourself? Who is more kindly disposed and nearer
to you than you are to yourself? How comes it,
then, that you have not persuaded yourself to learn?
Are not things now upside down? Is this what you
have been in earnest about? Not to learn how to
get rid of pain, and turmoil, and humiliation, and so
become free? Have you not heard that there is but
a single way which leads to this end, and that is to
give up the things which lie outside the sphere of
the moral purpose, and to abandon them, and to
admit that they are not your own? To what class
of things, then, does another's opinion about you
belong?—To that which lies outside the sphere of
the moral purpose.—And so it is nothing to you?—
Nothing.—So long, then, as you are stung and
disturbed by the opinions of others, do you still
fancy that you have been persuaded as to things
good and evil?

Will you not, then, let other men alone, and
become your own pupil and your own teacher? "All
other men shall see to it, whether it is profitable for
them to be in a state out of accord with nature and
so to live, but as for me no one is closer to myself
than I am. What does it mean, then, that I have
heard the words of the philosophers and assent to
them, but that in actual fact my burdens have

ἔργῳ δ᾽ οὐδὲν γέγονα κουφότερος; μή τι οὕτως
ἀφυής εἰμι ; καὶ μὴν περὶ τὰ ἄλλα, ὅσα ἐβου-
λήθην, οὐ λίαν ἀφυὴς εὑρέθην, ἀλλὰ καὶ γράμ-
ματα ταχέως ἔμαθον καὶ παλαίειν καὶ γεωμε-
13 τρεῖν καὶ συλλογισμοὺς ἀναλύειν. μή τι οὖν οὐ
πέπεικέ με ὁ λόγος ; καὶ μὴν οὐκ ἄλλα τινὰ
οὕτως ἐξ ἀρχῆς ἐδοκίμασα ἢ εἱλόμην καὶ νῦν
περὶ τούτων ἀναγιγνώσκω, ταῦτα ἀκούω, ταῦτα
γράφω· ἄλλον οὐχ εὑρήκαμεν μέχρι νῦν ἰσχυ-
14 ρότερον τούτου λόγον. τί οὖν τὸ λεῖπόν μοι
ἐστίν ; μὴ οὐκ ἐξῄρηται τἀναντία δόγματα ; μὴ
αὐταὶ αἱ ὑπολήψεις ἀγύμναστοί εἰσιν οὐδ᾽ εἰθισ-
μέναι ἀπαντᾶν ἐπὶ τὰ ἔργα, ἀλλ᾽ ὡς ὁπλάρια
ἀποκείμενα [1] κατίωται καὶ οὐδὲ περιαρμόσαι μοι
15 δύναται ; καίτοι οὔτ᾽ ἐπὶ τοῦ παλαίειν οὔτ᾽ ἐπὶ
τοῦ γράφειν ἢ ἀναγιγνώσκειν ἀρκοῦμαι τῷ μαθεῖν,
ἀλλ᾽ ἄνω κάτω στρέφω τοὺς προτεινομένους καὶ
16 ἄλλους πλέκω καὶ μεταπίπτοντας ὡσαύτως. τὰ δ᾽
ἀναγκαῖα θεωρήματα, ἀφ᾽ ὧν ἔστιν ὁρμώμενον
ἄλυπον γενέσθαι, ἄφοβον, ἀπαθῆ, ἀκώλυτον,
ἐλεύθερον, ταῦτα δ᾽ οὐ γυμνάζω οὐδὲ μελετῶ
17 κατὰ ταῦτα τὴν προσήκουσαν μελέτην. εἶτά
μοι μέλει, τί οἱ ἄλλοι περὶ ἐμοῦ ἐροῦσιν, εἰ φανοῦμαι αὐτοῖς ἀξιόλογος, εἰ φανοῦμαι εὐδαίμων ;"

18   Ταλαίπωρε, οὐ θέλεις βλέπειν, τί σὺ λέγεις
περὶ σαυτοῦ ; τίς φαίνῃ σαυτῷ ; τίς ἐν τῷ ὑπολαμβάνειν, τίς ἐν τῷ ὀρέγεσθαι, τίς ἐν τῷ ἐκκλί-
νειν· τίς ἐν ὁρμῇ, παρασκευῇ, ἐπιβολῇ, τοῖς ἄλλοις

---

[1] Reiske: ἐπικείμενα S.

become no lighter? Can it be that I am so dull?
And yet, indeed, in everything else that I have
wanted I was not found to be unusually dull, but I
learned my letters rapidly, and how to wrestle, and
do my geometry, and analyse syllogisms. Can it be,
then, that reason has not convinced me? Why,
indeed, there is nothing to which I have so given my
approval from the very first, or so preferred, and
now I read about these matters, and hear them, and
write about them. Down to this moment we have
not found a stronger argument than this. What is
it, then, that I yet lack? Can it be that the
contrary judgements have not all been put away?
Can it be that the thoughts themselves are unexer-
cised and unaccustomed to face the facts, and, like
old pieces of armour that have been stowed away, are
covered with rust, and can no longer be fitted to me?
Yet in wrestling, or in writing, or in reading, I am
not satisfied with mere learning, but I turn over and
over the arguments presented to me, and fashion
new ones, and likewise syllogisms with equivocal
premisses. However, the necessary principles, those
which enable a man, if he sets forth from them, to
get rid of grief, fear, passion, hindrance, and become
free, these I do not exercise, nor do I take the
practice that is appropriate for them. After all that,
am I concerned with what everyone else will say
about me, whether I shall appear important or happy
in their eyes?"

O miserable man, will you not see what you are
saying about yourself? What sort of a person are
you in your own eyes? What sort of a person in
thinking, in desiring, in avoiding; what sort of a
person in choice, preparation, design, and the other

τοῖς ἀνθρωπικοῖς ἔργοις; ἀλλὰ μέλει σοι, εἴ σε
19 ἐλεοῦσιν οἱ ἄλλοι;—Ναί· ἀλλὰ παρὰ τὴν ἀξίαν
ἐλεοῦμαι.—Οὐκοῦν ἐπὶ τούτῳ ὀδυνᾷ; ὁ δέ γε
ὀδυνώμενος ἐλεεινός ἐστιν;—Ναί.—Πῶς οὖν ἔτι
παρὰ ἀξίαν ἐλεῇ; αὐτοῖς γὰρ οἷς περὶ τὸν ἔλεον
πάσχεις κατασκευάζεις σεαυτὸν ἄξιον τοῦ ἐλεεῖ-
20 σθαι. τί οὖν λέγει Ἀντισθένης; οὐδέποτ᾽ ἤ-
κουσας; "βασιλικόν, ὦ Κῦρε, πράττειν μὲν εὖ,
21 κακῶς δ᾽ ἀκούειν." τὴν κεφαλὴν ὑγιᾶ ἔχω καὶ
πάντες οἴονται ὅτι κεφαλαλγῶ. τί μοι μέλει;
ἀπύρετός εἰμι καὶ ὡς πυρέσσοντί μοι συνάχθον-
ται· "τάλας, ἐκ τοσούτου χρόνου οὐ διέλειπες
πυρέσσων." λέγω καὶ ἐγὼ σκυθρωπάσας ὅτι
"ναί· ταῖς ἀληθείαις πολὺς ἤδη χρόνος, ἐξ οὗ μοι
κακῶς ἐστιν." "τί οὖν γένηται;" ὡς ἂν ὁ
θεὸς θέλῃ. καὶ ἅμα ὑποκαταγελῶ τῶν οἰκτει-
ρόντων με.

22 Τί οὖν κωλύει καὶ ἐνταῦθα ὁμοίως; πένης
εἰμί, ἀλλὰ ὀρθὸν δόγμα ἔχω περὶ πενίας. τί οὖν
μοι μέλει, εἴ μ᾽ ἐπὶ τῇ πενίᾳ ἐλεοῦσιν; οὐκ ἄρχω,
ἄλλοι δ᾽ ἄρχουσιν. ἀλλ᾽ ὃ δεῖ ὑπειληφέναι,
ὑπείληφα περὶ τοῦ ἄρχειν καὶ μὴ ἄρχειν.
23 ὄψονται οἱ ἐλεοῦντές με, ἐγὼ δ᾽ οὔτε πεινῶ οὔτε
διψῶ οὔτε ῥιγῶ, ἀλλ᾽ ἀφ᾽ ὧν αὐτοὶ πεινῶσιν ἢ
διψῶσιν οἴονται κἀμέ. τί οὖν αὐτοῖς ποιήσω;
περιερχόμενος κηρύσσω καὶ λέγω "μὴ πλα-
νᾶσθε, ἄνδρες, ἐμοὶ καλῶς ἐστιν· οὔτε πενίας

---

¹ So also Marcus Aurelius, 7, 36; and cf. Diogenes
Laertius, 6, 3.

activities of men? Yet you are concerned whether
the rest of mankind pity you?—Yes, but I do not
deserve to be pitied.—And so you are pained at
that? And is the man who is pained worthy of
pity?—Yes.—How, then, do you fail to deserve pity
after all? By the very emotion which you feel concerning pity you make yourself worthy of pity. What,
then, says Antisthenes? Have you never heard?
"It is the lot of a king, O Cyrus, to do well, but to
be ill spoken of."[1] My head is perfectly sound and
yet everybody thinks I have a headache. What do
I care? I have no fever, and yet everybody
sympathizes with me as though I had: "Poor
fellow, you have had a fever for ever so long." I
draw a long face too, and say, "Yes, it truly is a
long time that I have been in a bad way." "What
is going to happen, then?" As God will, I reply,
and at the same time I smile quietly to myself at
those who are pitying me.

What, then, prevents me from doing the same
thing in my moral life also? I am poor, but I have
a correct judgement about poverty. Why, then, am
I concerned, if men pity me for my poverty? I
do not hold office, while others do. But I have the
right opinion about holding office and not holding it.
Let those who pity me look to it,[2] but as for myself,
I am neither hungry, nor thirsty, nor cold, but from
their own hunger and thirst they think I too am
hungry and thirsty. What, then, am I to do for
them? Shall I go about and make proclamation,
and say, "Men, be not deceived, it is well with me.

[2] As in IV. 7, 23, and 8, 24, and Acts xviii. 15. Probably
ὄψει, in S, I. 4, 13, can be defended on the analogy of these
other cases.

ἐπιστρέφομαι οὔτε ἀναρχίας οὔτε ἁπλῶς ἄλλου
οὐδενὸς ἢ δογμάτων ὀρθῶν· ταῦτα ἔχω ἀκώλυτα,
24 οὐδενὸς πεφρόντικα ἔτι"; καὶ τίς αὕτη φλυαρία;
πῶς ἔτι ὀρθὰ δόγματα ἔχω μὴ ἀρκούμενος τῷ
εἶναι ὅς εἰμι, ἀλλ᾽ ἐπτοημένος ὑπὲρ τοῦ δοκεῖν;
25 Ἀλλ᾽ ἄλλοι πλειόνων τεύξονται καὶ προτι-
μηθήσονται.—Τί οὖν εὐλογώτερον ἢ τοὺς περί τι
ἐσπουδακότας ἐν ἐκείνῳ πλεῖον ἔχειν, ἐν ᾧ ἐσπουδάκασιν; περὶ ἀρχὰς ἐσπουδάκασιν, σὺ περὶ
δόγματα· καὶ περὶ πλοῦτον, σὺ περὶ τὴν χρῆσιν
26 τῶν φαντασιῶν. ὅρα, εἰ ἐν τούτῳ σου πλέον
ἔχουσιν, περὶ ὃ σὺ μὲν ἐσπούδακας, ἐκεῖνοι δ᾽
ἀμελοῦσιν· εἰ συγκατατίθενται μᾶλλον περὶ τὰ
φυσικὰ μέτρα, εἰ ὀρέγονταί σου ἀναποτευκτότερον,
εἰ ἐκκλίνουσιν ἀπεριπτωτότερον, εἰ ἐν ἐπιβολῇ,
ἐν προθέσει, εἰ ἐν ὁρμῇ μᾶλλον εὐστοχοῦσιν, εἰ
τὸ πρέπον σῴζουσιν ὡς ἄνδρες, ὡς υἱοί, ὡς γονεῖς,
εἶθ᾽ ἑξῆς κατὰ τὰ ἄλλα τῶν σχέσεων ὀνόματα.
27 εἰ δ᾽ ἄρχουσιν ἐκεῖνοι, σὺ δ᾽[1] οὐ θέλεις σαυτῷ
τὰς ἀληθείας εἰπεῖν, ὅτι σὺ μὲν οὐδὲν τούτου
ἕνεκα ποιεῖς, ἐκεῖνοι δὲ πάντα, ἀλογώτατον δὲ
τὸν ἐπιμελούμενόν τινος ἔλαττον φέρεσθαι ἢ τὸν
ἀμελοῦντα;
28 Οὔ,[2] ἀλλ᾽ ἐπειδὴ φροντίζω ἐγὼ δογμάτων
ὀρθῶν, εὐλογώτερόν μέ ἐστιν ἄρχειν.—Ἐν ᾧ

---

[1] Defended in apodosis by Reiske and Schenkl: Upton
added ἀνιᾷ after δ᾽ and Schweighäuser οὐ.

[2] Transferred to this position by s from before ἤ just
above.

I take heed neither of poverty, nor lack of office, nor, in a word, anything else, but only correct judgements; these I possess free from hindrance, I have taken thought of nothing further " ? And yet, what foolish talk is this? How do I any longer hold correct judgements when I am not satisfied with being the man that I am, but am excited about what other people think of me ?

But others will get more than I do, and will be preferred in honour above me.—Well, and what is more reasonable than for those who have devoted themselves to something to have the advantage in that to which they have devoted themselves ? They have devoted themselves to office, you to judgements ; and they to wealth, you to dealing with your sense-impressions. See whether they have the advantage over you in what you have devoted yourself to, but they neglect; whether their assent is more in accord with natural standards, whether their desire is less likely to achieve its aim than is yours, whether their aversion is less likely to fall into what it would avoid, whether in design, purpose, and choice they hit the mark better, whether they observe what becomes them as men, as sons, as parents, and then, in order, through all the other terms for the social relations. But if they hold office, will you not tell yourself the truth, which is, that you do nothing in order to get office, while they do everything, and that it is most unreasonable for the man who pays attention to something to come off with less than the man who neglects it ?

Nay, but because I greatly concern myself with correct judgements, it is more reasonable for *me* to

φροντίζεις, ἐν δόγμασιν· ἐν ᾧ δ' ἄλλοι μᾶλλόν
σου πεφροντίκασιν, ἐκείνοις παραχώρει. οἷον εἰ
διὰ τὸ δόγματα ἔχειν ὀρθὰ ἠξίους τοξεύων μᾶλλον
ἐπιτυγχάνειν τῶν τοξοτῶν ἢ χαλκεύων μᾶλλον
29 τῶν χαλκέων. ἄφες οὖν τὴν [1] περὶ τὰ δόγματα
σπουδὴν καὶ περὶ ἐκεῖνα ἀναστρέφου, ἃ κτήσασθαι θέλεις, καὶ τότε κλαῖε, ἐάν σοι μὴ προχωρῇ·
30 κλαίειν γὰρ ἄξιος εἶ. νῦν δὲ πρὸς ἄλλοις
γίνεσθαι λέγεις, ἄλλων ἐπιμελεῖσθαι, οἱ [2] πολλοὶ
δὲ τοῦτο καλῶς λέγουσιν, ὅτι ἔργον ἔργῳ οὐ
31 κοινωνεῖ. ὁ μὲν ἐξ ὄρθρου ἀναστὰς ζητεῖ, τίνα
ἐξ οἴκου τοῦ Καίσαρος [3] ἀσπάσηται, τίνι κεχα-
ρισμένον λόγον εἴπῃ, τίνι δῶρον πέμψῃ, πῶς τῷ
ὀρχηστῇ ἀρέσῃ, πῶς κακοηθισάμενος ἄλλον
32 ἄλλῳ χαρίσηται. ὅταν εὔχηται, περὶ τούτων
εὔχεται· ὅταν θύῃ, ἐπὶ τούτοις θύει· τὸ τοῦ
Πυθαγόρου

> μὴ δ' ὕπνον μαλακοῖσιν ἐπ' ὄμμασι προσ-
> δέξασθαι

33 ἐνταῦθα παρατέθεικεν. "'πῇ παρέβην' τῶν
πρὸς κολακείαν; 'τί ἔρεξα ;' [4] μή τι ὡς ἐλεύθερος, μή τι ὡς γενναῖος ;" κἂν εὕρῃ τι τοιοῦτον,
ἐπιτιμᾷ ἑαυτῷ καὶ ἐγκαλεῖ, "τί γάρ σοι καὶ

---

[1] τὴν supplied by Sb.
[2] Upton : καί S.
[3] τοῦ Καίσαρος added by Wolf : ἐξιόντα suggested by
Reiske.
[4] Salmasius : ἔρεξα S.

---

[1] Cf. IV. 10, 24.
[2] Golden Verses, 40. See III. 10, 2.

rule.—Yes, in what you greatly concern yourself
with, that is, judgements; but in that with which
other men have concerned themselves more greatly
than you have, give place to them. It is as though,
because you have correct judgements, you insisted
that you ought in archery to hit the mark better than
the archers, or to surpass the smiths at their trade.
Drop, therefore, your earnestness about judgements, and concern yourself with the things which
you wish to acquire, and *then* lament if you do not
succeed, for you have a right to do that. But as it is,
you claim to be intent upon other things, to care for
other things, and there is wisdom in what common
people say, " One serious business has no partnership
with another." [1] One man gets up at early dawn
and looks for someone of the household of Caesar to
salute, someone to whom he may make a pleasant
speech, to whom he may send a present, how he may
please the dancer, how he may gratify one person
by maliciously disparaging another. When he prays,
he prays for these objects, when he sacrifices, he
sacrifices for these objects. The word of Pythagoras,[2]

> Also allow not sleep to draw nigh to your languor-
> ous eyelids,

he has wrested to apply here. " ' Where did I go
wrong—' [3] in matters of flattery ? ' What did I do ? '
Can it be that I acted as a free man, or as a man of
noble character ? " And if he find an instance of the
sort, he censures and accuses himself : " Why, what

---

[3] The single quotation-marks enclose famous phrases from
the *Golden Verses*, which Epictetus, with bitter irony, repre-
sents such a self-seeker as employing in a sense appropriate
to his own contemptible behaviour.

τοῦτο εἰπεῖν; οὐ γὰρ ἐνῆν ψεύσασθαι; λέγουσιν
καὶ οἱ φιλόσοφοι, ὅτι οὐδὲν κωλύει ψεῦδος
34 εἰπεῖν." σὺ δ' εἴπερ ταῖς ἀληθείαις οὐδενὸς
ἄλλου πεφρόντικας ἢ¹ χρήσεως οἵας δεῖ φαντασιῶν, εὐθὺς ἀναστὰς ἔωθεν ἐνθυμοῦ "τίνα μοι
λείπει πρὸς ἀπάθειαν; τίνα πρὸς ἀταραξίαν;
τίς εἰμι; μή τι σωμάτιον, μή τι κτῆσις, μή τι
φήμη; οὐδὲν τούτων. ἀλλὰ τί; λογικόν εἰμι
35 ζῷον." τίνα οὖν τὰ ἀπαιτήματα; ἀναπόλει τὰ
πεπραγμένα. "'πῇ παρέβην' τῶν πρὸς εὔροιαν;
'τί ἔρεξα' ἢ ἄφιλον ἢ ἀκοινώνητον ἢ ἄγνωμον;
'τί μοι δέον οὐκ ἐτελέσθη' πρὸς ταῦτα;"
36   Τοσαύτης οὖν διαφορᾶς οὔσης τῶν ἐπιθυμουμένων, τῶν ἔργων, τῶν εὐχῶν ἔτι θέλεις τὸ ἴσον
ἔχειν ἐκείνοις, περὶ ἃ σὺ μὲν οὐκ ἐσπούδακας,
37 ἐκεῖνοι δ' ἐσπουδάκασιν; εἶτα θαυμάζεις, εἴ σ'
ἐλεοῦσιν, καὶ ἀγανακτεῖς; ἐκεῖνοι δ' οὐκ ἀγα-
νακτοῦσιν, εἰ σὺ αὐτοὺς ἐλεεῖς. διὰ τί; ὅτι
ἐκεῖνοι μὲν πεπεισμένοι εἰσίν, ὅτι ἀγαθῶν τυγ-
38 χάνουσιν, σὺ δ' οὐ πέπεισαι. διὰ τοῦτο σὺ
μὲν οὐκ ἀρκῇ τοῖς σοῖς, ἀλλ' ἐφίεσαι τῶν
ἐκείνων· ἐκεῖνοι δ' ἀρκοῦνται τοῖς ἑαυτῶν καὶ
οὐκ ἐφίενται τῶν σῶν. ἐπεί τοι εἰ ταῖς
ἀληθείαις ἐπέπεισο, ὅτι περὶ τὰ ἀγαθὰ σὺ ὁ
ἐπιτυγχάνων εἶ, ἐκεῖνοι δ' ἀποπεπλάνηνται, οὐδ'
ἂν ἐνεθυμοῦ, τί λέγουσι περὶ σοῦ.

¹ ἢ supplied by s.

---

[1] Cf. Stobaeus, *Ecl.* II. 7, 11ᵐ (vol. II. p. 111, 13 ff.
Wachsmuth): "They (the Stoics) think that he (the wise
man) will upon occasion employ falsehood in a number of
different ways."

business did you have to say that? For wasn't it possible to lie? Even the philosophers say that there is nothing to hinder one's telling a lie." [1] But if in all truth you have concerned yourself greatly with nothing but the proper use of sense-impressions, then as soon as you get up in the morning bethink you, "What do I yet lack in order to achieve tranquillity? What to achieve calm? What am I? I am not a paltry body, not property, not reputation, am I? None of these. Well, what am I? A rational creature." What, then, are the demands upon you? Rehearse your actions. "'Where did I go wrong?' in matters conducive to serenity? 'What did I do' that was unfriendly, or unsocial, or unfeeling? 'What to be done was left undone' in regard to these matters?"

Since, therefore, there is so great a difference between the things which men desire, their deeds, and their prayers, do you still wish to be on an equal footing with them in matters to which you have not devoted yourself, but they have? And after all that, are you surprised if they pity you, and are you indignant? But they are not indignant if you pity them. And why? Because they are convinced that they are getting good things, while you are not so convinced in your own case. That is why you are not satisfied with what you have, but reach out for what they have. Because, if you had been truly convinced that, in the case of the things which are good, you are the one who is attaining them, while they have gone astray, you would not even have taken account of what they say about you.

ζ'. Περὶ ἀφοβίας.

1 Τί ποιεῖ φοβερὸν τὸν τύραννον;—Οἱ δορυφόροι, φησίν, καὶ αἱ μάχαιραι αὐτῶν καὶ ὁ ἐπὶ
τοῦ κοιτῶνος καὶ οἱ ἀποκλείοντες τοὺς εἰσιόντας.
2 —Διὰ τί οὖν, ἂν παιδίον αὐτῷ προσαγάγῃς μετὰ
τῶν δορυφόρων ὄντι, οὐ φοβεῖται; ἢ ὅτι οὐκ
3 αἰσθάνεται τούτων τὸ παιδίον; ἂν οὖν τῶν
δορυφόρων τις αἰσθάνηται καὶ ὅτι μαχαίρας
ἔχουσιν, ἐπ' αὐτὸ δὲ τοῦτο προσέρχηται αὐτῷ
θέλων ἀποθανεῖν διά τινα περίστασιν καὶ ζητῶν
ὑπ' ἄλλου παθεῖν αὐτὸ εὐκόλως, μή τι φοβεῖται
τοὺς δορυφόρους;—Θέλει γὰρ τοῦτο, δι' ὃ φο-
4 βεροί εἰσιν.—Ἂν οὖν τις μήτ' ἀποθανεῖν μήτε
ζῆν θέλων ἐξ ἅπαντος ἀλλ' ὡς ἂν διδῶται,
προσέρχηται αὐτῷ, τί κωλύει μὴ δεδοικότα
5 προσέρχεσθαι αὐτόν;—Οὐδέν.—Ἂν τις οὖν καὶ
πρὸς τὴν κτῆσιν ὡσαύτως ἔχῃ καθάπερ οὗτος
πρὸς τὸ σῶμα, καὶ πρὸς τὰ τέκνα καὶ τὴν
γυναῖκα καὶ ἁπλῶς ὑπό τινος μανίας καὶ ἀπο-
νοίας οὕτως ἢ διακείμενος, ὥστ' ἐν μηδενὶ
ποιεῖσθαι τὸ ἔχειν ταῦτα ἢ μὴ ἔχειν, ἀλλ' ὡς
ὀστρακίοις τὰ παιδία παίζοντα περὶ μὲν τῆς
παιδιᾶς διαφέρεται, τῶν ὀστρακίων δ' οὐ πεφρόντικεν, οὕτως δὲ καὶ οὗτος τὰς μὲν ὕλας παρ'
οὐδὲν ἢ πεποιημένος, τὴν παιδιὰν δὲ τὴν περὶ
αὐτὰς καὶ ἀναστροφὴν ἀσπάζηται· ποῖος ἔτι
τούτῳ τύραννος φοβερὸς ἢ ποῖοι δορυφόροι ἢ
ποῖαι μάχαιραι αὐτῶν;

CHAPTER VII

Of freedom from fear

WHAT makes the tyrant an object of fear?—His guards, someone says, and their swords, and the chamberlain, and those who exclude persons who would enter.—Why, then, is it that, if you bring a child into the presence of the tyrant while he is with his guards, the child is not afraid? Is it because the child does not really feel the presence of the guards? If, then, a man really feels their presence, and that they have swords, but has come for that very purpose, for the reason that he wishes to die because of some misfortune, and he seeks to do so easily at the hand of another, he does not fear the guards, does he?—No, for what makes them terrible is just what he wants.—If, then, a man who has set his will neither upon dying nor upon living at any cost, but only as it is given him to live, comes into the presence of the tyrant, what is there to prevent such a man from coming into his presence without fear? —Nothing.—If, then, a man feel also about his property just as this other person feels about his body, and so about his children, and his wife, and if, in brief, he be in such a frame of mind, due to some madness or despair, that he cares not one whit about having, or not having, these things; but, as children playing with potsherds strive with one another about the game, but take no thought about the potsherds themselves, so this man also has reckoned the material things of life as nothing, but is glad to play with them and handle them—what kind of tyrant, or guards, or swords in the hands of guards can any more inspire fear in the breast of such a man?

361

6 Εἶτα ὑπὸ μανίας μὲν δύναταί τις οὕτως
διατεθῆναι πρὸς ταῦτα καὶ ὑπὸ ἔθους οἱ Γαλι-
λαῖοι· ὑπὸ λόγου δὲ καὶ ἀποδείξεως οὐδεὶς
δύναται μαθεῖν, ὅτι ὁ θεὸς πάντα πεποίηκεν τὰ
ἐν τῷ κόσμῳ καὶ αὐτὸν τὸν κόσμον ὅλον μὲν
ἀκώλυτον καὶ αὐτοτελῆ, τὰ ἐν μέρει δ' αὐτοῦ
7 πρὸς χρείαν τῶν ὅλων; τὰ μὲν οὖν ἄλλα πάντα
ἀπήλλακται τοῦ δύνασθαι παρακολουθεῖν τῇ
διοικήσει αὐτοῦ· τὸ δὲ λογικὸν ζῷον ἀφορμὰς
ἔχει πρὸς ἀναλογισμὸν τούτων ἁπάντων, ὅτι τε
μέρος ἐστὶ καὶ ποῖόν τι μέρος καὶ ὅτι τὰ μέρη
8 τοῖς ὅλοις εἴκειν ἔχει καλῶς. πρὸς τούτοις δὲ
φύσει γενναῖον καὶ μεγαλόψυχον καὶ ἐλεύθερον
γενόμενον ὁρᾷ, διότι τῶν περὶ αὐτὸ τὰ μὲν ἀκώλυτα
ἔχει καὶ ἐπ' αὐτῷ, τὰ δὲ κωλυτὰ καὶ ἐπ' ἄλλοις·
ἀκώλυτα μὲν τὰ προαιρετικά, κωλυτὰ δὲ τὰ
9 ἀπροαίρετα. καὶ διὰ τοῦτο, ἐὰν μὲν ἐν τούτοις
μόνοις ἡγήσηται τὸ ἀγαθὸν τὸ αὑτοῦ καὶ συμφέρον, τοῖς ἀκωλύτοις καὶ ἐφ' ἑαυτῷ, ἐλεύθερος
ἔσται, εὔρουν, εὔδαιμον, ἀβλαβές, μεγαλόφρον,
εὐσεβές, χάριν ἔχον ὑπὲρ πάντων τῷ θεῷ,
μηδαμοῦ μεμφόμενον μηδενὶ τῶν γενομένων,
10 μηδενὶ[1] ἐγκαλοῦν· ἂν δ' ἐν τοῖς ἐκτὸς καὶ
ἀπροαιρέτοις, ἀνάγκη κωλύεσθαι αὐτό, ἐμποδίζεσθαι, δουλεύειν τοῖς ἐκείνων ἔχουσιν ἐξουσίαν,

---

[1] Schweighäuser : μηδέν S.

---

[1] Obviously referring to the Christians, as the Scholiast
saw. Cf. also II. 9, 19–21 and note, and Introd. p. xxvi f.

Therefore, if madness can produce this attitude of mind toward the things which have just been mentioned, and also habit, as with the Galilaeans,[1] cannot reason and demonstration teach a man that God has made all things in the universe, and the whole universe itself, to be free from hindrance, and to contain its end in itself, and the parts of it to serve the needs of the whole? Now all other animals have been excluded from the capacity to understand the governance of God, but the rational animal, man, possesses faculties that enable him to consider all these things, both that he is a part of them, and what kind of part of them he is, and that it is well for the parts to yield to the whole. And furthermore, being by nature noble, and high-minded, and free, the rational animal, man, sees that he has some of the things which are about him free from hindrance and under his control, but that others are subject to hindrance and under the control of others. Free from hindrance are those things which lie in the sphere of the moral purpose, and subject to hindrance are those which lie outside the sphere of the moral purpose. And so, if he regards his own good and advantage as residing in these things alone, in those, namely, which are free from hindrance and under his control, he will be free, serene, happy, unharmed, high-minded, reverent, giving thanks for all things to God, under no circumstances finding fault with anything that has happened, nor blaming anything; if, however, he regards his good and advantage as residing in externals and things outside the sphere of his moral purpose, he must needs be hindered and restrained, be a slave to those who have control over these things

11 ἃ τεθαύμακεν καὶ φοβεῖται, ἀνάγκη δ' ἀσεβὲς
εἶναι ἅτε βλάπτεσθαι οἰόμενον ὑπὸ τοῦ θεοῦ
καὶ ἄνισον, ἀεὶ αὑτῷ τοῦ πλείονος περιποιη-
τικόν, ἀνάγκη δὲ καὶ ταπεινὸν εἶναι καὶ
μικροπρεπές.

12 Ταῦτα τί κωλύει διαλαβόντα ζῆν κούφως καὶ
εὐηνίως, πάντα τὰ¹ συμβαίνειν δυνάμενα πράως
ἐκδεχόμενον, τὰ δ' ἤδη συμβεβηκότα φέροντα;

13 " θέλεις πενίαν; " φέρε καὶ γνώσῃ, τί ἐστὶ πενία
τυχοῦσα καλοῦ ὑποκριτοῦ. " θέλεις ἀρχάς; "
φέρε. θέλεις ἀναρχίαν; φέρε. ἀλλὰ πόνους

14 θέλεις;² φέρε καὶ πόνους. " ἀλλ' ἐξορισμόν; "
ὅπου ἂν ἀπέλθω, ἐκεῖ μοι καλῶς ἔσται· καὶ
γὰρ ἐνθάδε οὐ διὰ τὸν τόπον ἦν μοι καλῶς, ἀλλὰ
διὰ τὰ δόγματα, ἃ μέλλω μετ' ἐμαυτοῦ ἀπο-
φέρειν. οὐδὲ γὰρ δύναταί τις ἀφελέσθαι αὐτά,
ἀλλὰ ταῦτα μόνα ἐμά ἐστι καὶ ἀναφαίρετα καὶ
ἀρκεῖ μοι παρόντα, ὅπου ἂν ὦ καὶ ὅ τι ἂν ποιῶ.

15 " ἀλλ' ἤδη καιρὸς ἀποθανεῖν." τί λέγεις ἀποθανεῖν; μὴ τραγῴδει τὸ πρᾶγμα, ἀλλ' εἰπὲ ὡς
ἔχει " ἤδη καιρὸς τὴν ὕλην, ἐξ ὧν συνῆλθεν, εἰς
ἐκεῖνα πάλιν ἀποκαταστῆναι." καὶ τί δεινόν;
τί μέλλει ἀπόλλυσθαι τῶν ἐν τῷ κόσμῳ, τί

16 γενέσθαι καινόν, παράλογον; τούτων ἕνεκα φοβερός ἐστιν ὁ τύραννος; διὰ ταῦτα οἱ δορυφόροι
μεγάλας δοκοῦσιν ἔχειν τὰς μαχαίρας καὶ

---

¹ τά supplied by *Sb*.
² These last seven words (with the change of ἔχεις before
ἀναρχίαν to θέλεις, by Schenkl) in the scholia a little below
this point were seen by Lindsay to belong here.

---

¹ See *Encheiridion*, 17, and frag. 11 for parallels.

which he has admired and fears; he must needs be
irreverent, forasmuch as he thinks that God is
injuring him, and be unfair, always trying to secure
for himself more than his share, and must needs be
of an abject and mean spirit.

When a man has once grasped all this, what
is there to prevent him from living with a light
heart and an obedient disposition; with a gentle
spirit awaiting anything that may yet befall, and
enduring that which has already befallen? "Would
you have me bear poverty?" Bring it on and you
shall see what poverty is when it finds a good actor
to play the part.[1] "Would you have me hold
office?" Bring it on. "Would you have me suffer
deprivation of office?" Bring it on. "Well, and
would you have me bear troubles?" Bring them on
too. "Well, and exile?" Wherever I go it will be
well with me, for here where I am it was well with
me, not because of my location, but because of my
judgements, and these I shall carry away with me;
nor, indeed, can any man take these away from me,
but they are the only things that are mine, and they
cannot be taken away, and with the possession of
them I am content, wherever I be and whatever I do.
"But it is now time to die." Why say "die"?
Make no tragic parade of the matter, but speak of it
as it is: "It is now time for the material of which
you are constituted to be restored to those elements
from which it came." And what is there terrible
about that? What one of the things that make up
the universe will be lost, what novel or unreasonable thing will have taken place? Is it for this
that the tyrant inspires fear? Is it because of
this that his guards seem to have long and sharp

365

ὀξείας; ἄλλοις ταῦτα· ἐμοὶ δ' ἔσκεπται περὶ
17 πάντων, εἰς ἐμὲ οὐδεὶς ἐξουσίαν ἔχει. ἠλευθέρω-
μαι ὑπὸ τοῦ θεοῦ, ἔγνωκα αὐτοῦ τὰς ἐντολάς,
οὐκέτι οὐδεὶς δουλαγωγῆσαί με δύναται, καρ-
18 πιστὴν ἔχω οἷον δεῖ, δικαστὰς οἵους δεῖ. "οὐχὶ
τοῦ σώματός σου¹ κύριός εἰμι;"¹ τί οὖν πρὸς
ἐμέ; "οὐχὶ τοῦ κτησιδίου;" τί οὖν πρὸς ἐμέ;
"οὐχὶ φυγῆς ἢ δεσμῶν;" πάλιν τούτων πάντων
καὶ τοῦ σωματίου ὅλου σοι αὐτοῦ ἐξίσταμαι,
ὅταν θέλῃς. πείρασαί μοί σου τῆς ἀρχῆς² καὶ
γνώσῃ, μέχρι τίνος αὐτὴν ἔχεις.
19 Τίνα οὖν ἔτι φοβηθῆναι δύναμαι; τοὺς ἐπὶ
τοῦ κοιτῶνος; μὴ τί ποιήσωσιν; ἀποκλείσωσί
με; ἄν με εὕρωσι θέλοντα εἰσελθεῖν, ἀπο-
κλεισάτωσαν.—Τί οὖν ἔρχῃ ἐπὶ θύρας;—Ὅτι
καθήκειν ἐμαυτῷ δοκῶ μενούσης τῆς παιδιᾶς
20 συμπαίζειν.—Πῶς οὖν οὐκ ἀποκλείῃ;—Ὅτι ἂν
μή τίς με δέχηται, οὐ θέλω εἰσελθεῖν, ἀλλ' ἀεὶ
μᾶλλον ἐκεῖνο θέλω τὸ γινόμενον. κρεῖττον γὰρ
ἡγοῦμαι ὃ ὁ θεὸς θέλει ἢ ὃ ἐγώ. προσκείσομαι
διάκονος καὶ ἀκόλουθος ἐκείνῳ, συνορμῶ, συνο-
ρέγομαι,³ ἁπλῶς συνθέλω. ἀποκλεισμὸς ἐμοὶ
21 οὐ γίνεται, ἀλλὰ τοῖς βιαζομένοις. διὰ τί οὖν
οὐ βιάζομαι; οἶδα γάρ, ὅτι ἔσω ἀγαθὸν οὐδὲν
διαδίδοται τοῖς εἰσελθοῦσιν. ἀλλ' ὅταν ἀκούσω

¹ Schweighäuser (after Wolf): μου and εἰ S.
² s and Schenkl, who adds μοί: πειράσομαί σου τὴν
ἀρχήν S.
³ Wolf (after Schegk): ὀρέγομαι S.

swords? Let others see to that; I have considered all this, no one has authority over me. I have been set free by God, I know His commands, no one has power any longer to make a slave of me, I have the right kind of emancipator, and the right kind of judges. "Am I not master of your body?" Very well, what is that to me? "Am I not master of your paltry property?" Very well, what is that to me? "Am I not master of exile or bonds?" Again I yield up to you all these things and my whole paltry body itself, whenever you will. Do make trial of your power, and you will find out how far it extends.

Who is there, then, that I *can* any longer be afraid of? Shall I be afraid of the chamberlains? For fear they do what? Lock the door in my face? If they find me wanting to enter, let them lock the door in my face!—Why, then, do you go to the gate of the palace?—Because I think it fitting for me to join in the game while the game lasts.—How, then, is it that you are not locked out?[1]—Because, if anyone will not receive me, I do not care to go in, but always I wish rather the thing which takes place. For I regard God's will as better than my will. I shall attach myself to Him as a servant and follower, my choice is one with His, my desire one with His, in a word, my will is one with His will. No door is locked in my face, but rather in the face of those who would force themselves in. Why, then, do I not force myself in? Why, because I know that within nothing good is distributed among those who have entered. But when I hear someone called blessed,

---

[1] That is, it cannot properly be said of a man that he is "locked out" if he does not "wish" to enter.

τινὰ μακαριζόμενον, ὅτι τιμᾶται ὑπὸ τοῦ Καίσαρος, λέγω "τί αὐτῷ συμβαίνει; μή τι οὖν
καὶ δόγμα, οἷον δεῖ ἐπαρχίᾳ;[1] μή τι οὖν καὶ
τὸ χρῆσθαι ἐπιτροπῇ; τί ἔτι διωθοῦμαι; ἰσχα-
22 δοκάρυά τις διαρριπτεῖ·[2] τὰ παιδία ἁρπάζει καὶ
ἀλλήλοις διαμάχεται· οἱ ἄνδρες οὐχί, μικρὸν
γὰρ αὐτὸ ἡγοῦνται. ἂν δ' ὀστράκια διαρριπτῇ
23 τις, οὐδὲ τὰ παιδία ἁρπάζει. ἐπαρχίαι διαδί-
δονται· ὄψεται τὰ παιδία. ἀργύριον· ὄψεται
τὰ παιδία. στρατηγία, ὑπατεία· διαρπαζέτω
τὰ παιδία· ἐκκλειέσθω, τυπτέσθω, καταφιλείτω
24 τὰς χεῖρας τοῦ διδόντος, τῶν δούλων· ἐμοὶ δ'
ἰσχαδοκάρυόν ἐστιν." τί οὖν, ἂν[3] ἀπὸ τύχης
ῥιπτοῦντος αὐτοῦ ἔλθῃ εἰς τὸν κόλπον ἰσχάς;
ἄρας κατέφαγον·[4] μέχρι τοσούτου γὰρ ἔστι καὶ
ἰσχάδα τιμῆσαι. ἵνα δὲ κύψω[5] καὶ ἄλλον
ἀνατρέψω ἢ ὑπ' ἄλλου ἀνατραπῶ καὶ κολακεύσω
τοὺς εἰσιέντας,[6] οὐκ ἀξία οὔτ' ἰσχὰς οὔτ' ἄλλο τι
τῶν οὐκ ἀγαθῶν, ἅ με ἀναπεπείκασιν οἱ φιλόσοφοι μὴ δοκεῖν ἀγαθὰ εἶναι.
25 Δείκνυέ μοι τὰς μαχαίρας τῶν δορυφόρων.
"ἰδοῦ, ἡλίκαι εἰσὶ καὶ πῶς ὀξεῖαι." τί οὖν
ποιοῦσιν αἱ μεγάλαι αὗται μάχαιραι καὶ ὀξεῖαι;
26 "ἀποκτιννύουσιν." πυρετὸς δὲ τί ποιεῖ; "ἄλλο
οὐδέν." κεραμὶς δὲ τί ποιεῖ; "ἄλλο οὐδέν."

---

[1] Schenkl : ἐπαρχίαν S. The passage is extremely condensed
if not actually lacunose. This comparatively simple change
enables one to secure the general sense required, whether
or not it was originally expressed in this form.
[2] Bentley and Schenkl[2] : διαρρίπτη S. But cf. *Trans. Amer.
Philol. Assoc.* 52 (1921) 51.
[3] ἂν added by Sc.   [4] κατάφαγε s and Schenkl.
[5] Wolf : κρύψω S.
[6] Elter : εἰσιόντας (" those who enter the palace ") S.

because he is being honoured by Caesar, I say, "What is his portion? Does he, then, get also a judgement such as he ought to have for governing a province? Does he, then, get also the ability to administer a procuratorship? Why should I any longer push my way in? Somebody is scattering dried figs and nuts; the children snatch them up and fight with one another, the men do not, for they count this a small matter. But if somebody throws potsherds around, not even the children snatch them up. Governorships are being passed around. The children shall see[1] to that. Money. The children shall see to that. A praetorship, a consulship. Let the children snatch them up; let the children have the door locked in their faces, take a beating, kiss the hands of the giver, and the hands of his slaves. As for me, it's a mere scattering of dried figs and nuts." But what, then, if, when the man is throwing them about, a dried fig chances to fall into my lap? I take it up and eat it. For I may properly value even a dried fig as much as that. But neither a dried fig, nor any other of the things not good, which the philosophers have persuaded me not to think good, is of sufficient value to warrant my grovelling and upsetting someone else, or being upset by him, or flattering those who have flung the dried figs among us.

Show me the swords of the guards. "See how large and how sharp they are!" What, then, do these large and sharp swords do? "They kill." And what does fever do? "Nothing else." And what does a tile do? "Nothing else." Do you

---

[1] See note on IV. 6, 23.

θέλεις οὖν πάντα ταῦτα θαυμάζω καὶ προσκυνῶ
καὶ δοῦλος πάντων περιέρχωμαι; μὴ γένοιτο·
27 ἀλλ' ἅπαξ μαθών, ὅτι τὸ γενόμενον καὶ φθαρῆναι
δεῖ, ἵνα ὁ κόσμος μὴ ἵστηται μηδ' ἐμποδίζηται,
οὐκέτι διαφέρομαι, πότερον πυρετὸς αὐτὸ ποιήσει ἢ κεραμὶς ἢ στρατιώτης, ἀλλ' εἰ δεῖ συγ-
κρῖναι, οἶδ' ὅτι ἀπονώτερον αὐτὸ καὶ ταχύτερον
28 ὁ στρατιώτης ποιήσει. ὅταν οὖν μήτε φοβῶμαί
τι ὧν διαθεῖναί με δύναται μήτ' ἐπιθυμῶ τινος
ὧν παρασχεῖν, τί ἔτι θαυμάζω αὐτόν, τί ἔτι
τέθηπα; τί φοβοῦμαι τοὺς δορυφόρους; τί
χαίρω, ἄν μοι φιλανθρώπως λαλήσῃ καὶ ἀπο-
δέξηταί με, καὶ ἄλλοις διηγοῦμαι, πῶς μοι
29 ἐλάλησεν; μὴ γὰρ Σωκράτης ἐστίν, μὴ γὰρ
Διογένης, ἵν' ὁ ἔπαινος αὐτοῦ ἀπόδειξις ἢ περὶ
30 ἐμοῦ; μὴ γὰρ τὸ ἦθος ἐζήλωκα αὐτοῦ; ἀλλὰ
τὴν παιδιὰν σῴζων ἔρχομαι πρὸς αὐτὸν[1] καὶ
ὑπηρετῶ, μέχρις ἂν ὅτου μηδὲν ἀβέλτερον κελεύῃ
μηδ' ἄρρυθμον. ἂν δέ μοι λέγῃ "ἄπελθε ἐπὶ
Λέοντα τὸν Σαλαμίνιον," λέγω αὐτῷ "ζήτει
31 ἄλλον· ἐγὼ γὰρ οὐκέτι παίζω." "ἄπαγε αὐτόν."
ἀκολουθῶ ἐν παιδιᾷ. "ἀλλ' ἀφαιρεῖταί σου ὁ
τράχηλος." ἐκείνου δ' αὐτοῦ ἀεὶ ἐπιμένει, ὑμῶν
δὲ τῶν πειθομένων; "ἀλλ' ἄταφος ῥιφήσῃ."
εἰ ἐγώ εἰμι ὁ νεκρός, ῥιφήσομαι· εἰ δ' ἄλλος

---

[1] s: ἐμαυτόν S.

---

[1] See note on IV. 1, 160.
[2] As was sometimes done as a last insult to the dead.
Epictetus may also have had in mind the celebrated remark of
Diogenes before his death, who, when his friends protested
against his request that he be thrown out unburied (Diogenes

want me, then, to respect and do obeisance to all
these things, and to go about as the slave of them
all? Far from it! But if once I have learned that
what is born must also perish, so that the world may
not stand still, nor be hampered, it makes no difference to me whether a fever shall bring that consumma-
tion, or a tile, or a soldier; but, if I must make a
comparison, I know that the soldier will bring it
about with less trouble and more speed. Seeing,
therefore, that I neither fear anything of all that the
tyrant is able to do with me, nor greatly desire anything of all that he is able to provide, why do I any
longer admire him, why any longer stand in awe of
him? Why am I afraid of his guards? Why do I
rejoice if he speaks kindly to me and welcomes me,
and why do I tell others how he spoke to me? He
is not Socrates, is he, or Diogenes, so that his praise
should be a proof of what I am? I have not been
ambitious to imitate his character, have I? Nay,
but acting as one who keeps the game going, I come
to him and serve him so long as he commands me
to do nothing foolish or unseemly. If, however, he
says, "Go and bring Leon of Salamis,"[1] I reply,
"Try to get someone else, for I am not playing any
longer." "Take him off to prison," says the tyrant
about me. "I follow, because that is part of the game."
"But your head will be taken off." And does the
tyrant's head always stay in its place, and the heads
of you who obey him? "But you will be thrown out
unburied."[2] If the corpse is I, then I shall be
thrown out; but if I am something different from

Laertius, 6, 79), ironically suggested that his staff be laid by
his side to keep away the dogs and carrion birds. Cicero,
Tusc. Disp. 1, 104 ; Ps.-Diog. *Epist.* 25.

εἰμὶ τοῦ νεκροῦ, κομψότερον λέγε, ὡς ἔχει τὸ
32 πρᾶγμα, καὶ μὴ ἐκφόβει με. τοῖς παιδίοις ταῦτα
φοβερά ἐστι καὶ τοῖς ἀνοήτοις. εἰ δέ τις εἰς
φιλοσόφου σχολὴν ἅπαξ εἰσελθὼν οὐκ οἶδεν, τί
ἐστὶν αὑτός, ἄξιός ἐστι φοβεῖσθαι καὶ κολακεύειν
οὕσπερ πρότερον[1] ἐκολάκευεν· εἰ μήπω μεμάθηκεν,
ὅτι οὐκ ἔστι σὰρξ οὐδ' ὀστᾶ οὐδὲ νεῦρα, ἀλλὰ
τὸ τούτοις χρώμενον, τὸ[2] καὶ διοικοῦν καὶ παρα-
κολουθοῦν ταῖς φαντασίαις.

33　Ναί· ἀλλ' οἱ λόγοι οὗτοι καταφρονητὰς
ποιοῦσι τῶν νόμων.—Καὶ ποῖοι μᾶλλον λόγοι
πειθομένους παρέχουσι τοῖς νόμοις τοὺς χρω-
34 μένους; νόμος δ' οὐκ ἔστι τὰ ἐπὶ μωρῷ. καὶ
ὅμως ὅρα, πῶς καὶ πρὸς τούτους ὡς δεῖ ἔχοντας
παρασκευάζουσιν, οἵ γε διδάσκουσιν μηδενὸς
ἀντιποιεῖσθαι πρὸς αὐτούς, ἐν οἷς ἂν ἡμᾶς
35 νικῆσαι δύνωνται.[3] περὶ τὸ σωμάτιον διδάσκουσιν ἐξίστασθαι, περὶ τὴν κτῆσιν ἐξίστασθαι,
περὶ τὰ τέκνα, γονεῖς, ἀδελφούς, πάντων παραχωρεῖν, πάντα ἀφιέναι· μόνα τὰ δόγματα ὑπε-
ξαιροῦνται, ἃ καὶ ὁ Ζεὺς ἐξαίρετα ἑκάστου
36 εἶναι ἠθέλησεν. ποία ἐνθάδε παρανομία, ποία
ἀβελτερία; ὅπου κρείττων εἶ καὶ ἰσχυρότερος,
ἐκεῖ σοι ἐξίσταμαι· ὅπου πάλιν ἐγὼ κρείττων,
37 σὺ παραχώρει μοι. ἐμοὶ γὰρ μεμέληκεν, σοὶ δ'
οὔ. σοὶ μέλει, πῶς ἐν ὀρθοστρώτοις οἰκῇς, ἔτι[4]
πῶς παῖδές σοι καὶ πιλλᾶτοι διακονῶσιν, πῶς

---

[1] οὕσπερ Capps (Schweighäuser οὖσ), πρότερον Oldfather
(in part after Page) : ὃ ὕστερον (sic) S.　Capps would prefer
οὕσπερ νῦν κολακεύεις.
[2] Schenkl : S uncertain.
[3] Schweighäuser : δύνανται S.
[4] Schenkl : οἰχήσεται S.

the corpse, speak with more discrimination, as the
fact is, and do not try to terrify me. These things
are terrifying to the children and the fools. But if
a man who has once entered a philosopher's lecture
does not know what he himself is, he deserves to be
in a state of fear, and also to flatter those whom he
used to flatter before;[1] if he has not yet learned
that he is not flesh, nor bones, nor sinews, but that
which employs these, that which both governs the
impressions of the senses and understands them.

Oh yes, but statements like these make men
despise the laws.—Quite the contrary, what statements other than these make the men who follow
them more ready to obey the laws? Law is not simply
anything that is in the power of a fool. And yet
see how these statements make us behave properly
even toward these fools, because they teach us to
claim against such persons nothing in which they
can surpass us. They teach us to give way when it
comes to our paltry body, to give way when it comes
to our property, to our children, parents, brothers, to
retire from everything, let everything go; they
except only our judgements, and it was the will of
Zeus also that these should be each man's special
possession. What do you mean by speaking of law-
lessness and stupidity here? Where you are superior
and stronger, there I give way to you; and again,
where I am superior, you retire in favour of me. For
I have made these matters my concern, and you
have not. It is your concern how to live in marble
halls,[2] and further, how slaves and freedmen are to

[1] That is, before he began to attend lectures in philosophy.
But the text is highly uncertain.
[2] Strictly speaking, walls covered with a veneer of varie-
gated marble.

ἐσθῆτα περίβλεπτον φορῇς, πῶς κυνηγοὺς πολ-
38 λοὺς ἔχῃς, πῶς κιθαρῳδούς, τραγῳδούς. μή τι
ἀντιποιοῦμαι; μή τι οὖν δογμάτων σοι μεμέ-
ληκε; μή τι τοῦ λόγου τοῦ σεαυτοῦ; μή τι
οἶδας, ἐκ τίνων μορίων συνέστηκεν, πῶς συνά-
γεται, τίς ἡ διάρθρωσις αὐτοῦ, τίνας ἔχει
39 δυνάμεις καὶ ποίας τινάς; τί οὖν ἀγανακτεῖς,
εἰ ἄλλος ἐν τούτοις σου πλέον ἔχει ὁ μεμελε-
τηκώς;—Ἀλλὰ ταῦτ' ἐστὶ τὰ μέγιστα.—Καὶ
τίς σε κωλύει περὶ ταῦτ' ἀναστρέφεσθαι καὶ
τούτων ἐπιμελεῖσθαι; τίς δὲ μείζονα ἔχει παρασκευὴν βιβλίων, εὐσχολίας, τῶν ὠφελησόντων;
40 μόνον ἀπόνευσόν ποτε ἐπὶ ταῦτα, ἀπόνειμον κἂν
ὀλίγον χρόνον τῷ σαυτοῦ ἡγεμονικῷ· σκέψαι τί
ποτ' ἔχεις τοῦτο καὶ πόθεν ἐληλυθός, τὸ πᾶσιν
τοῖς ἄλλοις χρώμενον, πάντα τἆλλα δοκίμαζον,
41 ἐκλεγόμενον, ἀπεκλεγόμενον. μέχρι δ' ἂν οὗ
περὶ τὰ ἐκτὸς ἀναστρέφῃ, ἐκεῖνα ἕξεις οἷα οὐδείς,
τοῦτο δ' οἷον αὐτὸ ἔχειν θέλεις, ῥυπαρὸν καὶ
ἀτημέλητον.

η'. Πρὸς τοὺς ταχέως ἐπὶ τὸ σχῆμα τῶν
φιλοσόφων ἐπιπηδῶντας.

1 Μηδέποτ' ἀπὸ τῶν κοινῶν τινὰ μήτ' ἐπαι-
νέσητε μήτε ψέξητε μήτε τέχνην τινὰ ἢ ἀτεχ-

---

[1] Those who sang to their own accompaniment on the harp.
[2] See IV. 4, 44.

serve you, how you are to wear conspicuous clothing, how to have many hunting dogs, citharoedes,[1] and tragedians. I do not lay claim to any of these, do I? You, then, have never concerned yourself with judgements, have you? Or with your own reason, have you? You do not know, do you, what are its constituent parts, how it is composed, what its arrangement is, what faculties it has, and what their nature is? Why, then, are you disturbed if someone else, the man, namely, who has concerned himself with these matters, has the advantage of you therein? —But these are the most important things that there are.—And who is there to prevent you from concerning yourself with these matters, and devoting your attention to them? And who is better provided with books, leisure, and persons to help you? Only begin some time to turn your mind to these matters; devote a little time, if no more, to your own governing principle; consider what this thing is which you possess, and where it has come from, the thing which utilizes everything else, submits everything else to the test, selects, and rejects. But so long as you concern yourself with externals, you will possess them in a way that no one else can match, but you will have this governing faculty in the state in which you want to have it, that is, dirty and neglected.

CHAPTER VIII

To those who hastily assume the guise of the philosophers

NEVER bestow either praise or blame upon a man for the things which may be either good or bad,[2] nor

νίαν προσμαρτυρήσητε· καὶ ἅμα μὲν προπετείας
2 ἑαυτοὺς ἀπαλλάξετε, ἅμα δὲ κακοηθείας. " οὗτος
ταχέως λούεται." κακῶς οὖν ποιεῖ ; οὐ πάντως.
3 ἀλλὰ τί ; ταχέως λούεται.—Πάντα οὖν καλῶς
γίνεται ;—Οὐδαμῶς· ἀλλὰ τὰ μὲν ἀπὸ δογμάτων ὀρθῶν καλῶς, τὰ δ' ἀπὸ μοχθηρῶν μοχ-
θηρῶς. σὺ δὲ μέχρις ἂν καταμάθῃς τὸ δόγμα, ἀφ'
οὗ τις ποιεῖ ἕκαστα, μήτ' ἐπαίνει τὸ ἔργον μήτε
4 ψέγε. δόγμα δ' ἐκ τῶν ἐκτὸς οὐ ῥᾳδίως κρίνεται.
" οὗτος τέκτων ἐστίν." διὰ τί ; " χρῆται σκε-
πάρνῳ." τί οὖν τοῦτο ; " οὗτος μουσικός· ᾄδει
γάρ." καὶ τί τοῦτο ; " οὗτος φιλόσοφος." διὰ
5 τί ; " τρίβωνα γὰρ ἔχει καὶ κόμην." οἱ δ'
ἀγύρται τί ἔχουσιν ; διὰ τοῦτο, ἂν ἀσχημο-
νοῦντά τις ἴδῃ τινὰ αὐτῶν, εὐθὺς λέγει " ἰδοὺ
ὁ φιλόσοφος τί[1] ποιεῖ." ἔδει δ' ἀφ' ὧν ἠσχη-
μόνει μᾶλλον λέγειν αὐτὸν μὴ εἶναι φιλόσοφον.
6 εἰ μὲν γὰρ αὕτη ἐστὶν ἡ τοῦ φιλοσόφου πρόληψις καὶ ἐπαγγελία, ἔχειν τρίβωνα καὶ κόμην,
καλῶς ἂν ἔλεγον· εἰ δ' ἐκείνη μᾶλλον, ἀναμάρτητον εἶναι, διὰ τί οὐχὶ διὰ τὸ μὴ πληροῦν τὴν
ἐπαγγελίαν ἀφαιροῦνται αὐτὸν τῆς προσηγορίας ;
7 οὕτως γὰρ καὶ ἐπὶ τῶν ἄλλων τεχνῶν. ὅταν
ἴδῃ τις κακῶς πελεκῶντα, οὐ λέγει " τί ὄφελος
τεκτονικῆς ; ἰδοὺ οἱ τέκτονες οἷα ποιοῦσι κακά,"
ἀλλὰ πᾶν τοὐναντίον λέγει " οὗτος οὐκ ἔστι

---

[1] τί added by Reiske.

---

[1] That is, no conclusion about right or wrong can be drawn
from an action, in itself indifferent, the moral purpose of
which one does not know.

credit him with either skill or want of skill; and by
so doing you will escape from both rashness and
malice. "This man is hasty about bathing." Does
he, therefore, do wrong? Not at all. But what
is he doing? He is hasty about bathing.—Is all
well, then?—That by no means follows;[1] but
only the act which proceeds from correct judgements is well done, and that which proceeds
from bad judgements is badly done. Yet until you
learn the judgement from which a man performs
each separate act, neither praise his action nor blame
it. But a judgement is not readily determined by
externals. "This man is a carpenter." Why?
"He uses an adze." What, then, has that to do
with the case? "This man is a musician, for he
sings." And what has that to do with the case?
"This man is a philosopher." Why? "Because he
wears a rough cloak and long hair." And what do
hedge-priests wear? That is why, when a man sees
some one of them misbehaving, he immediately says,
"See what the philosopher is doing." But he ought
rather to have said, judging from the misbehaviour,
that the person in question was not a philosopher.
For if the prime conception and profession of the
philosopher is to wear a rough cloak and long hair,
their statement would be correct; but if it is rather
this, to be free from error, why do they not take
away from him the designation of philosopher,
because he does not fulfil the profession of one? For
that is the way men do in the case of the other arts.
When someone sees a fellow hewing clumsily with
an axe, he does not say, "What's the use of carpentry? See the bad work the carpenters do!" but
quite the contrary, he says, "This fellow is no

8 τέκτων, πελεκᾷ γὰρ κακῶς." ὁμοίως κἂν ᾄδοντός
τινος ἀκούσῃ κακῶς, οὐ λέγει "ἰδοὺ πῶς
ᾄδουσιν οἱ μουσικοί," ἀλλὰ μᾶλλον ὅτι¹ "οὗτος
9 οὐκ ἔστι μουσικός." ἐπὶ φιλοσοφίας δὲ μόνης
τοῦτο πάσχουσιν· ὅταν τινὰ ἴδωσι παρὰ τὸ
ἐπάγγελμα τὸ τοῦ φιλοσόφου ποιοῦντα, οὐχὶ
τῆς προσηγορίας ἀφαιροῦνται αὐτόν, ἀλλὰ
θέντες εἶναι φιλόσοφον, εἶτ᾽ ἀπ᾽ αὐτοῦ τοῦ
γινομένου λαβόντες, ὅτι ἀσχημονεῖ, ἐπάγουσι
μηδὲν ὄφελος εἶναι τοῦ φιλοσοφεῖν.

10 Τί οὖν τὸ αἴτιον; ὅτι τὴν μὲν τοῦ τέκτονος
πρόληψιν πρεσβεύομεν καὶ τὴν τοῦ μουσικοῦ
καὶ ὡσαύτως τῶν ἄλλων τεχνιτῶν, τὴν τοῦ
φιλοσόφου δ᾽ οὔ, ἀλλ᾽ ἅτε συγκεχυμένην καὶ
11 ἀδιάρθρωτον ἀπὸ τῶν ἐκτὸς μόνον κρίνομεν. καὶ
ποία ἄλλη τέχνη ἀπὸ σχήματος ἀναλαμβάνεται
καὶ κόμης, οὐχὶ δὲ καὶ θεωρήματα ἔχει καὶ ὕλην
12 καὶ τέλος; τίς οὖν ὕλη τοῦ φιλοσόφου; μὴ
τρίβων; οὔ, ἀλλὰ ὁ λόγος. τί τέλος; μή τι
φορεῖν τρίβωνα; οὔ, ἀλλὰ τὸ ὀρθὸν ἔχειν τὸν
λόγον. ποῖα θεωρήματα; μή τι τὰ περὶ τοῦ
πῶς πώγων μέγας γίνεται ἢ κόμη βαθεῖα;
ἀλλὰ μᾶλλον ἃ Ζήνων λέγει, γνῶναι τὰ τοῦ
λόγου στοιχεῖα, ποῖόν τι ἕκαστον αὐτῶν ἐστὶ
καὶ πῶς ἁρμόττεται πρὸς ἄλληλα καὶ ὅσα
13 τούτοις ἀκόλουθά ἐστιν. οὐ θέλεις οὖν ἰδεῖν
πρῶτον, εἰ πληροῖ τὴν ἐπαγγελίαν ἀσχημονῶν,

---

¹ s: οὗτος ὅτι S.

---

¹ The technical terminology of syllogistic reasoning is employed. Men "assume" or "lay down" (θέντες) the general
principle in the major premiss; "take" (λαβόντες) from

carpenter, for he hews clumsily with the axe." And, similarly, if a man hears somebody singing badly, he does not say, "See how the musicians sing!" but rather, "This fellow is no musician." But it is only in the case of philosophy that men behave like this; when they see somebody acting contrary to the profession of the philosopher, they do not take away from him the designation of philosopher, but, assuming that he is a philosopher, and then taking [1] from what goes on that he is misbehaving, they conclude that there is no good in being a philosopher.

What, then, is the reason for this? It is because we respect the prime conception of the carpenter, and the musician, and so also of all the other artisans and artists, while we do not respect that of the philosopher, but as if it were confused and inarticulate in our minds we judge of it only from externals. And what other art is there that is acquired by guise and hair-dress, and does not have also principles, and subject-matter, and end? What, then, is subject-matter for the philosopher? It is not a rough cloak, is it? No, but reason. What is end for the philosopher? It is not to wear a rough cloak, is it? No, but to keep his reason right. What is the nature of his principles? They do not have to do with the question how to grow a long beard, or a thick head of hair, do they? Nay, rather, as Zeno says, to understand the elements of reason, what the nature of each one is, and how they are fitted one to another, and all the consequences of these facts. Will you not, therefore, observe first of all whether the philosopher fulfils his profession by misbehaving,

observation or experience a fact as a minor premiss; and then "induce" or "conclude" (ἐπάγουσι).

379

καὶ οὕτως τῷ ἐπιτηδεύματι ἐγκαλεῖν; νῦν δ᾽,
αὐτὸς ὅταν σωφρονῇς, ἐξ ὧν ποιεῖν σοι δοκεῖ
κακῶς, λέγεις "ὅρα τὸν φιλόσοφον" (ὡς [1] πρέ-
ποντος λέγειν τὸν τὰ τοιαῦτα [2] ποιοῦντα φιλόσοφον) καὶ πάλιν "τοῦτο φιλόσοφός ἐστιν;" [3]
"ὅρα" δὲ "τὸν τέκτονα" οὐ λέγεις, ὅταν μοι-
χεύοντά τινα γνῷς ἢ λιχνεύοντα ἴδῃς, οὐδὲ
14 "ὅρα τὸν μουσικόν." οὕτως ἐπὶ ποσὸν [4] αἰσθάνῃ
καὶ αὐτὸς τῆς ἐπαγγελίας τοῦ φιλοσόφου, ἀπο-
λισθάνεις δὲ καὶ συγχέῃ ὑπὸ ἀμελετησίας.

15 Ἀλλὰ καὶ αὐτοὶ οἱ καλούμενοι φιλόσοφοι ἀπὸ
τῶν κοινῶν τὸ πρᾶγμα μετίασιν· εὐθὺς ἀναλαβόντες τρίβωνα καὶ πώγωνα καθέντες φασὶν
16 "ἐγὼ φιλόσοφός εἰμι." οὐδεὶς δ᾽ ἐρεῖ "ἐγὼ
μουσικός εἰμι," ἂν πλῆκτρον καὶ κιθάραν ἀγο-
ράσῃ, οὐδ᾽ "ἐγὼ χαλκεύς εἰμι," ἂν πιλίον καὶ
περίζωμα περιθῆται, ἀλλ᾽ ἁρμόζεται μὲν τὸ
σχῆμα πρὸς τὴν τέχνην, ἀπὸ τῆς τέχνης δὲ τὸ
ὄνομα, οὐκ ἀπὸ τοῦ σχήματος ἀναλαμβάνουσιν.
17 διὰ τοῦτο καλῶς Εὐφράτης ἔλεγεν ὅτι "ἐπὶ
πολὺ ἐπειρώμην λανθάνειν φιλοσοφῶν καὶ ἦν
μοι," φησίν, "τοῦτο ὠφέλιμον. πρῶτον μὲν γὰρ
ᾔδειν, ὅσα καλῶς ἐποίουν, ὅτι οὐ διὰ τοὺς θεατὰς
ἐποίουν, ἀλλὰ δι᾽ ἐμαυτόν· ἤσθιον ἐμαυτῷ
καλῶς, κατεσταλμένον εἶχον τὸ βλέμμα, τὸν

---

[1] οὐ after ὡς deleted by *Sb.*
[2] τοιαῦτα added by Schenkl (after Wolf).
[3] Elter's punctuation.

and then, if that be the case, blame his way of acting?
But as it is, when you yourself are behaving decently,
you say, on the basis of the evil that he seems to you
to be doing, "Look at the philosopher," just as
though it were proper to call a man who acts like
that a philosopher; and again, "Is that what a
philosopher is?" But you do not say, "Look at
the carpenter," when you know that a man is an
adulterer, or see a man eating greedily, nor do you
say, under similar circumstances, "Look at the
musician." Thus to a certain degree you too realize
what the philosopher's profession is, but you back-
slide and get confused through carelessness.

But even those who are styled philosophers pursue
their calling with means which are sometimes good and
sometimes bad. For example, when they have taken
a rough cloak and let their beards grow, they say,
"I am a philosopher." But nobody will say, "I am
a musician," if he buys a plectrum and a cithara;
nor, "I am a smith," if he puts on a felt cap and an
apron; but the guise is fitted to the art, and they
get their name from the art, but not from the guise.
That is why Euphrates[1] was right when he used to
say: "For a long time I tried not to let people
know that I was a philosopher, and this," he says,
"was useful to me. For, in the first place, I knew
that whatever I did well, I did so, not on account of
the spectators, but on my own account; it was for my
own sake that I ate well, and kept my countenance

---

[1] See on III. 15, 8, and compare for the uncertainty in
men's minds how to classify Euphrates, Apollonius of Tyana,
Epistles, 1.

---

18 περίπατον· πάντα ἐμαυτῷ καὶ θεῷ. εἶτα ὥσπερ
μόνος ἠγωνιζόμην, οὕτως μόνος καὶ ἐκινδύνευον·
οὐδὲν ἐμοὶ δράσαντι τὸ αἰσχρὸν ἢ ἀπρεπὲς τὸ
τῆς[1] φιλοσοφίας ἐκινδυνεύετο, οὐδ' ἔβλαπτον
19 τοὺς πολλοὺς ὡς φιλόσοφος ἁμαρτάνων. διὰ τοῦτο
οἱ μὴ εἰδότες μου τὴν ἐπιβολὴν ἐθαύμαζον, πῶς
πᾶσι φιλοσόφοις χρώμενος καὶ συζῶν αὐτὸς
20 οὐκ ἐφιλοσόφουν. καὶ τί κακόν, ἐν οἷς ἐποίουν
ἐπιγιγνώσκεσθαι τὸν φιλόσοφον, ἐν δὲ τοῖς
συμβόλοις μή;"

Βλέπε, πῶς ἐσθίω, πῶς πίνω, πῶς καθεύδω, πῶς
ἀνέχομαι, πῶς ἀπέχομαι, πῶς συνεργῶ, πῶς ὀρέξει χρῶμαι, πῶς ἐκκλίσει, πῶς τηρῶ τὰς σχέσεις
τὰς φυσικὰς ἢ ἐπιθέτους ἀσυγχύτως καὶ ἀπαρα-
21 ποδίστως· ἐκεῖθέν με κρῖνε, εἰ δύνασαι· εἰ δ'
οὕτως κωφὸς εἶ καὶ τυφλός, ἵνα μηδὲ τὸν
Ἥφαιστον ὑπολαμβάνῃς καλὸν χαλκέα, ἂν μὴ
τὸ πιλίον ἴδῃς περὶ τὴν κεφαλὴν περικείμενον,
τί κακὸν ὑφ' οὕτως ἠλιθίου κριτοῦ ἀγνοεῖσθαι;
22 Οὕτως ἐλάνθανε[2] παρὰ τοῖς πλείστοις Σωκράτης καὶ ἤρχοντο πρὸς αὐτὸν ἀξιοῦντες φιλο-
23 σόφοις συσταθῆναι. μή τι οὖν ἠγανάκτει ὡς
ἡμεῖς καὶ ἔλεγεν, "ἐγὼ δέ σοι οὐ φαίνομαι
φιλόσοφος;" ἀλλ' ἀπῆγεν καὶ συνίστα ἑνὶ
ἀρκούμενος τῷ εἶναι φιλόσοφος, χαίρων δὲ καὶ
ὅτι μὴ δοκῶν οὐκ ἐδάκνετο· ἐμέμνητο γὰρ τοῦ
24 ἰδίου ἔργου. τί ἔργον καλοῦ καὶ ἀγαθοῦ; μα-

---

[1] τῆς supplied by Reiske.
[2] Sb in margin : ἐλάνθα S.

---

[1] See note on III. 23, 21.

and gait composed; it was all for myself and for God.
And, secondly, as the contest was mine alone, so
also I alone ran the risks; in no respect through
me, if I did what was disgraceful or unseemly,
did the cause of philosophy come into danger, nor
did I do harm to the multitude by going wrong
as a philosopher. For that reason those who were
ignorant of my purpose wondered how it was that,
although I was familiar with all the philosophers and
lived with them, I was myself not acting in the rôle
of a philosopher. And what harm was there in
having the philosopher that I was, recognized by
what I did, rather than by the outward signs?"

See how I eat, how drink, how sleep, how endure,
how refrain, how help, how employ desire and how
aversion, how I observe my relationships, whether
they be natural or acquired, without confusion and
without hindrance; judge me on the basis of all this,
if you know how. But if you are so deaf and blind
as not to regard even Hephaestus as a good smith
unless you see the felt cap resting on his head, what
harm can come from passing unrecognized by a judge
so foolish?

In this way the great majority of men failed to
recognize Socrates, and so they used to come to him
and ask to be introduced to philosophers![1] Was
he, then, irritated as we are, and would he say,
"And don't *I* look like a philosopher to you?"
No, but he used to take them and introduce them,
and was satisfied with one thing, that is, *being* a
philosopher, and glad that he was not annoyed at
not being taken for one; for he habitually bore in
mind his own proper function. What is the function
of a good and excellent man? To have many

θητὰς πολλοὺς ἔχειν; οὐδαμῶς. ὄψονται οἱ
περὶ τοῦτο ἐσπουδακότες. ἀλλὰ θεωρήματα
δύσκολα ἀκριβοῦν; ὄψονται καὶ περὶ τούτων
25 ἄλλοι. ποῦ οὖν αὐτὸς καὶ ἦν τις καὶ εἶναι
ἤθελεν; ὅπου βλάβη καὶ ὠφέλεια. "εἴ μέ
τις," φησίν, "βλάψαι δύναται, ἐγὼ οὐδὲν ποιῶ·
εἰ ἄλλον περιμένω, ἵνα με ὠφελήσῃ, ἐγὼ οὐδέν
εἰμι. θέλω τι καὶ οὐ γίνεται· ἐγὼ ἀτυχής εἰμι."
26 εἰς τοσοῦτο σκάμμα προεκαλεῖτο πάντα ὀντι-
ναοῦν καὶ οὐκ ἄν μοι δοκεῖ ἐκστῆναι οὐδενί—
τί δοκεῖτε; καταγγέλλων καὶ λέγων "ἐγὼ τοιοῦ-
τός εἰμι"; μὴ γένοιτο, ἀλλὰ ὢν τοιοῦτος.
27 πάλιν γὰρ τοῦτο μωροῦ καὶ ἀλαζόνος "ἐγὼ
ἀπαθής εἰμι καὶ ἀτάραχος· μὴ ἀγνοεῖτε, ὦ
ἄνθρωποι, ὅτι ὑμῶν κυκωμένων[1] καὶ θορυβου-
μένων περὶ τὰ μηδενὸς ἄξια μόνος ἐγὼ ἀπήλ-
28 λαγμαι πάσης ταραχῆς." οὕτως οὐκ ἀρκεῖ σοι
τὸ μηδὲν ἀλγεῖν, ἂν μὴ κηρύσσῃς "συνέλθετε
πάντες οἱ ποδαγρῶντες, οἱ κεφαλαλγοῦντες, οἱ
πυρέσσοντες, οἱ χωλοί, οἱ τυφλοί, καὶ ἴδετέ με
29 ἀπὸ παντὸς πάθους ὑγιᾶ"; τοῦτο κενὸν καὶ
φορτικόν, εἰ μή τι ὡς ὁ Ἀσκληπιὸς εὐθὺς ὑποδεῖξαι δύνασαι, πῶς θεραπεύοντες αὖθις[2] ἔσονται
ἄνοσοι κἀκεῖνοι, καὶ εἰς τοῦτο φέρεις παράδειγμα τὴν ὑγίειαν τὴν σεαυτοῦ.
30 Τοιοῦτος γάρ τίς ἐστιν ὁ Κυνικὸς τοῦ σκήπτρου
καὶ διαδήματος ἠξιωμένος παρὰ τοῦ Διὸς καὶ

---

[1] Reiske: κοιμωμένων S.　　　　[2] Reiske: εὐθύς S.

---

[1] See note on IV. 6, 23.
[2] Strictly speaking, the loosened and smoothed earth on

pupils? Not at all. Those who have set their
hearts on it shall see to that.[1] Well, is it to set
forth difficult principles with great precision? Other
men shall see to these things also. In what field
was he, then, somebody, and wished so to be? In
the field where there was hurt and help. "If,"
says he, "a man can hurt me, what I am engaged
in amounts to nothing; if I wait for somebody else
to help me, I am myself nothing. If I want something and it does not happen, it follows that I am
miserable." This was the mighty ring[2] to which
he challenged every man whomsoever, and therein
he would not, I believe, have given way before anyone in—what do you suppose?—in proclaiming and
asserting "I am such and such a man"? Far from
it! but in *being* such and such a man. For, again,
it is the part of a fool and blowhard to say, "I am
tranquil and serene; be not ignorant, O men, that
while you are tossed about and are in turmoil over
worthless things, I alone am free from every perturbation." So is it not enough for you yourself to
feel no pain without proclaiming, "Come together,
all you who are suffering from gout, headaches, and
fever, the halt, and the blind, and see how sound
I am, and free from every disorder"? That is a
vain and vulgar thing to say, unless, like Asclepius,
you are able at once to show by what treatment
those others will also become well again, and for this
end are producing your own good health as an
example.

Such is the way of the Cynic who is deemed
worthy of the sceptre and diadem of Zeus, and

which wrestling matches were held, the ancient equivalent
of our ring.

λέγων " ἵν' ἴδητε, ὦ ἄνθρωποι, ὅτι τὴν εὐδαιμονίαν καὶ ἀταραξίαν οὐχ ὅπου ἐστὶ ζητεῖτε,
31 ἀλλ' ὅπου μή ἐστιν, ἰδοὺ ἐγὼ ὑμῖν παράδειγμα
ὑπὸ τοῦ θεοῦ ἀπέσταλμαι μήτε κτῆσιν ἔχων
μήτε οἶκον μήτε γυναῖκα μήτε τέκνα, ἀλλὰ μηδ'
ὑπόστρωμα μηδὲ χιτῶνα μηδὲ σκεῦος· καὶ ἴδετε,
πῶς ὑγιαίνω· πειράθητέ μου κἂν ἴδητε ἀτάραχον,
ἀκούσατε τὰ φάρμακα καὶ ὑφ' ὧν ἐθεραπεύθην."
32 τοῦτο γὰρ ἤδη καὶ φιλάνθρωπον καὶ γενναῖον.
ἀλλ' ὁρᾶτε, τίνος ἔργον ἐστίν· τοῦ Διὸς ἢ ὃν
ἂν ἐκεῖνος ἄξιον κρίνῃ ταύτης τῆς ὑπηρεσίας,
ἵνα μηδαμοῦ μηδὲν παραγυμνώσῃ πρὸς τοὺς
πολλούς, δι' οὗ τὴν μαρτυρίαν τὴν αὑτοῦ, ἣν
τῇ ἀρετῇ μαρτυρεῖ καὶ τῶν ἐκτὸς καταμαρτυρεῖ,
αὐτὸς ἄκυρον ποιήσῃ·

οὔτ' ὠχρήσαντα[1] χρόα κάλλιμον οὔτε παρειῶν
δάκρυ' ὀμορξάμενον.

33 καὶ οὐ μόνον ταῦτα, ἀλλ' οὐδὲ ποθοῦντά τι ἢ
ἐπιζητοῦντα, ἄνθρωπον ἢ τόπον ἢ διαγωγήν, ὡς
τὰ παιδία τὸν τρυγητὸν ἢ τὰς ἀργίας, αἰδοῖ
που ταχοῦ κεκοσμημένον, ὡς οἱ ἄλλοι τοίχοις
καὶ θύραις καὶ θυρωροῖς.
34 Νῦν δ' αὐτὸ μόνον κινηθέντες πρὸς φιλοσοφίαν,
ὡς οἱ κακοστόμαχοι πρός τι βρωμάτιον, ὃ μετὰ
μικρὸν σικχαίνειν μέλλουσιν, εὐθὺς ἐπὶ τὸ σκῆπτρον, ἐπὶ τὴν βασιλείαν. καθεῖλκε τὴν κόμην,
ἀνείληφε τρίβωνα, γυμνὸν δεικνύει τὸν ὦμον,
μάχεται τοῖς ἀπαντῶσιν κἂν ἐν φαινόλῃ τινὰ

---

[1] Bentley : χωρήσαντα S.

[1] Homer, *Odyssey*, XI. 529 f.

says, "That you may see yourselves, O men, to be looking for happiness and serenity, not where it is, but where it is not, behold, God has sent me to you as an example; I have neither property, nor house, nor wife, nor children, no, not even so much as a bed, or a shirt, or a piece of furniture, and yet you see how healthy I am. Make trial of me, and if you see that I am free from turmoil, hear my remedies and the treatment which cured me." For this, at length, is an attitude both humane and noble. But see whose work it is; the work of Zeus, or of him whom Zeus deems worthy of this service, to the end that he shall never lay bare to the multitudes anything whereby he shall himself invalidate the testimony which it is his to give in behalf of virtue, and against externals.

"Never there fell o'er his beauteous features a
    pallor, nor ever
Wiped he the tears from his cheeks." [1]

And not merely that, but he must neither yearn for anything, nor seek after it—be it human being, or place, or manner of life—like children seeking after the season of vintage, or holidays; he must be adorned on every side with self-respect, as all other men are with walls, and doors, and keepers of doors.

But, as it is, being merely moved towards philosophy, like dyspeptics who are moved to some paltry foods, which they are bound in a short while to loathe, immediately these men are off to the sceptre, to the kingdom. One of them lets his hair grow long, he takes up a rough cloak, he shows his bare shoulder, he quarrels with the people he meets, and if he sees somebody in an overcoat he quarrels

35 ἴδῃ, μάχεται αὐτῷ. ἄνθρωπε, χειμάσκησον
πρῶτον· ἰδοῦ σου τὴν ὁρμήν, μὴ κακοστομάχου
ἢ κισσώσης γυναικός ἐστιν. ἀγνοεῖσθαι μελέτη-

36 σον πρῶτον, τίς εἶ· σαυτῷ φιλοσόφησον ὀλίγον
χρόνον. οὕτως καρπὸς γίνεται· κατορυγῆναι δεῖ
εἰς¹ χρόνον τὸ σπέρμα, κρυφθῆναι, κατὰ μικρὸν
αὐξηθῆναι, ἵνα τελεσφορήσῃ. ἂν δὲ πρὸ τοῦ
γόνυ φῦσαι τὸν στάχυν ἐξενέγκῃ, ἀτελές ἐστιν,

37 ἐκ κήπου Ἀδωνιακοῦ. τοιοῦτον εἶ καὶ σὺ φυτά-
ριον· θᾶττον τοῦ δέοντος ἤνθηκας, ἀποκαύσει σε

38 ὁ χειμών. ἰδοῦ, τί λέγουσιν οἱ γεωργοὶ περὶ τῶν
σπερμάτων, ὅταν πρὸ ὥρας θερμασίαι γένωνται;
ἀγωνιῶσιν, μὴ ἐξυβρίσῃ τὰ σπέρματα, εἶτα αὐτὰ
πάγος εἰς λαβὼν ἐξελέγξῃ. ὅρα καὶ σύ, ἄνθρωπε·

39 ἐξύβρικας, ἐπιπεπήδηκας δοξαρίῳ πρὸ ὥρας.
δοκεῖς τις εἶναι, μωρὸς παρὰ μωροῖς· ἀποπαγήσῃ,
μᾶλλον δ' ἀποπέπηγας ἤδη ἐν τῇ ῥίζῃ κάτω, τὰ
δ' ἄνω σου μικρὸν ἔτι ἀνθεῖ καὶ διὰ τοῦτο δοκεῖς

40 ἔτι ζῆν καὶ θάλλειν. ἄφες ἡμᾶς γε κατὰ φύσιν
πεπανθῆναι. τί ἡμᾶς ἀποδύεις, τί βιάζῃ; οὔπω
δυνάμεθα ἐνεγκεῖν τὸν ἀέρα. ἔασον τὴν ῥίζαν

---

¹ εἰς added by Schenkl.

---

¹ Suggesting a very serious effort. See note on I. 2, 32.

² Early spring house-gardens in honour of Adonis, where
seeds were thickly planted in porous earthenware, sponges,
and the like, sprouting luxuriantly, and of course quickly
fading (cf. the reference to them in Isaiah, 1. 29: "Ye shall
be confounded for the gardens that ye have chosen.") The
expression became proverbial for incompleteness and early
fading.

³ This metaphor is so preposterous, for it is always the
extremities of plants which are the first to be frostbitten, and
not the protected roots, that one is inclined to ask if the text

with him. Man, take a winter's training first;[1] look at your own choice, for fear it is like that of a dyspeptic, or a woman with the strange cravings of pregnancy. Practise first not to let men know who you are; keep your philosophy to yourself a little while. That is the way fruit is produced : the seed has to be buried and hidden for a season, and be grown by slow degrees, in order that it may come to perfection. But if it heads out before it produces the jointed stock, it never matures, it is from a garden of Adonis.[2] That is the kind of plant you are too; you have blossomed prematurely, and the winter will blight you utterly. See what the farmers say about their seeds, when the hot weather comes before its proper time. They are in utmost anxiety lest the seeds should grow insolently lush, and then but a single frost should lay hold of them and expose their weakness. Man, do you also beware; you have grown insolently lush, you have leaped forward to occupy some petty reputation before its due time; you think yourself somebody, fool that you are among fools; you will be bitten by the frost, or rather, you have already been bitten by the frost, down at the root, while your upper part still blooms a little, and for that reason you seem to be still alive and flourishing.[3] Allow *us* at least to ripen as nature wishes. Why do you expose us to the elements, why force us? We are not yet able to stand the open air. Let the root grow, next

be sound. Clearly it is, since a whole series of corrections would have to be made in order to avoid the difficulty. Epictetus, a city dweller, probably knew little directly about the effects of frost on garden plants. The words "flower," "tree," and "herb" do not occur in his conversations at all, and even "plant" but rarely.—See note on IV. 11, 1.

αὐξηθῆναι, εἶτα γόνυ λαβεῖν τὸ πρῶτον, εἶτα τὸ
δεύτερον, εἶτα τὸ τρίτον· εἶθ' οὕτως ὁ καρπὸς
ἐκβιάσεται τὴν φύσιν, κἂν ἐγὼ μὴ θέλω.

41 Τίς γὰρ ἐγκύμων γενόμενος καὶ πλήρης τηλικούτων δογμάτων οὐχὶ αἰσθάνεταί τε τῆς αὑτοῦ
42 παρασκευῆς καὶ ἐπὶ τὰ κατάλληλα ἔργα ὁρμᾷ ;
ἀλλὰ ταῦρος μὲν οὐκ ἀγνοεῖ τὴν αὑτοῦ φύσιν καὶ
παρασκευήν, ὅταν ἐπιφανῇ τι θηρίον, οὐδ' ἀνα-
μένει τὸν προτρεψόμενον, οὐδὲ κύων, ὅταν ἴδῃ
43 τι τῶν ἀγρίων ζῴων· ἐγὼ δ' ἂν ἴσχω τὴν ἀνδρὸς
ἀγαθοῦ παρασκευήν, ἐκδέξομαι, ἵνα με σὺ παρα-
σκευάσῃς ἐπὶ τὰ οἰκεῖα ἔργα ; νῦν δ' οὔπω ἔχω,
πίστευσόν μοι. τί οὖν με πρὸ ὥρας ἀποξηρᾶναι
θέλεις, ὡς αὐτὸς ἐξηράνθης ;

θ'. Πρὸς τὸν εἰς ἀναισχυντίαν μεταβληθέντα.

1 Ὅταν ἄλλον ἴδῃς ἄρχοντα, ἀντίθες, ὅτι σὺ
ἔχεις τὸ μὴ δεῖσθαι ἀρχῆς· ὅταν ἄλλον πλου-
2 τοῦντα, ἰδοῦ τί ἀντὶ τούτου ἔχεις. εἰ μὲν γὰρ
μηδὲν ἔχεις ἀντ' αὐτοῦ, ἄθλιος εἶ· εἰ δ' ἔχεις
τὸ μὴ χρείαν ἔχειν πλούτου, γίγνωσκε, ὅτι πλεῖον
3 ἔχεις καὶ πολλῷ πλείονος ἄξιον. ἄλλος γυναῖκα
εὔμορφον, σὺ τὸ μὴ ἐπιθυμεῖν εὐμόρφου γυναικός.
μικρά σοι δοκεῖ ταῦτα ; καὶ πόσου ἂν τιμή-
σαιντο οὗτοι αὐτοὶ οἱ πλουτοῦντες καὶ ἄρχοντες
καὶ μετ' εὐμόρφων διαιτώμενοι δύνασθαι πλούτου
καταφρονεῖν καὶ ἀρχῶν καὶ αὐτῶν τούτων τῶν

let it acquire the first joint, and then the second, and then the third; and so finally the fruit will forcibly put forth its true nature, even against my will.

For who that has conceived and is big with such great judgements is not aware of his own equipment, and does not hasten to act in accordance with them? Why, a bull is not ignorant of his own nature and equipment, when some wild beast appears, nor does he hang back for someone to encourage him; neither does a dog, when he sees some wild animal; and shall I, if I have the equipment of a good man, hang back, so that you may encourage me to do what is my own proper work? But as yet I do not have the equipment, believe me. Why, then, do you wish to have me wither away before my time, as you yourself have withered?

CHAPTER IX

To the man who had become shameless

WHENEVER you see another person holding office, set over against this the fact that you possess the ability to get along without office; whenever you see another person wealthy, see what you have instead. For if you have nothing instead, you are wretched; but if you are capable of feeling no need of wealth, know that you are better off, and have something worth far more than wealth. Another has a comely wife, you the ability not to yearn for a comely wife. Is all this small in your eyes? Yet how much would these men give, who are rich and hold office, and live with beautiful women, to be able to despise wealth and offices, and these very same women whom they

4 γυναικῶν, ὧν ἐρῶσιν καὶ ὧν τυγχάνουσιν ; ἀγνοεῖς
οἷόν τί ἐστι δίψος πυρέσσοντος ; οὐδὲν ὅμοιον
ἔχει τῷ τοῦ ὑγιαίνοντος. ἐκεῖνος πιὼν ἀποπέ-
παυται· ὁ δὲ πρὸς ὀλίγον ἡσθεὶς [1] ναυτιᾷ, χολὴν
αὐτὸ ποιεῖ ἀντὶ ὕδατος, ἐμεῖ, στροφοῦται, διψῇ
5 σφοδρότερον. τοιοῦτόν ἐστι μετ' ἐπιθυμίας πλουτεῖν, μετ' ἐπιθυμίας ἄρχειν, μετ' ἐπιθυμίας καλῇ
συγκαθεύδειν· ζηλοτυπία πρόσεστιν, φόβος τοῦ
στερηθῆναι, αἰσχροὶ λόγοι, αἰσχρὰ ἐνθυμήματα,
ἔργα ἀσχήμονα.

6 Καὶ τί, φησίν, ἀπολλύω ;—Ἄνθρωπε, ὑπῆρχες
αἰδήμων καὶ νῦν οὐκέτι εἶ· οὐδὲν ἀπολώλεκας ;
ἀντὶ Χρυσίππου καὶ Ζήνωνος Ἀριστείδην ἀναγιγνώσκεις καὶ Εὐηνόν ; [2] οὐδὲν ἀπολώλεκας ;
ἀντὶ Σωκράτους καὶ Διογένους τεθαύμακας τὸν
πλεῖστας διαφθεῖραι καὶ ἀναπεῖσαι δυνάμενον.
7 καλὸς εἶναι θέλεις καὶ πλάσσεις σεαυτὸν μὴ ὢν
καὶ ἐσθῆτα ἐπιδεικνύειν θέλεις στιλπνήν, ἵνα τὰς
γυναῖκας ἐπιστρέφῃς, κἄν που μυραφίου ἐπι-
8 τύχῃς, μακάριος εἶναι δοκεῖς. πρότερον δ' οὐδὲ [3]
ἐνεθυμοῦ τι τούτων, ἀλλὰ ποῦ εὐσχήμων λόγος,
ἀνὴρ ἀξιόλογος, ἐνθύμημα γενναῖον. τοιγαροῦν
ἐκάθευδες ὡς ἀνήρ, προῄεις ὡς ἀνήρ, ἐσθῆτα
ἐφόρεις ἀνδρικήν, λόγους ἐλάλεις πρέποντας ἀνδρὶ

---

[1] Reiske : ἤσθετο S.   [2] See explanatory note.
[3] Wendland (and perhaps S originally) : οὐδέν Sc.

---

[1] Typical erotic writers, the former the author of the
celebrated *Milesian Tales*, the latter of an erotic work
admired by Menander. Yet compare, on the Evenus of this
passage, von Wilamowitz, *Hermes*, 11 (1876), 300, who conjectures Eubius (Εὔβιον), whom Ovid, *Tristia*, 2. 416, calls

passionately love and win? Do you not know what
kind of thing the thirst of a man in fever is? It
is quite unlike that of a man in health. The latter
drinks and his thirst is gone, but the other gets a
momentary satisfaction, and then becomes nauseated,
turns the water into bile, throws up, has a pain in
his bowels, and suffers more violent thirst than
before. A similar thing it is to be rich and have
strong desire, to hold office and have strong desire,
to sleep by the side of a beautiful woman and have
strong desire; jealousy is added to one's lot, fear
of loss, disgraceful words, disgraceful thoughts,
unseemly deeds.

And what do I lose? says somebody.—Man,
you used to be modest, and are no longer so;
have you lost nothing? Instead of Chrysippus and
Zeno you now read Aristeides and Evenus;[1] have
you lost nothing? Instead of Socrates and Diogenes
you have come to admire the man who is able to
corrupt and seduce the largest number of women.
You wish to be handsome and make yourself up,
though you are not handsome, and you wish to
make a show of gay attire, so as to attract the
women, and you think yourself blessed if perchance
you light upon some trivial perfume. But formerly
you used never even to think of any of these
things, but only where you might find decent
speech, a worthy man, a noble thought. Therefore
you used to sleep as a man, to go forth as a man, to
wear the clothes of a man, to utter the discourse that
was suitable for a good man; and after all that do

impurae conditor historiae, and mentions together with
Aristeides, as here. On the question see Crusius, *Real-
Encyclopädie*[2], 6, 850–51.

ἀγαθῷ· εἶτά μοι λέγεις "οὐδὲν ἀπώλεσα";

9 οὕτως οὐδὲν ἄλλο ἢ κέρμα ἀπολλύουσιν ἄνθρωποι; αἰδὼς οὐκ ἀπόλλυται, εὐσχημοσύνη οὐκ ἀπόλλυται; ἢ οὐκ ἔστι ζημιωθῆναι ταῦτα

10 ἀπολέσαντα; σοὶ μὲν οὖν δοκεῖ τάχα τούτων οὐδὲν οὐκέτι εἶναι ζημία· ἦν δέ ποτε χρόνος, ὅτε μόνην αὐτὴν ὑπελογίζου καὶ ζημίαν καὶ βλάβην, ὅτε ἠγωνίας, μή τις ἐκσείσῃ σε τούτων τῶν λόγων καὶ ἔργων.

11 Ἰδού, ἐκσέσεισαι ὑπ' ἄλλου μὲν οὐδενός, ὑπὸ σαυτοῦ δέ. μαχέσθητι σαυτῷ, ἀφελοῦ σαυτὸν

12 εἰς εὐσχημοσύνην, εἰς αἰδῶ, εἰς ἐλευθερίαν. εἴ σοί τίς που ἔλεγεν περὶ ἐμοῦ ταῦτα, ὅτι μέ τις μοιχεύειν ἀναγκάζει, ὅτι ἐσθῆτα φορεῖν τοιαύτην, ὅτι μυρίζεσθαι, οὐκ ἂν ἀπελθὼν αὐτόχειρ ἐγένου τούτου τοῦ ἀνθρώπου τοῦ οὕτως μοι παραχρω-

13 μένου; νῦν οὖν οὐ θέλεις σαυτῷ βοηθῆσαι; καὶ πόσῳ ῥάων αὕτη ἡ βοήθεια; οὐκ ἀποκτεῖναί τινα δεῖ, οὐ δῆσαι, οὐχ ὑβρίσαι, οὐκ εἰς ἀγορὰν προελθεῖν, ἀλλ' αὐτὸν αὑτῷ λαλῆσαι, τῷ μάλιστα πεισθησομένῳ, πρὸς ὃν οὐδείς ἐστί σου πιθανώ-

14 τερος. καὶ πρῶτον μὲν κατάγνωθι τῶν γιγνομένων, εἶτα καταγνοὺς μὴ ἀπογνῷς σεαυτοῦ μηδὲ πάθῃς τὸ τῶν ἀγεννῶν ἀνθρώπων, οἳ ἅπαξ ἐνδόντες εἰσάπαν ἐπέδωκαν ἑαυτοὺς καὶ ὡς ὑπὸ

15 ῥεύματος παρεσύρησαν, ἀλλὰ μάθε τὸ τῶν παιδοτριβῶν. πέπτωκε τὸ παιδίον· "ἀναστάς," φησίν,

16 "πάλιν πάλαιε, μέχρις ἂν ἰσχυροποιηθῇς." τοιοῦτόν τι καὶ σὺ πάθε· ἴσθι γάρ, ὅτι οὐδέν ἐστιν

you still say, "I have lost nothing"? And is it nothing but small change that men lose in this way? Is not self-respect lost, is not decency lost? Or is it impossible that the loss of these things counts for anything? To you, indeed, the loss of none of these things, perhaps, seems any longer serious; but there once was a time when you thought it the only serious loss and harm, when you were in great anxiety lest anyone should dislodge you from these good words and deeds.

Behold, you *have* been dislodged, though by no one else but yourself. Fight against yourself, vindicate yourself for decency, for respect, for freedom. If anyone ever told you about me that someone was forcing me to commit adultery, to wear clothes like yours, or to perfume myself, would you not have gone and murdered the man who was so maltreating me? And now, therefore, are you not willing to come to your own rescue? Yet how much easier is the work of rescue in the latter case! It is not necessary to kill somebody, put him in bonds, or assault him; you do not have to come out into the market-place, but only to talk to yourself, the man most likely to be persuaded, to whom no one is more persuasive than yourself. And first of all condemn what you are doing; then, when you have passed your condemnation, do not despair of yourself, nor act like the spiritless people who, when once they have given in, surrender themselves completely, and are swept off by the current, as it were, but learn how the gymnastic trainer of boys acts. The boy he is training is thrown; "get up," he says, "and wrestle again, till you get strong." React in some such way yourself, for I would have

εὐαγωγότερον ἀνθρωπίνης ψυχῆς. θελῆσαι δ ἴ
καὶ γέγονεν, διώρθωται· ὡς πάλιν ἀπονυστάσαι
καὶ ἀπόλωλεν. ἔσωθεν γάρ ἐστι καὶ ἀπώλεια
17 καὶ [1] βοήθεια. — Εἶτα τί μοι ἀγαθόν; — Καὶ τί
ζητεῖς τούτου μεῖζον; ἐξ ἀναισχύντου αἰδήμων
ἔσῃ, ἐξ ἀκόσμου κόσμιος, ἐξ ἀπίστου πιστός, ἐξ
18 ἀκολάστου σώφρων. εἴ τινα ἄλλα τούτων μείζονα
ζητεῖς, ποίει ἃ ποιεῖς· οὐδὲ θεῶν σέ τις ἔτι σῶσαι
δύναται.

ι΄. Τίνων δεῖ καταφρονεῖν καὶ πρὸς τίνα
διαφέρεσθαι;

1 Ἀπορία πᾶσα ἐν [2] τοῖς ἀνθρώποις περὶ τὰ
ἐκτὸς γίνεται, ἀμηχανία περὶ τὰ ἐκτός. "τί
ποιήσω; πῶς γένηται; πῶς ἀποβῇ; μὴ τόδε
2 ἀπαντήσῃ, μὴ τόδε." πᾶσαι αὗται αἱ φωναὶ
περὶ τὰ ἀπροαίρετα στρεφομένων εἰσίν· τίς γὰρ
λέγει "πῶς μὴ συγκατατιθῶμαι τῷ ψεύδει;
3 πῶς μὴ ἀπονεύσω ἀπὸ τοῦ ἀληθοῦς;"; ἐὰν οὕτως
ᾖ εὐφυής, ὥστε περὶ τούτων ἀγωνιᾶν, ὑπομνήσω
αὐτὸν ὅτι "τί ἀγωνιᾷς; ἐπὶ σοί ἐστιν· ἀσφαλὴς
ἴσθι· μὴ πρὸ τοῦ ἐπάγειν τὸν φυσικὸν κανόνα
προπήδα ἐν τῷ συγκατατίθεσθαι."

[1] Schegk, and Upton's "codex": ἤ S.
[2] Schenkl: πᾶσαν (apparently) S.

you know that there is nothing more easily prevailed upon than a human soul. You have but to
will a thing and it has happened, the reform has
been made ; as, on the other hand, you have but to
drop into a doze and all is lost. For it is within
you that both destruction and deliverance lie.—But
what good do I get after all that?—And what
greater good than this are you looking for? Instead
of shameless, you will be self-respecting ; instead of
faithless, faithful ; instead of dissolute, self-controlled. If you are looking for anything else greater
than these things, go ahead and do what you are
doing ; not even a god can any longer save you.

CHAPTER X

*What ought we to despise and on what place a high
value ?*

MEN find all their difficulties in externals, their
perplexities in externals. " What shall I do?
How is it to take place? How is it to turn
out? I am afraid that this will befall me, or
that." All these are the expressions of men who
concern themselves with the things that lie outside
the sphere of the moral purpose. For who says,
" How am I to avoid giving assent to the false?
How am I to refuse to swerve aside from the
true?"? If a man is so gifted by nature as to be
in great anxiety about these things, I shall remind
him, " Why are you in great anxiety? It is under
your own control ; rest secure. Do not be in a
hurry to give your assent before applying the rule of
nature."

4 Πάλιν ἂν περὶ ὀρέξεως ἀγωνιᾷ,[1] μὴ ἀτελὴς
5 γένηται καὶ ἀποτευκτική, περὶ ἐκκλίσεως, μὴ
περιπτωτική, πρῶτον μὲν αὐτὸν καταφιλήσω,
ὅτι ἀφεὶς περὶ ἃ οἱ ἄλλοι ἐπτόηνται καὶ τοὺς
ἐκείνων φόβους περὶ τῶν ἰδίων ἔργων πεφρόν-
6 τικεν, ὅπου αὐτός ἐστιν· εἶτα ἐρῶ αὐτῷ "εἰ μὴ
θέλῃς ὀρέγεσθαι ἀποτευκτικῶς μηδ' ἐκκλίνειν
περιπτωτικῶς, μηδενὸς ὀρέγου τῶν ἀλλοτρίων,
μηδὲν ἔκκλινε τῶν μὴ ἐπὶ σοί. εἰ δὲ μή, καὶ
7 ἀποτυχεῖν καὶ περιπεσεῖν ἀνάγκη." ποία ἐνθάδ'
ἀπορία; ποῦ τόπον ἔχει "πῶς γένηται;" καὶ
"πῶς ἀποβῇ;" καὶ "μὴ ἀπαντήσῃ τόδε ἢ
τόδε";
8 Νῦν οὐχὶ τὸ ἐκβησόμενον ἀπροαίρετον ;—Ναί.
—Ἡ δ' οὐσία τοῦ ἀγαθοῦ καὶ κακοῦ ἐστιν ἐν
τοῖς προαιρετικοῖς ;—Ναί.—Ἔξεστιν οὖν σοι
παντὶ τῷ ἀποβάντι χρῆσθαι κατὰ φύσιν ; μή τις
9 σε κωλῦσαι δύναται ;—Οὐδείς.—Μηκέτι οὖν μοι
λέγε "πῶς γένηται ;" ὅπως γὰρ ἂν γένηται, σὺ
αὐτὸ θήσεις καλῶς καὶ ἔσται σοι τὸ ἀποβὰν
10 εὐτύχημα. ἢ τίς ἂν ἦν ὁ Ἡρακλῆς λέγων "πῶς
μοι μὴ μέγας λέων ἐπιφανῇ μηδὲ μέγας σῦς μηδὲ
θηριώδεις ἄνθρωποι ;"; καὶ τί σοι μέλει ; ἂν
μέγας σῦς ἐπιφανῇ, μεῖζον ἆθλον ἀθλήσεις· ἂν
κακοὶ ἄνθρωποι, κακῶν ἀπαλλάξεις τὴν οἰκου-

---

[1] μή before this word was deleted by Meibom.

Again, if a man is in great anxiety about desire, for fear lest it become incomplete and miss its mark, or about aversion, for fear lest it fall into what it would avoid, I shall first give him a kiss of congratulation, because he has got rid of what the rest of mankind are excited about, and their fears, and has turned his serious thought to his own true business in the realm where he himself is. And after that I shall say to him, " If you do not wish to desire without failing to get, or to avoid without falling into the object of your aversion, desire none of those things which are not your own, and avoid none of those things which are not under your control. If not, you are of necessity bound to fail in achieving your desires, and to fall into what you would avoid." Where is there any difficulty in that case? What room is there to ask, " How is it to take place?" and " How is it to turn out?" and to say, " I am afraid that this will befall me, or that"?

Is not the future outside the sphere of the moral purpose now?—Yes.—And is not the true nature of the good and evil inside the sphere of the moral purpose?—Yes.—Are you permitted, then, to make a natural use of every outcome? No one can prevent you, can he?—No one.—Therefore, say no longer to me, " How is it to take place?" Because, whatever takes place, you will turn it to good purpose, and the outcome will be a blessing for you. Or what would Heracles have been had he said " How am I to prevent a great lion from appearing, or a great boar, or savage men?"? And what do you care for that? If a great boar appears, the struggle in which you are to engage will be greater; if evil men appear, you will clear the world of evil men.—

11 μένην.—Ἂν οὖν οὕτως ἀποθάνω;—Ἀγαθὸς ὢν
ἀποθάνῃ, γενναίαν πρᾶξιν ἐπιτελῶν. ἐπεὶ γὰρ
δεῖ πάντως ἀποθανεῖν, ἀνάγκη τί ποτε ποιοῦντα
εὑρεθῆναι, ἢ γεωργοῦντα ἢ σκάπτοντα ἢ ἐμπο-
ρευόμενον ἢ ὑπατεύοντα ἢ ἀπεπτοῦντα ἢ διαρ-
12 ροιζόμενον. τί οὖν θέλεις ποιῶν εὑρεθῆναι ὑπὸ
τοῦ θανάτου; ἐγὼ μὲν τὸ ἐμὸν μέρος ἔργον τί
ποτε ἀνθρωπικόν, εὐεργετικόν, κοινωφελές, γεν-
13 ναῖον. εἰ δὲ μὴ δύναμαι τὰ τηλικαῦτα ποιῶν
εὑρεθῆναι, ἐκεῖνό γε τὸ ἀκώλυτον, τὸ διδόμενον,
ἐμαυτὸν ἐπανορθῶν, ἐξεργαζόμενος τὴν δύναμιν
τὴν χρηστικὴν τῶν φαντασιῶν, ἀπάθειαν ἐκπο-
νῶν, ταῖς σχέσεσι τὰ οἰκεῖα ἀποδιδούς·[1] εἰ οὕτως
εὐτυχής εἰμι, καὶ τοῦ τρίτου τόπου παραπτόμενος,
τοῦ περὶ τὴν τῶν κριμάτων ἀσφάλειαν.

14 Ἂν μετὰ τούτων με ὁ θάνατος καταλάβῃ,
ἀρκεῖ μοι ἂν δύνωμαι πρὸς τὸν θεὸν ἀνατεῖναι
τὰς χεῖρας, εἰπεῖν ὅτι "ἃς ἔλαβον ἀφορμὰς παρὰ
σοῦ πρὸς τὸ αἰσθέσθαι σου τῆς διοικήσεως καὶ
ἀκολουθῆσαι αὐτῇ, τούτων οὐκ ἠμέλησα· οὐ
15 κατήσχυνά σε τὸ ἐμὸν μέρος. ἰδού, πῶς κέχρη-
μαι ταῖς αἰσθήσεσιν, ἰδού, πῶς ταῖς προλήψεσιν.
μή ποτέ σε ἐμεμψάμην, μή τι τῶν γινομένων τινὶ
δυσηρέστησα ἢ ἄλλως γενέσθαι ἠθέλησα, μή τι

---

1 Reiske: ἀποδιδοῦν S.

---

[1] See III. 2, 1, and note.
[2] These imaginary last words of Epictetus have given much
offence to Elizabeth Carter (author of the most famous
of the English translations), and no doubt others, who find
them ostentatious and lacking in humility. They represent,
however, an ideal and not an actual condition, and as such are
entirely innocent. Epictetus, who was in fact the most humble

But if I die in so doing?—You will die as a good man, bringing to fulfilment a noble action. Why, since you have to die in any event, you must be found doing something or other—farming, or digging, or engaged in commerce, or holding a consulship, or suffering with dyspepsia or dysentery. What is it, then, you wish to be doing when death finds you? I for my part should wish it to be some work that befits a man, something beneficent, that promotes the common welfare, or is noble. But if I cannot be found doing such great things as these, I should like at least to be engaged upon that which is free from hindrance, that which is given me to to do, and that is, correcting myself, as I strive to perfect the faculty which deals with the external impressions, labouring to achieve calm, while yet giving to each of my human relationships its due; and, if I am so fortunate, striving to attain to the third field of study,[1] that which has to do with security in the formation of judgements.

If death finds me occupied with these matters, it is enough for me if I can lift up my hands unto God, and say,[2] "The faculties which I received from Thee to enable me to understand Thy governance and to follow it, these I have not neglected; I have not dishonoured Thee as far as in me lay. Behold how I have dealt with my senses, behold how I have dealt with my preconceptions. Have I ever blamed Thee? Have I been discontented with any of these things which happen, or wished it to have been otherwise? Have I at all violated my

of men (see Vol. I. pp. xviii–xx), does not say, "It is enough for me *because* I can lift up my hands unto God, and say," but, "*if* I can," which is a very different matter.

16 τὰς σχέσεις παρέβην;[1] χάριν ἔχω,[2] ὅ με σὺ
ἐγέννησας, χάριν ἔχω, ὧν ἔδωκας· ἐφ' ὅσον ἐχρησάμην τοῖς σοῖς, ἀρκεῖ μοι. πάλιν αὐτὰ ἀπόλαβε
καὶ κατάταξον εἰς ἣν θέλεις χώραν· σὰ γὰρ ἦν
17 πάντα, σύ μοι αὐτὰ δέδωκας." οὐκ ἀρκεῖ οὕτως
ἔχοντα ἐξελθεῖν; καὶ τίς βίων κρείττων ἢ εὐσχη-
μονέστερος τοῦ οὕτως ἔχοντος, ποία δὲ κατα-
στροφὴ εὐδαιμονεστέρα;

18 "Ἵνα δὲ ταῦτα γένηται, οὐ μικρὰ δέξασθαι
οὐδὲ μικρῶν ἀποτυχεῖν. οὐ δύνασαι καὶ ὑπατεῦσαι θέλειν καὶ ταῦτα καὶ ἀγροὺς ἔχειν ἐσπου-
δακέναι καὶ ταῦτα καὶ τῶν δουλαρίων φροντίζειν
19 καὶ σεαυτοῦ. ἀλλ' ἄν τι τῶν ἀλλοτρίων θέλῃς,
τὰ σὰ ἀπώλετο. αὕτη τοῦ πράγματος ἡ φύσις·
20 προῖκα οὐδὲν γίνεται. καὶ τί θαυμαστόν; ἂν
ὑπατεῦσαι θέλῃς, ἀγρυπνῆσαί σε δεῖ, περιδραμεῖν,
τὰς χεῖρας καταφιλῆσαι, πρὸς ταῖς ἀλλοτρίαις
θύραις κατασαπῆναι, πολλὰ μὲν εἰπεῖν, πολλὰ δὲ
πρᾶξαι ἀνελεύθερα, δῶρα πέμψαι πολλοῖς, ξένια
καθ' ἡμέραν ἐνίοις· καὶ τί τὸ γινόμενόν ἐστιν;
21 δώδεκα δεσμὰ ῥάβδων καὶ τρὶς ἢ τετράκις ἐπὶ
βῆμα καθίσαι καὶ κιρκήσια δοῦναι καὶ σπυρίσιν
δειπνίσαι.[3] ἢ δειξάτω μοί τις, τί ἐστὶ παρὰ
22 ταῦτα. ὑπὲρ ἀπαθείας οὖν, ὑπὲρ ἀταραξίας,
ὑπὲρ τοῦ καθεύδοντα καθεύδειν, ἐγρηγορότα
ἐγρηγορέναι, μὴ φοβεῖσθαι μηδέν, μὴ ἀγωνιᾶν

---

[1] Schweighäuser : παρεβῆναι S.
[2] χάοιν ἔχω here added by Reiske.
[3] Reiske : δειπνῆσαι S.

---

[1] The consular fasces.
[2] The *sportulae* which were distributed at Rome by a
patron among his clients.

relationships with others? For that Thou didst beget me I am grateful; for what Thou hast given I am grateful also. The length of time for which I have had the use of Thy gifts is enough for me. Take them back again and assign them to what place Thou wilt, for they were all Thine, and Thou gavest them me." Is it not enough for a man to take his departure from the world in this state of mind? And what among all the kinds of life is superior to this, or more seemly than his who is so minded, and what kind of end is more fortunate?

But that this may take place a man must accept no small troubles, and must miss no small things. You cannot wish for a consulship and at the same time wish for this; you cannot have set your heart upon having lands and this too; you cannot at the same time be solicitous for your paltry slaves and yourself too. But if you wish for any one of the things that are not your own, what is your own is lost. This is the nature of the matter: Nothing is done except for a price. And why be surprised? If you wish to be consul you must keep vigils, run around, kiss men's hands, rot away at other men's doors, say and do many slavish things, send presents to many persons, and guest-gifts to some people every day. And what is the outcome of it all? Twelve bundles of rods,[1] and the privilege of sitting three or four times on the tribune, and giving games in the Circus, and lunches in little baskets.[2] Or else let someone show me what there is in it beyond this. For calm, then, for peace of mind, for sleeping when you are asleep, and being awake when you are awake, for fearing nothing, for being in great

ὑπὲρ μηδενὸς οὐδὲν ἀναλῶσαι θέλεις, οὐδὲν
23 πονῆσαι; ἀλλ' ἄν τι ἀπόληταί σου περὶ ταῦτα
γινομένου ἢ ἀναλωθῇ κακῶς ἢ ἄλλος τύχῃ ὢν
ἔδει σε τυχεῖν, εὐθὺς [1] δηχθήσῃ ἐπὶ τῷ γενομένῳ;
24 οὐκ ἀντιθήσεις, τί ἀντὶ τίνος λαμβάνεις, πόσον
ἀντὶ πόσου; ἀλλὰ προῖκα θέλεις τὰ τηλικαῦτα
λαβεῖν; καὶ πῶς δύνασαι; ἔργον ἔργῳ.

25   Οὐ δύνασαι καὶ τὰ ἐκτὸς ἔχειν ἐπιμελείας
τετυχηκότα καὶ τὸ σαυτοῦ ἡγεμονικόν. εἰ δ'
ἐκεῖνα θέλεις, τοῦτο ἄφες· εἰ δὲ μή, οὔτε τοῦτο
ἕξεις οὔτ' ἐκεῖνα, περισπώμενος ἐπ' ἀμφότερα.
26 εἰ τοῦτο θέλεις, ἐκεῖνά σε ἀφεῖναι δεῖ. ἐκχε-
θήσεται τὸ ἔλαιον, ἀπολεῖται τὰ σκευάρια, ἀλλ'
ἐγὼ ἀπαθὴς ἔσομαι. ἐμπρησμὸς ἔσται ἐμοῦ μὴ
παρόντος καὶ ἀπολεῖται τὰ βιβλία, ἀλλ' ἐγὼ
χρήσομαι ταῖς φαντασίαις κατὰ φύσιν. ἀλλ'
27 οὐχ ἕξω φαγεῖν. εἰ οὕτως τάλας εἰμί, λιμὴν τὸ
ἀποθανεῖν. οὗτος δ' ἐστὶν ὁ λιμὴν πάντων, ὁ
θάνατος, αὕτη ἡ καταφυγή. διὰ τοῦτο οὐδὲν τῶν
ἐν τῷ βίῳ χαλεπόν ἐστιν. ὅταν θέλῃς, ἐξῆλθες
28 καὶ οὐ καπνίζῃ. τί οὖν ἀγωνιᾷς, τί ἀγρυπνεῖς;
οὐχὶ δὲ εὐθὺς ἀναλογισάμενος, ποῦ σου τὸ ἀγαθόν
ἐστι καὶ τὸ κακόν, λέγεις ὅτι " ἐπ' ἐμοὶ ἀμφότερα·
οὔτε τούτου τις ἀφελέσθαι με δύναται οὔτ' ἐκείνῳ
29 ἄκοντα περιβαλεῖν. τί οὖν οὐ ῥέγχω βαλών;

---

[1] μή after εὐθύς is deleted in S.

[1] Supply: "has no partnership." See IV. 6, 30, where
the proverb is given in full.
[2] The reference is to suicide. Cf. I. 25, 18 and 20.

anxiety about nothing, are you unwilling to spend anything, to make any exertion? But if something that belongs to you be lost while you are engaged in these affairs, or be spent to no purpose, or someone else get what you ought to have got, are you going to be vexed immediately at what has happened? Will you not balance off what you are getting in return for what, how much in return for how much? Nay, do you wish to get such valuable things for nothing? And how can you? " One serious business with another." [1]

You cannot be continually giving attention to both externals and your own governing principle. But if you want the former, let the latter go; otherwise you will have neither the latter nor the former, being drawn in both directions. If you want the latter, you must let the former go. The oil will be spilled, my paltry furniture will perish, but I shall be calm. There will be a fire when I am not at home, and my books will perish, yet I shall deal with my external impressions according to nature. But I shall have nothing to eat. If I am so badly off as all that, death is my harbour. And this is the harbour of all men, even death, and this their refuge. That is why no one of the things that befall us in our life is difficult. Whenever you wish, you walk out of the house, and are no longer bothered by the smoke. [2] Why, then, are you consumed with anxiety? Why do you keep vigils? And why do you not forthwith reckon up where your good and your evil lie, and say, " They are both under my control; no man can either rob me of the one, or plunge me in the other against my will? Why, then, do I not throw myself down and

τὰ ἐμὰ ἀσφαλῶς ἔχει· τὰ ἀλλότρια ὄψεται αὐτὰ
ὃς ἂν φέρῃ, ὡς ἂν διδῶται παρὰ τοῦ ἔχοντος
30 ἐξουσίαν. τίς εἰμὶ ὁ θέλων αὐτὰ οὕτως ἔχειν ἢ
οὕτως ; μὴ γάρ μοι δέδοται ἐκλογὴ αὐτῶν ; μὴ
γὰρ ἐμέ τις αὐτῶν διοικητὴν πεποίηκεν ; ἀρκεῖ
μοι ὧν ἔχω ἐξουσίαν. ταῦτά με δεῖ κάλλιστα
παρασκευάσαι, τὰ δ' ἄλλα ὡς ἂν θέλῃ ὁ ἐκείνων
κύριος."

31   Ταῦτά τις ἔχων πρὸ ὀφθαλμῶν ἀγρυπνεῖ, καὶ
στρέφεται ἔνθα καὶ ἔνθα ; τί θέλων ἢ τί ποθῶν ;
Πάτροκλον ἢ Ἀντίλοχον ἢ Πρωτεσίλαον ;[1] πότε
γὰρ ἡγήσατο ἀθάνατόν τινα τῶν φίλων ; πότε
γὰρ οὐκ εἶχεν πρὸ ὀφθαλμῶν, ὅτι αὔριον ἢ εἰς
32 τρίτην δεῖ ἢ αὐτὸν ἀποθανεῖν ἢ ἐκεῖνον ; " ναί,"
φησίν, " ἀλλ' ᾤμην, ὅτι ἐκεῖνος ἐπιβιώσεταί μοι
καὶ αὐξήσει μου τὸν υἱόν." μωρὸς γὰρ ἦς καὶ τὰ
ἄδηλα ᾤου. τί οὖν οὐκ ἐγκαλεῖς σεαυτῷ, ἀλλὰ
33 κλαίων κάθησαι ὡς τὰ κοράσια ; " ἀλλ' ἐκεῖνός
μοι φαγεῖν παρετίθει." ἔζη γάρ, μωρέ· νῦν δ' οὐ
δύναται. ἀλλ' Αὐτομέδων σοι παραθήσει· ἂν δὲ
34 καὶ Αὐτομέδων ἀποθάνῃ, ἄλλον εὑρήσεις. ἂν δ'

---

[1] Oldfather : Μενέλαον S. See explanatory note.

[1] Homer, *Iliad*, XXIV. 5, referring to Achilles on his bed
when mourning for Patroclus.

[2] Patroclus and Antilochus were well-known friends of
Achilles, but "Menelaus" (the reading of S) must be wrong,
partly because he was not in any way a special friend, and
particularly because he was not killed, as the context requires. Some other friend of the hero, who was killed, must
be supplied, and that can hardly be anyone but Protesilaus,
who was one of his playmates under the tutelage of Cheiron.
Philostratus, *Her.* 176 K. Achilles leaped on shore im-

snore? What is mine is safe. What is not mine
shall be the concern of whoever gets it, according
to the terms upon which it may be given by Him
who has authority over it. Who am I to wish that
what is not mine should be either thus or so? For
it has not been given me to make a choice among
these things, has it? For no one has made me an
administrator of them, has he? I am satisfied with
the things over which I have authority. These I
ought to treat so that they may become as beautiful
as possible, but everything else as their master may
desire."

Does any man who has all this before his eyes
keep vigils, and does he "toss hither and thither"?[1]
What does he wish, or what does he yearn for?
For Patroclus, or Antilochus, or Protesilaus?[2] Why,
when did he regard any of his friends as immortal?
Yes, and when did he not have before his eyes the
fact that on the morrow or the day after either
he or his friend must die?[3] "Yes," he says, "but
I had thought he was going to survive me, and
bring up my son." No doubt, but then you were
a fool, and were thinking of things that were un-
certainties. Why, then, do you not blame yourself, instead of sitting and crying like little girls?
"Nay, but he used to set my food before me."
Yes, fool, for then he was alive; and now he cannot.
But Automedon[4] will set your food before you, and
if Automedon too die, you will find somebody else.

mediately after Protesilaus and avenged his death. See
Escher in the *Real-Encyclopädie*[2], I. 229, 9 ff.

[3] A kind of proverbial expression. Compare Marcus
Aurelius, 4. 47.

[4] Comrade and charioteer of both Patroclus and Achilles.

ἡ χύτρα, ἐν ᾗ ἥψετό σοι τὸ κρέας, καταγῇ, λιμῷ
σε δεῖ ἀποθανεῖν, ὅτι μὴ ἔχεις τὴν συνήθη
χύτραν; οὐ πέμπεις καὶ ἄλλην καινὴν ἀγο-
ράζεις;

35   οὐ μὲν γάρ τι,

φησίν,

κακώτερον ἄλλο πάθοιμι.

τοῦτο γάρ σοι κακόν ἐστιν; εἶτ' ἀφεὶς τοῦτο
ἐξελεῖν αἰτιᾷ τὴν μητέρα, ὅτι σοι οὐ προεῖπεν, ἵν'
ὀδυνώμενος ἐξ ἐκείνου διατελῇς;

36   Τί δοκεῖτε; μὴ ἐπίτηδες ταῦτα συνθεῖναι Ὅμη-
ρον, ἵν' ἴδωμεν, ὅτι οἱ εὐγενέστατοι, οἱ [1] ἰσχυρότα-
τοι, οἱ πλουσιώτατοι, οἱ [1] εὐμορφότατοι, ὅταν
οἷα δεῖ δόγματα μὴ ἔχωσιν, οὐδὲν κωλύονται
ἀθλιώτατοι εἶναι καὶ δυστυχέστατοι;

ια'. Περὶ καθαριότητος.

1   Ἀμφισβητοῦσί τινες, εἰ ἐν τῇ φύσει τοῦ
ἀνθρώπου περιέχεται τὸ κοινωνικόν· ὅμως δ'
αὐτοὶ οὗτοι οὐκ ἄν μοι δοκοῦσιν ἀμφισβητῆσαι,
ὅτι τό γε [2] καθάριον πάντως περιέχεται καὶ εἴ
2 τινι ἄλλῳ καὶ τούτῳ τῶν ζῴων χωρίζεται. ὅταν
οὖν ἄλλο τι ζῷον ἴδωμεν ἀποκαθαῖρον ἑαυτό,
ἐπιλέγειν εἰώθαμεν θαυμάζοντες ὅτι "ὡς ἄνθρω-

---

[1] οἱ added by s.   [2] τό γε Wolf : ποτέ S.

---

[1] Homer, *Iliad*, XIX. 321.
[2] The generalization is somewhat hasty. Many animals,
like cats (and the felidae in general), moles, most birds,
snakes, etc., are distinctly more cleanly than any but the

If the pot in which your meat used to be boiled gets broken, do you have to die of hunger because you do not have your accustomed pot? Won't you send out and buy a new one to take its place? He says,

> Ill no greater than this could befall me.[1]

Why, is this what you call an ill? And then, forbearing to get rid of it, do you blame your mother, because she did not foretell it to you, so that you might continue to lament from that time forth?

What do you men think? Did not Homer compose this in order for us to see that there is nothing to prevent the persons of highest birth, of greatest strength, of most handsome appearance, from being most miserable and wretched, when they do not hold the right kind of judgements?

CHAPTER XI

Of cleanliness

Some people raise the question whether the social instinct is a necessary element in the nature of man; nevertheless, even these people, as it seems to me, would not question that the instinct of cleanliness is most assuredly a necessary element, and that man is distinguished from the animals by this quality if by anything.[2] When, therefore, we see some other animal cleaning itself, we are in the habit of saying in surprise that it is acting "like a human

most civilized men. Epictetus was clearly not strong in natural history. Cf. notes on II. 24, 16; IV. 8, 39; IV. 11, 32, and *Ench.* 33, 16.

πος." καὶ πάλιν ἄν τις ἐγκαλῇ τινὶ ζῴῳ, εὐθὺς
εἰώθαμεν ὥσπερ ἀπολογούμενοι λέγειν ὅτι " οὐ
3 δήπου ἄνθρωπός ἐστιν." οὕτως ἐξαίρετόν τι
περὶ τὸν ἄνθρωπον εἶναι οἰόμεθα ἀπὸ τῶν θεῶν
αὐτὸ πρῶτον λαμβάνοντες. ἐπεὶ γὰρ ἐκεῖνοι
φύσει καθαροὶ καὶ ἀκήρατοι, ἐφ' ὅσον ἠγγίκασιν
αὐτοῖς οἱ ἄνθρωποι κατὰ τὸν λόγον, ἐπὶ τοσοῦτον
καὶ τοῦ καθαροῦ καὶ τοῦ καθαρίου εἰσὶν ἀνθεκτι-
4 κοί. ἐπεὶ δ' ἀμήχανον τὴν οὐσίαν αὐτῶν παντάπασιν εἶναι καθαρὰν ἐκ τοιαύτης ὕλης κεκρα-
μένην, ὁ λόγος παραληφθεὶς εἰς τὸ ἐνδεχόμενον
ταύτην καθάριον ἀποτελεῖν πειρᾶται.

5 Ἡ[1] πρώτη οὖν καὶ ἀνωτάτω καθαρότης ἡ ἐν
ψυχῇ γενομένη καὶ ὁμοίως ἀκαθαρσία. ψυχῆς
δ' ὡς σώματος μὲν ἀκαθαρσίαν οὐκ ἂν εὕροις,[2] ὡς
ψυχῆς δὲ τί ἂν ἄλλο εὕροις ἢ τὸ παρέχον αὐτὴν
6 ῥυπαρὰν πρὸς τὰ ἔργα τὰ αὐτῆς; ἔργα δὲ ψυχῆς
ὁρμᾶν, ἀφορμᾶν, ὀρέγεσθαι, ἐκκλίνειν, παρασκευάζεσθαι, ἐπιβάλλεσθαι, συγκατατίθεσθαι.
7 τί ποτ' οὖν ἐστι τὸ ἐν τούτοις τοῖς ἔργοις ῥυπαρὸν
παρέχον αὐτὴν καὶ ἀκάθαρτον; οὐδὲν ἄλλο ἢ τὰ
8 μοχθηρὰ κρίματα αὐτῆς. ὥστε ψυχῆς μὲν ἀκαθαρσία δόγματα πονηρά, κάθαρσις δ' ἐμποίησις
οἵων δεῖ δογμάτων. καθαρὰ δ' ἡ ἔχουσα οἷα δεῖ
δόγματα· μόνη γὰρ αὕτη ἐν τοῖς ἔργοις τοῖς
αὑτῆς ἀσύγχυτος καὶ ἀμόλυντος.
9 Δεῖ δέ τι ἐοικὸς τούτῳ καὶ ἐπὶ σώματος φιλο-

---

[1] ἡ added by Upton.   [2] Upton's "codex": εὕρηις S.

---

[1] Our idiom requires us to use both "clean" and "pure,"
and their derivatives, for what in the Greek is expressed
by a single word.

being." And again, if one finds fault with some beast, we are in the habit of saying immediately, as though in apology, "Well, of course it isn't a human being." So true it is that we consider cleanliness to be a special characteristic of man, deriving it in the first instance from the gods. For since they are by nature pure [1] and undefiled, in so far as men have approached them by virtue of reason, just so far are they attached to purity and cleanliness. But since it is impossible for the nature of men to be altogether pure, seeing that it is composed of such material as it is, the reason which they have received from the gods endeavours to render this material clean as far as is possible.

Therefore, the prime and highest purity is that which appears in the soul, and the same is true of impurity. But you would not find the same impurity in a soul as you would in a body, and as being soul, what else would you find impure about it than that which makes it dirty for the performance of its own functions? And the functions of a soul are the exercise of choice, of refusal, of desire, of aversion, of preparation, of purpose, and of assent. What, then, can that be which makes the soul dirty and unclean in these functions? Nothing but its erroneous decisions. It follows, therefore, that impurity of a soul consists of bad judgements, and purification consists in creating within it the proper kind of judgements; and a pure soul is the one which has the proper kind of judgements, for this is the only soul which is secure against confusion and pollution in its own functions.

Now one ought to be eager to achieve, as far

τεχνεῖν κατὰ τὸ ἐνδεχόμενον. ἀμήχανον ἦν
μύξας μὴ ῥεῖν τοῦ ἀνθρώπου τοιοῦτον ἔχοντος τὸ
σύγκραμα· διὰ τοῦτο χεῖρας ἐποίησεν ἡ φύσις
καὶ αὐτὰς τὰς ῥῖνας ὡς σωλῆνας πρὸς τὸ ἐκδι-
δόναι τὰ ὑγρά. ἂν οὖν ἀναρροφῇ τις αὐτάς, λέγω
10 ὅτι οὐ ποιεῖ ἔργον ἀνθρωπικόν. ἀμήχανον ἦν μὴ
πηλοῦσθαι τοὺς πόδας μηδὲ ὅλως μολύνεσθαι διὰ
τοιούτων τινῶν πορευομένους· διὰ τοῦτο ὕδωρ
11 παρεσκεύασεν, διὰ τοῦτο χεῖρας. ἀμήχανον ἦν
ἀπὸ τοῦ τρώγειν μὴ ῥυπαρόν τι προσμένειν τοῖς
ὀδοῦσι· διὰ τοῦτο "πλῦνον," φησίν, "τοὺς
ὀδόντας." διὰ τί; ἵν' ἄνθρωπος ᾖς καὶ μὴ θηρίον
12 μηδὲ συΐδιον. ἀμήχανον μὴ ἀπὸ τοῦ ἱδρῶτος καὶ
τῆς κατὰ τὴν ἐσθῆτα συνοχῆς ὑπολείπεσθαί τι
περὶ τὸ σῶμα ῥυπαρὸν καὶ δεόμενον ἀποκαθάρ-
σεως· διὰ τοῦτο ὕδωρ, ἔλαιον, χεῖρες, ὀθόνιον,
ξύστρα, νίτρον, ἔσθ' ὅθ' ἡ ἄλλη πᾶσα παρασκευὴ
13 πρὸς τὸ καθῆραι αὐτό. οὔ· ἀλλ' ὁ μὲν χαλκεὺς[1]
ἐξιώσει τὸ σιδήριον καὶ ὄργανα πρὸς τοῦτο ἕξει
κατεσκευασμένα, καὶ τὸ πινάκιον αὐτὸς σὺ πλυνεῖς, ὅταν μέλλῃς ἐσθίειν, ἐὰν μὴ ᾖς παντελῶς
ἀκάθαρτος καὶ ῥυπαρός· τὸ σωμάτιον δ' οὐ
πλυνεῖς[2] οὐδὲ καθαρὸν ποιήσεις ;—Διὰ τί ;
14 φησίν.—Πάλιν ἐρῶ σοι· πρῶτον μὲν ἵνα τὰ
ἀνθρώπου ποιῇς, εἶτα ἵνα μὴ ἀνιᾷς τοὺς ἐν-

---

[1] The words ὡς χαλκεύς following this word in S have
been deleted in the MS.
[2] C. Schenkl : πλύνεις S.

---

[1] A sort of scraper, generally of metal, much used by
athletes.
[2] The excesses, probably Oriental in origin, to which
Christian asceticism soon went in regard to despising clean-

as may be, something similar to this in the case of the body also. It was impossible that there should be no discharge of mucus from the nose, since man's body has been composed as it is; for that reason nature made hands, and the nostrils like tubes to discharge the humours. If, therefore, a man snuffs back these discharges of mucus, I say that he is not acting as a human being should. It was impossible that the feet should not get muddy, nor dirty at all, when they pass through certain such substances; for that reason nature has provided water, for that hands. It was impossible that some impurity from eating should not remain on the teeth; for that reason nature says, "Wash your teeth." Why? In order that you may be a human being, and not a beast or a pig. It was impossible that something dirty and needing to be cleaned off should not be left on the person from our sweat and the pressure of our clothes; for that reason we have water, oil, hands, a towel, a strigil,[1] nitre, and, on occasion, every other kind of equipment to cleanse the body. Not so you.[2] But the smith will remove the rust from his iron tool, and will have implements made for this purpose, and you yourself will wash your plate when you are going to eat, unless you are utterly unclean and dirty; but will you not wash nor make clean your poor body?—Why? says someone.—Again I will tell you: First, so as to do what befits a man; and second, so as not to offend those

liness, seem to have begun to manifest themselves already in the early second century among enthusiastic young Stoics and would-be Cynics. It is interesting to see how Epictetus, simple and austere as he was, vigorously maintained the validity of older Greek and Roman feeling in this regard.

15 τυγχάνοντας. τοιοῦτόν τι καὶ ἐνθάδε ποιεῖς καὶ
οὐκ αἰσθάνῃ. σαυτὸν ἄξιον ἡγῇ τοῦ ὄζειν· ἔστω,
ἴσθι ἄξιος. μή τι καὶ τοὺς παρακαθίζοντας, μή
τι καὶ τοὺς συγκατακλινομένους, μή τι καὶ τοὺς
16 καταφιλοῦντας; ἵα¹ ἄπελθ' εἰς ἐρημίαν πού
ποτε, ἧς ἄξιος εἶ, καὶ μόνος δίαγε κατόζων σεαυτοῦ.
δίκαιον γάρ ἐστι τῆς σῆς ἀκαθαρσίας σὲ μόνον
ἀπολαύειν. ἐν πόλει δ' ὄντα οὕτως ἀπερισκέπτως
καὶ ἀγνωμόνως ἀναστρέφεσθαι τίνος σοι φαίνεται ;
17 εἰ δ' ἵππον σοι πεπιστεύκει ἡ φύσις, περιεώρας
αὐτὸν καὶ ἀτημέλητον ; καὶ νῦν οἴου σου τὸ
σῶμα ὡς ἵππον ἐγκεχειρίσθαι· πλῦνον αὐτό,
ἀπόσμηξον, ποίησον, ἵνα σε μηδεὶς ἀποστρέφηται,
18 μηδεὶς ἐκτρέπηται. τίς δ' οὐκ ἐκτρέπεται ῥυπαρὸν ἄνθρωπον, ὄζοντα, κακόχρουν μᾶλλον ἢ τὸν
κεκοπρωμένον ; ἐκείνη ἡ ὀσμὴ ἔξωθέν ἐστιν
ἐπίθετος, ἡ δ' ἐξ ἀθεραπευσίας ἔσωθεν καὶ οἱονεὶ
διασεσηπότος.

19 Ἀλλὰ Σωκράτης ὀλιγάκις ἐλούετο.—Ἀλλὰ
ἔστιλβεν² αὐτοῦ τὸ σῶμα, ἀλλ' ἦν οὕτως
ἐπίχαρι καὶ ἡδύ, ὥστ' ἤρων αὐτοῦ οἱ ὡραιότατοι
καὶ εὐγενέστατοι καὶ ἐπεθύμουν ἐκείνῳ παρα-
κατακλίνεσθαι μᾶλλον ἢ τοῖς εὐμορφοτάτοις.
ἐξῆν ἐκείνῳ μήτε λούεσθαι μήτε πλύνεσθαι, εἰ

¹ Schenkl : ἤ S.

whom you meet. You are doing something of the
sort even here, and do not realize it. You think
that you are worthy of the smell.[1] Very well, *be*
worthy of it. Do you think, though, that those who
sit by your side, those who recline beside you, those
who kiss you, are worthy of it too?[2] Bah, go away
into a wilderness somewhere or other, a place worthy
of you, and live alone, smelling of yourself! For it
is only right that you should enjoy your uncleanliness
all by yourself. But since you are living in a city,
what kind of character do you fancy you are exhibiting, to behave so thoughtlessly and inconsiderately?
If nature had committed to your care a horse, would
you have utterly neglected it? And now I would
have you think that your body has been entrusted
to you like a horse; wash it, rub it down, make it
so that nobody will turn his back on you or move
aside. But who does not avoid a dirty fellow that
smells and has an unsightly skin, even more than a
man bespattered with dung? In this latter case
the smell is external and acquired, in the other it
comes from slovenliness that is internal, and is
characteristic of one who has grown rotten through
and through.

But Socrates bathed infrequently,[3] says someone.—
Why, his body was radiant; why, it was so attractive
and sweet that the handsomest and most high-born
were in love with him, and yearned to sit by his
side rather than beside those who had the prettiest

---

[1] That is, so good that his smell makes no real difference.
[2] That is, bad enough to deserve such treatment (ἄξιος
meaning both "good enough" and "bad enough").
[3] Plato, *Symposium*, 174 A.

---

[2] *Sb* in margin: ἔστι μέν *S*.

ἤθελεν· καίτοι καὶ τὸ ὀλιγάκις ἰσχὺν εἶχεν.[1]—

20 Ἀλλὰ λέγει Ἀριστοφάνης

τοὺς ὠχριῶντας, τοὺς ἀνυποδήτους λέγω.—

Λέγει γὰρ καὶ ἀεροβατεῖν αὐτὸν καὶ ἐκ τῆς
21 παλαίστρας κλέπτειν τὰ ἱμάτια. ἐπεί τοι πάντες
οἱ γεγραφότες περὶ Σωκράτους πάντα τἀναντία
αὐτῷ προσμαρτυροῦσιν, ὅτι ἡδὺς οὐ μόνον ἀκοῦσαι,
ἀλλὰ καὶ ἰδεῖν ἦν. πάλιν περὶ Διογένους ταῦτα
22 γράφουσι. δεῖ γὰρ μηδὲ κατὰ τὴν ἀπὸ τοῦ
σώματος ἔμφασιν ἀπὸ φιλοσοφίας ἀποσοβεῖν
τοὺς πολλούς, ἀλλ' ὥσπερ τὰ ἄλλα εὔθυμον καὶ
ἀτάραχον ἐπιδεικνύειν αὐτὸν οὕτως καὶ ἀπὸ τοῦ
23 σώματος. "ἴδετε, ὦ ἄνθρωποι, ὅτι οὐδὲν ἔχω,
οὐδενὸς δέομαι· ἴδετε πῶς ἄοικος ὢν καὶ ἄπολις
καὶ φυγάς, ἂν οὕτως τύχῃ, καὶ ἀνέστιος πάντων
τῶν εὐπατριδῶν καὶ πλουσίων ἀταραχώτερον
διάγω καὶ εὐρούστερον. ἀλλὰ καὶ τὸ σωμάτιον[2]
ὁρᾶτε ὅτι οὐ κακοῦται ὑπὸ τῆς αὐστηρᾶς διαίτης."
24 ἂν δέ μοι ταῦτα λέγῃ τις ἀνθρώπου σχῆμα
καταδίκου ἔχων καὶ πρόσωπον, τίς με πείσει θεῶν
προσελθεῖν φιλοσοφίᾳ, εἴ γε[3] τοιούτους ποιεῖ;
μὴ γένοιτο· οὐδ', εἰ σοφὸς ἔμελλον εἶναι, ἤθελον.

[1] The words κἂν θερμῷ μὴ θέλῃς, ψυχρῷ, here, I have transferred to § 32, where, as Schweighäuser saw, they clearly
belong.
[2] Wolf : ἱμάτιον S.
[3] εἴ γε Reiske, after Schegk : ὥστε S.

---

[1] Ibid., 217-18.
[2] λούεσθαι is properly of "bathing," as in the public
baths, especially, in this passage, the warm baths of Roman
times, which are clearly in mind ; πλύνεσθαι is properly of
cleaning clothes, as in a laundry, which was generally done

forms and features.[1] He might have neither bathed
nor washed,[2] had he so desired; yet even his infrequent
bathings were effective.— But Aristophanes says,

> The pallid men I mean, who shoeless go.[3]—

Oh, yes, but then he says also that Socrates " trod the
air," and stole people's clothes from the wrestling
school.[4] And yet all who have written about Socrates
unite in bearing testimony to the precise opposite
of this ; that he was not merely pleasant to hear, but
also to see.   Again, men write the same thing about
Diogenes.   For a man ought not to drive away the
multitude from philosophy, even by the appearance
of his body, but as in everything else, so also on the
side of the body, he ought to show himself cheerful
and free from perturbation.   " See, O men, that I
have nothing, and *need* nothing.   See how, although
I am without a house, and without a city, and an
exile, if it so chance, and without a hearth, I still
live a life more tranquil and serene than that of all
the noble and the rich.   Yes, and you see that even
my paltry body is not disfigured by my hard way of
living."   But if I am told this by a person who has
the bearing and face of a condemned man, what one
of all the gods shall persuade me to approach
philosophy, if she makes people like that ?   Far be
it from me ! I shouldn't be willing to do so, not
even if it would make me a wise man.

in ancient Greece, as in modern, and in the Orient, with cold
water.   All that is meant, as far as Socrates is concerned,
is that he generally washed at home in cold water, and very
seldom used public baths or hot baths.

[3] *Clouds*, 103, slightly modified.

[4] *Ibid.*, 179 and 225.   The argument is that the evidence
of Aristophanes is worthless anyway, because he also made
these two preposterously false statements about Socrates.

25 Ἐγὼ μὲν νὴ τοὺς θεοὺς τὸν νέον τὸν πρώτως κινούμενον θέλω μᾶλλον ἐλθεῖν πρός με πεπλασμένον τὴν κόμην ἢ¹ κατεφθινηκότα καὶ ῥυπαρόν. βλέπεται γάρ τις ἐν ἐκείνῳ τοῦ καλοῦ φαντασία, ἔφεσις δὲ τοῦ εὐσχήμονος. ὅπου δ' αὐτὸ εἶναι
26 φαντάζεται, ἐκεῖ καὶ φιλοτεχνεῖ. λοιπὸν ὑποδεῖξαι μόνον αὐτῷ δεῖ καὶ εἰπεῖν "νεανίσκε, τὸ καλὸν ζητεῖς καὶ εὖ ποιεῖς. ἴσθι οὖν, ὅτι ἐκεῖ φύεται, ὅπου τὸν λόγον ἔχεις· ἐκεῖ αὐτὸ ζήτει, ὅπου τὰς ὁρμὰς καὶ τὰς ἀφορμάς, ὅπου τὰς
27 ὀρέξεις, τὰς ἐκκλίσεις. τοῦτο γὰρ ἔχεις ἐν σεαυτῷ ἐξαίρετον, τὸ σωμάτιον δὲ φύσει πηλός ἐστιν. τί πονεῖς εἰκῇ περὶ αὐτό; εἰ μηδὲν
28 ἕτερον, τῷ χρόνῳ γνώσῃ, ὅτι οὐδέν ἐστιν." ἂν δέ μοι ἔλθῃ κεκοπρωμένος, ῥυπαρός, μύστακα ἔχων μέχρι τῶν γονάτων, τί αὐτῷ εἰπεῖν ἔχω, ἀπὸ ποίας αὐτὸν ὁμοιότητος ἐπαγαγεῖν; περὶ τί γὰρ
29 ἐσπούδακεν ὅμοιον τῷ καλῷ, ἵν' αὐτὸν μεταθῶ καὶ εἴπω "οὐκ ἔστιν ἐνθάδε τὸ καλόν, ἀλλ' ἐνθάδε"; θέλεις αὐτῷ λέγω "οὐκ ἔστιν ἐν τῷ κεκοπρῶσθαι τὸ καλόν, ἀλλ' ἐν τῷ λόγῳ"; ἐφίεται γὰρ τοῦ καλοῦ; ἔμφασιν γάρ τινα αὐτοῦ ἔχει; ἄπελθε καὶ χοίρῳ διαλέγου, ἵν' ἐν βορβόρῳ
30 μὴ κυλίηται. διὰ τοῦτο καὶ Πολέμωνος ἥψαντο οἱ λόγοι οἱ Ξενοκράτους ὡς φιλοκάλου νεανίσκου· εἰσῆλθεν γὰρ ἔχων ἐναύσματα τῆς περὶ τὸ καλὸν σπουδῆς, ἀλλαχοῦ δ' αὐτὸ ζητῶν.

¹ ἤ added by Schenkl.

---

¹ See III. 1, 14, and note.
² Much as Suetonius so admirably says of Nero (c. 55): *Erat illi aeternitatis perpetuaeque famae cupido, sed inconsulta.*

As for me, by the gods, I should rather have the young man who was experiencing the first stirrings towards philosophy come to me with his hair carefully dressed, than with it in a state of desperate neglect and dirty. For the first case shows that there exists in the young man a sort of imaging of beauty, and an aiming at comeliness, and where he fancies it to be, there also he devotes his efforts. With that as a starting-point, all that it is necessary to do is to show him the way, and say, "Young man, you are seeking the beautiful, and you do well. Know, then, that it arises in that part of you where you have your reason; seek it there where you have your choices and your refusals, where you have your desires and your aversions. For this part is something of a special kind which you have within you, but your paltry body is by nature only clay. Why do you toil for it to no purpose? If you learn nothing else, time at least will teach you that it is nothing." But if he comes to me bespattered with dung, dirty, his moustache reaching down to his knees, what have I to say to him, from what point of resemblance can I start so as to prevail upon him? For what is there to which he is devoted, that bears any resemblance to the beautiful, so that I may turn him about and say, "Beauty is not there, but here"? Do you want me to say to him, "Beauty does not consist in being bespattered with dung, but in reason"? For is he aiming at beauty? Has he any manifestation of it? Go and talk to a pig, that he may wallow no more in mud! That is why the words of Xenocrates laid hold even of a Polemo,[1] because he was a young man who loved beauty. For he came to Xenocrates with glimmerings of a zeal for the beautiful, but was looking for it in the wrong place.[2]

31 Ἐπεί τοι οὐδὲ τὰ ζῷα τὰ ἀνθρώποις σύντροφα
ῥυπαρὰ ἐποίησεν ἡ φύσις. μή τι ἵππος κυλίεται
ἐν βορβόρῳ, μή τι κύων γενναῖος ; ἀλλ' ὁ ὗς καὶ
τὰ σαπρὰ χηνίδια¹ καὶ σκώληκες καὶ ἀράχναι,
τὰ μακροτάτω τῆς ἀνθρωπίνης συναναστροφῆς
32 ἀπεληλασμένα. σὺ οὖν ἄνθρωπος ὢν οὐδὲ ζῷον
εἶναι θέλεις τῶν ἀνθρώποις συντρόφων, ἀλλὰ
σκώληξ μᾶλλον ἢ ἀράχνιον ; οὐ λούσῃ πού ποτε
ὡς θέλεις, οὐκ ἀποπλυνεῖς σεαυτόν, κἂν θερμῷ
μὴ θέλῃς, ψυχρῷ ;² οὐχ ἥξεις καθαρός, ἵνα σοι
χαίρωσιν οἱ συνόντες ; ἀλλὰ καὶ εἰς τὰ ἱερὰ
ἡμῖν συνέρχῃ τοιοῦτος, ὅπου πτῦσαι οὐ νενό-
μισται οὐδ' ἀπομύξασθαι, ὅλος ὢν πτύσμα καὶ
μύξα ;

33 Τί οὖν ; καλλωπίζεσθαί τις ἀξιοῖ ; μὴ γένοιτο,
εἰ μὴ ἐκεῖνο ὃ πεφύκαμεν, τὸν λόγον, τὰ δόγματα,
τὰς ἐνεργείας, τὸ δὲ σῶμα μέχρι τοῦ καθαρίου,
34 μέχρι τοῦ μὴ προσκόπτειν. ἀλλ' ἂν ἀκούσῃς,
ὅτι οὐ δεῖ φορεῖν κόκκινα, ἀπελθὼν κόπρωσόν
σου τὸν τρίβωνα ἢ κατάρρηξον.—Ἀλλὰ πόθεν
ἔχω καλὸν τρίβωνα ;—Ἄνθρωπε, ὕδωρ ἔχεις,
35 πλῦνον αὐτόν. ἰδοὺ νέος ἀξιέραστος, ἰδοὺ πρεσ-
βύτης ἄξιος τοῦ ἐρᾶν καὶ ἀντερᾶσθαι, ᾧ τις υἱὸν
αὑτοῦ παραδώσει παιδευθησόμενον,³ ᾧ θυγατέρες,

---

¹ Sb : ἡνίδια S.
² These last five words, which appear in § 19, actually
belong here, as Schweighäuser saw.
³ παρᾳδώσει Kronenberg ; παιδευθησόμενον Schenkl : παρα-
δοθησόμενον S.

---

¹ Of course a spider is not ordinarily a dirty animal in its
personal habits ; the most that can be said is that it is
frequently found in quiet and hence dusty spots. Cf. note
on § 1.

Why, look you, nature has not made dirty even the animals which associate with man. A horse doesn't roll around in the mud, does he? or a highly bred dog? No, but the hog, and the miserable rotten geese, and worms, and spiders, the creatures farthest removed from association with human beings. Do you, then, who are a human being, wish to be not even an animal of the kind that associates with men, but rather a worm, or a spider?[1] Will you not take a bath somewhere, some time, in any form you please? Will you not wash yourself? If you don't care to bathe in hot water, then use cold. Will you not come to us clean, that your companions may be glad? What, and do you in such a state go with us even into the temples, where it is forbidden by custom to spit or blow the nose, yourself being nothing but a mass of spit and drivel?

Well, what then? Is anyone demanding that you beautify yourself? Heaven forbid! except you beautify that which is our true nature[2]—the reason, its judgements, its activities; but your body only so far as to keep it cleanly, only so far as to avoid giving offence. But if you hear that one ought not to wear scarlet, go bespatter your rough cloak with dung—or tear it to pieces![3] Yet where am I to get a rough cloak that looks well?—Man, you have water, wash it! See, here is a lovable young man, here an elderly man worthy to love and to be loved in return, to whom a person will entrust the education of his son, to whom daughters and young men will come, if it

[2] *i.e.* a man really *is* not body, which he has in common with other animals, but mind, reason, or moral purpose. Cf. such passages as I. 1. 23; III. 1, 25–6; 13, 17; IV. 5, 12 and 23; 7, 31 f.; and § 27 above.

[3] That is, the young man carries the precept to extremes, the command being ironical.

ᾧ νέοι προσελεύσονται, ἂν οὕτως τύχῃ, ἵνα ἐν
36 κοπρῶνι λέγῃ τὰς σχολάς. μὴ γένοιτο. πᾶσα
ἐκτροπὴ ἀπό τινος ἀνθρωπικοῦ γίνεται, αὕτη
ἐγγύς ἐστι τῷ μὴ ἀνθρωπικὴ εἶναι.

ιβʹ. Περὶ προσοχῆς.

1 Ὅταν ἀφῇς[1] πρὸς ὀλίγον τὴν προσοχήν, μὴ
τοῦτο φαντάζου, ὅτι, ὁπόταν θέλῃς, ἀναλήψῃ
αὐτήν, ἀλλ᾽ ἐκεῖνο πρόχειρον ἔστω σοι, ὅτι παρὰ
τὸ σήμερον ἁμαρτηθὲν εἰς τἆλλα χεῖρον ἀνάγκη
2 σοι τὰ πράγματα ἔχειν. πρῶτον μὲν γὰρ τὸ πάντων χαλεπώτατον ἔθος τοῦ μὴ προσέχειν ἐγγίνε-
ται, εἶτα ἔθος τοῦ ἀναβάλλεσθαι τὴν προσοχήν·
ἀεὶ δ᾽ εἰς ἄλλον καὶ ἄλλον χρόνον εἴωθας ὑπερτίθεσθαι[2] τὸ εὐροεῖν, τὸ εὐσχημονεῖν, τὸ κατὰ
3 φύσιν ἔχειν καὶ διεξάγειν. εἰ μὲν οὖν λυσιτελὴς
ἡ ὑπέρθεσίς ἐστιν, ἡ παντελὴς ἀπόστασις αὐτῆς
ἐστι λυσιτελεστέρα· εἰ δ᾽ οὐ λυσιτελεῖ, τί οὐχὶ
διηνεκῆ τὴν προσοχὴν φυλάσσεις; "σήμερον
4 παῖξαι θέλω." τί οὖν κωλύει[3] προσέχοντα;
"ᾆσαι." τί οὖν κωλύει προσέχοντα; μὴ γὰρ
ἐξαιρεῖταί τι μέρος τοῦ βίου, ἐφ᾽ ὃ οὐ διατείνει
τὸ προσέχειν; χεῖρον γὰρ αὐτὸ προσέχων ποιήσεις, βέλτιον δὲ μὴ προσέχων; καὶ τί ἄλλο τῶν
5 ἐν τῷ βίῳ κρεῖσσον ὑπὸ τῶν μὴ προσεχόντων
γίνεται; ὁ τέκτων μὴ προσέχων τεκταίνει

---

[1] Kronenberg (after *Sb* and *s*): φησί *S*.
[2] Schenkl: ἴ*ωθι (or ἴ*ωθας) ὑπερτιθέμενος *S*.
[3] κωλύει added by C. Schenkl.

so chance—all for the purpose of having him deliver his lectures sitting on a dunghill? Good Lord, no! Every eccentricity arises from some human trait, but this trait comes close to being non-human.

CHAPTER XII

Of attention

WHEN you relax your attention for a little while, do not imagine that whenever you choose you will recover it, but bear this in mind, that because of the mistake which you have made to-day, your condition must necessarily be worse as regards everything else. For, to begin with—and this is the worst of all—a habit of not paying attention is developed; and after that a habit of deferring attention; and always you grow accustomed to putting off from one time to another tranquil and appropriate living, the life in accordance with nature, and persistence in that life. Now if the postponement of such matters is profitable, it is still more profitable to abandon them altogether; but if it is not profitable, why do you not maintain your attention continuously? "To-day I want to play." What is to prevent your playing, then,—but with attention? "I want to sing." What is to prevent your singing, then,—but with attention? There is no part of the activities of your life excepted, to which attention does not extend, is there? What, will you do it worse by attention, and better by inattention? And yet what other thing, of all that go to make up our life, is done better by those who are inattentive? Does the inattentive carpenter do his work more accur-

ἀκριβέστερον ; ὁ κυβερνήτης μὴ προσέχων [1]
κυβερνᾷ ἀσφαλέστερον ; ἄλλο δέ τι τῶν μικρο-
6 τέρων ἔργων ὑπὸ ἀπροσεξίας ἐπιτελεῖται κρεῖσσον ; οὐκ αἰσθάνῃ, ὅτι, ἐπειδὰν ἀφῇς τὴν γνώμην,
οὐκ ἔτι ἐπὶ σοί ἐστιν ἀνακαλέσασθαι αὐτήν, οὐκ
ἐπὶ τὸ εὔσχημον, οὐκ ἐπὶ τὸ αἰδῆμον, οὐκ ἐπὶ τὸ
κατεσταλμένον ; ἀλλὰ πᾶν τὸ ἐπελθὸν ποιεῖς,
ταῖς προθυμίαις ἐπακολουθεῖς.

7 Τίσιν οὖν δεῖ με προσέχειν ;—Πρῶτον μὲν
ἐκείνοις τοῖς καθολικοῖς καὶ ἐκεῖνα πρόχειρα
ἔχειν καὶ χωρὶς ἐκείνων μὴ καθεύδειν, μὴ ἀνίσ-
τασθαι, μὴ πίνειν, μὴ ἐσθίειν, μὴ συμβάλλειν
ἀνθρώποις· ὅτι προαιρέσεως ἀλλοτρίας κύριος
οὐδείς, ἐν ταύτῃ δὲ μόνῃ τἀγαθὸν καὶ κακόν.
8 οὐδεὶς οὖν κύριος οὔτ' ἀγαθόν μοι περιποιῆσαι
οὔτε κακῷ με περιβαλεῖν, ἀλλ' ἐγὼ αὐτὸς ἐμαυτοῦ
9 κατὰ ταῦτα ἐξουσίαν ἔχω μόνος. ὅταν οὖν
ταῦτα ἀσφαλῆ μοι ᾖ, τί ἔχω περὶ τὰ ἐκτὸς
ταράσσεσθαι ; ποῖος τύραννος φοβερός, ποία
νόσος, ποία πενία, ποῖον πρόσκρουσμα ;—Ἀλλ'
10 οὐκ ἤρεσα τῷ δεῖνι.—Μὴ οὖν ἐκεῖνος ἐμόν ἐστιν
ἔργον, μή τι ἐμὸν κρίμα ;—Οὔ.—Τί οὖν ἔτι μοι
μέλει ;—Ἀλλὰ δοκεῖ τις εἶναι.—Ὄψεται αὐτὸς
11 καὶ οἷς δοκεῖ, ἐγὼ δ' ἔχω, τίνι με δεῖ ἀρέσκειν,
τίνι ὑποτετάχθαι, τίνι πείθεσθαι· τῷ θεῷ καὶ
12 μετ' ἐκεῖνον ἐμοί.[2] ἐμὲ ἐκεῖνος συνέστησεν ἐμαυτῷ
καὶ τὴν ἐμὴν προαίρεσιν ὑπέταξεν ἐμοὶ μόνῳ δοὺς
κανόνας εἰς χρῆσιν αὐτῆς τὴν ὀρθήν, οἷς ὅταν

---

[1] These last six words are added, to fill an obvious lacuna,
in Upton's "codex." Something like them is certainly
needed.

[2] ἐμοί supplied by Diels.

ately? The inattentive helmsman steer more safely?
And is there any other of the lesser functions of life
which is done better by inattention? Do you not
realize that when once you let your mind go
wandering, it is no longer within your power to
recall it, to bring it to bear upon either seemliness,
or self-respect, or moderation? But you do anything that comes into your head, you follow your
inclinations.

What are the things, then, to which I ought to
pay attention?—First, these general principles, and
you ought to have them at your command, and
without them neither go to sleep, nor rise up, nor
drink, nor eat, nor mingle with men; I mean the
following: No man is master of another's moral
purpose; and: In its sphere alone are to be found
one's good and evil. It follows, therefore, that no
one has power either to procure me good, or to
involve me in evil, but I myself alone have authority
over myself in these matters. Accordingly, when
these things are secure for me, what excuse have I
for being disturbed about things external? What
kind of tyrant inspires fear, what kind of disease, or
poverty, or obstacle?—But I have not pleased So-
and-so.—He is not my function, is he? He is not
my judgement, is he?—No.—Why, then, do I care
any longer?—But he has the reputation of being
somebody.—He and those who think so highly of
him will have to see to that, but I have one whom
I must please, to whom I must submit, whom I
must obey, that is, God, and after Him, myself.
God has commended me to myself, and He has
subjected to me alone my moral purpose, giving me
standards for the correct use of it; and when I follow

κατακολουθήσω, ἐν συλλογισμοῖς οὐκ ἐπιστρε-
φομαι οὐδενὸς τῶν ἄλλο τι λεγόντων, ἐν μεταπίπ-
13 τουσιν οὐ φροντίζω οὐδενός. διὰ τί οὖν ἐν τοῖς
μείζοσιν ἀνιῶσί με οἱ ψέγοντες ; τί τὸ αἴτιον
ταύτης τῆς ταραχῆς ; οὐδὲν ἄλλο ἢ ὅτι ἐν τού-
14 τῳ τῷ τόπῳ ἀγύμναστός εἰμι. ἐπεί τοι πᾶσα
ἐπιστήμη καταφρονητική ἐστι τῆς ἀγνοίας καὶ
τῶν ἀγνοούντων καὶ οὐ μόνον αἱ ἐπιστῆμαι, ἀλλὰ
καὶ αἱ τέχναι. φέρε ὃν θέλεις σκυτέα καὶ τῶν
πολλῶν καταγελᾷ περὶ τὸ αὐτοῦ ἔργον· φέρε ὃν
θέλεις τέκτονα.

15   Πρῶτον μὲν οὖν ταῦτα ἔχειν πρόχειρα καὶ
μηδὲν δίχα τούτων ποιεῖν, ἀλλὰ τετάσθαι τὴν
ψυχὴν ἐπὶ τοῦτον τὸν σκοπόν, μηδὲν τῶν ἔξω
διώκειν, μηδὲν τῶν ἀλλοτρίων, ἀλλ' ὡς διέταξεν
ὁ δυνάμενος, τὰ προαιρετικὰ ἐξ ἅπαντος, τὰ δ'
16 ἄλλα ὡς ἂν διδῶται. ἐπὶ τούτοις δὲ μεμνῆσθαι,
τίνες ἐσμὲν καὶ τί ἡμῖν ὄνομα, καὶ πρὸς τὰς
δυνάμεις τῶν σχέσεων πειρᾶσθαι τὰ καθήκοντα
17 ἀπευθύνειν· τίς καιρὸς ᾠδῆς, τίς καιρὸς παιδιᾶς,[1]
τίνων παρόντων· τί ἔσται ἀπὸ τοῦ πράγματος·
μή τι καταφρονήσωσιν ἡμῶν οἱ[2] συνόντες, μή τι
ἡμεῖς αὐτῶν· πότε σκῶψαι καὶ τίνας ποτὲ κατα-
γελάσαι καὶ ἐπὶ τίνι ποτὲ συμπεριενεχθῆναι καὶ
τίνι, καὶ λοιπὸν ἐν τῇ συμπεριφορᾷ πῶς τηρῆσαι
τὸ αὑτοῦ. ὅπου δ' ἂν ἀπονεύσῃς ἀπό τινος τού-
18 των, εὐθὺς ζημία, οὐκ ἔξωθέν ποθεν, ἀλλ' ἐξ
αὐτῆς τῆς ἐνεργείας.

---

[1] Upton's "codex" and Wolf : παιδείας S.
[2] οἱ supplied by Sb.

---

[1] See note on I. 7, 1.

these standards, I pay heed to none of those who say
anything else, I give not a thought to anyone in arguments with equivocal premisses.[1] Why, then, in the
more important matters am I annoyed by those who
censure me? What is the reason for this perturbation of spirit? Nothing but the fact that in this
field I lack training. For, look you, every science
is entitled to despise ignorance and ignorant people,
and not merely the sciences, but also the arts. Take
any cobbler you please, and he laughs the multitude
to scorn when it comes to his own work; take any
carpenter you please.

First, therefore, we ought to have these principles
at command, and to do nothing apart from them,
but keep the soul intent upon this mark; we must
pursue none of the things external, none of the
things which are not our own, but as He that is
mighty has ordained; pursuing without any hesitation the things that lie within the sphere of the
moral purpose, and all other things as they have
been given us. And next we must remember who
we are, and what is our designation, and must endeavour to direct our actions, in the performance of
our duties, to meet the possibilities of our social
relations. We must remember what is the proper
time for song, the proper time for play, and in
whose presence; also what will be out of place;
lest our companions despise us, and we despise ourselves; when to jest, and whom to laugh at, and to
what end to engage in social intercourse, and with
whom; and, finally, how to maintain one's proper
character in such social intercourse. But whenever
you deviate from any one of these principles, immediately you suffer loss, and that not from anywhere
outside, but from the very nature of the activity.

19 Τί οὖν; δυνατὸν ἀναμάρτητον ἤδη εἶναι;
ἀμήχανον, ἀλλ' ἐκεῖνο δυνατὸν πρὸς τὸ μὴ ἁμαρτάνειν τετάσθαι διηνεκῶς. ἀγαπητὸν γάρ, εἰ
μηδέποτ' ἀνιέντες ταύτην τὴν προσοχὴν ὀλίγων
20 γε ἁμαρτημάτων ἐκτὸς ἐσόμεθα. νῦν δ' ὅταν
εἴπῃς " ἀπαύριον προσέξω," ἴσθι ὅτι τοῦτο λέγεις
" σήμερον ἔσομαι ἀναίσχυντος, ἄκαιρος, ταπεινός·
ἐπ' ἄλλοις ἔσται τὸ λυπεῖν με· ὀργισθήσομαι
21 σήμερον, φθονήσω." βλέπε ὅσα κακὰ σεαυτῷ
ἐπιτρέπεις. ἀλλ' εἴ σοι[1] αὔριον καλῶς ἔχει,
πόσῳ κρεῖττον σήμερον; εἰ αὔριον συμφέρει,
πολὺ μᾶλλον σήμερον, ἵνα καὶ αὔριον δυνηθῇς
καὶ μὴ πάλιν ἀναβάλῃ εἰς τρίτην.

ιγ΄.   Πρὸς τοὺς εὐκόλως ἐκφέροντας τὰ αὑτῶν.

1   Ὅταν τις ἡμῖν ἁπλῶς δόξῃ διειλέχθαι περὶ τῶν
ἑαυτοῦ πραγμάτων, πῶς[2] ποτε ἐξαγόμεθα καὶ
αὐτοὶ πρὸς τὸ ἐκφέρειν πρὸς αὐτὸν τὰ ἑαυτῶν
ἀπόρρητα καὶ τοῦτο ἁπλοῦν οἰόμεθα εἶναι·
2 πρῶτον μὲν ὅτι ἄνισον εἶναι δοκεῖ αὐτὸν μὲν
ἀκηκοέναι τὰ τοῦ πλησίον, μὴ μέντοι μεταδιδόναι
κἀκείνῳ ἐν τῷ μέρει τῶν ἡμετέρων. εἶθ' ὅτι
οἰόμεθα οὐχ ἁπλῶν ἀνθρώπων παρέξειν αὐτοῖς
3 φαντασίαν σιωπῶντες τὰ ἴδια. ἀμέλει πολλάκις
εἰώθασιν λέγειν " ἐγώ σοι πάντα τἀμαυτοῦ εἴρηκα,

---

[1] Schenkl: εἰσ S.   [2] Trincavelli: πῶς S.

What then ? Is it possible to be free from fault altogether ? No, that cannot be achieved, but it *is* possible ever to be intent upon avoiding faults. For we must be satisfied, if we succeed in escaping at least a few faults by never relaxing our attention. But now, when you say, "To-morrow I will pay attention," I would have you know that this is what you are saying : "To-day I will be shameless, tactless, abject; it will be in the power of other men to grieve me ; I will get angry to-day, I will give way to envy." Just see all the evils that you are allowing yourself! But if it is good for you to pay attention to-morrow, how much better is it to-day ! If it is to your interest to-morrow, it is much more so to-day, that you may be able to do the same to-morrow also, and not put it off again, this time to the day after to-morrow.

CHAPTER XIII

To those who lightly talk about their own affairs

WHEN someone gives us the impression of having talked to us frankly about his personal affairs, somehow or other we are likewise led to tell him our own secrets, and to think that is frankness ! The first reason for this is because it seems unfair for a man to have heard his neighbour's affairs, and yet not to let him too have, in his turn, a share in ours. Another reason, after that, is because we feel that we shall not give the impression to these men of being frank, if we keep our own private affairs concealed. Indeed, men are frequently in the habit of saying, "I have told you everything

σύ μοι οὐδὲν τῶν σῶν εἰπεῖν θέλεις ; ποῦ γίνεται
4 τοῦτο ;" πρόσεστι[1] δὲ καὶ τὸ οἴεσθαι ἀσφαλῶς
πιστεύειν τῷ ἤδη τὰ αὐτοῦ πεπιστευκότι· ὑπέρχε-
ται γὰρ ἡμᾶς, ὅτι οὐκ ἄν ποτε οὗτος ἐξείποι τὰ
ἡμέτερα εὐλαβούμενος, μήποτε καὶ ἡμεῖς ἐξείπω-
5 μεν τὰ ἐκείνου. οὕτως καὶ ὑπὸ τῶν στρατιωτῶν
ἐν Ῥώμῃ οἱ προπετεῖς λαμβάνονται. παρακεκά-
θικέ σοι στρατιώτης ἐν σχήματι ἰδιωτικῷ καὶ
ἀρξάμενος κακῶς λέγει τὸν Καίσαρα, εἶτα σὺ
ὥσπερ ἐνέχυρον παρ' αὐτοῦ λαβὼν τῆς πίστεως
τὸ αὐτὸν τῆς λοιδορίας κατῆρχθαι λέγεις καὶ αὐτὸς
6 ὅσα φρονεῖς, εἶτα δεθεὶς ἀπάγῃ. τοιοῦτόν τι καὶ ἐν
τῷ καθόλου πάσχομεν. οὐ γὰρ[2] ὡς ἐμοὶ ἐκεῖνος
ἀσφαλῶς πεπίστευκεν τὰ ἑαυτοῦ, οὕτως κἀγὼ
7 τῷ ἐπιτυχόντι· ἀλλ' ἐγὼ μὲν ἀκούσας σιωπῶ, ἄν
γε ὦ τοιοῦτος, ὁ δ' ἐξελθὼν ἐκφέρει πρὸς πάντας·
εἶτ' ἂν γνῶ τὸ γενόμενον, ἂν μὲν ὦ καὶ αὐτὸς
ἐκείνῳ ὅμοιος, ἀμύνασθαι θέλων ἐκφέρω τὰ
8 ἐκείνου καὶ φύρω καὶ φύρομαι. ἂν δὲ μνημονεύω,
ὅτι ἄλλος ἄλλον οὐ βλάπτει, ἀλλὰ τὰ αὐτοῦ
ἔργα ἕκαστον καὶ βλάπτει καὶ ὠφελεῖ, τούτου
μὲν κρατῶ τοῦ μὴ ὅμοιόν τι ποιῆσαι ἐκείνῳ,
ὅμως δ' ὑπὸ φλυαρίας τῆς ἐμαυτοῦ πέπονθα
ἃ πέπονθα.
9 Ναί· ἀλλ' ἄνισόν ἐστιν ἀκούσαντα τὰ τοῦ

---

[1] Wolf: προσέτι S.   [2] οὐ γάρ Schenkl: αὐτάρ S.

[1] It may possibly be, as Upton suggests, that this abuse
led John the Baptist to warn soldiers specifically, " Neither
accuse any falsely " (Luke iii. 14).

about myself, aren't you willing to tell me anything about yourself? Where do people act like that?" Furthermore, there is also the thought that we can safely trust the man who has already entrusted knowledge of his own affairs; for the idea occurs to us that this man would never spread abroad knowledge of our affairs, because he would be careful to guard against our too spreading abroad knowledge of his affairs. In this fashion the rash are ensnared by the soldiers in Rome. A soldier, dressed like a civilian, sits down by your side, and begins to speak ill of Caesar, and then you too, just as though you had received from him some guarantee of good faith in the fact that he began the abuse, tell likewise everything you think, and the next thing is—you are led off to prison in chains.[1] We experience something of the same sort also in the general course of our life. For even though this particular man has safely entrusted knowledge of his own affairs to me, I do not myself in like manner tell my affairs to any chance comer; no, I listen and keep still, if, to be sure, I happen to be that kind of a person, but he goes out and tells everybody. And then, when I find out what has happened, if I myself resemble the other person, because I want to get even with him I tell about his affairs, and confound him and am myself confounded. If, however, I remember that one person does not harm another, but that it is a man's own actions which both harm and help him, this much I achieve, namely, that I do not act like the other person, but despite that I get into the state in which I am because of my own foolish talking.

Yes, but it isn't fair to hear your neigbour's

πλησίον ἀπόρρητα αὐτὸν ἐν τῷ μέρει μηδενὸς
10 μεταδιδόναι αὐτῷ.—Μὴ γὰρ σε παρεκάλουν,
ἄνθρωπε; μὴ γὰρ ἐπὶ συνθήκαις τισὶν ἐξήνεγκας
τὰ σαυτοῦ, ἵν' ἀκούσῃς ἐν τῷ μέρει καὶ τὰ ἐμά;
11 εἰ σὺ φλύαρος εἶ καὶ πάντας τοὺς ἀπαντήσαντας
φίλους εἶναι δοκεῖς, θέλεις καὶ ἐμὲ ὅμοιόν σοι
γενέσθαι; τί δ', εἰ σὺ καλῶς μοι πεπίστευκας τὰ
σαυτοῦ, σοὶ δ' οὐκ ἔστι καλῶς πιστεῦσαι, θέλεις
12 με προπεσεῖν; οἷον εἰ πίθον εἶχον ἐγὼ μὲν
στεγνόν, σὺ δὲ τετρυπημένον καὶ ἐλθὼν παρακατέθου μοι τὸν σαυτοῦ οἶνον, ἵνα βάλω εἰς τὸν
ἐμὸν πίθον, εἶτ' ἠγανάκτεις ὅτι μὴ κἀγὼ σοὶ
πιστεύω τὸν ἐμαυτοῦ οἶνον· σὺ γὰρ τετρυπη-
13 μένον ἔχεις τὸν πίθον. πῶς οὖν ἔτι ἴσον γίνεται; σὺ πιστῷ παρακατέθου, σὺ αἰδήμονι, τὰς
ἑαυτοῦ ἐνεργείας μόνας βλαβερὰς ἡγουμένῳ καὶ
14 ὠφελίμους, τῶν δ' ἐκτὸς οὐδέν· ἐγὼ σοὶ θέλεις
παρακαταθῶμαι, ἀνθρώπῳ τὴν ἑαυτοῦ προαίρεσιν ἠτιμακότι, θέλοντι δὲ κερματίου τυχεῖν ἢ
ἀρχῆς τινος ἢ προαγωγῆς ἐν τῇ αὐλῇ, κἂν μέλλῃς
15 τὰ τέκνα σου κατασφάζειν, ὡς ἡ Μήδεια; ποῦ
τοῦτο ἴσον ἐστίν; ἀλλὰ δεῖξόν μοι σαυτὸν
πιστόν, αἰδήμονα, βέβαιον, δεῖξον, ὅτι δόγματα
ἔχεις φιλικά, δεῖξόν σου τὸ ἀγγεῖον ὅτι οὐ τέτρη-
ται καὶ ὄψει, πῶς οὐκ ἀναμενῶ[1] ἵνα μοι σὺ
πιστεύσῃς τὰ σαυτοῦ, ἀλλ' αὐτὸς ἐλθὼν σὲ
16 παρακαλῶ ἀκοῦσαι τῶν ἐμῶν. τίς γὰρ οὐ θέλει
χρήσασθαι ἀγγείῳ καλῷ, τίς ἀτιμάζει σύμβουλον
εὔνουν καὶ πιστόν, τίς οὐκ ἄσμενος δέξηται τὸν
ὥσπερ φορτίου μεταληψόμενον τῶν αὐτοῦ περι-

---

[1] Elter, after Wolf : ἀναμένω S.

secrets and then give him no share of your own in
return.—Man, I did not invite your confidences, did
I? You did not tell about your affairs on certain
conditions, that you were to hear about mine in
return, did you? If you are a babbler, and think
that every person you meet is a friend, do you also
want me to be like yourself? And why, if you did
well to entrust your affairs to me, but it is impossible
for me to do well in trusting you, do you wish me to
be rash? It is just as though I had a jar that was
sound, and you one with a hole in it, and you came
to me and deposited your wine with me, for me to
store it in my jar; and then you complained because
I do not entrust to you my wine also; why, *your* jar
has a hole in it! How, then, is equality any longer
to be found? You made your deposit with a faithful
man, with a respectful man, with a man who
regards only his own activities as either harmful or
helpful, and nothing that is external. Do you wish
me to make a deposit with you—a man who has
dishonoured his own moral purpose, and wants to
get paltry cash, or some office, or advancement at
court, even if you are going to cut the throats of
your children, as Medea did? Where is there
equality in that? Nay, show yourself to me as a
faithful, respectful, dependable man; show that
your judgements are those of a friend, show that
your vessel has no hole in it, and you shall see how
I will not wait for you to entrust the knowledge of
your affairs to me, but I will go of myself and ask you
to hear about mine. For who does not wish to use a
good vessel, who despises a friendly and faithful
counsellor, who would not gladly accept the man
who is ready to share his difficulties, as he would

433

στάσεων καὶ αὐτῷ τούτῳ κουφιοῦντα αὐτὸν τῷ
μεταλαβεῖν;

17 Ναί· ἀλλ' ἐγὼ σοὶ πιστεύω, σὺ ἐμοὶ οὐ
πιστεύεις.—Πρῶτον μὲν οὐδὲ σὺ ἐμοὶ πιστεύεις,
ἀλλὰ φλύαρος εἶ καὶ διὰ τοῦτο οὐδὲν δύνασαι
κατασχεῖν. ἐπεί τοι εἰ τοῦτό ἐστιν, ἐμοὶ μόνῳ
18 αὐτὰ πίστευσον· νῦν δ' ὃν ἂν εὐσχολοῦντα ἴδῃς,
παρακαθίσας αὐτῷ λέγεις "ἀδελφέ, οὐδένα σου
ἔχω εὐνούστερον οὐδὲ φίλτερον, παρακαλῶ σε
ἀκοῦσαι τὰ ἐμά"· καὶ τοῦτο πρὸς τοὺς οὐδέ τι
19 ὀλίγον ἐγνωσμένους ποιεῖς. εἰ δὲ καὶ πιστεύεις
ἐμοί, δῆλον ὅτι ὡς πιστῷ καὶ αἰδήμονι, οὐχ ὅτι
20 σοὶ τὰ ἐμαυτοῦ ἐξεῖπον. ἄφες οὖν, ἵνα κἀγὼ
ταὐτὰ ὑπολάβω. δεῖξόν μοι, ὅτι, ἄν τις τινὶ τὰ
αὐτοῦ[1] ἐξείπῃ, ἐκεῖνος πιστός ἐστι καὶ αἰδήμων.
εἰ γὰρ τοῦτο ἦν, ἐγὼ περιερχόμενος πᾶσιν ἀνθρώποις τὰ ἐμαυτοῦ ἂν ἔλεγον, εἰ τούτου ἕνεκα
ἔμελλον πιστὸς καὶ αἰδήμων ἔσεσθαι. τὸ δ'
ἐστὶν οὐ τοιοῦτον, ἀλλὰ δογμάτων δεῖ οὐχ ὧν
21 ἔτυχεν. ἂν γοῦν τινα ἴδῃς περὶ τὰ ἀπροαίρετα
ἐσπουδακότα καὶ τούτοις ὑποτεταχότα τὴν αὐτοῦ
προαίρεσιν, ἴσθι ὅτι ὁ ἄνθρωπος οὗτος μυρίους
ἔχει τοὺς ἀναγκάζοντας, τοὺς κωλύοντας. οὐκ
22 ἔστιν αὐτῷ χρεία πίσσης ἢ τροχοῦ πρὸς τὸ ἐξει-
πεῖν ἃ οἶδεν, ἀλλὰ παιδισκαρίου νευμάτιον, ἂν
οὕτως τύχῃ, ἐκσείσει αὐτόν, Καισαριανοῦ φιλο-
φροσύνη, ἀρχῆς ἐπιθυμία, κληρονομίας, ἄλλα

---

[1] s: αὑτῶι S.

---

[1] Means of torture among the ancients. See also II.
6, 18.

share a burden with him, and to make them light for him by the very fact of his sharing in them?

Yes, but I trust you, while you do not trust me.— First, you do not trust me, either, but you are a babbler, and that is the reason why you cannot keep anything back. Why, look you, if that statement of yours is true, entrust these matters to me alone; but the fact is that whenever you see anybody at leisure you sit down beside him and say, "Brother, I have no one more kindly disposed or dearer to me than you, I ask you to listen to my affairs"; and you act this way to people whom you have not known for even a short time. And even if you do trust me, it is clear you trust me as a faithful and respectful person, not because I have already told you about my affairs. Allow me also, then, to have the same thought about you. Show me that, if a man unbosoms himself to somebody about his own affairs, he is faithful and respectful. For if that were so, I should have gone about and told my own affairs to all men, that is, if that was going to make me faithful and respectful. But that is not the case; to be faithful and respectful a man needs judgements of no casual sort. If, therefore, you see someone very much in earnest about the things that lie outside the province of his moral purpose, and subordinating his own moral purpose to them, rest assured that this man has tens of thousands of persons who subject him to compulsion and hinder him. He has no need of pitch or the wheel[1] to get him to speak out what he knows, but a little nod from a wench, if it so happen, will upset him, a kindness from one of those who frequent Caesar's court, desire for office, or an inheritance, and thirty thousand

23 τούτοις ὅμοια τρισμύρια. μεμνῆσθαι οὖν ἐν τοῖς
καθόλου, ὅτι οἱ ἀπόρρητοι λόγοι πίστεως χρείαν
24 ἔχουσι καὶ δογμάτων τοιούτων· ταῦτα δὲ ποῦ
νῦν εὑρεῖν ῥᾳδίως; ἢ δειξάτω μοί τις τὸν οὕτως
ἔχοντα, ὥστε λέγειν " ἐμοὶ μόνων μέλει τῶν ἐμῶν,
τῶν ἀκωλύτων, τῶν φύσει ἐλευθέρων. ταύτην
οὐσίαν ἔχω τοῦ ἀγαθοῦ, τὰ δὲ ἄλλα γινέσθω ὡς
ἂν διδῶται· οὐ διαφέρομαι."

other things of the sort. Remember, therefore, in
general, that confidences require faithfulness and
faithful judgements; and where can one readily
find these things nowadays?[1] Or, let someone
show me the man who is so minded that he can say,
" I care only for what is my own, what is not subject
to hindrance, what is by nature free. This, which is
the true nature of the good, I have; but let everything else be as God has granted, it makes no
difference to me."

[1] Cf. " When the Son of man cometh, shall he find faith on
the earth?" (Luke xviii. 8).

FRAGMENTS

Introductory Note

THE genuine fragments of Epictetus are not very numerous, and since several of them are of unusual interest, it has seemed best to add them at this point. One fragment, No. 28 b, I have added to those listed by Schenkl, since its discovery was subsequent to his latest edition.

Earlier editions have included a large number of aphorisms gathered from Stobaeus, and from a gnomology purporting to contain excerpts from Democritus, Isocrates, and Epictetus. The researches of a group of scholars, principally H. Schenkl,[1] R. Asmus,[2] and A. Elter,[3] have thrown such doubt upon the authenticity of these aphorisms that it would scarcely serve any useful purpose to reproduce them in the present work.

---

[1] *Die epiktetischen Fragmente, Sitzungsberichte der philos.-hist. Classe der K. Akad. der Wiss.*, Wien, 115 (1888), 443–546. Also ed. maior 1916, Chapter III, pp. xlviii–lii.

[2] *Quaestiones Epicteteae*, Freiburg i. B., 1888.

[3] *Epicteti et Moschionis Sententiae*, Bonn, 1892.

FRAGMENTA

1 (175 [1]).   Stobaeus, *Eclogae*, II. 1, 31

Ἀρριανοῦ Ἐπικτητείου πρὸς τὸν περὶ οὐσίας
πολυπραγμονοῦντα [2]

Τί μοι μέλει, φησί, πότερον ἐξ ἀτόμων ἢ ἐξ
ἀμερῶν ἢ ἐκ πυρὸς καὶ γῆς συνέστηκε τὰ ὄντα;
οὐ γὰρ ἀρκεῖ μαθεῖν τὴν οὐσίαν τοῦ ἀγαθοῦ καὶ
κακοῦ καὶ τὰ μέτρα τῶν ὀρέξεων καὶ ἐκκλίσεων
καὶ ἔτι ὁρμῶν καὶ ἀφορμῶν καὶ τούτοις ὥσπερ
κανόσι χρώμενον διοικεῖν τὰ τοῦ βίου, τὰ δ' ὑπὲρ
ἡμᾶς ταῦτα χαίρειν ἐᾶν, ἃ τυχὸν μὲν ἀκατά-
ληπτά ἐστι τῇ ἀνθρωπίνῃ γνώμῃ, εἰ δὲ καὶ τὰ
μάλιστα θείη [3] τις εἶναι καταληπτά, ἀλλ' οὖν τί
ὄφελος καταληφθέντων; οὐχὶ δὲ διακενῆς πράγματα ἔχειν φατέον τοὺς ταῦτα ὡς ἀναγκαῖα τῷ
τοῦ φιλοσόφου λόγῳ προσνέμοντας; Μή τι οὖν
καὶ τὸ ἐν Δελφοῖς παράγγελμα παρέλκον ἐστί,
τὸ Γνῶθι σαυτόν;—Τοῦτο δὲ μὲν οὔ, φησί.—
Τίς οὖν ἡ δύναμις αὐτοῦ; εἰ χορευτῇ τις παρήγ-
γελλε τὸ γνῶναι ἑαυτόν, οὔκουν ἂν [4] τῇ προσ-
τάξει προσεῖχε τῷ ἐπιστραφῆναι καὶ τῶν συγ-
χορευτῶν καὶ τῆς πρὸς αὐτοὺς συμφωνίας;—
Φησίν.—Εἰ δὲ ναύτῃ; [5] εἰ δὲ στρατιώτῃ; πό-

---

[1] Numbers in parenthesis refer to Schweighäuser's edition,
which was followed by Long in his translation.
[2] The final word of the title added by Wachsmuth.
[3] Schweighäuser: θῇ MSS.

440

FRAGMENTS

1

From Arrian the pupil of Epictetus. To the man who was bothering himself about the problem of being

What do I care, says Epictetus, whether all existing things are composed of atoms, or of indivisibles, or of fire and earth? Is it not enough to learn the true nature of the good and the evil, and the limits of the desires and aversions, and also of the choices and refusals, and, by employing these as rules, to order the affairs of our life, and dismiss the things that are beyond us? It may very well be that these latter are not to be comprehended by the human mind, and even if one assume that they are perfectly comprehensible, well, what profit comes from comprehending them? And ought we not to say that those men trouble themselves in vain who assign all this as necessary to the philosopher's system of thought? Is, therefore, also the precept at Delphi superfluous, "Know thyself"?—That, indeed, no, the man answers.—What, then, does it mean? If one bade a singer in a chorus to "know himself," would he not heed the order by paying attention both to his fellows in the chorus and to singing in harmony with them?—Yes.—And so in the case of a sailor?

---

⁴ οὔκουν ἂν Schenkl (οὔκουν Wachsmuth) : οὐκ ἂν ἐν MSS.

⁵ Canter and Wachsmuth : εἶδεν αὐτῇ(ν) MSS.

τερον οὖν ὁ ἄνθρωπος αὐτὸς ἐφ᾽[1] αὑτοῦ πεποιῆ-
σθαί σοι δοκεῖ ζῷον ἢ πρὸς κοινωνίαν;—Πρὸς
κοινωνίαν.[2]—Ὑπὸ τίνος;—Ὑπὸ τῆς φύσεως.—
Τίνος οὔσης καὶ πῶς διοικούσης τὰ ὅλα καὶ
πότερον οὔσης ἢ μή, ταῦτα οὐκέτι ἀναγκαῖον
πολυπραγμονεῖν.

2 (135). Stobaeus, IV. 44, 65

Ἀρριανοῦ Ἐπικτητείου.

Ὁ τοῖς παροῦσι καὶ δεδομένοις ὑπὸ τῆς τύχης
δυσχεραίνων ἰδιώτης ἐν βίῳ, ὁ δὲ ταῦτα γενναίως
φέρων καὶ εὐλογιστῶν πρὸς τὰ[3] ἀπ᾽ αὐτῶν ἀνὴρ
ἀγαθὸς ἄξιος[4] νομίζεσθαι.

3 (136). Stobaeus, IV. 44, 66

Τοῦ αὐτοῦ.

Πάντα ὑπακούει τῷ κόσμῳ καὶ ὑπηρετεῖ καὶ
γῆ καὶ θάλασσα καὶ ἥλιος καὶ τὰ λοιπὰ ἄστρα
καὶ τὰ γῆς φυτὰ καὶ ζῷα· ὑπακούει δὲ αὐτῷ καὶ
τὸ ἡμέτερον σῶμα καὶ νοσοῦν καὶ ὑγιαῖνον, ὅταν
ἐκεῖνος θέλῃ, καὶ νεάζον καὶ γηρῶν καὶ τὰς ἄλλας
διερχόμενον μεταβολάς. οὐκοῦν εὔλογον καί, ὃ
ἐφ᾽ ἡμῖν ἐστί, τουτέστι τὴν κρίσιν, μὴ ἀντιτείνειν
μόνην πρὸς αὐτόν· καὶ γὰρ ἰσχυρός ἐστι καὶ
κρείσσων καὶ ἄμεινον ὑπὲρ ἡμῶν βεβούλευται

---

[1] Cobet : ὑφ᾽ MSS.
[2] πρὸς κοινωνίαν supplied by Heeren.
[3] Schenkl : εὐλογίστω τά MSS.
[4] Gesner : ἀξίως MSS.

or a soldier ? Does it seem to you, then, that man has been made a creature to live all alone by himself, or for society?—For society.—By whom?—By Nature.—What Nature is, and how she administers the universe, and whether she really exists or not, these are questions about which there is no need to go on to bother ourselves.

2

From Arrian the pupil of Epictetus

He who is dissatisfied by what he has and what has been given him by fortune is a layman in the art of living, but the man who bears all this in a noble spirit and makes a reasonable use of all that comes from it deserves to be considered a good man.

3

From the same

All things obey and serve the Cosmos,[1] both earth, and sea, and sun, and the other stars, and the plants and animals of earth ; obedient to it also is our body, both in sickness and in health, when the Cosmos wishes, both in youth and in old age, and when passing through all the other changes. There-fore it is reasonable also that the one thing which is under our control, that is, the decision of our will, should not be the only thing to stand out against it. For the Cosmos is mighty and superior to us, and has taken better counsel for us than we can, by uniting

---

[1] A pantheistic form of expression for God, common enough in Stoicism in general, but rare in Epictetus. Cf. also frag. 4, where, however, the expression may really belong to Rufus.

μετὰ τῶν ὅλων καὶ ἡμᾶς συνδιοικῶν. πρὸς δὲ
τούτοις καὶ ἡ ἀντίπραξις μετὰ τοῦ ἀλόγου καὶ
πλέον οὐδὲν ποιοῦσα πλὴν τὸ διακενῆς σπᾶσθαι
καὶ περιπίπτειν ὀδύναις καὶ λύπαις ποιεῖ.

4 (169). Stobaeus, II. 8, 30. Musonius, frag.
38 (H.)

Ῥούφου ἐκ τῶν Ἐπικτήτου περὶ φιλίας.

Τῶν ὄντων τὰ μὲν ἐφ' ἡμῖν ἔθετο ὁ θεός, τὰ
δ' οὐκ ἐφ' ἡμῖν. ἐφ' ἡμῖν μὲν τὸ κάλλιστον καὶ
σπουδαιότατον, ᾧ δὴ καὶ αὐτὸς εὐδαίμων ἐστί,
τὴν χρῆσιν τῶν φαντασιῶν. τοῦτο γὰρ ὀρθῶς
γιγνόμενον ἐλευθερία ἐστίν, εὔροια, εὐθυμία,
εὐστάθεια, τοῦτο δὲ καὶ δίκη ἐστὶ καὶ νόμος καὶ
σωφροσύνη καὶ ξύμπασα ἀρετή. τὰ δ' ἄλλα
πάντα οὐκ ἐφ' ἡμῖν ἐποιήσατο. οὐκοῦν καὶ ἡμᾶς
συμψήφους χρὴ τῷ θεῷ γενέσθαι καὶ ταύτῃ
διελόντας τὰ πράγματα τῶν μὲν ἐφ' ἡμῖν πάντα
τρόπον ἀντιποιεῖσθαι, τὰ δὲ μὴ ἐφ' ἡμῖν ἐπιτρέψαι
τῷ κόσμῳ καί, εἴτε τῶν παίδων δέοιτο εἴτε τῆς
πατρίδος εἴτε τοῦ σώματος εἴτε ὁτουοῦν,[1] ἀσμένους
παραχωρεῖν.

5 (67). Stobaeus, III. 19, 13. Musonius, frag.
39 (H.)

Ῥούφου ἐκ τοῦ Ἐπικτήτου περὶ φιλίας.

Τὸ δὲ Λυκούργου τοῦ Λακεδαιμονίου τίς ἡμῶν
οὐ θαυμάζει; πηρωθεὶς γὰρ ὑπό τινος τῶν

[1] Meineke: ὁτιοῦν MSS.

444

us together with the universe under its governance. Besides, to act against it is to side with unreason, and while accomplishing nothing but a vain struggle, it involves us in pains and sorrows.

4

Rufus.   From the remarks of Epictetus on friendship [1]

Of things that are, God has put some under our control, and others not under our control. Under our control He put the finest and most important matter, that, indeed, by virtue of which He Himself is happy, the power to make use of external impressions. For when this power has its perfect work, it is freedom, serenity, cheerfulness, steadfastness; it is also justice, and law, and self-control, and the sum and substance of virtue. But all other things He has not put under our control. Therefore we also ought to become of one mind with God, and, dividing matters in this way, lay hold in every way we can upon the things that are under our control, but what is not under our control we ought to leave to the Cosmos, and gladly resign to it whatever it needs, be that our children, our country, our body, or anything whatsoever.

5

Rufus.   From Epictetus on friendship

What man among us does not admire the saying of Lycurgus the Lacedaemonian? For when he had

The natural way to take this and the next few titles is to assume that Epictetus had quoted with approval a fairly long passage from his revered teacher Musonius Rufus.

πολιτῶν τῶν ὀφθαλμῶν τὸν ἕτερον καὶ παρα-
λαβὼν τὸν νεανίσκον παρὰ τοῦ δήμου, ἵνα
τιμωρήσαιτο, ὅπως ἂν[1] αὐτὸς βούληται, τούτου
μὲν ἀπέσχετο, παιδεύσας δὲ αὐτὸν καὶ ἀποφήνας
ἄνδρα ἀγαθὸν παρήγαγεν εἰς τὸ θέατρον. θαυ-
μαζόντων δὲ τῶν Λακεδαιμονίων "τοῦτον μέντοι
λαβών," ἔφη, "παρ' ὑμῶν ὑβριστὴν καὶ βίαιον
ἀποδίδωμι ὑμῖν ἐπιεικῆ καὶ δημοτικόν."

6 (69).   Stobaeus, III. 20, 60.   Musonius, frag.
40 (H.)

Ῥούφου ἐκ τοῦ Ἐπικτήτου περὶ φιλίας.

Ἀλλὰ παντὸς μᾶλλον τῆς μὲν φύσεως ἐκεῖνο
τὸ ἔργον συνδῆσαι καὶ συναρμόσαι τὴν ὁρμὴν τῇ[2]
τοῦ προσήκοντος καὶ ὠφελίμου φαντασίᾳ.[2]

7 (70).   Stobaeus, III. 20, 61.   Musonius, frag.
41 (H.)

Τοῦ αὐτοῦ.

Τὸ δὲ οἴεσθαι εὐκαταφρονήτους τοῖς ἄλλοις
ἔσεσθαι, ἐὰν μὴ τοὺς πρώτους ἐχθροὺς παντὶ
τρόπῳ βλάψωμεν, σφόδρα ἀγεννῶν καὶ ἀνοήτων
ἀνθρώπων.   φαμὲν γὰρ τὸν εὐκαταφρόνητον
νοεῖσθαι μὲν καὶ κατὰ τὸ ἀδύνατον εἶναι βλάψαι·
ἀλλὰ πολὺ μᾶλλον νοεῖται κατὰ τὸ ἀδύνατον
εἶναι ὠφελεῖν.

[1] ἄν added by C. Schenkl.

been blinded in one eye by one of his fellow-citizens, and the people had turned over the young man to him, to take whatever vengeance upon the culprit he might desire, this he refrained from doing, but brought him up and made a good man of him, and presented him in the theatre. And when the Lace-daemonians expressed their surprise, he said, "This man when I received him at your hands was insolent and violent; I am returning him to you a reasonable and public-spirited person."

6

Rufus. From Epictetus on friendship

But above all else this is the function of nature, to bind together and to harmonize our choice with the conception of what is fitting and helpful.

7

The same

To fancy that we shall be contemptible in the sight of other men, if we do not employ every means to hurt the first enemies we meet, is characteristic of extremely ignoble and thoughtless men. For it is a common saying among us that the contemptible man is recognized among other things by his incapacity to do harm; but he is much better recognized by his incapacity to extend help.

---

2 Bücheler: τῆς . . . φαντασίας MSS.

8 (134).   Stobaeus, IV. 44, 60.   Musonius, frag.
42 (H.)

Ῥούφου ἐκ τῶν Ἐπικτήτου περὶ φιλίας.

Ὅτι τοιαύτη ἡ τοῦ κόσμου φύσις καὶ ἦν καὶ
ἔστι καὶ ἔσται καὶ οὐχ οἷόν τε ἄλλως γίγνεσθαι
τὰ γιγνόμενα ἢ ὡς νῦν ἔχει· καὶ ὅτι ταύτης τῆς
τροπῆς καὶ τῆς μεταβολῆς οὐ μόνον οἱ ἄνθρωποι
μετειλήφασι καὶ τἆλλα ζῷα τὰ ἐπὶ γῆς, ἀλλὰ
καὶ τὰ θεῖα καὶ νὴ Δί᾿ αὐτὰ τὰ τέτταρα στοιχεῖα
ἄνω καὶ κάτω τρέπεται καὶ μεταβάλλει καὶ γῆ
τε ὕδωρ γίνεται καὶ ὕδωρ ἀήρ, οὗτος δὲ πάλιν εἰς
αἰθέρα μεταβάλλει· καὶ ὁ αὐτὸς τρόπος τῆς
μεταβολῆς ἄνωθεν κάτω.   ἐὰν πρὸς ταῦτά τις
ἐπιχειρῇ ῥέπειν τὸν νοῦν καὶ πείθειν ἑαυτὸν
ἑκόντα δέχεσθαι τὰ ἀναγκαῖα, πάνυ μετρίως καὶ
μουσικῶς διαβιώσεται τὸν βίον.

9 (180).   Gellius, XIX. 1, 14–21 [1]

14   *Philosophus in disciplina Stoica celebratus . . . ex
sarcinula sua librum protulit Epicteti philosophi quintum
Διαλέξεων, quas ab Arriano digestas congruere scriptis
15 Zenonis et Chrysippi non dubium est.   in eo libro,
graeca scilicet oratione scriptum ad hanc sententiam
legimus:* Visa animi (*quas* φαντασίας *philosophi ap-
pellant*), *quibus mens hominis prima statim specie
accidentis ad animum rei pellitur, non voluntatis*

[1] Also in abbreviated form (from Gellius) in Augustine,
Civ. Dei, 9, 4 (cf. 9, 5), and *Quaest. in Heptat.* 1, 30.

[1] That is, from the heavier to the lighter, and again from
the lighter to the heavier.

448

FRAGMENTS

8

Rufus. From the remarks of Epictetus on friendship

Such was, and is, and will be, the nature of the
universe, and it is not possible for the things that
come into being to come into being otherwise than
they now do. And not only has mankind participated
in this process of change and transformation, and all
the other living beings upon earth, but also those
which are divine, and, by Zeus, even the four
elements, which are changed and transformed up-
wards and downwards,[1] as earth becomes water, and
water air, and air again is transformed into ether ;
and there is the same kind of transformation also
downwards. If a man endeavours to incline his
mind to these things, and to persuade himself to
accept of his own accord what needs must befall
him, he will have a very reasonable and harmonious
life.

9

*A philosopher who is well known in the Stoic school
. . . brought out of his handbag the fifth book of the
Discourses of the philosopher Epictetus, which had been
arranged by Arrian, and agree, no doubt, with the
writings of Zeno and Chrysippus. In that book, written
of course in Greek, we find a passage to this purport :*
Things seen by the mind (*which the philosophers call*
φαντασίας),[2] whereby the intellect of man is struck
at the very first sight of anything which penetrates
to the mind, are not subject to his will, nor to his

---

[2] External impressions.

sunt neque arbitraria,[1] sed vi quadam sua inferunt
sese hominibus noscitanda;[2] probationes autem (*quas*
16 συγκαταθέσεις *vocant*), quibus eadem visa noscuntur,
17 voluntariae sunt fiuntque hominum arbitratu.   prop-
terea cum sonus aliquis formidabilis aut caelo aut ex
ruina aut repentinus nescio cuius[3] periculi nuntius
vel quid aliud est[4] eiusmodi factum, sapientis quoque
animum paulisper moveri et contrahi et pallescere
necessum est, non opinione alicuius mali praecepta,
sed quibusdam motibus rapidis et inconsultis officium
18 mentis atque rationis praevertentibus.   mox tamen
ille sapiens ibidem τὰς τοιαύτας φαντασίας (*id est visa
istaec animi sui terrifica*) non adprobat (*hoc est* οὐ
συγκατατίθεται οὐδὲ προσεπιδοξάζει), sed abicit re-
spuitque nec ei metuendum esse in his quicquam
19 videtur.   atque hoc inter insipientis sapientisque
animum differe dicunt quod insipiens, qualia sibi
esse primo animi sui pulsu visa sunt saeva et aspera,
talia esse vero putat et eadem incepta, tamquam[5] si
iure metuenda sint, sua quoque adsensione adprobat
20 καὶ "προσεπιδοξάζει" (*hoc enim verbo Stoici, cum super
ista re disserunt, utuntur*), sapiens autem, cum breviter
et strictim colore atque vultu motus est, οὐ συγκατατίθεται, sed statum vigoremque sententiae suae reti-
net, quam de huiuscemodi visis semper habuit, ut de

---

[1] L. Carrio: arbitrariae MSS.
[2] Salmasius: noscitandae MSS.
[3] Ed. Greifswald 1537: nescius MSS.
[4] J. Gronov: ex MSS (or omit)
[5] Edd.: quamquam MSS.

---

[1] Does not assent or confirm by approval.
[2] Such external impressions.
[3] Also confirms by his approval.
[4] The word seems to occur only here, and may be peculiar
to Epictetus.

control, but by virtue of a certain force of their own thrust themselves upon the attention of men; but the assents (*which they call* συγκαταθέσεις), whereby these same things seen by the mind are recognized, are subject to man's will, and fall under his control. Therefore, when some terrifying sound comes from the sky, or from the collapse of a building, or sudden word comes of some peril or other, or something else of the same sort happens, the mind of even the wise man cannot help but be disturbed, and shrink, and grow pale for a moment, not from any anticipation of some evil, but because of certain swift and unconsidered motions which forestall the action of the intellect and the reason. Soon, however, our wise man does not give his assent (*this is,* οὐ συγκατατίθεται οὐδὲ προσεπιδοξάζει)[1] to τὰς τοιαύτας φαντασίας[2] (*that is, these terrifying things seen by his mind*), but rejects and repudiates them, and sees in them nothing to cause him fear. And this, they say, is the difference between the mind of the fool and the mind of the wise man, that the fool thinks the cruel and harsh things seen by his mind, when it is first struck by them, actually to be what they appear, and likewise afterwards, just as though they really were formidable, he confirms them by his own approval also, καὶ προσεπιδοξάζει[3] (*the word the Stoics use when they discuss this matter*);[4] whereas the wise man, when his colour and expression have changed for a brief instant, οὐ συγκατατίθεται,[5] but keeps the even tenor and strength of the opinion which he has always had about mental impressions of this kind, as things

_____

[5] Does not give his consent.

minime metuendis, sed fronte falsa et formidine inani
territantibus.

21   *Haec Epictetum philosophum ex decretis Stoicorum
sensisse atque dixisse, in eo, quo dixi, libro legimus.*

10 (179).   Gellius, XVII. 19

*Favorinum ego audivi dicere Epictetum philosophum
dixisse* plerosque istos, qui philosophari viderentur,
philosophos esse eiuscemodi " ἄνευ τοῦ πράττειν, μέχρι
τοῦ λέγειν " *(id significat "factis procul, verbis tenus").*

2 *iam illud est vehementius, quod Arrianus solitum eum
dictitare in libris, quos de dissertationibus eius composuit,*

3 *scriptum reliquit.   nam, cum, inquit,* animadverterat
hominem pudore amisso, inportuna industria, cor-
ruptis moribus, audacem, confidentem lingua cetera-
que omnia praeterquam animam procurantem, istius-
modi, *inquit,* hominem cum viderat studia quoque et
disciplinas philosophiae contrectare et physica adire
et meditari dialectica multaque id genus theoremata
auspicari[1] sciscitarique: inclamabat deum atque
hominum fidem ac plerumque inter clamandum his
eum verbis increpabat: "῍Ανθρωπε, ποῦ βάλλεις; σκέψαι,
εἰ κεκάθαρται τὸ ἀγγεῖον.   ἂν γὰρ εἰς τὴν οἴησιν αὐτὰ
βάλῃς,[2] ἀπώλετο· ἢν[3] σαπῇ, οὖρον ἢ ὄξος ἐγένετο[4] ἢ εἴ
τι τούτων χεῖρον."   *nihil profecto his verbis gravius,*

4 *nihil verius: quibus declarabat maximus philosophorum
litteras atque doctrinas philosophiae, cum in hominem*

---

[1] Eussner: suspicari MSS.   [2] Usener: βάλλῃς MSS.
[3] H or HC the MSS.   [4] Usener: γένοιτο MSS.

---

[1] Without doing, as far as speaking.
[2] Man, where are you stowing all this? Look and see if
the vessel has been cleansed. For if you stow it in the

that do not deserve to be feared at all, but terrify
only with a false face and a vain fear.

*This is the sentiment and expression of the philosopher
Epictetus, derived from the doctrines of the Stoics, that
we have read in the book of which I spoke above.*

10

*I have heard Favorinus say that he had heard the
philosopher Epictetus say,* that most of those who gave
the appearance of philosophizing were philosophers
of this kind: ἄνευ τοῦ πράττειν, μέχρι τοῦ λέγειν [1] (*this
means, " apart from deeds, as far as words* "). *There
is a still more vigorous expression which he was accustomed to use, that Arrian has recorded in the books
which he wrote about his discourses.* For Arrian says
that when Epictetus had noticed a man lost to
shame, of misdirected energy, and evil habits, bold,
impudent in speech, and concerned with everything
else but his soul, when he saw a man of that kind,
continues Arrian, handling also the studies and pur-
suits of philosophy, and taking up physics, and
studying dialectics, and taking up and investigating
many a theoretical principle of this sort, he would
call upon gods and men, and frequently, in the
midst of that appeal, he would denounce the man
in these words : Ἄνθρωπε, ποῦ βάλλεις; σκέψαι, εἰ
κεκάθαρται τὸ ἀγγεῖον. ἂν γὰρ εἰς τὴν οἴησιν αὐτὰ βάλῃς,
ἀπώλετο· ἢν σαπῇ, οὖρον ἢ ὄξος ἐγένετο ἢ εἴ τι τούτων
χεῖρον.[2] *Surely there is nothing weightier, nothing
truer than these words, in which the greatest of philosophers declared that* the writings and teachings of
philosophy, when poured into a false and low-lived

vessel of opinion, it is ruined ; if it spoils, it turns into urine,
or vinegar, or, it may be, something worse.

falsum atque degenerem tamquam in vas spurcum
atque pollutum influxissent, verti, mutari, corrumpi
et (*quod ipse* κυνικώτερον *ait*) urinam fieri aut si quid
est urina spurcius.

5   *Praeterea idem ille Epictetus, quod ex eodem Favo-*
rino audivimus, solitus dicere est duo esse vitia multo
omnium gravissima ac taeterrima, intolerantiam et
incontinentiam, cum aut iniurias, quae sunt ferendae,
non toleramus neque ferimus aut, a quibus rebus
voluptatibusque nos tenere debemus, non tenemus.

6 "itaque," *inquit*, "si quis haec duo verba cordi habeat
eaque sibi imperando atque observando curet, is
erit pleraque inpeccabilis vitamque vivet tranquil-
lissimam."   *verba haec duo dicebat:* "ἀνέχου" *et*
"ἀπέχου."

10*a* (181).   Arnobius, *Adversus Gentes*, 2, 78

Cum de animarum agitur salute ac de respectu
nostri, aliquid et sine ratione faciendum est, *ut*
Epictetum dixisse adprobat Arrianus.

11 (174).   Stobaeus, IV. 33, 28

Ἐκ τῶν Ἀρριανοῦ προτρεπτικῶν ὁμιλιῶν.

Ἀλλὰ δὴ Σωκράτης Ἀρχελάου μεταπεμπο-
μένου αὐτὸν ὡς ποιήσοντος πλούσιον ἐκέλευσεν
ἀπαγγεῖλαι αὐτῷ διότι[1] "'Ἀθήνησι τέσσαρές εἰσι
χοίνικες τῶν ἀλφίτων ὀβολοῦ ὤνιοι καὶ κρῆναι

---

[1] Gesner : διὰ τί MSS.

---

[1] Somewhat after the fashion of the Cynics.

person, as though into a dirty and defiled vessel,
turn, change, are spoiled, and (*as he himself says*
κυνικώτερον) [1] become urine, or something, it may be,
dirtier than urine.

*The same Epictetus, moreover, as we have heard
from Favorinus, was in the habit of saying* that there
were two vices which are far more severe and
atrocious than all others, want of endurance and
want of self-control, when we do not endure or bear
the wrongs which we have to bear, or do not abstain
from, or forbear, those matters and pleasures which we
ought to forbear. " And so," he says, " if a man should
take to heart these two words and observe them in
controlling and keeping watch over himself, he will,
for the most part, be free from wrongdoing, and
will live a highly peaceful life." *These two words,
he used to say, were* ἀνέχου *and* ἀπέχου.[2]

10 a (181)

When the salvation of our souls and regard for our
true selves are at stake, something has to be done,
even without stopping to think about it, *a saying of
Epictetus which Arrian quotes with approval.*

11

From the homilies of Arrian, exhorting to virtue

Now when Archelaus [3] sent for Socrates with
the intention of making him rich, the latter bade
the messenger take back the following answer:
" At Athens four quarts of barley-meal can be
bought for an obol,[4] and there are running springs

---

[2] Bear and forbear.   [3] The king of Macedon.
[4] A penny and a half, or three cents; in other terms, the
sixth part of the day's wage of an ordinary labourer.

ὕδατος ῥέουσιν." εἰ γάρ τοι μὴ ἱκανὰ τὰ ὄντα
ἐμοί, ἀλλ' ἐγὼ τούτοις ἱκανὸς καὶ οὕτω κἀκεῖνα
ἐμοί. ἢ οὐχ ὁρᾷς, ὅτι οὐκ εὐφωνότερον οὐδὲ
ἥδιον [1] ὁ Πῶλος τὸν τύραννον Οἰδίποδα ὑπεκρί-
νετο ἢ τὸν ἐπὶ Κολωνῷ ἀλήτην [2] καὶ πτωχόν;
εἶτα χείρων Πώλου ὁ γενναῖος ἀνὴρ φανεῖται,
ὡς μὴ πᾶν τὸ περιτεθὲν ἐκ τοῦ δαιμονίου πρόσωπον ὑποκρίνασθαι καλῶς; οὐδὲ τὸν Ὀδυσσέα
μιμήσεται, ὃς καὶ ἐν τοῖς ῥάκεσιν οὐδὲν μεῖον
διέπρεπεν ἢ ἐν τῇ οὔλῃ χλαίνῃ τῇ πορφυρᾷ;

12 (note to frag. 71).   Stobaeus, III. 20, 47

Ἀρριανοῦ.

Μεγαλόθυμοι πράως εἰσί τινες ἡσυχῇ καὶ οἷον
ἀοργήτως πράττοντες ὅσα καὶ οἱ σφόδρα τῷ
θυμῷ φερόμενοι. φυλακτέον οὖν καὶ τὸ τούτων
ἀβλέπτημα ὡς πολὺ χεῖρον ὂν τοῦ διατεινόμενον
ὀργίζεσθαι. οὗτοι μὲν γὰρ ταχὺ κόρον τῆς
τιμωρίας λαμβάνουσιν, οἱ δὲ εἰς μακρὸν παρα-
τείνουσιν ὡς οἱ λεπτῶς πυρέττοντες.

13 (omitted).   Stobaeus, I. 3, 50

Ἐκ τῶν Ἐπικτήτου ἀπομνημονευμάτων.

Ἀλλ' ὁρῶ, φησί τις, τοὺς καλοὺς καὶ ἀγαθοὺς
καὶ λιμῷ καὶ ῥίγει ἀπολλυμένους.—Τοὺς δὲ μὴ

[1] Gaisford: δι' ὅν MSS.
[2] Schweighäuser: ἀλείτην MSS.

of water." For, look you, if what I have is not sufficient for me, still, I am sufficient for it, and so it too is sufficient for me. Or do you not see that Polus[1] was not accustomed to act Oedipus the King with any finer voice or more pleasure to his audience than Oedipus at Colonus, the outcast and beggar? And then shall the man of noble nature make a poorer showing than Polus, and not play well any rôle to which the Deity assigns him? And will he not follow the example of Odysseus, who was no less pre-eminent in his rags than in his rich and purple cloak?

12

From Arrian

There are certain persons who exhibit their high spirit rather gently,[2] and in a sort of passionless manner do everything that even those who are swept away by their anger do. We must be on our guard, therefore, against the error of these persons, as something much worse than violent anger. For those who give way to violent anger are soon sated with their revenge, but the others prolong it like men who have a light fever.

13

From the Memorabilia *of Epictetus*

But, says someone, I see the good and excellent perishing from hunger and cold.—And do you not see

---

[1] A famous actor of the fourth century. See J. B. O'Connor, *Chapters in the History of Actors and Acting* (1908), 128-30.

[2] Capps suggests that ἡσυχῇ is used here as it is in Menander, *Hero*, 20.

καλοὺς καὶ μὴ ἀγαθοὺς οὐχ ὁρᾷς τρυφῇ καὶ
ἀλαζονείᾳ καὶ ἀπειροκαλίᾳ ἀπολλυμένους; —
'Αλλ' αἰσχρὸν τὸ παρ' ἄλλου τρέφεσθαι.—Καὶ
τίς, ὦ κακόδαιμον, αὐτὸς ἐξ ἑαυτοῦ τρέφεται
ἄλλος γε ἢ ὁ κόσμος; ὅστις γοῦν ἐγκαλεῖ τῇ
προνοίᾳ, ὅτι οἱ πονηροὶ οὐ διδόασι δίκην, ὅτι
ἰσχυροί εἰσι καὶ πλούσιοι, ὅμοιόν τι δρᾷ ὥσπερ
εἰ τοὺς ὀφθαλμοὺς ἀπολωλεκότων αὐτῶν ἔλεγε
μὴ δεδωκέναι δίκην αὐτούς, ὅτι οἱ ὄνυχες ὑγιεῖς
εἶεν. ἐγὼ μὲν γάρ φημι πολὺ[1] διαφέρειν μᾶλλον
ἀρετὴν κτήσεως[2] ἢ ὀφθαλμοὶ ὀνύχων διαφέρουσιν.

14 (52). Stobaeus, III. 6, 57

'Εκ τῶν 'Επικτήτου ἀπομνημονευμάτων.[3]

. . .[4] τοὺς δυσχερεῖς δὲ φιλοσόφους εἰς μέσον
ἄγοντες, οἷς οὐ δοκεῖ κατὰ φύσιν ἡδονὴ εἶναι,
ἀλλ' ἐπιγίγνεσθαι τοῖς κατὰ φύσιν, δικαιοσύνῃ,
σωφροσύνῃ, ἐλευθερίᾳ. τί ποτ' οὖν ἡ ψυχὴ ἐπὶ
μὲν τοῖς τοῦ σώματος ἀγαθοῖς μικροτέροις οὖσι
χαίρει καὶ γαληνιᾷ, ὥς φησιν 'Επίκουρος, ἐπὶ δὲ
τοῖς αὑτῆς ἀγαθοῖς μεγίστοις οὖσιν οὐχ ἥδεται;
καίτοι καὶ δέδωκέ μοι ἡ φύσις αἰδῶ καὶ πολλὰ
ὑπερυθριῶ, ὅταν τι ὑπολάβω αἰσχρὸν λέγειν.
τοῦτό με τὸ κίνημα οὐκ ἐᾷ τὴν ἡδονὴν θέσθαι
ἀγαθὸν καὶ τέλος τοῦ βίου.

---

[1] αἱ (ἄν P²) after this word was deleted by Meineke.
[2] Suggested by Schenkl: κακίας MSS.
[3] The last word of the title added by Asmus.
[4] Schenkl indicated the lacuna.

those who are not good and excellent perishing from luxury, and bombast, and vulgarity?—Yes, but it is disgraceful to be supported by another.—And who, O miserable fellow, is supported by himself alone, except the Cosmos? Whoever accuses Providence, therefore, because the wicked are not punished, and because they are strong and rich, is acting just as though, when the wicked had lost their eyes, he said they were not being punished because their finger-nails were in good condition. Now, as for me, I assert that there is much more difference between virtue and property than there is between eyes and finger-nails.

14

From the Memorabilia of Epictetus

. . . bring forward the ill-natured [1] philosophers, who think that pleasure is not something natural, but a sequel of things that are natural, as justice, self-control, and freedom. Why indeed, then, does the soul take delight in the lesser goods of the body, and enjoy calm therein, as Epicurus says,[2] and yet not find pleasure in its own goods, which are very great? Verily nature has also given me a sense of shame, and frequently I blush, when I feel that I am saying something disgraceful. It is this emotion which does not allow me to lay down pleasure as the good and end of life.

[1] Or "morose," that is, from the point of view of the Epicureans. The reference is to the Stoics, who rejected the "pleasure" of Epicurus, and accepted only that which followed on virtuous conduct.

[2] Frag. 425 (Usener).

15 (53).   Stobaeus, III. 6, 58

Ἐκ τῶν Ἐπικτήτου ἀπομνημονευμάτων.

Ἐν Ῥώμῃ αἱ γυναῖκες μετὰ χεῖρας ἔχουσι τὴν
Πλάτωνος Πολιτείαν, ὅτι κοινὰς ἀξιοῖ εἶναι τὰς
γυναῖκας. τοῖς γὰρ ῥήμασι προσέχουσι τὸν νοῦν,
οὐ τῇ διανοίᾳ τἀνδρός, ὅτι οὐ γαμεῖν κελεύων καὶ
συνοικεῖν ἕνα μιᾷ εἶτα κοινὰς εἶναι βούλεται τὰς
γυναῖκας, ἀλλ᾽ ἐξαιρῶν τὸν τοιοῦτον γάμον καὶ
ἄλλο τι εἶδος γάμου εἰσφέρων. καὶ τὸ ὅλον οἱ
ἄνθρωποι χαίρουσιν ἀπολογίας τοῖς ἑαυτῶν ἁμαρ-
τήμασι πορίζοντες· ἐπεί τοι φιλοσοφία φησίν,
ὅτι οὐδὲ τὸν δάκτυλον ἐκτείνειν εἰκῇ προσήκει.

16 (78).   Stobaeus, III. 29, 84

Ἐκ τῶν Ἐπικτήτου ἀπομνημονευμάτων.

Εἰδέναι χρή, ὅτι οὐ ῥᾴδιον δόγμα παραγενέσθαι
ἀνθρώπῳ, εἰ μὴ καθ᾽ ἑκάστην ἡμέραν τὰ αὐτὰ
καὶ λέγοι τις καὶ ἀκούοι καὶ ἅμα χρῶτο πρὸς
τὸν βίον.

17 (15).   Stobaeus, III. 4, 91

Ἐπικτήτου.

Εἰς συμπόσιον μὲν οὖν παρακληθέντες τῷ
παρόντι χρώμεθα· εἰ δέ τις κελεύοι τὸν ὑποδεχό-

---

[1] The community of women which Plato proposed was,
first of all, restricted to a small, highly-trained, and devoted
band of warrior-saints ; and, second, such that no man and
woman should pair off for more than a very temporary "marriage," all such matings being carefully supervised by the
highest authorities. Instead of being more licentious than

FRAGMENTS

15

From the Memorabilia *of Epictetus*

At Rome the women have in their hands Plato's *Republic*, because he insists on community of women. For they pay attention only to the words, and not to the meaning of the man; the fact is, he does not bid people marry and live together, one man with one woman, and then go on to advocate the community of women, but he first abolishes that kind of marriage altogether, and introduces another kind in its place.[1] And in general people delight in finding excuses for their own faults; for, indeed, philosophy says we ought not to stretch out even our finger at random![2]

16

From the Memorabilia *of Epictetus*

One ought to know that it is not easy for a man to acquire a fixed judgement, unless he should day by day state and hear the same principles, and at the same time apply them to his life.

17

From Epictetus

Now when we have been invited to a banquet, we take what is set before us; and if a person should

ordinary monogamous marriage (which frequently deserves Bernard Shaw's jibe, that it is popular largely because it combines the maximum of temptation with the maximum of opportunity), Plato's proposal was relatively a denial of the flesh, and a marked move towards asceticism.

[2] See II. 11, 17. The remark in this connection is no doubt ironical, mockingly justifying the process of "rationalization" just described.

μενον ἰχθῦς αὐτῷ παρατιθέναι ἢ πλακοῦντας,
ἄτοπος ἂν δόξειεν. ἐν δὲ τῷ κόσμῳ αἰτοῦμεν
τοὺς θεούς, ἃ μὴ διδόασι, καὶ ταῦτα πολλῶν
ὄντων, ἅ γε ἡμῖν δεδώκασι.

18 (16). Stobaeus, III. 4, 92

Τοῦ αὐτοῦ.

Χαρίεντες, ἔφη, εἰσὶν οἱ μέγα φρονοῦντες ἐπὶ
τοῖς οὐκ ἐφ᾽ ἡμῖν. "ἐγώ," φησί, "κρείττων εἰμί
σου·[1] ἀγροὺς γὰρ ἔχω πολλούς, σὺ δὲ λιμῷ παρα-
τείνῃ." ἄλλος λέγει "ἐγὼ ὑπατικός εἰμι." ἄλλος
"ἐγὼ ἐπίτροπος." ἄλλος "ἐγὼ οὔλας τρίχας
ἔχω."[2] ἵππος δ᾽ ἵππῳ οὐ λέγει ὅτι "κρείττων
εἰμί σου· πολὺν γὰρ κέκτημαι χιλὸν καὶ κριθὰς
πολλὰς καὶ χαλινοί μοί εἰσι χρυσοῖ καὶ ἐφίππια
ποικίλα," ἀλλ᾽ ὅτι "ὠκύτερός σού εἰμι." καὶ
πᾶν ζῷον κρεῖττον καὶ χεῖρόν ἐστιν ἐκ τῆς
ἑαυτοῦ ἀρετῆς καὶ κακίας. ἆρ᾽ οὖν ἀνθρώπου
μόνου ἀρετὴ οὐκ ἔστιν, ἀλλὰ δεῖ ἡμᾶς εἰς τὰς[3]
τρίχας ἀφορᾶν καὶ τὰ ἱμάτια καὶ τοὺς πάππους;

19 (17). Stobaeus, III. 4, 93

Τοῦ αὐτοῦ.[4]

Τῷ μὲν ἰατρῷ μηδὲν συμβουλεύοντι ἄχθονται
οἱ κάμνοντες καὶ ἡγοῦνται ἀπεγνῶσθαι ὑπ᾽ αὐτοῦ.

---

[1] σου added here by Schenkl; after ἐγώ A man. alt., and
Gesner.
[2] ἔχω added by Gesner.

bid his host to set before him fish or cakes, he would be regarded as eccentric. Yet in the world at large we ask the gods for things which they do not give us, and that too when there are many things which they actually have given us.

18
From the same

Those are amusing persons, he said, who take great pride in the things which are not under our control. A man says, " I am better than you ; for I have many estates, and you are half-dead with hunger."[1] Another says, " I am a consular." Another, " I am a procurator." Another, " I have thick curly hair." But one horse does not say to another horse, " I am better than you, for I have quantities of fodder, and a great deal of barley, and my bridles are of gold, and my saddle-cloths are embroidered," but " I can run faster than you can." And every creature is better or worse because of its own particular virtue or vice. Can it be, then, that man is the only creature without a special virtue, but he must have recourse to his hair, and his clothes, and his grandsires ?

19
The same

When men are sick and their physician gives them no advice, they are annoyed, and think that

[1] The phrase is from Plato, *Symposium*, 207 B.

[3] τὰς added by Meineke.
[4] The superscription added by Gaisford.

πρὸς δὲ τὸν φιλόσοφον διὰ τί [1] οὐκ ἄν τις οὕτω
διατεθείη, ὥστε οἰηθῆναι ἀπεγνῶσθαι ὑπ' αὐτοῦ
σωφρονήσειν, εἰ μηδὲν λέγοι ἔτι [2] πρὸς αὐτὸν τῶν
χρησίμων;

20 (18). Stobaeus, III. 4, 94

Τοῦ αὐτοῦ.

Οἱ τὸ σῶμα εὖ διακείμενοι καὶ καύματα καὶ
ψύχη ὑπομένουσιν· οὕτω δὲ καὶ οἱ τὴν ψυχὴν
καλῶς διακείμενοι καὶ ὀργὴν καὶ λύπην καὶ περι-
χάρειαν καὶ τὰ ἄλλα πάθη φέρουσιν.

21 (56). Stobaeus, III. 7, 16

Ἐπικτήτου.

Διὰ τοῦτο ἐπαινεῖν Ἀγριππῖνον δίκαιον, ὅτι
πλείστου ἄξιος ἀνὴρ γενόμενος οὐδεπώποτε
ἐπῄνεσεν ἑαυτόν, ἀλλ' εἰ καὶ ἄλλος τις αὐτὸν
ἐπῄνει, ἠρυθρία. οὗτος δ', ἔφη, ὁ ἀνὴρ τοιοῦτος
ἦν, ὥστε τοῦ συμβαίνοντος ἀεὶ ἑαυτῷ δυσκόλου
ἔπαινον γράφειν· εἰ μὲν πυρέττοι, πυρετοῦ· εἰ δὲ
ἀδοξοῖ, ἀδοξίας· εἰ δὲ φεύγοι,[3] φυγῆς. καί ποτε
μέλλοντι, ἔφη, αὐτῷ [4] ἀριστήσειν ἐπέστη ὁ λέγων,
ὅτι φεύγειν αὐτὸν κελεύει Νέρων, καὶ ὃς [5] " οὐκοῦν,"
εἶπεν, " ἐν Ἀρικίᾳ ἀριστήσομεν."

---

[1] διὰ τί Gesner : διότι MSS.   [2] Bücheler : τι MSS.
[3] Meineke : φύγοι MSS.   [4] Gesner : τω or τῷ MSS.
[5] ἔφη after this word deleted by Schow.

---

[1] A distinguished Roman Stoic of the middle of the first
century after Christ. See I. 1, 28–30 ; I. 2, 12–13 ; frag. 22.

he has given them up.   And why should not a man
feel that way toward the philosopher, and so conclude
that he has given up hope of one's ever coming to a
sound state of mind, if he no longer tells one anything that is of any use?

20

The same

Those whose bodies are in good condition can
endure heat and cold; so also those whose souls are
in an excellent condition can endure anger, and grief,
and great joy, and every other emotion.

21

From Epictetus

For this reason it is right to praise Agrippinus,[1]
because, although he was a man of the very highest
worth, he never praised himself, but used to blush
even if someone else praised him.   His character
was such, said Epictetus, that when any hardship
befell him he would compose a eulogy upon it; on
fever, if he had a fever; on disrepute, if he suffered
from disrepute; on exile, if he went into exile.
And once, he said, when Agrippinus was preparing
to take lunch, a man brought him word that Nero
ordered him into exile; " Very well," said he, " we
shall take our lunch in Aricia." [2]

[2] The first stop outside Rome for persons travelling south
and east, the common direction, as in the well known
egressum magna me excepit Aricia Roma (Horace, *Sat.* I. 5, 1).
Compare the version of the same incident in I. 1, 30.

22. Stobaeus, IV. 7, 44

Ἀγριππίνου.[1]

Ὁ Ἀγριππῖνος ἡγεμονεύων ἐπειρᾶτο τοὺς καταδικαζομένους ὑπ' αὐτοῦ πείθειν, ὅτι προσήκει αὐτοῖς καταδικασθῆναι. οὐ γὰρ ὡς πολέμιος αὐτοῖς, ἔφη, οὐδ' ὡς λῃστὴς καταφέρω τὴν ψῆφον αὐτῶν, ἀλλ' ὡς ἐπιμελητὴς καὶ κηδεμών, ὥσπερ καὶ ὁ ἰατρὸς τὸν τεμνόμενον παραμυθεῖται καὶ πείθει παρέχειν ἑαυτόν.

23 (94). Stobaeus, IV. 53, 29

Ἐπικτήτου.

Θαυμαστὴ ἡ φύσις καί, ὥς φησιν ὁ Ξενοφῶν, φιλόζωος. τὸ γοῦν σῶμα, τὸ πάντων ἀηδέστατον καὶ ῥυπαρώτατον, στέργομεν καὶ θεραπεύομεν· εἰ γὰρ ἔδει πέντε μόναις ἡμέραις θεραπεῦσαι τὸ τοῦ γείτονος σῶμα, οὐκ ἂν ὑπεμείναμεν. ὅρα γὰρ οἷόν ἐστιν ἕωθεν ἀναστάντα τρίβειν τοὺς ὀδόντας τοὺς ἀλλοτρίους καί τι τῶν ἀναγκαίων ποιήσαντα ἀπονίζειν ἐκεῖνα τὰ μέρη. τῷ ὄντι θαυμαστόν ἐστι φιλεῖν πρᾶγμα, ᾧ τοσαῦτα λειτουργοῦμεν καθ' ἑκάστην ἡμέραν. νάττω τουτονὶ τὸν θύλακον· εἶτα κενῶ· τί τούτου βαρύτερον; ἀλλὰ θεῷ δεῖ με ὑπηρετεῖν. διὰ τοῦτο μένω καὶ ἀνέχομαι λούων τὸ δύστηνον

[1] See explanatory note.

---

[1] Ascribed to Epictetus by Gaisford and Asmus, but there is some doubt about the ascription, for the resemblance with I. 18 is not conclusive.

FRAGMENTS

22

From Agrippinus [1]

When Agrippinus was governor,[2] he used to try to persuade the persons whom he sentenced that it was proper for them to be sentenced. "For," he would say, "it is not as an enemy or as a brigand that I record my vote against them, but as a curator and guardian; just as also the physician encourages the man upon whom he is operating, and persuades him to submit to the operation."

23

From Epictetus

Nature is wonderful, and, as Xenophon [3] says, "fond of her creatures." At all events we love and tend our body, the most unpleasant and dirtiest thing that there is; why, if we had had to tend our neighbour's body for no more than five days, we could not have endured it. Just consider what a nuisance it is to get up in the morning and brush some other person's teeth, and then after attending to a call of nature to wash those parts. Truly it is wonderful to love a thing for which we perform so many services every day. I stuff this bag here;[4] and then I empty it; what is more tiresome? But I must serve God. For that reason I remain, and endure to wash this miserable paltry body, and to

---

[2] He was proconsul of Crete and Cyrenaica under Claudius. For all that is known about him see *Prosopographia Imperii Romani*, III. p. 4, No. 16.

[3] *Memorabilia*, I. 4, 7, where, however, the expression is used of a "wise Creator.'

[4] Pointing to his belly.

τοῦτο σωμάτιον, χορτάζων, σκέπων· ὅτε δὲ
νεώτερος ἦν, καὶ ἄλλο τι προσέταττέ μοι καὶ
ὅμως ἠνειχόμην αὐτοῦ. διὰ τί οὖν οὐκ ἀνέχεσθε,
ὅταν ἡ δοῦσα ἡμῖν φύσις τὸ σῶμα ἀφαιρῆται ;—
Φιλῶ, φησίν, αὐτό.—Οὐκ οὖν, ὃ νῦν δὴ ἔλεγον,
καὶ αὐτὸ τὸ φιλεῖν ἡ φύσις σοι δέδωκεν; ἡ δ᾽
αὐτὴ λέγει "ἄφες αὐτὸ ἤδη καὶ μηκέτι πρᾶγμα
ἔχε."

24 (95). Stobaeus, IV. 53, 30

Τοῦ αὐτοῦ.

Ἐὰν νέος τελευτᾷ τὸν βίον, ἐγκαλεῖ τοῖς
θεοῖς . . .,[1] ὅτι δέον αὐτὸν ἤδη ἀναπεπαῦσθαι
πρᾶγμα ἔχει, καὶ οὐδὲν ἧττον, ὅταν προσίῃ[2]
ὁ θάνατος, ζῆν βούλεται καὶ πέμπει παρὰ τὸν
ἰατρὸν καὶ δεῖται αὐτοῦ μηδὲν ἀπολιπεῖν προθυμίας καὶ ἐπιμελείας. θαυμαστοί, ἔφη, ἄνθρωποι μήτε ζῆν θέλοντες μήτε ἀποθνήσκειν.

25 (71). Stobaeus, III. 20, 67

Ἐπικτήτου.

Ὅτῳ μετὰ ἀνατάσεως καὶ ἀπειλῆς ἐπιχειρεῖς,
μέμνησο προλέγειν, ὅτι ἥμερος εἶ· καὶ οὐδὲν ἄγριον
δράσας ἀμετανόητος καὶ ἀνεύθυνος διαγενήσῃ.

---

[1] For the obvious lacuna the best suggestions seem to be:
ὅτι πρὸ τῆς ὥρας ἁρπάζεται (Cobet)· ἐὰν δὲ γέρων τις ὢν μὴ
τελευτᾷ τὸν βίον (Schweighäuser), καὶ οὗτος ἐγκαλεῖ τοῖς θεοῖς
(Cobet).
[2] Meibom: προσίῃ or προσίει MSS.

feed and shelter it; and when I was younger, there was still another behest which it laid upon me, yet nevertheless I endured it. Why, then, when Nature, which gave us our body, takes it away, do you not bear it?—I love it, says somebody.—Well, but as I was just now saying, is it not Nature that has given you this very affection? But the same Nature also says, "Let it go now, and have no more trouble with it."

24

The same

If a man dies young, he blames the gods ⟨because he is carried off before his time. But if a man fails to die when he is old, he too blames the gods⟩, because, when it was long since time for him to rest, he has trouble; yet none the less, when death draws nigh, he wishes to live, and sends for the doctor, and implores him to spare no zeal and pains. People are very strange, he used to say, wishing neither to live nor to die.

25

From Epictetus

When you attack someone with vehemence and threatening, remember to tell yourself beforehand that you are a tame animal;[1] and then you will never do anything fierce, and so will come to the end of your life without having to repent, or to be called to account.

[1] See IV. 5, 10.

26 (176).   Marcus Aurelius, 4, 41

Ψυχάριον εἶ βαστάζον νεκρόν, ὡς Ἐπίκτητος
ἔλεγεν.

27 (177).   Marcus Aurelius, 11, 37

Τέχνην ἔφη δὲ περὶ τὸ συγκατατίθεσθαι
εὑρεῖν καὶ ἐν τῷ περὶ τὰς ὁρμὰς τόπῳ τὸ
προσεκτικὸν φυλάσσειν, ἵνα μεθ' ὑπεξαιρέσεως,
ἵνα κοινωνικαί, ἵνα κατ' ἀξίαν, καὶ ὀρέξεως μὲν
παντάπασιν ἀπέχεσθαι, ἐκκλίσει δὲ πρὸς μηδὲν
τῶν οὐκ ἐφ' ἡμῖν χρῆσθαι.

28 (178).   Marcus Aurelius, 11, 38

Οὐ περὶ τοῦ τυχόντος οὖν, ἔφη, ἐστὶν ὁ ἀγών,
ἀλλὰ περὶ τοῦ μαίνεσθαι ἢ μή.

28 a.   Marcus Aurelius, 11, 39 [1]

Ὁ Σωκράτης ἔλεγεν "τί θέλετε; λογικῶν
ψυχὰς ἔχειν ἢ ἀλόγων;" "λογικῶν." "τίνων
λογικῶν; ὑγιῶν ἢ φαύλων;" "ὑγιῶν." "τί
οὖν οὐ ζητεῖτε;" "ὅτι ἔχομεν." "τί οὖν μάχεσθε
καὶ διαφέρεσθε;"

28 b.   Marcus Aurelius, 4, 49, 2–6 [2]

"'Ἀτυχὴς ἐγώ, ὅτι τοῦτό μοι συνέβη.' οὐμεν-
οῦν· ἀλλ' 'εὐτυχὴς ἐγώ, ὅτι τούτου μοι συμβε-

[1] Ascribed to Epictetus by Leopold and Breithaupt.
[2] Convincingly assigned to Epictetus for many reasons,
chiefly lexicographical, by H. Fränkel, *Philologus* 80 (1924),
221. I give the text of Schenkl (1913), with the quotation
marks adjusted to the new interpretation.

FRAGMENTS

26

You are a little soul, carrying around a corpse, as Epictetus used to say.

27

We must discover, said he, an art that deals with assent, and in the sphere of the choices we must be careful to maintain close attention, that they be made with due reservations, that they be social, and that they be according to merit; and from desire we must refrain altogether, and must exercise aversion towards none of the things that are not under our control.

28

It is no ordinary matter that is at stake, said he, but it is a question of either madness or sanity.

28 a

Socrates used to say, "What do you want? To have souls of rational or irrational animals?" "Of rational animals." "Of what kind of rational animals? Sound or vicious?" "Sound." "Why, then, do you not try to get them?" "Because we have them." "Why, then, do you strive and quarrel?"

28 b [1]

"Me miserable, that this has befallen me!" Say not so, but rather, "Fortunate that I am, because,

---

[1] This whole passage is taken to be a direct quotation from Epictetus, with the exception of the first two lines in the second paragraph, where Marcus Aurelius applies the doctrine to himself, and the last two lines, in which he characteristically condenses and summarizes it.

βηκότος ἄλυπος διατελῶ οὔτε ὑπὸ παρόντος
θρανόμενος, οὔτε ἐπιὸν φοβούμενος.' συμβῆναι
μὲν γὰρ τὸ τοιοῦτον παντὶ ἐδύνατο· ἄλυπος δὲ
οὐ πᾶς ἐπὶ τούτῳ ἂν διετέλεσεν. διὰ τί οὖν
ἐκεῖνο μᾶλλον ἀτύχημα ἢ τοῦτο εὐτύχημα ;
λέγεις δὲ ὅλως ἀτύχημα ἀνθρώπου, ὃ οὐκ ἔστιν
ἀπότευγμα τῆς φύσεως τοῦ ἀνθρώπου ; ἀπότευγμα δὲ τῆς φύσεως τοῦ ἀνθρώπου εἶναι δοκεῖ
σοι, ὃ μὴ παρὰ τὸ βούλημα τῆς φύσεως αὐτοῦ
ἐστί ; τί οὖν ; τὸ βούλημα μεμάθηκας. μή τι
οὖν τὸ συμβεβηκὸς τοῦτο κωλύει σε δίκαιον
εἶναι, μεγαλόψυχον, σώφρονα, ἔμφρονα, ἀπρό-
πτωτον, ἀδιάψευστον, αἰδήμονα, ἐλεύθερον, τἆλλα, ὧν συμπαρόντων ἡ φύσις ἡ τοῦ ἀνθρώπου
ἀπέχει τὰ ἴδια ;'

Μέμνησο λοιπὸν ἐπὶ παντὸς τοῦ εἰς λύπην
σε προαγομένου, τούτῳ χρῆσθαι τῷ δόγματι·
" οὐχ ὅτι τοῦτο ἀτύχημα, ἀλλὰ τὸ φέρειν αὐτὸ
γενναίως εὐτύχημα."

FRAGMENTA DUBIA ET SPURIA

29 (77). Stobaeus, III. 35, 10 [1]

Ἐκ τοῦ Ἐπικτήτου ἐγχειριδίου.

Μηδενὸς οὕτως ἐν παντὶ προνόει, ὡς τοῦ
ἀσφαλοῦς· ἀσφαλέστερον γὰρ τοῦ λέγειν τὸ
σιγᾶν· ἐὰν δὲ τὸ λέγειν, ὅσα δίχα ἔσται νοῦ
καὶ ψόγου μεστά.[2]

[1] These words are not found in the *Encheiridion*, and may
very possibly not be by Epictetus at all.

although this has befallen me, I continue to live untroubled, being neither crushed by the present nor afraid of the future." For something of this kind might have befallen anyone; but not everyone would have continued to live untroubled by it. Why, then, count the former aspect of the matter a misfortune, rather than this latter good fortune? And in general do you call a man's misfortune that which is not an aberration from man's nature? And does that seem to you to be an aberration from the nature of man which does not contravene the will of his nature? What then? This will of man's nature you have already learned; this, then, which has befallen you does not prevent you, does it, from being just, high-minded, self-controlled, self-possessed, deliberate, free from deceit, self-respecting, free, and everything else, the possession of which enables the nature of man to come into its own?

Remember for the future, whenever anything begins to trouble you, to make use of the following judgement: This thing is not a misfortune, but to bear it in a noble spirit is good fortune.

DOUBTFUL AND SPURIOUS FRAGMENTS

29

From the Encheiridion *of Epictetus*

Under all circumstances take thought of nothing so much as safety; for it is safer to keep silence than to speak; and refrain from saying what will be devoid of sense and full of censure.

---

[1] Supplied by Hense.

30 (89).   Stobaeus, IV. 46, 22 [1]

['Επικτήτου.]

Οὔτε ναῦν ἐξ ἑνὸς ἀγκυρίου οὔτε βίον ἐκ μιᾶς
ἐλπίδος ἁρμοστέον.

31 (90).   Stobaeus, IV. 46, 23

Τοῦ αὐτοῦ.

Καὶ τοῖς σκέλεσι καὶ ταῖς ἐλπίσι τὰ δυνατὰ
δεῖ διαβαίνειν.

32 (92).   Stobaeus, IV. 53, 27 [2]

['Επικτήτου.]

Ψυχὴν σώματος ἀναγκαιότερον ἰᾶσθαι· τοῦ
γὰρ κακῶς ζῆν τὸ τεθνάναι κρεῖσσον.

33 (54).   Stobaeus, III. 6, 59.   Democritus, frag.
232 (Diels)

[Τοῦ αὐτοῦ ('Επικλήτου)].[3]

Τῶν ἡδέων τὰ σπανιώτατα γινόμενα μάλιστα
τέρπει.

34 (55).   Stobaeus, III. 6, 60.   Democritus, frag.
233 (Diels)

Τοῦ αὐτοῦ.

Εἴ τις ὑπερβάλλοι τὸ μέτριον, τὰ ἐπιτερπέσ-
τατα ἀτερπέστατα ἂν γίνοιτο.[4]

---

[1] This and the next fragment probably belong to the
collection of Aristonymus.

[2] Variously ascribed elsewhere.

DOUBTFUL AND SPURIOUS FRAGMENTS

30

From Epictetus

We ought neither to fasten our ship to one small anchor nor our life to a single hope.

31

From the same

We ought to measure both the length of our stride, and the extent of our hope, by what is possible.

32

From Epictetus

It is much more necessary to cure the soul than the body; for death is better than a bad life.

33

From the same

Those of our pleasures which come most rarely give the greatest delight.

34

From the same

If a man should overpass the mean, the most delightful things would become least delightful.

---

³ So in *Florilegium*, Cod. Paris. 1168 [500 E]. The fragment belongs to Democritus.

⁴ Burchard: γίγνοιτο or γένοιτο MSS. The fragment belongs to Democritus.

35 (114).   *Florilegium*, Cod. Paris. 1168 [501 E]

Οὐδεὶς ἐλεύθερος ἑαυτοῦ μὴ κρατῶν.[1]

36 (140).   Antonius, 1, 21 [2]

Ἀθάνατον χρῆμα ἡ ἀλήθεια καὶ ἀΐδιον, παρέχει δὲ ἡμῖν οὐ κάλλος χρόνῳ μαραινόμενον οὔτε παρρησίαν ἀφαιρετὴν[3] ὑπὸ δίκης, ἀλλὰ τὰ δίκαια καὶ τὰ νόμιμα διακρίνουσα ἀπ' αὐτῶν τὰ ἄδικα καὶ ἀπελέγχουσα.

[1] In Stobaeus the maxim is ascribed to Pythagoras.
[2] The style of this fragment is alien to Epictetus.
[3] Kronenberg: ἀφαιρεῖτην MS.

DOUBTFUL AND SPURIOUS FRAGMENTS

35

No man is free who is not master of himself.

36

The truth is something immortal and eternal, and does not present us with a beauty that withers from the passage of time, nor a freedom of speech which can be taken away by justice, but it presents us with what is just and lawful, distinguishing the unlawful therefrom, and refuting it.

THE *ENCHEIRIDION*, OR *MANUAL*

THIS celebrated work is a compilation made by Arrian himself from the *Discourses*, and the great majority of those who know Epictetus at all have come to do so from this little book alone. That is a pity, because the necessary aridity and formalism of such a systematization obscure the more modest, human, and sympathetic aspects of the great teacher's character. Most of the unfavourable criticism which has been passed upon Epictetus— and there is some of this, although not much—is clearly based upon the occasionally somewhat inadequate impressions which any compendium must produce. For it may be doubted whether even so noble a statement as the Apostles' Creed has ever made a single convert.

Occasionally Arrian has modified to a slight degree the form of statement, as we may observe from the numerous instances, amounting to somewhat more than half of the book, where material from the first four books of the *Discourses* has been employed; but the substance seems to have been faithfully preserved, wherever it is possible to follow his procedure in detail.

The separate editions and translations of the *Encheiridion*[1] are extremely numerous. Few, how-

[1] Those who are curious about bibliographical information may be referred to a separate study, *Contributions toward a Bibliography of Epictetus*, Urbana, Illinois, 1927.

ever, have been of any notable value, except, perhaps, the celebrated translations by Politian and
Leopardi, and Schweighäuser's separate edition of
1798,[1] which is still the last independent critical
text,[2] and has been reprinted by most subsequent
editors, even Schenkl, although the latter has added
much useful critical material in his notes, especially
those which indicate the probable sources of such
passages as seem to be derived from the four
books of the *Discourses*, and in particular has
arranged the *apparatus criticus* in more convenient
terms.

The *sigla* which Schenkl has devised for Schweighäuser's apparatus, and which may occasionally be
employed below, are the following:

A MSS. in which portions of the *Encheiridion*
   precede the corresponding commentary of
   Simplicius.
V The ed. of 1528.

[1] For some unknown reason Schweighäuser in his
Epicteteae Philosophiae Monumenta, III. 1799, reproduced
Upton's much less satisfactory text.
[2] One reason for this delay is the extremely large number
of MSS. involved, not merely of the work itself, but of the
two Christian paraphrases and of the huge commentary by
Simplicius, which is more than ten times the bulk of the
original. The texts of these must first be critically determined before their value for the *Encheiridion* can be esti-
mated, so that in reality four works instead of one have
to be edited from the very foundations. Another is the
very slight probability that any really notable contributions
to knowledge might result therefrom. As an intellectual
problem the preparation of a new edition of the *Encheiridion*
presents certain interesting features, but as a practical
undertaking it is outranked by a good many other possible
investigations.

B   MSS. in which the entire *Encheiridion* precedes the commentary of Simplicius.

C   MSS. containing the *Encheiridion* alone.

v   The edition of Trincavelli (1535).

D   MSS. of Class B which exhibit the text of the *Encheiridion* (frequently abbreviated) as *lemmata* before the commentary of Simplicius.

un.   unus.

nonn.   nonnulli.

sing.   singuli.

Nil.   The *Encheiridion* in the paraphrase of St. Nilus (Schweighäuser, V. 95–138).

Par.   The *Encheiridion* in the anonymous Christian paraphrase (Schweighäuser, V. 1–94).

ΕΠΙΚΤΗΤΟΥ ΕΓΧΕΙΡΙΔΙΟΝ

1 c. 1. Τῶν ὄντων τὰ μέν ἐστιν ἐφ' ἡμῖν, τὰ δὲ
οὐκ ἐφ' ἡμῖν. ἐφ' ἡμῖν μὲν ὑπόληψις, ὁρμή, ὄρεξις,
ἔκκλισις καὶ ἑνὶ λόγῳ ὅσα ἡμέτερα ἔργα· οὐκ ἐφ'
ἡμῖν δὲ τὸ σῶμα, ἡ κτῆσις, δόξαι, ἀρχαὶ καὶ ἑνὶ
2 λόγῳ ὅσα οὐχ ἡμέτερα ἔργα. καὶ τὰ μὲν ἐφ'
ἡμῖν ἐστὶ φύσει ἐλεύθερα, ἀκώλυτα, ἀπαραπό-
διστα, τὰ δὲ οὐκ ἐφ' ἡμῖν ἀσθενῆ, δοῦλα, κωλυτά,
3 ἀλλότρια. μέμνησο οὖν, ὅτι, ἐὰν τὰ φύσει δοῦλα
ἐλεύθερα οἰηθῇς καὶ τὰ ἀλλότρια ἴδια, ἐμποδισθήσῃ, πενθήσεις, ταραχθήσῃ, μέμψῃ καὶ θεοὺς
καὶ ἀνθρώπους, ἐὰν δὲ τὸ σὸν μόνον οἰηθῇς σὸν
εἶναι, τὸ δὲ ἀλλότριον, ὥσπερ ἐστίν, ἀλλότριον,
οὐδείς σε ἀναγκάσει οὐδέποτε, οὐδείς σε κωλύσει,
οὐ μέμψῃ οὐδένα, οὐκ ἐγκαλέσεις τινί, ἄκων
πράξεις οὐδὲ ἕν, ἐχθρὸν οὐχ ἕξεις,[1] οὐδείς σε
βλάψει, οὐδὲ γὰρ βλαβερόν τι πείσῃ.

4 Τηλικούτων οὖν ἐφιέμενος μέμνησο, ὅτι οὐ δεῖ
μετρίως κεκινημένον ἅπτεσθαι αὐτῶν, ἀλλὰ τὰ

---

[1] This is the order for the last phrase in Nil. All other
authorities put it after βλάψει.

THE *ENCHEIRIDION* OF EPICTETUS

1. Some things are under our control, while others are not under our control. Under our control are conception, choice, desire, aversion, and, in a word, everything that is our own doing; not under our control are our body, our property, reputation, office, and, in a word, everything that is not our own doing. Furthermore, the things under our control are by nature free, unhindered, and unimpeded; while the things not under our control are weak, servile, subject to hindrance, and not our own. Remember, therefore, that if what is naturally slavish you think to be free, and what is not your own to be your own, you will be hampered, will grieve, will be in turmoil, and will blame both gods and men; while if you think only what is your own to be your own, and what is not your own to be, as it really is, not your own, then no one will ever be able to exert compulsion upon you, no one will hinder you, you will blame no one, will find fault with no one, will do absolutely nothing against your will, you will have no personal enemy, no one will harm you, for neither is there any harm that can touch you.

With such high aims, therefore, remember that you must bestir yourself with no slight effort to lay hold of them, but you will have to give up some

μὲν ἀφιέναι παντελῶς, τὰ δ' ὑπερτίθεσθαι πρὸς
τὸ παρόν. ἐὰν δὲ καὶ ταῦτ' ἐθέλῃς καὶ ἄρχειν
καὶ πλουτεῖν, τυχὸν μὲν οὐδ' αὐτῶν τούτων τεύξῃ
διὰ τὸ καὶ τῶν προτέρων ἐφίεσθαι, πάντως γε
μὴν ἐκείνων ἀποτεύξῃ, δι' ὧν μόνων ἐλευθερία καὶ
εὐδαιμονία περιγίνεται.

5　Εὐθὺς οὖν πάσῃ φαντασίᾳ τραχείᾳ μελέτα
ἐπιλέγειν ὅτι "φαντασία εἶ καὶ οὐ πάντως τὸ
φαινόμενον." ἔπειτα ἐξέταζε αὐτὴν καὶ δοκίμαζε
τοῖς κανόσι τούτοις οἷς ἔχεις, πρώτῳ δὲ τούτῳ
καὶ μάλιστα, πότερον περὶ τὰ ἐφ' ἡμῖν ἐστιν
ἢ περὶ τὰ οὐκ ἐφ' ἡμῖν· κἂν περί τι τῶν οὐκ ἐφ'
ἡμῖν ᾖ, πρόχειρον ἔστω τὸ διότι "οὐδὲν πρὸς
ἐμέ."

1　c. 2. Μέμνησο, ὅτι ὀρέξεως ἐπαγγελία ἐπιτυχία[1] οὗ ὀρέγῃ, ἐκκλίσεως ἐπαγγελία τὸ μὴ
περιπεσεῖν ἐκείνῳ ὃ ἐκκλίνεται, καὶ ὁ μὲν ἐν[2]
ὀρέξει ἀποτυγχάνων ἀτυχής, ὁ δὲ ἐν[3] ἐκκλίσει
περιπίπτων δυστυχής. ἂν μὲν οὖν μόνα ἐκκλίνῃς
τὰ παρὰ φύσιν τῶν ἐπὶ σοί, οὐδενί, ὧν ἐκκλίνεις,
περιπεσῇ· νόσον δ' ἂν ἐκκλίνῃς ἢ θάνατον ἢ
2　πενίαν, δυστυχήσεις. ἆρον οὖν τὴν ἔκκλισιν
ἀπὸ πάντων τῶν οὐκ ἐφ' ἡμῖν καὶ μετάθες ἐπὶ
τὰ παρὰ φύσιν τῶν ἐφ' ἡμῖν. τὴν ὄρεξιν δὲ
παντελῶς ἐπὶ τοῦ παρόντος ἄνελε· ἄν τε γὰρ
ὀρέγῃ τῶν οὐκ ἐφ' ἡμῖν τινός, ἀτυχεῖν ἀνάγκη,

---

[1] Nil. alone : ἐστὶν ἐπιτυχία AD, ἐστὶ τὸ ἐπιτυχεῖν C, τὸ
ἐπιτυχεῖν B (τυχεῖν Par., τὸ τυχεῖν Simpl.).
[2] Nil. C un.　　　[3] Nil. alone.

---

[1] The remark, as many others of the admonitions, is
addressed to a student or a beginner.

things entirely, and defer others for the time being.
But if you wish for these things also, and at the
same time for both office and wealth, it may be that
you will not get even these latter, because you aim
also at the former, and certainly you will fail to
get the former, which alone bring freedom and
happiness.

Make it, therefore, your study at the very outset
to say to every harsh external impression, " You
are an external impression and not at all what you
appear to be." After that examine it and test it
by these rules which you have, the first and most
important of which is this: Whether the impression
has to do with the things which are under our control, or with those which are not under our control; and, if it has to do with some one of the
things not under our control, have ready to hand
the answer, " It is nothing to me."

2. Remember that the promise of desire is the
attainment of what you desire, that of aversion is not
to fall into what is avoided, and that he who fails
in his desire is unfortunate, while he who falls into
what he would avoid experiences misfortune.   If,
then, you avoid only what is unnatural among those
things which are under your control, you will fall
into none of the things which you avoid; but if you
try to avoid disease, or death, or poverty, you will
experience misfortune.   Withdraw, therefore, your
aversion from all the matters that are not under our
control, and transfer it to what is unnatural among
those which are under our control.   But for the time
being [1] remove utterly your desire; for if you desire
some one of the things that are not under our control you are bound to be unfortunate; and, at the

485

τῶν τε ἐφ' ἡμῖν, ὅσων ὀρέγεσθαι καλὸν ἄν, οὐδὲν
οὐδέπω σοι πάρεστι. μόνῳ δὲ τῷ ὁρμᾶν καὶ
ἀφορμᾶν χρῶ, κούφως μέντοι καὶ μεθ' ὑπεξαιρέσεως καὶ ἀνειμένως.

c. 3. Ἐφ' ἑκάστου τῶν ψυχαγωγούντων ἢ
χρείαν παρεχόντων ἢ στεργομένων μέμνησο
ἐπιλέγειν, ὁποῖόν ἐστιν, ἀπὸ τῶν σμικροτάτων
ἀρξάμενος. ἂν χύτραν στέργῃς, ὅτι "χύτραν
στέργω"· κατεαγείσης γὰρ αὐτῆς οὐ ταραχθήσῃ.
ἂν παιδίον σαυτοῦ καταφιλῇς ἢ γυναῖκα, ὅτι
ἄνθρωπον καταφιλεῖς· ἀποθανόντος γὰρ οὐ
ταραχθήσῃ.

c. 4. Ὅταν ἅπτεσθαί τινος ἔργου μέλλῃς,
ὑπομίμνησκε σεαυτόν, ὁποῖόν ἐστι τὸ ἔργον.
ἐὰν λουσόμενος ἀπῇς, πρόβαλλε σεαυτῷ τὰ
γινόμενα ἐν βαλανείῳ, τοὺς ἀπορραίνοντας, τοὺς
ἐγκρουομένους, τοὺς λοιδοροῦντας, τοὺς κλέπτον-
τας. καὶ οὕτως ἀσφαλέστερον ἅψῃ τοῦ ἔργου,
ἐὰν ἐπιλέγῃς εὐθὺς ὅτι "λούσασθαι θέλω καὶ
τὴν ἐμαυτοῦ προαίρεσιν κατὰ φύσιν ἔχουσαν
τηρῆσαι." καὶ ὡσαύτως ἐφ' ἑκάστου ἔργου.
οὕτω γὰρ ἄν τι πρὸς τὸ λούσασθαι γένηται
ἐμποδών, πρόχειρον ἔσται διότι "ἀλλ' οὐ τοῦτο
ἤθελον μόνον, ἀλλὰ καὶ τὴν ἐμαυτοῦ προαίρεσιν
κατὰ φύσιν ἔχουσαν τηρῆσαι· οὐ τηρήσω δέ, ἐὰν
ἀγανακτῶ πρὸς τὰ γινόμενα."

c. 5. Ταράσσει τοὺς ἀνθρώπους οὐ τὰ πράγματα, ἀλλὰ τὰ περὶ τῶν πραγμάτων δόγματα·

---

[1] See M. Aurelius, 1, 4, where Mr. Haines (in *L.C.L.*)
suggests that the reference is to some such reservations as

same time, not one of the things that are under our control, which it would be excellent for you to desire, is within your grasp. But employ only choice and refusal, and these too but lightly, and with reservations,[1] and without straining.

3. With everything which entertains you, is useful, or of which you are fond, remember to say to yourself, beginning with the very least things, " What is its nature? " If you are fond of a jug, say, " I am fond of a jug "; for when it is broken you will not be disturbed. If you kiss your own child or wife, say to yourself that you are kissing a human being; for when it dies you will not be disturbed.

4. When you are on the point of putting your hand to some undertaking, remind yourself what the nature of that undertaking is. If you are going out of the house to bathe, put before your mind what happens at a public bath—those who splash you with water, those who jostle against you, those who vilify you and rob you. And thus you will set about your undertaking more securely if at the outset you say to yourself, " I want to take a bath, and, at the same time, to keep my moral purpose in harmony with nature." And so do in every undertaking. For thus, if anything happens to hinder you in your bathing, you will be ready to say, " Oh, well, this was not the only thing that I wanted, but I wanted also to keep my moral purpose in harmony with nature; and I shall not so keep it if I am vexed at what is going on."

5. It is not the things themselves that disturb men, but their judgements about these things. For

recommended in James iv. 15 : " For that ye ought to say is, If the Lord will, we shall live, and do this, or that."

example, death is nothing dreadful, or else Socrates
too would have thought so, but the judgement
that death is dreadful, *this* is the dreadful thing.
When, therefore, we are hindered, or disturbed,
or grieved, let us never blame anyone but ourselves, that means, our own judgements. It is
the part of an uneducated person to blame others
where he himself fares ill ; to blame himself is the
part of one whose education has begun ; to blame
neither another nor his own self is the part of one
whose education is already complete.

6. Be not elated at any excellence which is not
your own. If the horse in his elation were to say,
" I am beautiful," it could be endured ; but when
you say in your elation, " I have a beautiful horse,"
rest assured that you are elated at something good
which belongs to a horse. What, then, is your
own ? The use of external impressions. Therefore, when you are in harmony with nature in the
use of external impressions, then be elated ; for
then it will be some good of your own at which you
will be elated.

7. Just as on a voyage, when your ship has
anchored, if you should go on shore to get fresh
water, you may pick up a small shell-fish or little
bulb[1] on the way, but you have to keep your attention fixed on the ship, and turn about frequently for
fear lest the captain should call ; and if he calls, you
must give up all these things, if you would escape
being thrown on board all tied up like the sheep.
So it is also in life : If there be given you, instead
of a little bulb and a small shell-fish, a little wife
and child, there will be no objection to that; only,
if the Captain calls, give up all these things and run

to the ship, without even turning around to look back. And if you are an old man, never even get very far away from the ship, for fear that when He calls you may be missing.

8. Do not seek to have everything that happens happen as you wish, but wish for everything to happen as it actually does happen, and your life will be serene.

9. Disease is an impediment to the body, but not to the moral purpose, unless that consents. Lameness is an impediment to the leg, but not to the moral purpose. And say this to yourself at each thing that befalls you; for you will find the thing to be an impediment to something else, but not to yourself.

10. In the case of everything that befalls you, remember to turn to yourself and see what faculty you have to deal with it. If you see a handsome lad or woman, you will find continence the faculty to employ here; if hard labour is laid upon you, you will find endurance; if reviling, you will find patience to bear evil. And if you habituate yourself in this fashion, your external impressions will not run away with you.

11. Never say about anything, "I have lost it," but only "I have given it back." Is your child dead? It has been given back. Is your wife dead? She has been given back. "I have had my farm taken away." Very well, this too has been given back. "Yet it was a rascal who took it away." But what concern is it of yours by whose instrumentality the Giver called for its return? So long as He gives it you, take care of it as of a thing that is not your own, as travellers treat their inn.

12. If you wish to make progress, dismiss all

ἐπιλογισμούς. " ἐὰν ἀμελήσω τῶν ἐμῶν, οὐχ
ἕξω διατροφάς"· " ἐὰν μὴ κολάσω τὸν παῖδα,
πονηρὸς ἔσται." κρεῖσσον γὰρ λιμῷ ἀποθανεῖν
ἄλυπον καὶ ἄφοβον γενόμενον ἢ ζῆν ἐν ἀφθόνοις
ταρασσόμενον. κρεῖττον δὲ τὸν παῖδα κακὸν
εἶναι ἢ σὲ κακοδαίμονα. ἄρξαι τοιγαροῦν ἀπὸ
2 τῶν σμικρῶν. ἐκχεῖται τὸ ἐλάδιον, κλέπτεται
τὸ οἰνάριον· ἐπίλεγε ὅτι " τοσούτου πωλεῖται
ἀπάθεια, τοσούτου ἀταραξία"· προῖκα δὲ οὐδὲν
περιγίνεται. ὅταν δὲ καλῇς τὸν παῖδα, ἐνθυμοῦ,
ὅτι δύναται μὴ ὑπακοῦσαι καὶ ὑπακούσας μηδὲν
ποιῆσαι ὧν θέλεις· ἀλλ' οὐχ οὕτως ἐστὶν αὐτῷ
καλῶς, ἵνα ἐπ' ἐκείνῳ ᾖ τὸ σὲ μὴ ταραχθῆναι.

c. 13. Εἰ προκόψαι θέλεις, ὑπόμεινον ἕνεκα τῶν
ἐκτὸς ἀνόητος δόξας καὶ ἠλίθιος, μηδὲν βούλου
δοκεῖν ἐπίστασθαι· κἂν δόξῃς τις εἶναί τισιν,
ἀπίστει σεαυτῷ. ἴσθι γὰρ ὅτι οὐ ῥάδιον τὴν
προαίρεσιν τὴν σεαυτοῦ κατὰ φύσιν ἔχουσαν
φυλάξαι καὶ τὰ ἐκτός, ἀλλὰ τοῦ ἑτέρου ἐπι-
μελούμενον τοῦ ἑτέρου ἀμελῆσαι πᾶσα ἀνάγκη.

1 c. 14. Ἐὰν θέλῃς τὰ τέκνα σου καὶ τὴν γυναῖκα
καὶ τοὺς φίλους σου πάντοτε ζῆν, ἠλίθιος εἶ·
τὰ γὰρ μὴ ἐπὶ σοὶ θέλεις ἐπὶ σοὶ εἶναι καὶ τὰ
ἀλλότρια σὰ εἶναι· οὕτω κἂν τὸν παῖδα θέλῃς
μὴ ἁμαρτάνειν, μωρὸς εἶ· θέλεις γὰρ τὴν κακίαν

---

¹ That is, the slave-boy would be in a remarkable position
of advantage if his master's peace of mind depended, not
upon the master himself, but upon the actions of his
slave-boy.

reasoning of this sort: "If I neglect my affairs, I shall have nothing to live on." "If I do not punish my slave-boy he will turn out bad." For it is better to die of hunger, but in a state of freedom from grief and fear, than to live in plenty, but troubled in mind. And it is better for your slave-boy to be bad than for you to be unhappy. Begin, therefore, with the little things. Your paltry oil gets spilled, your miserable wine stolen; say to yourself, "This is the price paid for a calm spirit, this the price for peace of mind." Nothing is got without a price. And when you call your slave-boy, bear in mind that it is possible he may not heed you, and again, that even if he does heed, he may not do what you want done. But he is not in so happy a condition that your peace of mind depends upon him.[1]

13. If you wish to make progress, then be content to appear senseless and foolish in externals, do not make it your wish to give the appearance of knowing anything; and if some people think you to be an important personage, distrust yourself. For be assured that it is no easy matter to keep your moral purpose in a state of conformity with nature, and, at the same time, to keep externals; but the man who devotes his attention to one of these two things must inevitably neglect the other.

14. If you make it your will that your children and your wife and your friends should live for ever, you are silly; for you are making it your will that things not under your control should be under your control, and that what is not your own should be your own. In the same way, too, if you make it your will that your slave-boy be free from faults, you are a fool; for you are making it your will that vice be not

493

vice, but something else. If, however, it is your will not to fail in what you desire, this is in your power. Wherefore, exercise yourself in that which is in your power. Each man's master is the person who has the authority over what the man wishes or does not wish, so as to secure it, or take it away. Whoever, therefore, wants to be free, let him neither wish for anything, nor avoid anything, that is under the control of others; or else he is necessarily a slave.

15. Remember that you ought to behave in life as you would at a banquet. As something is being passed around it comes to you; stretch out your hand and take a portion of it politely. It passes on; do not detain it. Or it has not come to you yet; do not project your desire to meet it, but wait until it comes in front of you. So act toward children, so toward a wife, so toward office, so toward wealth; and then some day you will be worthy of the banquets of the gods. But if you do not take these things even when they are set before you, but despise them, then you will not only share the banquet of the gods, but share also their rule. For it was by so doing that Diogenes and Heracleitus, and men like them, were deservedly divine and deservedly so called.

16. When you see someone weeping in sorrow, either because a child has gone on a journey, or because he has lost his property, beware that you be not carried away by the impression that the man is in the midst of external ills, but straightway keep before you this thought: "It is not what has happened that distresses this man (for it does not distress another), but his judgement about it." Do

495

not, however, hesitate to sympathize with him so far as words go, and, if occasion offers, even to groan with him; but be careful not to groan also in the centre of your being.

17. Remember that you are an actor in a play, the character of which is determined by the Playwright : if He wishes the play to be short, it is short ; if long, it is long ; if He wishes you to play the part of a beggar, remember to act even this rôle adroitly ; and so if your rôle be that of a cripple, an official, or a layman. For this is your business, to play admirably the rôle assigned you; but the selection of that rôle is Another's.[1]

18. When a raven croaks inauspiciously, let not the external impression carry you away, but straightway draw a distinction in your own mind, and say, " None of these portents are for me, but either for my paltry body, or my paltry estate, or my paltry opinion, or my children, or my wife. But for me every portent is favourable, if I so wish ; for whatever be the outcome, it is within my power to derive benefit from it."

19. You can be invincible if you never enter a contest in which victory is not under your control. Beware lest, when you see some person preferred to you in honour, or possessing great power, or otherwise enjoying high repute, you are ever carried away by the external impression, and deem him happy. For if the true nature of the good is one of the things that are under our control, there is no place for either envy or jealousy; and you yourself will not wish to be a praetor, or a senator, or a consul, but a free man. Now there is but one way that leads to this, and that is to despise the things that are not under our control.

c. 20. Μέμνησο, ὅτι οὐχ ὁ λοιδορῶν ἢ ὁ τύπτων ὑβρίζει, ἀλλὰ τὸ δόγμα τὸ περὶ τούτων ὡς ὑβριζόντων. ὅταν οὖν ἐρεθίσῃ σέ τις, ἴσθι, ὅτι ἡ σή σε ὑπόληψις ἠρέθικε. τοιγαροῦν ἐν πρώτοις πειρῶ ὑπὸ τῆς φαντασίας μὴ συναρπασθῆναι· ἂν γὰρ ἅπαξ χρόνου καὶ διατριβῆς τύχῃς, ῥᾷον κρατήσεις σεαυτοῦ.

c. 21. Θάνατος καὶ φυγὴ καὶ πάντα τὰ δεινὰ φαινόμενα πρὸ ὀφθαλμῶν ἔστω σοι καθ' ἡμέραν, μάλιστα δὲ πάντων ὁ θάνατος· καὶ οὐδὲν οὐδέποτε οὔτε ταπεινὸν ἐνθυμηθήσῃ οὔτε ἄγαν ἐπιθυμήσεις τινός.

c. 22. Εἰ φιλοσοφίας ἐπιθυμεῖς, παρασκευάζου αὐτόθεν ὡς καταγελασθησόμενος, ὡς καταμωκησομένων σου πολλῶν, ὡς ἐρούντων ὅτι "ἄφνω φιλόσοφος ἡμῖν ἐπανελήλυθε" καὶ "πόθεν ἡμῖν αὕτη ἡ ὀφρύς;" σὺ δὲ ὀφρὺν μὲν μὴ σχῇς· τῶν δὲ βελτίστων σοι φαινομένων οὕτως ἔχου, ὡς ὑπὸ τοῦ θεοῦ τεταγμένος εἰς ταύτην τὴν χώραν· μέμνησό τε διότι,[1] ἐὰν μὲν ἐμμείνῃς τοῖς αὐτοῖς, οἱ καταγελῶντές σου τὸ πρότερον οὗτοί σε ὕστερον θαυμάσονται, ἐὰν δὲ ἡττηθῇς αὐτῶν, διπλοῦν προσλήψῃ καταγέλωτα.

c. 23. Ἐάν ποτέ σοι γένηται ἔξω στραφῆναι πρὸς τὸ βούλεσθαι ἀρέσαι τινί, ἴσθι ὅτι ἀπώλεσας τὴν ἔνστασιν. ἀρκοῦ οὖν ἐν παντὶ τῷ εἶναι φιλόσοφος, εἰ δὲ καὶ δοκεῖν βούλει,[2] σαυτῷ φαίνου καὶ ἱκανὸς ἔσῃ.

1 c. 24. Οὗτοί σε οἱ διαλογισμοὶ μὴ θλιβέτωσαν·

---

[1] τε διότι Nil. : δὲ ὅτι Ench.
[2] The words τῷ εἶναι at this point are omitted by Par.

20. Bear in mind that it is not the man who reviles or strikes you that insults you, but it is your judgement that these men are insulting you. Therefore, when someone irritates you, be assured that it is your own opinion which has irritated you. And so make it your first endeavour not to be carried away by the external impression; for if once you gain time and delay, you will more easily become master of yourself.

21. Keep before your eyes day by day death and exile, and everything that seems terrible, but most of all death; and then you will never have any abject thought, nor will you yearn for anything beyond measure.

22. If you yearn for philosophy, prepare at once to be met with ridicule, to have many people jeer at you, and say, "Here he is again, turned philosopher all of a sudden," and "Where do you suppose he got that high brow?" But do you not put on a high brow, and do you so hold fast to the things which to you seem best, as a man who has been assigned by God to this post; and remember that if you abide by the same principles, those who formerly used to laugh at you will later come to admire you, but if you are worsted by them, you will get the laugh on yourself twice.

23. If it should ever happen to you that you turn to externals with a view to pleasing someone, rest assured that you have lost your plan of life. Be content, therefore, in everything to *be* a philosopher, and if you wish also to be taken for one, show to yourself that you are one, and you will be able to accomplish it.

24. Let not these reflections oppress you: "I

"ἄτιμος ἐγὼ βιώσομαι καὶ οὐδεὶς οὐδαμοῦ." εἰ
γὰρ ἡ ἀτιμία ἐστὶ κακόν, οὐ δύνασαι ἐν κακῷ
εἶναι δι' ἄλλον, οὐ μᾶλλον ἢ ἐν αἰσχρῷ· μή τι
οὖν σόν ἐστιν ἔργον τὸ ἀρχῆς τυχεῖν ἢ παραληφθῆναι ἐφ' ἑστίασιν; οὐδαμῶς. πῶς οὖν ἔτι
τοῦτ' ἔστιν ἀτιμία; πῶς δὲ οὐδεὶς οὐδαμοῦ ἔσῃ,
ὃν ἐν μόνοις εἶναί τινα δεῖ τοῖς ἐπὶ σοί, ἐν οἷς
2 ἔξεστί σοι εἶναι πλείστου ἀξίῳ; ἀλλά σοι οἱ
φίλοι ἀβοήθητοι ἔσονται; τί λέγεις τὸ ἀβοήθητοι; οὐχ ἕξουσι παρὰ σοῦ κερμάτιον· οὐδὲ
πολίτας Ῥωμαίων αὐτοὺς ποιήσεις. τίς οὖν σοι
εἶπεν, ὅτι ταῦτα τῶν ἐφ' ἡμῖν ἐστιν, οὐχὶ δὲ
ἀλλότρια ἔργα; τίς δὲ δοῦναι δύναται ἑτέρῳ, ἃ
μὴ ἔχει αὐτός; "κτῆσαι οὖν," φησίν, "ἵνα ἡμεῖς
3 ἔχωμεν." εἰ δύναμαι κτήσασθαι τηρῶν ἐμαυτὸν
αἰδήμονα καὶ πιστὸν καὶ μεγαλόφρονα, δείκνυε
τὴν ὁδὸν καὶ κτήσομαι. εἰ δ' ἐμὲ ἀξιοῦτε τὰ
ἀγαθὰ τὰ ἐμαυτοῦ ἀπολέσαι, ἵνα ὑμεῖς τὰ μὴ
ἀγαθὰ περιποιήσησθε, ὁρᾶτε ὑμεῖς, πῶς ἄνισοί
ἐστε καὶ ἀγνώμονες. τί δὲ καὶ βούλεσθε μᾶλλον;
ἀργύριον ἢ φίλον πιστὸν καὶ αἰδήμονα; εἰς
τοῦτο οὖν μοι μᾶλλον συλλαμβάνετε καὶ μή, δι'
ὧν ἀποβαλῶ αὐτὰ ταῦτα, ἐκεῖνά με πράσσειν
ἀξιοῦτε.

4   "'Αλλ' ἡ πατρίς, ὅσον ἐπ' ἐμοί," φησίν,

---

¹ That is, every man is exclusively responsible for his own
good or evil.   But honour and the lack of it are things which
are obviously not under a man's control, since they depend
upon the action of other people. It follows, therefore, that

THE *ENCHEIRIDION* OF EPICTETUS

shall live without honour, and be nobody anywhere." For, if lack of honour is an evil, you
cannot be in evil through the instrumentality of
some other person, any more than you can be in
shame.[1] It is not your business, is it, to get office,
or to be invited to a dinner-party? Certainly not.
How, then, can this be any longer a lack of honour?
And how is it that you will be "nobody anywhere,"
when you ought to be somebody only in those
things which are under your control, wherein you
are privileged to be a man of the very greatest
honour? But your friends will be without assistance? What do you mean by being "without
assistance"? They will not have paltry coin from
you, and you will not make them Roman citizens.
Well, who told you that these are some of the
matters under our control, and not rather things
which others do? And who is able to give another
what he does not himself have? "Get money,
then," says some friend, "in order that we too may
have it." If I can get money and at the same time
keep myself self-respecting, and faithful, and high-
minded, show me the way and I will get it. But
if you require me to lose the good things that
belong to me, in order that you may acquire the
things that are not good, you can see for yourselves
how unfair and inconsiderate you are. And which
do you really prefer? Money, or a faithful and
self-respecting friend? Help me, therefore, rather
to this end, and do not require me to do those
things which will make me lose these qualities.

"But my country," says he, "so far as lies in me,

[1] lack of honour cannot be an evil, but must be something
indifferent.

501

"ἀβοήθητος ἔσται." πάλιν, ποίαν καὶ ταύτην
βοήθειαν; στοὰς οὐχ ἕξει διὰ σὲ οὔτε βαλανεῖα.
καὶ τί τοῦτο; οὐδὲ γὰρ ὑποδήματα ἔχει διὰ τὸν
χαλκέα οὐδ' ὅπλα διὰ τὸν σκυτέα· ἱκανὸν δέ, ἐὰν
ἕκαστος ἐκπληρώσῃ τὸ ἑαυτοῦ ἔργον. εἰ δὲ ἄλλον
τινὰ αὐτῇ κατεσκεύαζες πολίτην πιστὸν καὶ
αἰδήμονα, οὐδὲν ἂν αὐτὴν ὠφέλεις; "ναί."
οὐκοῦν οὐδὲ σὺ αὐτὸς ἀνωφελὴς ἂν εἴης αὐτῇ.
"τίνα οὖν ἕξω," φησί, "χώραν ἐν τῇ πόλει;"
ἣν ἂν δύνῃ φυλάττων ἅμα τὸν πιστὸν καὶ
5 αἰδήμονα. εἰ δὲ ἐκείνην ὠφελεῖν βουλόμενος
ἀποβαλεῖς ταῦτα, τί ὄφελος ἂν αὐτῇ γένοιο
ἀναιδὴς καὶ ἄπιστος ἀποτελεσθείς;

1 c. 25. Προετιμήθη σού τις ἐν ἑστιάσει ἢ ἐν
προσαγορεύσει ἢ ἐν τῷ παραληφθῆναι εἰς συμ-
βουλίαν; εἰ μὲν ἀγαθὰ ταῦτά ἐστι, χαίρειν σε
δεῖ, ὅτι ἔτυχεν αὐτῶν ἐκεῖνος· εἰ δὲ κακά, μὴ
ἄχθου, ὅτι σὺ αὐτῶν οὐκ ἔτυχες· μέμνησο δέ, ὅτι
οὐ δύνασαι μὴ ταὐτὰ ποιῶν πρὸς τὸ τυγχάνειν
2 τῶν οὐκ ἐφ' ἡμῖν τῶν ἴσων ἀξιοῦσθαι. πῶς γὰρ
ἴσον ἔχειν δύναται ὁ μὴ φοιτῶν ἐπὶ θύρας τινὸς
τῷ φοιτῶντι; ὁ μὴ παραπέμπων τῷ παραπέμ-
ποντι; ὁ μὴ ἐπαινῶν τῷ ἐπαινοῦντι; ἄδικος οὖν
ἔσῃ καὶ ἄπληστος, εἰ μὴ προϊέμενος ταῦτα, ἀνθ'
ὧν ἐκεῖνα πιπράσκεται, προῖκα αὐτὰ βουλήσῃ

will be without assistance." Again I ask, what
kind of assistance do you mean? It will not have
loggias or baths of your providing. And what does
that signify? For neither does it have shoes provided by the blacksmith, nor has it arms provided by
the cobbler; but it is sufficient if each man fulfil
his own proper function. And if you secured for it
another faithful and self-respecting citizen, would
you not be doing it any good? "Yes." Very well,
and then you also would not be useless to it.
"What place, then, shall I have in the State?"
says he. Whatever place you *can* have, and at the
same time maintain the man of fidelity and self-
respect that is in you. But if, through your desire
to help the State, you lose these qualities, of what
good would you become to it, when in the end you
turned out to be shameless and unfaithful?

25. Has someone been honoured above you at a
dinner-party, or in salutation, or in being called in
to give advice? Now if these matters are good,
you ought to be happy that he got them; but if
evil, be not distressed because you did not get
them; and bear in mind that, if you do not act the
same way that others do, with a view to getting
things which are not under our control, you cannot
be considered worthy to receive an equal share with
others. Why, how is it possible for a person who
does not haunt some man's door, to have equal
shares with the man who does? For the man who
does not do escort duty, with the man who does?
For the man who does not praise, with the man who
does? You will be unjust, therefore, and insatiable,
if, while refusing to pay the price for which such
things are bought, you want to obtain them for

nothing. Well, what is the price for heads of lettuce? An obol,[1] perhaps. If, then, somebody gives up his obol and gets his heads of lettuce, while you do not give up your obol, and do not get them, do not imagine that you are worse off than the man who gets his lettuce. For as he has his heads of lettuce, so you have your obol which you have not given away.

Now it is the same way also in life. You have not been invited to somebody's dinner-party? Of course not; for you didn't give the host the price at which he sells his dinner. He sells it for praise; he sells it for personal attention. Give him the price, then, for which it is sold, if it is to your interest. But if you wish both not to give up the one and yet to get the other, you are insatiable and a simpleton. Have you, then, nothing in place of the dinner? Indeed you have; you have not had to praise the man you did not want to praise; you have not had to put up with the insolence of his doorkeepers.

26. What the will of nature is may be learned from a consideration of the points in which we do not differ from one another. For example, when some other person's slave-boy breaks his drinking-cup, you are instantly ready to say, "That's one of the things which happen." Rest assured, then, that when your own drinking-cup gets broken, you ought to behave in the same way that you do when the other man's cup is broken. Apply now the same principle to the matters of greater importance. Some other person's child or wife has died; no one but would say, "Such is the fate of man." Yet when a man's own child dies, immediately the cry is, "Alas! Woe is me!" But we

ἐγώ." ἐχρῆν δὲ μεμνῆσθαι, τί πάσχομεν περὶ
ἄλλων αὐτὸ ἀκούσαντες.

c. 27. Ὥσπερ σκοπὸς πρὸς τὸ ἀποτυχεῖν οὐ
τίθεται, οὕτως οὐδὲ κακοῦ φύσις ἐν κόσμῳ γίνεται.

c. 28. Εἰ μὲν τὸ σῶμά σού τις ἐπέτρεπε τῷ
ἀπαντήσαντι, ἠγανάκτεις ἄν· ὅτι δὲ σὺ τὴν
γνώμην τὴν σεαυτοῦ ἐπιτρέπεις τῷ τυχόντι, ἵνα,
ἐὰν λοιδορήσηταί σοι, ταραχθῇ ἐκείνη καὶ συγ-
χυθῇ, οὐκ αἰσχύνῃ τούτου ἕνεκα;

1   c. 29. Ἑκάστου ἔργου σκόπει τὰ καθηγούμενα καὶ τὰ ἀκόλουθα αὐτοῦ καὶ οὕτως ἔρχου
ἐπ' αὐτό. εἰ δὲ μή, τὴν μὲν πρώτην προθύμως
ἥξεις ἅτε μηδὲν τῶν ἑξῆς ἐντεθυμημένος, ὕστερον
δὲ ἀναφανέντων δυσχερῶν τινων αἰσχρῶς ἀπο-
2   στήσῃ. θέλεις Ὀλύμπια νικῆσαι; κἀγώ, νὴ
τοὺς θεούς· κομψὸν γάρ ἐστιν. ἀλλὰ σκόπει τὰ
καθηγούμενα καὶ τὰ ἀκόλουθα καὶ οὕτως ἅπτου
τοῦ ἔργου. δεῖ σ' εὐτακτεῖν, ἀναγκοτροφεῖν,
ἀπέχεσθαι πεμμάτων, γυμνάζεσθαι πρὸς ἀνάγκην,
ἐν ὥρᾳ τεταγμένῃ, ἐν καύματι, ἐν ψύχει, μὴ
ψυχρὸν πίνειν, μὴ οἶνον, ὡς ἔτυχεν, ἁπλῶς ὡς
ἰατρῷ παραδεδωκέναι σεαυτὸν τῷ ἐπιστάτῃ, εἶτα
ἐν τῷ ἀγῶνι παρορύσσεσθαι,[1] ἔστι δὲ ὅτε χεῖρα
ἐκβαλεῖν,[2] σφυρὸν στρέψαι, πολλὴν ἁφὴν κατα-

---

[1] Upton from the *Disc.*: παρέρχεσθαι or παρέχεσθαι MSS.
[2] Upton from the *Disc.*: βαλεῖν, λαβεῖν, or βλαβεῖν MSS.

---

[1] That is, it is inconceivable that the universe should
exist in order that some things may go wrong; hence,
nothing natural is evil, and nothing that is by nature evil
can arise.—Thus in effect Simplicius, and correctly, it seems.
[2] This chapter is practically word for word identical with
III. 15. Since it was omitted in Par., and not com-
mented on by Simplicius, it may have been added in some
second edition, whether by Arrian or not.

ought to remember how we feel when we hear of the same misfortune befalling others.

27. Just as a mark is not set up in order to be missed, so neither does the nature of evil arise in the universe.[1]

28. If someone handed over your body to any person who met you, you would be vexed; but that you hand over your mind to any person that comes along, so that, if he reviles you, it is disturbed and troubled—are you not ashamed of that?

29.[2] In each separate thing that you do, consider the matters which come first and those which follow after, and only then approach the thing itself. Otherwise, at the start you will come to it enthusiastically, because you have never reflected upon any of the subsequent steps, but later on, when some difficulties appear, you will give up disgracefully. Do you wish to win an Olympic victory? So do I, by the gods! for it is a fine thing. But consider the matters which come before that, and those which follow after, and only when you have done that, put your hand to the task. You have to submit to discipline, follow a strict diet, give up sweet cakes, train under compulsion, at a fixed hour, in heat or in cold; you must not drink cold water,[3] nor wine just whenever you feel like it; you must have turned yourself over to your trainer precisely as you would to a physician. Then when the contest comes on, you have to "dig in"[4] beside your opponent, and sometimes dislocate your wrist, sprain your ankle, swallow

---

[3] That is, *cold* water not at all; while wine may be drunk, but only at certain times, *i.e.*, probably with one's meals. Such prohibitions are still common in Europe, particularly in popular therapeutics.

[4] See note on III. 15, 4.

πιεῖν, ἔσθ' ὅτε μαστιγωθῆναι, καὶ μετὰ τούτων [1]
3 πάντων νικηθῆναι. ταῦτα ἐπισκεψάμενος, ἂν ἔτι
θέλῃς, ἔρχου ἐπὶ τὸ ἀθλεῖν. εἰ δὲ μή, ὡς τὰ παιδία
ἀναστραφήσῃ, ἃ νῦν μὲν παλαιστὰς παίζει, νῦν
δὲ μονομάχους, νῦν δὲ σαλπίζει, εἶτα τραγῳδεῖ·
οὕτω καὶ σὺ νῦν μὲν ἀθλητής, νῦν δὲ μονομάχος,
εἶτα ῥήτωρ, εἶτα φιλόσοφος, ὅλῃ δὲ τῇ ψυχῇ
οὐδέν· ἀλλ' ὡς πίθηκος πᾶσαν θέαν, ἣν ἂν ἴδῃς,
μιμῇ καὶ ἄλλο ἐξ ἄλλου σοι ἀρέσκει. οὐ γὰρ
μετὰ σκέψεως ἦλθες ἐπί τι οὐδὲ περιοδεύσας,
ἀλλ' εἰκῇ καὶ κατὰ ψυχρὰν ἐπιθυμίαν.

4 Οὕτω θεασάμενοί τινες φιλόσοφον καὶ
ἀκούσαντες οὕτω τινὸς λέγοντος, ὡς Εὐφράτης [2]
λέγει (καίτοι τίς οὕτω δύναται εἰπεῖν, ὡς ἐκεῖνος ;),
5 θέλουσι καὶ αὐτοὶ φιλοσοφεῖν. ἄνθρωπε, πρῶτον
ἐπίσκεψαι, ὁποῖόν ἐστι τὸ πρᾶγμα· εἶτα καὶ τὴν
σεαυτοῦ φύσιν κατάμαθε, εἰ δύνασαι βαστάσαι.
πένταθλος εἶναι βούλει ἢ παλαιστής ; ἴδε
σεαυτοῦ τοὺς βραχίονας, τοὺς μηρούς, τὴν ὀσφὺν
6 κατάμαθε. ἄλλος [3] γὰρ πρὸς ἄλλο πέφυκε.
δοκεῖς, ὅτι ταῦτα ποιῶν ὡσαύτως δύνασαι
ἐσθίειν, ὡσαύτως πίνειν, ὁμοίως ὀρέγεσθαι,
ὁμοίως δυσαρεστεῖν ; ἀγρυπνῆσαι δεῖ, πονῆσαι,
ἀπὸ τῶν οἰκείων ἀπελθεῖν, ὑπὸ παιδαρίου
καταφρονηθῆναι, ὑπὸ τῶν ἀπαντώντων [4] καταγελασθῆναι, ἐν παντὶ ἧττον ἔχειν, ἐν τιμῇ, ἐν ἀρχῇ,
7 ἐν δίκῃ, ἐν πραγματίῳ παντί. ταῦτα ἐπίσκεψαι,

[1] Nil. and the *Discourses* : τῶν Ench.
[2] Wolf from the *Discourses* : ὡς εὖ Σωκράτης Ench. ; ὡς εὖ τις σοφῶν Nil.
[3] Nilus and the *Discourses* : ἄλλο Ench.
[4] Schweighäuser from the *Discourses* : ἀπάντων A un., Nil. ; the clause om. by other MSS.

quantities of sand, sometimes take a scourging, and along with all that get beaten. After you have considered all these points, go on into the games, if you still wish to do so; otherwise, you will be turning back like children. Sometimes they play wrestlers, again gladiators, again they blow trumpets, and then act a play. So you too are now an athlete, now a gladiator, then a rhetorician, then a philosopher, yet with your whole soul nothing; but like an ape you imitate whatever you see, and one thing after another strikes your fancy. For you have never gone out after anything with circumspection, nor after you had examined it all over, but you act at haphazard and half-heartedly.

In the same way, when some people have seen a philosopher and have heard someone speaking like Euphrates [1] (though, indeed, who can speak like him?), they wish to be philosophers themselves. Man, consider first the nature of the business, and then learn your own natural ability, if you are able to bear it. Do you wish to be a contender in the pentathlon, or a wrestler? Look to your arms, your thighs, see what your loins are like. For one man has a natural talent for one thing, another for another. Do you suppose that you can eat in the same fashion, drink in the same fashion, give way to impulse and to irritation, just as you do now? You must keep vigils, work hard, abandon your own people, be despised by a paltry slave, be laughed to scorn by those who meet you, in everything get the worst of it, in honour, in office, in court, in every paltry affair. Look these drawbacks over carefully, if you

---

[1] See note on III. 15, 8.

εἰ θέλεις ἀντικαταλλάξασθαι τούτων ἀπάθειαν,
ἐλευθερίαν, ἀταραξίαν· εἰ δὲ μή, μὴ προσάγαγε,
μὴ ὡς τὰ παιδία νῦν φιλόσοφος, ὕστερον δὲ
τελώνης, εἶτα ῥήτωρ, εἶτα ἐπίτροπος Καίσαρος.
ταῦτα οὐ συμφωνεῖ. ἕνα σε δεῖ ἄνθρωπον ἢ
ἀγαθὸν ἢ κακὸν εἶναι· ἢ τὸ ἡγεμονικόν σε δεῖ
ἐξεργάζεσθαι τὸ σαυτοῦ ἢ τὰ ἐκτός· ἢ περὶ τὰ
ἔσω φιλοτεχνεῖν ἢ περὶ τὰ ἔξω· τοῦτ' ἔστιν ἢ
φιλοσόφου τάξιν ἐπέχειν ἢ ἰδιώτου.

c. 30. Τὰ καθήκοντα ὡς ἐπίπαν ταῖς σχέσεσι
παραμετρεῖται. πατήρ ἐστιν· ὑπαγορεύεται ἐπιμελεῖσθαι, παραχωρεῖν ἁπάντων, ἀνέχεσθαι
λοιδορούντος, παίοντος. "ἀλλὰ πατὴρ κακός
ἐστι." μή τι οὖν πρὸς ἀγαθὸν πατέρα φύσει
ᾠκειώθης; ἀλλὰ πρὸς πατέρα. "ὁ ἀδελφὸς
ἀδικεῖ." τήρει τοιγαροῦν τὴν τάξιν τὴν σεαυτοῦ
πρὸς αὐτόν· μηδὲ σκόπει, τί ἐκεῖνος ποιεῖ, ἀλλὰ
τί σοὶ ποιήσαντι κατὰ φύσιν ἡ σὴ ἕξει προαίρεσις. σὲ γὰρ ἄλλος οὐ βλάψει, ἂν μὴ σὺ θέλῃς·
τότε δὲ ἔσῃ βεβλαμμένος, ὅταν ὑπολάβῃς
βλάπτεσθαι. οὕτως οὖν ἀπὸ τοῦ γείτονος, ἀπὸ
τοῦ πολίτου, ἀπὸ τοῦ στρατηγοῦ τὸ καθῆκον
εὑρήσεις, ἐὰν τὰς σχέσεις ἐθίζῃ θεωρεῖν.

1   c. 31. Τῆς περὶ τοὺς θεοὺς εὐσεβείας ἴσθι ὅτι
τὸ κυριώτατον ἐκεῖνό ἐστιν, ὀρθὰς ὑπολήψεις
περὶ αὐτῶν ἔχειν ὡς ὄντων καὶ διοικούντων τὰ
ὅλα καλῶς καὶ δικαίως, καὶ σαυτὸν εἰς τοῦτο
κατατετάχέναι,[1] τὸ πείθεσθαι αὐτοῖς καὶ εἴκειν
πᾶσι τοῖς γινομένοις καὶ ἀκολουθεῖν ἑκόντα ὡς

---

[1] κατατεταχότων suggested by Schweighäuser. The sense
would then be: "and have appointed you to," referring to
the gods.

are willing at the price of these things to secure tranquillity, freedom and calm. Otherwise, do not approach philosophy; don't act like a child—now a philosopher, later on a tax-gatherer, then a rhetorician, then a procurator of Caesar. These things do not go together. You must be one person, either good or bad; you must labour to improve either your own governing principle or externals; you must work hard either on the inner man, or on things outside; that is, play either the rôle of a philosopher or else that of a layman.

30. Our duties are in general measured by our social relationships. He is a father. One is called upon to take care of him, to give way to him in all things, to submit when he reviles or strikes you. "But he is a bad father." Did nature, then, bring you into relationship with a *good* father? No, but simply with a father. "My brother does me wrong." Very well, then, maintain the relation that you have toward him; and do not consider what he is doing, but what you will have to do, if your moral purpose is to be in harmony with nature. For no one will harm you without your consent; you will have been harmed only when you think you are harmed. In this way, therefore, you will discover what duty to expect of your neighbour, your citizen, your commanding officer, if you acquire the habit of looking at your social relations with them.

31. In piety towards the gods, I would have you know, the chief element is this, to have right opinions about them—as existing and as administering the universe well and justly—and to have set yourself to obey them and to submit to everything that happens, and to follow it voluntarily, in the

ὑπὸ τῆς ἀρίστης γνώμης ἐπιτελουμένοις. οὕτω
γὰρ οὐ μέμψῃ ποτὲ τοὺς θεοὺς οὔτε ἐγκαλέσεις
2 ὡς ἀμελούμενος. ἄλλως δὲ οὐχ οἷόν τε τοῦτο
γίνεσθαι, ἐὰν μὴ ἄρῃς ἀπὸ τῶν οὐκ ἐφ' ἡμῖν καὶ
ἐν τοῖς ἐφ' ἡμῖν μόνοις θῇς τὸ ἀγαθὸν καὶ τὸ
κακόν. ὡς, ἄν γέ τι ἐκείνων ὑπολάβῃς ἀγαθὸν
ἢ κακόν, πᾶσα ἀνάγκη, ὅταν ἀποτυγχάνῃς ὧν
θέλεις καὶ περιπίπτῃς οἷς μὴ θέλεις, μέμψασθαί
3 σε καὶ μισεῖν τοὺς αἰτίους. πέφυκε γὰρ πρὸς
τοῦτο πᾶν ζῷον τὰ μὲν βλαβερὰ φαινόμενα καὶ
τὰ αἴτια αὐτῶν φεύγειν καὶ ἐκτρέπεσθαι, τὰ δὲ
ὠφέλιμα καὶ τὰ αἴτια αὐτῶν μετιέναι τε καὶ
τεθηπέναι.[1] ἀμήχανον οὖν βλάπτεσθαί τινα
οἰόμενον χαίρειν τῷ δοκοῦντι βλάπτειν, ὥσπερ
4 καὶ τὸ αὐτῇ τῇ βλάβῃ χαίρειν ἀδύνατον. ἔνθεν
καὶ πατὴρ ὑπὸ υἱοῦ λοιδορεῖται, ὅταν τῶν δοκούντων ἀγαθῶν εἶναι τῷ παιδὶ μὴ μεταδιδῷ·
καὶ Πολυνείκην καὶ Ἐτεοκλέα τοῦτ' ἐποίησε
πολεμίους ἀλλήλοις τὸ ἀγαθὸν οἴεσθαι τὴν
τυραννίδα. διὰ τοῦτο καὶ ὁ γεωργὸς λοιδορεῖ
τοὺς θεούς, διὰ τοῦτο ὁ ναύτης, διὰ τοῦτο ὁ
ἔμπορος, διὰ τοῦτο οἱ τὰς γυναῖκας καὶ τὰ τέκνα
ἀπολλύντες. ὅπου γὰρ τὸ συμφέρον, ἐκεῖ καὶ
τὸ εὐσεβές. ὥστε, ὅστις ἐπιμελεῖται τοῦ ὀρέγεσθαι ὡς δεῖ καὶ ἐκκλίνειν, ἐν τῷ αὐτῷ καὶ
5 εὐσεβείας ἐπιμελεῖται. σπένδειν δὲ καὶ θύειν

---

[1] Vv: τεθαυμακέναι *Ench.* (Nil. ; Simpl.).

belief that it is being fulfilled by the highest in-
telligence. For if you act in this way, you will
never blame the gods, nor find fault with them
for neglecting you. But this result cannot be
secured in any other way than by withdrawing your
idea of the good and the evil from the things which
are not under our control, and placing it in those
which are under our control, and in those alone.
Because, if you think any of those former things
to be good or evil, then, when you fail to get what
you want and fall into what you do not want, it is
altogether inevitable that you will blame and hate
those who are responsible for these results. For
this is the nature of every living creature, to flee
from and to turn aside from the things that appear
harmful, and all that produces them, and to pursue
after and to admire the things that are helpful, and
all that produces them. Therefore, it is impossible
for a man who thinks that he is being hurt to take
pleasure in that which he thinks is hurting him,
just as it is also impossible for him to take pleasure
in the hurt itself. Hence it follows that even a
father is reviled by a son when he does not give
his child some share in the things that seem to be
good; and this it was which made Polyneices and
Eteocles enemies of one another, the thought that
the royal power was a good thing. That is why the
farmer reviles the gods, and so also the sailor, and
the merchant, and those who have lost their wives
and their children. For where a man's interest lies,
there is also his piety. Wherefore, whoever is
careful to exercise desire and aversion as he should,
is at the same time careful also about piety. But
it is always appropriate to make libations, and sacri-

fices, and to give of the firstfruits after the manner
of our fathers, and to do all this with purity, and
not in a slovenly or careless fashion, nor, indeed,
in a niggardly way, nor yet beyond our means.

32.[1] When you have recourse to divination, remember that you do not know what the issue is
going to be, but that you have come in order to
find this out from the diviner ; yet if you are indeed a
philosopher, you know, when you arrive, what the
nature of it is. For if it is one of the things which
are not under our control, it is altogether necessary
that what is going to take place is neither good
nor evil. Do not, therefore, bring to the diviner
desire or aversion, and do not approach him with
trembling, but having first made up your mind that
every issue is indifferent and nothing to you, but
that, whatever it may be, it will be possible for
you to turn it to good use, and that no one will
prevent this. Go, then, with confidence to the
gods as to counsellors ; and after that, when some
counsel has been given you, remember whom you
have taken as counsellors, and whom you will be
disregarding if you disobey. But go to divination
as Socrates thought that men should go, that is, in
cases where the whole inquiry has reference to the
outcome, and where neither from reason nor from
any other technical art are means vouchsafed for
discovering the matter in question. Hence, when
it is your duty to share the danger of a friend or of
your country, do not ask of the diviner whether you
ought to share that danger. For if the diviner
forewarns you that the omens of sacrifice have been
unfavourable, it is clear that death is portended, or
the injury of some member of your body, or exile ;

yet reason requires that even at this risk you are to stand by your friend, and share the danger with your country. Wherefore, give heed to the greater diviner, the Pythian Apollo, who cast out of his temple the man who had not helped his friend when he was being murdered.[1]

33. Lay down for yourself, at the outset, a certain stamp and type of character for yourself, which you are to maintain whether you are by yourself or are meeting with people. And be silent for the most part, or else make only the most necessary remarks, and express these in few words. But rarely, and when occasion requires you to talk, talk, indeed, but about no ordinary topics. Do not talk about gladiators, or horse-races, or athletes, or things to eat or drink —topics that arise on all occasions; but above all, do not talk about people, either blaming, or praising, or comparing them. If, then, you can, by your own conversation bring over that of your companions to what is seemly. But if you happen to be left alone in the presence of aliens, keep silence.

Do not laugh much, nor at many things, nor boisterously.

Refuse, if you can, to take an oath at all, but if that is impossible, refuse as far as circumstances allow.

Avoid entertainments given by outsiders and by persons ignorant of philosophy; but if an appropriate occasion arises for you to attend, be on the

---

The point of the story is that a man does not need to go to a diviner in order to learn whether he should defend his country or his friends. That question was long ago settled by the greatest of diviners, Apollo at Delphi, who ordered to be cast out of his temple an inquirer that had once failed to defend his own friend.

προσοχή, μήποτε ἄρα ὑπορρυῇς εἰς ἰδιωτισμόν.
ἴσθι γάρ, ὅτι, ἐὰν ὁ ἑταῖρος ᾖ μεμολυσμένος, καὶ
τὸν συνανατριβόμενον αὐτῷ συμμολύνεσθαι
ἀνάγκη, κἂν αὐτὸς ὢν τύχῃ καθαρός.

7 Τὰ περὶ τὸ σῶμα μέχρι τῆς χρείας ψιλῆς
παραλάμβανε, οἷον τροφάς, πόμα, ἀμπεχόνην,
οἰκίαν, οἰκετίαν· τὸ δὲ πρὸς δόξαν ἢ τρυφὴν
ἅπαν περίγραφε.

8 Περὶ ἀφροδίσια εἰς δύναμιν πρὸ γάμου κα-
θαρευτέον· ἁπτομένῳ δὲ ὧν νομίμον ἐστὶ με-
ταληπτέον. μὴ μέντοι ἐπαχθὴς γίνου τοῖς
χρωμένοις μηδὲ ἐλεγκτικός· μηδὲ πολλαχοῦ τὸ
ὅτι αὐτὸς οὐ χρῇ, παράφερε.

9 Ἐάν τίς σοι ἀπαγγείλῃ ὅτι ὁ δεῖνά σε κακῶς
λέγει, μὴ ἀπολογοῦ πρὸς τὰ λεχθέντα, ἀλλ'
ἀποκρίνου διότι "ἠγνόει γὰρ τὰ ἄλλα τὰ προ-
σόντα μοι κακά, ἐπεὶ οὐκ ἂν ταῦτα μόνα
ἔλεγεν."

10 Εἰς τὰ θέατρα τὸ πολὺ παριέναι οὐκ ἀναγκαῖον.
εἰ δέ ποτε καιρὸς εἴη, μηδενὶ σπουδάζων φαίνου
ἢ σεαυτῷ, τοῦτ' ἔστι θέλε γίνεσθαι μόνα τὰ
γινόμενα καὶ νικᾶν μόνον τὸν νικῶντα· οὕτω γὰρ
οὐκ ἐμποδισθήσῃ. βοῆς δὲ καὶ τοῦ ἐπιγελᾶν
τινι ἢ ἐπὶ πολὺ συγκινεῖσθαι παντελῶς ἀπέχου.
καὶ μετὰ τὸ ἀπαλλαγῆναι μὴ πολλὰ περὶ τῶν
γεγενημένων διαλέγου, ὅσα μὴ φέρει πρὸς τὴν
σὴν ἐπανόρθωσιν· ἐμφαίνεται γὰρ ἐκ τοῦ τοιούτου, ὅτι ἐθαύμασας τὴν θέαν.

518

alert to avoid lapsing into the behaviour of such laymen. For you may rest assured, that, if a man's companion be dirty, the person who keeps close company with him must of necessity get a share of his dirt, even though he himself happens to be clean.

In things that pertain to the body take only as much as your bare need requires, I mean such things as food, drink, clothing, shelter, and household slaves; but cut down everything which is for outward show or luxury.

In your sex-life preserve purity, as far as you can, before marriage, and, if you indulge, take only those privileges which are lawful. However, do not make yourself offensive, or censorious, to those who do indulge, and do not make frequent mention of the fact that you do not yourself indulge.

If someone brings you word that So-and-so is speaking ill of you, do not defend yourself against what has been said, but answer, "Yes, indeed, for he did not know the rest of the faults that attach to me; if he had, these would not have been the only ones he mentioned."

It is not necessary, for the most part, to go to the public shows. If, however, a suitable occasion ever arises, show that your principal concern is for none other than yourself, which means, wish only for that to happen which does happen, and for him only to win who does win; for so you will suffer no hindrance. But refrain utterly from shouting, or laughter at anyone, or great excitement. And after you have left, do not talk a great deal about what took place, except in so far as it contributes to your own improvement; for such behaviour indicates that the spectacle has aroused your admiration.

519

11 Εἰς ἀκροάσεις τινῶν μὴ εἰκῆ μηδὲ ῥαδίως
παρίθι· παριὼν δὲ τὸ σεμνὸν καὶ τὸ[1] εὐσταθὲς
καὶ ἅμα ἀνεπαχθὲς φύλασσε.

12 Ὅταν τινὶ μέλλῃς συμβαλεῖν, μάλιστα τῶν
ἐν ὑπεροχῇ δοκούντων, πρόβαλε σαυτῷ, τί ἂν
ἐποίησεν ἐν τούτῳ Σωκράτης ἢ Ζήνων, καὶ οὐκ
ἀπορήσεις τοῦ χρήσασθαι προσηκόντως τῷ

13 ἐμπεσόντι. ὅταν φοιτᾷς πρός τινα τῶν μέγα
δυναμένων, πρόβαλε, ὅτι οὐχ εὑρήσεις αὐτὸν
ἔνδον, ὅτι ἀποκλεισθήσῃ, ὅτι ἐντιναχθήσονταί[2]
σοι αἱ θύραι, ὅτι οὐ φροντιεῖ σου. κἂν σὺν
τούτοις ἐλθεῖν καθήκῃ, ἐλθὼν φέρε τὰ γινόμενα
καὶ μηδέποτε εἴπῃς αὐτὸς πρὸς ἑαυτὸν ὅτι " οὐκ
ἦν τοσούτου"· ἰδιωτικὸν γὰρ καὶ διαβεβλημένον
πρὸς τὰ ἐκτός.

14 Ἐν ταῖς ὁμιλίαις ἀπέστω τὸ ἑαυτοῦ τινῶν
ἔργων ἢ κινδύνων ἐπὶ πολὺ καὶ ἀμέτρως μεμνῆσθαι. οὐ γάρ, ὡς σοὶ ἡδύ ἐστι τὸ τῶν σῶν
κινδύνων μεμνῆσθαι, οὕτω καὶ τοῖς ἄλλοις ἡδύ
ἐστι τὸ τῶν σοὶ συμβεβηκότων ἀκούειν.

15 Ἀπέστω δὲ καὶ τὸ γέλωτα κινεῖν· ὀλισθηρὸς
γὰρ ὁ τρόπος[3] εἰς ἰδιωτισμὸν καὶ ἅμα ἱκανὸς
τὴν αἰδὼ τὴν πρὸς σὲ τῶν πλησίον ἀνιέναι.

16 ἐπισφαλὲς δὲ καὶ τὸ εἰς αἰσχρολογίαν προελθεῖν.
ὅταν οὖν τι συμβῇ τοιοῦτον, ἂν μὲν εὔκαιρον ᾖ,

---

[1] In Nil. only.   [2] Nil.: ἐκτιναχθήσονται MSS.
[3] C un., Nil., Simpl.: τόπος MSS.

---

[1] A favourite way of introducing a new work of literature
to the reading public, somewhat like our modern musical

Do not go rashly or readily to people's public readings,[1] but when you do go, maintain your own dignity and gravity, and at the same time be careful not to make yourself disagreeable.

When you are about to meet somebody, in particular when it is one of those men who are held in very high esteem, propose to yourself the question, "What would Socrates or Zeno have done under these circumstances?" and then you will not be at a loss to make proper use of the occasion. When you go to see one of those men who have great power, propose to yourself the thought, that you will not find him at home, that you will be shut out, that the door will be slammed in your face, that he will pay no attention to you. And if, despite all this, it is your duty to go, go and take what comes, and never say to yourself, "It was not worth all the trouble." For this is characteristic of the layman, that is, a man who is vexed at externals.

In your conversation avoid making mention at great length and excessively of your own deeds or dangers, because it is not as pleasant for others to hear about your adventures, as it is for you to call to mind your own dangers.

Avoid also raising a laugh, for this is a kind of behaviour that slips easily into vulgarity, and at the same time is calculated to lessen the respect which your neighbours have of you. It is dangerous also to lapse into foul language. When, therefore, anything of the sort occurs, if the occasion be suitable, go even so far as to reprove the person

recitals, or artists' exhibitions. See also III. 23 for similar public lectures given by a philosopher.

521

καὶ ἐπίπληξον τῷ προελθόντι· εἰ δὲ μή, τῷ γε
ἀποσιωπῆσαι καὶ ἐρυθριᾶσαι καὶ σκυθρωπάσαι
δῆλος γίνου δυσχεραίνων τῷ λόγῳ.

c. 34. Ὅταν ἡδονῆς τινος φαντασίαν λάβῃς,
καθάπερ ἐπὶ τῶν ἄλλων, φύλασσε σαυτόν, μὴ
συναρπασθῇς ὑπ᾽ αὐτῆς· ἀλλ᾽ ἐκδεξάσθω σε τὸ
πρᾶγμα, καὶ ἀναβολήν τινα παρὰ σεαυτοῦ λάβε.
ἔπειτα μνήσθητι ἀμφοτέρων τῶν χρόνων, καθ᾽ ὅν
τε ἀπολαύσεις τῆς ἡδονῆς, καὶ καθ᾽ ὃν ἀπολαύσας
ὕστερον μετανοήσεις καὶ αὐτὸς σεαυτῷ λοιδο-
ρήσῃ· καὶ τούτοις ἀντίθες ὅπως ἀποσχόμενος
χαιρήσεις καὶ ἐπαινέσεις αὐτὸς σεαυτόν. ἐὰν
δέ σοι καιρὸς φανῇ ἅψασθαι τοῦ ἔργου,
πρόσεχε, μὴ ἡττήσῃ σε τὸ προσηνὲς αὐτοῦ καὶ
ἡδὺ καὶ ἐπαγωγόν· ἀλλ᾽ ἀντιτίθει, πόσῳ ἄμεινον
τὸ συνειδέναι σεαυτῷ ταύτην τὴν νίκην νενικη-
κότι.

c. 35. Ὅταν τι διαγνούς, ὅτι ποιητέον ἐστί,
ποιῇς, μηδέποτε φύγῃς ὀφθῆναι πράσσων αὐτό,
κἂν ἀλλοῖόν τι μέλλωσιν οἱ πολλοὶ περὶ αὐτοῦ
ὑπολαμβάνειν. εἰ μὲν γὰρ οὐκ ὀρθῶς ποιεῖς,
αὐτὸ τὸ ἔργον φεῦγε· εἰ δὲ ὀρθῶς, τί φοβῇ τοὺς
ἐπιπλήξοντας οὐκ ὀρθῶς;

c. 36. Ὡς τὸ "ἡμέρα ἐστί" καὶ "νύξ ἐστι"
πρὸς μὲν τὸ διεζευγμένον μεγάλην ἔχει ἀξίαν,
πρὸς δὲ τὸ συμπεπλεγμένον ἀπαξίαν, οὕτω καὶ

---

[1] The ordinary person, to be sure, can no more call up a
blush off-hand than he can a sneeze or a hiccough, and the
observation of nature implied by the command is, therefore,
imperfect (cf. note in IV. 11, 1). But all Epictetus means is
that one should make no effort to conceal any natural expression of moral resentment under such circumstances.

who has made such a lapse; if, however, the occasion does not arise, at all events show by keeping silence, and blushing,[1] and frowning, that you are displeased by what has been said.

34. When you get an external impression of some pleasure, guard yourself, as with impressions in general, against being carried away by it; nay, let the matter wait upon *your* leisure, and give yourself a little delay. Next think of the two periods of time, first, that in which you will enjoy your pleasure, and second, that in which, after the enjoyment is over, you will later repent and revile your own self; and set over against these two periods of time how much joy and self-satisfaction you will get if you refrain. However, if you feel that a suitable occasion has arisen to do the deed, be careful not to allow its enticement, and sweetness, and attractiveness to overcome you; but set over against all this the thought, how much better is the consciousness of having won a victory over it.

35. When you do a thing which you have made up your mind ought to be done, never try not to be seen doing it, even though most people are likely to think unfavourably about it. If, however, what you are doing is not right, avoid the deed itself altogether; but if it is right, why fear those who are going to rebuke you wrongly?

36. Just as the propositions, "It is day," and "It is night," are full of meaning when separated, but meaningless if united;[2] so also, granted that for

[2] Compare I. 25, 11–13. It does not seem possible in our idiom to use the same expressions for ἀξία, "worth," or "value," which occurs three times in this section, and ἀπαξία, "lack of worth," or "lack of value," which occurs twice.

τὸ τὴν μείζω μερίδα ἐκλέξασθαι πρὸς μὲν τὸ
σῶμα ἐχέτω ἀξίαν, πρὸς δὲ τὸ¹ τὸ κοινωνικὸν
ἐν ἑστιάσει, οἷον δεῖ, φυλάξαι, ἀπαξίαν ἔχει.
ὅταν οὖν συνεσθίῃς ἑτέρῳ, μέμνησο, μὴ μόνον
τὴν πρὸς τὸ σῶμα ἀξίαν τῶν παρακειμένων ὁρᾶν,
ἀλλὰ καὶ τὴν πρὸς τὸν ἑστιάτορα αἰδῶ φυλάξαι.²

c. 37. Ἐὰν ὑπὲρ δύναμιν ἀναλάβῃς τι πρόσωπον, καὶ ἐν τούτῳ ἠσχημόνησας καὶ, ὃ ἠδύνασο
ἐκπληρῶσαι, παρέλιπες.

c. 38. Ἐν τῷ περιπατεῖν καθάπερ προσέχεις,
μὴ ἐπιβῇς ἥλῳ ἢ στρέψῃς τὸν πόδα σου, οὕτω
πρόσεχε, μὴ καὶ τὸ ἡγεμονικὸν βλάψῃς τὸ
σεαυτοῦ. καὶ τοῦτο ἐὰν ἐφ᾽ ἑκάστου ἔργου
παραφυλάσσωμεν, ἀσφαλέστερον ἁψόμεθα τοῦ
ἔργου.

c. 39. Μέτρον κτήσεως τὸ σῶμα ἑκάστῳ ὡς
ὁ ποὺς ὑποδήματος. ἐὰν μὲν οὖν ἐπὶ τούτου
στῇς, φυλάξεις τὸ μέτρον· ἐὰν δὲ ὑπερβῇς, ὡς
κατὰ κρημνοῦ λοιπὸν ἀνάγκη φέρεσθαι· καθάπερ
καὶ ἐπὶ τοῦ ὑποδήματος, ἐὰν ὑπὲρ τὸν πόδα
ὑπερβῇς, γίνεται κατάχρυσον ὑπόδημα, εἶτα
πορφυροῦν, κεντητόν. τοῦ γὰρ ἅπαξ ὑπὲρ τὸ
μέτρον ὅρος οὐθείς ἐστιν.

c. 40. Αἱ γυναῖκες εὐθὺς ἀπὸ τεσσαρεσκαίδεκα
ἐτῶν ὑπὸ τῶν ἀνδρῶν κυρίαι καλοῦνται. τοιγαροῦν ὁρῶσαι, ὅτι ἄλλο μὲν οὐδὲν αὐταῖς
πρόσεστι, μόνον δὲ συγκοιμῶνται τοῖς ἀνδράσι,
ἄρχονται καλλωπίζεσθαι καὶ ἐν τούτῳ πάσας

---

¹ τό added by Schweighäuser from Simplicius.
² αἰδῶ φυλάξαι Schweighäuser : οἵαν δεῖ φυλαχθῆναι MSS.

---

¹ That is, property, which is of use only for the body,
should be adjusted to a man's actual bodily needs, just as a

you to take the larger share at a dinner is good for your body, still, it is bad for the maintenance of the proper kind of social feeling. When, therefore, you are eating with another person, remember to regard, not merely the value for your body of what lies before you, but also to maintain your respect for your host.

37. If you undertake a rôle which is beyond your powers, you both disgrace yourself in that one, and at the same time neglect the rôle which you might have filled with success.

38. Just as you are careful, in walking about, not to step on a nail or to sprain your ankle, so be careful also not to hurt your governing principle. And if we observe this rule in every action, we shall be more secure in setting about it.

39. Each man's body is a measure for his property,[1] just as the foot is a measure for his shoe. If, then, you abide by this principle, you will maintain the proper measure, but if you go beyond it, you cannot help but fall headlong over a precipice, as it were, in the end. So also in the case of your shoe; if once you go beyond the foot, you get first a gilded shoe, then a purple one, then an embroidered one. For once you go beyond the measure there is no limit.

40. Immediately after they are fourteen, women are called "ladies" by men. And so when they see that they have nothing else but only to be the bedfellows of men, they begin to beautify themselves,

---

[1] shoe is (or at least should be) adjusted to the actual needs of a man's foot. The comparison seems to have been a commonplace; see Demophilus, *Similitudines*, 20 (Mullach); Horace, *Epist.* I. 7, 98 and 10, 42 f.

ἔχειν τὰς ἐλπίδας. προσέχειν οὖν ἄξιον, ἵνα
αἴσθωνται, διότι ἐπ' οὐδενὶ ἄλλῳ τιμῶνται ἢ τῷ
κόσμιαι φαίνεσθαι καὶ αἰδήμονες.[1]

c. 41. Ἀφυΐας σημεῖον τὸ ἐνδιατρίβειν τοῖς
περὶ τὸ σῶμα, οἷον ἐπὶ πολὺ γυμνάζεσθαι, ἐπὶ
πολὺ ἐσθίειν, ἐπὶ πολὺ πίνειν, ἐπὶ πολὺ ἀπο-
πατεῖν, ὀχεύειν. ἀλλὰ ταῦτα μὲν ἐν παρέργῳ
ποιητέον· περὶ δὲ τὴν γνώμην ἡ πᾶσα ἔστω
ἐπιστροφή.

c. 42. Ὅταν σέ τις κακῶς ποιῇ ἢ κακῶς λέγῃ,
μέμνησο, ὅτι καθήκειν αὐτῷ οἰόμενος ποιεῖ ἢ
λέγει. οὐχ οἷόν τε οὖν ἀκολουθεῖν αὐτὸν τῷ σοὶ
φαινομένῳ, ἀλλὰ τῷ ἑαυτῷ, ὥστε, εἰ κακῶς αὐτῷ[2]
φαίνεται, ἐκεῖνος βλάπτεται, ὅστις καὶ ἐξη-
πάτηται. καὶ γὰρ τὸ ἀληθὲς συμπεπλεγμένον
ἄν τις ὑπολάβῃ ψεῦδος, οὐ τὸ συμπεπλεγμένοι·
βέβλαπται, ἀλλ' ὁ ἐξαπατηθείς. ἀπὸ τούτων
οὖν ὁρμώμενος πράως ἕξεις πρὸς τὸν λοιδοροῦντα.
ἐπιφθέγγου γὰρ ἐφ' ἑκάστῳ ὅτι "ἔδοξεν αὐτῷ."

c. 43. Πᾶν πρᾶγμα δύο ἔχει λαβάς, τὴν μὲν
φορητήν, τὴν δὲ ἀφόρητον. ὁ ἀδελφὸς ἐὰν
ἀδικῇ, ἐντεῦθεν αὐτὸ μὴ λάμβανε, ὅτι ἀδικεῖ
(αὕτη γὰρ ἡ λαβή ἐστιν αὐτοῦ οὐ φορητή), ἀλλὰ
ἐκεῖθεν μᾶλλον, ὅτι ἀδελφός, ὅτι σύντροφος, καὶ
λήψῃ αὐτὸ καθ' ὃ φορητόν.

---

[1] C un., Nil.: αἰδήμονες ἐν σωφροσύνῃ other MSS.
[2] C un., Nil. (ed. Rom.): om. other MSS.

---

[1] Two judgements connected with "and." Zeller, *Philosophie der Griechen*,[4] III. 1 (1909), 106, and note 3. Compare also I. 26, 14 ; II. 9, 8. An example of an inconsistent composite judgement is given in *Ench.* 36.

and put all their hopes in that. It is worth while for us to take pains, therefore, to make them understand that they are honoured for nothing else but only for appearing modest and self-respecting.

41. It is a mark of an ungifted man to spend a great deal of time in what concerns his body, as in much exercise, much eating, much drinking, much evacuating of the bowels, much copulating. But these things are to be done in passing ; and let your whole attention be devoted to the mind.

42. When someone treats you ill or speaks ill of you, remember that he acts or speaks thus because he thinks it is incumbent upon him. That being the case, it is impossible for him to follow what appears good to you, but what appears good to himself ; whence it follows, that, if he gets a wrong view of things, the man that suffers is the man that has been deceived. For if a person thinks a true composite judgement[1] to be false, the composite judgement does not suffer, but the person who has been deceived. If, therefore, you start from this point of view, you will be gentle with the man who reviles you. For you should say on each occasion, " He thought that way about it."

43. Everything has two handles, by one of which it ought to be carried and by the other not. If your brother wrongs you, do not lay hold of the matter by the handle of the wrong that he is doing, because this is the handle by which the matter ought not to be carried ; but rather by the other handle—that he is your brother, that you were brought up together, and then you will be laying hold of the matter by the handle by which it ought to be carried.

c. 44. Οὗτοι οἱ λόγοι ἀσύνακτοι· "ἐγώ σου πλουσιώτερός εἰμι, ἐγώ σου ἄρα κρείσσων"· "ἐγώ σου λογιώτερος, ἐγώ σου ἄρα κρείσσων" ἐκεῖνοι δὲ μᾶλλον συνακτικοί· "ἐγώ σου πλουσιώτερός εἰμι, ἡ ἐμὴ ἄρα κτῆσις τῆς σῆς κρείσσων"· "ἐγώ σου λογιώτερος, ἡ ἐμὴ ἄρα λέξις τῆς σῆς κρείσσων." σὺ δέ γε οὔτε κτῆσις εἶ οὔτε λέξις.

c. 45. Λούεταί τις ταχέως· μὴ εἴπῃς ὅτι κακῶς, ἀλλ' ὅτι ταχέως. πίνει τις πολὺν οἶνον· μὴ εἴπῃς ὅτι κακῶς, ἀλλ' ὅτι πολυν. πρὶν γὰρ διαγνῶναι τὸ δόγμα, πόθεν οἶσθα, εἰ κακῶς; οὕτως οὐ[1] συμβήσεταί σοι ἄλλων[2] μὲν φαντασίας καταληπτικὰς λαμβάνειν,[3] ἄλλοις δὲ συγκατατίθεσθαι.

1   c. 46. Μηδαμοῦ σεαυτὸν εἴπῃς φιλόσοφον μηδὲ λάλει τὸ πολὺ ἐν ἰδιώταις περὶ τῶν θεωρημάτων, ἀλλὰ ποίει τὸ ἀπὸ τῶν θεωρημάτων· οἷον ἐν συμποσίῳ μὴ λέγε, πῶς δεῖ ἐσθίειν, ἀλλ' ἔσθιε, ὡς δεῖ. μέμνησο γάρ, ὅτι οὕτως ἀφῃρήκει πανταχόθεν Σωκράτης τὸ ἐπιδεικτικόν, ὥστε[4] ἤρχοντο πρὸς αὐτὸν βουλόμενοι φιλοσόφοις ὑπ' αὐτοῦ συσταθῆναι, κἀκεῖνος ἀπῆγεν αὐτούς. οὕτως 2 ἠνείχετο παρορώμενος. κἂν περὶ θεωρήματός τινος ἐν ἰδιώταις ἐμπίπτῃ λόγος, σιώπα τὸ πολύ· μέγας γὰρ ὁ κίνδυνος εὐθὺς ἐξεμέσαι, ὃ οὐκ

---

[1] Nil.: οὖν *Ench.*
[2] C un., Nil., Simpl.: ἄλλας other MSS.
[3] C un., Nil.: καταλαμβάνειν other MSS.
[4] C un., Nil., Simpl.: om. here but placed before κἂν (below) by other MSS.

44. The following statements constitute a *non sequitur*: "I am richer than you are, therefore I am superior to you"; or, "I am more eloquent than you are, therefore I am superior to you." But the following conclusions are better: "I am richer than you are, therefore my property is superior to yours"; or, "I am more eloquent than you are, therefore my elocution is superior to yours." But *you* are neither property nor elocution.

45. Somebody is hasty about bathing;[1] do not say that he bathes badly, but that he is hasty about bathing. Somebody drinks a good deal of wine; do not say that he drinks badly, but that he drinks a good deal. For until you have decided what judgement prompts him, how do you know that what he is doing is bad? And thus the final result will not be that you receive convincing sense-impressions of some things, but give your assent to others.

46. On no occasion call yourself a philosopher, and do not, for the most part, talk among laymen about your philosophic principles, but do what follows from your principles. For example, at a banquet do not say how people ought to eat, but eat as a man ought. For remember how Socrates had so completely eliminated the thought of ostentation, that people came to him when they wanted him to introduce them to philosophers, and he used to bring them along. So well did he submit to being overlooked. And if talk about some philosophic principle arises among laymen, keep silence for the most part, for there is great danger that you will spew up immediately what you have not digested.

---

[1] The implication must be that a hurried bath, like a hurried shave, is apt to leave something to be desired.

ἔπεψας. καὶ ὅταν εἴπῃ σοί τις, ὅτι οὐδὲν οἶσθα, καὶ σὺ μὴ δηχθῇς, τότε ἴσθι, ὅτι ἄρχῃ τοῦ ἔργου. ἐπεὶ καὶ τὰ πρόβατα οὐ χόρτον φέροντα τοῖς ποιμέσιν ἐπιδεικνύει πόσον ἔφαγεν, ἀλλὰ τὴν νομὴν ἔσω πέψαντα ἔρια ἔξω φέρει καὶ γάλα· καὶ σὺ τοίνυν μὴ τὰ θεωρήματα τοῖς ἰδιώταις ἐπιδείκνυε, ἀλλ' ἀπ' αὐτῶν πεφθέντων τὰ ἔργα.

c. 47. Ὅταν εὐτελῶς ἡρμοσμένος ᾖς κατὰ τὸ σῶμα, μὴ καλλωπίζου ἐπὶ τούτῳ μηδ', ἂν ὕδωρ πίνῃς, ἐκ πάσης ἀφορμῆς λέγε, ὅτι ὕδωρ πίνεις. κἂν ἀσκῆσαί ποτε πρὸς πόνον θέλῃς, σεαυτῷ καὶ μὴ τοῖς ἔξω· μὴ τοὺς ἀνδριάντας περιλάμβανε· ἀλλὰ διψῶν ποτὲ σφοδρῶς ἐπίσπασαι ψυχροῦ ὕδατος καὶ ἔκπτυσον καὶ μηδενὶ εἴπῃς.[1]

1 c. 48. Ἰδιώτου στάσις καὶ χαρακτήρ· οὐδέποτε ἐξ ἑαυτοῦ προσδοκᾷ ὠφέλειαν ἢ βλάβην, ἀλλ' ἀπὸ τῶν ἔξω. φιλοσόφου στάσις καὶ χαρακτήρ· πᾶσαν ὠφέλειαν καὶ βλάβην ἐξ ἑαυτοῦ προσδοκᾷ.

2 Σημεῖα προκόπτοντος· οὐδένα ψέγει, οὐδένα ἐπαινεῖ, οὐδένα μέμφεται, οὐδενὶ ἐγκαλεῖ, οὐδὲν περὶ ἑαυτοῦ λέγει ὡς ὄντος τινὸς ἢ εἰδότος τι. ὅταν ἐμποδισθῇ τι ἢ κωλυθῇ, ἑαυτῷ ἐγκαλεῖ. κἄν τις αὐτὸν ἐπαινῇ, καταγελᾷ τοῦ ἐπαινοῦντος αὐτὸς παρ' ἑαυτῷ· κἂν ψέγῃ, οὐκ ἀπολογεῖται. περίει-

---

[1] That is, in cold weather (see III. 12, 2 and 10), because this takes a person out of doors where people can see him.
[2] See III. 12, 17, and note.

So when a man tells you that you know nothing, and you, like Socrates, are not hurt, then rest assured that you are making a beginning with the business you have undertaken. For sheep, too, do not bring their fodder to the shepherds and show how much they have eaten, but they digest their food within them, and on the outside produce wool and milk. And so do you, therefore, make no display to the laymen of your philosophical principles, but let them see the results which come from these principles when digested.

47. When you have become adjusted to simple living in regard to your bodily wants, do not preen yourself about the accomplishment ; and so likewise, if you are a water-drinker, do not on every occasion say that you are a water-drinker. And if ever you want to train to develop physical endurance, do it by yourself and not for outsiders to behold ; do not throw your arms around statues,[1] but on occasion, when you are very thirsty, take cold water into your mouth, and then spit it out, without telling anybody.[2]

48. This is the position and character of a layman : He never looks for either help or harm from himself, but only from externals. This is the position and character of the philosopher : He looks for all his help or harm from himself.

Signs of one who is making progress are : He censures no one, praises no one, blames no one, finds fault with no one, says nothing about himself as though he were somebody or knew something. When he is hampered or prevented, he blames himself. And if anyone compliments him, he smiles to himself at the person complimenting ; while if anyone censures him, he makes no defence. He goes

σι δὲ καθάπερ οἱ ἄρρωστοι, εὐλαβούμενός τι κινῆσαι τῶν καθισταμένων, πρὶν πῆξιν λαβεῖν.
3 ὄρεξιν ἅπασαν ἦρκεν ἐξ ἑαυτοῦ· τὴν δ' ἔκκλισιν
εἰς μόνα τὰ παρὰ φύσιν τῶν ἐφ' ἡμῖν μετατέθεικεν.
ὁρμῇ πρὸς ἅπαντα ἀνειμένῃ χρῆται. ἂν ἠλίθιος
ἢ ἀμαθὴς δοκῇ, οὐ πεφρόντικεν. ἑνί τε λόγῳ, ὡς
ἐχθρὸν ἑαυτὸν παραφυλάσσει καὶ ἐπίβουλον.

c. 49. "Οταν τις ἐπὶ τῷ νοεῖν καὶ ἐξηγεῖσθαι
δύνασθαι τὰ Χρυσίππου βιβλία σεμνύνηται, λέγε
αὐτὸς πρὸς ἑαυτὸν ὅτι " εἰ μὴ Χρύσιππος ἀσαφῶς
ἐγεγράφει, οὐδὲν ἂν εἶχεν οὗτος, ἐφ' ᾧ ἐσεμνύ-
νετο."

Ἐγὼ δὲ τί βούλομαι; καταμαθεῖν τὴν φύσιν
καὶ ταύτῃ ἕπεσθαι. ζητῶ οὖν, τίς ἐστιν ὁ ἐξηγού-
μενος· καὶ ἀκούσας, ὅτι Χρύσιππος, ἔρχομαι
πρὸς αὐτόν. ἀλλ' οὐ νοῶ τὰ γεγραμμένα· ζητῶ
οὖν τὸν ἐξηγούμενον. καὶ μέχρι τούτων οὔπω
σεμνὸν οὐδέν. ὅταν δὲ εὕρω τὸν ἐξηγούμενον,
ἀπολείπεται χρῆσθαι τοῖς παρηγγελμένοις· τοῦτο αὐτὸ μόνον σεμνόν ἐστιν. ἂν δὲ αὐτὸ τοῦτο
τὸ ἐξηγεῖσθαι θαυμάσω, τί ἄλλο ἢ γραμματικὸς
ἀπετελέσθην ἀντὶ φιλοσόφου; πλήν γε δὴ ὅτι
ἀντὶ Ὁμήρου Χρύσιππον ἐξηγούμενος. μᾶλλον
οὖν, ὅταν τις εἴπῃ μοι "ἐπανάγνωθί μοι[1] Χρύσιππον," ἐρυθριῶ, ὅταν μὴ δύνωμαι ὅμοια τὰ
ἔργα καὶ σύμφωνα ἐπιδεικνύειν τοῖς λόγοις.

c. 50. "Οσα προτίθεται, τούτοις ὡς νόμοις, ὡς

[1] In A alone.

about like an invalid, being careful not to disturb, before it has grown firm, any part which is getting well. He has put away from himself his every desire, and has transferred his aversion to those things only, of what is under our control, which are contrary to nature. He exercises no pronounced choice in regard to anything. If he gives the appearance of being foolish or ignorant he does not care. In a word, he keeps guard against himself as though he were his own enemy lying in wait.

49. When a person gives himself airs because he can understand and interpret the books of Chrysippus, say to yourself, "If Chrysippus had not written obscurely, this man would have nothing about which to give himself airs."

But what is it I want? To learn nature and to follow her. I seek, therefore, someone to interpret her; and having heard that Chrysippus does so, I go to him. But I do not understand what he has written; I seek, therefore, the person who interprets Chrysippus. And down to this point there is nothing to justify pride. But when I find the interpreter, what remains is to put his precepts into practice; this is the only thing to be proud about. If, however, I admire the mere act of interpretation, what have I done but turned into a grammarian instead of a philosopher? The only difference, indeed, is that I interpret Chrysippus instead of Homer. Far from being proud, therefore, when somebody says to me, "Read me Chrysippus," I blush the rather, when I am unable to show him such deeds as match and harmonize with his words.

50. Whatever principles are set before you, stand fast by these like laws, feeling that it would be

ἀσεβήσων, ἂν παραβῇς, ἔμμενε. ὅ τι δ᾽ ἂν ἐρῇ
τις περὶ σοῦ, μὴ ἐπιστρέφου· τοῦτο γὰρ οὐκ ἔτ᾽
ἐστὶ σόν.

1   c. 51. Εἰς ποῖον ἔτι χρόνον ἀναβάλλῃ τὸ τῶν
βελτίστων ἀξιοῦν σεαυτὸν καὶ ἐν μηδενὶ παρα-
βαίνειν τὸν διαιροῦντα λόγον; παρείληφας τὰ
θεωρήματα, οἷς ἔδει σε συμβάλλειν, καὶ συμβέ-
βληκας. ποῖον οὖν ἔτι διδάσκαλον προσδοκᾷς,
ἵνα εἰς ἐκεῖνον ὑπερθῇ τὴν ἐπανόρθωσιν ποιῆσαι
τὴν σεαυτοῦ; οὐκ ἔτι εἶ μειράκιον, ἀλλὰ ἀνὴρ
ἤδη τέλειος. ἂν νῦν ἀμελήσῃς καὶ ῥαθυμήσῃς
καὶ ἀεὶ προθέσεις[1] ἐκ προθέσεως[2] ποιῇ[3] καὶ
ἡμέρας ἄλλας ἐπ᾽ ἄλλαις ὁρίζῃς, μεθ᾽ ἃς προ-
σέξεις σεαυτῷ, λήσεις σεαυτὸν οὐ προκόψας,
ἀλλ᾽ ἰδιώτης διατελέσεις καὶ ζῶν καὶ ἀποθνήσκων.

2 ἤδη οὖν ἀξίωσον σεαυτὸν βιοῦν ὡς τέλειον καὶ
προκόπτοντα· καὶ πᾶν τὸ βέλτιστον φαινόμενον
ἔστω σοι νόμος ἀπαράβατος. κἂν ἐπίπονόν τι
ἢ ἡδὺ ἢ ἔνδοξον ἢ ἄδοξον προσάγηται, μέμνησο,
ὅτι νῦν ὁ ἀγὼν καὶ ἤδη πάρεστι τὰ Ὀλύμπια καὶ
οὐκ ἔστιν ἀναβάλλεσθαι οὐκέτι καὶ ὅτι[4] παρὰ
μίαν ἡμέραν καὶ ἐν πρᾶγμα[5] καὶ[6] ἀπόλλυται

3 προκοπὴ καὶ[6] σῴζεται. Σωκράτης οὕτως ἀπε-
τελέσθη, ἐπὶ πάντων τῶν προσαγομένων αὐτῷ[7]
μηδενὶ ἄλλῳ προσέχων ἢ τῷ λόγῳ. σὺ δὲ εἰ καὶ
μήπω εἶ Σωκράτης, ὡς Σωκράτης γε εἶναι βουλόμενος ὀφείλεις βιοῦν.

---

[1] A un., Nil.: ὑπερθέσεις the other MSS.
[2] A un., Nil.: ὑπερθέσεως (—εων) the other MSS.
[3] Nil.: ποιῇς Ench.
[4] C (several), Nil.: ἔτι the other MSS.
[5] ἡμέραν καὶ ἐν πρᾶγμα Simpl.: ἥτταν καὶ ἔνδοσιν Ench.
[6] C un., Nil., Simpl.: ἤ the other MSS. (except in the
second case ἤ καί B A sing.).

impiety for you to transgress them. But pay no attention to what somebody says about you, for this is, at length, not under your control.

51. How long will you still wait to think yourself worthy of the best things, and in nothing to transgress against the distinctions set up by the reason? You have received the philosophical principles which you ought to accept, and you have accepted them. What sort of a teacher, then, do you still wait for, that you should put off reforming yourself until he arrives? You are no longer a lad, but already a full-grown man. If you are now neglectful and easy-going, and always making one delay after another, and fixing first one day and then another, after which you will pay attention to yourself, then without realizing it you will make no progress, but, living and dying, will continue to be a layman throughout. Make up your mind, therefore, before it is too late, that the fitting thing for you to do is to live as a mature man who is making progress, and let everything which seems to you to be best be for you a law that must not be transgressed. And if you meet anything that is laborious, or sweet, or held in high repute, or in no repute, remember that *now* is the contest, and here before you are the Olympic games, and that it is impossible to delay any longer, and that it depends on a single day and a single action, whether progress is lost or saved. This is the way Socrates became what he was, by paying attention to nothing but his reason in everything that he encountered. And even if you are not yet a Socrates, still you ought to live as one who wishes to be a Socrates.

---

⁷ τῶν προσαγομένων αὐτῷ Meibom : προσάγων ἑαυτόν *Ench.*

1 c. 52. Ὁ πρῶτος καὶ ἀναγκαιότατος τόπος
ἐστὶν ἐν φιλοσοφίᾳ ὁ τῆς χρήσεως τῶν θεωρημάτων, οἷον τὸ¹ μὴ ψεύδεσθαι· ὁ δεύτερος ὁ τῶν
ἀποδείξεων, οἷον πόθεν ὅτι οὐ δεῖ ψεύδεσθαι;
τρίτος ὁ αὐτῶν τούτων βεβαιωτικὸς καὶ διαρθρω-
τικός, οἷον πόθεν ὅτι τοῦτο ἀπόδειξις; τί γάρ
ἐστιν ἀπόδειξις, τί ἀκολουθία, τί μάχη, τί ἀληθές,
2 τί ψεῦδος; οὐκοῦν ὁ μὲν τρίτος τόπος ἀναγκαῖος
διὰ τὸν δεύτερον, ὁ δὲ δεύτερος διὰ τὸν πρῶτον·
ὁ δὲ ἀναγκαιότατος καὶ ὅπου ἀναπαύεσθαι δεῖ, ὁ
πρῶτος. ἡμεῖς δὲ ἔμπαλιν ποιοῦμεν· ἐν γὰρ τῷ
τρίτῳ τόπῳ διατρίβομεν καὶ περὶ ἐκεῖνόν ἐστιν
ἡμῖν ἡ πᾶσα σπουδή· τοῦ δὲ πρώτου παντελῶς
ἀμελοῦμεν. τοιγαροῦν ψευδόμεθα μέν, πῶς δὲ
ἀποδείκνυται ὅτι οὐ δεῖ ψεύδεσθαι, πρόχειρον
ἔχομεν.

1 c. 53. Ἐπὶ παντὸς πρόχειρα ἑκτέον² ταῦτα·

ἄγου δέ³ μ᾽, ὦ Ζεῦ, καὶ σύ γ᾽⁴ ἡ Πεπρωμένη,
ὅποι ποθ᾽ ὑμῖν εἰμι διατεταγμένος·
ὡς ἕψομαί γ᾽ ἄοκνος· ἢν δέ γε μὴ θέλω,
κακὸς γενόμενος, οὐδὲν ἧττον ἕψομαι.

2 "ὅστις δ᾽ ἀνάγκῃ συγκεχώρηκεν καλῶς,
σοφὸς παρ᾽ ἡμῖν, καὶ τὰ θεῖ᾽⁵ ἐπίσταται."

3 "ἀλλ᾽, ὦ Κρίτων, εἰ ταύτῃ τοῖς θεοῖς φίλον,
4 ταύτῃ γενέσθω."

"ἐμὲ δὲ Ἄνυτος καὶ Μέλητος⁶ ἀποκτεῖναι μὲν
δύνανται, βλάψαι δὲ οὔ."

¹ C un., and perhaps Simpl.: ὁ τοῦ the other MSS.
² C nonn., Par., Simpl.: εὐκτέον the other MSS.
³ Meibom (from the *Disc.*): ἄγε δή με *Ench.*
⁴ Meibom (from *s* in three of the four quotations in the
Disc.); καί A un., and S generally. The other MSS. omit.
⁵ C nonn., Plutarch: θεῖα the other MSS. ⁶ Μέλιτος MSS.

52. The first and most necessary division in philosophy is that which has to do with the application of the principles, as, for example, Do not lie. The second deals with the demonstrations, as, for example, How comes it that we ought not to lie? The third confirms and discriminates between these processes, as, for example, How does it come that this is a proof? For what is a proof, what is logical consequence, what contradiction, what truth, what falsehood? Therefore, the third division is necessary because of the second, and the second because of the first; while the most necessary of all, and the one in which we ought to rest, is the first. But we do the opposite; for we spend our time in the third division, and all our zeal is devoted to it, while we utterly neglect the first. Wherefore, we lie, indeed, but are ready with the arguments which prove that one ought not to lie.

53. Upon every occasion we ought to have the following thoughts at our command:

Lead thou me on, O Zeus, and Destiny,
To that goal long ago to me assigned.
I'll follow and not falter; if my will
Prove weak and craven, still I'll follow on.[1]

" Whoso has rightly with necessity complied,
We count him wise, and skilled in things divine." [2]

" Well, O Crito, if so it is pleasing to the gods, so let it be." [3]

" Anytus and Meletus can kill me, but they cannot hurt me." [4]

---

[1] From Cleanthes. See note on II. 23, 42.
[2] Euripides, frag. 965 Nauck.
[3] Plato, *Crito*, 43 D (slightly modified).
[4] Plato, *Apology*, 30 C–D (somewhat modified).

INDEX

539

INDEX

INDEX

INDEX

INDEX

INDEX

INDEX

INDEX

Hephaestus, 383
Hera, 89
Heracleitus, 88, 495
Heracles, 151, 188–9, 237, 335, 399
Herald, 127, 155
Herd, 167
Hermes, 19, 121
Hides, 137
Hierophant, 127–9
High brow, 499; spirit, 457
High-minded and High-mindedness, 63, 119, 187, 283, 363, 473, 501
Hindrance, 31, 79, 91, 99, 185, 197, 207, 245, 267–71, 279, 289, 313, 325, 351–3, 363, 383, 435–7, 483, 489
Hippias, 45
Hive, 167
Hog, 421
Holiday, 279–81, 323, 387
Holy rites, 129
Home, 147
Homer, 159, 191, 409, 533; quoted, 19, 79, 141, 155, 159, 163, 169, 189–93, 387, 409
Honey, 323
Honour, 59, 103, 115, 119, 125, 169, 275, 295, 301, 355, 369, 501, 509; position of, 347
Hope, 475, 527; give up, 465
Horse, 5, 7, 13, 33, 43, 99, 107, 267, 273, 283, 309, 323, 335, 415, 421, 463, 489; -race, 517
Hospital, 181
Host, one's, 463
Hot weather, 389
House, 77, 135, 153, 229, 267–9, 387, 405, 417
Household, 157, 197, 207–9, 345; head of, 217; of Caesar, 223; of one, 187
Human being. See *Man*.
Humane, 387
Humiliation, 185, 349
Hunger, 75, 191, 227–9, 233, 353, 409, 457, 463, 493
Hunting, 33; dog, 21, 33, 159, 375
Hurt, 341–3, 385, 447, 513, 525
Husband, 55
Hymn of praise, 237, 281
Hypothesis, 29
Hypothetical premisses, 23, 209, 319

Ignoble, 119, 203, 205, 231, 239, 291, 447
Ignorance and Ignorant, 343, 427

Ilium, 133
Ill (evil), 409, 519, 527
Illness, 39–43, 109, 119–23, 153, 221, 239, 257, 295, 345, 425, 443, 485, 491
Ill-omened, 213–5
Imagination, 219
Imitation, 37, 509
Immortality, 187
Immutability, 231; of nature, 449
Impediment, 319, 491
Imperishable, 341
Impertinence, 159, 329
Imperturbability, 317
Impiety, 35, 113, 535
Implement, 235
Important things, 375
Impossible, 191
Impressions, external, 401, 405, 445, 449–51, 485, 489, 491, 497–9, 523; intellectual, 117. See also *Sense-impression*.
Imprint, 337
Imprisonment, 291
Improvement, 519
Impudent of speech, 453
Impulse to act, 31
Impunity, 285, 411
Inattention, 311, 423 ff.
Incantation, 213
Incapacity, 169, 447
Inclinations, 425
Income, 161
Inconsiderate, 501
Inconstancy, 117
Indifferent, 291
Indigestion, 229
Indignation, 359
Individual, 345
Indivisible, 441
Indulgence, 519
Industry, 329
Infant, 203
Inferior and Inferiority, 111, 167
Inheritance, 25, 435
Initiates in the mysteries, 281
Injury, 59, 61, 113–15, 335, 365
Injustice, 237, 335
Inn, 491
Insatiable, 503–5
Insensibility, 167
Insolence and Insolent, 295, 447, 505
Instruction, 129, 183
Insult, 167, 499; gesture of, 25
Intellect, 449–51

INDEX

550

INDEX

INDEX

INDEX

INDEX

INDEX

INDEX

INDEX

557

INDEX

INDEX